# Footprint
# Croatia
## Handbook

*Jane Foster*

*To travel hopefully is a better thing than to arrive*

Robert Louis Stevenson

1st edition

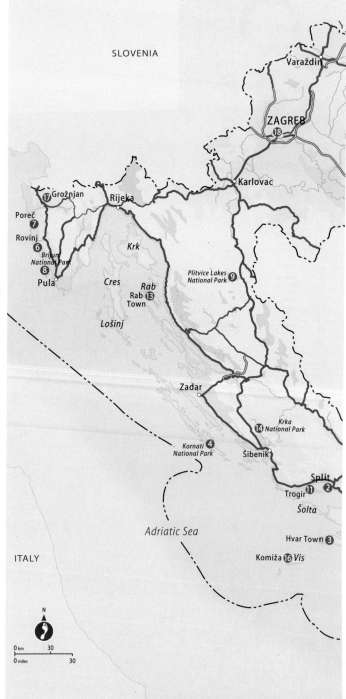

# Croatia

**1 Dubrovnik :**
The 'Pearl of the Adriatic': a UNESCO-listed medieval walled city

**2 Split**
A city within the walls of an impressive Roman palace

**3 Hvar Town**
The islands' most fashionable resort: yachts and late-night bars

**4 Kornati National Park**
A vast seascape of scattered islands, best explored by yacht

**5 Korčula Town**
A beautifully preserved medieval fortified town on a small peninsula

**6 Rovinj**
A Colourful fishing town much loved by artists and writers

**7 Poreč**
Croatia's most visited seaside resort, noted for its Byzantine mosaics

**8 Brijuni National Park**
Glorious landscaped parkland on an island that was once Tito's private residence

**9 Plitvice Lakes National Park**
A series of emerald-blue lakes connected by cascades and waterfalls

SLOVENIA

Varaždin

ZAGREB
18

Karlovac

17 Grožnjan
Rijeka
Poreč
7
Rovinj
6
Brijuni
National Park
8
Pula

Krk

Plitvice Lakes
National Park 9

Cres
Rab
Rab 13
Town

Lošinj

Zadar

Krka
National Park
14

Kornati 4
National Park

Šibenik

Split
Trogir 11 2
Šolta

Adriatic Sea

Hvar Town 3

Komiža 16 Vis

ITALY

N

0 km        30
0 miles        30

**⑩ Zlatni Rat**
Croatia's most-photographed beach

**⑪ Trogir**
Medieval city on a small island, accessed from the mainland by bridge

**⑫ Mljet National Park**
Two connected salt-water lakes surrounded by dense pine forest

**⑬ Rab Town**
Medieval stone town with four elegant bell towers

**⑭ Krka National Park**
A series of waterfalls running through a steep sided wooded canyon

**⑮ Biokovo Mountain**
Climb to the top for stunning views, west to Italy and east to Bosnia

**⑯ Komiža**
An unspoilt fishing village on the island of Vis

**⑰ Grožnjan**
A medieval walled hill town colonized by artists

**⑱ Zagreb**
The sober Austro-Hungarian style capital: home to one in four Croats

4

# Contents

5

Inland Croatia

Kvarner

Istria

North
Dalmatia

Central
Dalmatia

South
Dalmatia

## North Dalmatia

174 **Zadar**
181 Nin
183 **Island of Pag**
183 Pag Town
184 Novalja
185 Paklenica National Park
186 Dugi Otok and the Zadar Archipelago
188 Biograd-na-Moru
189 Kornati National Park

## Central Dalmatia
194 **Split**
210 **Trogir**
214 Salona
216 Klis
217 Sinj
218 Omiš
220 **Island of Hvar**
221 Hvar Town
226 Stari Grad
228 Jelsa
230 Vrboska
231 South side of Hvar
233 **Island of Vis**
234 Vis Town
236 Komiža
238 **Island of Brač**
239 Supetar
241 Bol
243 Milna
244 Island of Šolta
246 Markarska
249 Markarska Rivijera
251 **Sibenik**
255 Skradin and Krk National Park
256 Islands of Zlarin and Prvić
257 Vodice
258 Island of Murter
260 Primošten
261 Knin

## South Dalmatia
266 **Dubrovnik**
279 Trsteno Arboretum
279 Elafiti Islands
281 Cavtat
283 **Island of Korčula**
284 Korčula Town
289 Lumbarda
290 Vela Luka
291 Blato
292 **Island of Lastovo**
294 Lastovo Town and around
295 **Island of Mljet**
298 **Pelješac Peninsula**
299 Orebić
301 Ston

## Background
304 **History**
323 Modern Croatia
324 **Economy**
325 **Culture**
325 Architecture
329 Art
331 Literature
334 Language
335 Music
337 **Land and environment**
337 Geography
338 Wildlife and vegetation
339 **Books**
340 **Cinema**

## Footnotes
342 Useful words and phrases
345 Food glossary
347 Index
350 Shorts
351 Map index
352 Map symbols
353 Credits
354 Acknowledgements

**Inside cover**
Overview
Price guide

**Back cover**
Author

A foot in the door

*Rovinj* (previous page) *A medieval town on the Istrian coast, Rovinj is a popular choice for tourists to visit and artists and musicians to settle in. It's easy to see why*
**Market day in Dubrovnik** (right) *Fresh, seasonal ingredients are used in Croatian cooking. A visit to the market, as well as enjoying its wares, is a highlight*
**Island of Mljet** (below) *Steep, rocky slopes and dense forests, the island is visited by a few in search of peace and tranquility*

**Cavtat** (above) *A fishing village at the very south of Croatia with a seafront promenade lined with bars and cafés, palms and plants*
**Rovinj** (right) *A labyrinth of steep, narrow cobbled streets leads to the hilltop church of Sv Eufemija (pictured on the previous page)*

# Introducing Croatia

They dress like Italians and aspire to doing business like Austrians. They look to the Pope in Rome for spiritual guidance, but their country sits perched precariously on the edge of the Balkan peninsula. At sea (some 35,000 sailors now work on foreign ships) and on the football pitch (many play in Italy, Germany and the UK), Croatians entered the 21st century determined to become acknowledged as part of Western Europe. Before they succeed however they will have to overcome almost an entire millennium of political and cultural development influenced by four great cities – Venice, Vienna, Budapest and Istanbul. "You are what you eat", the saying goes. In Zagreb its *schnitzel*, in Slavonia goulash, and in Pula pasta and risotto. But at home, everyone prepares Turkish coffee. And so we arrive at the delicate issue of the Balkan question.

It goes back to AD 395, when the Romans divided their Empire into East and West, effectively drawing a line down the middle of the Balkan peninsula. In 1054, the Christian church split along the same border, leaving Catholics to the west, and Orthodox to the east. Then, in the 16th century the expansion of the Ottoman empire brought an influx of Orthodox Serb refugees onto Croatian territory, plus a third faith, Islam. The minarets were hastily demolished when the Turks retreated two centuries later, but the Orthodox settlers remained and became an integral part of society. It was then the fate of the region that the powers of the Austro-Hungary empire, and later within Yugoslavia itself, would promote potential tensions between Croats and Serbs to weaken national integrity and leave Croatia open to manipulation. In the early 1990s, some 350,000 Serbs fled and Zagreb hastily claimed that Croatia was not a Balkan country and in fact never had been.

Hugging a long, meandering stretch of the sunny East Adriatic coast, lined with blissful islands, today Croatia appears the epitome of peace and tranquillity. Relations with neighbouring countries have improved and the Serb population is returning. Economically, the country's future lies largely in tourism, so if you come here your money will be well spent. Judging from current trends, the days of cheap mass tourism are over. Instead Croatia offers visitors the chance to relate more directly to the land, the sea, the people and their culture. As you wander through winding cobbled streets, you will be greeted by wafts of grilled red peppers and chopped garlic, barbecued sardines and freshly squeezed lemon. This is Croatia, here and now.

**Dobrovnik** (left)  A fortified city backed by limestone mountains and jutting out into the Adriatic Sea

**Poreč** (below)  A seaside resort, home to the sixth-century Euphrasius Basilica which is decorated with golden Byzantine mosaics so stunning as to earn it a place on the UNESCO list of world heritage sites

**Arena in Pula** (above)  This first-century Roman amphitheatre was built to host gladiator fights for a capacity of 22,000 spectators. This number was way beyond the city's population at that time

**Streets of Split** (right)  The glitterati might be visiting in their droves but traditional life continues

**Sestine** (next page)  With its castles, forests and rolling hills, inland Croatia sometimes has a fairy-tale appearance

# Highlights

In Croatia stone prevails. It is difficult to imagine how man managed to carve out a living from such a barren, apparently inhospitable environment. From the rugged karst mountains of Velebit and Biokovo, rising well over 1,000 m from the coast, to the countless scattered islands, such as the Kornati and Pag, vegetation is scanty and it has taken many years of hard labour to clear meagre patches of soil for cultivation. But visit a traditional *konoba* (wine cellar) in Dalmatia or Istria, and the steady flow of wine from aged oak barrels will be enough to assure you that this land can be generous, indeed that Bacchus may be lurking close at hand.

**A lion's share**

The Romans arrived some 2,000 years ago, and promptly set about colonizing the East Adriatic, building military camps and trading ports. Their most remarkable surviving monuments are the imposing amphitheatre in Pula, where gladiators and early Christians once confronted lions, and Diocletian's Palace in Split, where subjects would fall to their knees upon the appearance of their former Emperor. Today Pula amphitheatre still arouses cheers from the public, though now through more peaceful forms of entertainment – rock concerts and an annual film festival – and Diocletian's Palace is a labyrinth of medieval streets, which are lined with Renaissance town houses, coffee bars and chic boutiques stocking imported designer labels.

**Wall to wall treasures**

The popular coastal resorts of Poreč, Hvar and Korčula owe their present appearance to the Venetians, who built them to serve as ports of call for trade ships en route to the Black Sea, though today their harbours are filled with fishing boats, water taxis and flashy yachts. Their historic centres, surrounded by defensive walls, take you back through the centuries. The town gates are too narrow to allow for the passage of vehicles, so areas within the fortifications remain the exclusive domain of the pedestrian, with flagstone streets opening out onto piazzas of white marble, invariably given over to open-air cafés and night-time concerts below the stars. The undisputed queen of all the walled cities is Dubrovnik, built not by Venice, but by the skill and cunning of her own citizens.

**Draw of the deep blue sea**

With 1,778 km of mainland coast (and a staggering 5,790 km if you count the islands), finding a place to lie in the sun and swim in crystal clear sea won't be too much of a problem. During the 20th century, when tourists first started to visit Croatia, it wasn't the cultural attractions of churches and museums that brought them to these shores, but the shores themselves. The golden shingle beach of Zlatni Rat on the island of Brač and the curving sands of Baška on the island of Krk, with their hire-by-the-hour sun-beds and coloured umbrellas, are featured in all the glossy brochures, and indeed they are splendid. But better still the undiscovered coves, backed by terraces of vineyards and olive groves on some of the lesser-known islands, where the rocky shoreline gives way to smooth white pebbles, and the only sound you'll hear will be the gentle lapping of the sea.

14

**Trsteno Arboretum** (right)
One of the oldest and most beautiful
landscaped parks in the country, just
a stone's throw from Dubrovnik
**Island of Hvar** (below)  An island of
Venetian villages, lavender fields and
vineyards as well as hidden coves and bays

**Plitvice Lakes** (left)  The lakes and falls of this national park are
spectacular, as is the karst landscape that forms the backdrop
**Ocean bed** (above)  There are many opportunities for
adventures at the bottom of the Adriatic
**Dubrovnik** (next page)  Church of Saint Blaise
amidst the terracotta roofs of Dubrovnik

# At one with nature

Croatia is unspoilt: the sea is crystal clear and the mountains are sublime. With a long indented coastline, over 1,000 islands, a warm, sunny Mediterranean climate and only one third of the UK population density, this is a place you can really escape the crowds and return to nature.

**In the pink**

Naturists believe that naked bathing is the ultimate way to find harmony with the elements, and Croatia is Europe's top naturist destination. Naturism began in the early 20th century on the island of Rab, coming of age so to speak in the 1960s. Although during the 1990s it decreased quite significantly, perhaps due to the influence of the Catholic Church, it still has a large following by visitors and Croatians alike. Infact during the presidential campaign of 2000, Stipe Mesić declared himself a naturist and won. There are over 30 official nudist beaches, however, on the Adriatic, you are free to hike to a secluded cove, where the emerald sea meets a pebble beach, and literally bare all to the sea and sunshine. If you haven't done it before, try it here: you'll experience a wonderful sense of freedom and finally get that all over tan.

**Sail of the century**

Hardly the most restful way to spend your holiday, but exploring the Croatian coast on the deck of a sailing boat is one of the most enjoyable ways. A day at the mercy of the wind and waves is exhausting but enjoying the sheer vastness of the open sea, eating in the open air and slumbering to the gentle movements of the tide is guaranteed to replenish body and soul. There is also the unbeatable feeling of freedom when travelling in this way. You are able to anchor where you wish, be it in an upbeat seaside resort where you can feast on lobster and wine, or an isolated island where all you will be assured of is peace and solitude.

**Adventures in the Adriatic**

Anthropologists claim that man originated from the sea and the experience of diving can give some credence to this theory. The mystic silence and serenity of the underwater world is stirring. Don the gear and swim down into the depths of the Adriatic. Croatia isn't world renowned for its diving but there are some magical spots: the *Modra Spilja* (Blue Cave) near Vis is one of the finest but there are vast coral reefs inhabited by shoals of fish and ancient shipwrecks complete with broken amphorae dotted all along the coastline.

**The road less travelled**

For those who prefer *terra firma*, Croatia offers some excellent hiking routes. Some, such as Velika Paklenica canyon in Paklenica National Park, lead upwards into the rugged karst mountains for stunning views over the sea, while others take you inland to meet the thundering rapids and cascades of Krka and Plitvice waterfalls. Official routes are clearly marked, while many of the islands are criss-crossed by old-fashioned donkey paths, running from rural villages through vineyards and olive groves: if you're lucky you may find one that leads to a deserted bay.

**Castaway**

Away from the main resorts there are plenty of isolated holiday retreats. Lighthouses, perched on a rocks far out to sea, can be rented where you won't see a soul, save maybe a fisherman. Or try living Robinson Crusoe style, with just a gas lamp and water from a well, in a simple stone cottage on the uninhabited Kornati islands. Still pretty rustic but a little more homely with some creature comforts, is agrotourism. You can spend your days on a working farm gaining an insight into rural life and feasting on locally produced cheeses, hams, wines and olive oils.

Essentials

# Planning your trip

## Where to go

Croatia offers a wide variety of landscapes and each region has its own unique charac-
teristics. However, for most people the real pull is the coast, and above all the islands. If
you are short of time and planning to spend a week or less here it is best to concentrate
on one area. Take either Istria, Central Dalmatia or South Dalmatia, and use a coastal
town as a main regional base.

**One week**  In Istria, the most popular region with the best tourist facilities, Pula, Poreč or Rovinj each
warrant a visit. You could choose one of them your base, and use it for making day trips to
the islands of Brijuni national park and the inland hill towns of Motovun and Grožnjan.

In Central Dalmatia, the monumental Roman city of Split is an ideal starting point for
exploring the islands of Brač, Hvar and Vis, as well the nearby coastal towns of Trogir
and Makarska and the inland village of Klis.

In South Dalmatia, the walled city of Dubrovnik will undoubtedly absorb two or
three days of sightseeing, as well as serving as a launching pad for visiting the Elaphiti
islands, Mljet National Park, the coastal resort of Cavtat and Trsteno Arboretum.

**Two weeks**  If you have two weeks at your disposal, the number of options opens up considerably.
To understand the country's complexity, spend some time in the capital, Zagreb, a city
culturally and geographically closer to Vienna and Budapest than to the Venetian influenced coastal region. Having visited the city's museums and churches, devote a couple
of days to the rural villages and medieval castles of Zagorje, and the small Baroque city
of Varaždin.

From Zagreb, you could then take the overnight train directly down to Split to visit
Dalmatia, and follow the itineraries mentioned above. Alternatively take a bus or train
to Rijeka in the Kvarner region. Close by lie the restful seaside resorts of Opatija and
Lovran, made up of elegant Vienna Secession style hotels and villas, and from Rijeka
port there are direct boat lines to the islands of Rab and Cres (summer only), both of
which offer unspoilt nature and endless opportunities for bathing, watersports and
hiking. From Rijeka there are regular overnight ferries and daytime buses down the
coast to Zadar, Split and Dubrovnik in Dalmatia.

**Three weeks**  North Dalmatia is in many ways less attractive than Central and South Dalmatia, but if
you have three weeks in Croatia it may be worth a visit, particularly if you enjoy unspoilt
nature parks. The chief city, Zadar, is renowned for its Romanesque churches. Close by,
Kornati National Park is a haven of small uninhabited rocky islands, while day hiking in
Paklenica National Park, will give you a taste of the mountains. The region's most interesting island is Pag, home to the delicious *Paški sir* (sheeps cheese).

Finally, Slavonia, the eastern most region of Croatia, has little of great interest to holiday makers, but if you want to get a complete picture of the country and its recent
tragic history, the largely devastated town of Vukovar, sitting on the west bank of the
River Danube, illustrates better than anywhere else the suffering caused by the war for
independence. Neighbouring Osijek is a more cheerful place to spend the night, and
makes an ideal starting point for visiting Kopa čki Rit Nature Park.

## When to go

Peak-season runs July to August, which is when most Germans and Italians take their
summer holidays. On the plus side, nightlife is at its most animated, with open-air

cultural performances – the top events being the Summer Festivals in Dubrovnik and Split – and outdoor discos along the coast. On the down side, the beaches can be horribly crowded, and restaurants and bars so busy you may have to queue for a table. Accommodation prices also rise steeply during this period, and availability may be scarce, so you should really book a place to stay in advance.

Mid-season, May to June and September to October, is probably the most rewarding time to visit. Through June and September the sea is warm enough to swim (hardier types will also manage in May and October) and the beaches reasonably peaceful. Hotels and restaurants are working but not overly busy, so you'll tend to get more personalized service. As temperatures are not unbearably hot, this is an ideal time for active land sports such as hiking and biking. Spring and autumn are also the best moments to catch local delicacies: wild asparagus and cherries in late-April, and mushrooms, truffles and chestnuts in early-October.

During low season, November to April, many restaurants and hotels on the islands close down completely. Although you can't be guaranteed good weather, if you do visit Croatia during this period you can be almost certain there will be few foreigners around.

The Adriatic Coast is blessed with a Mediterranean climate. The summers are warm, dry and brilliantly sunny, with July temperatures averaging 25°C in Dubrovnik, while winters are mild and rainy, with January temperatures averaging 9°C. In contrast, Inland Croatia has a continental climate, with hot summers – July temperatures average 24°C in Zagreb – and cold winters, averaging 0°C through January.

## Tours and tour operators

*Balkan Holidays*, T0845 1301114, www.balkanholidays.co.uk  Arrange holidays to the **In the UK** seaside resorts of Dubrovnik, Makarska and Brela. *Capitvating Croatia*, T0870 1203561, www.captivating-croatia.co.uk  Arrange holidays to Poreč, Rovinj, Makarska, Brela, Brač, Tučepi, Hvar, Korčula, Dubrovnik, Lopud, Mljet and Cavtat.

*Croatia for Travellers*, 63 Therberton St, London N1 0QY, T020 72264460, www.croatiafortravellers.co.uk  Offers programmes for independent travellers. One-week itineraries include tailor-made cultural tours of Dalmatia and the islands, UNESCO heritage tour and national parks, wine tour, scuba diving in Dalmatia, and Robinson Crusoe cottage accommodation on the Kornati islands.

*Explore Worldwide*, 1 Frederick St, Aldershot, Hants, GU11 1LQ, T01252 760000, www.exploreworldwide.com  Offer a selection of adventure tours, including an 11-day exploration of Dubrovnik and the Dalmatian mainland, and an eight-day cruise covering Split and the surrounding islands.

*Holiday Options*, T0870 0130450, www.holidayoptions.co.uk  Arrange holidays to Poreč, Rovinj and Vrsar in Istria, Opatija in Kvarner, Makarska, Baška Voda and Brela on the mainland coast in Central Dalmatia, Dubrovnik and Cavtat on the mainland coast in South Dalmatia, and to the Dalmatian islands of Brač, Hvar, Korčula and Mljet.

*Neilson Active Holidays*, Locksview, Brighton Marina, Brighton, BN2 5HA, T0870 3333356, www.neilson.co.uk  Offer a one-week surf-sail-cycle holidays, based in Pomena on the island of Mljet, South Dalmatia.

*Ramblers Holidays*, Box 43, Welwyn Garden City, AL8 6PQ, T01707 331133, www.ramblersholidays.co.uk  Offer a one-week sightseeing break based in Dubrovnik, with trips to Cavtat and Čilipi.

*Saga Holidays*, T0800 300600, www.saga.co.uk/travel  Organize seven-day breaks for the 50 plus age group in Poreč and Rabac in Istria, and Makarska and Dubrovnik in Dalmatia. They also run a Heart of the Mediterranean Saga Rose Cruise from Southampton to Venice, calling at Dubrovnik and Hvar en route.

*Thompson Holidays*, T0870 1650079, www.thompson-holidays.com  Arrange packages to Poreč and Rovinj in Istria.

*Transun*, T0870 4444747, www.transun.co.uk Arrange packages to Poreč and Rovinj in Istria, Opatija in Kvarner, Primošten, Bol, Jelsa, Hvar, Baška Voda, Brela, Makarska, Orebić, Korčula, Mljet, Lopud. Mlini, Cavtat and Dubrovnik in Dalmatia.

*Voyages Jules Verne*, 21 Dorset Sq, London NW1 6QG, T020 76161000, www.vjv.com Offer a seven-day 1001 Dalmatian Islands package covering Venice, Pula, Dubrovnik, the island of Korčula, and Montenegro.

**In the US**    *Remote Odysseys Worldwide*, PO Box 579, Coeur d'Alene, ID 83816. T0208 7650841, www.rowinternational.com Offer a Jewels of the Adriatic two-week tour, from Venice to Dubrovnik by private yacht, combining sailing, walking, history, culture and wine tasting.

*Smithsonian Study Tours*, PO Box 23293, Washington DC 20026-3293, T202 3574700, F6339250, www.smithsonianstudytours.org Offer a two-week cruise, Voyage from Venice to the Dalmatian Coast, departing from Venice and calling at Pula, Opatija, Zadar, Kornati National Park, Split, Korčula and Dubrovnik.

**Specialist tour operators**
*See also the entries above*

**Cycling** Agencies specializing in adventure sports, such as *Big Blue*, Podan Glavice 2, Bol, island of Brač, T021 635614, www.big-blue-sport.hr; *Huck Finn*, Vukovarska 271, Zagreb, T01 6183333, www.huck-finn.hr; and *Marco Polo*, Istarska 2, T052 816616, Rovinj, www.marcopolo.hr, include organized cycling tours in their programmes.

**Diving** *Dive Tours*, Total Diving Solutions Ltd, 46 Watergate St, Chester, CH1 2LA, T01244 401177, www.divetours.co.uk Organize diving holidays throughout the world, with a Korčula base in Croatia. See the listings of individual towns throughout the book for details of local diving outfits.

**Hiking and climbing** *Biokovo Active Holidays*, Makarska, T021 611688. Organize group walks, hiking and climbing, on Mount Biokovo and the island of Brač in Central Dalmatia. In addition, agencies specializing in adventure sports, such as *Active Holidays*, Knezova Kačića bb, Omiš, T021 863015, www.activeholidays-croatia.com and *Marco Polo*, Istarska 2, T052 816616, Rovinj, www.marcopolo.hr Include free climbing in their programmes, and Paklenica National Park, Jadranska cesta bb, Starigrad Paklenica, T023 369202, www.paklenica.hr Can arrange guided hiking tours of Velebit.

**Rafting** The bigger travel agents such as *Atlas*, Ćira Carića 3, Dubrovnik, T020 442222, www.atlas-croatia.com and *Generalturist*, Praška 5, Zagreb, T01 4810033, www.generalturist.com, organize one-day rafting trips and one-week adventure trips including rafting. Smaller companies specializing in adventure sports, such as *Huck Finn*, Vukovarska 271, Zagreb, T01 6183333, www.huck-finn.hr and *Active Holidays*, Knezova Kačića bb, Omiš, T021 863015, www.activeholidays-croatia.com, also include rafting in their programmes.

**Sailing** *Activity Holidays*, 48 Canada Rd, Cobham, Surrey, KT11 2BA, T01932 867418, www.activity-holidays.co.uk Specialize in sailing in Greece and Croatia. Offer one-week sailing instruction, as well as skippered charter, both bareboat (one yacht) and flotilla sailing (groups of five-10 yachts). Based in Betina on the island of Murter, close to Kornati National Park, in Croatia.

*Adriatic Holidays Ltd*, 1 Victoria St, Oxford OX2 6BT, T01865 516577, www.adriaticholidaysonline.com Operate with three charter companies in Croatia with bases in Pula, Biograd, Trogir, Split and Dubrovnik.

*Cosmos Yachting*, 6 Rocks Lane, Barnes, London SW13 0DB, T020 88780880, www.cosmosyachting.com Specialize in bareboat and crewed yacht charters in various parts of Europe and the Caribbean. Bases in Pula and Split in Croatia.

## Croatia Tourist Boards

**Austria,** Am Hof 13, 1010 Wien, T43 1 5853884.
**Belgium,** Vieille Halle aux Bles 38, 1000 Brussels, T32 2 550188.
**Croatia,** Iblerov trg 10/IV, 10000 Zagreb, T385 1 4699333, www.croatia.hr
**Czech Republic,** Krakovská 25, 110 00 Praha 1, T420 2 22211812.
**France,** 48 Avenue Victor Hugo, 75116 Paris, T33 1 45009955.
**Germany,** Rumfordstrasse 7, 80469 Mčnchen, T49 89 223344.
**Hungary,** Magyar u 36, 1053 Budapest, T36 1 2666505.
**Italy,** Via Umbria 15, 00187 Roma, T39 06 42010525 and Piazzetta Pattari 1/3, 20122

Milano, T39 02 86454443.
**Netherlands,** Hoge Gouwe 93, 2801 LD Gouda, T0900 20 22102.
**Poland,** Chmielna 16 lok. 2, 00-020 Warszawa, T48 22 8285193.
**Slovakia,** Trenčianska 5, 821 09 Bratislava, T421 7 55562054.
**Slovenia,** Gosposvetska 2, 1000 Ljubljana, T386 1 2307400.
**Sweden,** Kungsgatan 24, 11135 Stockholm, T46 8 53482080.
**UK,** 2 Lanchesters, 162-164 Fulham Palace Road, W6 9ER London, T44 208 5637979.
**USA,** 350 Fifth Avenue, Suite 4003, 10118 New York, T1 212 2798672.

*Essentials*

*Nautilus Sailing*, 4 Church St, Edenbridge, Kent, TN8 5BD, T01732 867445, www.nautilus-yachting.com   Specialize in sailing in various parts of the world, with yacht charter bases in Pula, Zadar, Split and Dubrovnik in Croatia. Also offer Learn to Sail holidays, with four beginners aboard in the company of one instructor.

*Sailing Holidays Ltd*, 105 Mount Pleasant Rd, London NW10 3EH, T020 84598787, www.sailingholidays.co.uk   Specialize in sailing in Greece and Croatia. Organize flotilla holidays with base marinas at Kremik (Primošten), Dubrovnik and Tučepi in Croatia. Possibility of opting for one week afloat and one week ashore.

**Naturism**  *Dune Leisure*, 25 High St, Edwinstowe, Nottinghamshire, NG21 9QP, T0870 751 8866, www.dune.uk.com   Specialize in naturist holidays around the world, focusing on the Rovinj-Poreč area in Croatia.

*Peng Travel*, 86 Station Rd, Gidea Park, Romford, Essex, RM2 6DB, T0845 3458345 (in UK) or T01708 471832 (from outside the UK), www.pengtravel.co.uk   Specialize in naturist holidays around the world, focusing on the Rovinj-Pore č area in Croatia.

## Finding out more

The best way of finding out more information for your trip is to contact the Croatian National Tourist Board in your country or write direct to the head office in Zagreb (see box, page 21 for contact details of embassies and page 59 for the Zagreb office).

Croatian homepage, www.hr
Croatian government, www.mvp.hr (links to various ministries)
Croatian information centre, www.hic.hr
Croatian news agency, www.hina.hr
General cultural information, www.croatia.net
Food and restaurants, www.gastronaut.hr (in Croatian only)
Croatia Naturally, www.cronatur.hr (naturism)
Croatian telecom phone directory http://imenik.hinet.hr

# Language

*See page 342 for a list of useful words and phrases and page 334 for background information*

The official language is Croatian. Most people working in tourism, as well as the majority of younger Croatians, speak good English, however, so you won't have much of a problem in communicating unless you get off-the-beaten track. If you do make the effort to learn a few words and phrases though your efforts are likely to be rewarded with a smile of appreciation and probably a new found respect. If you are serious about learning the language a self-study course is a good option, but better still, is a language course completed in the country itself.

*Colloquial Croatian and Serbian: The Complete Course for Beginners*, Celia Hawkesworth (Routledge). An easy to use and up-to-date pack including a book and cassette, this course includes concise grammar notes, a useful vocabulary and pronunciation guide plus interactive exercises.

Zagreb University together with the Croatian Heritage Foundation organizes four-week Croatian **language courses** through both July and August, primarily intended for people of Croatian origin born outside the country, but also open to anyone else who is interested in learning the language. The courses take place in the Gornji Grad area of Zagreb. Students are divided into small groups (six-10 participants per class) catering for various levels from beginner to advanced. Besides the Monday to Friday language lessons, the school organizes weekend cultural trips. For further information, Sveučilište u Zagrebu (University of Zagreb), University School of Croatian Language and Culture, Trg maršala Tita 14, 10000 Zagreb, T385 1 4564251, F4830602, www.unizg.hr See page 74 for private language schools also offering courses in Croatian for foreigners in Zagreb.

# Disabled travellers

As a consequence of the increase in the number of physically disabled people after the war, Croatians have become more aware of the problems faced by those with mobility difficulties. In the past many public buildings such as airports, hotels, railway stations and bus stations did not make special provision for wheelchair access, but projects to rectify the situation are now underway, and in some cases are already complete. The problem of facilitating access onto ferries has yet to be resolved, but you will normally find a steward who is ready to help. The more expensive, modern hotels are generally better equipped – when choosing a place to stay ask exactly what provisions they have. It's often a good idea to request a ground floor room or a room close to the lift.

*Savez Organizacija Invalida Hrvatske* (Association of Organisations of Disabled People in Croatia), Savska Cesta 3, 10000 Zagreb, T385 01 4829394, publishes guides for disabled travellers to Zagreb, Split, Pula, Rijeka, Varaždin and Koprivnica, available in both Croatian and English.

*Holiday Care*, T0845 1249971, www.holidaycare.org.uk, can give basic information about facilities for disabled people in various countries and can also help you find a tour operator who specializes in travel for people with mobility difficulties.

*Tripscope*, T08457 585641 (UK), T44 117 9397782 (outside UK), www.tripscope.org.uk, run a telephone helpline providing general information about travel for the disabled.

# Gay and lesbian travellers

Homosexuality has been legal in Croatia since 1977, though it remains taboo among the older generation and is only now beginning to be accepted in the more alternative youth circles. On 2 July 2002 the country had its first ever Gay Pride March in which some 200 people paraded through central Zagreb, with police with riot shields on hand to intervene in case of trouble. Relatively few on lookers hurled insults at the marchers, but undoubtedly Croatia still has a long way to go before gays and lesbians can feel free to openly express themselves here.

The website, www.gaytimes.co.uk, has short country guides, including Croatia. For a listing of gay-friendly clubs and bars in Zagreb, Rijeka and Split, visit www.cro-lesbians.com (in Croatian only) and click on 'Vodic'. For general information about tours for lesbian and gay travellers, check out the website of the **International Gay and Lesbian Travellers Association**, www.iglta.org

## Student travellers

If you are a full-time student, an **International Student Identity Card** (ISIC) will entitle you to reductions at Youth Hostels, museums and certain international trains and air-fares. They are available at student travel offices and travel agents around the world in over 100 countries, to find your nearest office, check out www.isic.org

If you are already in Croatia, and have proof that you are a student, you can get an ISIC through the travel section of the **Hrvatski Ferijalni i Hostelski Savez** (Croatian Youth Hostel Association). In summer 2002 this service costs 40Kn. For more information contact them at Dežmanova 9, 10000 Zagreb, T01 4847474, www.hfhs.hr

## Travelling with children

Like all South Europeans, Croatians love children and give a lot of time and attention to them. They also let their kids stay up late, so through summer it's quite usual to turn up at a restaurant around 2200 for dinner with the little ones in tow.

Very few Croatian **hotels** go along with the idea of putting an extra bed for a young child in the parents' double room. Some hotels have rooms with three or four beds that are designed to accommodate a family, though there are no cheap rates for kids in this case. Likewise, few hotels offer baby-sitting facilities. If you have very young children, private accommodation is probably your best bet. This way you can agree directly with the person from whom you are renting on how best to arrange rooms and beds to suit your needs, and as you will probably also have a kitchen, you can prepare meals when and as you like.

Ask any Croatian child what their favourite **food** is and the reply will more than likely be pizza. This is a good starting point, and it's quite normal in pizzerias to ask for an extra plate then cut up the pizzas and share. Pasta dishes and barbecued meats also go down well with kids, though fish is obviously more tricky: one of the parents is going to have to sort out the bones. If you opt for self-catering, you'll find an endless range of yoghurts and biscuits, which make good snacks, as well as wholesome, locally produced fruit juices.

*Croatia Airlines* and *Croatian Railways* both offer a 50% discount on **tickets** for children under the age of 12. Regarding buses, each bus company has its own rules, which can even vary depending on the route. Some offer free travel for children up to the age of 4, others offer a 50% discount up to the age of 6, and some a 20% discount up to the age of 12. For exact details, ask when buying tickets.

Children love the freedom of running around on **beaches** and splashing in the sea, but bear in mind that there's not much sand here. Most of the beaches are pebbly, so plastic sandals are recommended for those with sensitive feet. Sea urchins can be a stumbling block (literally): while local children have an inexplicable ability to pluck them off the rocks with their fingers, these black prickly monsters can seriously upset those who are not in the know. Once again, plastic sandals are the best solution.

## Women travellers

Croatian society is basically patriarchal, and local men, like most South European males, will be quite open about expressing their interest in a woman. Advances are normally totally harmless – a few flattering comments then it's up to you to respond. If you are not impressed, ignore them and they will more than likely go away. Local women are quite head strong and don't stand any nonsense – act the same way and you'll be fine. However, some bars are frequented almost exclusively by men: these are best avoided by a woman travelling alone as her presence could be interpreted as an open invitation.

## Working in the country

*The options are generally teaching a language or volunteer work*

Unemployment rates in Croatia are over 22%, so opportunities for foreign workers are obviously very limited. Anyone wishing to take on a full-time paid job must apply to the Croatian Embassy for an appropriate visa: to do this you should present a copy of the employment contract for the job you intend to take, plus details of the type of work you will be doing, in Croatian.

*Euroclub*, Vrh Lučac 5, Split 21000, T385 21 483238, www.euroclub.hr, run a summer holiday camp for children on the island of Šolta, and take on young enthusiastic people to teach English, Italian and German – you need to be a native speaker or to have a university degree in the language you hope to teach. The idea is that the kids have fun and learn at the same time, so you'll be expected to join in games and sports activities after class. Paid employment is on a weekly basis and full board is provided. *Lancon*, Kumičićeva 10, Zagreb 10000, T385 1 4854985, www.lancon.hr, run business English language courses for companies in the Zagreb area, and are always on the look out for qualified TEFL teachers to take on one-year contracts. Salaries (including healthcare and pension) are gauged on the candidate's educational background and teaching experience.

*Eco-centre Caput Insulae*, Beli 4, Beli, Island of Cres, T385 51 840525, www.caput-insulae.com, takes on volunteers to help with the upkeep of the centre (see page 158). Activities include maintaining ecotrails, repairing drystone walls and clearing ponds, as well as work in the interpretation centre. Cost includes accommodation in a shared, fully furnished house. *Plavi Svijet* (Blue World), Zad Bone 11, Veli Lošinj, Island of Lošinj, T385 51 236406, www.blue-world.org, takes on volunteers to help with the **Adriatic Dolphin Project** (see page 164). Activities include observing the dolphins at sea and collecting and analysing data. Cost includes accommodation in a shared, fully furnished house.

# Before you travel

## Getting in

Visas  EU, US, Canadian, Australian, New Zealand and Israeli passport holders can enter Croatia without a visa and stay for up to 90 days. South Africans, however, require a visa, which can be obtained at the Croatian Embassy in Pretoria. For further details, visit the Croatian Government website, www.mvp.hr (in Croatian and English), or contact the Croatian embassy in your country.

Foreigners are required to register with the local police within 24 hours of arrival. If you are staying in a hotel or renting a room, it is the owner's responsibility to do this for you. If you are staying with friends, they should by law register you, though in reality people are quite relaxed about this. However, theoretically failure to comply with this rule risks deportation.

## Croatian embassies

◀

*Australia*, 14 Jindalee Crescent, O'Malley Act 2606, Canberra, T61 2 62866988.

*Austria*, Heuberggasse 10, 1170 Vienna, T43 1 4802083.

*Belgium* (and Luxembourg), Avenue Louise 425, 1050 Brussels, T32 2 6446510.

*Bosnia Herzegovina*, Mehmeda Spahe 16, 71000 Sarajevo, T387 33 444330.

*Bulgaria*, Veliko Trnovo 32, 1504 Sofia, T359 2 9433225.

*Canada*, 229 Chapel St, Ottawa, Ontario K1N 7Y6, T613 5627820, www.croatiaemb.net

*Czech Republic*, V Pruhledu 9, 16200 Prague 6, T42 02 33340479.

*Denmark*, Dronningens Tvaergade 5/2, 1302 Copenhagen, T45 33 919095.

*Finland*, Eteläesplanadi 12, 0013 Helsinki, T358 9 6222232.

*France*, 39 Avenue Georges Mandel, 75116 Paris, T33 1 53700280.

*Germany*, Ahornstrasse 4, 10787 Berlin, T49 30 21915514.

*Greece*, Tzavela 4, Neo Psychico, 15451 Athens, T30 210 6777059.

*Hungary*, Munkacsy Mihaly utca 15, 1065B udapest, T36 1 3541315.

*Iceland*, Fosshals 27, 110 Reykjavik, T35 4 5674437.

*Ireland*, Adelaide Chambers, Peter St, Dublin 8, T353 1 4983018.

*Israel*, Canion Ramat Aviv, 40 Einstein St, PO Box 6-7, Tel Aviv 69101, T97 23 6438654.

*Italy*, Via Luigi Bodio 74/76, 00191 Roma, T39 06 36304630.

*Japan*, 3-3-10 Hiroo, Shibuya-ku, Tokyo 150-0012, T81 3 54693014.

*FYROM*, Mitropolit Teodosij Gologanov 59, 91000 Skopje, T389 2 127350.

*Netherlands*, Amalistraat 16, NL-2514 JC the Hague, T31 70 3623638.

*New Zealand* (Consulate), 131 Lincoln Road, Henderson PO Box 83-200, Edmonton, Auckland, T64 9 8365581.

*Norway*, Drammensveien 82, 0271 Oslo, T47 22 442233.

*Poland*, Ignacego Krasickiego 10, 02-628 Warsaw, T48 22 8441225.

*Portugal*, Rua D Lourenco de Almeida 24, 1400 Lisbon, T351 1 3021033.

*Romania*, Dr Burghelea 1, Sector 2, Bucharest, T40 21 3130457.

*Russia*, Korobeynikov pereulok 16/10, 119034 Moscow, T70 95 2013222.

*Serbia and Montenegro*, Kneza Miloša 62, 11000 Belgrade, T381 11 3610535.

*Slovakia*, Mišikova 21, Bratislava, T42 12 54433647.

*Slovenia*, Gruberjevo nabrežje 6, 1000 Ljubljana, T386 1 4256220.

*South Africa*, 1160 Church Street, 0083 Colbyn Pretoria, T27 12 3421206.

*Spain*, c/Claudio Coello 78/2, 28001 Madrid, T34 91 5776881.

*Sweden*, Birger Jarlsgatan 13/I, 11145 Stockholm, T46 8 6788310.

*Switzerland*, Thunstrasse 45, 3005 Bern, T41 31 3520275/9, www.croatia.ch

*UK*, 21 Conway St, W1T 6BN, London, T020 73872022, www.croatianembassy.co.uk

*USA*, 2343 Massachusetts Avenue NW, Washington DC, 20008-2853, T202 5885899, F5888936, www.croatiaemb.org

*See individual town and city directories for details of embassies in Croatia*

**Essentials**

You can bring into Croatia, free of duty, 200 cigarettes or 50 cigars, one litre of wine, one litre of spirits, 60 ml of perfume or 250 ml of toilet water. Valuable professional and technical equipment, such as expensive cameras and laptop computers, should be declared at the *carina* (customs) upon entry at the border – this way you can be sure to get them out again. Boats and yachts do not need to be reported, but you should have proof of ownership. Before launching a boat of over 3 m you should notify the harbour office, and you need a special permit for transporting boats on trailers of over 18 m. Pets need to have a recent vet's certificate. Foreign currency can be brought in and out of the country freely. When leaving Croatia, you can take up to 2000Kn.

**Customs**

No particular vaccinations are compulsory but some are recommended as a matter of course. See page 54 for details.

**Vaccinations**

## What to take

If you're visiting in summer bring light clothes and swimwear. Be sure to include a few long sleeved tops and trousers or skirts: even in July and August temperatures can drop significantly at night, and you'll need to have arms and legs reasonably covered for entering churches. Many of the medieval town centres are paved or cobbled, so make sure you have a pair of comfortable walking shoes, and if you're planning on serious hiking in the mountains, you'll need some good strong walking boots. Besides clothing, other useful travel items include a plug adaptor, a Swiss army knife, a torch (especially useful on the more remote islands), an alarm clock (for those early morning departures), pre-moistened wipes, sun cream, a small first-aid kit, toilet paper and a beach towel.

However, there's nothing worse than being loaded down with unnecessary luggage. Remember that just about anything you could possibly require will be available in local shops. If you're planning on renting a private room or apartment, essentials such as bedding, bath towels, soap and cooking utensils will be supplied by your host, and beach gear – roll-up mats, plastic sandals and snorkels – can be bought in all the main seaside resorts. If visiting in late autumn, winter or early spring, be prepared for rain and cold winds, plus the most unexpected warm sunny spells: hat, gloves and sunglasses.

# Money

Currency   The official currency is the Kuna (Kn), which is divided into 100 lipa. The word kuna means 'pine marten' (there's a picture of one on the coins), and refers back to medieval times when the animals' pelts were used as a way of exchange. When the Kuna was reintroduced as a form of currency in May 1994 (replacing the Croatian Dinar, which had replaced the Yugoslav Dinar in December 1991) it aroused protests from local Serbs, Jews and gypsies, as it was last used under the fascist Ustaše government that controlled Croatia during the Second World War from 1941 to 1945.

The Kuna is still not fully convertible so you can't buy it at your bank at home before arriving in Croatia, or sell it back when you return, though you can exchange small amounts at border points in neighbouring countries, eg the ferry port in Ancona and the train station in Trieste.

A limit of 2000Kn can be taken out of the country. Before leaving Croatia, you can exchange unused Kune for foreign currency in a bank, but officially you need a receipt showing where you got the Kune from in the first place.

The euro is the most readily accepted foreign currency and can be changed easily in banks and bureaux de change. By law in shops, restaurants, hotels etc, you should pay in Croatian Kuna.

Credit cards   Most hotels, restaurants and shops now accept the major credit cards (American
& ATMs   Express, Diners Club, MasterCard and Visa) though some of the smaller establishments take cash only. Until recently it was advisable to take plenty of liquid money when travelling to the islands, but now even the small towns in remote places, such as Komiža on the island of Vis, are equipped with an ATM. Don't rely on this completely however, as some towns literally have one ATM and if this is out of service, or money, and the bank is closed you will be caught short unless you have a reserve of cash.

Make sure you know the correct procedure if you lose your card – it's normally easier to call the 24-hour helpline of the issuer in your home country than to try to sort things out from here.

## Money matters

*Recent exchange rates in March 2003.*
| 11.45Kn | £1.00 |
| 7.60Kn | €1.00 |
| 7.10Kn | US$1.00 |

**Traveller's cheques** The safest way to carry money is in traveller's cheques, though with the rise in availability of ATMs and the ever-wider acceptance of credit cards, traveller's cheques are accepted less frequently and exchanged at less favourable rates.

**Banks & bureaux de change** Most towns and villages, even on the islands, have a *banka* (bank), which will generally be open Monday to Friday 0700-1900 and Saturday 0700-1300. All the main towns have a *mjenjačnica* (bureaux de change), which is normally located close to the bus or train station. In smaller towns it is often possible to change money at the post office or the local travel agents. Larger hotels will also change money, though their rates are normally pretty bad .

**Money transfers** If you are stranded in a remote place and need money urgently, the easiest way is to receive it is to have it wired via Western Union, www.westernunion.com, to the nearest post office. Hrvatska Pošta (Croatian Post) is an agent for Western Union and even the smallest post offices on the islands offer this service.

**Cost of living** The average monthly salary in Croatia is around 3000Kn (£260), roughly a third of an average salary earned in neighbouring Italy, but around double an average salary in Hungary. The average pension stands at about 1600Kn (£140), though almost 176,000 pensioners are said to receive less than 1000Kn (£87) per month. Given the fact that a recent survey showed that the monthly shopping basket for a family of four amounts to 5000Kn (£435), everyday life for local people is obviously not easy. However, Croatians dress well and are extremely proud and generous, so from the outside it's difficult to realize how big the current economic crisis is.

**Cost of travelling** Croatia is much more expensive than former Eastern bloc countries such as the Czech Republic and Hungary. Some Western Europeans come here with the idea that it's a cheap option and then complain about the prices, not taking into consideration the high quality of locally produced food and the fact that most manufactured goods are imported from Western Europe in the first place.

Hotels and restaurants are reasonably cheaper by EU standards, though prices rise significantly through July and August with an influx of Italian and German tourists. Private rooms are the best source of low-cost, clean comfortable accommodation – expect to pay anything between 200Kn and 600Kn for a double, depending on the place, time of year and furnishing. There are not many really top-class luxury hotels in Croatia – the rich and famous who turn up here are normally aboard a private yacht – even the most expensive hotels in Dubrovnik and Zagreb rarely charge over 1500Kn for a double room. In some fashionable resorts on the islands, such as Hvar Town on the island of Hvar, prices for everything (even a cup of coffee) are hiked up through July and August, but drop again in September.

Public transport – buses, trains and ferries – is very cheap by Western European standards. The exception is cabins on ferries and sleeping cars on the overnight trains, which cost around the same as a night in a lower to mid-range hotel, but are optional in any case.

Essentials

Essentials

# Getting there

## Air

International flights to Croatia usually arrive in Zagreb, Split or Dubrovnik, though through summer there are also lines direct to Pula, Zadar, Rijeka, and Bol on the island of Brač. Fares vary greatly from airline to airline and according to the time of year. To get the best deals avoid peak time travel (Monday mornings, Friday evenings and Bank Holidays) when tickets are at the most expensive. Generally cheaper flights depart mid-morning or mid-afternoon. Check out the following websites for cheap deals: www.bargainflights.com; www.flynow.com; www.lastminute.co.uk; www.statravel.co.uk

From the UK & Europe
Through winter, *Croatia Airlines*, www.croatiaairlines.hr, T020 85630022, offers direct flights from London Heathrow and London Gatwick to Zagreb, Split and Dubrovnik. Flights cost from £260-280 throughout the year. It is advisable to book early during the summer months as availability is limited. Approximate flight time from London to Zagreb is 2½ hours. In summer, there are additional flights from Heathrow to Pula, Zadar and Rijeka. Flight time is approximately two hours. In addition, through summer flights are available from Manchester to Zagreb, Split, Dubrovnik and Pula. From the UK, the cheapest (but not the most direct) way to get to Croatia is with *Ryanair*, www.ryanair.com, taking a bargain flight to Trieste, Venice, Treviso, Ancona and Pescara in neighbouring Italy, and then continuing your journey either by bus, train or ferry. See below for details of journey times and costs.

*Croatia Airlines* offer direct flights to Zagreb from Amsterdam, Barcelona, Berlin, Brussels, Copenhagen, Dusseldorf, Frankfurt, Gothenburg, Istanbul, Madrid, Moscow, Mostar, Munich, Paris, Prague, Rome, Sarajevo, Skopje, Stockholm, Stuttgart, Tel Aviv, Warsaw, Vienna and Zurich. The same company also offers direct flights to Split and Dubrovnik from Amsterdam, Berlin, Brussels, Dusseldorf, Frankfurt, Istanbul, Ljubljana, Munich, Paris, Prague, Rome, Skopje, Tel Aviv, Warsaw, Vienna and Zurich.

From North America, New Zealand & Australia
There are no direct lines from Australia, Canada, New Zealand, South Africa or the US to Croatia. For *Croatia Airlines* (Sales Agents) in the USA contact T1 973 8843401, Toll Free Go-Croatia T888 4627628, in Australia T61 3 96999355 and New Zealand T64 9 8387700. The most common routes are via Rome, Frankfurt, Paris or London. Flight times and prices vary enormously depending on the route, availability etc.

## Road

Car
There are good road links to Croatia from the neighbouring countries of Slovenia, Hungary, Bosnia Herzegovina, and Serbia and Montenegro. Visitors arriving from Italy or Austria will pass through Slovenia.

Bus
There are regular international buses to Croatia from major towns in Italy, Slovenia, Hungary, Austria, Germany, Bosnia Herzegovina, Serbia and Montenegro, and the Former-Yugoslav Republic of Macedonia. Buses depart from Trieste (Italy) to Rijeka taking 2½ hours and costing €7.30 one way. Buses also depart from Trieste for Pula taking 3¾ hours and costing €11.70 one way.

Slightly less frequent services (once or twice a week) run from France, Belgium, the Netherlands, Great Britain, Switzerland, Slovakia and the Czech Republic. *Eurolines*, T08705 808080, www.eurolines.com, run a direct weekly service from London Victoria

## Croatia Airlines

◀

**Zagreb**, Savska 41, T385 1 6160066.
**Split**, Obala Hrvatskog Narodnog
Perporoda 9, T385 21 362055.
**Dubrovnik**, Brslaje 9, T385 20 413776.
**Pula**, Ulica Carrarina 8, T385 52 218909.

**Rijeka**, Trg Republike Hrvatske 9, T385 51
330207.
**Zadar**, Poljana Natka Nodila 7, T385 23
250101.

Essentials

to Zagreb (journey time 31 hours, return ticket £133). The bus leaves London at 2200
and arrives in Zagreb at 0500 two days later, having passed through Paris and Frankfurt, where occasionally it is necessary to change. From Zagreb it continues south to
Split in Central Dalmatia, stopping at Šibenik en route. If you're heading for Istria, you'll
need to change in Zagreb. With two nights on the road, the journey is pretty exhausting and you'll probably need another day to recuperate. *Eurolines* agent in Croatia is
the Rijeka-based company **Autotrans**, www.autotrans.hr

## Sea

Croatia is well connected to Italy by overnight ferry lines the year through, and by fast
daytime catamarans during summer. Services increased through Summer 2002 as
tourism picked up, and the number of companies operating and the routes covered
could expand further in Summer 2003.

**Ferry**
*Tickets can be
purchased in the port
of departure, though
through summer and
over Easter cabins may
be fully booked*

**From Italy to Dalmatia** The main route is Ancona-Split, though Ancona-Zadar,
Bari-Dubrovnik and Pescara-Split are possible options. During high season, some ser-
vices call en route at the more popular islands such as Hvar and Korčula a couple of
times a week, though for exact information you should check with the companies
(websites are not totally reliable as schedules are liable to last minute alterations).
*Jadrolinija* run regular overnight services Ancona-Split, Ancona-Zadar and Dubrovnik-
Bari. *SEM* and *Adriatica* also cover the line Ancona-Split. During summer, both
*Jadrolinija* and *SEM* sail Ancona-Split every evening, but through winter services are
slightly reduced.

Exact times vary from day to day and season to season, but in general ferries leave
Ancona at 2100 to arrive in Split at 0700, then depart from Split at 2100 to arrive in
Ancona at 0700. Others leave Ancona at 2200 to arrive in Zadar at 0600, then leave
Zadar at 2300 to return to Ancona at 0700. The ferry from Bari normally leaves at 2200
to arrive in Dubrovnik at 0600, and leaves Dubrovnik at 2300 to arrive in Bari at 0800.

Through high season, expect to pay around €80 for a return ticket without a cabin
(many people sleep rough on the deck), or €145 for a return ticket with a bed in a double
cabin. A return ticket for a car is an extra €95, and bicycles travel free of charge.

**From Italy and Slovenia to Istria** During summer it is possible to arrive in Istria by
boat from either northern Italy or Slovenia. *Adriatica* operate the Linea della Costa
Istriana, running from Trieste to Brijuni National Park, stopping at Grado and Rovinj
en route. The total journey takes just over four hours and costs €19.40 one-way (foot
passengers only). *Lošinjska Plovidba* run a line from Koper (in Slovenia) to Zadar, stopping at Pula, Unije, Mali Lošinj and Silba en route. This journey takes 14 hours and costs
€23 one-way (foot passengers) and €67 one-way (with a car).

The following companies have services: *Adriatica*, Venice, Italy, T39 041 781861
www.adriatica.it *Jadrolinija*, Rijeka, Croatia, T385 51 666111, www.jadrolinija.hr
*Lošinjska Plovidba*, Mali Lošinj, Croatia, T385 51 231524, www.losinjska-plovidba.hr *Mia
Tours*, Zadar, Croatia, T385 23 254300, www.miatours.hr *SANMAR*, Pescara, Italy, T39

085 65247, www.sanmar.it *SEM*, Split, Croatia, T385 21 338292, www.sem-marina.hr *SNAV*, Naples, Italy, T39 081 7612348, www.snavali.com

Catamaran **From Italy to Dalmatia** During summer (roughly mid-June to late September), fast daytime catamarans run between Italy and Croatia. *SNAV* operate a daily catamaran service (taking passengers and vehicles), leaving Ancona at 1100 to arrive in Split at 1500, then departing from Split at 1700 to return to Ancona at 2100. Expect to pay €78.50 one-way. The same company also operates a service from Pescara, stopping at various places on the islands, such as Stari Grad (on Hvar), Vela Luka (on Korčula) and Bol (on Brač), on certain days of the week, though for exact details you should check with the ticket office.

Hydrofoil **From Italy to Dalmatia** *SANMAR* run a Pescara-Split hydrofoil (passenger only, no vehicles), calling at Bol (on Brač), Vela Luka (on Korčula), Hvar Town (on Hvar) and Vis Town (on Vis) on certain days, for exact details check with the ticket office. Expect to pay €114 for a one-way ticket and €180 for a return ticket in high season. *Mia Tours* run an Ancona-Zadar hydrofoil (passenger only, no vehicles), calling at Božava (on Dugi Otok) on certain days. Departure time from Ancona varies though it's normally in the late afternoon, and the direct run to Zadar takes three hours. Expect to pay €70 for a one-way ticket and €120 for a return ticket in high season.

## Train

Regular daily international trains run direct to Zagreb from Italy (Venice, 6½ hours), Slovenia (Ljubljana, 2½ hours), Austria (Vienna, 6½ hours), Hungary (Budapest, 6½ hours), Germany (Munich, 8½ hours) and Serbia (Belgrade, 6½ hours).

From the UK The cheapest and fastest route is London-Paris-Venice-Zagreb, taking Eurostar through the Channel Tunnel. The entire journey takes about 39 hours and requires two overnight trains. Depart from London at 1353 to arrive in Paris at 1753; leave Paris at 2001 to arrive in Venice at 0825, and finally depart from Venice at 2120 to arrive in Zagreb at 0507. The best return fare for this journey totals £328.00, taking a 'Leisure Apex 14' ticket London-Paris (which must be booked at least 14 days in advance, is non refundable and subject to availability), and a bed in a six-berth couchette for both the Paris-Venice and Venice-Zagreb overnight hauls. For further details or information about alternative routes, contact *Rail Europe*, T08705 848848, www.raileurope.co.uk

*The Eurail pass is not valid in Croatia* **Inter Rail pass** The Inter Rail pass offers unlimited second class train travel in 29 countries throughout Europe and parts of North Africa. The entire area has been divided into eight zones: Croatia is in Zone D, together with Hungary, Slovakia, the Czech Republic and Poland. If you are 26 or under, an Inter Rail pass for one zone costs £125 for 12 days or £149 for 22 days, and an open pass for all 29 participant countries £265. If you are over 26, a 12-day pass for one zone costs £182, a 22-day pass for one zone £219, and an open pass for all countries £379. For further details check out the website, www.interrailnet.com

# Touching down

## Airport information

Croatia's main airports are Zagreb (ZAG), Split (SPU) and Dubrovnik (DBV). Flights from most European capital cities land in **Zagreb Airport**, T01 6265222, www.tel.hr/

## Touching down

◀

*Opening hours*  *Open-air markets normally work Monday-Saturday 0700-1300 and Sunday 0700-1100. General stores tend to stay open all day Monday-Friday 0700-2000 and in most towns at least one will be open Sunday 0700-1100. Clothes shops and bookshops are normally open Monday-Friday 0900-1300 and 1700-1930 and Saturday 0900-1300. Shops may work extended hours in tourist areas during summer.*

*Official time*  *Croatia is one hour ahead of GMT.*
*Electricity*  *The electric current is 220 volts AC, 50Hz. Plugs have two round pins (as in the rest of continental Europe). Pack an adaptor for things you bring from home.*
*Weights and measures*  *Weights and measures are metric.*
*Emergencies*  *Police 92; Fire brigade 93; Ambulance 94; Road assistance 987.*

Essentials

zagreb-airport There is no tourist office here, but the travel agency *Atlas*, T01 4562248, is located in the passenger terminal building and works daily 0700-1830. There are two banks, *Zagrebačka banka*, T01 4562414, and *Privredna banka*, T01 4562032, both of which work daily 0900-2100 and are located in the landside transit area of the Passenger Terminal Building. The post office is next to the banks and works the same hours. Other facilities include a duty-free shop, a newsagents, and a bar and restaurant. All the major international rent-a-car companies have bases here (*Avis*, *Budget* and *Hertz*). An airport bus makes regular runs between the airport and the city centre (see page 58 for further details). Taxis are also available – expect to pay 150-200Kn over the same route.

It's also possible to take flights from most European capital cities to Split Airport, T021 203171, www.split-airport.hr There is no tourist office in the airport. In the passenger terminal area you will find *Splitska banka*, a bank working daily 0600-1300 and 1400-2100. Close by, the post office works 0700-2100 daily through peak season, and Monday-Friday 0700-2000 and Saturday 0700-1700 during the rest of the year. Other facilities include a duty-free shop, a newsagents, and a bar and restaurant. The international rent-a-car companies *Avis*, *Budget* and *Hertz* all have bases here. An airport bus makes regular runs between the airport and the city centre (see page 194 for further details). Taxis are also readily available.

Many European capital cities also have direct flights to Dubrovnik Airport, T020 773377, www.airport-dubrovnik.hr There is no tourist office here, but you will find the travel agency *Atlas*, T020 773383. Airport facilities include a bank, a post office, a duty-free shop, a bar and *Avis*, *Budget* and *Hertz* car hire offices. An airport bus makes regular runs between the airport and the city centre (see page 266 for further details). Taxis are also readily available.

**Pula Airport** (PUY; T052 530105) and **Zadar Airport** (ZAD; T023 205800) also have flights to and from several European capitals the year round, though the number of destinations and frequency of flights is reduced in winter. **Rijeka Airport** (RJK; T051 842040), **Brač Airport** (BWK; T021 648615) and **Osijek Airport** (OSI; T031 514400) all work in summer only, and offer restricted timetables to suit the mainsteam tourist traffic.

Airport tax for flights to and from Croatia is included in the price of the ticket.      Airport tax

## Tourist information

All the major cities and most smaller towns along the coast and on the islands have a *turistički ured* (tourist office). Their addresses and telephone numbers can be found in the relevant sections of this book. Opening hours vary depending on the time of year, with

Essentials

# ▶ How big is your footprint?

**Fires**   During summer, especially along the coast, when the vegetation is bone dry, there is a constant danger of forest fire. On no account at all throw away glowing cigarette stubs, and do not light fires anywhere except in purpose-built barbecues.

**Hiking paths**   Leave paths as you find them. If you get lost do not tramp through other people's vineyards and olive groves unnecessarily.

**Beaches**   In spring it may be warm enough to sunbathe, or even swim, but many beaches will be strewn with waste. This has not been dumped intentionally, but has been washed up by the sea currents, and is usually cleaned up by locals once the holiday season gets underway. Do not leave picnic litter on beaches, no matter what state they are in when you arrive.

**Rubbish**   Getting rid of rubbish on the islands is a major problem, and on some of the tinier, more remote islands, people are expected to take their litter back to the mainland by ferry when they leave. If there are no bins in sight, check whether this is the correct procedure.

**Cars**   Try to avoid taking a car to the islands – if you really want to appreciate nature to its fullest, walk or cycle instead. Alternatively, use public transport, which is cheap and (relatively) efficient, and in any case gives you a chance to meet the locals.

**National parks**   Entrance fees are payable to national parks. Although they may seem steep, this money goes towards the upkeep of the natural environment, and is therefore money well spent.

**Date shells**   Known in Croatian as prstaci (and in Italian as datteri), date shells are similar to mussels but have a more refined flavour. There is a national campaign against collecting and eating them, as they grow inside rocks along the coast, and can only be obtained by smashing open the rocks, which leads to the erosion of the coast. By law restaurants are not allowed to sell them: although they will not be listed on menus, they may be on offer, at a price. However, the environmental damage caused in collecting them far outweighs the pleasure of eating them.

many of the smaller offices working mornings only through winter. All tourist offices provide information about local hotels, sports facilities and public transport, and most can also help you find self-catering accommodation. The larger ones provide maps and sightseeing information. See page 21 for addresses tourist boards overseas.

## Local customs and laws

Clothing   For business, like anywhere else, appearance counts: a smart suit, with a tie for men, or stylish accessories for women. In all other situations you can get away with casual wear, though scanty clothing is frowned upon in churches – cover your legs and shoulders before entering, even if it's just for a quick peek at the interior. Very few restaurants or nightclubs demand a shirt and tie, but remember that Croatians, and especially Dalmatians, are quite style conscious, so you may receive some withering looks if you turn up in a smart restaurant in shorts and a grubby T-shirt.

   Croatia is well known for its nudist beaches, which are marked 'FKK' (from the German, Freie Kunst und Kulture). In secluded bays it's also acceptable to bare all, but on crowded family beaches you should definitely wear swimming trunks or bikini bottoms. At beachside bars and eateries it's normally acceptable to sit at a table in a swimsuit, but never, ever topless.

A formal greeting takes the form of a handshake – social kissing is reserved for friends and family. Croatians are generally friendly and hospitable, though they are not ones for false smiles: shop assistants can be a little dour, and waiters and waitresses in over-crowded bars and restaurants are quite open about displaying exasperation.

Conduct

People here like to discuss politics and religion, but following the recent war there are a few thorny issues that should be treated with care. The extradition of war criminals remains a matter of concern, as does the return of people who were displaced during the 1990's. A lot of Croats have heart-rending stories to tell, but remember that many families have mixed marriages somewhere down the line, so do not be too blatant about displaying personal views about who was right and who was wrong.

It's usual to 'clink' glasses when making a toast and you should look the person you're clinking with straight in the eyes so as not to seem evasive. Croatians often eat cheese at the beginning of a meal as an appetizer rather than at the end, so if you order everything at once the cheese will probably arrive first. In informal eateries along the coast, it is quite normal for people to eat barbecued fish with their hands, which is actually far more practical than struggling with a knife and fork.

Eating

Croatians are very proud and when they go out to eat it's a matter of 'no expense spared'. They therefore find it very odd when a table of foreigners divides up a bill pro-portionally according to who has eaten what – stinginess is regarded very badly here. Worse still, on some menus the basic cover charge is listed as *kruh* (bread). Occasionally foreign visitors dispute this tiny sum at the end of the meal, telling their waiter or waitress they never touched the bread. Such penny-pinching only serves to give foreigners a bad name, especially if they come from countries where the average monthly salary is several times more than that of a Croatian.

Tips are not included in bills. At the end of a good meal at a restaurant it is customary to leave 10% extra if you were satisfied with the service, but it is not normal to tip waiters and waitresses in bars. There are no particular rules regarding taxis.

Tipping

Historically, religion has always been the main defining factor between Croats and Serbs: the former adhering to the Roman Catholic faith, the latter to the Eastern Orthodox church. Religion therefore forms an important factor in ethnic identity – during the recent war many Croats underwent hasty baptisms, and the numbers attending church soared. Also during the 1990's, most Orthodox churches ceased to function, but today in larger cities such as Zagreb, Rijeka, Zadar and Dubrovnik, and in many smaller towns which once had a large Serb population, they are working once more. Many Croats (even tourist guides) refuse to enter them, though visitors are quite welcome and if the doors are open you can freely take a look inside.

Religion

Prohibitions are the same as for any other European country. Penalties for the possession, use, or trafficking of illegal drugs (from marijuana to heroin) are strict, and convicted offenders can expect prison sentences and hefty fines. The carrying of firearms is also banned.

Prohibitions

## Responsible tourism

Fortunately Croatian tourism has not been commercialized to the extent of that in Greece and Spain, and most people who come here on holiday are interested in more than drinking cheap beer and lounging by a pool.

Package tourism to the region reached its peak during the 1970's and 1980's, when large state-owned resorts were constructed along the Adriatic Coast. As the boom appeared unstoppable, many locals who had traditionally lived from wine making and

Essentials

the production of olive oil abandoned their fields and invested in building concrete seaside villas with rooms and apartments to let to foreign visitors. Easy money indeed, but in many families an entire generation consequently lost the know-how of cultivating grapes and olives. Fortunately today things are changing, and with agrotourism slowly but surely catching on, Croatians are re-evaluating the small scale production of traditional local specialities: wine, various types of *rakija*, olive oil and cheeses.

The potential for agrotourism is enormous, though to date it's only really taken off in Istria, where the tourist board have laid down certain rules, requiring farms that register themselves under this category to be built of traditional materials, ie natural stone. Grants are also becoming available, through various European organizations, for the restoration of old farm buildings and diversification into agrotourism and ecotourism.

## Safety

Despite the negative image created by the war, Croatia has a lower crime rate than most other European countries. Foreigners do not appear to be singled out, though as in any other country, crimes such as pickpocketing are more likely to occur in crowded public spaces such as bus or train stations. The loss or theft of a passport should be reported immediately to the local police and your nearest embassy or consulate.

Rare cases of violent crime are usually targeted at specific persons or property as a result of organized criminal activity or actions prompted by ethnic tensions left over from the war for independence.

Although military action connected to the war ended in 1995, the problem of land mines, mostly along the former confrontation lines in eastern Slavonia and the Krajina, remains. De-mining is not complete: if you are passing through such areas, exercise caution and do not stray from known safe roads and paths.

# Where to stay

Along the coast private accommodation, either in a rented room or apartment, is the best choice in terms of coast, facilities and insight into the way the locals live. However, if you feel like splashing out and being pampered here and there, the hotels listed in this guide have been selected fro their authentic atmosphere and central location.

There aren't any central websites listing private accommodation but lcoal tourist offices often have details and their websites are listed throughout the book.

Hotels  Croatian tourism dates back to the late 19th century when the region was under Austro-Hungary and so along the coast you'll find a number of Vienna Secession-style hotels built for the Central European aristocracy of the time, the best examples being in Opatija.

However, during the tourist boom of the 1970's and 1980's, many of the older hotels were neglected in favour of large modern complexes, which sprung up in popular resorts such as Poreč, Rovinj, Bol, Hvar Town, Korčula Town and Dubrovnik. Although they tend to be vast and somewhat impersonal, these socialist-era hotels are equipped with excellent sports facilities, and generally lie overlooking the sea, discreetly hidden by careful landscaping, a short walk from the centre of town.

The third, and most recent, breed of hotel are the small, private, family-run establishments, often in refurbished town houses, which have opened over the last decade, the best examples being in Pula.

All hotels are officially graded by the Ministry of Tourism into five categories: 5-star, luxury; 4-star, deluxe; 3-star, first class; 2-star, moderate and 1-star, budget. Classified hotels are listed on the Croatian National Tourist Board website, www.croatia.hr, under their respective regions.

## A bed for the night

◀

Essentials

*Accommodation price codes in this book are based on the cost per person for two people sharing a double room with an en-suite bathroom during the high season with breakfast. Be aware that many hotels offer substantial discounts during low season. Here is an idea of what to expect at each level:*

***LL-L*** *(over 700Kn)  These are the top notch hotels, only existing in Zagreb and Dubrovnik. They should offer all the pampering extras such as sauna and massage, business facilities (including internet), several bars and restaurants. Credit cards are always accepted and they will usually change foreign currency for you.*

***AL-A*** *(500-700Kn)  This category includes some of the best recently refurbished hotels, generally offering comfortable, tastefully furnished rooms with all*

*modcons. You can expect a generous breakfast and good dining facilities. Credit cards are always accepted.*

***B-D*** *(150-400Kn)  These are the average-priced hotels, which vary greatly in quality, but all rooms should have an en-suite bathroom, TV and telephone, and most also have a minibar. Generally there is a hotel restaurant, but the standard of the food is not guaranteed. Credit cards are normally accepted.*

***E-G*** *(150Kn and under)  This category includes anything from 'B&B' type accommodation to youth hostels. At this level you may be down to a shared bathroom on the corridor, and although most supply towels, you might need to bring your own soap. Very few have restaurants, and you will probably have to pay in cash.*

When referring to price lists, you will find that some hotels list half-board and full-board only. Simple 'bed and breakfast' works out only very slightly cheaper than half-board, but is recommended as by and large hotel restaurants lack atmosphere, and the standard of the food unfortunately reflects the savings made in order to be able to offer cheap package deals. You are far better eating out in local restaurants at night, and snacking or picnicking at lunchtime.

Last but not least, if you are staying on the coast it is well worth asking for a room with a sea view (most of which have balconies): it may cost a little more, but makes all the difference when you wake up in the morning.

Along the coast you will find a plethora of families offering *sobe* (rooms) and *apartmani* (apartments) for rent, usually with en-suite bathrooms and simple self-catering facilities provided (see page 45). These can be in anything from quaint, old stone cottages with gardens, to modern concrete block three-storey houses with spacious balconies. Hosts are generally welcoming and hospitable, and many visitors find a place they like and then return each summer. Local tourist offices and travel agents have lists of recognized establishments and can arrange bookings for you. In busy areas, you'll also find people waiting for travellers at the ferry ports and bus stations, and offering rooms by word of mouth, but in this case you're not guaranteed to find the best standards.

Prices vary enormously depending on location and season, but you can expect to pay anything from 100-180Kn (€15-25) per person per day for a double room with an en-suite bathroom, and anything from 300-600Kn (€42-84) per day for a four-person apartment with a kitchen and dining area. Note that there is normally a 30% surcharge for stays of less than three nights.

British-based operators specializing in private accommodation in Croatia include Interhome Ltd, 383 Richmond Rd, Twickenham, TW1 2EF, T020 88911294,

**Private accommodation**

www.interhome.co.uk, who have a database of almost 500 private homes to let on a weekly basis in Croatia, and *Croatian Villas Ltd*, 102 Maidstone Rd, London N11 2JP, T020 83689978, www.croatianvillas.com, who specialize in quality villas and apartments for holiday rentals in top Croatian resorts.

So-called **'Robinson Crusoe' style accommodation** started out on the Kornati islands, though it is gradually spreading to other isolated locations. As the term implies this type of accommodation consists of a simple stone cottage, basically furnished and offering minimum modern comforts: gas lighting and water from a well. The beauty of these cottages lies in their detachment from the rest of the world – they are normally found on small unpopulated islands with no regular ferry links to the mainland, no shops, and no cars. They are generally for rent on a weekly basis, and transport to them is arranged by the agencies responsible for letting them. Croatian agencies specializing in Robinson cottages include *Coronata*, Žrtava Ratova 17, Murter, T385 22 435089, www.coronata.hr, and *Kornat Turist*, Hrvatskih vladara 2, Murter, T385 22 435854/5, www.kornatturist.hr  The British-based operator *Croatia for Travellers*, 63 Therberton St, London N1 0QY, T020 72264460, www.croatiafortravellers.co.uk, can also book a cottage for you.

Another novel and highly popular form of accommodation is the **lighthouse**. Along the Croatian coast, there are now 11 carefully restored lighthouses with apartments to rent on a weekly basis. Nine of these are on islands (you will be taken there and brought back by boat), and three on peninsulas along the mainland coast. In Istria, these include Savudrija (Umag), Rt Zub (Novigrad), Sv Ivan (Rovinj) and Porer (Pula), while in Dalmatia there are Prišnjak (Murter), Sv Petar (Makarska), Palagruža (Vis), Pločica (Vela Luka), Sušac (Lastovo), Struga (Lastovo) and Sv Andrija (Elafiti). Most lighthouses have one or two apartments sleeping anything from two to eight people, and several are still home to a resident lighthouse keeper. However, you can be sure of extreme isolation and minimum contact with the outside world, as most of them are located on lonely islets far out to sea. Each apartment has electricity, running water, TV and a fully equipped kitchen. Bed linen and blankets are provided, but be sure to take a week's provisions as there will be no chance of shopping once you are there, unless you manage to make a special agreement with local fishermen or the lighthouse keeper. Prices vary greatly depending on the size of the apartment, location and season, but as an indicator the cost of renting a four-person apartment in the lighthouse of Sv Ivan, near Rovinj, for one week, are as follows: July to August 6285Kn (€880); June and September 5040Kn (€706) and during the rest of the year 3810Kn (€533). However, as this has become a hugely popular alternative, be sure to book several months in advance. For further details contact *Adriatica Net*, Selska 34, Zagreb, T385 1 3644461, www.adriatica.net (online booking service).

**Agrotourism**  An increasingly popular option is so-called agrotourism: farmhouses offering overnight accommodation and home cooking. This is a great solution for families with young children, as exploring the farm and getting to know the farm animals is guaranteed to go down well with kids. To date, the idea has only really taken off in Istria, but the potential is enormous.

Most of these establishments are off-the-beaten track (you normally need a car to reach them) and offer bed and breakfast deals in simply furnished rooms with en-suite bathrooms. Many also have a restaurant area, generally done out in rustic style, serving authentic local dishes (generally far superior to the food served in commercial restaurants), along with their own wine, cheese and olive oil. Some of the larger agrotourism centres also offer a range of sporting activities such as horse riding and mountain biking.

Prices vary greatly depending on the type of room, the location and season, but expect to pay anything from 180-320Kn (€25-45) per person per day for a double room (with an en-suite bathroom) with breakfast in August.

For a list of farms and rural homes offering overnight accommodation and meals in Istria, check out, www.istra.com/agroturizam

**Camping**

The sunny, dry climate and unspoilt nature make Croatia an ideal place for camping. Of the 127 registered campsites, about 90% are on the mainland coast or on the islands, many backed by pinewoods overlooking the sea. Most operate from early-May to early-October, are well run and offer basic facilities such as showers and WC's and a small bar, while the larger ones may include restaurants and extensive sports facilities, such as scuba diving courses and mountain bike rentals. The most developed regions in terms of capacity and facilities provided are Istria and Kvarner, while Dalmatia is in many ways more attractive thanks to its rugged, untamed natural beauty. As in other European countries, camping outside of designated areas is prohibited.

For further information contact **Kamping Udruženje Hrvatske** (Croatian Camping Union), Pionirska 1, Poreč, T052 451324 and 451292, www.camping.hr   This excellent website lists all official campsites, complete with contact details, facilities and prices. Naturist campsites are also listed and marked 'FKK'.

**Naturist camps**
*See also page 48*

Naked bathing was first pioneered in Croatia in the early 20th century, and Europe's first naturist camp ground opened here in 1953. Today there are 20 naturist campsites, almost all along the coast and on the islands, attracting visitors from Germany, Austria, the Netherlands, Italy and Slovenia, as well as other countries around the world. Europe's largest naturist camp, Koversada, is in Istria, and can provide accommodation for up to 7,000 visitors.

For more information about naturism in Croatia, including a list of naturist camps accompanied by comments from people who have stayed at them, check out the *Croatia Naturally* website, www.cronatur.hr

**Youth hostels**

There are youth hostels in Pula, Zagreb, Punat and Krk (both on the island of Krk), Veli Lošinj (on the island of Lošinj), Zadar and Dubrovnik. These provide basic but comfortable dormitory style overnight accommodation (expect to pay around 70Kn per person per night), and some offer the option of half or full board. The Zagreb hostel has been omitted from this book as it is in a very poor state of repair and is due to close for refurbishment, but a good alternative during summer is renting a room in the Zagreb University student halls of residence, see page 68. The old hostel in Šibenik has closed and looks unlikely to reopen.

For further information about hostels contact the **Hrvatski Ferijalni i Hostelski Savez** (Croatian Youth Hostel Association), Savska 5, 10000 Zagreb, T/F 01 4829294/6, www.hfhs.hr

# Getting around

## Air

If you plan a short stay, the fastest way to move quickly from city to city is obviously to fly. The airports, with the exception of Rijeka, are all close to the town centres adding little to the journey time. In summer 2002, *Croatia Airlines*, www.croatiaairlines.hr, offered the following internal flights from the capital: Zagreb to Split (45 minutes); Zagreb to Dubrovnik (50 minutes); Zagreb to Pula (40 minutes); Zagreb to Zadar (50 minutes); Zagreb to Rijeka (35 minutes); Zagreb to Bol (Bra č) (one hour).

Prices for one-way, midday, midweek flights in winter 2002-2003 were quoted Zagreb-Split 244Kn and Zagreb-Dubrovnik 439Kn. However, prices vary greatly depending on season, time of day and availability.

## Road

Croatia has an extensive road network with frequent bus services. There are limited stretches of motorway, although new routes are currently under construction. Tolls are payable on the following roads: Zagreb-Karlovac, Zagreb-Krapina, Varaždin-Čakovec and Zagreb-Slavonski Brod, as well as for passage through the Učka tunnel and over Krk Bridge.

The coastal road from Rijeka to Dubrovnik offers truly stunning views over the sea, but is twisty and tiring, and gets notoriously slippery after rain. The inland road from Zagreb to Dalmatia, passing through Lika, is occasionally blocked by snow during winter, and Maslenica bridge (north of Zadar) and Krk bridge (from the mainland to the island of Krk) are apt to short closures when the bura (northeast) wind is very strong. On the islands roads tend to be narrow and less well maintained.

**Bus** Buses tend to be slightly faster and marginally more expensive than trains, though they are generally less comfortable. While train services are limited, by using the bus you can get from any major city to the most remote village, albeit having to change several times en route. There are numerous private companies, each operating on their own terms, so there's no such thing as an unlimited travel pass. Prices and quality of buses vary from company to company, and a return ticket is sometimes, but not always, cheaper than two one-way tickets. Expect to pay around 130Kn for a one-way ticket Zagreb-Split (seven hours), or 120Kn for a one-way ticket Zagreb-Pula (5½ hours). For national information contact (Zagreb Bus Station), T060 313333, www.akz.hr (buses to and from Zagreb only).

**Car** Having a car obviously makes you more independent so you can plan your itinerary more freely. However, it also creates various problems that one would not encounter if using public transport. Medieval walled cities such as Split and Dubrovnik are traffic free so you'll have to park outside the walls – even then, finding a place can be difficult as the more central parking spots are reserved for residents with permits. Having a car can also make ferry transfers to the islands extremely problematic: during high season be prepared to sit in queues for hours on end to get a place on the boat (there is no reservation system for vehicles: you buy a ticket and then it is a case of first come, first aboard).

**Rules and regulations** Croatians drive on the right. A national and international driving licence is required and you should also have a passport or identity card close at hand. If you are from outside the EU, and entering Croatia with your own vehicle, you will need a Green Card. The maximum legal alcohol to blood ratio is 0.05%.

**Speed limits** Maximum speeds are 50 kph (30 mph) in towns; 80 kph (50 mph) out of town; and 130 kph (80 mph) on motorways. Heavy fines are imposed for exceeding these limits.

**Motoring organizations** Hrvatska Autoclub (Croatian Automobile Club) provides a 24-hour breakdown service, T987 (staffed by multi-lingual operators), www.hak.hr

**Car hire** Expect to pay in the region of 370Kn per day for a small car such as a Fiat Uno 45 SL; 480Kn for a VW Polo 1.0L or 580Kn for a Fiat Punto. Payments can be made by credit card, and your credit card number will be taken in lieu of a deposit. Most companies require drivers to be 21 or over. Car hire companies include *Avis*, www.avis.hr; *Budget*, www.budget.hr; *Hertz*, www.hertz.hr; and *Sixt*, www.sixt.hr

**Petrol stations**  Normally open daily 0700-1800, and often until 2200 in summer. The larger cities and major international roads have 24-hour petrol stations.

On the smaller islands where public transport is limited, it is quite normal for drivers to   **Hitching** stop and offer a lift to someone who is walking, even if they are not thumbing a lift.

## Sea

The Croatian Adriatic has 66 inhabited islands, many of which can be reached by ferry.   **Ferries** There are regular connections between the mainland ports and the major islands: Rijeka serves Rab; Zadar serves Dugi Otok; Split serves Šolta, Brač, Hvar, Vis, Korčula and Latovo, and Dubrovnik serves the Elafiti islands and Mljet. Prices are reasonable as the state-owned ferry company *Jadrolinija* has been subsidized by the government in an attempt to slow down depopulation of islands. Timetables are normally geared towards the islanders, enabling them to work or attend school on the mainland. In low season there may be only one boat per day, leaving the island in the early morning and returning in the early evening. This can be inconvenient for brief visits in the opposite direction, as visitors from the mainland have to take the evening ferry to the island, stay a couple of nights, and return home in the early morning.

As well as connecting the islands, *Jadrolinija* operates an overnight coastal service (with cabins available) running from Rijeka to Dubrovnik, stopping at Zadar, Split, Stari Grad (island of Hvar), Korčula and Sobra (island of Mljet) en route.

*Jadrolinija* also runs a number of catamaran services between the mainland and the   **Catamaran** islands. On the plus side these are much faster than ferries, while on the minus side they are slightly more expensive, do not take cars and do not allow passengers on the deck.

Sample prices are: Rijeka-Split by ferry, one-way, passenger 142Kn, car 382Kn; Rijeka-   **Prices** Rab Town by catamaran, one way 40Kn (passengers only); Split-Stari Grad (Hvar) by ferry, one way, passenger 27Kn, car 180Kn; Dubrovnik-Sobra (Mljet) by ferry, one way, passenger 27Kn, car 180Kn. There is no discount on return tickets.

Besides *Jadrolinija*, a number of smaller local companies run ferries and catamarans   **Companies** on certain routes. *Lošinjska Plovidba*, based in Mali Lošinj on the island of Lošinj in Kvarner, operates a summer service from Pula to Zadar, stopping at Unije, Mali Lošinj and Silba en route. *Mediteranska Plovidba*, based in Korčula Town on the island of Korčula in South Dalmatia, run a daily passenger service from Korčula Town to Orebić, and a summer service from Korčula Town to Drvenik on the mainland, just south of

Makarska. *Rapska Plovidba*, based in Rab Town on the island of Rab in Kvarner, run regular daily ferry services from Mišnjak on the island of Rab to Jablanac on the mainland, and between Rab Town and Lun on the island of Pag. *SEM*, based in Split in Central Dalmatia, operates daily catamarans from Split to the islands of Vis and Šolta. Through summer, *SEM* also organizes a number of excursions by catamaran to surrounding islands.

*Jadrolinija*, Rijeka-based head office, T051 666111, www.jadrolinija.hr UK agent *Dalmatian and Istrian Travel*, T44 20 87495255. *Jadrolinija* offices along the coast and on the islands: Rijeka, T051 666100; Mali Lošinj, T051 231765; Zadar, T023 254800; Brbinj, T023 378713; Šibenik, T022 213468; Split, T021 338333; Supertar, T021 631357; Hvar Town, T021 741132; Stari Grad, T021 765048; Korčula Town, T020 715410; Vela Luka, T020 812015; Vis Town, T021 711032; Dubrovnik, T020 418000. Other companies include *Lošinjska Plovidba*, based in Mali Lošinj, T051 231524, www.losinjplov.hr; *Mediteranska Plovidba*, based in Korcula Town, T020 711156; *Rapska Plovidba*, based in Rab Town, T051 724122, www.rapska-plovidba.hr; *SEM*, based in Split, T021 338292, www.sem-marina.hr

## Train

All major Croatian cities, except Dubrovnik, are connected by rail. Train travel into more remote regions has been limited by topography, the rocky Dinaric Alps making it extremely difficult to build railways. The most useful long-distance routes covered by train are Zagreb-Osijek (3½ hours), Zagreb-Rijeka (four hours) and Zagreb-Split (eight hours), the latter being covered by both a day train and an overnight service with comfortable sleeping cars.

For a one-way ticket, expect to pay: Zagreb-Osijek 92Kn; Zagreb-Rijeka 81Kn and Zagreb-Split 138Kn. A return ticket is sometimes, but not always, cheaper than two one-way tickets. For further information contact **Hrvatske Zeljeznice, HZ** (Croatian Railways), www.hznet.hr

The Zone D **Inter Rail pass** (see page 30) gives you free second class train travel throughout Croatia, as well as in Hungary, Slovakia, the Czech Republic and Poland. There are no national discount rail passes.

## Maps

An excellent source of maps is *Stanfords*, 12-14 Longacre, London, WC2E 9LP, T0207 8361321, www.standfords.co.uk As well as stocking maps of the country you will also be able to acquire *Imray* and *British Admiralty* charts for sailing maps. Branches also in Bristol and Manchester. See also page 52. *Freytage & berndt* Croatia map 1:500 000 and Adriatic Coast 1:250 000 is recommended.

# Keeping in touch

## Communications

**Internet cafés** Internet cafés are springing up all over the place. Even on the islands, if you ask around you'll often find a bar with a computer set up in a corner, though it may not be signed as an internet café from the outside. Well-established internet cafés are listed in this book in individual town directories under Communications. Expect to pay 10-15Kn per hour.

In Zagreb, the main *pošta* (post office) next to the train station is open 24 hours. In other towns, most post offices work Monday-Friday 0700-2000 and Saturday 0700-1300, while in villages on the islands you may find them open mornings only, Monday to Friday 0930-1200.

**Post**

The postal service is run by **Hrvatska Pošta** and is pretty reliable. Airmail letters and postcards take about five days to reach EU countries and two weeks to get to the US, Canada and Australia. *Marke* (stamps) can be bought at post offices and newspaper kiosks. To send a postcard to the EU expect to pay 4Kn, to Canada or the US 5.50Kn and to Australia 6Kn. Letters cost 7.20Kn to the EU, 10.20Kn to Canada and the US and 11.20Kn to Australia. Larger post offices also have a facility whereby you can send and receive faxes.

*Essentials*

Public payphones are blue and operate with a *telekarta* (phonecard) which can be bought at newspaper kiosks. Phonecards are available with 25, 50, 100 and 200 units, and cost 13Kn, 24Kn, 38Kn and 67Kn respectively. As many payphones are on busy streets, which tend to be noisy, you may find it more comfortable to telephone from a cabin at the post office, where your call will be timed and you pay when finished. Cheap rates are in force Monday-Saturday 1900-0700 and all day Sunday.

**Telephone**
*Phone codes are listed throughout the book by each town heading*

To call Croatia from abroad, dial 00 from the UK, Ireland and New Zealand, 011 from the US and Canada, 0011 from Australia, followed by 385, then the area code minus the first zero, then the number. To call abroad from Croatia dial 00 followed by the country code: UK 44; Ireland 353; Australia 61; New Zealand 64; US and Canada 1. International directory enquiries: 902. Local directory enquiries: 988.

Mobile phones are as popular in Croatia as anywhere else in Europe. System dialing codes are 091and 098. If you are going to stay in the country for a longer period it may be worth subscribing to a Croatian 'pay as you go' network.

## Media

Speaking at a conference in Zagreb in early 2002, the Croatian President, Stipe Mesić, said that in the countries of the former Yugoslavia "the lack of media freedom in the 1980's was followed by government control of the media in the 1990's that disseminated intolerance and hatred".

His predecessor, Franjo Tudjman, was renowned for having made **HRT**, the state radio and television company and the primary news source for the majority of Croatians, a mere mouthpiece of the government. Television was certainly a major player in encouraging ethnic violence during the war of independence, with many news reports being no more than downright propaganda. When Tudjman died, he left hundreds of lawsuits pending against publications and journalists who had spoken against the state apparatus. In 1996 he had made a new law, forcing district attorneys to prosecute any individuals suspected of libelling the president; the speaker of the parliament; the prime minister, or the chief justices of the Supreme and Constitutional courts. Such was the degree of state interference in media matters. The present government is now reforming media laws and opening up the way for freedom of speech.

The most widely distributed dailies are *Večernji List*, *Vjesnik* and *Jutarnji List*, all from Zagreb, and *Slobodna Dalmacija* from Split. *Novi List* is a respected independent daily from Rijeka, and *La Voce del Popolo*, also from Rijeka, is an Italian-language daily published for the Italian minorities living in Croatia and Slovenia. In addition, you will find British, American, Italian, German and Slovenian newspapers and magazines readily available in all the main tourist destinations.

**Newspapers**

**Magazines**   The most talked about magazine is *Feral Tribune*, a Split-based satirical weekly, which has won more journalism awards than any other Croatian publication over the last decade, but has also incurred the most lawsuits (mainly during the Tudjman years). The former government's repeated attempts to close the magazine left it in financial crisis, at which point the Hungarian-born multimillionaire George Soros stepped in and offered *Feral* considerable financial support in the interest of free press. *Globus* and *Nacional* are weekly magazines reviewing current national and international news and events, while *Klik* and *Nomad* are aimed at the late-teen and early-20's market, and concentrate on music, fashion and contemporary cultural trends.

**Television & radio**   **Hrvatska radiotelevizija**, www.hrt.hr, is the state-run national TV and radio company, which airs three channels: HRT1 shows mainly Croatian-made programmes including news, documentaries, educational, scientific and cultural transmissions; HRT2 broadcasts mainly foreign light entertainment and comedies plus regional news, and HRT3 concentrates on sports and music. In addition, there are a great number of local TV channels, which vary greatly in quality, some being no more than mere advertising networks.

Foreign productions are shown in original version with subtitles. British comedies such as *Allo Allo*, *Only Fools and Horses*, and *Men Behaving Badly* have an astonishing cult-following here, as do David Attenborough BBC wildlife documentaries. However, over the last decade, cheap American films have started to hog a fair chunk of viewing time.

All that said, most hotels have satellite TV so you can tune in to foreign channels. In addition, Hrvatska Radio 1, on 92.1 MHz, broadcasts news in English every day at 8.03am, 10.03am, 2.03pm and 8.03pm.

# Food and drink

Croatian cuisine can be divided into two main groups: Mediterranean along the coast and Continental in the inland regions. That said, each region has its own particular specialities reflecting its unique geography, history and culture. Croatia's highly complex past is clearly evident in its cooking, which displays the traces left by centuries of occupation by three foreign empires: the Venetians brought pasta and risotto to the coast, Austro-Hungary introduced paprika-flavoured goulash and strudel inland, and the Ottoman Turks bequeathed the region with *sarma* (stuffed sauerkraut rolls) and *baklava*.

## Cuisine

**Coastal Croatia Dalmatia**   Along the Dalmatian Coast, simple, honest fish and seafood dishes top the menu. All ingredients are fresh and seasonal, so there's little attention paid to fussy preparation. The classic favourite is fresh fish, barbecued and served with olive oil and lemon, plus *blitva sa krumpirom* (swiss chard and potatoes with garlic and olive oil) as a side dish. Likewise, shellfish such as *kucice* (clams) and *škampi* (shrimps) are flashed over a hot flame with garlic, white wine and parsley, a method known as *na buzaru*, which cooks the flesh to a turn and produces a delicious rich sauce to mop up with bread. Worth mentioning here is that some of the best shellfish, notably *ostrige* (oysters) and *dagnje* (mussels), can be found in Ston on Pelješac Peninsula in South Dalmatia.

In summer, a popular and refreshing starter is *salata of hobotnice* (octopus salad) made from octopus, boiled potatoes, onion and parsley, dressed with olive oil and vinegar. Venetian influence is apparent in the abundance of risottos, the most popular being *crni rižot* (black risotto) made from cuttlefish ink, as well as *rižot frutti di mare*

## Dining out

◀

Essentials

*Remember that fish (especially Class I white fish such as bass, bream and John Dory) is sold by the kilogram and is expensive, while seafood risotto and pasta dishes are fairly economical. Therefore, you can pay almost as much for a portion of fresh fish in a cheap restaurant as you would for a portion of risotto in an expensive restaurant. The price coding used here is for a three-course meal with house wine.*

*Zagreb) or the yachting fraternity (along the coast).*

*Mid-range (80-200Kn) Most restaurants fall into this category. However, if you choose large quantities of fresh fish in a mid-range restaurant you can easily exceed the 200Kn mark.*

*Cheap (20-80Kn) Mainly pizzerias and informal eateries serving fixed-menu lunch and dinner.*

*Expensive (over 200Kn) High-class restaurants with food, wine, service and setting that warrant inflated prices. Often either geared to business people (in*

*Seriously cheap (under 20Kn) Mainly small shops doing take-away food such as sandwiches and pastries.*

---

(seafood risotto), normally combining mussels, clams and prawns, and *rižot sa škampima* (shrimp risotto) invariably served with a splash of cream at the end. Pasta dishes are also served with a variety of seafood sauces, though the pasta is often over-cooked by Italian standards. Another classic Dalmatian dish is *brodet*, a hearty mixed fish stew made with onions and tomatoes, and normally served with polenta. On the island of Hvar a local version of *brodet* is *gregada*, made with onions, potatoes and fresh herbs but no tomato.

Regarding meat dishes, locals rave about *dalmatinski pršut*, smoked dried ham on a par with Italian prosciutto. It's normally served as an appetizer on a platter together with *Paški sir* (sheep's cheese from the island of Pag) and a few olives. Meats such as steak, sausages and homemade burgers are invariably prepared on a charcoal fire and served with chips and a side salad (lettuce, cucumber and tomato). Another classic Dalmatian dish, brought to the area by the Venetians, is *pasticada*, beef stewed in sweet wine and served with *njoki* (gnocchi).

Lamb has a cult following throughout the Balkans, and in Croatia you'll see many roadside restaurants serving *janjetina* – whole lamb roast on a spit – especially in inland Dalmatia. A special mention also needs to be given to the *peka*, a metal dome dating back to Illyrian times. Food is placed in a terracotta pot and covered entirely with a *peka*, which in turn is buried below white embers. Delicious casseroles of either octopus, veal or lamb can be prepared using this long slow cooking method, though most restaurants that offer it stipulate that you should order a day in advance.

Desserts are limited, the standard offering being *palacinke* (pancakes), served either *sa orasima* (with walnuts), *sa marmeladom* (with jam) or *sa cokoladom* (with choco-late). In Dubrovnik, look out for *rožata*, similar to crème caramel.

If you visit the island of Vis, *pogaca* makes a perfect snack – similar to Italian focaccia (from which it takes its name), it consists of a light bread base filled with tomato, onion and anchovy: you can buy it in several local bakeries.

Besides the forementioned, in Istria you can expect slightly more adventurous dishes  Istria
with extra care given to presentation, probably due to Italian influence. Look out for the regional speciality, *tartufi* (truffles), usually served with pasta or steak, and risotto and pasta dishes *mare monti*, literally meaning 'sea and mountains', which combine shellfish and mushrooms. The best oysters and mussels are to be found in

Essentials

▶ **Brodet**

*Ingredients*
1 kg mixed fresh fish
1 onion
4 or 5 cloves of garlic
1 tablespoon of concentrated tomato
puree or two ripe tomatoes
1 tablespoon of chopped parsley
10 cl water
10 cl dry white wine
3 tablespoons of vinegar
8 tablespoons of olive oil
Salt and freshly ground black pepper

*Method*
Clean and gut the fish, removing the scales
and head but leaving the back bone. Dice
the onion and fry in oil until translucent,
add the chopped garlic and continue to fry
to a light golden colour. Add the tomato
and fish, and cook for five minutes. Add the
water, wine and vinegar, salt and pepper.

Cook for 30 minutes over a gentle flame
(without a lid so the juice thickens) until
the fish is falling freely from the bone.
Do not stir – to stop the brodet sticking
to the bottom of the pan, shake it
occasionally with a sharp side to side
rotating movement. Take off the heat,
add the parsley and leave to stand for
5-10 minutes. Eat warm, served with
polenta, and use fresh crusty bread to
mop up the juices.

This is an old-fashioned dish originally
invented by fishermen to use up the fish
they had not sold by the end of the day.
It is best made with a mixture of several
types of fish, preferably from the Adriatic.
If you are in Croatia ask the fishmonger's
advice, otherwise consider including
snapper, bream, perch, shark, mullet, as
well as octopus and squid.

Limski Kanal, between Rovinj and Poreč. On the meat front, Istrians prepare delicious *srnetina* (venison) stew, normally served with *njoki* (gnocchi) or *fuži*, a local form of pasta. As in Dalmatia, rich casseroles can be prepared under a *peka*, but in Istria it's known as a *cirepnja*. Regarding side dishes, you'll find colourful flavoursome salads combining mixed leaves such as rukola (rocket) and radicchio.

**Inland Croatia** Moving inland, food is generally heavier, with lard or dripping used in place of olive oil for frying and roasting. The Zagreb area, and especially Zagorje, is known for *štrukli*, dumplings filled with curd cheese, which can either be boiled or baked. The most popular meats are roast turkey, duck or goose, classically served with *mlinci*, wafer thin pastries cooked in dripping. The best bread is made from maize flour rather than wheat, giving it a yellow colour and a heavier consistency.

In Slavonia, pork is used to make *kulen*, a delicious spicy salami often served as an appetizer. Hungarian influence is apparent in meat specialities such as *gulaš* (goulash) and *fiš paprikaš* (a rich stew made from river fish), both of which are generously seasoned with hot paprika.

In Lika, the inland area between Zagreb and Dalmatia, look out for *škripavac* cheese, roast lamb, and hearty peasant dishes employing *kiseli kupus* (sauerkraut), *grah* (beans) and *krumpir* (potatoes).

Throughout the country you will come across Turkish inspired dishes, which make tasty and filling snacks: *burek* (filo pastry filled with either minced meat and onions or curd cheese) and *cevapcici* (meat rissoles served in pita bread with *ajvar* - a relish made from red peppers and aubergines). Also of Turkish origin are *sarma* (cabbage leaf rolls filled with minced meat and rice), better known as *arambašici* in Sinj, which are often eaten for special celebrations. Last but not least, *baklava* is a delicious syrup-drenched sweet made from filo pastry and ground walnuts.

## How to prepare Turkish coffee

*For each person you need:*
*1 coffee cup of water*
*1 teaspoon of sugar*
*2 teaspoons of ground coffee*
*Put the water and sugar in the džezver*
*and heat till simmering. Take off the flame,*
*stir in the coffee, put back on the flame*
*and heat till just before simmering point.*
*Take off the heat and allow to sit for 2-3*
*minutes before serving (so the coffee can*
*start to settle). Pour and drink immediately*
*without stirring.*

## Eating out

For a full blown lunch or dinner, visit a *restoran* (restaurant), where you can expect formal service and a menu including a wide range of Croatian dishes. Most restaurants work 1200-1500 and 1900-2300, and many, especially along the coast, have a large terrace for open-air dining through summer. For a simpler meal, try a *gostionica*, a place you can also go just to drink. There may not be a written menu, but many *gostionice* in Dalmatia serve *merenda* (a hearty cut-price brunch), offer daily specials chalked up on a board, and sometimes have a set three-course meal, which works out very cheap. Service will be less formal, but you can often land some excellent home cooking, and they tend to stay open all day, Monday to Saturday 0800-2300. The terms *konoba* (in Dalmatia) and *klet* (in Zagorje) were originally associated with places for making and storing wine, but the names are now used by many rustic style restaurants serving local specialities. Some open in the evenings only and may stay open for late-night drinking. Most towns have a pizzeria, and some serve surprisingly good pizza, comparable to the best in Italy. A few also offer a choice of substantial salads and a limited selection of pasta dishes.

For something sweet, call at a *slasticarnica*. Many are run by Albanians (who made up one of former-Yugoslavia's ethnic minorities) and they offer eastern goodies such as *baklava* (see above), along with a selection of *sladoled* (ice cream). Most work 0800-2000, and serve coffee, tea and fruit juices, but no alcohol.

If you are travelling in inland Istria, look out for agrotourism centres where you can expect quality local produce such as home-made cheese and wine, as well as unusual seasonal specialities such as *šparoge* (wild asparagus) in spring, and *tartufi* (truffles) and *gljive* (mushrooms) in autumn.

## Eating in

If you opt for private accommodation you will be able to eat in occasionally, which is a great solution for longer stays and families with children, and gives you the added pleasure of shopping at the open-air markets. Along the coast, all apartments (and even some rooms) come with a small cooking space, including a fridge and hot-plates (but not always an oven) and a sink. Some larger apartments and houses also have a built-in barbecue on the terrace or in the garden, in which case you'll have great fun preparing fresh fish over charcoal, just as the locals do.

All cooking utensils and kitchen equipment such as pans, bowls, plates, glasses, cups and cutlery will be provided: if anything is missing ask your host and they will give you anything extra you require. Occasionally basics such as sugar, salt and pepper are provided – normally left by the people that were there before you.

You will probably also be supplied with a *džezver* – a small metal coffee pot with a handle, used for preparing Turkish-style coffee, which is usually drunk here rather than instant, filter or espresso coffee. Vacuum packed ground coffee can be bought in packs of 100 or 250g in general stores.

Essentials

## Drinks

Meeting friends for *kava* (coffee) is something of a morning ritual. Many bars open as early as 0600, and are busy all day. While most people prepare Turkish coffee at home, cafés and bars serve Italian-style espresso and cappuccino. If you ask for *čaj* (tea) you will automatically be given *šipak* (rosehip) served with lemon; if you want English-style tea ask for *indijski čaj sa mlijekom* (Indian tea with milk). Most cafés have tables outside, even in winter where possible, and there is no extra charge for sitting down.

Wine    Croatian wines are little known abroad as they are exported in relatively small quantities, though some of them, such as the highly esteemed *Dingač*, are truly excellent. By and large the north produces whites and the south reds, though there are some exceptions.

Among the whites, names to look out for are: *Pošip* and *Grk* (from the island of Korčula), *Vugava* (island of Vis), *Žlahtina* (island of Krk), *Malvazija* (Istria), *Graševina* and *Traminac* (Slavonia). Of the reds, be sure to try: *Dingač* (Pelješac peninsula), *Plavac* (islands of Hvar and Vis), *Babić* (Primošten) and *Teran* (Istria). Dalmatia also produces a rich sweet wine known as *Prošek*, similar to sweet sherry.

To buy top wines at better prices, go direct to the producer. You will find vineyards open to the public on Pelješac Peninsula and the island of Hvar. On the island of Vis, some producers have opened small shops where you can sample wine and then buy bottles to take home. In Istria, the regional tourist board has drawn up a series of wine routes with a list of producers who receive visitors, for an interactive map check out the website, www.istra.com/vino

Lower grade wines are bottled in one-litre bottles with a metal cap, while better wines come in 0.75 l with a cork. Sometimes you will find the same label on both, but the 0.75 l bottle will be more expensive and of much higher quality. Most bars serve wine by the glass, either by the dec (1 dl) or dva deca (2 dl). In Dalmatia, bevanda (half white wine, half water) is a refreshing summer drink.

Beer    Beer was introduced to Croatia under Austro-Hungary, when the Hapsburgs built the first breweries to supply their soldiers. Light-coloured lager, served well chilled, is the most common sort of beer, with popular brands being *Karlovačko*, *Kaltenburg*, *Laško Zlatorog* and *Ožujsko*. *Tomislav* is a stout (dark beer) brewed in Zagreb. When you buy beer by the bottle, you pay a small deposit, which you can get back upon return of the empties and display of the receipt. Imported draught *Guinness* is popular but tends to be about three times the price of local beer.

Spirits    *Rakija*, a distilled spirit usually made from a grape base, was introduced to the region by the Turks, and is normally drunk as an aperitif before eating, but can also be taken as a digestive at the end of a meal. The most popular types are: *loza* (made from grapes), *travarica* (flavoured with aromatic grasses), *šljivovica* (made from plums) and *pelinkovac* (flavoured with juniper berries and bitter herbs, similar to Italian amaro). In addition, there are various regional specialities such as *biska* (flavoured with mistletoe) in inland Istria and *rogoš* (flavoured with carob) on the island of Vis. Imported spirits such as whisky and gin are popular but expensive.

# Shopping

Croatia is hardly a shoppers' paradise, a state of affairs clearly illustrated by the number of organized shopping buses to Trieste in Italy and Graz in Austria. As manufacturing industries struggle to recover from the crisis of the 1990's, clothes and household goods are largely imported from Western Europe, and come with the predictable mark-up price.

However, the open-air fruit and vegetable markets are animated, colourful affairs, well worth a look round to check out local seasonal produce. If you opt for private accommodation with self-catering facilities you will find shopping for food gives closer insight into the way people live, and eat. There are very few large supermarkets in Croatia, the nearest thing being small general stores, where you can shop for basics. But remember that fresh bread is best bought from a *pekarna* (bakery), meat from a *mesnica* (butchers), and fruit, vegetables and fish from the open-air morning market.

Top of the list, both during your stay and when it's time to go home, should be Croatian **wine** and **rakija** (see Food and drink). Each region makes its own wines, and even though they are all available in general stores throughout the country, it is worth tasting local wines while you travel from region to region. Better still, in some areas it's possible to visit cellars for wine tasting sessions and then buy direct from the producer.

**What to buy**
*See also individual town and city sections for listings*

Essentials

Throughout Europe, **olive oil** varies greatly from country to country. Although Croatia is not big on preserving olives to eat, Istrian and Dalmatian farmers produce some excellent *maslinovo ulje* (olive oil): when selecting a bottle, be sure to choose *djevičansko* (virgin), which is slightly more expensive but has a fuller flavour.

If you like **truffles**, look out for *tartufi* (truffles) and truffle-based products in Istria. On a slightly more sober note, Croatia produces some excellent **herbal teas**, available freshly dried on the open-air market, or in packages in the shops: the most popular varieties are *šipak* (rosehip), *menta* (mint) and *kamilica* (camomile).

Other ideas for gifts include **handmade lace** (the best being from the island of Pag), **natural sponges** (the best being from the tiny island of Krapanj, near Sibenik), **lavender** (either dried or distilled, from the island of Hvar), and an original **Croatian tie** (in a presentation box complete with a brief history of the tie). See also page 70.

# Entertainment and nightlife

Nightlife along the coast is great through summer with extended hours: open-air bars working till 0300 and open-air discos till 0500 at weekends. Holiday-makers are the main spenders, but young locals also dress up and stay out late, especially on Friday and Saturday nights. When Croatian bands play live, Croatian youngsters make up the major part of the audience, as the music is slightly inaccessible to foreigners.

*See also page 52, Spectator sports*

Winter tends to be a bit miserable: the police are quite strict about bars closing at 2300 Sunday-Thursday and 2400 Friday-Saturday, and most young Croatians are short of money so they either go out rarely or go out often but don't drink much. Young married couples with kids do not go out much – mainly because of financial problems. Of the older generation, 50 and over, it is normal for the man to go out drinking occasionally but for the wife to stay at home.

Cinema is quite popular, though most cinemas just show the current American box-office successes – the only really good place for alternative art films is *Kinoteka* in Zagreb. The open-air cinemas through summer are wonderful – the atmosphere is great, even if the films are not always fantastic. Theatre and opera tend to be the domain of the middle-aged middle-class class. The Summer Festivals in Dubrovnik and Split are perfect for older holiday-makers, offering a range of open-air musical and theatrical performances – here again, the atmosphere can be more memorable than the spectacle itself.

# Holidays and festivals

*See individual towns and cities for details of local festivals and holidays*

Festivals aren't celebrated with the same flamboyancy as in some other European countries. The most striking thing is the number of Croatian flags that are hoisted up on national holidays – above churches and town halls, in shops windows, and even hanging from people's balconies. Croatians celebrate Christmas and Easter at home with their families, so there's very little activity on the streets and most bars and restaurants are shut. However, midnight mass on 24 December is quite a big event, with churches probably seeing their biggest turn out of the year that night. New Year's day is seen in with massive fireworks displays in most places – surprisingly, despite the traumas of the war, Croatians still love big bangs and flashing lights. All Saint's Day is known as Day of the Dead in Croatia – people visit the family grave and fresh flowers are on sale in extraordinary quantities in the days leading up to 1 November.

**Public holidays**

Various towns have local public holidays to celebrate their respective Saint's Day, eg Sveti Vlaho in Dubrovnik on 3 February, Sudamja in Split on 6 May and Sveti Nikola in Komiža on the island of Vis on 6 December. The national public holidays are as follows: New Year's Day (1 January), Epiphany (6 January), Easter Sunday and Monday, May Day (1 May), National Day (30 May), Anti-fascist Day (22 June), National Thanksgiving Day (5 August), Assumption Day (15 August), Independence Day (8 October), All Saints Day (1 November), Christmas (25 and 26 December).

# Sport and special interest travel

## Participatory sports

**Beaches & bathing**

With a rugged indented coastline, countless islands and a pleasant Mediterranean climate, Croatia is a great place for sunbathing and swimming. The water is crystal clear, has a classic emerald-blue colour, and can reach temperatures of up to 27°C in summer. Most of the beaches are of pebbles (there is very little sand) and many are backed by pinewoods or typical Mediterranean planting such as tamarisks and agaves.

Along the coast and on the islands, 33 beaches have been awarded the Blue Flag, www.blueflag.org, a European eco-label indicating high environmental standards as well as good sanitary and safety facilities.

Croatia's most-photographed beach has to be Zlatni Rat at Bol on the island of Brač, a natural spit made up of tiny pebbles, while the country's largest sand beach is at Baška on the island of Krk. Beware of large modern hotels that claim to have a beach out front – in reality this is often no more than a concrete bathing area giving easy access into the water. The general rule with Croatian beaches is the more difficult it is to reach, the more worth while the journey: many of the most stunning beaches are found in isolated coves accessible only by boat.

*An estimated 15% of all tourists to Croatia are naturists*

Organized **naturist bathing** began on the island of Rab in the early 20th century, and the real naturist expansion started in the 1960's when the first naturist camps opened in Istria and Dalmatia, making Croatia the first country in Europe to commercialize naked bathing. Most naturists are from Germany, Austria, the Netherlands, Italy and Slovenia (Croats themselves make up less than 5% of nudists here). During the 1990's, naturism decreased significantly, a trend that many put down to the influence of the Catholic Church in society. However, naturism is still strongly supported by official Croatian government bodies: during the presidential campaign of 2000, Stipe Mesić declared himself a naturist. And he won.

## Top ten dive sites

◀

**1** *Baron Gautsch* (near Rovinj)
A passenger ferry wreck from 1914,
suitable for advanced divers only,
depth 28-42 m.
**2** *Lina* (island of Cres)
A merchant shipwreck, suitable for
advanced divers only, depth 22-55 m.
**3** *Margarina* (island of Susak, close to
the island of Mali Lošinj)
An underwater reef and canyon with
amphorae and a shipwreck, beginner to
advanced levels, depth 5-40 m.
**4** *Rasip* (Kornati islands)
An underwater cliff with corals, sponges
and schools of fish, excellent visibility up
to 40 m, beginner to advanced levels,
depth 3-65 m.
**5** *Stambedar* (Pakleni otoci, near
Hvar Town)
A sea wall with red and violet gorgonians
(type of coral), beginner to advanced levels,
depth 5-45 m.

**6** *Te Vega* (island of Sušac, between
Korčula and Lastovo)
A small sea lake entered through a
2-m-long tunnel at a depth of 5 m,
beginner to advanced levels, depth 5-35 m.
**7** *Modra Spilja* (island of Biševo, close
to the island of Vis)
A sea cave, beginner to advanced levels,
depth 3-40 m.
**8** *S57* (Pelješac peninsula)
A well-preserved German torpedo
shipwreck from 1944, suitable for
advanced divers only, depth 25-39 m.
**9** *Taranto* (Dubrovnik)
A merchant shipwreck from 1943, suitable
for advanced divers only, depth 23-55 m.
**10** *Sv Andrija* (Elafiti islands, near
Dubrovnik)
A sea wall with red coral and a cave at a
depth of 26 m, beginner to advanced levels,
depth 3-78 m.

Essentials

There are about 30 official naturist resorts and beaches, marked 'FKK' (from the German freikörperkultur meaning 'free body culture'), as well as countless unofficial naturist beaches, usually found in more secluded areas. For a region by region listing, check out the *Croatia Naturally* website at, www.cronatur.hr

Bird watching remains a relatively undeveloped field of tourism here, though there are certainly some excellent opportunities of spotting rare species in beautiful natural surroundings. In Inland Croatia, the top sites are Kopački Rit Nature Park (near Osijek in Slavonia) and Lonjsko Polje Nature Park (southeast of Zagreb, close to the border with Bosnia Herzegovina). Both parks offer vast expanses of unspoilt wetlands inhabited by herons, storks, geese, ducks, kingfishers and woodpeckers, and Lonjsko Polje is reputed to have the highest concentration of storks in Europe with 600 nesting couples.

**Bird watching**
*See page 19 for specialist tour operators*

Along the coast, the top bird watching destination is the Island of Cres, noted for its Eurasion griffon vultures, as well as eagles, peregrines and buzzards: although the birds are under special protection, the *Eco-Centar Caput Insulae*, www.caput-insulae.com will occasionally organize guided tours for small groups of enthusiasts. Likewise, Paklenica National Park, www.paklenica.hr (near Zadar), is a natural habitat for various birds of prey, and bird watching tours headed by a qualified ornithologist can be arranged through the national park office upon request.

Local tourist boards have begun designating bike routes, though there is plenty of scope for further development. The best established routes to date start out from the coastal towns of Rovinj, Novigrad and Labin in Istria, for further details check out www.istria.com   Bike routes have also been devised on the islands of Rab, Hvar and Mljet: further information is available from their respective tourist offices. Mountain bikes are generally available for rent in places suitable for cycling, either from agencies

**Cycling & mountain biking**
*See page 19 for specialist tour operators*

▶ **Stipe Božić**

*Born in Split in 1951, Božić is Croatia's best known mountaineer. In 1979 he climbed to the summit of Mount Everest via the previously unconquered west ridge, and he is the second European, after the Italian Reinhold Messner, to have reached the summit of the highest peak in the world twice. He has also reached the North Pole, and climbed the Seven Summits – the highest peaks on all seven continents: Mount Everest (Asia), Aconcagua (South America), Mount McKinley (North America), Kilimanjaro (Africa), Mount Vinson (Antarctica), Mont Blanc and Elbrus (Europe) and Mount Kosciusko (Australia). What makes his Himalayan trips especially interesting is that he filmed most of them: he has made a series of films and documentaries about climbing, and stood with camera in hand on K2, Kangchenjunga and Manaslu.*

that specialize in hiring bikes, mopeds and boats, or from large hotels with extensive sporting facilities. Expect to pay around €15 for a day or €80 for a week.

If you are planning on taking your own bicycle, it is worth noting that on overnight ferries from Italy to Croatia bikes travel free (you just pay the passenger ticket), but in summer 2002 the local ferries between the mainland and the islands started to add a small surcharge for bikes. This may however be cut again in summer 2003.

**Diving**
*See page 19 for specialist tour operators*

Along the coast you will find numerous diving clubs offering lessons (with multilingual instructors), guided tours and rental equipment. To dive in Croatia, you need to hold a valid diver's card issued by the **Hrvatski Ronilački Savez** (Croatian Diving Federation). These can be obtained from all recognized Croatian diving clubs, are valid for one year as of the date of issue, and were priced at 100Kn (€15) in summer 2003.

For a full list of recognized diving clubs in Croatia, contact either **Hrvatski Ronilački Savez**, Dalmatinska 12, Zagreb, T01 4848765, www.diving-hrs.hr, or **Pro Diving Croatia**, Bulevar Oslobodjenja 23, Rijeka, T051 219111, www.diving.hr

Expect to pay 1850-2250Kn (€250-300) for a one-week diving educational programme, or if you are already experienced, 320Kn (€43) for an organized group dive with a qualified guide (including equipment rental) or 185Kn (€25) for the same tour using your own equipment.

Within the waters of Kornati and Mljet national parks, diving is restricted to organized groups, and diving is totally prohibited in the waters of Brijuni and Krka national parks.

**Hiking & climbing**
*See page 19 for specialist tour operators*

Croatia's unspoilt nature, varied landscapes ranging from slopes supporting meadowland and forests ideal for gentle hiking, to steep grey cliffs ideal for free climbing, plus a pleasant mild and reasonably dry climate through spring and autumn, make it a great place to explore on foot. The majority of mountains belong to the Dinaric range, and although none are over 2,000 m, they require the same efforts from the climber as many much higher mountains thanks to their rugged rocky karst landscape and sparse population. The number of marked trails and *planinarski dom* (mountain refuges) serving simple food and offering overnight accommodation are a proof of a long tradition of mountain-climbing.

All official hiking paths are signed at regular intervals by a red circle with a white dot in the middle, or occasionally two parallel red lines with a white line between them. The more popular routes are clearly marked while those that are rarely used are less well maintained. The islands have been little exploited by walkers, but the potential is certainly there. The highest mountains on the islands are: Vidova Gora on Brač, 778 m; Sv Nikola on Hvar, 626 m; Gorica on Cres, 650 m and Osorčića on Lošinj, 588 m. The best

## Ten highest mountains

**Dinara**, *Central Dalmatia, 1831 m.*
**Kamesnica**, *Central Dalmatia, 1809 m.*
**Biokovo**, *Central Dalmatia, 1762 m*
*(peak Sv Jure).*
**Velebit**, *North Dalmatia, 1758 m*
*(peak Vaganski Vrh).*
**Lička Pljesivica**, *Lika, 1657 m (peak Ozeblin).*

**Velika Kapela**, *Gorski kotar, Kvarner,*
*1534 m (peak Bjelolasica).*
**Risnjak**, *Gorski kotar, Kvarner, 1528 m.*
**Svilaja**, *Central Dalmatia, 1508 m.*
**Snježnik**, *Gorski kotar, Kvarner, 1506 m.*
**Učka**, *Istria, 1400 m (peak Vojak).*

*Essentials*

places for free climbing are in inland Istria, Paklenica National Park near Zadar in North Dalmatia, and the Cetina Valley near Omiš in Central Dalmatia.

**Hrvatski Planinarski Savez** (Croatian Hiking Association), Kozarčeva 22, Zagreb, T01 4824142, http://hps.inet.hr, is an umbrella group for some 170 local walking clubs and can supply maps and information about mountain huts throughout the country. The association is also responsible for the Mountain Rescue Service, which can be called out through the police, T92.

Of all the so-called extreme sports that have emerged over the last decade, whitewater rafting is probably the most accessible to complete beginners. The best rivers for rafting in Croatia are the Dobra and the Kupa near Karlovac in Inland Croatia, the Zrmanja near Zadar in North Dalmatia, and the Cetina near Omiš in Central Dalmatia.

**Rafting**
See page 19 for specialist tour operators

With a myriad of islands, deep clean sea and moderate winds, Croatia is a sailor's paradise. A total of 48 fully equipped modern marinas line the coast all the way from Umag in the north to Dubrovnik in the south, while temporary mooring facilities are available along the seafront in most coastal towns and villages, and there are plenty of deserted bays, ideal for dropping anchor and bathing in total solitude. The most crowded period is July-August, when sailing enthusiasts from all over Europe flock to the Adriatic, and fashionable resorts, such as Hvar Town, are inundated with yachts and yachters. The mid-season periods of May-June and September-October are more peaceful, and the weather still fairly reliable.

**Sailing**
See page 19 for specialist tour operators

**Renting a yacht**   There are 75 registered charter companies in Croatia, which have about 14,000 vessels, of which 10,100 are yachts, and the rest motorboats. Most companies rent yachts on a weekly basis from 1700 Saturday to 0900 the following Saturday. When you charter a yacht this can be bareboat (meaning you are alone) or with a skipper (a qualified yachtsman who normally knows the area well). To go bareboat you, or one of the crew, must have a sailing licence and at least two years' sailing experience. Prices vary greatly depending on the size and type of yacht, as well as the season. For example, the British company *Nautilus Yachting* ask between £769 and £1330 for one week on a *Bavaria 34* (10.8 m long, sleeps six) while the Croatian company *Club Adriatic* ask between €770-1540 for one week on a *Sun Odyssey 32* (9.6 m long, sleeps 6). You can expect to pay an extra €100 per day for a skipper. The other possibility is to join part of a flotilla, a group of yachts (normally between five and 10) crewed by people with mixed levels of sailing experience, lead by an expert sailor.

*Club Adriatic*, www.clubadriatic.com, is an online charter service with special low-season offers and last-minute deals on over 700 yachts. They also run an online marine guide, the VIP Adriatic Navigator, www.adriatic-navigator.com, has detailed information about harbours, restaurants etc in lesser known places along the coast.

**Marinas**  Croatia's largest nautical tourism company is *Adriatic Croatia International (ACI)*, M Tita 151, Opatija, T051 271288, www.aci-club.hr, which manages 21 of the country's 48 marinas. For full information, check out the website.

**Sailing schools**  *Adriatic Nautical Academy (ANA)*, T051 711967, www.sailing-ana.hr, run an annual sailing school from late March to early November based at the ACI Marina in Jezera on the island of Murter, offering intensive courses at all levels with multilingual instructors. In addition, some tour operators such as *Activity Holidays* and *Nautilus Yachting* offer one-week sailing courses for beginners. Expect to pay between £423-615 (including flight from the UK, transfer and yacht).

**Maps**  Croatian sea charts are available from *Plovput*, Obala Lazareta 1, Split, T021 355900, www.plovput.hr If you rent a yacht, the maps will be supplied.

Watersports  Jet-skiing, para-sailing and water-skiing are only available at the more commercial resorts such as Bol on the island of Brač, but they will probably become more widespread as tourism picks up further.

Windsurfing  Croatia's top windsurfing locations are Bol on the island of Brač in Central Dalmatia and Viganj on Pelješac Peninsula in South Dalmatia, both of which catch the *jugo* (wind from the south) through summer. Further north, the coast is less suitable for windsurfing as the main wind is the bura (wind from the northeast), which blows mainly through winter.

In Bol, close to Zlatni Rat beach, there are two windsurfing clubs, *Big Blue*, Podan Glavice 2, Bol, T021 635614, www.big-blue-sport.hr, and *Orca Sport*, Račić 9, Bol, T021 321771, www.orca-sport.com, both of which offer courses at all levels from beginner to advanced and rent equipment to experienced surfers. Bol is also home to the *Croatian Open Cup*, staged in July, which attracts competitors from Croatia, Slovenia, Hungary and Italy.

In Viganj, near Orebić, the windsurfing club *Bofor*, Viganj 74, Kučište, T020 719072, offers courses and rental equipment, and organizes the one-week *Adria Championship* in late July, attracting surfers from the Czech Republic, Hungary, Austria, Italy, Slovenia and Croatia.

The above mentioned windsurfing clubs work from early April to late October. Courses are normally arranged in blocks of two hour lessons: expect to pay €100 for eight hours at beginner level or €150 for 10 hours at advanced level. If you just want to rent a board, expect to pay €10 for one hour or €80 for 10 hours, including surf shoes, harness and wetsuits.

## Spectator sports

For a country of only four million, Croatia has scored outstanding success in international sporting events over the last decade. Before the country's break up in 1991, Yugoslavia was a force to be reckoned with in sports such as football, basketball, handball and water polo, all of which remain favourite team games in Croatia today.

Football  As in most countries, football is the most popular spectator sport. During the late
(Nogomet)  1990's the Croatian national team was extremely strong, reaching the quarter-final in the European Championship 1996, and coming third in the World Cup in France in 1998, having beaten Germany with an unforgettable 3-0 in the quarter-final, only to be knocked out by the eventual victors, France, in the semi-final. The team fared less well in the World Cup 2002, having played a tremendous match against Italy to win 2-1, but failing to pull through to the later stages.

The current national team is made up mainly of youngsters, the old stars of the late 1990's such as Davor Šuker, Robert Prosinečki, Igor Štimac and Zvonimir Boban having retired. Middlesborough striker Alen Boksić is still playing, though he too looks set to withdraw from the game sometime during 2003. For more information about the Croatian national team check out the Croatian Football Federation website at www.hns-cff.hr

There are 12 teams in the Croatian premier league, the top names being Hajduk, www.hnkhajduk.hr, from Split, three times quarter-finalist in the European League of Champions (the last time being in 1995) and once semi-finalist of the UEFA cup. Hajduk's arch-rivals are Dinamo, www.nk-dinamo.hr, from Zagreb.

Croatia's best known sportsman is probably tennis player Goran Ivanišević (born in **Tennis (Tenis)** Split in 1971) who ranked second in the world in 1992 and won the much coveted Wimbledon tournament in summer 2001, see box, page 200. Among women players, Iva Majoli (born in Zagreb in 1977) ranked sixth in the world in 1997, but has had little outstanding success of late. The country's top annual tournaments are the ATP Croatia Open, www.croatiaopen.hr, held at Umag, and the WTA Croatia Bol Ladies Open, www.bolladies.hr, staged in Bol, on the island of Bra č.

The Croatian team won the silver medal at the 1992 Olympics in Barcelona, and came **Basketball** third in the European Cup in both 1993 and 1995, and also third in the World Cup in **(Košarka)** Toronto in 1994. Recent Croatian players on the NBA include Tony Kukoč, Jan Tabak and Dino Rada, all from Split. Two Croats have joined the Basketball Hall of Fame: Krešimir Cosić (Zagreb 1948-95, enshrined 1996) and Dražen Petrović (Šibenik 1964-93, enshrined 2002).

The country's two top basketball teams are Split, www.kksplit.hr, from Split (formerly known as Jugoplastika), who were European champions in 1989, 1990 and 1991, and Cibona, www.cibona.com, from Zagreb.

The Croatian men's team scored their first World Championship victory in 2003 at Lis- **Handball** bon, having come second in the World Championship in 1995 and taking the gold **(Rukomet)** medal at the 1996 Olympics in Atlanta. The local club Podravka from Koprivnica won the Women's European Championship in 1996. Croatia will host the 2003 Women's World Championship.

The Croatian team won the silver medal in water polo at the 1996 Olympics in Atlanta. **Water polo** The game is especially popular in South Dalmatia: the country's top club is Jug from **(Vaterpolo)** Dubrovnik, which won the European Champions League in 2001, closely followed by Mladost from Zagreb, which won the European Champions League for the seventh occasion in 1996, giving it more wins than any other European club to date. Jadran from Split was once a highly regarded club, winning the European Champions League in 1992 and 1993, but has not fared so well of late.

Croatia is not a country particularly noted for skiing, but it has however produced one **Skiing** of the world's top skiers: Janica Kostelić (born in Zagreb in 1982), who became the first **(Skijanje)** alpine skier ever to win four medals at a single Olympic Winter Games when she took three golds (in the combined race, the slalom and the giant slalom) and a silver (in the super-G) at the 2002 Winter Games in Salt Lake City, US. Also in 2002, she was named 'Sports Woman of the Year'.

Essentials

# Health

*See individual town and city directories for details of medical services*

The popularity of the Dalmation Coast is at no real cost to your health. Make sure you are up to date with the most basic **vaccines** such as tetanus, diphtheria and polio. It is still wise to be up to date with hepatitis A vaccine and Typhoid even for this relatively safe destination.

**Tap water** is safe to drink throughout the country. Most EU countries have a reciprocal healthcare agreement with Croatia, meaning that you pay a basic minimum for consultation and hospital treatment is free if you can show your E111 from (available from the Post Office). If your country doesn't have such an agreement, you will have to pay in accordance with listed prices. For minor complaints visit a *ljekarna* (pharmacy): most are open Monday-Friday 0800-1900 and Saturday 0800-1400, and in larger cities they have a rota system whereby at least one should be open at night and weekends. For something more serious, visit the local doctor's surgery – most doctors speak some English. Outside surgery hours or in the case of an emergency, go to *hitno pomoć* (casualty). Dial 94 for an ambulance. You can also check with clinics and hospitals are used by British Diplomats for their own ailments.

**Common complaints**

**Sun burn** Avoid extensive exposure to the sun, wear a hat and sunglasses and use a high protection factor sun cream, especially during the hottest part of the day (1100-1500). Drink plenty of water to avoid dehydration.

**Sea sickness** Even on short trips out to the islands, the movement of the sea can be unsettling. Try Kwells or other sea-sickness tablets.

**Insect bites** The insects you will come across here are more unpleasant than dangerous, unless you have a specific allergy. Mosquitoes are rarely a problem, except in the Osijek and Kopački Rit wetland area. To ward them off, buy insect repellent at a local pharmacy.

**Sea urchins** Black spiky sea urchins are common along the rocky shorelines. If you step on one, do not try to remove the spikes yourself as this can result in infection. To avoid the problem altogether, invest in a pair of plastic sandals for getting in and out of the water.

**Snake bites** The best way to protect yourself from snake bites is to be well dressed and to keep to marked roads and paths. Snakes only bite if they feel threatened, and very few here are poisonous. However, if you are bitten, you should immediately immobilize the bitten part and bind the arm or leg to slow down the circulation. If it is poisonous the bite will normally swell within 30 minutes. Send someone for help at once.

**Sexual health** The range of visible and invisible diseases is awesome. Unprotected sex can spread HIV, Hepatitis B and C, Gonorrhea (green discharge), chlamydia (nothing to see but may cause painful urination and later female infertility), painful recurrent herpes, syphilis and warts, just to name a few. You can cut down the risk by using condoms, a femidom or avoiding sex altogether. Consider getting a sexual health check on your return home if you do have intercourse.

Adapted by **Dr Charlie Easmon** MBBS MRCP MSc Public Health DTM&H DOccMed Director of Travel Screening Services.

Inland Croatia

# Inland Croatia

Quite another world from the open seascapes and sun-soaked medieval stone towns of the coast, Inland Croatia is flatter, damper and infinitely more central European. Nowhere is the Hapsburgian influence felt so strongly as in **Zagreb**, the country's economic, political and cultural capital. Northwest from here, the rolling hills of **Zagorje** offer woodland, vineyards and rural villages, as well as several proud castles, monuments to the days when local peasants were held in the grip of a harsh feudal system.

North of Zagreb, close to the Hungarian border, **Varaždin** is noted for its well-preserved Baroque old town, while northeast of the capital, the village of **Hlebine** is home to several galleries displaying the unusual works of Croatia's so-called Naïve artists.

Moving east, the flat, fertile plains of Slavonia extend all the way to the border with Serbia. The main town here is **Osijek**, built on the south bank of the River Drava and worth visiting to see **Tvrđa**, a complex of 18th-century buildings erected by the Austrians to defend the region from the Turks. Close by, **Kopački Rit Nature Park** is a vast wetland supporting protected birds such as storks and herons.

South of Zagreb, on the road to Dalmatia, you will pass through **Lika**, an area still recovering from the after effects of the war: in the past many Serbian families lived here, and having fled during the early 1990s they are only now beginning to return. The main sight here is **Plitvice National Park**, a paradise of emerald-green lakes and thundering waterfalls set amid a dense forest, close to the border with Bosnia Herzegovina.

# Zagreb

*Inland Croatia*

Phone code: 01
Colour map 1,
grid B5/6
Population: 1 million

*With most holiday makers heading straight for the sea and sunshine of the coast, the Mitteleuropean-style capital, Zagreb, is often overlooked as a tourist destination. However, as Croatia's economic and administrative centre, and home to one in four Croats (including most of the country's politicians, businessmen and intellectuals) it's certainly worth devoting a few days to if you want to understand what (or who) makes the nation tick.*

*The city centre is composed of two main areas, the hilltop **Gornji Grad** (Upper Town), and the lower-lying **Donji Grad** (Lower Town), which meet at **Trg Bana Jelačića**, the main square. Medieval Gornji Grad, home to the Cathedral and the Croatian Parliament, is reminiscent of old Prague, thanks to its romantic winding **cobbled streets**, **red-tiled rooftops** and **church spires**. In contrast, Donji Grad, where you'll finds the **museums**, the National Theatre and the university, was laid out on a strict grid system during the 19th century, and is made up of grandiose **Hapsburgian buildings** interspersed between a series of green squares linked by **tree-lined boulevards**. Beyond the city centre lie the standard suburbs of high-rise apartment blocks, constructed during the latter half of the 20th century.*

*Despite the economic crisis caused by the recent war, the city centre is looking surprisingly good. A plethora of privately owned general stores and boutiques have opened up (albeit selling imported goods), and apart from peeling paint here and there, most of the buildings still manage to carry off their proud Austro-Hungarian image pretty well. Unfortunately, high living costs, low wages and mass unemployment are still a harsh reality for the people who live here, but as a visitor you can spend a pleasant enough few days exploring the city's museums, parks and churches.*

## Ins and outs

**Getting there**
See Transport, page
73, for further details

Zagreb is 182 km from
Rijeka, 365 km from
Split and 581 km from
Dubrovnik

Through summer, *Croatia Airlines* operate regular international flights to and from Amsterdam, Barcelona, Berlin, Brussels, Copenhagen, Dusseldorf, Frankfurt, Gothenburg, Istanbul, London (Gatwick and Heathrow), Madrid, Manchester, Moscow, Mostar, Munich, Paris, Prague, Rome, Sarajevo, Skopje, Stockholm, Stuttgart, Tel Aviv, Warsaw, Vienna and Zurich. Internal flights link the capital with Brač (island of Bol), Dubrovnik, Pula, Rijeka, Split and Zadar. The number of destinations and the frequency of flights are reduced in winter. The airport is at Pleso, 17 km from the city centre. Shuttle buses run to the city centre. There are frequent connections with all the main cities and also daily international connnections with Slovenia, Hungary, Serbia and Montenegro, Austria, Germany and Switzerland. There are train connections to the major cities and some international connections. The train station is at Trg Kralja Tomislava 12, a 10-min walk from the main square.

**Getting around**
The city centre is compact and reasonably manageable on foot. An amusing (though rather unnecessary) funicular links Donji Grad to Gornji Grad, operating 0630-2100, tickets 2.5Kn. To reach more outlying sights you may need to rely on public transport. Regular tram and bus services operate through the day 0400-2345, with slightly less frequent services at night 2335-0345. Tickets cost 6Kn when bought from a kiosk or 7Kn from the driver, a day ticket costs 16Kn. You can find taxis in front of the bus and train stations, near the main square and in front of the larger hotels.

## 24 hours in the city

Watch the city wake up over coffee and a croissant at **Mala Kavana**, seated at an outdoor table overlooking the main square, Trg Bana Jelačića. Five minutes away, stallholders at Dolac open-air market will be setting up their fruit and vegetable stands – certainly worth a peep.

Spend the morning in Gornji Grad, taking a look in the **Cathedral** to see a 12th-century inscription in the little-known Glagolitic script, and visiting the **Church of St Mark's** with its much-photographed red-white-and-blue tile roof. Lovers of modern sculpture should also reserve an hour for the **Meštrović Atelier**.

Try to arrive at **Lotrščak Tower** just before noon for the firing of the cannon at 1200, then enjoy stunning panoramic views over the city rooftops from **Strossmayer Šetalište**. For an early lunch, stop at the nearby **Pod Gričkim Topom** for seafood risotto and a salad on the summer terrace, then take a short funicular ride down to Donji Grad.

Spend the afternoon in Donji Grad checking out the **Mimara Museum** and the **Arts and Crafts Museum**, pausing for tea at the Viennese-style **Kavana Palace**. If you tire of the sightseeing lark, get back in touch with nature amid the beautifully landscaped **Maksimir Park**.

Whet your appetite with an early evening aperitif at an open-air café on **Tkalčićeva**, then head to the old-fashioned **Stari Fijaker** for dinner, where you're guaranteed to sample the best of traditional Zagrebian roast meat and game dishes.

Round off the evening in a club: the young and rebellious should head for either **Tvornica** or **Močvara**, while mature and/or glamorous types will feel infinitely more comfortable at **Saloon**.

**Tourist Information Centres**

The main Tourist Information Centre (TIC), T4814051, www.zagreb-touristinfo.hr, is on the main square, at Trg Bana Jelačića 11. Open Mon-Fri 0830-2000, Sat 0900-1700, Sun 1000-1400. A smaller TIC, T4921645, is at Trg Nikole Šubiᵃa Zrinskog 14, close to the train station. Open Mon, Wed and Fri 0900-1700, Tue and Thu 0900-1800. Head office is at Kaptol 5, T 4898555, F4814340. The centres are helpful and all the staff speak English. They can provide information about accommodation, events, public transport etc plus maps and promotional material. The TIC close to the train station deals specifically with organizing guided tours of the city.

**Best time to visit**

Being the capital, Zagreb is fairly animated the year through. Two major cultural events, the *Summer Festival*, with open-air classical music concerts and theatre in Gornji Grad, and the *Folk Festival*, with displays of regional costume, singing and dancing on the main square, both take place in Jul.

The city is notoriously cold and foggy through winter (there are even songs about it) and can be extremely hot in summer (when most Zagrebians pack up and head for the coast). It's probably best visited in spring or autumn, when the parks and gardens are at their prettiest and temperatures are ideal for exploring on foot and enjoying the open-air bars and cafés.

**Orientation**

Orientating yourself around the city is not difficult. The basic urban layout is clear, with Gornji Grad and Donji Grad meeting at Trg Bana Jela čića, the main square.

Inland Croatia

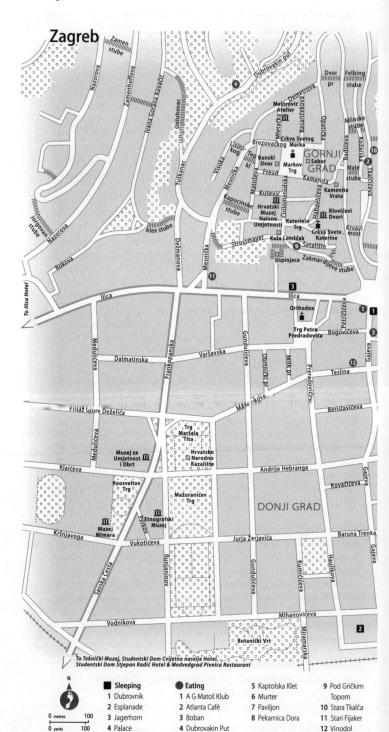

Inland Croatia

**Zagreb**

| | |
|---|---|
| **Sleeping** | |
| 1 Dubrovnik | |
| 2 Esplanade | |
| 3 Jagerhorn | |
| 4 Palace | |

| | |
|---|---|
| **Eating** | |
| 1 A G Matoš Klub | |
| 2 Atlanta Café | |
| 3 Boban | |
| 4 Dubrovakin Put | |

5 Kaptolska Klet
6 Murter
7 Paviljon
8 Pekarnica Dora

9 Pod Gričkim
   Topom
10 Stara Tkalča
11 Stari Fijaker
12 Vinodol

# Sights

## Gornji Grad

The loveliest part of Zagreb is, undoubtedly, Gornji Grad (Upper Town). A two-hour stroll through peaceful cobbled streets will take you to the Cathedral and several other notable churches, the Sabor (Croatian Parliament) and a handful of good museums.

Lying between Gornji Grad and Donji Grad, Trg Bana Jelačića, the main square, makes an ideal starting place for exploring Zagreb. A vast paved space, it's closed to cars but plays the role of the city centre's main tram intersection, making it an important public meeting place and providing the surrounding cafés with a steady influx of customers. Buildings lining the square date from 1827 onwards, and include several fine examples of Vienna Secessionist architecture. In the centre of the square stands a **bronze equestrian statue** of Ban Jelačić (19th-century Croatian viceroy, see page 317) created by the Viennese sculptor Antun Fernkorn and first erected in 1866. In 1945, Tito, who regarded Jelačić as a symbol of Croatian nationalism, renamed the square Trg Republika, and had the statue dismantled. In 1991, when the HDZ came to power, the square reverted to its former name and a campaign was launched for the return of the statue. Several months later, accompanied by a spectacular firework display, the new president, Franjo Tudjman, performed a triumphant re-inauguration ceremony, the Ban reassembled and back in his former position, having spent 44 years in pieces, hidden away in a cellar.

**Trg Bana Jelačića**

Inland Croatia

**Dolac**   On the northern edge of the square lies Dolac, the city's main market since 1930. Arranged on two levels, it's a colourful and entertaining affair, with farmers from the surrounding countryside setting up stalls of fruit and vegetables on a raised piazza, while meats and dairy products are sold in an indoor area below. Behind the fruit and vegetable section, you'll find people selling handmade items such as lace, hats and jewellery, and to each side of the piazza a conglomeration of snack bars serving cheap eats. ■ *Mon-Fri 0700-1600, Sat-Sun 0700-1200.*

**Katedrala**   From Dolac, it's just a couple of minutes walk to the Katedrala (Cathedral). Much of the original structure, dating back to the 12th century, was destroyed by the Tartars in 1242. While reconstruction and extension work took place between the 13th and 16th centuries, this in turn was badly damaged by the 1880 earthquake, thus the neo-Gothic façade and twin steeples we see today were designed by an Austrian architect, Herman Bolle. Inside, the north wall bears an inscription of the Ten Commandments in 12th-century Glagolitic script (see page 129), and nearby, a touching relief by Ivan Meštrović portrays the late Archbishop Alojzije Stepinac kneeling before Christ, and marks the controversial bishop's final resting place. In front of the Cathedral, a gilded statue of the Virgin, protected by four angels, stands on a high stone column. Like the Ban Jelačić statue, it is the work of Antun Fernkorn. ■ *0800-2000. Kaptol 31.*

**Tkalčićeva**   From the Cathedral, proceed along the street of Kaptol, then take the first left, followed by the first right, pass through a walled public garden and descend a short flight of steps to arrive on Tkalčićeva. Until 1898, when it was filled in, this street was a channel forming the boundary between Kaptol and Gradec, and was known as 'Potok' (The Brook). Today it's a pretty pedestrian zone lined with 19th-century town houses, most of which host popular street-level café-bars with open-air seating: an amusing place for morning coffee or an early evening drink, perfect for people-watching.

**Kamenita**   From Tkalčićeva, a flight of steep wooden steps leads to the parallel street of
**Vrata (Stone**   Radićeva, where you'll find a number of small private galleries and gift shops.
**Gate)**   From here, it's five minutes to Kamenita Vrata, formerly one of four entrances into the walled town of Gradec. In 1731, after a devastating fire had consumed the surrounding wooden buildings, a painting of the Virgin Mary was found in the ashes, remarkably undamaged. Kamenita Vrata was reconstructed and became regarded as a place of miracles. Today locals come here to pray and pay tribute to the Virgin: there's a delightful shrine adorned with flickering candles and the walls are hung with small plaques saying 'Hvala', or 'Thank you' (so it obviously works). Close by, at Kamenita 9, stands a pharmacy dating back to the mid-14th century and still functioning today. On the wall, a memorial stone records that the grandson of the Italian poet Dante Alighieri worked here in 1399.

**Crkva**   Kamenita Ulica leads to Trg Svetog Marka, for centuries the centre of Zagrebian
**Svetog Marka**   political, cultural and commercial life. A daily market used to be held here, and
**(St Mark's**   it was the main public meeting place until Trg Bana Jelačića took over the role
**Church)**   during the 19th century. The centrepiece is Crkva Svetog Marka, erected in the 13th century as the parish church of Gradec. Its most remarkable feature is the steeply pitched roof, added during reconstruction in 1880 and decorated in red-white-and-blue tiles depicting the coats of arms for Zagreb (on the right) and the Kingdom of Croatia, Dalmatia and Slavonia (on the left). Inside, the

walls are frescoed with biblical scenes, painted by Jozo Kljaković between 1936 and 1938. During the Middle Ages, a pole of shame was erected in front of the church, where local lawbreakers were punished with a public whipping. One such 'offender', Matija Gubec, was less fortunate: having organized an unsuccessful peasant uprising in 1573, he was brought to Markov Trg and 'crowned with molten iron for his impertinence'. Local myth has it that a stone face carved on the corner building between Čirolmetodska ulica and Kamenita ulica is a monument to him. ■ *0800-2000. Markov Trg.*

**Sabor (Croatian Parliament)**

Facing the main entrance to the church stands the Sabor, housed within a neoclassical building completed in 1910. On 25 June 1991, this was the very place where members of the Sabor voted in favour of national independence, thus marking the beginning of the end of the Socialist Federal Republic of Yugoslavia. On 7 October 1991 the building was hit by a bomb: the next day Croatia cut off all state and legal links with Belgrade. On the opposite side of the square stands a single-storey Baroque building, **Banski Dvori** (Ban's Court Palace), where the Croatian viceroy resided from 1809 to 1918.

**Meštrović Atelier**

A short walk north of the square will bring you to the charming Meštrović Atelier. During the 1920's, the Dalmatian sculptor Ivan Meštrović (see page 330) refurbished this 17th-century building to serve as a home and studio. Dividing his time between Zagreb and Split, he lived and worked here on and off until fleeing the country during the Second World War. When he died in 1962 it was turned into a memorial museum with a beautifully presented exhibition of his sculptures and drawings. ■ *Tue-Fri 0900-1400, Sat 1000-1800. 15Kn. T4851123, Mletačka 8.*

**Hrvatski Muzej Naivne Umjetnosti (Croatian Naïve Art Museum)**

Returning to Trg Sv Marka, Čirilmetodska, the street running south of the square, leads to this museum. You may not consider Croatian Naïve art (see pages 87 and 330) aesthetically pleasing, but it certainly is unusual. During the 1930's, a group of farmers from the village of Hlebine in Slavonia took up painting (with no previous tuition), and the canvasses on display here show what they produced. Several of them, most notably Ivan Generalić, went on to receive international recognition. When it first opened in 1952, this was known as the Peasant Art Gallery. ■ *Tue-Fri 1000-1800, Sat-Sun 1000-1300, closed Mon, 10Kn. T4851911, www.hmnu.org, Čirilmetodska 3.*

**Crkva Svete Katerine (St Catherine's Church)**

Čirilmetodska leads to Katerinin Trg, overlooked by the Baroque church. Built for the Jesuit order between 1620 and 1632, it was modelled on Giacomo da Vignola's Il Gesu in Rome. The vaulted ceilings are encrusted with sugary pink-and-white stuccowork, and there's a clever 18th-century illusionist fresco above the main altar. ■ *0800-2000. Katerinin Trg.*

**Klovićevi Dvori**

Close by, most major international exhibitions are staged at Klovićevi Dvori, a 17th-century Jesuit College that was reconstructed in 1982 to form a large art gallery. There isn't a permanent collection. Recent temporary exhibitions include '2000 years of Nigerian Art' and 'Jewels of Ottoman Art from the Topkapi Museum'. During the Zagreb Summer Festival, concerts are staged in the internal courtyard. The museum café makes an ideal stopping point for weary legs. ■ *Tue-Sun 1100-1900, admission prices vary depending on the exhibition. T4852117, www.galerijaklovic.hr, Jezuitski Trg 4.*

Inland Croatia

▶ **Tesla the inventor**

*Nikola Tesla was born in 1856 to a Serbian family in Smiljan, Croatia, and educated in Graz and Prague. Having completed his studies in 1881, he worked as electrical engineer for a telephone company in Budapest, before emigrating to the US in 1884 at the age of 28. There he was briefly employed by Thomas Edison, but soon decided to work alone on research and inventions, and the two thus became archrivals.*

*In 1888, Tesla designed the first system of generating and transmitting alternating current, though the patent rights to this revolutionary invention were bought by the American scientist George Westinghouse. In 1891 he invented the Tesla coil, a transformer still used today in radios and television sets. In 1895, he designed the first hydroelectric power plant on the Niagara Falls. However, in the same year his laboratory was destroyed by fire, and he began a series of economic and mental ups and downs that were to taint his later years.*

*An eccentric loner, he lived almost exclusively in hotels. From 1897 to 1933 he resided at the luxury Waldorf-Astoria Hotel, where he entertained New York celebrities: 6ft 6in tall, dark and handsome, many women are said to have been intrigued by him, but he remained a lifelong bachelor.*

*In 1915 he was nominated for the Nobel Prize for physics, which he was to share with Thomas Edison, but he refused to divide it with his former employee so in the end neither of them received the award. On 10 July 1931, his 75th birthday, he was featured on the cover of Time Magazine. However, by this time he had become totally solitary and had developed an unusual obsession with rescuing pigeons from Central Park. In 1933, due to financial problems, he moved from the Waldorf-Astoria to the far less glamorous Hotel New Yorker in Manhattan where he died in 1943. In 1956, the Tesla (T), a unit for measuring magnet flux density, was named after him.*

**Strossmayer Šetalište (Strossmayer Promenade)**   Returning to Čirilmetodska then turning left, you will arrive on Strossmayer Šetalište, a pleasant walkway following the line of Gradec's former south-facing wall, offering stunning views over the city rooftops. Pride of place is taken by **Kula Lotrščak** (Lotrščak Tower), part of the 13th-century fortification system. The tower now houses a gallery, and it is possible to climb to the top for dramatic views across the city to Novi Zagreb, on the south side of the River Sava. Each day at noon, a small (but extremely loud) cannon is fired from the top of the tower, in memory of the times when it was used to warn off the possibility of an Ottoman attack. ■ *Tue-Sun 1100-1900. 10Kn. Strossmayer Šetalište 9.*

**Uspinjaca**   Opposite the tower stands the upper station of the Uspinjaca (funicular railway), connecting Gornji Grad and Donji Grad. Built in 1891, it ran on steam until 1934, and makes an amusing way to descend 40 m (130 ft) to Tomićeva, just off Ilica. From here it's just a five-minute walk back to Trg Bana Jelačića, the main square. ■ *0630-2100. 2.5Kn. Strossmayer Šetalište.*

## Donji Grad

While Gornji Grad is made up of higgledy-piggledy cobbled streets which evolved spontaneously over the centuries, Donji Grad (Lower Town) was built on a formal grid during the late 19th century. The urban plan was drawn up by Milan Lenuci, who proposed a succession of adjoining squares with central gardens, laid out to form a 'U', now known as Lenuci's Green Horseshoe.

Inland Croatia

About five minutes southwest of Trg Bana Jelačića (and equally accessible from Ilica) lies Trg Petra Predradovića, better known to locals as Cvijetni Trg (Flower Square), in reference to the flower sellers who used to set up stalls here. Alas, the stalls are no longer, but there are a couple of colourful kiosks vending fresh bouquets. At the north end of the square stands the Orthodox Church, still frequented by Zagreb's (seriously depleted) Serb community.

**Trg Petra Predradovića**

From Trg Petra Predradovića, the street of Preradovićeva leads south, and if you follow this then take the first right onto Masarykova, you arrive at the vast green Trg Maršala Tita (Marshall Tito Square). This is the first of a series of three squares that make up one side of Lenuci's Green Horseshoe. The centre-piece is the monumental neo-Baroque **Hrvatsko Narodno Kazalište** (Croatian National Theatre), designed by two Viennese architects, Hellmer and Fellner, in 1894. Construction work was completed in record time, so as to be ready for an official opening by Emperor Franz Josef on his state visit in 1895. In front of the theatre lies the slightly neglected '*Zdenac Života*' (Well of Life) by Ivan Meštrović, dating from 1912. ■ *The theatre season runs Sep-Jun. T4828532, www.hnk.hr, Trg Maršala Tita 15.*

**Trg Maršala Tita (Marshall Tito Square)**
*Muzej za Umjetnost i Obrt is probably the best museum in Zagreb, after the Meštrović Atelier*

On the western side of the square stands the **Muzej za Umjetnost i Obrt** (Arts and Crafts Museum), a pleasant purpose-built 19th-century structure designed by Herman Bolle. The interior is refreshingly light and airy, providing a visitor-friendly exhibition space for a vast collection of furniture, laid out in chronological order and illustrating how Croatian design has been influenced by Austrian and Italian tastes, from the Baroque period up to the Modern Movement. ■ *Tue-Fri 1000-1800, Sat-Sun 1000-1300, closed Mon. 15Kn. T4826922, www.muo.hr, Trg Maršala Tita 10.*

Across the busy main road of Savska Cesta lies Roosevelt Trg, dominated by this renowned museum, housed within a neo-Renaissance former grammar school building. This phenomenal private collection was donated to the city by Ante Topić-Mimara. No one is quite sure how Mimara amassed such a treasure trove of art works: born in Dalmatia in 1898, he spent most of his life abroad, where he made his fortune, supposedly as a merchant. In 1973 he began transferring his collection to Zagreb and arranged for the founding of a museum, which opened in 1987, the year he died. On display are canvases attributed to Old Masters such as Raphael, Rembrandt and Rubens, as well as modern paintings by Manet, Degas and Renoir (though whether all these pieces are genuine remains a matter of controversy). The collection also includes an astounding hoard of ancient Egyptian glassware, Chinese porcelain and Persian carpets – all well worth seeing but of little relevance to Croatian culture. ■ *Tue-Wed, Fri-Sun 1000-1700, Thu 1000-1900, closed Mon. 15Kn. T4828100, www.mimara.hr, Rooseveltov trg 4.*

**Muzej Mimara (Mimara Museum)**

Further down Savska Cesta lies the Tekničke Muzej (Technical Museum), best visited in mid-afternoon when three highly enlightening 30-minute guided tours are on offer. While the ground floor displays a slightly mystifying selection of engines and turbines (appreciated almost exclusively by children and mechanical engineers), the star attraction is the Nikola Tesla demonstration, performed daily at 1530 in an area arranged to look like the early 20th-century scientist's laboratory. If you arrive a little earlier, there's a guided visit of a reconstructed mine at 1500, and then a Planetarium visit at 1600. ■ *Tue-Fri 0900-1700, Sat-Sun 0900-1300, closed Mon, 15Kn. T4844050, Savska Cesta 18, near Cibona Stadium.*

**Tekničke Muzej (Technical Museum)**

*Inland Croatia*

**Etnografski Muzej (Ethnographic Museum)** Returning to Trg Maršala Tita, the next square in the Green Horseshoe series is Mažuranićev Trg, home to this museum. Worth a look in if you're interested in traditional folk costumes – the variety of colours, materials and styles on display illustrates the cultural diversity of Croatia's contrasting inland and coastal regions. The lace from the island of Pag and the gold embroidered scarves from Slavonia are particularly worth seeing. There's also a section devoted to artefacts from the South Pacific, Asia and Africa, collected by 19th-century Croatian explorers and travellers. ■ *Tue-Thu 1000-1800, Fri-Sun 1000-1300, closed Mon. 15Kn. T4826220, Mažuranićev trg 14.*

**Botanički Vrt (Botanical Gardens)** Founded in 1889 as research grounds for the Faculty of Botany at Zagreb University, the gardens are small but well kept, and offer a welcome retreat from the bustle of the city. The main section is an arboretum, arranged informally in the style of an English garden, beside two artificial ponds with stunning water lilies and an ornamental bridge. ■ *0900-1800. Mon closed. Trg M Marilića 9a.*

**Trg Kralja Tomislava** Five minutes from the gardens stands the **Glavni Kolodvor** (main train station). From 1919 to 1977 the Orient Express used to stop here. The James Bond film *From Russia with Love* (1963) features Sean Connery in Zagreb Station, as one of the train's illustrious passengers, en route to Istanbul. Glavni Kolodvor overlooks Trg Kralja Tomislava, named after Tomislav (the first King of the medieval state of Croatia), and bears an equestrian statue of him. In the centre of the square stands the **Umjetnički Paviljon** (Art Pavilion), originally built to celebrate '1,000 years of Hungarian Culture' in Budapest in 1896, then dismantled and reassembled here, under the initiative of the Croatian artist Vlaho Bukovac (see page 329). Today it is used for temporary exhibitions. ■ *Mon-Sat 1100-1900, Sun 1000-1300. 20Kn. T4841070, www. umjetnicki-paviljon.hr, Trg Kralja Tomislava 22.*

**Trg Nikole Šubića Zrinskog** You are now are the second set of three leafy squares that make up the remaining side of Lenuci's Green Horseshoe. Proceeding back towards the city centre, the next square is overlooked by the 19th-century Croatian Academy of Sciences and Arts (formerly named the Yugoslav Academy of Sciences and Arts) housing the **Strossmayerova Galerija Starih Majstora** (Strossmayer Gallery of Old Masters). Founded by Bishop Strossmayer in 1884, the collection has expanded gradually over the last 120 years and now includes many notable canvases by Venetian Renaissance and Baroque painters such as Bellini and Carpaccio, and Dutch masters Brueghel and Van Dyck. Worth a special mention is a small *Mary Magdalene* by El Greco. ■ *Tue 1000-1300 and 1700-1900, Wed-Sun 1000-1300, closed Mon. 15Kn. T4895111, www.mdc.hr/strossmayer   Trg Nikole Šubića Zrinskog 11.*

Across the road, the **Arheoloski Muzej** (Archaeological Museum) exhibits finds from prehistoric times up to the Tartar invasion. Pride of place is taken by the Vučedol Dove, a three-legged ceramic vessel in the form of a bird, dating back to the fourth millennium BC and found in Vukovar, Eastern Slavonia. ■ *Tue-Fri 1000-1700, Sat-Sun 1000-1300. 15Kn. T4873101, www.amz.hr, Trg Nikole Šubića Zrinskog 19.*

# Excursions

If you plan to stay more than three days in the Zagreb area, an excursion into the surrounding countryside will give you a clearer picture of what inland Croatia is all about. Zagrebians love walking and most would probably nominate **Mount Medvenica** as their favourite out-of-town trip. See page 75 for further details.

**Maksimir Park**

East of the city centre lies the green expanse of Maksimir Park, animated by joggers, lovers and families with kids. Founded as a city garden by Archbishop Maximilian Vrhovac (after whom it is named) in 1784, Maksimir claims to be the first public park in southeast Europe. During the 19th century, Archbishop Juraj Haulik extended the park to its present 18 hectares, and proposed the English-style landscaping with lawns, woods, tree-lined avenues, artificial lakes and romantic follies. The zoo was added in 1925. Opposite the park stands the **Dinamo Football Stadium**, home ground to the city football team and the main venue for international matches played in Croatia. ■ *Sunrise to sunset, 3 km east of the city centre, tram no11 and no12 (direction Dubrava) from Trg Bana Jelačića, the main square.*

**Mirogoj Cemetery**

North of the city centre lies Mirogoj Cemetery, designed by Herman Bolle in 1876. The west side of the cemetery is enclosed within a protective wall sheltering a neo-Renaissance arcade, while the monumental main entrance is crowned with a copper cupola. Over the decades citizens of varying religious and political persuasion have been laid to rest here, as can be seen by the stylistic range of tombs: the elongated pentagonal Muslim headstones, the Orthodox stones bearing Cyrillic script, the Jewish with the six-point star, Socialists the five-point red star and of course the majority Catholics. ■ *0800-2000, 2 km northeast of the city centre, bus 106 from Kaptol, opposite the Cathedral.*

**Samobor**

Cake lovers might opt for a leisurely afternoon in Samobor where the local delicacy is *kremšnita* (custard pie). See page 76.

**Zagorje**

Another popular excursion is a drive through Zagorje, a region north of the capital, noted for its undulating hills, vineyards and *klets*. Here you can visit Tito's birthplace and Staro Selo (Old Village Farm Museum) at **Kumrovec**, plus the romantic castle of **Trakošćan** and the imposing but sadly neglected **Veliki Tabor** fortress. See page 78.

**Varaždin**

Last but by no means least, architectural fanatics are advised to make a trip to the well-preserved Baroque town and former capital, Varaždin. See page 83. Those interested in modern art may be intrigued (or reviled) by the Hlebine Art Gallery, displaying works by local Naïve artists, at **Hlebine**. See further, page 87.

Inland Croatia

# Essentials

## Sleeping

**Donji Grad**
■ *on map, page 60*

*As there are no hotels in Gornji Grad, all the lodgings listed here are found in Donji Grad*

**L** *Hotel Esplanade*, Mihanovićeva 1, opposite the train station, T4566666, F4577907, www.esplanade.hr  Built in 1925 for travellers on the Orient Express, the grandiose interior of this 179-room hotel has retained its old-fashioned charm, while modern facilities include a business centre, plus massage, sauna and beauty salon. Closed for renovation in the New Year, due to open in Sep 2003.

**A** *Hotel Dubrovnik*, Gajeva 1, just off the main square, T4873555, F4818447, www.tel.hr/hotel-dubrovnik  The most centrally located hotel in town is best known for its unfortunately garish mirrored-glass façade. However, its 275 rooms are modern and comfortable, and some offer views of the Cathedral. **A** *Hotel Palace*, Strossmayerov Trg 10, between the train station and the main square, T4814611, F4811358, www.palace.hr  Overlooking a leafy square, this Secessionist building was converted to the become city's first hotel in 1907. There are 132 rooms, plus a pleasant street-level Viennese-style café.

**B** *Jagerhorn*, Ilica 14, 100 m west of the main square, T4833877, F4833446. Adjoining a well-known game restaurant of the same name, *Jagerhorn* is tucked away in a passageway off Ilica, and offers 13 simply furnished cosy rooms. **B** *Vila Tina*, Bukovačka Cesta 213, 20 mins from the main square, close to Maksimir Park, T445138, F2445204, www.vilatina.com  This delightful family-run hotel comprises 16 tastefully furnished rooms, adorned with extras such as fresh fruit and flowers. There's an excellent restaurant, plus a small indoor pool, solarium and sauna.

**C** *Hotel Sliško*, Supilova 13, 200 m from the bus station, T/F6184777, www.slisko.hr  This small hotel has 12 smartly furnished rooms, each with a private bathroom. There's a bar and breakfast room (but no restaurant) and ample parking space.

**D** *Ilica*, Ilica 102, a 15-min walk west of the main square, T3777622, F3777722, www.hotel-ilica.hr  This friendly modern hotel comprises 14 rooms and 2 apartments, but no restaurant.

**E** *Studentski Dom Cvijetno naselje*, Odranska 8, off Savska cesta, 2 km south west of the centre, T6191245, F4593592, turizam@sczg.hr  Student halls of residence open to visitors from mid-Jul to late-Sep. 407 rooms. Double rooms with en-suite facilities. Reduced rates for students. **E** *Studentski Dom Stjepan Radić*, Jarunska 2, close to Jarun Lake, 3 km southwest of the centre, T3634255, turizam@sczg.hr  Student halls of residence open to visitors from mid-Jul to late-Sep. 500 rooms. Double rooms with shared facilities. Reduced rates for students.

**F** *Ravnice*, Ravnice 38d, 20 mins from the main square, close to Maksimir Park, T2332325. This clean and genuinely friendly hostel remains open all year and offers 9 rooms, each with 2, 3 or 4 beds.

*Evistas*, Šenoina 28, T4839554, F4839543, evistas@zg.tel.hr  This agency that can arrange short-term apartment rentals or rooms with local families.

Inland Croatia

# Eating

**Mid-range** *Atlanta Café Restaurant*, Tkalčićeva 65, T4813848. One of the few restaurants in a street lined with busy cafés, *Atlanta* is fun and stylish. Inside, terracotta coloured walls are hung with gigantic gilt-framed mirrors, and the menu features pastas, risottos and a range of creative meat dishes. *Baltazar*, Nova Ves 4, T4666824. Located north of the Cathedral, *Baltazar* specializes in classic Balkan dishes such as *ražnjić* (mixed grilled meat), *Čevapčići* (kebabs) and *zapečeni grah* (oven-baked beans). In summer there are tables outside in a pretty courtyard. Closed Sun. *Dubrovakin Put*, Dubrovkin put bb, in Tuškanac Park, 10 mins from the main square, T4834975. Considered by many to be the best fish restaurant in town, *Dubravkin Put* comprises a light and airy dining room decorated with colourful modern canvasses by Edo Murtić, plus outdoor seating on a leafy terrace. The house speciality is *brodet* (fish stew) prepared with fresh herbs. *Kaptolska Klet*, Kaptol 5, T4814838. Opposite the Cathedral, this popular rustic eatery offers extensive seating both indoors and out. The menu features reasonably priced hearty local dishes like *purica sa mlincima* (turkey with savoury pastries) and *zagorski štrukli* (baked cheese dumplings). *Murter*, Kaptol 27, T4817745. Set in a vaulted brick cellar, this highly regarded restaurant specializes in classic Dalmatian fish dishes, but also does an excellent peppered steak. There's an open-plan kitchen so you can watch the cooks while they work. Closed Sun and all Aug. *Pod Gričkim Topom*, Za kmardijeve stube 5, T4833607. This small, homely restaurant, lying just below Strossmayer Šetalište, offers stunning views over the city rooftops. Dalmatian fish dishes predominate: try the *ligne na žaru* (barbecued squid).

**Cheap** *Stara Tkalča*, Tkalčićeva 70, T4813235. Fun and informal, students come here to eat barbecued meats and sausages and drink cheap beer. Rustic wooden tables and rock music set the scene.

**Expensive** *A G Matoš Klub*, Gajeva 2, T4872544. A chic modern restaurant affording fantastic 1st-floor views down onto the main square, perfect for dinner on a cold winter's night. The menu includes sophisticated dishes such as grilled fillet of bass in scampi and lemon sauce, or veal stuffed with goose liver in tarragon sauce. *Paviljon*, Trg kralja Tomislava 22, T4813066. Occupies the ground floor of the charming 19th-century Art Pavilion, close to the train station. Choose from delights such as grilled salmon on wild rice, or crispy roast duck on red cabbage with figs. Through summer it is possible to eat outside. Closed Sun.

**Mid-range** *Klub Maksimir*, Oboj 1, T2341189. Lying on the edge of Maksimir Park, this 'club' doubles as a restaurant and exhibition space. The menu changes frequently, but you can expect imaginative risotto, gnocchi and mushroom dishes, plus an unusual dining room decorated with modern sculpture and a leafy summer terrace. *Stari Fijaker*, Mesnička 6, T4833829. Located a 5-min walk along Ilica from the main square, *Stari Fijaker* serves up traditional Zagrebian fare such as roast meats and *zagorski štrukli* (baked cheese dumplings) in an old-fashioned dining room with wooden panelled walls and crisp white table linens. *Vinodol*, Nikole Tesle 10, T4811341. A good choice for meat lovers, the speciality here are lamb and veal prepared under a *peka*. There's outdoor seating on a large summer terrace, with whole lamb turning on a spit.

**Gornji Grad**
● *on map, page 60*

All the restaurants listed here are open daily for lunch and dinner, unless otherwise stated

Inland Croatia

**Donji Grad**
● *on map, page 60*

▶ **The place where ties began**

Around the world an estimated 600 million businessmen wake up each morning and put on a tie before setting off to work. What many of them probably don't realise is that the tie originates from Croatia.

During the early 17th century, Croatian soldiers began wearing narrow scarves, tied loosely around the neck. Those worn by officers were of coloured silk or fine cotton, while those worn by lower ranking soldiers were of a coarser material.

In 1635, when France entered the Thirty Year's War as an ally of Sweden and the protestant princes of Germany against the Hapsburgs, some 6,000 foreign soldiers and knights came to Paris to give their support to King Louis XIII and

Cardinal Richelieu. And among them were a group of Croatian mercenaries.

The chic French were immediately impressed by the Croatian soldiers' stylish neck ties, and by 1650 the new style 'a la croate' had arrived in the court of Louis XIV, who was well known for his love of ornamentation and grandeur.

The expression, 'a la croate', soon evolved into a new French word, which still exists today: la cravate. When the exiled English King Charles II (also noted for extravagant taste) returned home in 1660 he brought this new fashion accessory to Britain, and over the following decades the cravat came to symbolize the height of culture and elegance through out Europe.

**Cheap** *Medvedgrad Pivnica*, Savska 56, T6177110. A popular micro brewery, *Medvedgrad* also serves up generous portions of roast meats, goulash, and beans and sausage, accompanied by a range of salads. You'll find it close to the Cibona stadium, taking tram no4 from the train station or tram no17 from the main square. *Restoran Boban*, Gajeva 9, just off the main square, T4811549. Owned by Zvonimir Boban (captain of the Croatian national football team during the 1998 World Cup), this basement level restaurant specializes in pasta dishes. It's extremely popular, so be prepared to queue for a table.

**Seriously cheap** *Pekarnica Dora*, 8 Trg Strossmayerova. A 24-hr bakery close to the train station selling *burek* (cheese or meat baked in filo pastry), bread, cold drinks and yoghurt.

## Cafés

**Gornji Grad**  For informal café-bars, head for the pretty street of Tklačićeva, where you'll find a wide choice of laid-back studenty haunts: *Sun³ani Sat*, at number 27, with tables and comfy wicker chairs outside is as good as any. If you're doing a round of the museums in Gornji Grad, *Gallery Klovićevi Dvori museum café* at Jezuitski trg 4 offers a peaceful, cultural ambience.

**Donji Grad**  Of several cafés overlooking Trg Bana Jelačića, the main square, *Gradska Kavana* at number 10 and *Mala Kavana* at number 5 are the largest and most popular, and both offer outdoor seating through summer. *Kavana Palace*, on the ground floor of *Hotel Palace* at Strossmayerov trg 10, close to the train station, has a Viennese-style interior and a summer terrace.

## Bars and clubs

**Gornji Grad**  *Tolkein*, Vraničanijeva 8. A tiny bar hidden away in an old stone building in Gornji Grad, with a few tables outside when the sun shines. *Gjuro II*, Medveščak 2, T4683381.

Wed-Sun 2100-0200. Young professionals with an alternative streak meet up here to drink, chat and dance. Music predominantly techno. *Saloon*, Tuškanac 1a, T4834903. Tue-Sat 2200-0400. The place to be seen, especially if you want to hit the gossip magazines. It can get very busy, but in summer the crowds spill out onto an open-air terrace. Commercial disco predominates, with a smattering of Croatian hits.

*Bulldog Pub*, Bogovićeva 6, T4817393. Very popular with young Croatians and English-speaking visitors alike, this large pub lies just 5 mins from the main square. Through summer tables spill onto the pedestrian area out front. *Old Pharmacy*, Andrije Hebranga 11a, T4554367. A peaceful pub with a collection of English-language newspapers, TV and a non-smoking side room. *Pivnica Medvedgrad*, Savska 56, T6177110, www.pivinca-medvedgrad.hr  The best choice in town for a beer, this spacious microbrewery serves 4 of its own brews. There's an adjoining dining hall (see Eating) if you feel peckish. *Aquarius*, Aleja Mira bb, T3640231, www.aquarius.hr Closed Mon. Undoubtedly Zagreb's top club for dance, commercial and techno, plus occasional concerts by popular Croatian bands. Overlooking Lake Jarun, 4 km from the city centre. *BP Jazz Club*, Nikole Tesle 7, T4814444, www.bpclub.hr  A friendly jazz club located in a basement. Can get very crowded when there are live concerts. *Močvara* (The Swamp), Trnjanski Nasip bb, T6159668, www.urk.hr  Mon-Thu 2000-0100, Fri-Sun 2200-0400. A very popular alternative youth club, located in a disused factory on the banks of the River Sava. Founded in 1999 by a cultural association that wanted a venue for off-beat Croatian and foreign music and drama. *Tvornica*, Šubićeva 2, T4655007. Fri-Sat 0900-0400, closes earlier through the week. Another alternative venue, attracting some of Europe's top DJ's as well as staging rock concerts and theatre. Open day and night, located close to the bus station.

**Donji Grad**

## Entertainment

*Broadway Tkalča*, in the Centar Kaptol complex at Nova Ves 17, in Gornji Grad behind the Cathedral, is the city's largest cinema, with 3 screens, T4860241. The best cinema for alternative arty films is *Kinoteka*, Kordunska 1, west of the main square, close to Ilica, T3771753. *Zagreb*, Trg Petra Predradovića 4, is the most centrally located cinema.

**Cinemas**

**Hrvatsko Narodno Kazalište** (Croatian National Theatre) at Trg Maršala Tita 15, stages classical, contemporary and Croatian drama, opera and ballet, Sep-Jun. For information, T4828532, or visit their excellent website, www.hnk.hr  *Komedija*, Kaptol 9, T4814566, www.komedija.hr  A small theatre in Gornji Grad, close to the Cathedral, staging operettas and Croatian musicals.

**Theatre**

**Hrvatski Glazbeni Zavod** (Croatian Music Institute), Gundulićeva 6, T4830822. Stages chamber music recitals and occasional performances of Dalmatian *klapa* (see page 335). **Koncertna Dvorana Vatroslav Lisinski** (Vatroslav Lisinski Concert Hall), Stjepana Radića 4, T6121166, www.lisinski.hr  A modern complex with 2 auditoriums, this is the home to the Zagreb Philharmonic Orchestra. It also hosts occasional musicals and jazz concerts.

**Classical music**

**Dinamo Stadium**, Maksimirska 128, T2334111. Tickets 40Kn. The Croatian national football team, and the Zagreb city football team, Dinamo, play here. **Dražen Petrović Basketball Centre**, Savska 30, T4843333. Tickets 10-30Kn. The Zagreb basketball team, Cibona, play here.

**Spectator sports**

## Festivals

*Folklore Festival*, **late-Jul**. A 5-day celebration of music and dance, with performers from Croatia and other southeast European countries dressed in traditional folk costumes. Main events take place on Trg Bana Jelačića and in the Gallery Klovićevi Dvori courtyard in Gornji Grad. For information check out the website, www.msf.hr

*Summer Festival*, **mid-Jul to mid-Aug**. Evening musical performances by Croatian and foreign orchestras and soloists. Main events are staged in the Cathedral, St Catherine's Church and the Gallery Klovićevi Dvori courtyard in Gornji Grad. For information check out the website, www.kdz.hr

*St Martin's Day*, **Nov 11**. Celebrated in the rural area of Zagorje, north of Zagreb. A feast of food and drink culminates with the blessing of the season 's new wine.

## Shopping

*Algoritam*, Gajeva 1, just off the main square, T4818672. The best **bookshop** for foreign language publications, including novels, travel guides and maps. *Croata*, Kaptol 13, close to the Cathedral in Gornji Grad, T4814600, www.croata.hr  Sells original **Croatian ties** in presentation boxes, along with a history of the tie. **Dolac**, the **open-air market**, just off the main square, is the best place to shop for fresh fruit and vegetables. There is also a small arts and crafts section. *Galerija Bil Ani*, Radieva 37, parallel to Tkalčićeva in Gornji Grad, T4852345. Throughout Croatia you'll find souvenir shops selling hand-made miniature **ceramic replicas** of traditional Dalmatian, Istrian, Slavonian and Zagrebian houses. This gallery was the first to start producing them. **Tourist Information Centre**, Trg Bana Jelačića 11, T4814051. Other than picking up maps and leaflets, here you can buy a **liṭsitarsko srce** (gingerbread heart decorated with icing) and *paška čipka* (handmade lace from the island of Pag). *Vinoteka Bornstein*, Kaptol 19, close to the Cathedral in Gornji Grad, T4812363. A beautiful vaulted brick cellar stocked with quality **Croatian wines**, olive oils and truffle products: ideal as presents to take home.

## Sport

**Ice-skating**  Ice-skating Rink, Paviljon 40, Zagrebački Velesajam, inside the Trade Fair Centre complex in Novi Zagreb, south of the River Sava, T6554357. Mon-Fri 1000-2200, Sat-Sun 1000-1200, 1800-1930 and 2030-2200.

**Fitness centres**  Mladost Sports Complex, Jarunska 5, T3658555. Mon-Fri 1100-1500 and 1800-2000, Sat 1300-1700, Sun 1000-1400. This vast sports complex comprises an indoor Olympic swimming pool, 16 tennis courts and a fitness centre. *Sheraton Hotel fitness centre*, Kneza Borne 2, T4552655. Mon-Fri 0700-2200, Sat-Sun 0900-2200. The hotel fitness club, swimming pool, solarium, sauna and massage facilities are open to non-residents at 60Kn per day or 380Kn per month.

**Tennis**  *Maksimir Tennis Club*, Ravnice 1, close to Maksimir Park, T2910429. Mon-Fri 1000-1800, Sat 1000-1500. The centre comprises 4 indoor and 22 outdoor tennis courts, plus a bowling alley and table tennis facilities.

## Tour operators

*Atlas*, Zrinjevac 17, T4873064, www.atlas-croatia.com  Organize a wide variety of cultural and sporting excursions, primarily in Dalmatia, plus yacht charters from Split and Dubrovnik. *Croatia Express*, Nikola Tesle 4, T4811842, www.croatiaexpress.com Provide public transport information and tickets for the entire country. *Generalturist*, Praška 5, T4810033, www.generalturist.com One of the largest Croatian travel agencies, *Generalturist* specialize in tailor-made trips both with and without guides, pilgrimage tours and yacht charters. *Globtour Zagreb*, Zrinjevac 1-1, T4810020, www.globtour.hr, offer guided tours in Zagreb and the surrounding area. *Kompas*, Gajeva 6, T4811536, www.kompas.hr, arrange hotel bookings and trips, primarily in Zagreb. *Zagrebtours*, Zrinjevac18, T4873305, www.zagrebtours.hr, specialize in Zagreb and the surrounding area.

## Transport

Through summer, there are regular flights to and from **Amsterdam**, **Barcelona**, **Berlin**, **Brussels**, **Copenhagen**, **Dusseldorf**, **Frankfurt**, **Gothenburg**, **Istanbul**, **London** (Gatwick and Heathrow), **Madrid**, **Manchester**, **Moscow**, **Mostar**, **Munich**, **Paris**, **Prague**, **Rome**, **Sarajevo**, **Skopje**, **Stockholm**, **Stuttgart**, **Tel Aviv**, **Warsaw**, **Vienna** and **Zurich**. Internal flights link the capital with **Brač** (island of Bol), **Dubrovnik**, **Pula**, **Rijeka**, **Split** and **Zadar**. The number of destinations and the frequency of flights are reduced in winter. Sample prices for Zagreb: London Heathrow with *Croatia Airlines*, departing daily through August vary from one-way at US$726 to special economy return at US$269. Zagreb Airport, Pleso bb, T6265222 (information), T4562229 (lost and found), www.tel.hr/zagreb-airport Airport bus service, T6157992. It is 17 km from the city centre. A shuttle bus, T6157992, runs from the airport to Zagreb bus station every 30 mins 0700-2000, and from Zagreb bus station to the airport 0600-1930. The journey takes approximately 25 mins and a one-way ticket costs 25Kn. Expect to pay 150-200Kn to make the same journey by taxi.

**Air**

Internal services include about 20 buses daily to **Rijeka** in Kvarner (3½ hrs); 16 buses to **Pula** in Istria (5½ hrs); 10 to **Osijek** in Slavonia (4 hrs); 20 to **Zadar** in North Dalmatia (5½ hrs); 30 to **Split** in Central Dalmatia (7 hrs) and 6 to **Dubrovnik** in South Dalmatia (10½ hrs). There are also daily international bus lines to **Ljubljana** (Slovenia); **Barcs** and **Nagykanisza** (Hungary); **Belgrade** (Serbia and Montenegro); **Graz** (Austria); **Munich**, **Stuttgart**, **Frankfurt**, **Dortmund**, **Cologne**, and **Dusseldorf** (Germany) and **Zurich** (Switzerland). The bus station is at Avenija M Držića bb, a 15-min walk from the main square. Left luggage costs 1.20Kn per item per hr, open non-stop 24 hrs.

**Bus**
*For all information about buses to and from Zagreb, T060-313333, www.akz.hr*

*Avis*, T6265840, www.avis.hr, is at the airport and in the city centre at *Hotel Opera*, Kršnjavoja 1, T4836006; *Budget*, T6265854, www.budget.hr, is at the airport and in the city centre at Praška 5, T4805687; *Hertz*, www.hertz.hr, T4562635, is at the airport and in the city centre at Mažuranićev trg 2, T4847222. *Sixt*, T6219900, www.sixt.hr, is at the airport and in the city centre at Roosevelt trg 4, T4828385. Expect to pay 400Kn per day for a small car such as a Fiat Uno, 800Kn per day for a large car such as an Opal Astra Automatic.

**Car hire**

*Radio Taxi*, T6682505/6682558. 24-hr service, usually arrive within 5-10 mins.

**Taxi**

Internal services includes 5 trains daily to and from **Rijeka** in Kvarner (approx 3½ hrs), 4 trains daily to **Split** in Dalmatia (8 hrs) and 4 trains daily to **Osijek** in Slavonia (4 hrs). Daily international trains run direct to and from **Budapest** (Hungary), **Belgrade** (Serbia and Montenegro), **Munich** (Germany), **Vienna** (Austria) and **Venice** (Italy). International train information, T4811892. Left luggage costs 12Kn per item per day, open non-stop 24 hrs.

**Train**
*National train information T060 333444, www.hznet.hr*

Inland Croatia

# Directory

**Airlines offices** *Adria Airways*, Praška 9, T4810011. *Aeroflot*, Varšavska 13, I4872055. *Air Canada*, Mihanovićeva 1, *Hotel Esplanade*, T4577924. *Air France*, Kršnjavoga 1, *Hotel Opera*, T4837100. *Alitalia*, *Generalturist*, Praška 5, T4810413. *Austrian Airlines*, Zagreb Airport, T6265900. *Avioimpex*, Savska 1, T4829439. *Bosna Air*, Zagreb Airport, T4562672. *British Airways*, Kneza Borne 2, *Hotel Sheraton*, T4553336. *Croatia Airlines*, Trg Nikole Šubića Zrinskog 17, T4819633. *CSA*, Trg Nikole Šubića Zrinskog 17, T4873301. *Delta*, Mihanovićeva 1, *Hotel Esplanade*, T4577277. *KLM*, Mihanovićeva 1, *Hotel Esplanade*, T4573133. *LOT*, Trg Bana Jelačića 2, T4837500. *Lufthansa*, Zagreb Airport, T4562187. *Malaysia Airlines*, Strossmazerov Trg 7/1, T4810777. *Malev* (Hungarian Airlines), Kršnjavoga 1, *Hotel Opera*, T4836935. *Turkish Airlines*, Zagreb Airport, T4562008.

**Communications** Internet café: *Ergonet*, Centar Kaptol, Nova Ves 11, T4860105, Gornji Grad, www.ergo2000.hr Mon-Sat 0900-2300, Sun 1500-2300. The following are in Donji Grad: *Art Net Club*, Preradovićeva 25, T4558471, www.haa.hr Mon-Sat 0900-2300; *Charlie Net*, Gajeva 4, T4880233, Mon-Sat 0800-2200; *Cyber Café Sublink*, Teslina 12, T4811329, www.sublink.hr Mon-Sat 0900-2300, Sun 1500-2200; *Iskoninternet*, Preradovićeva 5, T4811758, www.kic.hr Mon-Sat 0900-2300, Sun 0012-2400 and *Net Kulturni Klub Mama*, Preradovićeva 18, T4856400, 0012-2400. **Post offices**: the main post office is at Branimirova 4, next to the train station, and is open 24 hrs. The central post office is at Jurišićeva 4, close to the main square, and works Mon-Fri 0700-2100, Sat 0800-1800, Sun 0800-1400. **Telephone**: if you prefer to telephone from a peaceful phone booth, rather than calling on the street, go to the main post office (see Post Offices, above). Otherwise, if you don't mind the traffic noise, you'll find countless blue phone kiosks dotted around the city.

**Cultural centres** British Council, Ilica 12, T4813700. Mon-Tue and Thu-Fri 1000-1600, Wed 1330-1830. French Cultural Institute, Preradovićeva 40, T4855222. Mon-Fri 0900-1700. Goethe Institute (German), Ulica Grada Vukovara 64, T6195000. Mon-Thu 0830-1700, Fri 0830-1630. Italian Cultural Institute, Preobraženska 4, T4830208. Mon-Thu 1200-1500, Fri 0012-1400.

**Embassies** Austria, Jabukovac 39, T4834459; Australia, Centar Kaptol, Nova Ves 11 III Kat, T4891200; Belgium, Pantovčak 125b, T4578901; Bosnia and Herzegovina, Torbarova 9, T4683761; Canada, Prilaz Gjure Deželića 4, T4881200; Czech Republic, Savska cesta 41, T6177246; Denmark (Consulate), Pantovčak 35, T3760536; France, Schlosserove stube 5, T4557767; Germany, Ulica grada Vukovara 64, T6158105; Great Britain, Vlaška 121-III, T4555310; Hungary, Krležin Gvozd 11a, T4834990; Italy, Medulićeva 22, T4846386; Japan, Ksaver 211, T4677755; Macedonia, Petrinjska ulica 29, T4922902; Netherlands, Medveščak 56, T4684880; Norway, Petrinjska 9, T4922829; Poland, Krležin Gvozd 3, T4899444; Slovakia, Prilaz Gjure Deželića 10, T4848941; Slovenia, Savska 41, T6311014; Spain, Medulićeva 5, T4848607; Sweden, Frankopanska 22, T4849322; Switzerland, Bogovićeva 3, T4810891; US, Hebrangova 2, T6612200; Union of Serbia and Montenegro, Mesićeva 19, T4680552.

**Medical services** Doctors and hospitals: Ignjata Djordjica 26, T4600911, for emergencies. Casualty, Draškovićeva 19, T4610011. Pharmacies: all pharmacies are marked by a glowing green cross. Pharmacies at Ilica 43, T4848450, and Ilica 301, T3774423, stay open 24 hrs.

**Languages schools** *Berlitz*, Amruševa 10, T4812116, www.berlitz.com *Inlingua*, Vlaška 40, T4921877. *Centar za strane jezike*, Vodnikova 12, 10000 Zagreb, T 3851 4829222, F 385 1 4829149.

Run year-round courses in Zagreb as well as a Dubrovnik-based summer school. *Sokrates*, Pavla Hatza 21, 10000 Zagreb, T 385 1 4923400, F 385 1 4923400.

*Petecin*, Kaptol 11, T4814802. *Predom*, Draškovićeva 31, T4612900.  **Laundry**

**City Library**, Trg Ante Starčevića 6, T4572344, www.kgz.hr (website not in English)  **Libraries** Mon-Fri 0800-2000, Sat 0800-1400. **National Public Library**, Hrvatske bratske zajednice bb, T6164111. Mon-Fri 0800-2100, Sat 0800-1500. **British Council**, Ilica 12, T4813700, www.britishcouncil.hr  Mon-Tue and Thu-Fri 1000-1600, Wed 1330-1830. **French Cultural Institute**, Preradovićeva 40, T4855222. Mon-Fri 0900-1700. **Goethe Institute** (German), Ulica Grada Vukovara 64, T6195000. Mon-Thu 0830-1700, Fri 0830-1630. **Italian Cultural Institute**, Preobraženska 4, T4830208. Mon-Thu 1200-1500, Fri 1200-1400.

Ambulance 94; Fire 93; Police 92.  **Useful numbers**

*Inland Croatia*

## Medvednica Nature Park

Lying just north of Zagreb – in fact the city's suburbs extend on to the lower slopes – Medvednica Mountain has long been a popular hiking destination for the people of Zagreb, with the first organized walking groups setting out to scale its heights in the late 19th century. Still today it's a popular destination, especially on Sundays, when the early morning tram is literally heaving with hikers – many well past retirement age – setting out to climb to Sljeme, the 1033 m summit, many decked in appropriate walking gear and armed with a picnic lunch.  *Phone code: 01 Colour map 1, grid B5/6*

Nature Park office, Bliznec bb, Zagreb, T4580699, www.hinet.hr/park-prirode-medvednica can supply maps and information about which mountain huts are working. Open Mon-Fri 0800-1600.  **Ins & outs** *See Transport, page 76, for details*

Medvednica was declared a nature park in 1981, with marked walking paths winding their way across the slopes, 64% of which are covered with deciduous and coniferous woods of oak, beech, chestnut and fir. The park is at its prettiest in spring, when the woodland paths are dense with wild flowers, and in autumn, when the trees take on golden and russet hues. In winter there are basic skiing facilities.  **Sights**

The highest peak, **Sljeme**, which can be reached by cable car, is crowned by a TV tower and a small chapel, and on a fine day it's possible to see Zagreb to the south, Zagorje to the north and the Slovenian Alps to the west from this fine vantage point.

Traces of prehistoric man have been found in **Veternica Cave**, on the mountain, which was first mentioned as *Mons Ursi* (Bear Mountain) in 1209. Its present name is derived from the Croatian *medvjed*, meaning 'bear', and indeed the slopes were once populated by bears.

Medvednica is ideal for picnicking, with several designated areas equipped with wooden tables and benches, though cheap substantial food is also available at several mountain huts. Alternatively, if you can hold out till the homeward journey, there are a number of good traditional restaurants on the road between the park and the capital.

**Sleeping & eating**

**D** *Tomislavov Dom*, Sljemenska cesta bb, T4555833, F4555834. Just a 5-min walk from the cable car, this mountain-top hotel set in pretty woodland offers 67 basic but comfortable rooms, plus a café, restaurant, sauna, bowling alley, and conference facilities. **Mid-range** *Stari Puntijar*, Gračanka cesta 65, on the road between Zagreb and Medvednica, T4675500. A charming restaurant well-known for traditional 19th-century Zagreb dishes such as *podolac* (ox) medallions in cream and saffron, *zagorski štruki* (baked cheese dumplings), *orehnjača* (walnut loaf) and *makovnjača* (poppy seed cake).

**Transport**

Take **tram** no14 from the city centre, all the way to the terminal stop, Mihaljevac. From there, take tram no15 to its terminal stop, Dolje. From Dolje a **funicular** runs hourly 0800-2000, bringing you close to Sljeme, in 23 mins. Return ticket 15Kn. If you're driving, head out of the city centre north along Medveščak, passing through the village of Gračani to arrive at the funicular.

## Samobor and Žumberak i Samobor Gorje Nature Park

*Phone code: 01*
*Colour map 1, grid B5*
*Population: 36,206*
*20 km west of Zagreb*

Lying close to the hills of the recently designated Žumberak i Samobor Gorje Prirodni Park, Samobor has a somewhat Alpine feel. Narrow cobbled streets meet at the large main square, Trg kralja Tomislava, surrounded by palatial 19th-century town houses and open-air cafés. Just off the square you'll find Mala Venecija (Little Venice), a pretty area built along the banks of Gradna Brook, traversed by a series of wooden bridges. Samobar provides well for Zagrebian's favourite pastimes – hiking and dining (see box) – so it's a popular weekend retreat. If you are arriving from the Slovenian border there is a lovely, reasonably priced, old-fashioned hotel, making it an ideal first-night base.

**Ins & outs**
*See Transport, page 78, for further details*

**Getting there** There are 50 buses a day from Zagreb. **Getting around** The town is easily navigable on foot. **Tourist office** The town tourist office is at Trg kralja Tomislava 5, T3360044, www.samobor.hr (in Croatian only).

**History**

The town dates back to 1270, when supporters of the Czech king, Otokar, built Stari Grad fortress on Tepec Hill. A settlement grew up below the fortress, expanding rapidly during the 16th century with the opening of copper mines in the nearby village of Rude, plus the arrival of Franciscan monks. Stari Grad was abandoned during the late 18th century and now lies derelict, though the remaining walls and defence tower are worth the uphill hike if you're a ruins fan. In 1797 fire destroyed much of the town below, hence most of today's buildings are post-18th century.

**Sights**

A five-minute walk from the main square stands Livadićev Dvor, dating back to 1764. Members of the Illyrian Movement (see page 317) used to meet here during the mid-19th century, and in 1949 the building was turned into the **Gradski Muzej** (Town Museum). Inside you'll find various exhibits relating to Samobor's past, ranging from a small archaeological collection to the history of the local mountaineering club. ■ *Tue-Fri 0900-1400, Sat-Sun 0900-1300. 8 Kn. T3361014. Livadićev Dvor, Livadićeva 7.*

Leave the main square by Sv Ane, a winding pathway leading through wooded parkland up to **Anindol Šetalište** (Anindol Promenade) on **Tepec Hill**. From here there are wonderful views over the town and surrounding countryside. If you reach the top you'll come to the ruins of Stari Grad, and close by you'll find two small Baroque chapels, **Kapelica Sv Ane** and **Kapela Sv Jurja**, joined together by a pilgrimage path known as **Križni Put** (Stations of the Cross).

## Savouries, sweets and shots ◀

You'll find plenty of small traditional restaurants serving up excellent local dishes in Samobor and its surroundings. Look out for cesnjofke *(garlic flavoured sausages)* and rudarska gredlica, *a concoction of egg, flour, oil, cheese and walnuts, known as* miner's pie *after the men who used to work the copper mines at Rude. If you have a sweet tooth, be sure to try* samoborska kremšnita, *a delicious custar dpie made with flaky pastry. In* May 2001, the people of Samobor were nominated for the *Guinness Book of Records, having just knocked up the 'world's largest custard pie', weighing 1.1 tons. Last but not least, the local liquor, Bermet, and* muštarda *(mustard) make unusual presents to take home. They are both based on recipes brought here by the French between 1809 and 1813, when Samobor was part of Napoleon's Illyrian Provinces.*

Inland Croatia

The people of Samobor have long been known as keen hikers, with organized walks going back to the late-19th century. In 1999, the hills of Samobor Gorje and Žumberak were declared **Žumberak i Samobor Gorje Prirodni Park** (Žumberak i Samobor Gorje Nature Park). Displaying typical *karst* features such as caves and gorges, the region is covered with dense forests of beech and chestnut, interspersed with sub-Alpine meadows, isolated hamlets and a series of well-marked footpaths. You can pick up a hiking map at the nature park office in Bregana. Many of the **village churches** of the Žumberak region belong to a community of *Grkokatolici* (Greek Catholics), descendants of Orthodox *Uskoks* (see page 149) who were invited by the Hapsburgs to repopulate the region in the early 17th century, and were allowed to continue practising Orthodox rites on the condition that they acknowledged papal supremacy. ■ *Nature Park Office, Grdnjaci 57, Bregana, 10 km from Samobor. T3323848. Getting there: there isn't any public transport.*

**Sleeping** **C** *Hotel Livadić*, Trg Kralja Tomislava 1, T3365850, F3365851, www.hotel-livadic.hr Overlooking the main square, this romantic, family-run hotel occupies a building dating back to 1800. The 17 rooms are truly luxurious – wooden antique furniture, parquet flooring and oriental rugs – without being astronomically expensive. Well worth staying at.

**Eating** **Mid-range** *Pri Staroj Vuri*, Giznik 2, T3360548. This highly regarded restaurant serves up all-but-forgotten local dishes, recorded in a cookery book by Canon Birling from 1812. It's close to the main square, in an 18th-century town house with a cosy dining room decorated with traditional folk objects and a collection of old clocks. Closed late-Jul to mid-Aug.

**Cheap** *Samoborska Pivnica*, Šmidhenova 3, T3361623. Centrally located beer hall serving excellent ale plus good inexpensive local dishes. *Izletište Anindol*, Sv Ane 71, T3367020. This delightful old wooden building, on the path up to Anindol Šetalište, has been converted into a small restaurant specializing in barbecued meats. On a sunny day you can eat in the garden. Closed Mon. *Kavana Livadić*, Trg Kralja Tomislava 1. The best place in town to try *samoborske kremšnita*, this old-fashioned café occupies the ground floor of *Hotel Livadić* (see Sleeping). Indoors it's furnished with beautiful antiques, and in summer there are tables outside in a pretty courtyard.

**Festivals** *Fašnik*, 2 weeks of bawdy carnival celebrations, climaxing with the lighting of a bonfire, a firework display and the burning of Prince Fašnik. Locals suitably attired in masks and costume. Feb-Apr, depending when Easter falls. *Salami Festival*, Mar. *Old Timer Rally*, early-May. *Chestnut Festival*, Oct.

**Shopping**   *Podrum Obitelj Filipec*, Stražnicka 1a, 20 m off the main square. T3364835. Family-run wine cellar. The best place to buy *Bermet* (local vermouth liquor) and *muštarda* (spicy grape mustard), both typical Samobor souvenirs. *Oslaković Craft Shop*, Perkovčeva 17, T3360032. Family-run craft shop where you can buy a *lisitarsko srce* (traditional ginger-bread heart) and handmade candles.

**Sport**   *Konjički Klub Samobor – Žumberačko Eco Selo*, (Samobor Riding Club – Žumberak Eco Village). Located within the Žumberak i Samobor Gorje Nature Park, 18 km east of Samobor, this small mountainside sports centre offers pony trekking, hiking, waterfall tours and simple overnight accommodation. Open all year. Krovljak bb, Kalje, T3387472.

**Transport**   Bus station, T3366634. 50 **buses** daily to **Zagreb**, 40 mins, one-way ticket Kn16. You need private transport to reach **Žumberak i Samobor Gorje Nature Park.**

# Zagorje

*Northwest of Zagreb, beyond Medvednica Nature Park, lies the rural area of Zagorje. The scenery is calm and enchanting: rolling hillsides are planted with* **vineyards** *and* **orchards**, *and narrow country roads meander their way through a succession of villages of* **red-brick cottages** *and* **open-sided wooden barns** *filled with maize. Zagorjians are renowned for their drinking habits, and there is a local song that says "There is no man from Zagorje who can produce as much wine as his friends can drink", or words to that effect. Indeed, St Martin's Day on 11 November is a big event throughout the region, when the ritual blessing of the season's young wine is accompanied by copious festivities until the early hours.*

*Public transport is slow and sporadic, but if you have a car and are prepared to devote an entire day to Zagorje, you can visit a* **modern sculpture gallery** *in Klanjec, an* **open-air ethnological museum** *in Kumrovec, the* **medieval hilltop castles** *of Veliki Tabor and Trakošćan, and an unusual museum dedicated to prehistoric man in Krapina.*

## Klanjec

*Phone code: 049*
*Colour map 1, grid A5*
*55 km northwest*
*of Zagreb*

This picturesque small town sits on the east bank of the River Sutla, which forms the natural border with Slovenia. The main reason for coming here is to visit the Augustinčić Gallery. Klanjec also produced another noted artist, the poet Antun Mihanović (1796-1861), who wrote the words to *Lijepa Naša* (the Croatian national anthem). Some 3 km north of Klanjec, on the road to Kumrovec, you will pass the Lijepa Naša Monument, recording that it was this particular stretch of countryside that inspired Mihanović.

**Sights**   **Augustinčić Gallery** is devoted to the works of this local born 20th-century sculptor, Antun Augustinčić. Born in Klanjec in 1900, he studied Fine Art in Paris, then became student to another noted Croatian sculptor, Ivan Meštrović. During the Tito years he was made the official state artist: works from that time, such as the *Heroic Worker*, one of many works on show here, portray the appropriate socialist ideals of the period. Later the *Pieta* and *Carrying the Wounded* became favourite themes – his best known sculpture is *Peace*, erected in front of the United Nations building in New York in 1954. In 1970, Augustinčić donated his works to the state. When he died in 1979, he was buried next to his wife in the garden surrounding the gallery, below one of his most moving pieces, *Carrying the*

*Wounded.* ■ *Mon-Sat 0900-1600, Sun by appointment. 10Kn. T550343. Trg A Mihanovića 10.*

**Mid-range** *Zelenjak*, Rizvica 1, 3 km north of Klanjec, close to the *Lijepa Naša* monument on the road to Kumrovec, T550747, www.zelenjak.com   This popular restaurant and café is housed in a traditional Zagorje building with a glass conservatory overlooking the garden. Its main claim to fame is that it did the catering for one of Tito's parties, attended by Richard Nixon, Jacqueline Kennedy, Richard Burton and Elizabeth Taylor during the 1960's. Closed 1-15 Aug.

**Eating**

There are 4 **buses** daily from **Zagreb** (1¼ hrs).

**Transport**

# Kumrovec

The sleepy village of Kumrovec, like Klanjec, sits on the east bank of the River Sutla. It was here that the late President Josip Broz Tito was born in 1892, and his home and several houses in the old quarter surrounding it have been turned into an open-air ethnological museum, known as Staro Selo (Old Village).

*Phone code: 049*
*Colour map 1,*
*grid A5*
*40 km from Zagreb,*
*6 km from Klanjec*

Consisting of about 20 carefully restored 19th- and 20th-century thatched cottages and wooden farm buildings, **Staro Selo** is set amid orchards and with a stream flowing through animated by ducks.The quarter offers a lifelike reconstruction of 19th-century Zagorje rural life. Tito's childhood home, which was the first brick house in the village, built in 1860, was turned into a small memorial museum in 1953. The furniture inside is just as it would have been when Tito was a child, and there's a small room displaying letters and gifts sent to the Yugoslav leader by foreign allies. In the garden stands an imposing bronze statue of the man himself, created by Antun Augustinčić from neighbouring Klanjec in 1948. Reconstruction of the surrounding building started in 1977, so that today you can see a blacksmith's shop, and potter's studio and a candlemaker's workshop, where demonstrations are laid on by respective craftsmen at weekends. ■ *Summer 0800-1800, winter 0900-1500. 10Kn. T553107.*

**Sights**

**Cheap to mid-range** *Zagorska Klet*, within Staro Selo complex, T553107. Unashamedly set up for the tourists who visit Staro Selo, this small eatery nontheless does good basic Zagorje fare such as *zagorski štrukli* (baked cheese dumplings) and *kobasice* (sausages). It's also possible to come here just for a drink.

**Eating**

There are 4 **buses** daily to Kumrovec from **Zagreb** (1½ hrs). From there it is a 20-min walk to Staro Selo.

**Transport**

# Veliki Tabor

Sitting on a hill close to the small village of **Desinić** the lofty ochre-coloured castle of Veliki Tabor is quite impressive seen from a distance. Closer inspection reveals a medieval structure with high-pitched terracotta roofs in a poor state of repair, though if you don't mind cobwebs and creaky floorboards it certainly merits a stop. Close by, an informal farm restaurant serves delicious reasonably priced local goodies.

*Phone code: 049*
*Colour map 1, grid A5*
*15 km north of*
*Kumrovec*

Although some people believe that Veliki Tabor stands on the site of a second-century Roman fortress, the main pentagonal form of the castle dates

▶ **Tito**

The seventh of 15 children, Josip Broz was born on May 7, 1892, in Kumrovec (then part of Austria-Hungary) to a Slovenian mother and a Croatian blacksmith father. Although he only attended school between the age of 7 and 12, he was to become one of the 20th century's most extraordinary world leaders.

During the First World War he served with the Austrian army in Russia and was wounded and taken prisoner – a turn of events he used to his advantage, learning Russian and discovering the ideals of the Bolshevik movement. He returned to his homeland (by this time the Kingdom of the Serbs, Croats, and Slovenes) in 1920 and joined the Communist Party. After a series of arrests and a six-year stint in prison (the Communist Party was outlawed here at that time) he adopted the pseudonym of Tito and went to work for the Balkan sector of Comintern in Moscow. In 1937 he returned home and became Secretary General of the Yugoslavian Communist Party.

When Germany attacked Yugoslavia in 1941, Tito formed the Partizan resistance movement, fighting the German Nazis and their allies, the Croatian Ustaše, as well another anti-fascist group, the pro-royalist Serbian Chetniks, who were initially backed by the British. In 1944, however, the allies switched their backing to the Partisans, and at the end of the Second World War Tito set up the new Yugoslav government, based on Communist ideology.

After a series of disagreements over foreign policy, Tito broke with Stalin in 1948 and began to govern Yugoslavia along socialist lines, decentralising the economy and setting up workers' self-management organisations. This gained him considerable favours from the west, which began giving Yugoslavia massive loans. When Stalin died in 1953, Tito forged good relations with Kruschev, making Yugoslavia a 'midway country' between the Communist USSR and the capitalist west. In the 1960s he founded the Non-Alligned Nations together with leaders of African and Asian countries.

Undoubtedly a colourful character, he went through four wives and had a marked penchant for Scotch whisky, Cuban cigars and fast cars - the collection he left behind includes a 1960 Rolls Royce Phantom and several Mercedes limousines. His circle of glamorous friends included Elizabeth Taylor and Richard Burton, who played Tito in The Fifth Offensive, a 1972 production based on a true story from the Second World War.

At 1505 on May 4 1980, sirens sounded through out Yugoslavia. Tito was dead, and the entire country came to a stand still. His funeral, in Belgrade, was attended by representatives from over 125 countries – possibly the largest state funeral ever.

On 4 May 2000, his passing away was openly commemorated in Croatia for the first time since 1991, when 10,000 people gathered in Kumrovec to celebrate the great man who, on his deathbed, prophetically described himself as the last of the Yugoslavs.

back to the 12th century when it was the property of the Counts of Celje (in present-day Slovenia). In the 16th century the castle passed to the Ratkaj family, who added four semicircular side towers as protection against the Turks and enhanced the internal courtyard with three levels of open-arched galleries. During the Second World War, Franciscan nuns used the building as an orphanage to host 80 children who had lost their families, after which the castle became state property.

The custodians of Veliki Tabor are happy to recount a love story connected to the castle, which may or may not be true. According to hearsay, during the 15th century, Freidrich, the son of Count Herman II Celjski, who resided in the castle at the time, fell in love with a pretty peasant girl, named Veronika, from the nearby village of Desinić. Deeming the fair maiden unworthy of his son, the Count prohibited the affair, upon which the two young lovers ran away together. Count Herman sent his soldiers in hot pursuit: Freidrich was captured, and locked up in a tower in the castle, and Veronika was tried for witchcraft – she had, after all, enchanted the young man. When judges found Veronika innocent, the enraged Count had her drowned and her body bricked up in a wall in the castle. Strangely, during renovation work in 1982, a woman's skull was found here. It is now on show in the castle chapel on the first floor, and is said to be the last trace of the unfortunate Veronika.

■ *May-Sep 1000-1800, Oct-Apr 1000-1500. 20Kn. T343052. Desinić, www.veliki-tabor.hr*

**Cheap** *Grešna Gorica*, Desinić, T343001, www.gresna-gorica.com This homely rustic eatery serves up typical Zagorje dishes such as *zagorski štrukli* (baked cheese dumplings) and *pura s mlincima* (turkey with savoury pastries). Everything is made from local produce supplied by neighbouring farms. From the garden there's a good view of Veliki Tabor. **Eating**

There are 8 buses daily from Zagreb to Desinić (1 hr 50 mins). From there it is a 30-min walk to the castle. **Transport**

*Inland Croatia*

# Trakošćan

Dvor Trakošćan (Trakošćan Castle) is one of the most visited castles in Croatia and probably the most popular sight in Zagorje. A white fairy-tale fortress complete with turrets and a drawbridge, it stands on a small hill overlooking a small lake, and is undoubtedly at its most magical at night, when it is floodlit. *Phone code: 042 Colour map 1, grid A5 40 km south of Varazdin and 36 km north of Veliki Tabor*

The first castle on this site was built in the 13th century as an observation point above the road between Ptuj (in present-day Slovenia) and the Bednja Valley. It then passed on to various feudal lords, until being presented to the Drašković family, as a way of thanks for their dedication to defending the region against the Ottoman Turks, in the late 16th century. Over the following 200 years various defence towers and a drawbridge were added, until the castle fell into disuse (the Turks long since gone) and abandon. However, in the mid-19th century the Romanticist movement became fashionable among Central European aristocracy, and Vice-Marshall Juraj Drašković had the building restructured in neo-Gothic style and turned into a sumptuous country residence. He also landscaped the surrounding parkland, and created an artificial lake surrounded by a mixed forest of beech and fir, by damming up the River Bednja. Following the events of the Second World War, the Drašković family moved to Austria in 1944 and the property was nationalized and opened to the public in 1953.

On the first floor you can visit the luxurious wooden-panelled living quarters, complete with late 19th-century furniture and solemn family portraits, while the bedrooms, mainly furnished in Baroque style, are on the second floor. There is also an arms collection on display, consisting of rifles, pistols and Turkish weapons from between the 15th and 19th centuries. The grounds are especially pretty in spring and autumn. In summer a floating café operates on the lake, and it is also possible to rent boats for rowing.

■ *May-Sep 0900-1800, Oct-Apr 0900-1500. 20Kn. T796422. www.trakoscan.net*

**Sleeping**
**& eating**
**D** *Motel Coning*, Trakošćan 5, T796224, F796205, www.hotel.hr-coning  Lying just across the road from the castle, this modern hotel complex comprises 80 guest rooms, a restaurant, gym, tennis courts, sauna and solarium.

**Transport**  There is no public transport to Trakošćan, so you really need a car.

## Krapina

*Phone code: 049*
*Colour map 1, grid A5*
*Population: 4,647*
*57 km north*
*of Zagreb*
Nestled in a valley, sits the peaceful market town of Krapina. It's known throughout the country as the home of the *Krapinksi Čovjek* (Krapina man), a tribe of Neanderthals, who lived here some 30,000 years ago, the remains of which were dug up by a Croatian archaeologist in 1899. The settlement itself was first recorded as a castle, no longer in existence, during the 12th century, and since then it's been the administrative and cultural centre of rural Zagorje. During the 17th century, a Franciscan Monastery and the Baroque Church of St Catherine were built, giving Krapina the airs of a sedate and prosperous provincial town.

Krapina's second most noted citizen is Ljudevit Gaj, who was born here in 1809 and founded the Illyrian Movement in 1835, campaigning for the union of the South Slavs (Croats and Serbs) as an alternative to Austro-Hungarian hegemony. Aided by Ban Jelačić, the Croatian Viceroy at the time, Gaj secured the recognition of Serbo-Croatian as the nation's official language, and helped bring an end to the feudal system. You can see a monument to him, by the Dalmatian sculptor Ivan Rendić, on the main square.

**Sights**  A short walk west of the centre, the **Muzej Evolucije** (Museum of Evolution) records the work of Dragutin Gorjanović-Kramberger, who discovered the *Krapinksi Čovjek* in a nearby cave on Hušnjakovo Hill. From the museum, a path leads through woods to the cave in question, where you can see life-size sculptures of these prehistoric people and the animals that would have lived at that time. The actual bones of the 20-odd Neanderthals that were discovered here are now kept in the Croatian Museum of Natural Sciences in Zagreb. ■ *Jun-Sep 0800-1800, Oct-May 0800-1600. 15Kn. T371491. Šetalište V Sluge.*

**Festivals**  *Kajkavian Festival*, **Sep**. A festival celebrating Zagorje folk music.

**Transport**  There are 8 **buses** daily from **Zagreb** (1½ hrs). Krapina bus station T315018. There are 10 **trains** daily from **Zagreb** (1½ hrs). Krapina train station T371012.

# North of Zagreb

*Lying close to the Hungarian border and easily reached by public transport from Zagreb, the neighbouring provincial towns of Varaždin and Čakovec are both presided over by 16th-century castles, open to the public as museums. Close by, Koprivnica and Hlebine are worth the trek for their well-arranged galleries displaying paintings by local naïve artists.*

# Varaždin

Varaždin, with its 18th-century Baroque churches and town houses, makes a manageable day trip from the capital. Stari Grad, a well-preserved 16th-century castle surrounded by grassy ramparts, now housing a museum, is the main attraction. The best time to visit is autumn, when the trees take on russet hues complementing the pink and ochre façades. If you're lucky, you'll also catch the renowned *Varaždin Baroque Evenings* music festival, staged late-September to early-October.

*Phone code: 042*
*Colour map 1, grid A6*
*Population: 49,075*
*77 km northeast of Zagreb*

**History**

The town evolved from its most beautiful and best loved monument, the castle, which was first mentioned in 1181, in a document sealed by King Bela III of Hungary. In 1209, King Andreas II of Hungary and Croatia declared Varaždin a 'Free Royal City' (33 years before Zagreb was granted a similar honour, as locals proudly point out), and from that date onwards citizens were free to choose their own city governor. The Tartars besieged the town in 1242, plundering and burning much of it, but the townsfolk were undeterred and soon rebuilt it into an important trade centre, albeit amid ongoing conflicts between the local noble families.

During the Hapsburg era, Varaždin became an important military stronghold in their battle against Ottoman expansion. The town was enclosed within a sturdy fortification system, and though the Turks never succeeded in capturing it, they frequently plundered the surroundings.

In the 17th century, in reply to the emergence of a budding protestant movement, Rome sent in Jesuit monks to revive and reinforce the Catholic faith in the region. It was the Jesuits who brought Baroque architecture to Varaždin, for which the town is now noted.

The city became the capital of Croatia in 1756 – a short-lived period of joy which came to an abrupt end when more than half of the town (including the government building) was destroyed by fire in 1776. According to records, the fire was started by a young man who was smoking, tripped over a sow and dropped his cigarette in a haystack. After the disaster, smoking was banned and the unfortunate culprit was whipped 12 times in his native village of Sračinec, and 12 times more in front of Varaždin Town Hall.

Although an unfortunate event, the fire brought about a major period of development, and during the 18th century the town was rebuilt in Baroque style, as seen today. In 1997 Varaždin became the seat of a diocese.

**Sights**

Start a tour of the town from Trg Kralja Tomislava, the main square. The most impressive building here is undoubtedly the 15th-century **Gradska Vijećnica** (Town Hall), which has been the seat of the town council since 1523, making it one of the oldest buildings of it's type in Europe. The slightly incongruous clock tower was added in 1793. If you're here in summer (early-May to mid-October) on a Saturday morning between 1000 and 1200, you can see the *Purgari* (Varaždin guards), dressed in blue military uniforms dating back to 1750, keeping watch outside the main door. ■ *Trg Kralja Tomislava 3.*

Officially taking on the title of cathedral in 1997, when Varaždin became the seat of a diocese, **Katedrala** (Cathedral of the Assumption) was the first Baroque building in town. It dates back to the mid-17th century, when the style was brought here by Jesuit monks, who besides erecting the church, also constructed the neighbouring three-storey monastery and former grammar school building, now used as the Bishop's residence. Inside the cathedral, the

*Inland Croatia*

richly gilded main altar fills the central nave and bears paintings of the Virgin. The space is said to have exceptional acoustic qualities, and during the *Varaždin Baroque Evenings* music festival, concerts are held here. ■ *0800-1200 and 1600-1800. Pavlinska ulica, just off Trg Kralja Tomislava.*

Founded in 1954 and occupying the ground floor of **Dvor Herzer** (Herzer Palace), the slightly quirky **Entomološki Odjel** (Entomological Museum) is worth a look in for its beautifully presented collection of butterflies and drawings of insects. ■ *Tue-Fri 1000-1500, Sat-Sun 1000-1300. 10Kn. T210474. Franjevački trg 6.*

Just a five-minute walk from the centre stands Varaždin's top attraction, an impressive **castle** surrounded by lofty fortifications and ringed by a moat (now unfortunately empty). There's been a castle on the site for over 800 years, but the building's present appearance dates largely from the 16th century, when the existing structure was heavily reinforced against the possibility of a Turkish attack. The main entrance is an imposing gatehouse with a central tower and a wooden drawbridge, which leads into an internal courtyard ringed with three levels of open-arched galleries, designed by the Italian architect Domenico dell'Allio in the 1560's. In 1925 the castle was given to the town and turned into a **museum**. It now houses a splendid collection of period furniture, with individual rooms devoted to particular epochs, following on one from another in chronological order. Just outside the main entrance is *Sermaš*, a pleasant café with a summer terrace, ideal for coffee or a beer either before or after your visit. ■ *Tue-Fri 1000-1500, Sat-Sun 1000-1300. 15Kn. T210399. Strossmayerovo Šetalište 7.*

Most guided tours of Varaždin begin from the **Gradsko Groblje** (City Cemetery), partly because of its exceptional landscaping, and partly because there's a large car park nearby. Founded in 1773, the cemetery that you see today was laid out in 1905 by Herman Haller. Haller had studied various cemeteries in Europe, and wanted to create a place of rest for the dead that would not put off the living, but actually attract them. The result is a romantic garden filled with trees and shrubs, and immense hedges trimmed and shaped around ornate memorial stones. ■ *Hallerova Aleja, 400 m from the castle.*

**Sleeping** If you arrive in the morning you can probably exhaust the town's sights in a single day. However, the *Varaždin Baroque Evenings* music festival may give you reason to prolong your stay. In which case you may need accommodation. **D** *Hotel Turist*, Aleja K Zvonimira 1, close to the bus station, T395395, F215028, www.hotel-turist.hr, is Varaždin's principal hotel, with 100 rooms. It is a modern, rather impersonal establishment, but comfortable enough and well equipped with extras such as a fitness centre, and kennels for 4-legged visitors. Close by, **D** *Pansion Maltar*, Prešernova 1, T 311100, F211190, is a slightly cheaper and more homely option. All rooms have a TV and minibar, and road-weary travellers will welcome the laundry service.

**Eating** **Expensive** The most expensive restaurant in town is the highly regarded *Royal*, Uska ulica 5, T213477. Red carpets and wooden-panelled walls set a formal atmosphere in the dining room, while the chef takes similar care in turning out elegantly presented dishes. The house speciality is *Filesteak Royal* (fillet steak with Madeira sauce), and there's a wide choice of good Croatian wines. **Mid-range** Slightly less pricey is *Restoran Zlatna Guska*, J Habdelića 4, T213393. Set in a vaulted cellar space, it's relaxed during the day and romantic at night. They do delicious chicken and mushroom filled pancakes, and there's a help-yourself salad bar and excellent house wine. **Cheap to mid-range** Close by *Pivnica Raj*, Gundulića 11, T213146, is a microbrewery serving up *Knaput* beer and barbecued meat dishes. Most Fri and Sat nights there's live *tamburaška* music.

Since 1971, *Varaždin Baroque Evenings* has attracted international musicians and **Festivals** hailed as being one of the country's most important cultural events: each evening, for 2 weeks between **late-Sep and early-Oct**, Baroque music concerts are held in the Cathedral and the *Varaždin theatre auditorium*.

Regular **bus** and **train** services from **Zagreb**. Approximately 2 hrs. Bus station **Transport** T407888. 26 buses daily to **Zagreb**, 1-way ticket 45Kn. Train station, T210444. 14 trains daily to Zagreb, 1-way ticket Kn 45.

# Čakovec

Čakovec is a proud though rather uninspiring provincial town, centring on Trg Kralja Tomislava, the main square, a pleasant pedestrian area surrounded by two-storey pastel-coloured Baroque town houses with steep sloping tile roofs. Throughout the rest of the country, Čakovec is known for its castle, textile industry and hard-working citizens. A world away from the *fjaka* (easy-going laziness combined with an appreciation of all things good in life) of Dalmatia, this is a region where people actually claim to enjoy work, some holding down full-time jobs plus participating in out-of-hours voluntary activities.

*Phone code: 040*
*Colour map 1, grid A6*
*Population: 30,455*
*82 km northeast of Zagreb*

Inland Croatia

On the main road to Hungary, it is hardly a big tourist destination. However, the castle, *medimurska pita* (a delicious pie made of poppy seeds, cream cheese and walnuts, unique to the area) and the region's excellent white wines make it worth a half-day visit. Čakovec lies just 15 km northeast of its neighbour and arch-rival, Varaždin, so the two can be comfortably combined as a day trip from the capital.

There's been a castle here for centuries, though things didn't really take off **History** until 1547, when Nikola Šubić Zrinski became owner of the area. As Zrinski's major preoccupation was protecting the Hapsburg territories from the Turks, he rebuilt the existing *castrum* into an impressive Renaissance fortress with strong defensive walls and a moat, intended to oversee the permanently unstable border with the Ottoman Empire to the southeast.

A settlement of simple wooden craftsmen's houses grew up around the castle, gaining the status of free market town in 1579. During the 17th century, when the Zrinskis were one of most powerful Croatian noble families, Čakovec saw a period of significant economic and cultural development.

In the 19th century, Čakovec became an important traffic intersection point for the new railways linking Slovenia, Hungary and the Adriatic ports. Mills and distilleries were set up here, and by the early 20th century the town had developed into a small but prosperous industrial centre.

In the centre of town, on the main square, first-time visitors to Čakovec are **Sights** invariably struck by this extraordinary red brick and white stucco Secessionist building, the **Dom Sindikata** (Trade Union Hall). It was erected in 1904, by the Hungarian architect Odon Horvath, and was originally intended as a meeting place for local tradesmen. ■ *Trg Kralja Tomislava.*

Located on the edge of town, set amid carefully tended parkland, stands the **castle complex**. A generous section of the old 16th-century walls, complete with three semicircular bastions, is still standing, though the original Renaissance castle, built by the Zrinskis, was devastated by an earthquake in 1738. The 'New Castle', as it stands today, is a four-storey Baroque structure, based on a quadrangular ground plan with an inner courtyard, built by the Czech Counts of Althan during the 18th century. From 1855 to 1870 part of the complex was used as a sugar factory, and during the Second World War the northern wing was badly damaged. However, post-war restoration work saw the castle return to its former glory, and the **Muzej Medimurja** (Museum of Medimurje) opened here in 1954. Inside, you'll find an Ethnographic Department, with a fine display of local costumes, on the first floor, and an Archaeological Department and Art Gallery, with a collection of paintings by 20th-century artists who were born, lived or worked in the region, on the second floor. The ground floor is devoted to heavy stone pieces, tombstones and sculpture, from the first to 20th centuries. ■ *Tue-Fri 1000-1500, Sat-Sun 1000-1300. 15Kn. T313499. Trg Republike 5.*

**Wine tasting**  A pleasant drive 20 km northwest of town, through undulating countryside planted with vineyards, brings you to the sleepy village of Štrigova, close to the Slovenian border. Here the **Lovrec** family run a small high- quality **vineyard** producing a variety of award-winning white wines: Chardonnay, Pinot, Rizling, Graševina, Sauvignon and Trminac. In an authentic wooden outbuilding, complete with rustic furnishing, you can take part in an amusing and informative wine-tasting session (available in Croatian, Slovenian, English and German). Expect to sample six different wines, ranging from dry to sweet, accompanied by homemade bread, local cheese and salami. At the end, it is possible to buy wine to take home. ■ *Open daily for wine tasting, but better to telephone first to arrange a time. T830171. Sv Urban 133, Štrigova.*

**Sleeping**  D *Hotel Park*, Zrinsko Frankopanska bb, T311255, F311244. Centrally located 1960's building with comfortable rooms.

**Eating**  **Expensive**  One of the best places to eat in the area is *Mala I liža,* Mačkovec 107, 5 km north of Čakovec, on the main road to Mursko Središće, T341101. Antique furniture and an open fireplace set a homely atmosphere in the dining room. Guests tuck into large platters of roast meats, along with local specialities such as fresh curd cheese and boiled ham. There's live music on Fri and Sat evenings.

**Mid-range to cheap**  A cheaper option in the centre of town is *Pilka Pivnica*, Josip Kozarca 15, T395899. This popular microbrewery serves excellent beer, plus pizzas and a selection of local fare if you feel peckish. For coffee and a cake overlooking the main square, call at *Slastičarna Cvek*, Kralja Tomislava 14, T310401. They have a tempting range of gateaux and strudels, and reputedly do the best *medimurska pita* in the region.

**Festivals**  *Fašnik*, traditional carnival celebrations held the weekend before **Shrove Tuesday**, with locals disguised in bizarre costumes and masks. *Čakovačko Ljeto*, **Jul**, is the Summer Festival, theatrical performances and concerts in the castle courtyard.

**Transport**  Bus station, T313947. 14 **buses** daily to **Zagreb** (2 hrs 20 mins), one-way ticket 55Kn. Train station, T384333. Eight **trains** daily to **Zagreb** (about 2 hrs or 3½ hrs (local)). One-way ticket, 55Kn. One train daily to **Budapest** in Hungary (5 hrs). You need private transport to reach Vinska Kuća Lovrec, on the edge of Štrigova.

# Koprivnica

Koprivnica is a provincial town on the left bank of a small river of the same name in the Podravina region. The main attraction is a number of small museums and galleries, both in Koprivnica and neighbouring Hlebine, displaying works by local artists who have been working in **Naïve Style**, characterized by rural landscapes and scenes from peasant life painted in vivid colours on glass, since the 1930's.

*Phone code: 048*
*Colour map 2, grid A2*
*Population: 24,809*
*98 km northeast of Zagreb and 70 km southeast of Varaždin*

Koprivnica was fortified against the Turks in the 16th century, though little of the old walls can be seen today. There are a number of notable Baroque buildings, such as the 17th-century **Franciscan monastery** and **Church of St Anthony of Padua**, but the main sight is undoubtedly the **Koprivnica Gallery** housing a collection of Naïve paintings and sculpture. ■ *Closed Sun, 10Kn. T622564, Zrinski Trg 9*. During the 20th century the town expanded with the founding of the Podravka food processing factory, which today employs several thousand people and is one of the few Croatian companies to be floated on the world stock market. While in the area, be sure to try local culinary specialities such as *prge* (dried smoked cheese) and *gorički gulas* (a variation of Hungarian goulash).

**C** *Hotel Podravina*, Hrvatske Državnosti 9, T621025, F621178. This centrally located, 4-storey, modern white hotel offers 62 basic but comfortable rooms, each with an en-suite bathroom, TV and minibar, plus a large restaurant with a summer terrace. **E** *Agroturizam Tara*, Teofila Hana 8, Starigrad, 3 km from Koprivnica, T634091. This friendly bed and breakfast has 7 double rooms. It's very popular so try to book at least a week in advance. The owner occasionally prepares dinner for guests, otherwise *Restoran Podravska Klet* (see Eating) is just down the road.

**Sleeping**

**Mid-range** *Pivnica Kraluš*, Zrinski Trg 10, T622302. Standing next door to the Koprivnica Gallery, this large beer hall serves local specialities such as *punjena puritina sa sviježem sirom* (turkey stuffed with curd cheese), *govedeg kuhanog jezika s prgama sira* (tongue with *prge* cheese) and *pivski kobasica* (beer sausage). There are tables outside on the square in summer. *Restoran Podravska Klet*, Starogradska cesta, Starigrad, T634069. This highly regarded eatery lies 3 km from Koprivnica, in a thatched cottage with a homely, old-fashioned dining room. Top dishes include *gorički gulaš* (a local version of Hungarian goulash) and *telaći kotleti s vrganjima* (veal cutlets with mushrooms). There is live folk music Fri and Sat nights till 0200.

**Eating**

*Podravski Motivi*, second weekend of **Jul**. Celebration of local arts and crafts, folk customs, naïve art and regional cuisine.

**Festivals**

From **Zagreb**, there are 7 **buses** (2½ hrs) and 15 **trains** daily to Koprivnica (1 hr 20 mins) . From **Varaždin** there are 10 **buses** (1hr) and 9 **trains** daily to Koprivnica (¾ hr). Koprivinca bus station, T621282. Koprivnica train station, T621122.

**Transport**

# Hlebine

The true birthplace of Croatian Naïve Art is the rural village of Hlebine. The so-called Hlebine School was founded here in 1930 when Professor Krsto Hegedušić met the untutored peasant-painter Ivan Generalić and was highly impressed by his work. Hegedušić gave much encouragement to Generalić and another peasant-painter Franjo Mraz, and the pair went on to hold several exhibitions in Zagreb and Sofia (Bulgaria) between 1931 and 1935. Generalić, Mraz

*Phone code: 048*
*Colour map 2, grid A2*
*13 km east of Koprivinca*

**Inland Croatia**

and a third artist, Mirko Virko Virius, became known as the first generation of Croatian Naïve art painters. After the Second World War, Ivan Generalić himself began teaching more local peasants to paint, and the second generation of Croatian Naïve artists evolved: Franjo Filipović, Dragan Gazi, Josip Generalić (Ivan's son), Mijo Kovačić, Ivan Večenaj, Stjepan Večenaj and Martin Mehkek. The best place for a general overview of their work is the **Hlebine Art Gallery**. ■ *Closed Sun and Sat afternoons. 10Kn. T836075, Trg Ivana Generalića 15.* Also well worth a visit are **Stara Kuća Ivana Generalića** (Former home of Ivan Generalić) and the **Galerija Josip Generalić** (Josip Generalić Gallery), both of which are owned and managed by the Generalić family. ■ *Visits by appointment, Gajeva 75, T836071.*

■ *Getting there: from Koprivnica to Hlebine there are 6* **buses** *daily (Mon-Fri), 2 buses (Sat) but no buses Sun.*

# East of Zagreb

*Seldom visited by tourists, other than those arriving from Serbia, the flat fertile plains of Slavonia spent several centuries under the Turks until being reclaimed by the Hapsburgs. Up until the Second World War a sizeable German minority lived here, and still today there are many Hungarian families. The region is known throughout Croatia for its excellent* kulen *(spicy salami) and* fiš paprikaš *(fish stew flavoured with paprika).*

## Lonjsko Polje Nature Park

*Phone code: 044*
*Colour map 2,*
*grid B1/2, C1/2*
*82 km southeast*
*of Zagreb*

In the village of Čigoč lies the main entrance to Lonjsko Polje Nature Park, occupying a flood plain on the east bank of the River Sava, between the provincial towns of Sisak and Nova Gradiška. This vast area of wetland and oak woods is best known for its storks, which come here to nest between April and October, then spend the rest of the year in South Africa. Čigoč is also noted for its lovely Posavina-style wooden houses, complete with finely carved balconies and thatched roofs.

**Ins & outs**
*See Transport, page*
*89, for further details*

The nature park information centre is located in a traditional wooden house in Čigoč, on the west side of the park, close to the main entrance, T715115. It is open Apr-Oct 0800-1600 and can supply maps and information. The nature park head office at Trg Kralja Petra Svačića bb in Jasenovac (on the border with Bosnia), T672080, is open all year Mon-Fri 0800-1600, and can supply maps of the park and basic information. If you call in at Jasenovac, look out for the giant concrete tulip, which is a memorial monument to the Serbs, Jews and gypsies killed in the town's infamous Ustaše concentration camp during the Second World War.

**Sights**

Declared a nature park in 1990, Lonjsko Polje is one of largest wetlands in Europe, displaying a landscape typical of large parts of Central Europe 150 years ago, before the advent of modern land drainage systems. Each year come spring, as the surrounding rivers swell, the oak woods and meadows of the river basin flood, providing a perfect natural habitat for some 240 bird species. While the best known visitors to the park are storks – some 600 couples, the highest concentration of storks in Europe – other endangered species such as herons, egrets, cormorants and eagles can also be spotted. The marshy meadows, woods of ash, willow and poplar, host more than 10,000 ducks through winter. Other indigenous species include the spotted Turopolje pig, who feeds on freshwater mussels and acorns, the semi-wild Posavac horse, wild boar, deer, otters, beavers and wild cats.

Several small agrotourism centres, offering locally produced food and (**E**) overnight accommodation, have popped up in the area. The two listed here are happy to receive visitors, but you should call first so they can have a meal and/or a room ready for you. **Mid-range** *Obitelj Ravlić*, Mužilovčica, village next to Čigoć, T710151. This traditional wooden house was restored by the Ravlić family and done out with old-fashioned furniture. There is a taverna, a small private ethnological museum and several rooms available for overnights stays. *Stara Hiža,* Čigoć, T715321. This friendly family-run farmstead occupies one of the traditional wooden houses in Čigoć. If you come for lunch or dinner, expect hearty fish-based dishes such as *riblji paprikaš* (fish stew with paprika). They have 6 Posavac horses for riding, as well as a boat and bikes for hire. The 2 guest rooms are done out with old-fashioned furniture.

*Sleeping & eating*

Public transport facilities in the area are poor, so you really need a car. From Zagreb it takes 1¼ hrs to drive here.

*Transport*

**Inland Croatia**

# Požega

Požega is slightly off-the-beaten track and of little interest to tourists, but worth a brief mention for its charming Baroque main square, **Trg Sv Trojstvo**. The oldest building on the square is **Crkva Sv Duha** (Church of the Holy Spirit), founded by Franciscan monks in 1280 – when Požega came under the Ottomans (1537-1688) it was used as a mosque. The adjoining Franciscan monastery was built during the 18th century, and the Church of the Holy Spirit restored following a fire in 1842. Also overlooking the square, the gothic **Crkva Sv Lovre** (Church of St Lawrence) dates back to 1300, and was taken over by the Jesuits, who in turn also built themselves a monastery here, in the 18th century. At the west end of the square lurks the **Gradski Muzej** (Civic Museum) housing a modest collection of archaeological finds, Romanesque reliefs and 18th-century Baroque paintings. Most of the other buildings surrounding Trg Sv Trojstvo are elegant Baroque town houses decorated with stuccowork, while a plague column in the centre dates from 1749. One block north from here, on Trg Sv Terezije, the late-Baroque **Sv Terezija** (St Theresa's) was built in 1763 and was one of a number of Croatian churches to be promoted to the status of cathedral in 1997. In the park in front of the cathedral stands a monument to Luka Ibrišimović Sokol, a Franciscan monk who was instrumental in liberating Požega from the Turks.

*Phone code: 034*
*Colour map 2, grid C3*
*Population: 20,943*
*175 km southeast of Zagreb and 67 km west of Osijek*

**E** *Hotel Grgin Dol*, Grgin dol 20, T/F273222. A 5-min walk east of the main square, *Grgin Dol* offers 18 comfortable rooms, each complete with en-suite bathroom, TV and minibar. There's a hotel bar and restaurant. Pets welcome.

*Sleeping & eating*

*Grgurevo* (Feast of St Gregory), **12 Mar**. A display of cannons and mortars on the main square commemorates a local victory over the Turks in 1688. *Music Festival Zlatne Zice Slavonije* (Golden Strings of Slavonia), **Sep**. Folk festival featuring Slavonian *tambura* music and traditional regional costumes.

*Festivals*

There are 4 **buses** daily from **Zagreb** (2½ hrs) and 6 buses daily from **Slavonski Brod** (1 hr). Požega bus station, Industrijska 2, T273133. There is 1 **train** daily from **Zagreb** (3½ hrs). Požega train station stands close to the bus station, T273911.

*Transport*

## Slavonski Brod

*Phone code: 035*
*Colour map 2, grid C4*
*Population: 58,642*
*197 km southeast of Zagreb and 47 km southwest of Osijek*

On the north bank of the River Sava, which forms the natural border with Bosnia, you'll pass by Slavonski Brod if driving along the main road (E70) from Zagreb to eastern Slavonia. It's by no means a tourist destination, but makes a decent stopping place for lunch, where you might also check out the 18th-century fortress and take a riverside stroll to the Franciscan Monastery.

The settlement was originally founded by the Romans as Marsonia. The Ottoman Turks occupied the area from 1526 to 1691, after which it was incorporated into the Military Border. The spectacular star-shaped **Brodska Tvrdjava** (Brod Fortress) complete with bastions and moats, designed to protect Slavonia from the Ottoman forces across the river, could accommodate 4,000 soldiers. Construction work, carried out largely by local peasants under forced labour, was completed in 1741. It ceased to function as a military base in 1860 – today there are plans to restore some of the buildings and you can walk a circuit of the ramparts to get an idea of the scale of the place.

Just east of the fortress, **Trg I B Mažuranić**, functions as the main square, with a number of open-air cafés offering views of the river. From here, a 10-minute walk along the riverside promenade will bring you to the 18th-century Baroque **Franjevački Samostan** (Franciscan Monastery) centring on a fine cloistered courtyard.

During the 19th century the town developed in the area between the fortress and the monastery, and soon became an important craft and trading centre due to its position on the river. The Tito years saw Slavonski Brod further industrialized and the modern high-rise suburbs were constructed to house workers. During the war for independence, the town was badly shelled. Its sister town, Bosanski Brod, lies just across the river and is now part of the Republika Srpska, the Serb-dominated area of Bosnia Herzegovina.

**Sleeping & eating** D *Hotel Park*, Trg Pobjede 1, T410228/9, F442306. Ideally located close to the tourist office, between the bus station and the main square, the *Park* offers 20 en-suite guest rooms and a hotel restaurant. **Mid-range** *Slavonski Podrum*, Andrije Štampa 1, T444856. A 15-min walk east of the fortress, close to the Franciscan Monastery, this highly popular restaurant occupies a charming 18th-century building with a beamed dining room. The house speciality is *teletina ispod peke* (veal prepared under a peka).

**Festivals** *Brodsko Kolo*, mid-Jun. The oldest and largest folk dance festival in Croatia, dating back over 30 years.

**Transport** If you are planning on driving to Slavonski Brod from Zagreb, remember that the main road (E70) incurs a 45Kn toll for this stretch. There are 14 **buses** daily from **Zagreb** (2 hrs 20 mins) and 6 buses daily from **Požega** (1 hr). Slavonski Brod bus station, Trg Hrvatskog Proljeća, T444300. There are 15 **trains** daily from **Zagreb** (2 hrs 10 mins). Slavonski Brod train station stands opposite the bus station, T441082.

## Đakovo

*Phone code: 031*
*Colour map 2, grid C5*
*Population: 20,912*
*38 km southwest of Osijek*

Đakovo is a small provincial town best known for its towering red-brick cathedral and quality white wines produced in the surrounding vineyards, which were originally owned by the Bishop. Đakovo is also home to a Lipizzaner stud farm – you can call by in the morning to see the horses in their stables, and at weekends they lay on occasional dressage performances for pre-arranged group visits.

Đakovo was first mentioned as a Bishop's See in 1244, with far-reaching influ- **History** ence extending over most of Slavonia and Bosnia. By the 14th century, the town had developed in two distinct parts. *Castrum Dyaco*, consisting of the Bishop's Palace and the Cathedral, protected by defensive walls (a 40-m long stretch of the medieval wall still stands today), and *Civitas Dyaco*, with a local secular community. However, in 1536 Đakovo was conquered and largely destroyed by the Turks, who then rebuilt it as a Muslim centre with three mosques, one of which is still standing today, albeit as a Catholic church. The Turks were finally pushed out in 1687, and Đakovo resumed its role as the seat of a Bishop and grew into a prosperous market town.

Today the old town centres on the pedestrian **Ulica Hrvatskih Velikana**, **Sights** known to locals as the Korzo, lined with 18th-century town houses with steep pitched tile roofs, many of which host cafés and shops at street level.

The imposing red-brick, neo-Gothic **Katedrala** (Cathedral) was commissioned by Bishop Josip Juraj Strossmayer in 1866, and the design work carried out by two Viennese architects, Karl Rosner and Friedrich Schmidt. The façade is flanked by two 84-m bell towers, and the interior decorated with late-19th-century Romantic religious frescoes by Alexander and Ljudevit Seitz, in a style reminiscent of the British Pre-Raphaelites. ■ *0800-1200 and 1500-1900. Strossmayerov Trg.*

A 10-minute walk north of the cathedral, along the Korzo, will bring you to the small, charming, white **Crkva Svi Sveti** (Church of All Saints). It started out as Hagipasha's Mosque, based on a square ground plan with a dome. When the Turks left Đakovo, the minaret was pulled down and it was converted into a small Catholic church. The classicist façade was added in the 19th century. ■ *Normally closed, but if you ask at the tourist office they can have it opened on request.*

From the cathedral, walk for 15 minutes east along Ulica Matije Gupca, then turn right on Ulica A Senoe to reach the small but welcoming **Državna Ergela Lipicanaca** (State Lipizzaner Stud Farm). Founded by the Hapsburgs in 1506 for the breeding of high quality horses for the Court of Vienna, it is one of several farms in Central Europe that still produce Lipizzaners for the Spanish Riding School of Vienna. Brown at birth, the horses later turn white, and are renowned for their intelligence and ability to learn complex semi-acrobatic movements with an able rider. Queen Elizabeth II visited the Đakovo stud in 1972 and a team of four Lipizzaners from here took part in the opening ceremony of the Olympic Games in Munich in 1972. ■ *Mon-Fri 0800-1400. Sat-Sun group visits by arrangement. T813286. Ulica A Senoe 45.*

If you're interested in the sculptor Ivan Meštrović a visit to the village of **Vrpolje**, 10 km south of Đakovo, is well worthwhile. Although Meštrović is always considered a Dalmatian (his family were from Otavice in Dalmatia and he grew up there), he was by chance born here in Vrpolje in 1883, when his parents were visiting Slavonia for the summer harvest. The small **Spomen Galerija** (Memorial Gallery) contains about 30 works by Meštrović, donated to the village by the artist himself. ■ *Mon-Sat 0800-1400. 10Kn. T (035)439075.*

**Mid-range** *Croatia Turist*, Petra Preradovića 25, T813391. Lying just 200 m from the **Eating** Cathedral, this is good a place to try *slavonski kulen* (sausages and salami flavoured with paprika), ham and game dishes. Be sure to order a bottle of local white wine: the *Riesling* or *Graševina* are both recommended. The dining room is vast and somewhat impersonal, but in summer there are tables outside on the terrace.

Inland Croatia

**Festivals**   *Đakovački Vezovi* (Đakovo Embroidery), first week of **Jul**. One of the largest folk festivals in Croatia, presenting traditional costumes, folk music and folk dancing from the regions of Slavonia and Baranja.

**Transport**   Bus station, T811390. 6 **buses** daily to **Zagreb** (3 hrs 20 mins). 20 **buses** daily to **Osijek** (40 mins).

## Osijek

*Phone code: 031*
*Colour map 2, grid B5*
*280 km from Zagreb;*
*30 km from the*
*Hungarian border;*
*20 km from the*
*Serbian border*

Osijek is the largest town in Slavonia and an important road and rail intersection point. Strung along the south bank of the River Drava, the three distinct parts of town are interspersed by tree-lined avenues and green parks, giving it an airy and relaxed feel. You can probably cover the main sights, notably the 18th-century Tvrda complex, in a day, after which you might visit the nearby Kopački Rit Nature Park.

**History**   The town was founded by the Romans as the fortified military camp of Mursa in the first century AD, in the area that is now Tvrda, and was last mentioned in 591, after which it was destroyed by invading Goths and Huns and sunk into oblivion. By the 12th century a new settlement had grown up in the area that is now Gornji Grad: it was a market town and river port, owned by a Cistercian Abbey and known by the Hungarian name of Eszek. However, the medieval town was ransacked by the Turkish leader Sultan Suleiman II the Magnificent in 1526, and an important Ottoman administrative centre, complete with mosques, built in its place. The Turks linked Osijek to Darda in the north with an 8-km long wooden bridge, which ran across the River Drava and the Baranja marshes.

In 1687, the Hapsburgs pushed the Turks out of the area, and set the town up as one of the principal army barracks on the Slavonian Miltary Border, based in the purpose-built Tvrda fortress complex. Almost a century later, in 1786, the three town boroughs of Tvrda, Gornji Grad and Donji Grad were united, and Osijek became the administrative centre of the wealthy agricultural region of Slavonia.

In the 20th century, industries such as food processing, chemicals, agricultural machinery, textiles and footwear grew up here, mainly due to the town's location on a transport crossroads between Zagreb and Belgrade, and Hungary and Bosnia Herzegovina. During the war for independence Osijek came under siege for several months in 1991 and 1992, lying dangerously close to the front line after the Serbs took Vukovar, just 35 km to the southeast. The theatre and the old rooftops of Tvrda were hit several times, though subsequent restoration work has repaired the worst of the damage.

**Sights**
*The reference to
'upper town' means
'up the river', not
'up the hill'*

Osijek can be divied into Gornji Grad (Upper Town), the main commercial centre, Donji Grad (Lower Town), a residential area, and Tvrda, a picturesque 18th-century quarter originally built by as a military barracks. Of these, Gornji Grad and Tvrdja are of prime interest to sightseers. One of the nicest aspects of Osijek is its relation to the river. A pleasant 2-km waterside walkway, known to locals as the promenada, leads along the south bank from Gornji Grad to Tvrda, while a pedestrian suspension bridge connects Gornji Grad to Copacabana, the 'town beach', where bathing is possible through summer.

**Gornji Grad**'s main sight, this red-brick, neo-Gothic church, **Crkva Sv Petra i Pavla** (Church of St Peter and Paul), was erected in 1894 to designs by the German architect Fritz Langenberg. Apparently the people of Osijek wanted something to rival the cathedral in neighbouring oakovo, and today locals call this the *Katedrala* (Cathedral) though officially it is not one. The interior is adorned with stained-glass windows, and frescoes painted by the Croatian artist Mirko Racki during the 1930's. ■ *0800-1200 and 1600-1900. Trg A Starčevića.*

The building of the **Hrvatsko Narodno Kazalište** (Croatian National Theatre), by the local architect Carlo Klausner in 1866, was an important landmark in Osijek's cultural development. In November 1991, during the recent war, it was hit by a grenade, and the auditorium and part of the stage were consequently destroyed by fire. Restoration of the theatre was carried out by the fast food chain MacDonalds, on the condition that they could occupy part of the building at street level. It reopened in December 1994. ■ *Županijska 9. T220700.*

The pleasant, leafy **Europska Avenija** is lined with some of Croatia's finest Art Nouveau buildings, including a succession of three-storey town houses designed by local architects for wealthy merchants between 1903 and 1906, a post office, and the charming **Urania Cinema**, added by the Osijek-born architect Victor Axmann in 1912. Incidentaly, the Urania is still working, being one of only two cinemas in town.

Tracing Croatian art from the 18th century up to the present day, the **Muzej Moderne Umjetnosti** (Museum of Modern Art) houses a horde of painting and sculptures, from Baroque portraits of local nobility up to 20th century abstract canvasses. It also hosts occasional temporary exhibitions dedicated to one particular artist or movement. ■ *Tue-Sat 0900-1200 and 1700-2000, Sat-Sun 1000-1300. 10Kn. T213587, Europska Avenija 9.*

**Tvrda** is especially lovely at night, when the cobbled streets are lamplit and a number of popular bars and cafés, plus an excellent little restaurant (see Eating), attract the local student community. Osijek town council has put forward Tvrda as a candidate for the UNESCO world cultural heritage list, and there are plans to restore many of the old buildings and turn them over to educational and cultural institutions. Work on Tvrda began in 1712, when the Austrians set about constructing a large army barracks surrounded by eight bastions linked by defensive walls (now only partly visible). Besides military and public buildings, civilian town houses were erected within the complex, along with several fine churches and monasteries, which cared for the centre's spiritual welfare as well as providing schools and a printing press. Today Tvrda is something of an open-air musuem, looking now much as it would have done in the 18th century. The complex centres on a main square, Trg Sv Trojstvo, lined by ochre-coloured Baroque buildings with steep pitched tile roofs, overlooking a plague monument erected in 1729 and flanked by two identical marble fountains from 1761. Also on the square you'll find the **Muzej Slavonije** (Museum of Slavonia), housing a collection of stone finds from Roman *Mursa*, and staging temporary exhibitions devoted to local history. ■ *Tue-Fri 1000-1300, Sat 1900-2200. 12Kn. Trg Sv.Trojstva 6. T208501.* Close by, the **Crkva Sv Mihovila** (Church of St Michael) with twin towers topped by onion domes, was built in Baroque style by the Jesuits in 1748 on the site of the former Kasim Pasha Mosque. ■ *Trg Juraj Križanica. 0800-1200 and 1600-1900.*

■ *Getting there: you can reach Tvrda on foot, either down Europska Avenija or along the riverside promenade. Alternatively, take tram no 1 from the main square, Trg Trg A Starčevića.*

Inland Croatia

**Sleeping**  **C** *Hotel Osijek*, Šamačka 4, T201333, F212135. This colossal high-rise concrete block stands just a 5-min walk from the main square, overlooking the river. The 178 rooms are functional, if somewhat impersonal, and each has a TV, bathroom and minibar. There's also a hotel bar and restaurant. Pets welcome. **D** *Hotel Central*, Trg A Starčevića 2, T283399, F283891. Located in a prime position on the main square, this 19th-century hotel looks rather rundown from the outside. However, the 27 rooms are comfortable enough and there's a street-level café and restaurant.

**Eating**  **Mid-range**  *Slavonska Kuća*, Kamila Firingera 26, T208277. Lying within the Tvrda complex, this cosy, rustic eatery specializes in traditional local dishes. Try the *riblja kobasica*, a type of sausage made from smoked fish, as an unusual starter, followed by the house speciality *riblji paprikaš* (fish stew with paprika), which comes to the table in a large bowl with a ladle.

**Bars & clubs**  The main concentration of bars (and cafés) is found along the riverside promenade and in the trendy student area of Tvrda. Osijek's most happening club is *Oxygene*, Županijska 7, opposite the tourist office. It's open for late night dancing Fri-Sat 2200-0500, with techno and house music predominating. There's an internet café open daily (see Directory) in the same building.

**Festivals**  *Croatian Tambura Music Festival*, **May**. A folk music festival, attended by groups from throughout the country. *Osijek Summer Nights*, **Jun-Aug**. Open-air cultural events.

**Sport**  Across the river from town, the waterside Copacabana recreation centre offers a large open-air pool, a sand beach and a number of pleasant bars and cafés.

**Tour operators**  *Hobby Tours*, Kapučinska 23, T201070, organize guided tours of Osijek, Kopački Rit and Đakovo, as well as wine-tasting sessions at local vineyards.

**Transport**  **Air**  Osijek Airport, T514400, lies 7 km from town. Through summer 2002 the only flights were internal lines to Dubrovnik (1 hr 20 mins). There are no flights at all in winter.

**Bus**  The bus station lies a 10-min walk from the centre at Bartula Kašića bb, T214355. There are 6 buses daily to **Zagreb** (4 hrs); 20 daily to **Đakovo** (40 mins) and 20 daily to **Vukovar** (¾ hr). An international bus also departs from **Osijek** for **Pecs** in Hungary, Mon-Sat (3 hrs). **Car hire**  *Hertz*, Gundulićeva 32, T200422, www.hertz.hr  **Taxi**  There is a taxi rank in front of the train station at Trg Ružičke, T200100. **Train**  The train station lies a 10-min walk from the centre, next to the bus station, at Trg Ružičke, T205155. There are 4 trains daily to **Zagreb** (4 hrs), and 2 international trains daily for **Pecs** in Hungary (3 hrs).

**Directory**  **Communications**  Post office: Županijska 8, Mon-Fri 0700-2000, Sat 0700-1400. Internet cafés: *Internet Klub Ukrik*, Sunčana 18, www.ukrik.hr  *Cybercaffe Oxygene*, Županska 7, www.oxygene.com.hr  **Consulate**  There is only one consulate in Osijek. *Hungarian*, S Radića 15, T250150. **Medical services**  Doctors and hospitals: Osijek Hospital, J Huttlera 4, T511511. Casualty, T506920. **Pharmacies**: *Ljekarna Centar*, Trg A Starcevica 7, T205722, works regular hours and also covers nights shifts. *Ljekarna Park*, Park Kralja P Kresimira IV 6, T208323, works regular hours and also covers Sat and Sun afternoons.

# Kopački Rit Nature Park

Kopački Rit Nature Park is a vast expanse of marshland prized for its wealth of rare birds. Lying between the River Drava and the River Danube, the park is part of Baranja, a region of flat, fertile agricultural land, which until the war for independence hosted a mixed farming community of Croats, Serbs and Hungarians. It was taken by the Serb military at the beginning of the war in 1991, was designated a UN-protected zone from 1992 to 1996, and then came under UN transitional administration until it was incorporated into Croatia in January 1998.

*Phone code: 031*
*Colour map 2, grid B5*
*12 km northeast*
*of Osijek*

**Getting there** Visits to the park by appointment only as part of a guided tour. 20Kn. The main entrance to the park is at Kopačevo, 3 km from Bilje. **Getting around** Guided visits to the park can be given by boat or on foot – access to certain areas is still restricted as the park was heavily mined during the war. **Tourist office** Bilje is the headquarters of the park. The nature park tourist information centre is at Petefi Šandora 35 in Bilje, T750855, www.bilje.hr  The office is open 0800-1600.

**Ins & outs**
*See Transport, page 95, for further details*

Said to be one of the largest and most beautiful wetlands in Europe, the park's waters, flora and fauna attract experts and scientists from far a field, as well as a curious day-trippers. Around 260 wild bird species nest here, including geese, ducks, herons, storks, coots, gulls, terns, kingfishers and woodpeckers, and in spring and autumn many other migratory species use the area as a temporary shelter. The waters are abundant in fish – hence why so many birds are attracted to the park – including pike, tench, bream, carp, catfish and perch, while the surrounding oak woods host deer, wild boar, wild cats, pine martens, stone martens and weasels. Some of the willow-lined ponds are home to otters.

**Sights**

Several families offer (**E**) bed and breakfast style accommodation in Bilje, 3 km from the park. Try either the Sklepić family at Dubrovačka 30, Bilje, T750243, or the Galić family at Ritska 1, Bilje, T750393. Both have 2 double bedrooms and serve up hearty breakfasts with home-made local salami and cheeses, and can also arrange fishing trips by boat.

**Sleeping**

**Mid-range** *Restoran Kod Varge*, Kralaja Zvonimira 37a, Bilje, T750031. Just outside the park in Bilje, *Kod Varge* is known for tasty fish dishes and home-made sausage. The house speciality is *šaran s kajmakom i krumpirom* (carp with sour cream and potatoes). *Restoran Komoran*, Podunavlje, Bilje, T753099. Located within the park, this highly regarded restaurant is housed in a traditional hunting lodge. The dining room is decorated with hunting and fishing equipment and trophies, and favourite dishes are *sakadaški fiš paprikaš* (hearty fish stew prepared with paprika) and *ražnjići od divljaći* (wild boar and venison kebabs).

**Eating**

Local **buses** leave **Osijek** for Bilje every hour. From Bilje you have to walk the final 3 km to the park entrance.

**Transport**

# Vukovar

On the west bank of the River Danube, which forms a natural border with Serbia, Vukovar was once a prosperous market town famed for its elegant 18th-century Baroque architecture. Since 1991, it has become better known as an image of the suffering and devastation caused by the war for independence. Many who fled at this time remain in other parts of Croatia or abroad. An eerie silence pervades in a town still divided between Croats and Serbs.

*Phone code: 032*
*Colour map 2, grid B6*
*Population: 30,126*
*303 km east of Zagreb and 35 km southeast of Osijek*

Inland Croatia

▶ **Casualties of war**

*Some people say the war started and ended in Vukovar. When Croatia claimed independence, Serbs from the surrounding villages were adamant that they would rather remain part of Yugoslavia. A group of Croatian activists (among them members of Tudjman's HDZ ruling party) provoked the situation by firing three rockets at the Serb-populated village of Borovo Selo. Tensions escalated and the situation soon ran out of control. By 1 August 1991 Vukovar lay under siege, surrounded by Yugoslav army reinforcements and Serb irregulars. On 19 November 1991, the town fell, by this time devastated, buildings lying in rubble and the streets lined with corpses. Of those who remained, the women and children were spared, but many of the men disappeared and have never been found, though several bodies have been identified in a mass grave at nearby Ovčara.*

*Vukovar officially came back under Croatian administration in January 1998 and a lengthy reconstruction programme was initiated in the hope that former-residents, both Croats and Serbs, would return. The process of rebuilding and reintegration is slow and will take many years to complete. Today there are two football teams, two radio stations: two separate communities that live side by side but ignore one another. At the nursery school, two separate playgroups are held under one roof, one for Croats, one for Serbs. And at the secondary school, Croatian and Serbian teenagers alternate morning and afternoon classes so as not to be in the same room at the same time. Nowhere else in the country are the physical and psychological traumas caused by the war so apparent.*

**History**  People lived in the area as long ago as the Bronze Age: the renowned Vučedol Dove, a three-legged vessel in the form of a bird from around 2000BC (now in Zagreb Archaeological Museum) was found at Vučedol, an archaeological site 5 km from Vukovar.

The town itself grew up at the confluence of the River Vuka and the River Danube. It became a free royal town in 1231 and the chief settlement of the *županija* (country) of Vukovo, an area of rich arable farmland dotted with noble fortresses and villages of serfs. In 1526, after Vukovar fell to the Ottoman Turks lead by Sultan Suleiman the Magnificent, mosques and public baths were built, and the town had a population of around 3,000, until the Turks were finally driven out in 1687. In 1736, a German nobleman, Philipp Karl zu Eltz (1665-1743), bought the Lordship of Vukovar, which covered 23 villages and some 31,000 serfs, and from then on the Eltz family played a crucial role in the town's development. Most of the population were employed in farming, notably the production of cereals and wine, but craftsmen's guilds also sprung up, and goods were exported along the River Danube by steamship. At the end of the Second World War, the Eltz family lost their property and returned to Germany, as did many other German settlers in the region, but following the declaration of Croatian independence in 1991, Jakob Graf zu Eltz moved back to Croatia and now sits as a member of parliament in Zagreb.

During the Tito years the area surrounding Vukovar was rapidly industrialized: the *Borovo* factory produced rubber goods such as footwear and tyres; *Vuteks* manufactured textiles and *Vupik* was a larger producer of wheat, maize, sugar-beet, wine, livestock and milk. The standard of living was high, and by 1991 Vukovar had a population of almost 45,000, of which 44% were Croats, 37% Serbs, and the remainder members of various minorities such as Hungarian, Slovaks and Ruthenians. The war of independence tragically changed the fortunes of Vukovar, see box.

**Gradski Muzej** (Town Museum) suffered the same fate as the rest of Vukovar – the Baroque Dvorac Eltz (Eltz Manor), in which it was housed, was shelled and badly damaged. Built in 1751 by the Eltz family, the manor is now under restoration and the ground floor has already reopened. Many of the original exhibits were looted or destroyed, but a new collection is gradually being built up, largely with donations from abroad. The museum also stages temporary art exhibitions. ■ *Mon-Sat 0800-1500. 10Kn. T441270, L Ribara 2.*

On raised ground a short distance southeast of the centre stands the three-story **Franjevački Samostan** (Franciscan Monastery), centring on a charming 18th-century cloistered courtyard. The complex includes the monastery church and a museum housing a collection of religious paintings. At the time of writing, the complex was still undergoing restoration. However, there are plans to reopen it to the public in the near future. For current information enquire at the tourist office, or call the monastery directly, T442641.

**Sights**

**D** *Hotel Dunav*, Trg Republike 1, T441285, F441762. As the only hotel in town, this is probably where you'll be sleeping if you decide to stay a night in Vukovar. It's a functional 8-storey 1970's concrete block, with 58 rooms, a bar and restaurant.

**Sleeping**

**Mid-range** *Tri Vrske*, Parobrodska 3, T441788. Accessed across a footbridge, this charming informal riverside restaurant is one of the few places that managed to keep functioning during the war. Freshwater fish tops the menu, with local dishes such as *riblji paprikaš* (fish stew with paprika) and smoked carp highly recommended.

**Eating**

There are 20 **buses** daily to Osijek (¾ hrs) and 5 to **Zagreb** (4½ hrs). Four daily international buses also depart from Vukovar for **Belgrade** in Serbia, and there are 2 buses weekly to **Berlin** and **Hamburg** in Germany. The bus station lies a 10-min walk from the centre at Olajnic bb, T441829.

**Transport**

**Communications  Post office**: M Pijade 4, Mon-Fri 0700-2000, Sat 0700-1400. **Consulates** There is only 1 consulate in Vukovar. Serbia and Montenegro, Ul Borisa Kidiriča 1, T441016. **Doctors and hospitals**: at Županijska 37, T452111.

**Directory**

*Inland Croatia*

# South of Zagreb

*Southwest of Zagreb lies the provincial town of Karlovac, probably best known today for its beer, Karlovačko pivo, though during the 16th century it was an important military base marking the border between Austro-Hungary and the Turkish empire. Moving further south, on the inland road to Dalmatia, you will come Plitvice national park, well worth a stop for its spectacular waterfalls.*

## Karlovac

Karlovac lies on a major road junction between Zagreb, with Rijeka to the west and Split to the south. It's not a town you'd specially set out to visit, but you're bound to pass through en route from the capital to either the Kvarner region or Dalmatia, and it's a great place to stretch your legs, with tree-lined promenades following the old town walls, and a pleasant riverside path leading to a small castle hotel. The town tourist office is at Ulica Petra Zrinskog 3, T615115, www.karlovac-touristinfo.hr

*Phone code: 047*
*Colour map 1, grid B5*
*Population: 59,395*
*55 km southwest of Zagreb*

**History**   Founded by the Hapsburgs in 1579 as a military base, for some time Karlovac marked the southern border of the Austro-Hungarian Empire. As a defence post against Ottoman expansion, the settlement was built to a sturdy Renaissance plan based on a six-point star with bastions and a moat, which was filled with water from the nearby rivers, the Korana and the Kupa. During the late 17th century, as the Turks were pushed further south and the settlement no longer served as a military base, it developed into a provincial town filled with Baroque architecture.

**Sights**   Today, the main square, Trg Bana Jelačića, is overlooked by the late 17th-century Baroque **Sv Trojstvo** (Holy Trinity Church), while café life centres on the **Korzo**, a pedestrian street lined with cafés and shops. Although the walls were demolished during the 19th century, the basic star plan can still be clearly seen in aerial views. The moats have been turned into a 2.5-km string of promenades lined by horse chestnut trees, with the loveliest part being the former Maria Valeria Promenade, recently renamed after the late President, Franjo Tudman.

Close to the main square, housed within the Baroque Frankopan Palace, the **Gradski Muzej** (Town Museum) displays archaeological finds, such as clay figures from an Illyrian shrine, scale models showing the development of the town, period furniture, finely embroidered traditional folk costumes, and local craftwork such as pottery, woodwork and basketry. ■ *Mon-Fri 0800-1500, Sat-Sun 1000-1200. 10Kn (Wed free). T615980, Strossmayerov Trg 7.*

Managed by the Town Museum, the **Galerija Vjekoslav Karas** (Vjekoslav Karas Gallery), located in a modern building opened in 1976, is named after the local artist Vjekoslav Karas (1821-58) and highlights Croatian painters from late 19th and early 20th centuries. ■ *Mon-Fri 0800-1500, Sat-Sun 1000-1200. 10Kn (Wed free). T412381, Ljudevita Šestica 3.*

East of town, a pleasant 30-minute stroll along the banks of the River Kupa brings you to the **Stari Grad Dubovac** (Dubovac Castle), complete with three towers and a triangular courtyard, built by the Frankopan family from the island of Krk in the 13th century. The dungeon and the main defence tower are open to the public, and part of the building now houses a hotel and restaurant. A brochure, available in English and Croatian, is available at the entrance. ■ *Open to visitors at any time as it also functions as a hotel. T416331. 10Kn. Zagrad 10.*

**Foginovo Kupalište** (Foginovo bathing area), on the bank of the River Korana, is known as the 'town beach', complete with a diving platform, an area set aside for beach volleyball, and a number of waterside bars and cafés. It's just a 10-minute walk from the centre, and bathing is possible from mid-June to early-September.

**Sleeping & eating**   D *Dubovac Castle Hotel*, Zagrad 11, T416331. Part of Stari Grad Dubovac (see Sights) has been converted into an 11-room hotel. *Stari Grad Restaurant* is part of the complex, and non-residents are welcome to eat here. Alternatively, the tourist office website includes a list of families offering private accommodation in Karlovac.

**Eating**   **Mid-range to expensive** *Restoran Srakovčić*, Put Davorina Trstenjaka 1, T614080. This large, highly regarded restaurant lies in the centre of town, close to the bus station and the River Korana. The interior is filled with plants, and the menu features hearty meat dishes such as smoked pork with prunes, veal stuffed with ham, cheese and mushrooms, and venison prepared in stout ale. See also *Dubovac Castle Hotel*, above.

*Ivanski Krijes*, St John's Day Bonfire, **23 Jun**. Festivities, organized by the tourist office, **Festivals**
take place on the banks of the River Kupa.

If you are planning to **drive** from **Zagreb** to Karlovac on the main road (E65), remem- **Transport**
ber that a 15Kn toll is payable. The 30 daily **buses** from **Zagreb** to **Split** stop in
Karlovac, as do the 20 buses from **Zagreb** to **Rijeka** (50 mins). Karlovac bus station,
T614700. Four daily **trains** from **Zagreb** to **Split** pass through Karlovac (30 min). The
12 daily local trains from Zagreb to Karlovac are far slower (1 hr) due to numerous stops
in small stations. Karlovac train station, T432233.

## Plitvice Lakes National Park

Travelling south on the road for Dalmatia, the remote Plitvice Lakes are *Phone code: 053*
Croatia's most popular inland destination. As the country's oldest and largest *Colour map 1, grid C6*
national park, Plitvice is home to 16 emerald-green lakes connected by a series *128 km from Zagreb*
of spectacular waterfalls, stretching 8 km in length. The surrounding slopes *and 73 km from*
are covered with dense forests of beech and fir, and visitors can explore the *Karlovac*
area following a series of marked paths and wooden bridges. If you enjoy
walking you may well want to spend a couple of days here – there are several
good hotels within the park and private accommodation is available in the
surrounding villages.

The national park tourist information centre is at Entrance 2, in the village of Plitvička **Ins & outs**
Jezera, T751014/5, www.np-plitvicka-jezera.hr The park is open daily Jun-Sep *See Transport, page*
0700-2000, 90Kn. Oct-May 0900-1700, 70Kn. The price of the ticket includes free use of *100, for further details*
national park buses and boats. The local tourist office lies south of the park in the village of Korenica at Trg Sv Jurja 6, T776798. Open summer only.

Making up part of a spectacular karst landscape, the lakes and falls of Plitvice **Sights**
developed over the last 10,000 years, and the process is continuing today. *The area was turned*
Such features are formed when limestone rock, consisting largely of calcium *into a national park in*
carbonate ($CaCO_3$), dissolves in water, which then becomes super-saturated *1928, and designated*
and deposits the $CaCO_3$ in the form of microcrystals. In the case of Plitvice, *a UNESCO world*
the deposits have built up to make rapids and travertine barriers that form *heritage site in 1979*
the waterfalls. It's beautiful the year through, though bear in mind that the
area is often covered by snow November to March, and the lakes may well be
frozen from December to January.

The lakes here are rich in trout (though fishing is prohibited within the
park), while the surrounding forests are home to foxes and badgers, as well as
the seldom sighted lynx, wolf and bear. Birdwatchers should look out for
woodpeckers and herons, plus rare species such as grey eagles and peregrine
falcons. Owls are plentiful, though rarely see in daylight hours.

The best way to explore the lakes is to begin at Entrance 2 (close to the
national park office and the village of Plitvička Jezera) then take the national
park bus to **Labudovac Falls**, where the water from **Prošćansko Jezero**, the
highest of the lakes (639 m above sea level) begins a spectacular journey, cas-
cading down through a succession of smaller basins to reach the park's largest
lake, **Jezero Kozjak**. The stretch from Labudovac Falls to Jezero Kozjak is
comfortably completed on foot, after which you can ride a national park boat
the length of the lake, then follow a series of wooden bridges and walkways
over and around a number of smaller pools to arrive at the park's largest and
most spectacular waterfall, **Veliki Slap**, where water thunders down to the
lowest lake, **Kaluderovac** (503 m). You are now just a 10-minute walk from

*Inland Croatia*

Entrance 1, where you might stop for a meal or refreshments at *Lička Kuća* (see Eating), and then take a national park bus back to your starting point at Entrance 2. This entire circuit takes about six hours. A map and information about alternative routes are available from the national park office.

**Sleeping**   **B** *Hotel Jezero*, Plitvička Jezera bb, close to Entrance 2, T751400, F751015, www.np-plitvicka-jezera.hr  The most luxurious hotel in the park is a large mountain lodge built on high ground overlooking the lakes. The 210 rooms and 7 suites are panelled in natural pine and have matching wooden furniture. Facilities include tennis courts, a fitness centre and sauna, and a bowling alley. **C** *Hotel Bellevue*, Plitvička Jezera bb, close to Entrance 2, T751700, F751013, www.np-plitvicka-jezera.hr  This slightly cheaper option offers 70 basic rooms, including 6 singles (ideal for the lone traveller) with en-suite bathrooms but few extras. Popular with excursion groups. Both the national park office and local tourist office can help you find private accommodation close to the park.

**Eating**   **Mid-range** *Lička Kuća*, opposite Entrance 1, T751024. This large, highly regarded restaurant is done out in rustic style with heavy wooden tables and benches. The menu features traditional Lika dishes such as *lička juha* (soup made from lamb's innards and vegetables) and *teletina ispod peke* (veal prepared under a *peka*). Closed Nov-Apr.

**Transport**   30 **buses** daily running from **Zagreb** to **Dalmatia** all pass through the village of Plitvička Jezera, but make sure the driver knows you want to get off there (2½ hrs).

Inland Croatia

Istria

# Introducing Istria

A large, triangular peninsula in northwest Croatia, Istria has an identity all of its own. Historically it has close ties with Italy, and still today many towns, especially on the western side, are bilingual. It's notably ahead of the rest of the country regarding current trends: restaurants serve beautifully presented creative cuisine, farmhouses dish up local specialities and offer overnight accommodation (agrotourism), and the tourist board has set up a series of bike paths and wine roads.

Lying on the tip of the peninsula, the region's principal city and port is **Pula**, with a first-century Roman forum as the main square and an ancient amphitheatre dominating the skyline.

Istria

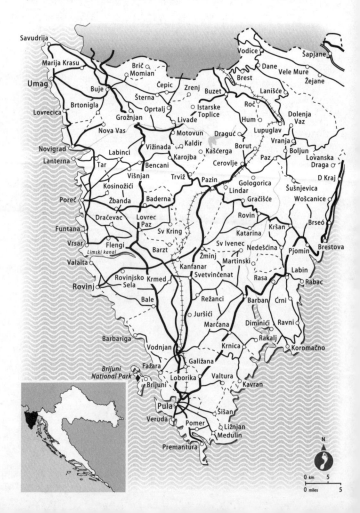

Close by, the islands of **Brijuni National Park** once served as the summer residence of the late President Tito: today visitors can stroll freely through the beautifully landscaped parkland, complete with fallow deer, and even stay overnight in a high-class hotel.

Croatia's most popular seaside resorts lie on the Istrian **west coast**: **Poreč**, home to a splendid sixth-century basilica decorated with stunning golden Byzantine mosaics, and neighbouring **Rovinj**, made up of ochre and russet coloured houses clustered around a pretty fishing harbour, crowned by a hilltop church. Thankfully, during the tourist boom of the 1970s, the vast new hotel complexes were constructed along the coast and hidden by landscaping, leaving the old town centres perfectly intact. Besides its cultural wealth, this area is renowned for nudist resorts, with the largest one in Europe, **Koversada**, lying in **Vrsar**, between Poreč and Rovinj.

Moving **inland** to the Srce Istre (Heart of Istra), narrow country roads meander through a gently rolling landscape of woodland and vineyards. Many rural villages lie semi-abandoned, though it's fast becoming fashionable to have a restored stone holiday cottage in the area. The romantic fortified hilltop towns of **Motovun** and **Grožnjan** have established themselves as alternative cultural centres, the former with an annual festival of avant guarde film, the latter with its community of artists and craftsmen plus an annual music summer school. **Buzet** and its surrounding villages are much prized for rustic eateries serving dishes with locally found truffles.

Less visited than the west coast, the **eastern side** of Istria faces on to the Kvarner Gulf. The main resort is **Rabac**, a modern settlement with a decent pebble beach and several good fish restaurants. It's not the sort of place you'd want to spend very long, but combined with neighbouring hilltop **Labin**, a former mining town, it offers a seaside-inland experience all in one. Nearby Brestova serves as the mainland port for ferries to the island of Cres (see Kvarner).

Istria

# Pula

Phone code: 052
Colour map 1, grid C1
Population: 58,594

*Pula is something of an enigma. Here magnificent ancient Roman **ruins** stand side by side with a declining **industrial port**, in a city that is Istria's administrative and economic centre. Somewhat surprisingly, it's also one of the top places in Croatia for small high-class family-run hotels and chic seafood restaurants serving beautifully presented **creative cuisine**. With two well-equipped **marinas**, one directly in front of the city centre and the other at Veruda, it's a popular destination for yachters, as well as sightseers who come to visit the monumental first-century **Roman amphitheatre** and the nearby **Brijuni National Park**, and holiday-makers on **package deals**, who normally sleep in the large seaside hotels south of the centre at Verudela and Medulin.*

## Ins and outs

**Getting there**
*Pula is 193 km from Zagreb, 98 km from Rijeka, 448 km from Split and 664 km from Dubrovnik*
Through summer there are regular flights to most European capitals. The airport lies 12 km northeast of Pula city centre. There is no airport bus connection, but taxis are readily available. The new bus station is at Trg 1 Istarska Brigade, 1 km northeast of the centre. The old bus station, close to centre, closed in autumn 2002. There are daily connections with the major cities in Croatia and Trieste, Italy. The train station is at Kolodvorska bb, 1 km north of centre. Services only cover the Istria Region.

**Getting around**
*See Transport, page 111, for further details*
The historic centre is quite compact, and the sights listed can comfortably be visited on foot. Verudela Peninsula, where many of the large commercial hotels and several good restaurants are located, is served by bus no 7.

**Tourist office**
The tourist information centre is in the heart of the old town at Forum 3, T219197, www.istra.com/pula

**Best time to visit**
Being Istria's economic and cultural centre, Pula is fairly lively the year through, though the most popular time to visit is Jul, when the *Pula Film Festival* and the *Istra Etno Jazz Festival* both take place.

## Background

Sometime during the fifth century BC, the Illyrian tribe of the Histri built a hilltop fortress on the present-day site of Kaštel. However, it was not until the time of the Roman general and statesman Julius Caesar (100-44BC) that Pula was founded as a Roman colony, *Colonia Julia Pollentia Herculanea*. During the reign of the first Roman Emperor, Augustus (63BC-AD14), it developed into an important administrative and commercial centre of about 5,000 inhabitants, complete with a forum and temples, town walls and 12 monumental gates, and a water supply and sewer system. In 539 the region was absorbed into the Byzantine Empire, and during the sixth and seventh centuries Pula became the main base of the Byzantine fleet on the Adriatic.

However, the tide of fortune was reversed in the late 13th century, when the city was hit by the plague: people were dying on the streets so fast that the corpses could not all be buried, inspiring the Italian poet Dante Alighieri (1265-1321) to mentioned Pula city graveyard in the *Divine Comedy* in the ninth cycle of *Hell*. Shortly afterwards, in 1331, the city fell to Venice. Losing

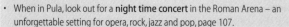

## Things to do in Istria

- When in Pula, look out for a **night time concert** in the Roman Arena – an unforgettable setting for opera, rock, jazz and pop, page 107.
- Spend a leisurely day visiting **Brijuni National Park** – check out the Tito exhibition and the animals in the safari park then take time off to walk and swim, page 112.
- See the glittering religious mosaics of **St Euphrasius Basilica** in Poreč, page 120.
- Splash out on a night in a luxury hotel at the unforgettable *Villa Angelo d'Oro* in Rovinj, page 116.
- Visit the crafts workshops and artists studios in the isolated hill town of **Grožnjan**, page 126.
- Order a dish prepared with locally **unearthed truffles** – undoubtedly an acquired taste, but this is a perfect time and place to start, page 127.

Istria

its role as a major port, a period of decline set in, and by the time the Venetians left, in 1797, the population stood at only 600.

Under the Hapsburgs from 1813 to 1918, Pula was made the chief base and arsenal of the Imperial Austrian Navy, and thus entered its second golden age. The small city of fading antique splendour was transformed into an industrial port with a prosperous middle class, though apparently it did little to impress the Irish novelist James Joyce, who worked here briefly in 1904, teaching English to Austrian naval officers, and referred to Pula as a "godforsaken nest" and "Siberia upon sea".

Under Italy in the run up to the Second World War, Mussolini came here in person to make a speech in the theatre, and as the war drew to a close the city was badly damaged by Anglo-American bombing.

During the Yugoslav years Pula lived through a period of intense industrial development, with the shipyard becoming a major source of employment. The *Pula Film Festival* was born in the 1950's, regularly attended by Tito and his celebrity friends such as Sofia Loren, Elizabeth Taylor and Richard Burton. Today, although it's a popular sightseeing destination thanks to its Roman monuments, unemployment is high and it is still struggling to recover from the economic and social damage caused by the recent war.

## Sights

**Forum** The vast paved piazza has been the city's most important public meeting space since Roman times. It's closed to traffic and overlooked by popular open-air cafés and the city tourist office, and on the north side you can still see the well-preserved **Augustov Hram** (Temple of Augustus) with an open portico supported by six tall columns with Corinthian capitals. It was built in the early first century AD to celebrate the cult of Augustus, who founded the Roman Empire in 27BC. Under Byzantine rule it was converted into a church, and later used as a granary. Today it houses a **lapidarium**, displaying pieces of Roman sculpture.

In Roman times, next to the Temple of Augustus, stood the **Temple of Diana**, dedicated to the goddess of hunting. It has long since disappeared, though during the 13th century the back wall was incorporated into the **Gradska Vijećnica** (Town Hall), which was later renovated to gain its present appearance with a Renaissance façade. ■ *Jun-Sep 0900-1300 and 1800-2100. Oct-May by appointment. Augustov Hram. T218603.*

**Katedrala (Cathedral)** From the north end of the Forum, Kandlerova ulica leads to the Cathedral, with a 17th-century Renaissance façade concealing a three-nave early Christian basilica, built on the foundations of a Roman temple during the fifth century. In front of the cathedral, the freestanding bell tower was built in the late 17th century, partly from stone blocks taken from the Arena (Roman amphitheatre). The complex was badly damaged by bombing during the Second

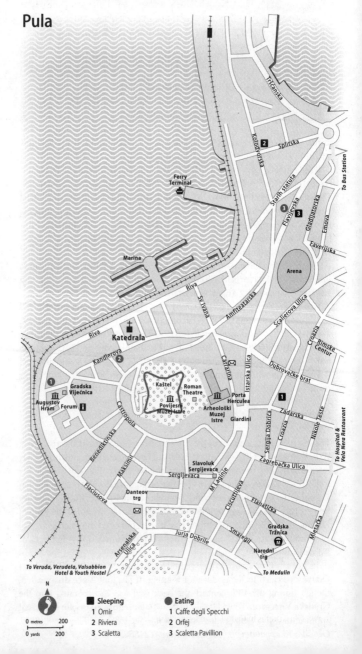

## Pula

Istria

| Sleeping | Eating |
|----------|--------|
| 1 Omir | 1 Caffe degli Specchi |
| 2 Riviera | 2 Orfej |
| 3 Scaletta | 3 Scaletta Pavillion |

0 metres 200
0 yards 200

To Veruda, Verudela, Valsabbion Hotel & Youth Hostel

To Medulin

To Hospital & Vela Nera Restaurant

To Bus Station

World War, but was fully restored in 1946. ■ *Jun-Sep 0900-1200 and 1800-2100, Oct-May open for mass only. Obala Maršala Tita.*

Continue to the end of Kandlerova ulica then take Amfiteatarska ulica to arrive in front of the Arena, a first-century Roman amphitheatre. Designed to host gladiator fights and able to accommodate 22,000 spectators, way beyond the city population of that time, it is the sixth largest building of its type in the world (after the Colosseum in Rome, and the amphitheatres in Verona, Catania, Capua and Arles). The outer walls are remarkably well preserved, though through the centuries stones from the inside have been carried off for use on other buildings. Originally the interior would have been encircled by tiers of stone seats, the central floor would have been covered with sand, and a *velarium* (large awning) would have been used as a temporary roof structure, to shelter spectators from the sun and rain.

**Arena**
*Today it is used for open-air concerts: recent performers include Sting, James Brown and Alanis Morissette. The annual Pula Film Festival is also held here*

The Arena fell into disuse in the sixth century, when gladiator games were forbidden. During the 16th century the Venetians planned to transfer it, stone by stone, to Venice, though fortunately a local senator, Gabriele Emo, protested and the project was abandoned. The building was restored in the early 19th century by General Marmont under Napoleon's Illyrian provinces. The underground halls house a musty and rather disappointing display of wooden oil presses and amphorae.

■ *May-Sep 0800-2100, Oct-Apr 0900-1500. 16kn. Flavijevska ulica.*

From the Arena, retrace your steps along Amfiteaterska ulica, then take the first left to arrive on Cararina ulica. Here, the second-century **Porta Gemina** (Twin Gate) is one of two surviving gates (originally there were 12) that led into the Roman walled town. Today it serves as the main entrance to the Arheološki Muzej Istre, housing an extensive but rather uninspiring display of local finds. The ground floor is dedicated to heavy stone pieces such as Roman gravestones and sarcophagi, and medieval stone altars from early Christian churches. On the first floor you'll find the prehistoric collection, including early daggers, axes, bracelets and pendants, and necklaces made of amber beads. Directly behind the museum, a path leads to the remains of a small semicircular second-century Roman theatre, which is still used for small open-air concerts through summer: the Portuguese band, Madre Deius, played here recently. A few doors down from the museum, still on Cararina ulica, stands **Porta Herulea** (Hercules Gate), a simple arch in the only surviving section of the original city walls from the first century BC. ■ *Jun-Sep 0900-2000, Oct-May Mon-Sat 0900-1500. 10Kn. T218603, Cararina 3.*

**Arheološki Muzej Istre (Archaeologica l Museum of Istria)**

Continue along Cararina ulica and across Giardini to reach Slavoluk Sergijevaca, a monumental arch built in the first century BC to honour the local Sergi family for their role at the Battle of Actium, fought between the Roman fleet of Octavian and the Roman-Egyptian fleet of Mark Antony and Cleopatra in 31BC. The Sergis were on the side of Octavian, who was victorious and consequently went on to become the first Roman emperor under the name of Augustus. Next to the arch and marked with a small plaque stands the house where the Irish author James Joyce (1882-1941) lived briefly during a spell in Istria. West of the arch lies Ulica Sergijevaca, the city's main street in Roman times and today a pedestrian area lined with Pula's highest concentration of clothes shops. East of the arch, Flanatička leads to Nardoni Trg, where the daily market is held. ■ *Ulica Sergijevaca.*

**Slavoluk Sergijevaca (Triumphal Arch of the Sergi)**

Istria

| | |
|---|---|
| **Gradska Tržnica (Main Market)** | Built as a covered market in 1903, this iron and glass structure was revolutionary in its time. The daily fish and meat market is still held inside, while fruit and vegetable stands are set up outside, in the shade of a fine row of chestnut trees. ■ *Mon-Sat 0700-1330, Sun 0700-1200. Narodni Trg.* |
| **Kaštel (Venetian Fortress)** | For the best views over the city, climb any one of several steep flights of steps off Ulica Sergijevaca to arrive on Ulica Castropola, leading up to the hilltop Kaštel. The present fortress was built by the Venetians in 1630, and later renovated by the Austrians in 1840. Today it houses the rather disappointing **Povijesni Muzej Istre** (Historical Museum of Istria). In summer, the central courtyard is used for **open-air cultural events** including the *Pula Film Festival* and the *Istra Etno Jazz Festival*. ■ *Jun-Sep 0800-2000, Oct-May 0800-1500. 10Kn. T211740. Kaštel.* |
| **Beaches** | The nearest beaches to the city centre are at **Veruda** and **Verudela**, 3 km south of the centre, where most big modern hotels are located. However, the most stunning beaches are on **Kamenjak Peninsula**, on the very southern tip of Istria, within Donji Kamenjak Nature Park. Some 9.5 km long and 1.5 km wide, Kamenjak is ringed by an indented 30-km coastline, with countless coves and secluded beaches. ■ *Getting there: 9 buses leave Pula daily for the small village of Premantura, on Kamenjak.* |

## Excursions

| | |
|---|---|
| **Vodnjan (It Dignano)**<br>*Phone code: 052*<br>*Colour map 1, grid C1*<br>*Population: 3,406* | Lying just 10 km north of Pula, on the main road to Rijeka, Vodnjan makes a good half-day trip from Pula. It warrants a visit for two reasons: a church containing an unusual collection of mummified saints, and an excellent little restaurant where you can try authentic local cuisine. The town itself is worth an amble, with charming medieval buildings tightly packed onto a hillside, surrounded by vineyards and olive groves. |

The Baroque **Crkva Svetog Blaža** (Church of St Blaise) was built in the 18th century on the site of a Romanesque basilica, while the 65-m bell tower was added in 1882. Inside, in glass cases hidden by a curtain behind the main altar, lie the extraordinary mummified bodies of three saints: St Leon Bembo, St Giovanni Olini and St Nicolas Bursa. Although their skin and nails have dried, giving them the quality of weathered wood, experts are unable to explain why they never decomposed, and they are said to be among the best preserved human relics in Europe. What's more, ailing believers who have prayed to them have been cured, and have left votive offering (such as wedding rings) as a way of thanks. ■ *Jun-Sep 0900-1900; winter by appointment. Trg Zagreb bb.*

The restaurant **Vodnjanka**, at Istarska bb, Vodnjan, has an open-air terrace in summer where guests can sit out, moving indoors to the cosy dining room, complete with beamed ceilings and an open fire, through winter. Seasonal specialities are on offer the year round: quiches and omelettes made from wild asparagus in spring, and snails with polenta in the last week of August. It closes each Sunday in winter.

■ *Getting there: 8 trains daily from Pula to Vodnjan (15 mins). Train station, Ulica Željeznička, is a 10-min walk from the centre. Ten buses leave daily from Pula to Vodnjan (20 mins).*

On the regional road between Vodnjan and Pazin, 26 km north of Pula, the tiny hilltown of Svetvinčenat is named after its oldest building, the **Crkva Sv Vinčenata** (Church of St Vincent). Standing on the town cemetery, the interior of this 12th-century Romanesque structure is adorned with three layers of wall paintings from different periods, the most valuable being the Romanesque frescoes attributed to Master Ognobenus Trivisanus. In the centre of town, the Renaissance main square, known as Placa, is overlooked by the **medieval castle**, a quadrangular stone structure with corner towers, now used to stage open-air cultural events through summer. The *Istra Ethno Jazz*, held in early-July, is a three-day festival which takes place in three castles, one being here in Svetvinčenat (the others are in Pula and Pazin). In late July the *Festival of Dance and Nonverbal Theatre*, is held over six days again within the castle walls.

Svetvin-čenat (It Sanvincenzo)
*Phone code: 052*
*Colour map 1, grid C1*

Just a kilometre from the centre is *Peresiji*, Peresiji 15, T214910, F211735, a lovely old stone farmhouse that has been converted to provide three apartments sleeping a total of 14 guests. The restaurant, open to overnight guests only, features home-produced food and wine from the family vineyard.

*Istria*

■ *Getting there: 19 buses daily from Pula to Svetvinčenat (45 mins).*

This national park, with beautiful parkland, deer and peacocks, and a colourful history can comfortably be visited in a day from Pula or you can stay overnight on the only inhabited island. See page 112 for details.

**Brijuni National Park**

The small historic town of Labin and its seaside neighbour Rabin can both be visited on a day trip from Pula. See page 131 for details.

**Labin & Rabac**

## Essentials

Many of Pula's hotels and restaurants are located in Medulin, which started out as a fishing village lying 11 km from the city centre, but has now been incorporated into the suburbs thanks to urban sprawl along the coast. **A-B** *Valsabbion*, Pješčana uvala IX/26, 4 km from city centre, Medulin, T/F218033, www.valsabbion.com Overlooking the sea, this small luxury hotel boasts 10 cheerful guest rooms adorned with pine furniture and primary coloured fabrics, plus fresh fruit and flowers. There's a swimming pool on the top floor, and beauty treatments are also available. **B** *Riviera*, Splitska 1, between the train station and the Arena, T211166, F219117. This rather down at heel Austro-Hungarian building dates back to the early 20th century. Behind the grandiose exterior are 89 simple but comfortable guest rooms. Pets welcome.

**Sleeping**
■ *on map, page 106*

**C** *Hotel Scaletta*, Flavijevska 26, T541025, F541026, www.hotel-scaletta.com Standing close to the Arena, this 12-room family-run hotel occupies a tastefully refurbished old town house. Rooms are decorated in sunny shades of ochre and green, and come with spanking new bathrooms. Open all year. **D** *Omir*, Sergija Dobrića 6, T210614, F213944. Another small family-run hotel close to the Arena, with 14 plain but comfortable guest rooms. Pets welcome. Open all year. **G** *Youth Hostel*, Valsaline 4, Veruda. T391133, F391106. 140-bed youth hostel in a bay with its own beach. To get there, take bus no 7 for Verudela and get off at Ulica Veruda, then follow a signed path through a field. Open all year.

*Porer Lighthouse*, Islet of Porer, 20 km from Pula, 2 km from Premantura Bay. *Adriatica Net*, Selska 34, Zagreb, T01 3644461, F3644463, www.adriatica.net Built on a tiny islet of bare rock in 1833, this lighthouse has been converted to 2 apartments, each sleeping 4. Daily trips to the village on the mainland can be arranged with the lighthouse keeper.

The following agencies can help you find private accommodation: *Activatravel*, Scalierova 1, T215497, www.activa-istra.com *Agenzia Europa Istra*, Splitska 1A, T529483, www.arenatursit.hr *Uniline*, Dobriceva 16/II, T213720, www.uniline.hr For a list of families offering agrotourism (farmhouse meals and accommodation), check out, www.istra.com/agroturizam

**Eating**
● *on map, page 106*

**Expensive** *Vela Nera*, Pješčana uvala bb, Medulin, T219209, www.velanera.hr Voted the best restaurant in Croatia on several occasions, *Vela Nera* occupies a modern concrete and glass pavilion with a large terrace overlooking Marina Veruda. The house speciality is *Rižoto Vela Nera* (risotto prepared with shrimps, peaches and champagne) but they also do excellent pasta dishes with lobster and truffles, and fresh fish.

**Mid-range to expensive** *Valsabbion*, Pješčana uvala IX/26, Medulin, T218033, www.valsabbion.com Surpassing *Vela Nera* to be voted Istria's top restaurant in 2002, this was one of the first Croatian restaurants to specialize in slow food (a concept which began in Italy in the 1990's as a reaction against fast food and globalization – it means making the most of local seasonal produce, giving extreme care to preparation, and then eating the food in a relaxed and appreciative manner). The menu changes daily depending on fresh produce, but you can expect beautifully presented dishes such as tagliatelli with pine nuts, and frogfish in vine leaves. *Restaurant Scaletta*, Flavijevska 26, T541025. Taking up the ground floor of *Hotel Scaletta* (see Sleeping), this highly regarded restaurant serves sophisticated dishes such as ravioli filled with shrimps, and breaded fillet mignon with dates and croquettes. Closed Sun in winter.

**Mid-range** *Caffe degli Specchi* (Kavana Ogledala), Flaciusova 20, on the seafront, west of the centre, T210663. This renowned café doubles as a restaurant, serving refined dishes such as tagliatelli with shrimps and rocket, and veal medallions with pine nut sauce. Open daily.

**Cheap to mid-range** *Scaletta Pavillion*, Flavijevska 26, T541025. Across the street from *Hotel Scaletta* (see Sleeping) but under the same management, this wood and glass pavilion offers good pizzas, salads, and grilled meat and fish dishes. Closed Sun in winter.

**Cheap** *Orfej*, Konzula Istranina 1, T214405. Lying just off the Forum, this small pizzeria is friendly and reasonably priced.

**Cafés**

*Caffe degli Specchi* (Kavana Ogledala), Flaciusova 20, on the seafront, east of the centre, T210663. This old-fashioned café dates back to the early 20th century, when it was frequented by distinguished visitors such as the Irish author James Joyce and German novelist Thomas Mann. *Cvajner*, Forum 2, T853465. This trendy but unpretentious café has open-air seating on the Forum square through summer. The interior bears frescoes uncovered during restoration, plus minimalist modern furniture and contemporary art.

**Bars & clubs**

*Uliks*, Trg Portarata 1. A popular, little bar looking onto the Triumphal Arch of the Sergi, next door to the house where James Joyce once lived, hence the name. *Bounty Pub*, Veronska 8. A buzzing English-style pub close to the covered market. *Rock Club Uljanik*, Dobrilina 2. A thriving venue for alternative rock concerts, in a disused building overlooking the shipyard, close to the city centre. *Aquarius*, Fucane bb, Medulin. Lying 10 km from the city centre, this open-air disco is one of the largest summer nightclubs in Croatia. Open Jun-Sep.

**Entertainment**

**Cinema** Zagreb, Giardini 1, is centrally located and Pula's only cinema. **Theatre** Istarsko Narodno Kazaliste (Istrian National Theatre), Laginjina 5, T212677, www.ink.hr

*Istra Etno Jazz*, **early-Jul**. A 3-day festival taking place in 3 Istrian castles: **Pazin**, **Svetivinčenat** and **Pula**. For information check out, www.istraetnojazz.com *Pula Film Festival*, **late-Jul**. Founded in 1954, this 5-day competitive festival is held in the Roman Arena and at Kaštel and features films from both Croatia and other European countries. For information check out www.pulafilmfestival.com *Bikers' Festival*, **late-Jul to early-Aug**. Over the last 8 years this annual 5-day festival has attracted several thousand motorcyclists. In summer 2002 it was held south of Pula by the sea at Puntižela and Motorhead were among the guest bands. **Festivals**

**Main Market**, Narodni Trg. Meat and fish for sale within a steel and glass pavilion, fruit and vegetables at stalls on the square. Mon-Sat 0700-1330, Sun 0700-1200. *Zigante Tartufi*, Smareglina 7, close to the covered market, www.zigantetartufi.com Stock an excellent range of truffles and truffle products from the Mirna Valley, plus Istrian olive oil and wines. **Shopping**

**Diving** *DC Puntizela*, Stinjan Kascuni 61, T517474, www.wreck-diving-craotia.com *Gratsch Diving*, Verudela bb, T505994, www.Pula.ScubaDivers.net *KL Sub*, Liburnijska 17, T573658, www.divingindie.com **Sport**

**Golf** There is a 9-hole golf course on the island of Veli Brijun, within Brijuni National Park. See page 112.

**Sailing** ACI Marina, Riva 1, T219142, www.aci-club.hr Located directly in front of the city centre, within sight of the Roman Arena. 200 berths, open all year. The following charter companies are based here: *Euromarine*, contact Holjevca 20, Zagreb, T (01) 6528201; *Nautica Adria*, T215150 and *Vinkomar*, T216872; *Marina Veruda*, Cesta prekomrskih brigada 12, Veruda Bay, T211033, www.marverudacom 610 berths; *Pivatus*, T212155; and *RR Nautika*, contact Kranjce Viceva 23, Zagreb, T(01) 3820470.

*Activatravel*, Scalierova 1, T215497, www.activa-istra.com Agrotourism in Istria, plus cultural sightseeing packages, wine tasting, and golf on Brijuni. *Atlas*, Ulica Starih Statuta 1, T214172, www.atlas-croatia.com Various services throughout the country, including guided tours. *Generalturist*, Carrarina 4, T218487, www.generalturist.com Tailor-made trips both with and without guides throughout the country. *Uniline*, Dobrićeva 16/II, T213720, www.uniline.hr Accommodation plus excursions throughout Istria. **Tour operators**

**Air** Through summer, *Croatia Airlines* operate regular international flights to and from **Amsterdam**, **Berlin**, **Brussels**, **Dusseldorf**, **Frankfurt**, **Istanbul**, **London** (Gatwick and Heathrow), **Manchester**, **Mostar**, **Munich**, **Paris**, **Prague**, **Rome**, **Sarajevo**, **Skopje**, **Tel Aviv**, **Warsaw**, **Vienna** and **Zurich**. Internal flights link **Pula** with **Dubrovnik**, **Split**, **Zadar** and **Zagrab**. The number of destinations and the frequency of flights are reduced in winter. Pula airport, T530105. **Transport**

**Bus** Internal services include about 16 buses daily to **Zagreb** (5½ hrs); 17 to **Rijeka** in Kvarner (2½ hrs); 3 to **Zadar** in North Dalmatia (7 hrs); 3 to **Split** in Central Dalmatia (10½ hrs) and 1 to **Dubrovnik** in South Dalmatia (14 hrs). There are also 3 international buses daily to **Trieste** (Italy). Pula bus station, T502997. Left luggage costs 10Kn per item, open 0430-2300.

**Car hire** *Avis* in the city centre at S Dobrića 1, T223739, www.avis.hr; *Budget* in the ACI Marina at Riva 1, T218252, www.budget.hr and *Hertz* in *Hotel Histria*, Verudela bb, T210868, www.hertz.hr

Istria

**Ferry** *Lošinjska Plovidba*, Splitska 2/4, Rijeka, T(051) 319000, www.losinjplov.hr Operate a summer ferry service from **Koper** (Slovenia) to **Zadar**, stopping at **Pula**, **Unije**, **Mali Lošinj** and **Silba** en route. Tickets can be bought in Pula from *Jadroagent*, Riva 14, T210431.

**Taxi**   Taxis are usually available at the bus station. The most central taxi rank is at Giardini, between the Arena and the Triumphal Arch of the Sergi. Taxi, T223228.

**Train**   Internal services cover the Istria region only, with regular daily trains from **Pula** to **Buzet**, stopping in **Vodnjan**, **Kanfanar**, **Pazin** and **Lupoglav** en route. From **Lupoglav**, *Croatian Railways* run a connecting bus to Rijeka. Pula train station, T541733. National train information, T060 333444, www.hznet.hr

**Directory**   **Airlines offices** *Croatia Airlines*, Carrarina 8, T218943. **Communications** Internet café: *Multimedia Centre*, Istarska 30. With art and photography exhibitions. **Post office**: Danteov Trg 4, Mon-Fri 0700-2000, Sat 0700-1400. Ćirilmetodske Družbe 1, Mon-Fri 0700-2000, Sat 0700-1400. **Telephone**: if you prefer to telephone from a peaceful phone booth, rather than calling on the street, go to the post office (see above). Otherwise, you'll find numerous phone kiosks dotted round town. **Medical services** Doctors and hospitals: Hospital, Zagrebačka 30, T214433 (24 hr casualty). **Pharmacies**: all pharmacies are marked by a glowing green cross. The centrally located pharmacy at Giardini 15, T222551, works non-stop 24 hrs. **Useful numbers** Ambulance 94; Fire 93; Police 92.

## Brijuni National Park

*Phone code: 052*
*Colour map 1, grid C1*

Brijuni went down in history as Tito's summer residence: between 1949 and 1979 the charismatic Yugoslav President used it for entertaining countless world leaders, as well as glamorous friends such as Richard Burton and Elizabeth Taylor. After Tito died, the Brijuni archipelago, made up of 14 islands and islets, was made a national park, and the largest island, Veli Brijun, opened to the public. This low-lying island, with its beautifully tended parkland, herds of deer and strutting peacocks, makes a good day trip from Pula. If you stay for any longer, in one of the hotels, then you'll have the place to yourself for walking, bathing, playing tennis and golf. It's a place for total relaxation.

**Ins & outs**
*See Transport, page*
*113, for further details*

**Getting there**   The only way to visit the island is as part of an organized group. National park boats leave from Fažana (10 km northwest of Pula), ferrying visitors back and forth to the island. Reserve in advance, T521880, Mon-Fri 0700-1500. Tickets cost 160Kn which includes the boat ride and a tour of the grounds. **Getting around** The tour is conducted by a professional guide. It is possible to stay overnight (see Sleeping): hotels provide space for 320 guests, who have the island all to themselves as no one lives here. **Tourist office** The national park tourist office is in Fažana opposite the quay, T525888, www.np-brijuni.hr

**History**   Ancient ruins and archaeological finds show that the Romans used to summer here, though the islands were later abandoned for centuries due to an infestation of malaria-carrying mosquitoes. Finally, in 1893 Brijuni was bought by Paul Kupelweiser, an Austrian industrial magnate who employed the German scientist Robert Koch (founder of modern medical bacteriology, 1843-1910) to purge the place of the disease. Kupelweiser then set about creating a prestigious health resort: he laid out the parkland, tree-lined avenues and exotic planting, had fresh water and electricity brought to the island and

## Non-Aligned Nations

◀

*Founded during the Cold War by Josip Broz Tito of Yugoslavia, Gamal Abdel Nasser of Egypt and Jawaharlal Nehru of India, the Non-Aligned Nations was an association of countries that declined to take the side of either of the two world super powers of that time, the capitalist USA and the Communist USSR. Many of the countries that joined the alliance were former colonies that had recently freed themselves from foreign domination and were against forming new ties with any big power. Key issues were politics, defence and economics, and though the organization was made up of members of vastly differing political persuasions, it formed an important buffer between the Communist East and capitalist West. Today it numbers 114 members, including Indonesia, Egypt, Ghana, Guinea, Cuba and Libya.*

Istria

built a heated seawater swimming pool. Brijuni fast became a haven for Vienna's nobility and high society, with elite guests including Archduke Franz Ferdinand and the German writer Thomas Mann. In the 1920's, under Italian rule, a casino, polo club and tennis courts were built. Brijuni fared badly during the Second World War, so that by the time Tito made it his official summer residence it was in need of extensive renovation: the war-ravaged hotels were rebuilt, the old villas restored, and the neighbouring island of Vanga planted with orchards, tangerine groves and vineyards.

**Sights** Today a **museum** houses a photography exhibition *Tito on Brijuni* showing the great man enjoying his summer retreat with friends and colleagues, and the signing of a pact marking the birth of the Non-Aligned Nations, which took place here in 1956.

Visitors can also see the **safari park**, with zebras, antelopes, lamas and elephants, many of which were given to Tito as presents, such as two Indian elephants, Sony and Lenka, a gift from Indira Ghandi. Brijuni is a lovely place to walk, but other options are renting a bike or an electric buggy, and it's even possible to hire (at a price) Tito's 1953 **Cadillac**.

Tito's former favourite residence, the sumptuous **Bijela Vila** (White Villa) now serves as the setting for important state functions and international meetings between the Croatian president and his foreign counterparts.

**Sleeping** **AL** *Hotel Neptun-Istra*, T525100, F212110, www.np-brijuni.hr  A large modern hotel with 66 rooms and 22 suites, overlooking the harbour on Veli Brijuni. Guests with cars leave their vehicles in the guarded parking area in Fažana and have unlimited ferry travel to and from the island. There's a large restaurant serving fish and meat dishes, plus a café for coffee and cakes.

**Eating** **Cheap to mid-range** Other than the hotel restaurants, there is nowhere to eat on Veli Brijuni. Alternatively, stop for lunch or dinner at *Feral*, on the quay in Fažana, where you'll find value-for-money pasta dishes, plus barbecued fish and meat, served up on a summer terrace overlooking the sea.

**Sports** The national park lays on facilities for **horse riding** and **cycling**. There are also 4 **tennis courts** (floodlit by night), and a 9-hole **golf course**, built by the Austrians in 1922.

**Transport** **Bus** There are 16 buses daily from **Pula** to Fažana (20 mins), and 8 national park passenger boats from Fažana to Brijuni. **Boat** The Venice-based Italian company

*Adriatica*, T 0039 041781861, www.adriatica.it Run a summer ferry service from **Trieste** in Italy to Brijuni National Park, stopping in **Grado**, **Lignano**, **Piran** (Slovenia), **Poreč** and **Rovinj** en route.

# West Coast

*The most visited resorts here are Poreč and Rovinj, both well worth seeing, though they do get extremely crowded in peak season. They are separated by Limski Kanal, a spectacular 12-km long, steep-sided sea channel renowned for its excellent restaurants serving locally produced oysters and mussels. North of Poreč lie the commercial resorts of Novigrad and Umag, noted respectively for big international sailing and tennis events.*

## Rovinj (It Rovigno)

*Phone code: 052*
*Colour map 1, grid C1*
*Population: 13,467*
*35 km northwest*
*of Pula*

On the west coast, Rovinj is composed of densely packed medieval town houses, built into a hillside and crowned by a church and elegant bell tower. Down below, Venetian-style coloured façades curve their way around a pretty fishing harbour, rimmed with open-air cafés, restaurants and ice cream parlours. Out to sea lie a scattering of 14 small islands, while south of town, the green expanse of Zlatni Rt Park has tree-lined avenues and an indented shoreline with several pebble coves for bathing. The town's beauty and easy-going atmosphere have long made it popular with Croatian and Italian artists, writers, musicians and actors.

**Ins & outs**
*See Transport, page*
*117, for further details*

**Getting there** There are regular daily buses from Pula and a ferry service during the summer (originating from Trieste, Italy, on its way to Brijuni National Park stopping en route in Rivinj). **Getting around** The historic centre is a small compact area, closed to traffic and easily manageable on foot. However, the rough cobbled streets and steep

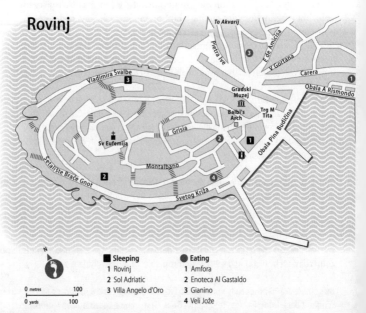

Rovinj

**Sleeping**
1 Rovinj
2 Sol Adriatic
3 Villa Angelo d'Oro

**Eating**
1 Amfora
2 Enoteca Al Gastaldo
3 Gianino
4 Veli Jože

uphill climb make high-heeled shoes impractical. **Tourist office** The town tourist office is at Obala P Budičina 12, T811566, www.tzgrovinj.hr

Rovinj started out as a small village founded on an island by the Romans. During the Middle Ages it was fortified with double walls and seven gates, and in 1283 it fell to Venice. Although it was placed under a Venetian governor, who imposed heavy trade taxes, citizens retained a certain amount of communal freedom and enjoyed relative prosperity. During the 16th century, the number of inhabitants increased as refugees fleeing the Turks arrived from Dalmatia, Bosnia, Albania and Greece, and in the late 17th century a bridge was built connecting the island to the mainland, and the town expanded along the coast. In 1763, the narrow channel separating the island from the coast was filled in, and thus Rovinj became a peninsula.

With the demise of Venice, the town entered a more difficult period under Austria: while Trieste in Italy became the Hapsburg's main trade port, and Pula their main military port and shipyard, Rovinj was seriously neglected, causing many families to leave and seek work in Pula. However, in 1872 the tobacco factory opened: still today it's the largest producer of Croatian cigarettes, and a warm, sweet smell of cured tobacco hangs in the air. A railway linking Rovinj with Kanfanar was built in 1876, but unfortunately closed in 1966 as it was considered unprofitable. Since the 1960's Rovinj has lived primarily from tourism, winning the prize for the 'best-kept resort' on several occasions.

**Background**

*The town is still home to a sizeable Italian majority, who have their own schools and cultural associations, and it is not unusual to hear Italian spoken*

Istria

The main square, **Trg M Tita**, opens out on one side on to the harbour. The principal building here is the 17th-century Town Hall, which now houses the **Gradski Muzej** (City Museum) which exhibits a collection of archaeological finds, Old Master paintings from between the 15th and 19th centuries, and contemporary works by Croatian painters and sculptors, many originating from Rovinj itself. ■ *Jun-Sep Mon-Sat 0900-1230 and 1830-2200, Oct-May Tue-Sat 0900-1230. 10Kn. Trg M Tita 11. T840471.*

**Sights**

Standing next to the Town Museum, this Baroque **Balbi's Arch** was built in 1680 on the site of a former town gate. The outer side of the arch is crowned by a stone relief of the head of a Turk, while the inner side bears the head of a Venetian. The architrave bears two coats of arms of the Balbi family and the Lion of St Mark's.

From Trg M Tita, a labyrinth of steep, narrow cobbled streets run up to the hilltop church of **Sv Eufemija** (St Euphemia). The building gained its Baroque appearance in 1736, though there had been a church here (originally dedicated to St George) for centuries. The 61-m Venetian bell tower, topped by a gleaming bronze weather vane of St Euphemia, was erected in 1677. Euphemia, who lived in the region that is now northwest Turkey, was thrown to the lions in 304, during one of Emperor

Diocletian's anti-Christian purges. According to legend, her remains were placed in a sixth-century marble sarcophagus, which floated out to sea from Constantinople and was washed ashore in Rovinj in AD800. The sarcophagus in question is now kept within the church, bearing Euphemia's bones, covered by a finely embroidered gold cloth. ■ *1000-1200 and 1600-1900.*

Dating back to 1891, the **Akvarij** (Aquarium) is one of the oldest in Europe. Marine life such as octopuses, poisonous scorpion fish, sea horses and large turtles are on display, plus other underwater life such as sponges and sea anemones. ■ *Summer 0900-2100. Winter by appointment. 10Kn. T804700. Obala G Paliage 5.*

**Zlatni Rt** (Punta Currente), laid out between 1890 and 1910 by Georg Huetteroth, is a vast expanse of parkland planted with avenues of holm oaks, alpine pines, cedar and cypresses, and criss-crossed by footpaths leading down to a series of pebble coves ideal for bathing. Other places for a dip, are the islands of **Sv Katarina** (St Catherine) and **Crveni Otok** (Red Island), both of which have pleasant rocky coastlines offering easy access to the water and through peak season, boats from the harbour leave every half an hour.

**Sleeping**
■ *on map, page 114*

**AL** *Villa Angelo d'Oro*, V Švalbe 38-42, T840502, F840111, www.rovinj.at  This small, luxury hotel is hidden away in the old town, one block back from the seafront, in the beautifully restored 17th-century Bishop's Palace. The 20 guest rooms are each individually furnished with antiques, and breakfast is served on a delightful rooftop garden terrace. Extras include a jacuzzi, sauna and solarium, plus a hotel boat at the guests' disposal. **B** *Sol Adriatic*, P Budicin 2, T815088, F813573. Bang in the centre, just off the main square and close to the harbour, this old-fashioned hotel has 27 basic but comfortable rooms. Through summer, breakfast is served on an open-air terrace out front. **C-B** *Hotel Rovinj*, Svetog Kriza 59, T811288, F840757. Lying close to the tip of the old town, this 68-room modern hotel is made up of a series of terraces overlooking the sea.

*St Ivan Lighthouse*, Otok Sv Ivan na Pučini (organized through *Adriatica Net*, Selska 34, Zagreb, T01-3644461, F3644463, www.adriatica.net) is on a tiny islet just 4 km from Rovinj. This lighthouse built in 1853 has been renovated to form 2 apartments, each sleeping 4.

The following agencies can help you find private accommodation: *Anetta Tours*, Carrera 59, T840414, www.anetta.hr  *Marco Polo*, Istarska 2, T816616, www.marcopolo.hr  *Uniline*, Palih Boraca bb, T816159, www.uniline.hr  For a list of families offering agrotourism (farmhouse meals and accommodation), check out www.istra.com/agroturizam

**Eating**
● *on map, page 114*

**Mid-range to expensive** *Enoteca Al Gastaldo*, Iza Kasarne 14, T814109. With an open log fire, walls stacked with wine bottles, and candlelight, this is a great place to come on a cold winter night. Try the spaghetti with either truffles or crab, accompanied by a delicious fresh salad of rocket and radicchio, then round off with a glass of local *rakija*. *Restaurant Amfora*, A Rismondo 23, T816663. With a small summer terrace overlooking the harbour, *Amfora* turns out beautifully presented seafood and pasta dishes. Closed Mon. *Restaurant Gianino*, A Ferri 38, T813402. Lying in a narrow side street, just back from the harbour, *Gianino* has long been popular with the yachting fraternity. House specialities include *tagliatelli mare-monti* (pasta with shrimps and mushrooms), rigatoni with lobster, and sole with truffles. Closed Mon.

**Mid-range**  *Veli Jože*, Sv Križa 1, T816337. This highly popular, informal eatery serves old-fashioned local dishes such as *bakalar in bianco* (dried cod prepared with onions, potatoes and white wine) and roast lamb with potatoes.

**Cheap**  *Vieccia Batana*, Trg M Tita 8. The oldest and most atmospheric café in town stands on the main square, close to the harbour. Perfect for morning coffee.

**Bars**  *Bethlehem*, Vodnjanska 1. This friendly pub offers low lighting, good rock music and a young crowd. *Valentino*, Sv Križa 28. Extremely popular bar overlooking the sea in the old town, with good music, several tables outside and underwater lighting. *Zanzi Bar*, Obala Pino Budicin. Ultra chic and verging on the pretentious, *Zanzi Bar* offers outdoor seating on a covered terrace, cocktails and cigars.

**Festivals**  *Chioggia-Rovinj-Chioggia*, open sailing regatta, **late-Apr**. *Pesaro-Rovinj-Pesaro*, open sailing regatta, **late-Apr**. *Grisia*, open-air art exhibition, **early-Aug**. *Rovinj Nights*, **Jul-Aug**, classical music concerts held in the Church of St Euphemia and the Franciscan Monastery. *Feast of St Euphemia*, **16 Sep**.

**Sport**  **Biking**  A marked bike path runs along the coast south of town from the ACI Marina, passing through Zlatni Rt, Rt Kuvi, Veštar and Cisterna to arrive in Sv Damijan. A map, *Bike Track Rovinj*, is available from the tourist office. **Diving**  Croatia's top diving site, recommended for advanced divers only, is the Baron Gausch wreck, just off the Rovinj Coast. This former passenger ship was en route from Koter (in present-day Montenegro) to Trieste (Italy) when it hit a mine and sunk in 1914. *Diving Center Valdaliso*, T815992, www.scuba-rovinj.com  *Nadi Scuba*, J Dobrile 11, T813290, www.scuba.hr  *DSC Rovinj*, based in Rijeka at Šetalište XIII divizije 28, T219111, www.diver.hr  organize a diving school here from early-Apr to mid-Nov. **Sailing**  *ACI Marina*, T813133, www.aci.club.hr  380 berths. Open all year. The charter company *WPT International* is based here, T815670.

**Tour operators**  *Marco Polo*, Istarska 2, T816616, www.marcopolo.hr  Organize sports activities such as cycling, paragliding, free-climbing and scuba diving. *Uniline*, Palih Boraca bb, T816159, www.uniline.hr  Organize excursions in the surrounding area.

**Transport**  **Boat**  *Adriatica*, the Venice-based Italian company, T 0039 041 781 861, www.adriatica.it  run a summer ferry service from **Trieste** in Italy to **Brijuni National Park**, stopping in **Grado**, **Lignano**, **Piran** (Slovenia), **Poreč** and **Rovinj** en route. Tickets are available in Rovinj from *Eurostar Travel*, Obala P Budicina 1, T813144. **Bus**  There are 12 buses daily to **Pula** (1 hr)and 6 to **Poreč** (1½ hrs). To reach Italy, an early morning service runs from Pula to **Padova**, stopping at **Rovinj**, **Trieste** and **Venice** en route, while a slightly later morning bus runs from Pula to **Trieste**, stopping in Rovinj, and **Poreč** en route. The bus station is at Trg na Lokvi bb, T811453. **Car hire**  *Budget*, Trg na Lokvi 6, T812561, www.budget.hr  (early-Apr to late-Oct). **Taxi**  There are normally several taxis available at the bus station. Taxi, T811100.

**Directory**  **Communications**  **Post office**: M Benussia 4, Mon-Fri 0700-2000, Sat 0700-1400. **Medical services**  **Doctors and hospitals**: a 24-hr tourist first aid centre operates in the casualty department of Rovinj doctors' surgery at Istarska ulica bb, T813004. **Pharmacies**: Gradska Ljekarna at Matteo Benussia, T813589.

Istria

## Vrsar (It Orsera)

*Phone code: 052*
*Colour map 1, grid C1*
*Population: 1,872*
*Between Poreč*
*(10 km) and Rovinj*
*(25 km)*

The fishing village of Vrsar is backed by gently undulating hills covered with pinewoods and vineyards. During the Middle Ages, stone cottages were built around the hilltop castle and church, and the entire complex fortified; it was not until the 19th century that the town expanded outside the walls and down to the bay. The Venetians exploited the area's quarries, and stone from here was used to construct several palaces overlooking Venice's Grand Canal; still today the nearby Montraker quarry is an important element, attracting contemporary artists and providing quality material for an annual sculpture summer school. In 1960, Europe's largest naturist resort, Koversada, opened here, and in the years that followed several large modern hotels were built along the coast.

**Sights**

Built in the 12th century as the summer residence of the Bishop of Poreč, the hilltop **Kaštel** (Castle) was continually reconstructed and extended over the centuries. A document from 1577 decrees, 'They [the peasants of Vrsar] are obliged to carry the Bishop's luggage without any charge whenever the Bishop comes to the castle or leaves it'. In 1778 it became Venetian state property. Today the ground floor houses a permanent exhibition of large canvasses painted with brightly coloured oils, created by **Edo Murtić** (see page 330), one of Croatia's most respected 20th-century artists, who now divides his time between Zagreb and Vrsar. ■ *Opening times variable.*

*From behind the church, there are spectacular views over the town and sea below*

Standing next to the Kaštel, the 19th-century **Church of St Martin** is best known for its prominent (some would say obtrusive) freestanding bell tower, added in 1991. The interior was decorated with religious frescoes by Antonio Macchi, from Rovinj, in 1946. Through summer, classical music concerts are held here each Thursday evening. ■ *1000-1200 and 1600-1900.*

On a hill above the sea, just north of town on the road to Poreč, **Dušan Đžamonja Sculpture Park** displays over 20 large abstract sculptures in metal and stone, created by Dušan Đžamonja. Born in what is now the Former Yugoslav Republic of Macedonia in 1928, he graduated from the Academy of Fine Arts in Zagreb. He now has two homes, one is Brussels and one in Vrsar, and has works displayed in various galleries around the world, including the Museum of Modern Art in New York and the Tate Gallery in London. ■ *Jun-Sep, Tue-Sun 0900-1100 and 1800-2100.*

**Sleeping**

*Koversada Naturist Settlement*, T441378, F441761, www.anita.hr Located 1.5 km south of Vrsar, close to the mouth of Limski Kanal, *Koversada* is Europe's largest nudist colony. A complex of pavilions and a campsite stretch 5 km along the coast, providing space for 7,000, and facilities including 2 supermarkets, 10 restaurants, pizzerias and snack bars, bathing areas, sports facilities and a post office. Pets welcome. Open mid-May to mid-Sep.

Vrsar-based agencies, *Bovi*, Jadranska 18, T441590, www.bovi.hr, and *Legović Tours*, Brostolade 7, T442262, www.nol-vrsar.com, will help you find private accommodation.

**Eating**

**Mid-range** *Kod Ilva*, Obala M Tita 1a, T441987. This large, highly regarded restaurant lies on the seafront, overlooking the harbour. Favourite dishes are pasta with asparagus, truffles and smoked ham, pasta with lobster, oven-baked fish and steaks. *Vrsaranka*, Sv Martin 1, T441197. On the edge of town, on the road to Poreč, house specialities at this large restaurant include pasta with truffles, and large platters of either mixed fish or mixed meats for 2.

*Summer Concerts*, **Jul-Aug**. Classical music concerts held in the hilltop Church of St **Festivals**
Martin, Thu evenings. *International Sculpture School*, **late-Aug to mid-Sep**. Held
each summer since 1991 at Montraker Quarry, on a peninsula close to the centre.
Works remain property of the town. Contact the tourist office for details.

**Biking**   Vrsar is the starting point for 3 well-marked bike routes: a short trail (5 km) tak-   **Sports**
ing you to the *Dušan Džamonja Sculpture Park*, a circular trail (18 km) passing alongside
Limski Kanal, and a long trail (27 km). Ask at the tourist office for details and a map or
check out the website, www.istra.com **Diving** *Morska Zvijezda*, AC Porto Sole,
T442119. *Ugor*, Obala M Tita bb, T441386. **Sailing** *Marina Vrsar*, Obala M Tita 1a,
T441064. 220 berths, open all year.

There are 12 **buses** daily from **Poreč** (20 mins) and 4 from **Rovinj** (25 mins). For infor-   **Transport**
mation, contact Poreč bus station, T432153.

Just 3 km north of Vrsar lies the mouth of Limski Kanal, a 12- km long flooded   **Limski Kanal**
canyon, edged in part by dramatic limestone cliffs rising 120 m above the   **(Lim Fjord)**
water, and in part by green slopes covered with woods of holm oak, ash and
pines. Underwater springs give the seawater a low salt content, making it ideal
for farming oysters and mussels, and several excellent fish restaurants have
opened here, taking advantage of both the locally produced shellfish and the
spectacular setting. Due to its resemblance to the Norwegian fjords, it was
used as the set for some parts of the two films about Vikings: *The Vikings*
(USA, 1958) starring Kirk Douglas and Tony Curtis, and *The Long Ships*
(UK/Yugoslavia, 1963). The Vrsar-based agency *Legović Tours* at Brostolade
7, T442262, www.nol-vrsar.com, organize full-day excursions by boat from
Vrsar, including a visit of Rovinj, a ride up Limski Kanal and a meal at one of
the restaurants.

**Mid-range to expensive**   *Viking*, Limski Kanal, T448223. Ranked among the Top 10   **Eating**
Istrian restaurants in 2002, this large establishment is best-known for fresh oysters,
pasta with shrimps and mushrooms, and barbecued fish dishes. *Lim Fjord*, Limski
Kanal, Sv Lovreč, T448222. With a vast open-air terrace overlooking the fjord, this
popular restaurant serves up pasta dishes, fresh lobster, oven-baked fish, and steak
with mushrooms.

# Poreč (It Parenzo)

*Backed by a low-lying, fertile plain planted with vineyards and olives groves,*   Phone code: 052
*Poreč is Istria's most visited seaside resort. The old town itself is quite tiny, a*   Colour map 1, grid C1
*cluster of Venetian-style* **terracotta roof houses** *lying compact on a small pen-*   Population: 10,448
*insula, though the interior of its main attraction, the sixth-century* **Euphrasius**   45 km northwest
**Basilica***, is decorated with golden Byzantine mosaics so stunning to have*   of Pula
*earned it a place on the UNESCO list of world heritage sites. Café life centres on*
*the seafront promenade overlooking the harbour, filled with fishing boats and*
*water-taxis, which shuttle holiday-makers back and forth to beaches on the*
*nearby islet of* **Sv Nikola** *(St Nicholas). South of the centre, Plava Laguna and*
*Zelena Laguna make up a 6-km stretch of modern hotel complexes, cleverly*
*hidden by landscaping and dense pinewoods.*

Istria

Ins & outs
See Transport, page
122, for further details **Getting there** There is a summer ferry service from Trieste to Brijuni National Park stopping en route here and daily buses from Pula. **Getting around** The old town is closed to traffic and can comfortably be explored on foot in an hour or so. **Tourist office** The city tourist office is at Zagreba čka 9, T451293, www.istra.com-porec

## History

Founded as a Roman *castrum* (military camp) in the second century BC, Poreč was later granted the status of a municipality, to become *Colonia Julia Parentium* in the first century BC. The layout of the old town still follows the original Roman plan, though most of the present buildings date from between the 13th and 18th centuries. The settlement became the seat of a diocese in the late third century AD, the first Bishop of Poreč being the martyr St Mauro, who like so many early Christians met a bloody end during the reign of Emperor Diocletian.

Following the collapse of the Western Roman Empire, Poreč passed successively under the Ostrogoths, the Byzantine Empire, the Franks and the Aquilean patriarch. In 1267, it was the first of the cities on the Istrian coast to come under the Venetian Republic. Despite its rather grand past, it gradually sank into decline, mainly due to several severe outbreaks of the plague, which decimated the population between the 14th and 17th centuries, so that by 1646 there were only about 100 inhabitants. During the second half of the 17th century, Venice repopulated the city and its surroundings with settlers from Dalmatia, Albania and the Greek island of Crete.

After the fall of the Venetian Republic, along with the rest of Istria, it came under Austria. In 1844, the steamship society Austrian Lloyd from Trieste set up a line for day trippers to Poreč, and in 1845 the first tourist guide to the city was published. During the 1970's it became Istria's principal resort, following the construction of several vast hotel complexes along the coast.

## Sights

Decumanus   Laid out by the Romans in the first century BC, this wide, paved street still forms the main thoroughfare through the old town, running the length of the peninsula to Trg Marafor. Today it's lined with fine Romanesque and Gothic town houses, several of which have been converted into boutiques and cafés at street level.

Trg Marafor   Lying on the tip of the peninsula, Trg Marafor was once the site of a small Roman forum. The ruins of two Roman temples, dedicated to Mars and Neptune, can still be seen today.

Eufrazijeva   Half way down Decumanus, a narrow side street leads to this well-signed
Basilica   complex consisting of a magnificent sixth-century basilica, a delightful
(Euphrasius   atrium, an octagonal baptistery, a 16th-century bell tower and the bishop's
Basilica)   palace. The interior of the church is decorated with stunning golden mosaics above, behind and around the main apse, making it one of the most important Byzantine monuments on the Adriatic, comparable to San Vitale in Ravenna. Above the altar, the central mosaic depicts the Virgin and Child, with the first Bishop of Poreč, St Mauro, to their right, and Bishop Euphrasius, who was responsible for the mosaic project, on their left. In front of the apse stands a 13th-century ciborium supported by four marble columns. The former bishop's palace now houses a museum of religious art, displaying a modest

collection of paintings, sculpture, embroidered vestments and crucifixes. ■ *0700-1900. Eufrazijeva bb.*

Housed within the 18th-century Baroque Sinčić Palace, the city museum displays Roman stone and ceramic finds on the ground floor, and 18th-century furniture and portraits belonging to the Carli family on the first and second levels. ■ *Jun-Sep 1000-1300 and 1800-2100, Oct-May by request. 10Kn. T431585. Dekumanus 9.*

**Gradski Muzej (City Museum)**

The best beaches lie on **Otok Sv Nikola** (St Nicholas' Island), which can be reached by regular taxi boats, leaving the harbour every half an hour through peak season.

**Beaches**

## Essentials

The majority of Poreč's hotels are found within the modern complexes of Zelena Laguna and Plava Laguna, south of town. However, the hotels listed here are small-scale and centrally located.

**Sleeping**
■ *on map, page 121*

*Istria*

**B** *Hotel Neptune*, Obala M Tita 15, T400800, F431351, www.riviera.hr  Fully renovated in 2001, this early 20th-century hotel offers 109 smart and comfortable guest rooms, and a bar and restaurant overlooking the seafront promenade in the old town. **B** *Depandance Parentino*, Obala M Tita 18, T400800, F431351, www.riviera.hr  Managed by *Hotel Neptune*, the *Parentino* offers 14 rooms in an ochre-coloured early 20th-century building with a sunny terrace overlooking the harbour.

**C** *Depandance Jadran*, Obala M Tita 24, T400800, F431351, www.riviera.hr  Managed by *Hotel Neptune*, the *Jadran* offers 22 rooms overlooking the seafront promenade plus a ground floor restaurant.

The following agencies can help you find private accommodation: *Adriatic dd*, Obala M Tita, T451499, and Trg Slobode 2a, T452655, www.adriatic-istra.com (also excursions to Plitvice, Brioni and Lim Fjord); *Arlen*, Vukovarska 26, T/F4819, www.arlen.hr; *Di-Tours*, Prvomajska 2, T/F2018, www.di-tours.hr;  *Lucky Travel*, Bracka 39, T434050,

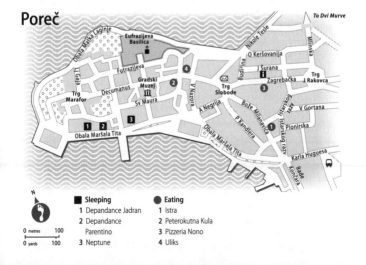

Poreč

**Sleeping**
1 Depandance Jadran
2 Depandance Parentino
3 Neptune

**Eating**
1 Istra
2 Peterokutna Kula
3 Pizzeria Nono
4 Uliks

0 metres 100
0 yards 100

www.lucky-travel.hr  For a list of families offering agrotourism (farmhouse meals and accommodation), check out, www.istra.com/agroturizam

**Eating**
● on map, page 121

*The main concentration of cafés is found on the sunny seafront promenade, Obala M Tita*

**Mid-range to expensive** *Peterokutna Kula*, Decumanus 1, in the old town, T451378. Set in a 15th-century pentagonal tower, cleverly converted to form dining spaces on various levels, *Peterokutna Kula* serves up all that is best in Istria: fish, seafood, steak and truffles. *Dvi Murve*, Grožnjanska 17, outside the centre, T434115. In Vranići, just north of Poreč, this highly regarded *konoba* serves ups specialities such as beefsteak Dvi Murve (steak with cream, mushroom and ham sauce), and fish baked in a salt crust. The ample summer terrace is shaded by two mulberry trees, after which the establishment is named. *Istra*, B Milanoviᵃa 30, between the bus station and the main square, Trg Slobode. T434636. Popular with locals and visitors alike, the house specialities here are *jastog sa rezancima* (pasta with lobster), and fish prepared under a *peka*.

**Mid-range** *Uliks*, Decumanus 2, in the old town, T451132. This tiny rustic *konoba* offers a good choice of local wines, seafood dishes, salads and platters of *pršut* (smoked ham) and *sir* (cheese).

**Cheap** *Pizzeria Nono*, Zagrebačka 4, opposite the tourist office, T453088. Busy with locals the year through, *Nono* serves up delicious pizzas baked in a brick oven, plus pasta and gnocchi dishes, steaks and colourful mixed salads.

**Bars**
A romantic option in the evening, is *Lapidarij*, Svetog Maura 10, in the old town, where you'll find an unusual Baroque bar space, plus tables outside in a large courtyard through summer.

**Festivals**
*Classical Music Festival*, **Jul-Aug**. Sacral and secular music in the Basilica of St Euphrasius. *Jazz Festival*, **Jul-Aug**. Held in the courtyard of the Town Museum. *Festival of St Mauro*, 21 Nov.

**Sport**
**Biking** Poreč is the starting point for two well-marked bike routes, one north to Tar (45-km round route) and the other south to Funtana (47 km). Ask at the tourist office for details and a map or check out the website, www.istra.com It is possible to rent bikes from *Vetura*, Trg J Rakovca 2, T434700. Expect to pay 80Kn for a whole day or 50Kn for a half day. **Diving** The following diving centres are in Poreč: *Plava Laguna*, Partizanska 5, T 098 367619 (mob), www.plava-laguna-diving.hr *RC Zelena Laguna*, Mihe Supaniᵃa 12, T451659, www.calimero-divingcenter.de *Vodeni Svijet*, Kamp Lanterna, T405045, www.rollis-waterworld.de **Sailing** *Marina Parentium*, in the tourist complex of Zelena Laguna, T452210. 200 berths, open all year. The charter company, *AMS Istra*, is based here, T452206. **Tennis** The 18 tennis courts at *Hotel Albatros*, Zelena Laguna, are open to non-residents, T410561.

**Transport**
**Boat** The Venice-based Italian company *Adriatica*, T 0039 041 781 861, www.adriatica.it, run a summer ferry service from **Trieste** in Italy to **Brijuni National Park**, stopping in **Grado**, **Lignano**, **Piran** (Slovenia), **Poreč** and **Rovinj** en route.

**Bus** There are 12 buses daily to **Pula** (1½ hrs) and 6 to **Rovinj** (45 mins). To reach Italy, a morning service runs from **Pula** to **Trieste**, stopping in **Rovinj** and **Poreč** en route. The bus station is at Rade Končara 1, a 5-min walk from the old town, T432153.

**Car hire** *Budget*, Zagrebacka 17, T453570, www.budget.hr and *Hertz*, Hotel Parentium, Zelena Laguna, T 091 3108691 (mob), www.hertz.hr

**Communications** Internet cafés: *Internet-Centar-Cybermac*, Mira Grahalica 1, **Directory**
T427075, www.cybermac.hr  **Post offices**: Vukovarska 17, Mon-Fri 0700-2000, Sat
0700-1400. **Medical services**  Emergency medical treatment: *Hitna Pomoc*, Dom
Zdravlja, M Gioseffija 2, T451611. **Pharmacies**: 2 central pharmacies take turns in working
extended hours – *Centralna Ljekarna*, M Gioseffija 2, T434950, and *Gradska
Ljekarna*, Trg Slobode 12, T432362.

## Novigrad (It Cittanova)

The ancient town of Novigrad is now a busy package resort with the standard    *Phone code: 052*
selection of large hotels, seaside restaurants, cafés and ice cream parlours. The    *Colour map 1, grid C1*
old town as it stands today was developed under Venice in the 13th century,    *Population: 2,629*
when it was fortified and used as a port for shipping oak from Motovun For-    *41 km northwest*
est. Much of the original medieval architecture was destroyed during a Turk-    *of Pazin*
ish attack in 1687, and new buildings were reconstructed in Venetian-Gothic
style. Everyday life centres on **Veliki Trg**, the main square, overlooked by an
18th-century Venetian **loggia** and the Baroque **Crkva Sv Pelagija** (Church of
St Pelagius), known by locals as the *Katedrala* (Cathedral), constructed on the
site of an 11th-century Romanesque **crypt** and presided over by a freestanding
bell tower.

Istria

Just north of town, on the Karpinjan Peninsula, stands the late-Baroque
**Palazzo Rigo** with a lapidarium displaying ancient Roman tombstones and
Byzantine finds. Rather unappealling concrete **bathing areas** lie in front of
the large hotels southeast of town. However, there are plans for the creation of
a pebble beach, which may be ready for summer 2003.

**C** *Hotel Cittar*, Prolaz Venecija 5, T757737, F757340. This modern, family-run hotel    **Sleeping**
lies in the centre, next to a remaining section of the old town wall. There are 14
rooms, each with a TV, telephone and mini bar. **D** *Hotel Emonia*, Mandrač bb,
T757322, F757314. Located in the old town, overlooking the harbour, this unassuming modern hotel has 21 basic but comfortable rooms, a bar and restaurant. *Rt Zub
Lighthouse*, Lanterna Peninsula. Contact *Adriatica Net*, Selska 34, Zagreb, T (01)
3644461, F3644463, www.adriatica.net  Lying on a peninsula between two pleasant
bays with beaches, 13 km south of Novigrad, this lighthouse dating back to 1872 was
recently converted to form 1 large apartment sleeping 8. Shops and restaurants lie
close at hand.

**Mid-range to expensive**  *Damir and Ornella*, Zidine 5, T758134. Despite its tiny din-    **Eating**
ing room seating only 28 (and no terrace) this friendly, family-run fish restaurant is definitely worth checking out. It lies in the old town, close to the main square, and serves
up delicious raw fish (sushi style), shrimps and lobster. *Mandrač*, Mandrač 6, T757120.
Considered by many to be the best restaurant in town, *Mandrač* is renowned for excellent tagliatelli with lobster, and barbecued fish and meat dishes. The ample summer
terrace looks onto the harbour.

*Venice-Novigrad-Venice*, open sailing regatta, **late-May**. *Rimini-Novigrad-Rimini*,    **Festivals**
open sailing regatta, **early-Jun**. *Caorle-Novigrad-Caorle*, open sailing regatta,
**early-Jun**. *Music Nights Novigrad*, **late-Jul**. Founded in 1995 by the Croatian jazz
musician Boško Petrović, in recent years this festival has attracted international performers such as the Temptations, Dan Gilespie, Scott Henderson and Hiram Bullock.
Open-air evening concerts take place on Veliki Trg, the main square. *Festival of St
Pelagius*, **28 Aug**.

Sport **Biking** Six marked bike paths lead from Novigrad, through the surrounding vineyards and old stone villages to inland Buje (see page 128) and Grožnjan (see page 126). It is possible to rent bikes (and mopeds) from *Hotel Maestral*, T757557, and the tourist office can supply a map of suggested routes.

Transport There are 3 **buses** daily from **Pula** (2 hrs 10 mins) and 8 from **Poreč** (30 mins) and **Umag** (20 mins). Bus station, T757660.

## Umag (It Umago)

*Phone code: 052*
*Colour map 1, grid C1*
*Population: 7,769*
*On the west coast,*
*83 km northwest*
*of Pula*

In 2002 Umag won a national competition for the best-kept and best-equipped resort on the mainland. Indeed, today it is well geared to the more commercial brand of tourism, with a string of vast modern hotels overlooking concrete bathing areas north of the centre. However, the compact old town, built on a peninsula next to a large semicircular bay, is worth a look for its narrow medieval streets and pretty squares. Umag hits the news each summer when it hosts the international *ATP Croatia Open* tennis tournament. The town tourist office is at Obala J B Tita 3/II, T741363, www.istra.com/umag

There are no decent beaches in Umag, so many visitors make do with the man-made concrete bathing areas in front of the larger hotels. You're better off renting a bike (see below) and peddling 5 km up the coast to Savudrija, where you'll find a rocky stretch of coast interspersed with pebble beaches and backed by pinewoods.

Sleeping **A** *Hotel Kristal*, Obala J B Tita 9, T700000. This large, modern pink hotel commands a prime position, on the tip of the peninsula, in the old town. There are 85 rooms and facilities include indoor and outdoor pools, a sauna, bike rental, and a bowling alley. *Svjetionik Savudrija*, Savudrija. Contact *Adriatica Net*, Selska 34, Zagreb, T (01) 3644461, F2611163, www.adriatica.net Lying on the mainland 9 km north of Umag, this lighthouse dating back to 1818 was recently converted to form 2 apartments, each sleeping 4. A small boat is at guests' disposal. Pets welcome.

Eating **Mid-range to expensive** *Restoran Allegro*, *Hotel Kristal*, Obala J B Tita 9, T700000. Housed within the *Hotel Kristal* (see Sleeping), this restaurant is popular with non-residents who are attracted by refined dishes – shrimps with artichoke mousse, and duck breast in basil sauce – served on a summer terrace overlooking the sea. *Restoran Badi*, Umaška, Lovrečića bb, T756293, www.restaurant-badi.com Lying 6 km from Umag, *Badi* is popular with Italian day trippers who drive over two borders especially to savour its excellent fish and seafood. Closed Wed and Oct-Easter.

Festivals *Feast of St Pelegrin*, last Sun in **May**. *ATP Croatia Open*, international tennis tournament, **late-Jul**. *Summer Festival*, **Jul-Aug**. Classical music concerts in the 18th-century Baroque Church of the Assumption of the Blessed Virgin Mary, plus contemporary art exhibitions in a number of small galleries.

Sports **Biking** It is possible to rent bikes from *Hotel Kristal* (see Sleeping). **Sailing** ACI Marina, Umag, T741066. 518 berths. Open all year. **Tennis** Each Jul the *ATP Croatia Open* tennis tournament is staged in the Stella Maris sports complex at *Savudriska Cesta bb*, north of town. There are 18 courts, which visitors are welcome to use. Expect to pay 40kn per hr, T741704.

Transport There are 4 buses daily from **Pula** (2 hrs 25 mins) and 8 from **Poreč** (45 mins) and **Novigrad** (20 mins). Bus station, T741817.

Istria

## Verne's vision

◀

*The old town grew up around the castle, above a 120-m deep gorge, carved out in rock by the River Pazinčica. In winter, the gorge fills to form a 3-km long lake.*

*The founder of modern science fiction, the French writer Jules Verne (1822-1905), mentioned this phenomenon in the novel Mathias Sandorf. Verne never visited Pazin, but based his vision of the gorge on pictures sent to him by the mayor.*

*The story takes place in 1867; three Hungarian noblemen organize a conspiracy from Trieste against the Austrian government, in the hope of overturning the Austro-Hungarian monarchy and regaining Hungary's*

*independence. After being caught, they are imprisoned in Pazin Castle. Two of them escape through a window and jump into the river below, and are carried by the current into a cave. After six hours, an underground river brings them out 20 km southwest, in Limski Kanal (Lim Channel), close to Poreč.*

*In 1934, an Italian scientist made an experiment with marked eels. After they were released in the gorge, a couple of days later they were found in water springs 20 km southeast of Pazin. Thus Verne's hypothesis of an underground river was partly correct, although in reality the water flows in the opposite direction.*

Istria

# Inland Istria

*Frequently overlooked by tourists but much-loved by Croatians, inland Istria is sometimes compared to Tuscany, thanks to its undulating green landscapes and medieval walled hilltowns. This is the country's top area for agrotoursim (farms offering meals and overnight accommodation) and is at it prettiest in spring or autumn.*

## Pazin

Located in the centre of Istria, Pazin is the region's largest inland town and a major road and rail intersection point. Although it dates back to the ninth century, it's hardly a charming place, with a dreary industrial suburb and little of interest, other than the castle. However, the one place that does warrant a visit is the nearby medieval **Church of St Mary**, in Beram, decorated with a memorable cycle of 15th-century frescoes.

*Phone code: 052
Colour map 1, grid C2
Population: 9,227
35 km north of Pula
and 32 km east of
Poreč*

Perched above the gorge and entered across a drawbridge, the medieval **castle** here was founded in the ninth century. However, its present appearance, with four wings grouped around a large interior courtyard, dates from between the 14th and 16th centuries. Inside you'll find the Ethnographic Museum, displaying traditional Istrian folk costumes, farm and fishing tools, musical instruments and an old-fashioned kitchen. The adjoining Town Museum shows local archaeological finds from prehistoric times up to the Middle Ages, plus a collection of church bells. ■ *May-Oct Mon-Sat 0900-1800, Sun 0900-1500; Nov-Apr Mon-Sat 0900-1600, Sun closed. 15Kn. Kastel, Trg Istarskog razvoda 1, T624351.*

The sleepy hilltop village of **Beram** is 7 km west of Pazin, just off the main road to Poreč. From the village, a 1-km track leads to a wood, where you'll find the cemetery church of **Sv Marija na Škriljinah** (St Mary's Church). The interior is totally covered by a cycle of extraordinary frescoes, dated 1474 and executed by Vincent of Kastav and his pupils. Biblical scenes are portrayed against a backdrop of Istrian countryside, giving an amusing interpretation of the New

Testament, as well as a record of how people lived here during the 15th century. The church is kept locked, but you can find the key in Beram: try either house number 22 or 33 and ask for a member of the Gortan family.

■ *Getting there: there are 10 buses daily from Pula to Pazin (1 hr), 5 from Poreč (1¼ hr) and 4 from Rovinj (1 hr 20 mins). Bus station, T624437. There are 8 trains daily from Pula to Pazin (1 hr). Train station, T624310. There is no bus to Beram, so you need a car or to take a taxi.*

## Motovun (It Montana)

*Phone code: 052*
*Colour map 1, grid B1*
*Population: 531*
*Altitude: 277 m*
*25 km northeast*
*of Poreč*

Lying, on the road to Buzet, this well-preserved fortified hilltown is frequently included on tours of inland Istria as a model example of local architecture. There are no outstanding buildings, but the complex as a whole is exceptionally pretty, with medieval stone houses and a Venetian loggia surrounded by defensive walls, towers and town gates. It is possible to walk a complete circuit of the ramparts, offering sweeping views of the oak forests and vineyards of the Mirna Valley. The informal summer *Film Festival* is very 'in', and probably Croatia's most enjoyable cultural event: in 2002 more than 70 films were shown in five venues and it attracted 40,000 cinema buffs from all over Europe.

**Sleeping & eating**

**D** *Hotel Kastel*, Trg Andrea Antico 7, T681607, F681652, www.hotel-kastel-motovun.hr Occupying an 18th-century building just outside the town walls, this peaceful old-fashioned hotel has 29 rooms and a restaurant with open-air dining in the garden through summer. Pets welcome. *Restaurant Mcotić*, Zadrugarska 19, T681758, located in New Motovun, below the old town, is a popular, mid-range restaurant serving up delicious pasta, steak and truffle dishes on a vast summer terrace.

**Festivals**

*Motovun Film Festival*, late-Jul Five-day international festival of avant-garde cinema, founded in 1999. In 2002 it was attended by the British director Stephen Daldry and producer Jeremy Thomas, and raised 25,000Kn for the restoration of the town walls, by putting aside 5Kn for each ticket sold. For up-to-date information about the forthcoming festival, check out the website, www.motovunfilmfestival.com

**Transport**

Five buses leave daily from **Pazin** (45 mins), 2 daily go from **Pula** (2 hrs) and 1 from **Poreč** (45 mins). For further information, contact the respective bus stations – there is no bus station in Motovun itself.

## Grožnjan (It Grisignana)

*Phone code: 052*
*Colour map 1, grid C1*
*Population: 185*
*26 km northeast of*
*Poreč and 8 km*
*southeast of Buje*

This charming medieval hilltown was all but abandoned until the mid-1960's, when it was rediscovered by painters, potters and sculptors, and proclaimed a 'Town of Artists'. They restored the crumbling medieval buildings, converting them into studios, workshops and galleries. Today it's a truly lovely place to visit, with partly preserved 14th-century town walls hugging a warren of narrow winding cobbled streets and old stone cottages.

Look out for the **Venetian loggia** adjoining the town gate, the Baroque **Church of Saints Mary**, **Vitus** and **Modest** with a freestanding bell tower on the main square, and the tiny 16th-century **Chapel of Saints Cosmas and Damian**, decorated with frescoes by Ivan Lovrenčić in 1990, in front of the town gate. There are some well-marked footpaths lead to the surrounding villages making good walks.

Each year Jeunesses Musicales Croatia, an international federation of young musicians, meets here for a summer school run by well-known

## Funny about fungus

The truffle is a subterranean European fungus, generally found in damp soils on or near the roots of oak trees. It can be white, brown or black, and although it grows approximately 30 cm below the soil, its scent is so strong that dogs and pigs can be trained to detect it. Fetching prices of up to €3,000 per kg, the truffle is among the most expensive foodstuffs in the world: it is used in foie gras, and can also be eaten grated on pasta or steak, or made into rich creamy sauce. Undoubtedly an acquired taste, past aficionados include Winston Churchill and Marilyn Monroe.

In Istria, about 500 registered truffle-hunters have a legal right to dig for this gnarled, tuberous fungus. However, each year between October and December an estimated 3,000 people and three times as many dogs (usually a cross between a retriever and a hound) wander through Istria's forests and meadows searching for this prestigious delicacy, making it one of region's top sources of income and main reasons why many people come here.

The largest truffle in the world, listed in the Guinness Book of Records, was unearthed in the Mirna Valley, Istria, on 2 November 1999. It was found by Giancarlo Zigante and his dog Diana, weighed 1.31 kg and measured 19.5 cm x 12.4 cm x 13.5 cm. Zigante decided not to sell it but prepared a dinner for 100 guests, and had the original cast in bronze. He now runs Zigante Tartufi, a small chain of shops specializing in truffles and truffle-based products, which you can visit in Buzet, Buje and Pula.

Truffles are also found in the Perigord region in southwest France and in Piedmont in northwest Italy.

European and Japanese professors, such as Geoffry Wharton, violin concert-master of the Cologne Philharmonic Orchestra, and the world-renowned trombonist Branimir Slokar. Each day, the old streets are filled with the sounds of brass, woodwind and stringed instruments of varying tones and pitches, and come evening live performances are staged beneath the stars.

*Hotel Ladonija*, Trg Poiani 2, in the old town, T/F776125. Although it was closed for refurbishment at the time of writing, this charming old-fashioned hotel should reopen for summer 2003. It's often fully booked through Aug, but even if you don't stay the night it's worth calling by for lunch or dinner in the excellent *konoba*. **Sleeping & eating**

*Jeunesse Musicales Croatia (JMC)*, **mid-Jun to mid-Sep**. International summer school of music, modern dance and theatre, founded in 1969. Contact Hrvatska Glazbena Mladež, Trg Stjepana Radića 4, Zagreb, T (01) 6111566, www.hgm.hr **Festivals**

**Buses** running between **Pazin** and **Buje** pass on the main road below Grožnjan – get off at the junction and walk the final 2 km up an unsurfaced track. **Transport**

## Buzet

Overlooking the fertile Mirna Valley, close to the Slovenian border in north-ern Istria, the fortified hilltop settlement of Buzet is frequently referred to as the 'Town of Truffles'. Indeed, many people visit the region specifically to indulge in this peculiar smelling earthy delicacy: you'll find countless small restaurants lying on the country roads between Buzet, Motovun and Pazin, several of which are listed below.

Although the town itself can be traced back to Roman times, when it was known as *Pinguentum*, it owes its present appearance to the centuries spent

*Phone code: 052*
*Colour map 1, grid B2*
*Population: 1,721*

under Venice (1421-1797), when it gained the town walls and gates, two of which have been preserved – the main gate from 1547 and the northern gate from 1592 – and the parish church on the main square. For a better picture of how locals once lived, call at the **Gradski Muzej** (Town Musuem), displaying a collection of antique farm tools, kitchen utensils and traditional folk costumes, along with a space devoted to temporary exhibitions of Croatian and foreign artists. ■ *Mon-Fri 0800-1100. 10Kn. T622792. Trg Rasporski Kapetana 1.*

The town tourist office is at Trg Fontana 7, T662343, www.istra.com/buzet

**Eating**    **Mid-range**    *Mlini*, Milinić 54, Buzet. T669057. In Buzet itself, this tiny *konoba* with several tables both indoors and out, serves a range of local dishes, the speciality being trout in truffle sauce. The following restaurants are out of town. *Konoba Draguć*, Draguć, T690018. Lying south of Buzet, on the road to Pazin, *Draguć* specializes in lamb and kid (young goat) prepared under a *peka*, served with copious portions of crusty homemade bread. *Restoran Vrh*, Vrh 2, 10 km southwest of Buzet, off the main road to Motovun, T667123. This friendly eatery serves up meat and truffle dishes, many accompanied by *fuñi*, a local variant of pasta. Closed Mon. *Toklarija*, Sovinjsko Polje, T663031. This tiny but highly regarded *gostiona* lies 8 km southwest of Buzet, off the main road to Motovun. Look out for homemade ravioli with prosciutto and cheese, ravioli with wild asparagus, rabbit, and mushroom and truffle dishes. Closed Tue. No credit cards.

**Truffle**    *Activatravel Istra*, based at Scalierova 1, Pula, T215497, www.activa-istra.com,
**gathering**    organize 1-day truffle gathering tours Jun-Dec. Participants should dress appropriately for a 3-hr (8-km) walk through Motovun Forest, which concludes with dinner at a local farm. Expect to pay 500Kn per person.

**Shopping**    *Zigante Tartufi*, Trg Fontana, www.zigantetartufi.com, stock an excellent range of truffles and truffle products from the Mirna Valley, plus Istrian olive oil and wines.

**Transport**    There are 2 **buses** (2½ hrs) and 4 **trains** (2 hrs) daily from **Pula**.

## Buje (It Buie)

*Phone code: 052*
*Colour map 1, grid B1*
*Population: 3,001*
*8 km northwest*
*of Grožnjan*

The medieval hilltown of Buje makes a pleasant outing for its sleepy cobbled streets, romantic old buildings and stunning views over the surrounding countryside, coupled with a number of informal eateries serving locally produced food and wine.

Formerly referred to as the 'Watchtower of Istria' due to its elevated position overlooking two important transit routes – situated where the road from Pula to Trieste intersects with that from Umag to Buzet – it was founded by the Romans as *Bullea*. The historic centre, protected by defensive walls and a series of towers - of which two remain, one square, the other pentagonal – date from the period spent under Venice (1412-1797).

On the main square stands a **16th-century loggia** with a frescoed façade and the 18th-century Baroque **Church of St Servelus**, constructed on the site of a 13th-century **Romanesque-Gothic church**: on the outer wall note a Roman *stele* (burial monument) featuring the busts of two men, said to be the Valeri brothers. Also worth seeing is the **Gradski Muzej** (Town Museum), housing a collection of local arts and crafts, plus the reconstruction of several rooms from a traditional Istrian house.

■ *Summer, Tue, Thu and Sat 0900-1300 pm, Mon, Wed and Fri 1600-1900; Winter by request. 10Kn. T772023. Trg Slobode 4. The tourist office is at Istarska 2, T773353, www.buje.hr (website in Croatian and Italian only).*

## Glagolitic script

*Invented by St Cyril (827-69) from Thessaloniki (Greece), the glagolitic script was the forerunner to Cyrillic, today used in Russia, Serbia and Montenegro, Bulgaria and Ukraine.*

*Cyril devised the 38-letter glagolitic alphabet (based on Greek characters) upon the request of the Moravian leader to the Byzantine Emperor, who wanted a form of writing that would more closely represent the sounds of the Slavic languages. Cyril and his brother St Methodius (826-884) then proceeded to translate books of the New Testament and develop a Slavonic liturgy, earning themselves the title of the 'Apostles of the Slavs'. At the time, Pope Nicholas I was against the use of the vernacular in church services, but it was later approved by his successor, Adrian II.*

*The script was used in many churches along the Croatian Adriatic coast right until the 19th century, though it met resistance from certain members of the clergy who favoured Latin as a way of forging closer ties with Rome. However, Croatian secular literature was traditionally written in Latin script, as the majority of the elite were educated at universities in Italy or Austro-Hungary.*

Istria

**B** *Hotel Miro*, Plovanija bb, T777050, F777051. This modern, 20-room hotel lies 1.5 km **Sleeping** from the Slovenian border crossing at Plovanija, on the road to Buje. Facilities include a restaurant, indoor swimming pool, sauna and gym, and casino. Open all year. **E** *Volpia*, Volpia 3, T/F777425, www.agriturizam-volpia.com   Just 3 km outside Buje, this beautifully restored old stone farmhouse has 16 comfortable guest rooms and a large dining room and summer terrace. Everything on the menu, including the wine, is organically produced on local farms.

**Mid-range**   *Pod Voltom*, A Bibić bb, T772232. Lying in the heart of the old town, this **Eating** small restaurant and café serves up pasta, meat and truffle dishes on a summer terrace offering fantastic views over the surrounding countryside. *Konoba Pjero*, Kremenje 99, T779200. Lying 3 km north of Buje, on the road to the Slovenian border crossing at Kaštel, this small, friendly *konoba* serves local specialities such as homemade Istrian sausages, roast pork and truffle dishes. Closed Mon.

*Zigante Tartufi*, J B Tita 12, www.zigantetartufi.com, stock an excellent range of truffles **Shopping** and truffle products from the Mirna Valley, plus Istrian olive oil and wines.

There are 5 **buses** daily from **Pula**, 7 from **Poreč**, and 3 from **Rovinj**. For information **Transport** contact the respective bus stations – there is no bus station in Buje itself.

## Glagolitic Alley – Hum and Roč

Glagolitic Alley was built in 1977 to record the historic importance of the *Phone code: 052* glagolitic script in this region. Lying between Roč and Hum, it stretches 7 km *Colour map 1, grid B2* and includes 11 monuments celebrating important events and people associated with this all-but-forgotten form of writing.

Despite its size (population 146), during the Middle Ages this unassuming lit- **Roč** tle town was an important economic, cultural and religious centre, and many glagolitic codices, manuscripts and Gospels, today found in museums in Zagreb and Vienna, were created here. The 16th-century **town walls** are still visible in part, as is the town gate, with a guard's room on the upper floor. The centre is dominated by the parish **Church of St Bartholomew**, which is of no great significance, but to its left stands the priest's home, where you can ask for the keys to two smaller churches: the adjacent **Church of St Anthony**, bearing a glagolitic alphabet from the 12th century carved into a votive cross on the right-hand wall, and the **Church of St Roč**, next to the town gate, where you can see fragments of 14th-century frescoes and glagolitic carvings.

**Eating** Mid-range: *Ročka Konoba*, Roč, T666451. A small *konoba* serving typical Istrian dishes such as *gulaš sa njokima* (goulash with gnocchi) along with homemade wine by the carafe. In summer it's possible to eat outside on the terrace. Closed Mon.

**From Roč to Hum: the Glagolitic Alley** In Roč, at the junction for Hum, you can see the **Pillar of the Čakav Parliament**, a reference to Croatian self-rule and the *Čakav* dialect (one of three variants of the Croatian language, see page 334). The second monument shows the **Three-legged Table before Two Cypresses**, with the trees symbolizing the apostles of the Slavs, St Cyril and St Methodius. Monument three is dedicated to the **Assembly of Kliment of Ohrid** – Kliment was a pupil of Cyril and Methodius, and he founded the first Slav university near Lake Ohrid, in the present-day Former Yugolsav Republic of Macedonia. The fourth monument, in front of the village church in Brnobici, is a **Lapidarium** displaying glagolitic inscriptions from various regions of former Yugoslavia. Monument five portrays **Mount Učka** partly hidden by clouds – in the Middle Ages it was regarded as the Croatian equivalent of Mount Olympus in Greece. The sixth monument is the **Grgur Ninski Observation Point**, featuring a block of stone engraved with the glagolitic, Latin and Cyrillic alphabets. Monument seven represents the **Istarski Razvod**, the historic document defining Istria's borders, while monument eight is dedicated to **Croatian Protestants and Heretics**. The ninth monument is a huge stone block recording the first glagolitic missal, dating from 1483. Monument ten, at the entrance to Hum, is devoted to **Resistance and Freedom** over the centuries, with three stone blocks representing the three historic periods of Antiquity, the Middle Ages and the Modern Age. The eleventh and final monument is the copper town gate of Hum, decorated with 12 medallions, each representing a month of the year and typical activities that take place at that time.

**Hum** Claiming to be the smallest town in the world (population 17), with weekly mass held in the parish church and annual elections for a mayor, Hum was once a strategically important border station between the Venetian and Hapsburg territories. Today there are only about a dozen old stone houses intact, and most people come here specifically to eat at the renowned **Humska Konoba**. Besides eating here, you can also ask for the key to the tiny Romanesque **Church of St Jerome**, decorated with 12th-century frescoes, standing on the cemetery on the edge of town.

**Eating** Mid-range: *Humska Konoba*, Hum 2, T660005. A tiny, old-fashioned *konoba* serving typical homemade Istrian dishes such as *fuži* (a type of pasta) with truffles, roast meats, and *biska*, a local liquor made from mistletoe. Nov-May Sat-Sun, Jun-Oct daily.

**Transport** **Buses** from **Buzet** to **Rijeka** (1 hr) stop on the main road just below Roč (20 mins), which is also served by 4 trains daily from Pula (1¾ hrs). There are no buses to **Hum**, but the trains from Pula stop at Hum station (1½ hrs), which is confusingly located 5 km from Hum itself, close to the village of **Erkovići**. There is no public transport along the Glagolitic Alley, so unless you have private transport you should be prepared to walk.

Istria

# East Coast

*The east coast offers few surprises and is far less rich in cultural sights and beaches than the west. The most interesting part, to the north, officially lies within the Kvarner region (see page 135), though geographically it is part of the Istrian peninsula.*

## Labin (It Albona)

Labin, 40 km northeast, of Pula can be visited in conjunction with its seaside neighbour, Rabac. Today's town is divided into two distinct parts: old Labin, the original hilltop settlement, and the newer Podlabin, founded in the early 20th century as a housing estate for local coal miners, and now surrounded by modern residential development. Many houses in the old town have remained derelict since walls started cracking due to subsidence in the 1960s, though people are gradually buying them up to restore as holiday cottages. The bus station lies in Podlabin, so first impressions are daunting, but a 15-minute walk brings you to the old town, a compact nucleus of stone buildings, walled by the Venetians in the 15th century.

*Phone code: 052*
*Colour map 1, grid C2*
*Population: 7,904*

*Istria*

The main tourist office, covering both Labin and Rabac, is at Aldo Negri 20 in Labin, T855560, www.istra.com/rabac  Through summer there is also a small tourist information point on Titov Trg, the main square, just outside the town walls, in Labin.

**Ins & outs**
*See Transport, page 132, for details*

The Illyrians, who were particularly partial to hilltop sites, founded the settlement around 2000BC and called it *Alvona*. Like the rest of Istria, it then passed to the Romans. The Venetians arrived in 1422, leaving a hallmark loggia overlooking Titov Trg, the main square, which was used for court verdicts, the annual election of a Mayor, and reading out the news. They also fortified Labin with walls and a gate, now known as Uskoška Vrata (Uskok Gate), after a failed attempt by 800 Uskoks to raid the town in 1599. Organized coal mining began in the area in 1785, to supply fuel to Rijeka, and increased under Austria during the 19th century. During the Mussolini period, Labin's miners went down in history on 2 March 1921 when they proclaimed the *Republica Albonessi* (Republic of Labin) as an independent workers' state, which held out 34 days, until the Italian army was sent in. After the Second World War, when Istria became part of Yugoslavia, a lot of Italians left the area, and a wave of Bosnian migrants arrived in their place to work the mines. During the 1960's many houses in the old town were abandoned due to subsidence caused by mining, but fortunately a number of artists moved in to save the old houses, carrying out restoration work and opening several small ateliers. The last mine closed in 1999 – although there are still seams of underlying coal, it has a high sulphur content (up to 12%) making it unacceptable by modern environmental standards (sulphur burns to form sulphur dioxide, which becomes diluted in the atmosphere and returns to earth as acid rain).

**History**

Standing next to the Church of the Birth of the Blessed Virgin Mary, easily identified by its 17th-century façade with a winged Lion of St Marks and a rose window, the **Gradski Muzej** (Town Museum) contains a modest collection of Roman stones, amphorae, wooden farming tools and local folk costumes. However, the undisputed highlight is the mock coal mine: visitors don hard hats and walk through dimly lit tunnels, stooping under beams to get some idea of how difficult life was for local miners. It's an amusing experience and

**Sights**

children will love it. ■ *Summer Mon-Sat 1000-1300 and 1700-1900; winter Mon-Fri 0700-1500. 10Kn. T855477, Trg 1 Maja.*

The collection in the **Galerija Matije Vlačića Ilirika** (Matthias Flacius Illyricus Gallery) commemorates Matthias Flacius Illyricus (1520-75), a Labin-born theologian who helped promote Protestantism in Germany. He studied in Venice where he was influenced by his uncle, Baldo Lupetina (also from Labin), who was eventually executed by drowning in 1562 for his anti-papal ideas. Illyricus then went to Wittenburg in Germany where he became involved with Martin Luther's movement. He wrote almost 300 books, the best known being an anti-papal history of the Christian church called *Historia Ecclesiae Christi* (also known as the *Magdeburg Centuries*). He had 12 children with his first wife and six more with a second, and eventually died in Germany, poor and practically destitute. Here you can see a collection of his books and manuscripts, mainly in Latin. ■ *Summer Mon-Sat 1000-1300 and 1700-1900; winter Mon-Fri 0700-1500. 10Kn. G Martinuzzi bb.*

Just north of Labin, on the main road to Rijeka, the **Forma Viva Sculpture Park** displays over 70 pieces of modern sculpture, created by artists from all over the world who have attended the Dubrova Mediterranean Sculptors' Symposium, held here each summer for over 30 years. ■ *Free. Dubrova bb.*

**Sleeping** There are no hotels in Labin, though a number of stone cottages have been restored to provide holiday homes in the old town. *Veritas*, Sv Katarine 8, T854428, can help you find private accommodation.

**Eating** **Mid-range to expensive** *Restaurant Dubrova*, Dubrova bb, T851706. This highly regarded restaurant lies on the main road between Pula and Rijeka, on the edge of the Forma Viva Sculpture Park. With tastefully furnished dining rooms on 2 floors, one with an open-fire, and a couple of open-air terraces, it can seat over 200. The menu features delicacies such as Italian and French style truffle dishes, fresh fish and steak. The pizza makes a cheaper alternative.

**Mid-range** *Gostionica Kvarner*, Šetalište San Marco bb, T852336. Located just outside the town walls, with a small summer terrace offering fantastic views over the Kvarner Gulf, this down-to-earth eatery stays open the year through. The kitchen turns out simple local dishes, the house speciality being *salat od rakovica* (crab salad).

**Sport** **Biking** A network of local bike paths centre on Labin and Rabac. It is possible to rent mountain bikes from *Hotel Neptune*, Rabac bb, T862520.

**Transport** Seven **buses** daily run between **Pula** and **Rijeka**, stopping in Labin en route. From Pula the journey takes 1 hr, from Rijeka the journey takes 1½ hrs. Labin bus station, T855220.

**Directory** **Communications** **Post office**: Trg 2 Ožujka bb, Mon-Fri 0700-2000, Sat 0800-1200. Titov Trg bb, Mon-Fri 0800-1500. **Medical services** Pharmacy: Ljekarna, T855474.

## Rabac

*Phone code: 052*
*Colour map 1, grid C2*
*Population: 1,472*

Built into the slopes overlooking a narrow bay, 4 km below the hilltop settlement of Labin, Rabac is the most popular resort on the east coast of Istria. Since the 1960's, this small fishing village has seen the construction of 14 large hotels and a plethora of holiday apartments, and can now accommodate up to 10,000 guests at a time. There's little of cultural interest, the main attraction being a decent pebble beach and a number of good fish restaurants. The main beach lies on the northern side of the bay where it is possible to rent sunbeds and umbrellas. The tourist office in Labin at Aldo Negri 20, T855560, www.istra.com/rabac, covers both Rabac and Labin.

Rabac's modern package hotels are uninspiring. You're better off contacting either **Sleeping**
*Temark*, Katuri 17, T854500 or *Top Tours*, Rabac bb, T872488, both agencies based in Rabac which can help you find private accommodation.

**Mid-range to expensive** *Nostromo*, Obala M Tita 7, T872601. Located 1 block back **Eating** from the seafront, *Nostromo* is considered the best restaurant in town. It's a little pricier than the others, but worth it. The house specialities are sea bass fillets with truffle sauce, frogfish carpaccio, and frogfish in wine with polenta. Open all year. *Rapčanka*, Obala M Tita 31, T872784. Arranged on 2 floors, with a classic fish restaurant in a beamed dining room on the upper level, and a pizzeria with a large brick oven downstairs, *Rapčanka* has been on the go since the 1970's. The house specialities are *fuižna pastirski način* (pasta with wild asparagus, mushrooms and ham) and *grdobina na partlonski* (fish prepared with wine and shellfish). Closed Dec-Feb.

**Cheap to mid-range** *Restoran Zelen Draga*, Plominska 17, T872988. Opposite the bus stop for Labin, this unassuming modern restaurant knocks up delicious *frigne lignje* (fried squid), *špinat* (spinach) and *fuži sa istarskom slaninom* (pasta with Istrian bacon). Ask to try the excellent homemade *travarica* at the end of your meal. Open all year.

**Biking** A network of local bike paths centre on Labin and Rabac. It is possible to rent **Sports** mountain bikes from *Hotel Neptune*, Rabac bb, T862520.

Rabac is not served by regional buses. However, a local service connects it to **Labin**, **Transport** with 14 **buses** daily. It is also possible to walk from Labin down to Rabac, following a well-marked 4-km footpath. *Budget*, Obala M Tita bb, T872357, www.budget.hr Car hire.

There is a **bank** with an ATM. There is no **pharmacy** in Rabac, the nearest one being **Directory** in Labin.

Istria

Istria

Kvarner

# Introducing Kvarner

The seaside resorts nearest to Zagreb lie packed around the Kvarner Gulf, a large deep bay sheltered by mountains of up to 1500 m. The Kvarner region separates the Istrian Peninsula from Dalmatia, and its chief city is the hard-working and slightly austere industrial port of **Rijeka**. Half an hour west of Rijeka, is **Opatija**, Croatia's oldest coastal resort. Packed with grandiose late-19th-century Austro-Hungarian style hotels it was once frequented by Central European aristocracy, who would trundle southwards to sun themselves, inhale the health-promoting seaside air and wade in the warm saline waters. Things haven't changed a great deal, with the town still drawing an elderly clientele of middle-class Europeans.

Kvarner also has its share of islands. The largest and easiest to reach is **Krk** – linked to the mainland by bridge – which has a string of best-avoided package resorts along the west coast, compensated for by a pretty monastery on the islet of **Košljun** and a stunning sand beach on the southeast coast at **Baška**.

Slightly more up-market, the island of **Rab** is best known for **Rab Town**, a romantic medieval settlement built on a walled peninsula with four bell towers creating a distinctive skyline. There is no shortage of good beaches here, with **Lopar Peninsula** to the north offering long stretches of sand and pebble, and plenty of space reserved for nudism, which Rab pioneered in the early 20th century.

West of Rab lies **Cres**, a long, thin island of scanty pastures, dry stonewalls and more sheep than people. With few memorable cultural monuments it remains firmly off-the-beaten track, but for those who enjoy hiking and wildlife, the pine forests of the **Tramuntana** on the northern tip offer blissful walks and great opportunities for bird watching.

South of Cres, and linked to it by a bridge, the island of **Lošinj** pulls tourists in droves through summer. Most people flock to the pretty but possibly overrated town of **Mali Lošinj**, renowned for a string of villas built by retired sea captains, each set amid a garden filled with exotic plants. However, just a half-an-hour hike over the hill, the sister town of **Veli Lošinj** is smaller, quieter and undeniably more authentic.

Returning to the mainland, east of Rijekja lie the rugged heights of **Gorski Kotar**, part of which is contained within **Risnjak National Park**, offering well-marked hiking paths, dense pine forests and bracing mountain air.

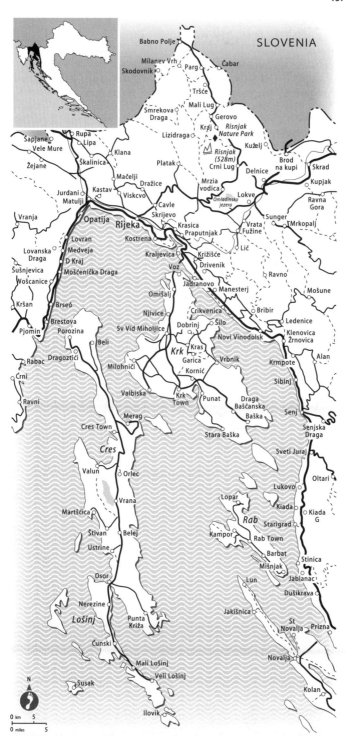

Kvarner

# Rijeka

Phone code: 051
Colour map 1, grid C3
Population: 143,800

*Overlooking the Kvarner Gulf, Rijeka is Croatia's largest **port**, with a **shipyard**, massive dry dock facilities, refineries and other heavy industries. Architecturally, the centre is remarkably similar to Trieste in Italy, with a grid of grandiose 18th-century **Austro-Hungarian buildings** on the seafront, and a sprawling suburb of **high-rise apartment blocks** from the 1960's. The main public meeting place is the **Korzo**, a pedestrian street a couple of blocks back from the port, lined with shops and open-air cafés. There are few memorable sights here, other than the lovely hilltop **castle** and pilgrimage **church of Trsat**, and the city has very few hotels, as most visitors to the area stay in the nearby seaside resort of **Opatija**. Rijeka receives national television coverage each year with the staging of Croatia's largest **Carnival**.*

## Ins and outs

**Getting there** Through summer, *Croatia Airlines* run regular flights to and from Zagreb and London Heathrow. The airport is at Omišalj on the island of Krk, 26 km from Rijeka city centre. An airport bus leaves 1½ hrs before flight departures. The journey takes about 40 mins. Through winter there are no flights from Omišalj, but *Croatia Airlines* operate a daily bus connecting Rijeka to Zagreb airport, 100Kn. Airport bus information T330207/ 336757. The city port is on the Riva, a 10-min walk south of the city centre. *Jadrolinija* run a coastal ferry from Rijeka to Dubrovnik, plus a service to the island of Rab. The bus station is at Žabica 1, a 5-min walk west of the city centre. The train station is at Krešimirova 5, a 10-min walk west of the city centre.

*See Transport, page 144, for further details*

*Rijeka is 98 km from Pula; 182 km from Zagreb; 350 km from Split and 566 km from Dubrovnik*

**Getting around** The centre can be explored entirely on foot. It's possible to walk up to Trsat, using the pilgrimage path, though bus no 1 will also get you there. If you're staying in Opatija and visiting Rijeka, the 2 town centres are connected by bus no 32 which runs every 20 mins.

**Tourist office** The new walk-in tourist information centre is at Korzo 33, T335882. Mon-Fri 0800-2000, Sat 0800-1400. The city tourist board office is at Užarska 14, T213145, www.tz-rijeka.hr

**Best time to visit** Like all the coastal towns, Rijeka is at its busiest Jun-Sep. However, Carnival celebrations (in late-Feb or early-Mar, depending when Easter falls) also pull the crowds, notably on the Sun before *Shrove Tuesday*, when the *International Carnival Parade* takes place.

## History

Founded as the Roman Tarsatica, Rijeka only really began to develop in 1466, when it came under Austrian rule. It fast became a major trading centre, with iron, oil, wood, wool, cattle and leather passing through the port by the 16th century. In 1723 it was awarded the status of a free port, and during the later half of the 18th century expanded, spreading beyond the old town walls when a large strip of land was reclaimed from the sea, extending the seafront by several hundred metres. In 1779 it passed to Hungary, and so while the rest of the coast came under Venice and therefore those towns were filled with Venetian-style architecture, Rijeka was developed under Hungary and so is distinct in that the buildings were designed by architects from Budapest.

## Things to do in Kvarner

- In Rijeka, visit the **hilltop bar in Trsat** for a drink overlooking the city below, page 141.
- Walk the 12-km **Lungomare coastal promenade** between the fishing villages of Volosko to Lovran, passing through Opatija, Croatia's oldest seaside resort, page 147.
- Climb to the top of **Učka Mountain** for spectacular views over Kvarner Bay, page 146.
- Skinny dip at **Kandarola Beach** on the island of Rab, page 168.
- Explore **Tramuntane Forest** on the island of Cres – if you're lucky you may see a griffon vulture in flight, page 158.

The world's first self-propelled torpedoes were produced here in 1866, though strangely they are now on display in Split Maritime Museum (see page 202), not in Rijeka. In the 1960's it became Yugoslavia's largest port, with a thriving shipyard and new heavy industries offering large-scale employment. Families moved in from rural areas of the country to find work here, and the modern high-rise suburbs came into being. During the Croatian war of independence Rijeka was noted for its tolerance, and many non-Croats were able to remain here safely. Today it is Croatia's largest seaport, and despite a national economic crisis, traditional industries such as shipbuilding, oil refining, paper milling and engine building continue to function.

## Sights

**Korzo**
A couple of blocks inland from the Riva (seafront), this main pedestrian thoroughfare follows the line given by the architect Arthur Gnamb at the end of the 18th century, when the city extended beyond the medieval city walls. Today, lined with clothes shops and open-air cafés, it is Rijeka's main shopping street and public meeting space. The name Korzo comes directly from the Italian, Corso.

**Gradski Toranj (City Tower)**
Half way down the Korzo, the Gradski Toranj forms an arched entrance into the Stari Grad (Old Town), which was once walled. The lower section of the tower dates back to the 13th century, while the upper level was rebuilt in Baroque style and decorated with the busts of two Austrian emperors and the Hapsburg coat of arms featuring the double-headed eagle in the 17th century. The clocks were added in 1784.

**Katedrala Svetog Vida (St Vitus Cathedral)**
From the City Tower, walk straight across the Stari Grad (Old Town), through Trg Ivana Koblena and Grivica, to arrive at the cathedral. Work on this Baroque rotunda (a building with a circular ground plan), built on the site of an even older church, began in 1638 and was completed in 1744. It was designed by the Jesuit architect Giacomo Briano, and is said to have been inspired by the church of Santa Maria della Salute in Venice. Inside, above the main altar, stands a **13th-century wooden Gothic Crucifix**, which was also kept in the former church. Local myth has it that during the 13th century one Petar Lončarić was playing cards here with two friends. He was losing, and out of anger threw a rock at the crucifix, hitting the body of Christ, which immediately began to bleed. The unfortunate gambler was swallowed up by the ground, and the crucifix consequently proclaimed miraculous. Sceptics

comment that the cult of the miraculous crucifix was supported by the Jesuits, as a counterbalance to the pilgrimage church, Our Lady of Trsat. ■ *0800-1200, 1600-1900. Trg Grivica 11.*

**Povijesni i Pomorski Muzej (History & Marine Museum)** A five-minute walk northeast of the Stari Grad (Old Town), on the hillside facing down towards the port, stands the Guvernerova Palača (Governor's Palace), built in neo-Renaissance style in 1896 to designs by the Budapest architect, Alajos Haussmann. This is where the Hungarian governor used to reside: the building clearly conveys the grandeur of authority, and D'Annunzio obviously thought so too, as he chose this as his base during his one year bid to rule the city. The ground floor is made up of a spacious atrium, imposing drawing rooms and a Marble Hall, all still furnished as they would have been in the late 19th century. The second floor is devoted to local shipping, with a display of model ships, navigational instruments, anchors, charts and old photos. ■ *Tue-Sat 0900-1300. 10Kn. Guvernerova Palača, Muzejski trg 1/1, T213578.*

**Muzej Grada Rijeka (Rijeka City Museum)** In the gardens of the Guvernerova Palača, and linked to it by an arcade, stands a modern pavilion built in 1976 to accommodate the Rijeka City Museum. Inside is a permanent display of ancient stone finds, periodically supplemented by temporary exhibitions relating to the region's history. ■ *Mon-Sat 1000-1300. 10Kn. Muzejski trg 1/1, T336711.*

**Prirodoslovni Muzej Rijeka (Natural History Museum)** Close by, an impressive late 19th-century villa houses the Natural History Museum, with a display of rocks and fossils illustrating the geological history of the Adriatic and an aquarium dedicated to the marine life of the same area. A multimedia presentation allows visitors to experience the depths of the sea through video, and three tanks display various fish, invertebrates, algae and marine flowering plants. ■ *Mon-Fri 0900-1900, Sat 0900-1400. 10Kn. Lorenzov prolaz 1, off Šetalište Vladimira Nazora, T334988, www.prirodoslovni.com*

**Gradska Tržnica (Main Market)** South of the Old Town, close to the port, this market complex is made up of three pavilions. Stalls selling fresh fruit and vegetables lie within two identical stone, steel and glass pavilions, designed by Isidor Vauching and completed in 1881. A third pavilion, designed by Karlo Pergoli in Liberty style, opened to the public in 1914. It houses the fish market and is decorated with stone carvings of fish and shells, by the Venetian sculptor Urbano Bottasso. ■ *0600-1400. Between Trninina and Vatroslava Lisinskog.*

**Kazalište Ivana Zajca (Ivan Zajc Theatre)** Across the square from the market complex stands the theatre. It was built by Fellner and Helmer, two architects from Vienna who also designed the Croatian National Theatre in Zagreb. It was completed in 1885. Lovers of **Gustav Klimt** will be interested to know that some of Klimt's early work can be seen here – together with Franz Matsch, he painted three of the six oval frescoes on the theatre ceiling. The building is not generally open to the public other than for performances, but if you telephone first you can arrange to see the frescoes. In the garden in front of the theatre stands Belizar Bahorić's statue of the Rijeka-born composer Ivan Zajc. ■ *Uljarska 1, T355900.*

**Pilgrimage path to Trsat** Up on the hill (139 m), above the town, stand the Church of Our Lady of Trsat and Trsat Castle. The most rewarding way to arrive in Trsat is to follow the pilgrimage path (though bus no 1 will get you there too), which starts from Titov Trg on the left back of the River Rječina. A Baroque gateway topped with a

◀

## Taken by a poet

*After the First World War, Italy and Yugoslavia both put forward claims to Rijeka, firing a dispute that was to last for the following three decades. In 1915, at the Treaty of London, the city had been promised to Yugoslavia, but at the Paris Peace Conference Italy claimed it on the grounds that Italian-speaking inhabitants formed a majority of the population. Meanwhile, Gabriele D'Annunzio (1863-1938), an Italian soldier, Romantic poet and outspoken supporter of Fascism, took control of the city in September 1919, along with a gang of some 300 legionaries. The situation became increasingly embarrassing for Rome, and over Christmas 1920 the Italian navy bombed the city from the sea in a successful bid to force out D'Annunzio. Rijeka was consequently established as a free city, a status it was to enjoy for only one year, as Italian troops, this time under the command of Benito Mussolini, occupied the city once again in 1922. In 1924 the Treaty of Rome awarded Rijeka to Italy, but declared the eastern suburb of Sušak, south of the River Rječina where the Slav majority resided, as part of Yugoslavia. After the Second World War, an Allied peace treaty with Italy handed Rijeka back to Yugoslavia in 1947, whereupon a large segment of the Italian population left the city.*

Kvarner

relief of the Virgin marks the beginning of the **Petar Kružić Stairway**, named after the Uskok captain from Klis, who had the lower part of the stairway built in 1531. A steep but worthwhile climb of over 500 steps brings you up through the dramatic **Rječina Gorge**. At the top, turn left and follow the busy road of Šetalište Joakima Rakovca uphill until you arrive at Frankopanski Trg, home to the 15th-century church and Franciscan Monastery complex.

The church was built by the wealthy Frankopan family to commemorate the 'Miracle of Trsat', when angels were said to have carried the house of the Virgin Mary from Nazareth and delivered it on this spot in 1291. As the story goes, it remained here for three years and was then moved (by the angels again) to Loreto, near Ancona in Italy. Inside the church, above the altar, an icon of the Virgin Mary, sent as a present from Pope Urban V in 1367 to console the people of Trsat for the loss of the holy house, is hung with offerings from pilgrims such as pearl necklaces and trinkets. Next to the church, the Baroque cloister of the Franciscan Monastery leads to the **Chapel of Votive Gifts**, displaying an extraordinary collection of offerings brought here by pilgrims, including a silver Gothic sculpture of the Virgin, countless religious portraits, and even discarded crutches, proof of the Virgin's miraculous healing powers. ■ *0700-1900. Frankopanski Trg, T217018.*

**Gospa Trsat (Church of our Lady of Trsat)** *Close by there's a decent restaurant, Trsatika (see Eating, page 143), should you decide to stop for lunch*

A five-minute walk from Frankopanski Trg lies Trsat Castle, built in the Middle Ages by the Frankopans on the foundations of a Roman observation point. In 1826 the remains of the castle were bought by Laval Nugent (1777-1862), an eccentric Irishman who had served as Field Marshall in the Austrian army. He had it restored in romantic style, and added a Classical Greek temple with four Doric columns brought in from Pula, intended as the family mausoleum.
The former dungeon is now used as an **art gallery**, and from early-April to late-October the castle hosts an **open-air café**, offering views over the city and across the Kvarner Bay to the islands of Cres and Krk. See also page 143. On summer evenings, **outdoor theatrical events**, concerts and fashion shows are held here.
■ *Jun-Sep 0900-2200, Oct-May 0900-1500. Ulica Zrinskog, T217714.*

**Gradina Trsat (Trsat Castle)**

## Essentials

**Sleeping**
■ *on map, page 142*

*Very few tourists stay overnight in Rijeka usually using the seaside resort town of Opatija, 15 km away, as a base for exploring the city*

**AL** *Hotel Bonavia*, Dolac 4, 1 block back from the Korzo, T357100, F335969, www.bonavia.hr Reopened in 2000 after extensive renovation, this smart luxury hotel lies in the city centre, a 10-min walk from the ferry port. The high-rise exterior conceals 114 plush rooms and 7 even plusher suites, a restaurant, jazz bar and fitness centre. There's even a hotel limousine and chauffeur service. **C** *Costabella*, Opatijska cesta 17, between Rijeka and Opatija, T623010, F623002, www.vior.hr Pleasant pension and restaurant overlooking the sea, 7 km from Rijeka city centre. 11 smartly furnished rooms and 2 apartments. Open-air tennis court, floodlit at night, beach at the bottom of the garden. **D** *Hotel Continental*, Šetalište Andrije Kačića-Miošića 1, across the river from Titov Trg, T372008, F372009. Built in 1888, the *Continental* lies at the foot of the pilgrimage path up to Trsat. The 38 rooms and 4 suites are extremely basic. There's a restaurant and café, and a pleasant summer terrace shaded by chestnut trees. The agencies *Maremonti*, Korzo 40/1, T212911, www.maremonti.hr and *Tours*, Rudolfa Strohala 2, T214915, www.tours.hr, can help you find private accommodation throughout the Kvarner region, though rooms in Rijeka itself are extremely limited.

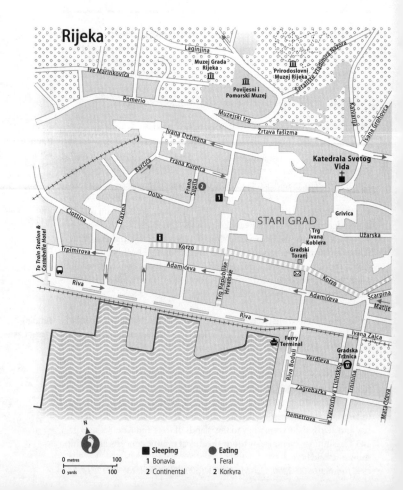

Kvarner

**Sleeping**
1 Bonavia
2 Continental

**Eating**
1 Feral
2 Korkyra

**Mid-range to expensive** *Feral*, M Gupca 6, T212274. This highly regarded fish restaurant is up a side road close to the theatre. House specialities are *crni rižot* (black risotto prepared with cuttlefish ink) and *fuži sa šparogama i škampima* (pasta with asparagus and shrimps).

**Mid-range** *Korkyra*, Slogin Kula 5, behind *Hotel Bonavia*, T339528. The interior of this *konoba* is hung with fishing nets decorated with shells. There's a wide choice of meat and fish dishes, and the house speciality is *njoki od krumpira* (gnocchi). *Trsatika*, J Rakovca 33, Trsat, T217455. High up on Trsat, below the pilgrimage church, this popular restaurant has a large summer terrace offering fantastic views over Rijeka. Favourite dishes include *gulaš* (goulash) and *škampi na buzaru* (shrimps prepared with onion and tomato). Closed Wed.

**Eating**
● *on map, page 142*

**Cafés**

The city's most popular cafés are concentrated along the Korso. Of these, *Filodramatica*, Korzo 28, is probably the most renowned. Built in 1819, it has a ground floor café plus a beautifully frescoed coffee-lounge on the 2nd floor, where you can indulge in delicious cakes and pastries. In Trsat, inside the castle complex, there's a lovely summer café offering fantastic views over the Kvarner Bay. Open 1 Apr-30 Oct.

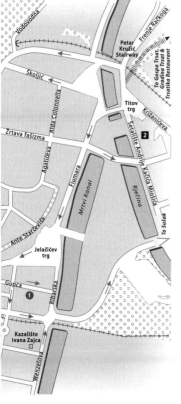

**Kvarner**

**Bars & clubs**

*Palach*, Kružna 6, T215063, www.mmc.hr Lying in a side street off the Korzo, *Palach* has been hosting live concerts for over 20 years and as the birthplace of many new bands has built up a cult following. It's named after Jan Palach, the Czech philosophy student who burnt himself to death in Prague in 1968 out of protest against Soviet occupation. It stays open daily until late, and there's also an internet centre. *Python*, Guvernerova Palača, Muzejski Trg 1. Located in the History and Marine Museum building, this underground café serves good cocktails, hosts a range of concerts and art exhibitions, and stays open late.

**Entertainment**

**Cinema** Rijeka has 2 cinemas: **Croatia**, Krešimirova 2, T335219, and **Teatro Fenice** at Dolac 13, T335225. **Theatre and classical music** Hrvatsko Narodno Kazalište Ivana Zajca (Croatian National Theatre Ivan Zajc), Uljarska 1, T355900, www.hnk-zajc.hr Stages ballet and opera, and dramas in both Croatian and Italian. **The Symphony Orchestra** of the Rijeka Philharmonic perform here, with a particular emphasis on 20th-century music.

**Festivals**

*Riječki Karneval* (Rijeka Carnival). Rijeka stages Croatia's largest Carnival celebrations. The main event is the *International Carnival Parade*, attracting several thousand participants in costumes and masks,

▶ **Zvončari**

*Unique to Carnival in Rijeka and the surrounding villages, Zvončari are young men dressed in bizarre costumes consisting of a sheepskin slung over the shoulders, a mask of a grotesque animal head with horns, and a large iron bell tied around the waist. During the afternoons and evenings, in the week preceding Shrove Tuesday, they go from village to* *village and house to house in large groups, regardless of the weather, acting roguishly and making a dreadful din with their bells. Traditionally, locals offer them* fritule *(similar to small doughnuts) and wine, then see them on their way. Their purpose is to chase away the forces of evil and invite the coming of spring and new life.*

notably the bizarre Zvončari, see also page 144. The parade is held the afternoon of the Sun before **Shrove Tuesday** and attracts over 100,000 spectators. For more information check out, www.ri-karneval.com.hr

**Shopping** A popular (though rather gimmicky) souvenir from Rijeka is morčići gold jewellery – earrings, pendants and brooches featuring the head of a dark man swathed in a white turban. Apparently they date back to the 16th century, but first became fashionable in 1845 after the Austrian Empress Maria-Anna, wife of Ferdinand I, ordered a pair of morčići earrings. Since 1991 they have been adopted as a symbol of Rijeka. They are available from *Grabušić*, M Gupca 15a, T333989, and *Mala Galerija*, Užarska 12, T335403.

**Sport** **Hiking** A series of marked footpaths criss-cross the wooded slopes of Risnjak National Park, see page 145, 15 km inland from Rijeka.

**Tour operators** *Da Riva*, Maršala Tita 162, Opatija, T272990, www.da-riva.hr Can organize minibus excursions to Risnjak National Park for groups of 6 to 8 people, departing from Opatija with the possibility of a pick-up point in Rijeka. *Generalturist*, Trg Republike Hrvatske 8a, T212900, www.generalturist.com One of the largest Croatian travel agencies, *Generalturist* specialize in tailor-made trips both with and without guides, pilgrimage tours and yacht charters.

**Transport** **Air** Through summer, there are regular flights to and from **London Heathrow** and **Zagreb**. Through winter there are no flights, but *Croatia Airlines* operate a daily bus connecting Rijeka to Zagreb airport. Rijeka airport, T842040.

**Bus** Internal services include 20 buses daily to **Zagreb** (3½ hrs); 17 buses to **Pula** in Istria (2½ hrs); 11 to **Zadar** in North Dalmatia (4½ hrs); 12 to **Split** in Central Dalmatia (8 hrs) and 5 to **Dubrovnik** in South Dalmatia (12 hrs). There are also daily international bus lines to **Trieste** (Italy), **Ljubljana** (Slovenia) and **Munich** and **Stuttgart** (Germany). For information about buses to and from Rijeka, T660360. Left luggage 0530-1030, 10Kn per piece per day.

**Car hire** *Avis*, Riva 22, T337917, www.avis.hr; *Budget*, Hotel Bonavia, Dolac 4, T214668, www.budget.hr and *Hertz*, Riva 6, T311098, www.hertz.hr

**Ferry** *Jadrolinija*, T211444, run a regular overnight coastal service between Rijeka and **Dubrovnik** in South Dalmatia, stopping at **Zadar**, **Split**, **Stari Grad** (island of Hvar), **Kor³ula** and **Sobra** (island of Mljet) en route. Through winter the service is reduced to two departures a week. The same company run a ferry direct to Rab Town (island of Rab), departing 1430 Tue and Thu.

**Taxi**   There are taxi ranks at both the train station, T332893, and bus station, T335138.

**Train**   Internal services include 5 trains daily to **Zagreb** (3½ hrs) and 1 train daily to **Osijek** (7½ hrs). Daily international trains run direct to **Budapest** (Hungary) and **Ljubljana** (Slovenia). Rijeka train station, T213333. National train information, T060 333444, www.hznet.hr   Left luggage 0900- 2100, 10Kn per piece per day.

**Airlines offices**   *Croatia Airlines*, Trg Republike Hrvatske 9, T330207. **Communica-**   **Directory**
**tions** Internet: *Internet Club Cont*, Šetalište andrije Kačića Miošića 1, T371630, www.internet-cont.com   *Palach*, Kružna 6, T215063, www.mmc.hr (see Bars & clubs). **Post office**: the main post office, at Krešimirova 7, beyond the train station, is open daily 24 hrs. The most central post office is on the Korzo, and is open Mon-Fri 0700-2100 and Sat 0700-1400. **Telephone**: if you prefer to telephone from a peaceful phone booth, rather than calling on the street, go to one of the post offices (see above). Otherwise, you'll find numerous phone kiosks dotted round town. **Consulates** Austria, Stipana Konzula Istranina 2, T338554. **Denmark**, Splitska 2, T212522. **Hungary**, Riva Boduli 1/IV, T213494. **Italy**, Riva 16, T212454. **Netherlands**, Veslarska 1b, T213126. **Norway**, Žrtava fašizma 2/II, T335827. **Sweden**, Riva 16, T212287. **Turkey**, Križaniᵃeva 2/II, T373503. **Serbia and Montenegro**, Erazma Barčića 9, T337420/1. **Medical ser-**
**vices**  Doctors and hospitals: **Rijeka Hospital**, Krešimirova 42, beyond the train station, T658111 (24-hr casualty). **Pharmacies**: all pharmacies are marked by a glowing green cross. **Ljekarna Centar**, Jadranski Trg 1 (T213101) works non-stop 24 hrs. **Use-**
**ful telephone numbers**   Ambulance 94; Fire 93; Police 92.

# Risnjak National Park

The forested heights of Risnjak National Park make a pleasant contrast to   *Phone code: 051*
Kvarner's seascapes. In summer the air is cool and pine scented, and through   *Colour map 1, grid B3*
winter the craggy peaks are snow-covered. This is the most densely forested   *30 km northeast*
region in the country, and two-thirds of the park is covered with beech and fir,   *of Rijeka*
which fare well up to an altitude of 1,200 m.

The park can be visited as an excursion from the coast, or en route from Rijeka to   **Ins & outs**
Zagreb. Information and maps are available from the park administration building,   *See Transport, page*
adjacent to *Motel Risnjak* at Bijela Vodica 48, in Crni Lug, T836133.   *146, for details*

Just north of Rijeka, the limestone mountains of **Gorski Kotor** form a natural   **Sights**
boundary between Croatia and Slovenia. In 1953, an area of 64 sq km was declared a national park to protect the indigenous forests and mountain meadows. The highest peak, **Veliki Risnjak** (1,528 m), is a rugged rocky mass unable to support plant life.

The Risnjak forests form a natural habitat to the **lynx**, after which the park is named (lynx in Croatian is *ris*). However, the last indigenous lynx were shot in the mid-19th century, while those that now live here arrived from the mountains of neighbouring Slovenia in 1974. Other wild animals still here include the **brown bear**, **wildcat**, **roe deer**, **red deer** and **chamois**, plus the seldom sighted **wolf** and **wild boar**. In addition, Risnjak claims to be the home to over 50 **bird** species, including the capercaillie, the largest type of European grouse.

The best place to start exploring the park is the picturesque little village of **Crni Lug** (726 m), where you might also decide to stay a night or two. Here, just a few minutes west of the park administration building, you'll find the beginning of the **Poučna Staza Leska** (Leska Educational Trail), a 4.5-km circular route with information points in both Croatian and English. Also from Crni Lug, a well-marked hiking path leads to the peak of Veliki Risnjak. Allow three hours each way, wear substantial walking boots and take plenty of water.

**Sleeping & eating**  **Mid-range  D** *Motel Risnjak*, Bijela Vodica 48, Crni Lug, T836133, F836116. Adjoining the national park office, this friendly 9-room hotel stays open all year, and has an excellent restaurant serving local specialities such as venison stew and škripavac cheese. **D** *Lovački Dom*, Japelniski vrh 2, Delnice, T812440, F812019. This large restaurant specializes in game, notably venison. Open all year and there are 10 guest rooms upstairs.

**Transport**
*The best way to reach Risnjak is by car, as public transport is limited*

Several buses and trains daily **Delnice** (50 mins), and from here it's just 12 km to **Crni Lug**, a route covered twice daily by a school bus during term time (call the national park administration building in advance to check the situation). Alternatively, contact the Opatija-based agency, *Da Riva*, Maršala Tita 162, T272482, www.da-riva.hr, which can organize minibus excursions to the national park.

## Opatija

*Phone code: 051*
*Colour map 1, grid C2*
*Population: 7,850*
*15 km west of Rijeka*

This is Croatia's longest-standing tourist resort with its old-fashioned hotels and an ageing clientele – through winter and spring at least half the guests are over 60. The seafront hotels, built largely in Vienna Secession style, offer neatly kept gardens and sunny terraces where you can drink coffee and watch the world go by during the day, and through summer dinner is also served outside, invariably to the accompaniment of live music.

Opatija owes much of its success to its wonderful microclimate, recommended for convalescence and people suffering from stress. Mount Učka shelters the coast from the cold *bura* wind, so that winters are mild, and summers never unreasonably hot.

**Ins & outs**
*See Transport, page 148, for further details*

**Getting there**  Regular buses from Rijeka and Pula. **Getting around** It's a small place and easy to get around on foot. The main street, Šetalište Maršala Tita, runs parallel to the coast for the length of the resort, and you can walk from one end to the other in half an hour. **Tourist office**  The tourist office is at Vladimira Nazora 3, T271710, www.opatija-tourism.hr and www.opatija.hr

**Background**  Opatija was named after a Benedictine Abbey (*opatija* means 'abbey' in Croatian) that was built here in the 15th century, though all that remains of it today is the reconstructed chapel of Sveti Jakov (St James), on the seafront. The settlement that grew up around the abbey was no more than a sleepy fishing village until 1844 when a wealthy Rijeka businessman, Iginio Scarpa, bought a piece of land close to the church and built a villa there. He named it Villa Angiolina, after his wife, and used it for entertaining the Central European elite of that time, including the Hapsburgs.

In 1882, with the opening of a railway linking Rijeka to Budapest and Vienna, the Society of Southern Railways bought Villa Angiolina and built the *Hotel Kvarner* next door, thus establishing the area as a winter health resort. They also initiated the building of the 12-km-long coastal promenade, Šetalište Franza Josefa. By the early 20th century, Opatija had become one of Europe's most elegant and fashionable seaside destinations, with a string of villas and hotels built in extravagant Vienna Secession style. Illustrious visitors included royalty and artists: Emperor Franz Josef, Wilhelm II of Germany and Prussia, Ferdinand I of Bulgaria, Carol I of Romania, Oscar II of

Sweden, and the Italian opera composer Giacomo Puccini, the Irish novelist James Joyce, the Russian novelist Anton Chekhov and the American dancer Isadora Duncan.

**Sights**

**Lungomare**, a 12-km coastal footpath, lined with century-old oaks and cypress trees, runs from **Volosko** to Lovran, passing through the seaside towns of Opatija, Ičići and Ika en route. Construction began in 1885, coinciding with the opening of Opatija's first hotels. It makes a lovely walk, with plenty of places to stop for a drink or a snack on the way. ■ *Šetalište Franza Josefa.*

**Villa Angiolina** is still standing and in excellent condition, though at present it is up for sale and so its future as a tourist attraction is uncertain. The grounds were landscaped by the Viennese architect Carl Schubert at the end of the 19th century, and planted with exotic trees and shrubs, grown from seeds brought home from East Asia, India, Australia, and North and South America by local sailors. The Botanički Vrt (Botanical Garden) centres on colourful flowerbeds and borders laid out with geometric precision, backed by fragrant camellias and magnolia trees, and dense clusters of bamboo grasses and palms. ■ *Tue-Sun from sunrise to sunset. Free. Park Prvi Maj, between Šetalište Maršala Tita and the seafront.*

There aren't real beaches in Opatija, though the concrete **bathing areas** along the seafront allow you to dip in and out of the sea. However, there are some pleasant pebble beaches south of Opatija at Medveja (10 km) and Mošćenićka Draga (16 km). ■ *Through summer a regular shuttle boat service runs 3 times daily from Opatija to Mošćenićka Draga, stopping at Lovran and Medveja en route.*

**Excursion**

Some 45 km from Opatija, the rugged mountains and dense pine forests of the **Risnjak National Park**, see page 145, can be visited in a day. If you are without private transport, contact *Da Riva*, Maršala Tita 162, T272482, www.da-riva.hr, who arrange trips by minibus.

**Sleeping**

**A** *Grand Hotel Kvarner-Amalia*, Park 1 Maja 4, T271233, F271202, www.liburnia.hr Next to the botanical garden and *Villa Angiolina*, this ochre-coloured neoclassical building first opened its doors to guests in 1884. There's a lovely café terrace beside the gardens overlooking the sea. Facilities include indoor and outdoor pools filled with seawater, sauna and massage. 86 rooms and suites. **B** *Villa Ariston*, Maršala Tita 179, T271379, F272429, www.villa-ariston.net This late-19th century villa, set in a lovely garden running down to the seafront promenade, attained its present appearance during the 1920's when it was renovated by Carl Seidl. Today it has 8 luxury guest rooms, each with parquet flooring and antique furniture. There's an excellent restaurant on the ground floor, and many non-residents come here solely to eat. There are no budget hotels in Opatija, but the following agencies can help you find private accommodation: *Da Riva*, Maršala Tita 162, T272482, www.da-riva.hr, *Katarina Line*, Maršala Tita 75/I, T272110, www.katarina-line.hr and *Maremonti*, Stube Valvasora 3, T272933, www.maremonti.hr

**Eating**

The best restaurants lie outside Opatija, 4 km along the coast in Volosko, a small town built around a pretty fishing harbour, walkable along the coastal promenade. The eateries of Opatija are made up mostly of large hotels offering half- or full-board.

**Opatija** Mid-range: *Bistro Yacht Club*, Zert 1, Opatija harbour, T272345. Overlooking the marina, on the coastal path to Volosko, this simple eatery is done out in blues and whites. The menu features risotto, squid, fish and salads.

*Kvarner*

**Volosko** Expensive: *Bevanda*, 51410 Opatija, T712722. On the road above the coast, this upmarket fish restaurant offers a wide assortment of quality fresh fish such as *orada* (gilt-head bream), *zubatac* (dentrix) and *brancin* (bass). Those who prefer meat could opt for beef stroganoff. Closed mid-Jun to mid-Jul. **Mid-range**: *Bevandica*, Supilova Obala 12, T701357. Run by the daughter of the owner of Bevanda, this easy-going fish restaurant has a sunny terrace looking out onto a pretty harbour. They do delicious seafood pasta dishes and a value-for-money 'mixed fish platter for two'.

Clubs    *Colosseum discoteque*, www.colosseum-opatija.com, plays techno and disco music into the early hours. Slightly out of place in Opatija, but it attracts hordes of youngsters from Rijeka.

Festivals    *Opatija Summer Stage*, **May-Aug**, cultural events staged in the open-air theatre. *Opatija Week Galijola*, **Jul**, 4-day international sailing regatta.

Sport    **Sailing**  *ACI Marina*, lying between Opatija and Ičići, T704004. 300 berths, open all year. The ACI headquarters (for the entire country) are at Maršala Tita 151, T271288, www.aci-club.hr

Tour operator    *Katarina Line*, 272110, F271372, www.katarina-line.hr, have a range of sailing ships for hire. Also organize accommodation and excursions.

Transport    Opatija is linked to **Rijeka** by local **bus** no 32 which runs every 20 mins and takes 30 mins. Intercity buses travelling between **Rijeka** and **Pula** also stop here taking 2 hrs to get from Pula to Opatija.

Crikvenica    Before reaching Senj, the first place of any real cultural interest driving south-
& Novi    cast of Rijeka on the coastal road for Dalmatia, you pass through the rather
Vinodolski    rundown seaside resorts of Crikvenica (37 km) and Novi Vinodolski (46 km). Both towns became popular vacation centres in the late 19th century under Austro-Hungary but today they offer little more than concrete bathing areas and large modern hotels catering for groups on cheap package holidays.

## Senj

*Phone code: 053*    Senj, built around a cove, is watched over by a hilltop castle once occupied by
*Colour map 1, grid C3*    Uskok pirates (see box) and today has a museum dedicated to them. Some-
*Population: 5,531*    thing of a backwater until the 16th century, the town became notorious as the
*63 km southeast*    headquarters of the fearsome Uskoks, who instated themselves as its military
*of Rijeka*    guardians from 1527 to 1617. However, the Uskoks' excessive exploits on the high seas eventually saw them deported inland, and Senj was absorbed into the *Vojska Krajina* (Military Border), a buffer zone between Ottoman territories to the southeast and Hapsburg lands to the north, set up by the Austrians. When the inland area of Lika was liberated from the Turks in 1689, Senj developed into a small but busy port town. South from here, between the mainland coast and the island of Rab, lies **Goli Otok**, an island turned into an infamous political prison at the end of the Second World War.

**Ins & outs**    The town is located at an important road junction, so you will pass through it if travel-
*See Transport, page*    ling from Rijeka to Plitvice National Park, or from Zagreb to the island of Rab. The town
*149, for further details*    tourist office is at Stara Cesta 2, T881068, www.lickosenjska.com/senj

## Uskoks

*During the 16th century, as the Ottoman Empire expanded westwards, groups of Slavs abandoned the eastern inland areas and fled towards the coast. One particular group, which settled in Klis (Central Dalmatia) in 1532, became known as the Uskoks (a name probably derived from uskočiti meaning 'to jump into' in Croatian). They defended Klis fortress for five years until it too fell to the Turks, then migrated north along the coast, finally settling in Senj in 1537.*

*The Hapsburgs, seeing them as hardened fighters ready to confront further Turkish expansion, allowed them to remain in the area as irregular soldiers, but offered them very limited financial support. Forced partly by poverty and partly by a latent*

*loathing of the Turks, the Uskoks turned to piracy, carrying out grizzly raids on Ottoman ships. Despite being men of no seafaring experience, they designed shallow galleys, with 10 oarsmen each side, which were notoriously speedy and particularly hard to catch.*

*The Austrians turned a blind eye to their antics, delighted to have an extra hand on their side, and even profited from them, allowing them to sell their captured goods in the international market in Trieste. The church also gave the gruesome pirates its blessing, celebrating the Uskoks as Catholic freedom fighters and taking a one-tenth cut of their loot, which was paid to the Franciscan and Dominican monasteries in Senj.*

**Sights**  Located on a hilltop 82 m above town, the **Nehaj Castle** (from *nehaj* meaning 'fear not') was built in 1558 by Captain Ivan Lenović of Senj, in order to defend the town against the Turks. Based on a square ground plan, this three-floor structure afforded views over the Kvarner Bay and the surrounding mountains, and was defended by 11 cannons. The Uskoks set up their main base in the castle, and after they were relocated inland in 1617 the Austrian navy was installed here. It was restored in 1977 and now houses an enlightening Uskok Museum, displaying a well-presented collection of costumes and weaponry, with texts in both Croatian and English. ■ *Jun-Sep 0700-1500 and 1800-2000. Closed Oct-May. 15Kn. T881141.*

**Eating**  **Mid-range**  *Konoba Lavlji Dvor*, P Preradovića 2, T881738. A 5-min walk from the seafront, this restaurant centres on a pleasant courtyard with outdoor dining. Barbecued meat and fish dishes top the menu, with pizza as a cheap alternative. Open early-Apr to late-Sep.

**Transport**  All **buses** running along the coast south from **Rijeka** to **Dalmatia** stop at Senj (1½ hrs). The bus station is at Ulica Kralja Zvonimira 8, T881235.

# Island of Krk (It Veglia)

*Linked to the mainland by a 1,430-m bridge, and home to Rijeka Airport, Krk is one of the most accessible of all the Croatian islands. It also happens to be the largest (38 km long and 20 km wide) and one of the most populous. While the northwest part of the island is low lying, fertile and fairly developed, the southeast part is mountainous and in places quite barren. It's certainly not the most beautiful island on the Adriatic, but its accessibility and wealth of tourist facilities make it very popular. The chief centre is **Krk Town**, which dates back to Roman times with a 12th-century seafront **castle** and a **cathedral**. The best beaches are found in **Baška**, **Malinska** and **Omišalj**, though unfortunately the*

*Phone code: 051*
*Colour map 1, grid C3*
*Population: 16,402*

Kvarner

*latter two are spoilt by the nearby petrochemical industry. **Punat**, with its vast marina, is a haven for yachters, while **Vrbnik** is known for its excellent white wine, Vrbnička Žlahtina.*

## Ins and outs

**Getting there**
*See Transport, pages 152 and 154, for further details*

Rijeka Airport is at Omišalj close to the northern tip of the island of Krk. The airport works in summer only, when *Croatia Airlines* run regular flights to and from Zagreb and London Heathrow. If you're thinking of driving to Krk, remember that there's a 10Kn toll for crossing the bridge, and that in winter, when the *bura* (northeast wind) is exceptionally strong, it is occasionally closed. Through summer there are 12 buses daily from Rijeka to Baška on Krk, stopping at Krk Town and Punat en route. The service is slightly reduced in winter. The year through, regular ferries operate between Valbiska on the southeast coast of Krk and Merag on the island of Cres taking about 30 mins. During summer there are also 5 ferries daily from Baška to Lopar to the island of Rab taking 50 mins.

**Getting around**

The main road runs the length of the island from the bridge in the north down to Baška in the southeast. Towns on this road – Omišalj, Njivice, Krk Town and Punat are connected by regular local buses. Towns off the main road are served by less frequent buses.

**Tourist office**

The island's main tourist office is in Krk Town at Trg Sv Kvirina 1, T221359, www.krk.hr

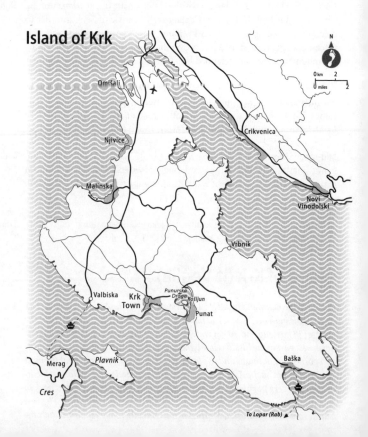

# Island of Krk

## Background

First settled by the Illyrian tribe of the Liburni, the island was later taken by the Romans, who established the municipality of *Curicum* on the site of present-day Krk Town. During the 12th century the Frankopan family came on the scene. Originally from Vrbnik, they built a castle in Krk Town, and gradually expanded their large hereditary estates to the mainland. At the height of their power they possessed territory equal to half of today's Croatia, which they defended boldly against Venice and the Turks. Krk was the last Croatian island to fall to Venice, when Count Ivan Frankopan was deceived and taken prisoner in 1480.

*Tourism began early here. In 1866 the first picture postcard of Krk Town was issued*

Krk was connected to the mainland in 1980 with the opening of a monumental bridge, incorporating two reinforced concrete arches and carrying 20 pipelines for water and oil. This is the only Adriatic island that has never suffered from depopulation. People here have always had work, be it in farming, industry or tourism, so very few families have moved away.

## Krk Town

Krk Town is, and always has been, the island's economic and administrative centre. While the old town is a compact cluster of terracotta roof houses built close up to the seafront, recent development has extended the settlement well beyond its former walls, not least to provide modern hotels for mass tourism.

*Phone code: 051*
*Colour map 1, grid C3*
*Population: 3,364*
*25 km south of Krk Bridge*

Few traces remain of the Roman municipality of *Curicum* which once stood here, though it was certainly a place of some importance, complete with a thermal baths decorated with mosaics, fragments of which can be seen in a side chapel in the **Katedrala Uznesenja** (Cathedral of Our Lady of the Assumption). Taking on its present form during the 12th century, the cathedral was built on the site of an early Christian basilica, which grew up over the first-century baths. Ancient stone columns, topped with finely carved capitals, were incorporated into the structure, and a gothic chapel dedicated to the Frankopans was added in the 15th century. ■ *1000-1300 and 1700-1900. Trg Sv Kvirina.*

**Sights**

Next to the cathedral stands the **Crkva Sv Kvirina** (Church of St Quirinus), a 12th-century Romanesque church built of white stone and dedicated to the town's patron saint. It's actually split into two levels, with a lower crypt area where prisoners sentenced to death attended a final mass before execution. The adjoining 18th-century bell tower really belongs to the cathedral, but was built here due to lack of space on the square. ■ *1000-1300 and 1700-1900. Trg Sv Kvirina.*

The Church of St Quirinus is crowned with a curvaceous onion dome, and houses the **Riznica** (Treasury) containing works of religious art including a stunning silver-plated altarpiece depicting Virgin Mary in Glory (1477) made in Venice as a gift for the cathedral, upon the request of Ivan Frankopan. ■ *Summer Mon-Sat 1000-1300. 10Kn. T221341.*

On the seafront, behind the cathedral, stands the **Frankopanski Kaštel** (Frankopan Castle), a sturdy, square structure with corner towers, from 1191. Besides building the castle, this powerful local family was responsible for the construction of the 12th-century town walls, part of which can still be seen today. ■ *Open only for cultural events during the summer festival. Kamplin Trg.*

There are no real beaches here, concrete **bathing areas** substituting the long stretches of unspoilt shoreline you might be dreaming of, but will only find in **Baška**, on the southeast tip of the island.

Kvarner

**Sleeping**   **B** *Hotel Marina*, Obala hrvatske mornarice 6, T221128, F221357, www.hotelikrk.com This old white building lies close to the Cathedral, overlooking the seafront. There are 18 simple but comfortable guest rooms, several with balconies, and a café and restaurant with tables outside through summer. Pets welcome. **F** *Youth Hostel*, OH Krk, Vinka Vitezića 32, T220212. This late 18th-century building once housed the island's first hotel. It reopened in 2001 as a 60-bed youth hostel with a restaurant. Open all year.

**Eating**   **Mid-range** *Konoba Nono*, Strossmayera 39, T222221. This friendly *konoba* serves up typical local dishes such as *šurlice z žgvacetom* (pasta with goulash). In summer it's possible to eat outside on the terrace. Closed 1 Jan-15 Jan.

**Festivals**   *Summer Festival*, **mid-Jul to late-Aug**, classical music, opera, ballet and drama take place in the Cathedral and the Frankopan Castle in Krk Town, and in the Franciscan Monastery on the Islet of Košljun close to Punat (see Excursions). *Kamplin Jazz Festival*, **mid-Aug**, 1-week open-air jazz festival held within the walls of the Frankopan Castle.

**Sport**   **Diving** *Aurea International*, Vršanska 26 L, T222277, www.aurea-krk.hr

**Transport**   Through summer there are 12 **buses** daily from **Rijeka** on the mainland to **Krk Town** (1 hr 40 mins). Seven of these continue across the **island to Baška**, stopping at **Punat** en route. Krk Town to Punat takes 10 mins. Punat to Baška takes 30 mins. In winter the service is slightly reduced. Krk Town bus station, T222149.

**Directory**   **Banks** There are 2 banks in town. **Communications** Post office: Bodulska bb, Mon-Fri 0700-2000, Sat 0700-1400. **Internet**: *Multilink Internet Centar*, T221088. **Medical services**   Doctor: Dom zdravlja, T222029. **Pharmacy**: Ljekarna, T221133.

## Punat

*Phone code: 051*
*Colour map 1, grid C3*
*4 km east of Krk Town*

On the southwest coast, Punat lies in a wide, sheltered bay called Puntarska Draga. Home to the largest and one of the best-equipped marinas on the Adriatic, it's a popular wintering hole for hardened yachters. People holidaying on the island flock to Punat on day trips to visit the nearby Islet of Košljun with its 15th-century Franciscan Monastery.

**Islet of Košljun**   Planted with dense woodland, this islet was first settled by Benedictine monks in the 11th century. The Franciscans took their place in the 15th century, building the **Franjevački Samostan** (Franciscan Monastery). Inside, a museum display includes a Hebrew Bible from the 11th century, one of only three preserved Ptolemaic Atlases dating back to 1511, and a collection of folk costumes, with a set of ladies scarves from the island of Krk, each one discreetly indicating which village the wearer came from and whether she was married, unmarried or widowed. ■ *Mon-Sat 0830-1200 and 1500-1700, Sun 1030-1200. 10Kn. T854017.*

Košljun was home to one of the first European financial institutions, the so-called *Košljunska Posujilnica* (Košljun Lending House), which was set up to protect the poor from usurers, and functioned between the 17th and 19th centuries. During the **Krk Summer Festival** (mid-July to late August), classical music concerts are held here in a lovely cloistered courtyard. ■ *Getting there: through summer regular taxi boats run from the seafront in Punat to the islet of Košljun (expect to pay 20Kn return).*

**G** *Youth Hostel*, Novi Put 8, T854037. This centrally located hostel offers overnight **Sleeping**
accommodation with prices depending on the room type. There are 90 beds and a restaurant. Half and full-pension are available. Open May-Sep.

**Mid-range**  *Marina*, Puntica 9, T854132. Based in the marina with a view over the bay  **Eating**
and the Islet of Košljun, this highly regarded restaurant serves up local specialities such
as *ražnjić od morskih plodova* (seafood kebabs) and *janjeća jetrica i palenta* (lambs liver
with polenta). Closed 15 Jan-30 Jan.

*Croatia Cup*, **late-May**, 4-day sailing regatta.                                               **Festivals**

**Sailing**  *Marina Punat*, Puntica 7, T654111, www.marina-punat.hr  830 berths plus  **Sport**
a dry dock with space for 300 boats on land. Open all year. The following charter
companies are based here: *Daranji Sailing*, T654111; *Ecker Yachting*, T654330; and
*Puntica*, T654320.

Through summer there are 7 **buses** daily from **Rijeka** on the mainland to Baška, stopping  **Transport**
at **Krk Town** and **Punat** (1 hr 50 mins) en route. In winter the service is slightly reduced.

# Baška

Thanks to its spectacular beach, Baška is the oldest and best-known resort on
the island. What was once a compact little fishing village now straggles almost
3 km along the coast, due to the restaurants, apartment blocks and the vast
*Hotel Corinthia* complex, which have sprung up over the last 30 years. Behind
town lies a fertile plain of cultivated fields, and behind that a band of rugged
limestone hills.

*Phone code: 051*
*Colour map 1, grid C3*
*Population: 901*
*19 km southeast of Krk Town and 43 km from Krk Bridge*

On the cultural front, the Romanesque **Crkva Sv Lucije** (Church of St Lucy),  **Sights**
lies 2 km inland in the tiny village of Jurandvor. It was here that the renowned
**Bašćanska Ploča** (Baška Tablet) was discovered, set in the church floor, in
1851. This white limestone slab, 2 m wide and 1 m high, was engraved with
13 lines (about 100 words) in Glagolitic characters (see page 129) sometime in
the late 11th century. It records, in Old Slavonic language, the donation of
land (probably the site the church is built on) from the early Croatian King,
Zvonimir, to the local parish. Although it is not the oldest surviving
Glagolithic text, it is regarded as the most important due to its graphic style,
language and historic content. In 1934, despite strong resistance from the
people of Jurandvor, who tried to hide the slab in the village school, the original was transferred to Zagreb, where it can now be seen in the Croatian Academy of Arts and Sciences. What you will see in the church here is a replica.
■ *Jul-Aug 0900-1100 and 1700-2200, Sep-Jun 1600-2000.*
     This 2-km stretch of pebble beach, which lies directly in front of town, is
spectacular and one of Croatia's loveliest beaches. The downside is that it can
also be one of the busiest, with the tourist office ambitiously estimating space
for 5,000 bathers at a time. If you prefer something more peaceful, take a
taxi-boat to any one of the succession of small, secluded bays (accessible only
from the sea) west of town.
     The tourist office is at Kralja Zvonimira 114, T856544, www.tz-baska.hr

The agencies *Šiloturist*, S Radića 26, T856171/856357, www.siloturist.hr, and *Splendido*  **Sleeping**
at Kralja Zvonimira 148, T856116, www.splendido.hr, can help you find private accommodation in Baška.

**Eating**   **Mid-range to expensive**  *Ribar*, Palada bb, T856461. Just 20 m from the quay, this large restaurant has a long-standing reputation for excellent seafood. If you've already had your fill of fish, try the *Baška Ploče*, a generous mixed meat platter for two. **Cheap to mid-range**  *Cicibela*, Emila Geistlicha bb, T856013. This cosy restaurant is known for its discreet waiters and romantic evening atmosphere. There's a good selection of fish and seafood dishes, with pizza providing a cheaper option.

**Sport**   **Diving**  *Rare Bird*, Kricon 12, T856536. **Hiking**  14 well-marked hiking paths criss-cross their way over the surrounding countryside. Hiking maps are available from the town tourist office. **Tennis**  Within the *Hotel Corinthia* complex there are 13 tennis courts, open to non-residents from early-Apr to late-Oct. Expect to pay 40Kn per hr.

**Transport**   **Bus**  Through summer there are 7 buses daily from **Rijeka** on the mainland to Baška (2 hrs 20 mins), stopping at **Krk Town** and **Punat** en route. Krk Town to Baška takes 40 mins). In winter the service is slightly reduced. For bus times contact Krk Town bus station, T222149. **Ferries**  *Jadrolinija* (Rijeka office, T211444) run a summer service of 5 ferries daily from Baška to Lopar to the island of Rab.

**Directory**   **Bank**  There is 1 bank. **Communications**  Post office: Zdenka Čermakova bb, Mon-Fri 0700-1900, Sat 0700-1400. **Internet:** *Primaturist*, T856971. **Medical services**  Doctor: Dom zdravlja, T856815. **Pharmacy:** Ljekarna, T856900.

## Vrbnik

*Phone code: 051*
*Colour map 1, grid C3*
*Population: 944*
*37 km from Krk Bridge*

*Off the beaten track,*
*it is worth going for*
*a wander around the*
*town and specifically*
*for the wine cellars*

Vrbnik is a tiny, tightly packed medieval settlement standing on the edge of a limestone cliff, 48 m above the sea. Below the town there's a small sheltered harbour, while the plain behind town is planted with the vineyards that produce the highly esteemed *Vrbnička Žlahtina*, a dry white wine which you should certainly try while here. First mentioned in 1100, Vrbnik was fortified during the Middle Ages, and part of the town walls can still be seen today, hugging a maze of narrow winding streets and old stone buildings. Northeast facing, it is fully exposed to the cold *bura* wind and can be extremely gusty in winter. The tourist office is at Trg Sv Ivana 2, T/F857479, www.multilink.hr/ vrbnik

**Sleeping**   **D** *Hotel Argentum*, Supec 68, T857370, F857352, www.vrbnik.net/argentum This 10-room modern hotel lies a short walk from the old town. It may not be very inspiring from the outside, but it has a good restaurant with a large terrace overlooking the sea and it makes an ideal base if you want to spend a couple of days here. Pets welcome.

**Eating**   **Mid-range to expensive**  *Nada*, Ulica Glavača 22, T857065, www.vrbnik.net/nada Lying close to the harbour, *Nada* doubles as a restaurant, where you can eat fresh fish and seafood on a wonderful terrace with views out to sea, and a *konoba* (wine cellar), where you can sample the excellent *Žlahtina Nada* along with nibbles such as *ovči sir* (sheeps cheese) and *pršut* (smoked ham). It's possible to buy bottles of wine and *rakija* in presentation boxes to take home.

**Transport**   There are 2 **buses** daily from **Krk Town** to **Vrbnik** (30 mins). For further information, contact Krk Town bus station, T222149.

**Directory**   **Bank**  There is 1 in town. **Communications**  Post office: Varoš 21, Mon-Fri 0800-1500. **Medical services**  Doctor and emergency treatment: T857010. There is no pharmacy.

# Island of Cres (It Cherso)

*Sparsely populated and little explored by the average tourist, this long, skinny, mountainous island is joined to a second island, **Lošinj**, by a bridge. The northern end is covered by a dense deciduous forest of beech and oak, known as the **Tramunatana**, which gradually gives way to meagre pastures and barren landscapes in the south. More for those in search of unspoilt nature, rather than culture, Cres offers good opportunities for **hiking** and **bird watching** (the rare Eurasion griffon vulture nests here), but little in the way of art and architecture. The islanders live primarily from sheep farming: Creška janjetina (Cres lamb) is especially tasty thanks to the ecologically clean pastures, rich in wild herbs such as kadulja (sage). In the middle of the island, **Vransko Jezero** (Lake Vrana) is an unusual natural phenomenom. This 6-km long freshwater lake is 74 m deep and its bottom lies 61 m below sea level: a godsend for the islanders, it supplies drinking water to both Cres and Lošinj and is also used to irrigate the surrounding olive groves.*

*Phone code: 051*
*Colour map 1/3,*
*grid C2/A1*
*Population: 2,959*

## Ins and outs

Buses leave daily from Rijeka to Mali Lošinj, stopping at towns en route. In summer, a daily catamaran service runs between Rijeka and Cres Town. The year through, regular ferries operate between Brestova on the mainland (in Istria) and Porozina on Cres (30 mins), and between Valbiska on the island of Krk and Merag on Cres (30 mins).

**Getting there**
*See Transport, page 157, for further details*

A main road runs the length of the island, from Porozina on the northern tip all the way to Osor in the south, where there is a bridge to Lošinj. Towns on this road, such as Cres Town and Osor, are connected by regular local buses. However, smaller villages off the main road are very poorly served by public transport.

**Getting around**

The island's main tourist office is in Cres Town, Conc 10, T571535, www.tzg-cres.hr At Osor, during summer, a small tourist office works on the main square, T237007. Outside season in Osor, contact the Mali Lošinj tourist office for further information.

**Tourist office**

## Background

Ancient sources record the islands of Cres and Lošinj under a common name, the *Apsyrtides*, connecting them with the Greek myth of Jason and the Golden Fleece. According to legend, the fleece was kept in the possession of King Aeetes, but when his daughter, Medea, fell in love with Jason, she agreed to help him steal it in return for eternal fidelity. Mission accomplished, the lovers set sail together with Medea's younger brother, Apsyrtos. When the King appeared in hot pursuit, Medea killed her brother, scattering his remains on the sea so as to slow down their father, who stopped to pick up the pieces. From Apsyrtos' body came into being the Apsyrtides, Cres and Lošinj.

Mythology aside, it seems Cres was originally settled by the Illyrian tribe of the Liburni around 1600BC. No one is quite sure who dug the channel between Cres and Lošinj. Some historians attribute it to the Liburni, while others claim it was the work of the Romans, who arrived sometime in the first century BC and developed *Apsoros* (present-day Osor), overlooking the channel, into a major trading centre.

Under Venice from 1409 to 1797, Cres was considerably wealthier and more developed than neighbouring Lošinj, but the tables were turned during the 19th century under the Hapsburgs when Lošinj became an important shipping centre, while Cres fell into relative obscurity. At the end of the First World War the Treaty of Versailles awarded both Cres and Lošinj to Italy, and it was only in 1947 that they were reunited with Yugoslavia.

## Cres Town

*Phone code: 051*
*Colour map 1, grid C2*
*Population: 2,333*

Located on the north side of a sheltered bay on the west coast, the island's chief settlement is made up of pastel-coloured houses giving onto a broad seafront promenade, which cuts its way around a deep triangular harbour filled with small fishing boats. Backed by terraces of olive groves, it's a pleasant enough place with a down-to-earth atmosphere and a handful of restaurants serving home-produced food and wine.

**Sights** During the 16th century it was fortified with town walls, five towers and several gates, most of which was pulled down in the early 20th century, though three gates, **Gradska Vrata** (Town Gate), **Mala Vrata** (Little Gate) and **Vrata Sv Mikule** (St Michel's Gate) and one round tower can still be seen. Within these limits, the old town is made up of a maze of winding streets opening out onto small squares. Traditionally homes were built on two levels: the ground floor would be used as either a *butiga* by artisans or a *konoba* by farmers, with the family living quarters upstairs.

Outside the former walls, south of the centre stands the 14th-century **Frančevaski Samostan** (Franciscan Monastery) built in late- Gothic and Renaissance styles. The covered arcade of the cloister displays the gravestones and busts of prominent local families, and there's also a small museum with a modest selection of 16th- and 17th-century religious paintings and furniture. ■ *Summer Mon-Sat 0900-1200 and 1600-1830. 5Kn. T571217.*

Kvarner

Islands of Cres & Lošinj

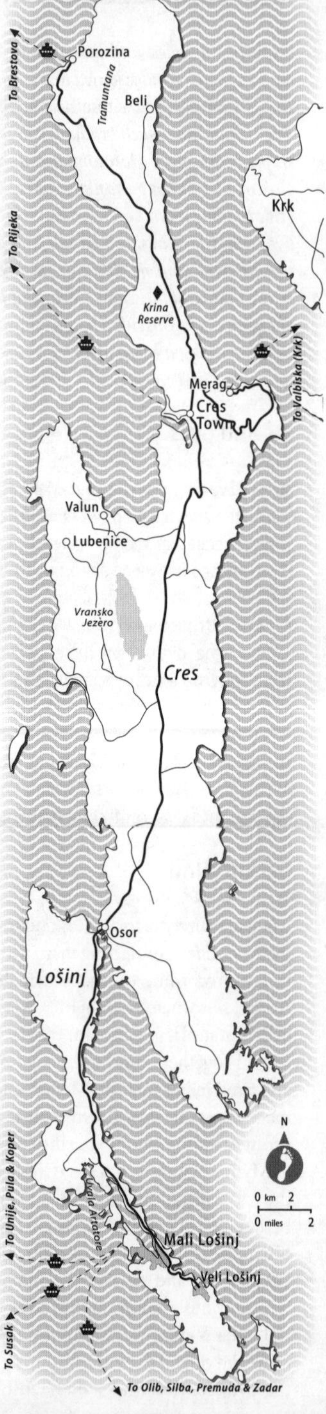

The seafront promenade leads west of town to a stretch of coast offering a series of small secluded **coves** ideal for sunbathing and swimming.

**Valun**, 13 km south of Cres Town (5 km off the main road), is a peaceful fishing village with pastel-coloured cottages built around a small harbour on the edge of Valun Bay, with a population of 62. A path on the seafront leads to blissful pebble beaches each side of the bay, and if you come outside peak season you may well have the place to yourself. The main sight here is the **Valunska Ploča** (Valun Tablet), a stone bearing an 11th-century inscription in both Glagolitic (see page 129) and Latin scripts. It was found in the tiny Church of St Mark in the village cemetery, but is now on display in the parish Church of St Mary. *Konoba Toš* is a small eatery with a vine-covered terrace overlooking the bay that is popular with yachters, who put down anchor here to indulge in the house specialities, *škampi* (shrimps) and Cres lamb. ■ *Getting there: unfortunately Valun is very poorly served by public transport, with only 3 buses a week to Cres Town, so you really need a car to get here.*

Perched on a cliff, 387 m above the sea, 5 km south of Valun and with a population of 24, **Lubenice** is worth a visit for its romantic crumbling charm and spectacular views. Made up of medieval stone cottages built around a square and a 15th-century parish church, the village is semi-abandoned, but comes to life each year in summer when the *Lubenice Music Evenings* are held here. Open-air classical music concerts, performed by renowned Croatian and foreign musicians, take place on the central square, July to August on Friday evenings. Ask at the Cres Town tourist office for details. ■ *Getting there: Lubenice is also badly served by public transport, with only 3 buses a week to Cres Town.*

**Excursions**
*Both Valun and Lubenice are well worth a visit*

*Hotel Cres*, Creskih kapetana bb, T571108, F571163. This small family-run hotel lies in the centre of town overlooking the harbour. The agency *Cresanka*, Varozina 25, Cres Town, T571161, www.cresanka.hr, can help you find private accommodation. They also organize hiking and culinary tours of the island.

**Sleeping**

*Mid-range   Riva*, Creskih kapetana 13, Cres, T571107. With a large terrace overlooking the harbour, this small fish restaurant serves up delicious octopus salad, barbecued scampi, and oven baked fish with potatoes, plus house wine, **Malvazija** by the carafe. *Belona*, Šetalište 20 Aprila 24, Cres, T571203. Popular with locals, this small old-fashioned eatery is known for oven-baked **arbun** (sea bream), pasta with lobster, and oven-baked lamb with potatoes, all of which come with generous portions of homemade bread. In warm weather it's possible to eat outside on the terrace.

**Eating**

*EMS European Championship*, 1-week sailing regatta, last week of **Jun**.

**Festivals**

*Sailing   Cres ACI Marina*, Jadranska obala 22, in the southern part of the bay, T571622, www.aci-club.hr, has 460 berths. Open all year. The marina also has 8 comfortable apartments.

**Sport**

*Boat   Lošinj Plovidba*, at Privalaka bb in Mali Losinj, T231524, www.losinjplov.hr, run regular ferries between **Brestova** on the mainland and **Porozina** (population 20) on Cres, with 19 crossings daily in summer, and 15 in winter. The same company also operates a service between **Valbiska** on the island of Krk and **Merag** (population 3) on Cres, with 13 crossings daily in summer, and 9 in winter. In addition, *Jadrolinija* (Rijeka office, T211444) run a once daily catamaran service between **Rijeka** and Cres Town the year through.

**Transport**

Kvarner

**Bus** There are 3 buses daily from **Rijeka** to **Mali Lošinj**, stopping at Cres Town (2½ hrs) and **Osor** en route. In addition 5 local buses daily cover the route from Cres Town to **Mali Lošinj** (1 hr) passing through **Osor** en route. Cres Town bus station, T571810.

**Taxi** It's often possible to find a taxi at the bus station. Taxi, T571664.

**Directory** **Banks** There is a bank in town. **Communications** Post offices: Cres Town, Cons 3, Mon-Fri 0700-1900, Sat 0700-1400. Beli, Beli 66, Mon-Fri 0930-1200. **Medical services** Pharmacies: Cres Town, Trg Frane Petrića 4, T571243. **Doctor and emergency treatment**: Cres Town, T571116.

## Beli

*Phone code: 051*
*Colour map 1, grid C2*
*20 km north of*
*Cres Town*

Beli stands on a hill, 130 m above a tiny harbour and pleasant pebble beach, on the northeast coast. Isolated and semi-abandoned with a population of 35, this cluster of old stone cottages is popular with hikers and nature lovers, who use it as a base for exploring the surrounding forests of the **Tramuntane**.

**Sights** Before setting off to walk through the Tramuntane, be sure to call at the well-run **Eco-centre Caput Insulae**. There's an informative exhibition, *Biodiversity of the Archipelago of Cres and Lošinj*, and a reserve for injured Eurasian griffon vultures. It's also possible to pick up an illustrated booklet, which will help you identify the trees and plants in the surrounding forests. From here, the most popular short walk is a 5-km eco-educative trail known as the *Tramuntana 1*, which takes you past 10 stations of natural and cultural significance. As you go, look out for birds such as the golden eagle, snake eagle, honey buzzard and of course, the griffon vulture. ■ *0900-1900. T840525, www.caput-insulae.com From mid-Feb to mid-Nov they run 1-day educational programmes.*

Almost 200 bird species are found on Cres, of which 90 breed here, making the island one of the richest ornithological areas on the Adriatic. The **Kruna Reserve**, between Beli and Merag, protects birds of prey such as the golden eagle, short-toed eagle, peregrine, honey buzzard and griffon vulture. Besides birds of prey, other species such as the eagle owl reside here. Visits to the ornithological reserve are restricted, but those interested in bird watching can contact the Eco-Centar Caput Insulae for guided tours in small groups.

**Sleeping** **E** *Pansion and Restoran Tramunata*, T/F840519, www.diving-beli.com Close to the
**& eating** eco-centre, this friendly *pansion* has 8 double rooms and a small restaurant serving hearty homemade meals. The diving centre is also based here. Open all year.

**Sport** **Diving** *Diving Club Beli*, *Pansion Tramunata*, T840519, www.diving-beli.com

**Transport** During the school summer break there are only 2 **buses** a week from **Cres Town** to Beli (30 mins). During term time a school bus covers the route, but you should check at the Cres Town tourist office for full details.

## Osor

*Phone code: 051*
*Colour map 3, grid A1*
*Population: 73*

Osor is a compact settlement of old stone buildings, located on a small peninsula on the southwest end of the island, overlooking **Kavuada**, an 11-m wide and 100-m-long sea channel (now traversed by a swing bridge) separating Cres from Lošinj. It is the oldest, and was once the most important, settlement

## Eurasian griffon vultures

*The Eurasian griffon vulture is one of the world's largest flying birds, with a wingspan of up to 2.8 m, a body weight of up to 15 kg, a maximum speed of 120 kph and eyesight nine times better than a human. It feeds on animal carcasses but never attacks living animals, and has long been respected by the farmers of Cres as it prevents disease by eating the bodies of dead sheep. However, as the island has seen a gradual but continual trend of depopulation, so the number of farmers and sheep has declined, and the griffon has been left with little in the way of food.*

*During the 1980s, when the number of griffon vultures had dropped to less than 50, the Eco-centre Caput Insulae established several feeding sites, where they deposit carcasses of slaughtered sheep and rescue injured birds so they can be taken to the centre and treated.*

*Their numbers have since risen, and there are now about 70 couples nesting in colonies on the vertical cliffs on the northeast side of the island. The female lays one egg per year, and during the two-month period of incubation both*

*parents sit on the egg. After hatching, the chick grows in the nest for four months, then spends another couple of months learning to fly with it parents, after which it leaves for several years roving, travelling as far afield as Greece, Israel and Spain. At the age of five, the griffon returns to the cliff where it was born, finds a mate and builds a nest, and then lives in the vicinity of its birthplace for up to 60 years.*

*However, modern-day life remains a constant threat to these spectacular birds. They occasionally chance upon carcasses of vermin that have been intentionally poisoned, they have a tendency to fly into electric cables, and young birds may even lose control of their wings and fall into the sea if disturbed by tourists during the summer season.*

*The Nature Conservation Act has declared the Eurasian griffon vulture a protected species. The killing or disturbing of griffon vultures, and the stealing of their eggs or chicks, are offences liable to a penalty of up to 40,000Kn. The public display of stuffed griffon vultures is also illegal.*

on either of the islands. Today Osor is often referred to as an open-air museum. Indeed, part of the ancient walls still exist, though the early settlement was largely destroyed by the Saracens in 841.

**History**  Founded by the Illyrian tribe of the Liburnians and named *Apsoros* by the Greeks, Osor lived its golden age under Roman rule, when it became a municipality and prosperous trading centre with a population of several thousand. Lying on the ancient land-sea Amber Route between the Baltic and the Aegean, it developed into an important transit point for merchants shipping amber from the north and silk and spices from the east. At that time ships sailed only with 'fair winds' (with the wind behind the vessel), and as the winds in this area frequently change direction ships kept close to the shores and were often forced to seek refuge in sheltered bays and inlets. Kavuada provided safe passage and shortened considerably the journey from the North Adriatic to Dalmatia.

During the 15th century, as ships became larger and navigational techniques more advanced, captains were able to sail their vessels more on the open sea. Kavuada consequently lost the bulk of its traffic and Osor fell into a period of decline from which it never recovered. Bouts of malaria and a plague epidemic only made matters worse, and under Venice Osor lost its role as the island's administrative centre, which passed to Cres Town.

**Sights**
*The most notable monuments date from the 15th century and are concentrated on the main square, once the site of the Roman forum*

On the south side of the square, the 15th-century Renaissance **Crkva Uznesenja** (Church of the Assumption) features a trefoil façade bearing an early-Renaissance portal topped with a statue of the *Mother of God*, attributed to Juraj Dalmatinac. Inside, a Baroque altar displays the relics of St Gaudencius, who was Bishop of Osor during the 11th century and is said to have banished all the snakes from the island. He died in Rome, but his body was miraculously transported back to Osor in a casket washed up by the sea. (The local Bishopric was founded in the sixth century but ceased to exist in 1828).

On the opposite side of the square stands the 15th-century **Gradska Vijećnica** (Town Hall), a two-storey building with a large semi-circular arch on the ground floor leading into an open-fronted space that once functioned as the loggia. Today it houses a *lapidarium* with early-Christian and Venetian stone carvings. On the first floor, where local patricians used to meet, is a small Archaeological Collection, with scale models of ancient Osor and first and second-century Roman gravestones. In a side street just off the square, the rather insignificant **Biskupova Palača** (Bishop's Palace) houses another *lapidarium* with more stone carvings from early Croatian churches. In summer it also hosts exhibitions of contemporary painting and sculpture.

The closest **beach** lies a few hundred metres north of the village in **Bijar Bay**.

**Sleeping & eating**
E *Restoran Osor*, Osor 28, T237221. A tiny dining room opens out onto a large summer terrace where guests tuck into local favourites such as pasta with shrimps, oven-baked fish and roast lamb. The owner also has 8 double rooms to rent, with an optional breakfast.

**Festivals**
*Osorske Večeri* (*Osor Musical Evenings*), **Jul-Aug**, classical music concerts have been held in the Church of the Assumption on the main square each summer since 1976.

**Transport**
Three **buses** daily from Rijeka to Mali Lošinj pass through **Cres Town** and Osor en route. In addition, 5 local buses cover the same route between **Cres Town** and **Mali Lošinj**, also stopping in Osor. Osor to Mali Lošinj. Cres Town to Osor it takes 40 mins, Osor to Mali Lošinj takes 20 mins.

# Island of Lošinj (It Lussino)

*Phone code: 051*
*Colour map 3, grid A1*
*Population: 8,388*

*Smaller but much more densely populated and certainly more touristy than neighbouring Cres, Lošinj is known for its mild climate, lush green vegetation and the long-established seaside resort of Mali Lošinj.*

## Ins and outs

**Getting there**
*See Transport, pages 162 and 163, for further details*

There are 3 buses daily from Rijeka to Mali Lošinj and Veli Lošinj, with stops at Cres Town and Osor on the island of Cres on the way. A local service covers the same route from Cres Town to Mali Lošinj and Veli Lošinj 5 times daily. A once-weekly ferry from Zadar to Mali Lošinj stops at the small islands of Olib, Silba and Premuda en route. Through summer, an additional ferry service from Koper (Slovenia) to Zadar stops at Pula, Unije, Mali Lošinj and Silba en route.

**Getting around**
Buses arriving in Mali Lošinj from the north then continue the 4-km stretch to Veli Lošinj, linking the towns 8 times daily.

**Tourist office**
The tourist office is on the seafront at Riva Lošinjskih Kapetana 29, Mali Lošinj, T231884, www.tz-malilosinj.hr

# History

In ancient times, known together with Cres as *Apsyrtides*, Lošinj seems to have remained unpopulated until the Middle Ages. The first settlers from the mainland were mentioned in 1280, and in 1389 they made an agreement with the people of Osor on Cres, who owned Lošinj, for self-rule. The name Lošinj, probably derived from the Croatian *loš* meaning poor or weak, appeared around the same time. Under Venice (1409-1797), Lošinj was neglected in favour of neighbouring Cres, the island's golden age finally dawning under the Hapsburgs when it developed into an important seafaring and shipbuilding centre. Shipping declined in the late 19th century, only to be superseded by tourism: with their mild Mediterranean climates, lush vegetation and crystal clean sea, both Mali Lošinj and Veli Lošinj were proclaimed health resorts in 1892. The demise of Austro-Hungary in 1918 saw the island awarded to Italy. During and after the Second World War, when the political future looked uncertain, many Italians left: the population declined dramatically, plummeting from 9,738 in 1910 to 5,449 just after the war. Lošinj was reunited with Yugoslavia in 1947.

## Mali Lošinj

Lying at the end of a sheltered, elongated bay on the southwest coast of the island of Lošinj, Mali Lošinj is the largest settlement on all the Croatian islands. Despite its name (*mali* means small, *veli* large), it's far bigger than neighbouring Veli Lošinj. Everyday life focuses on the harbour, skirted by a seafront promenade lined with cream, ochre and russet façades, many housing street level cafés with open-air seating under colourful awnings through summer. The town's loveliest houses, set in lush gardens filled with Mediterranean planting, were built by retired sea captains during the 19th century. Through peak season the place is packed with visitors, most of whom sleep in the large, modern hotels on ² ikat Peninsula, joined to the centre by a coastal path which meanders its way between the turquoise blue sea and scented pinewoods.

*Phone code: 051*
*Colour map 3, grid A1*
*Population: 6,296*

During the 15th century the Church of St Martin was built overlooking the large sheltered bay. A small village grew up around it, and three centuries later the locals set up a shipping company: the village became a town and by 1870 the port of Mali Lošinj was second only to Trieste on the Adriatic in terms of registered tonnage handled per annum, and Lošinj ship owners accounted for 170 cargo ships. However, the late 19th century saw the advent of the steamship: Lošinj's wind-powered vessels could no longer compete, shipping declined and many families emigrated. Around the same time, a study of the local climate, emphasizing its health-giving properties, was published in Vienna by Ambroz Hara³iᵃ, a nature-loving professor at the Naval Academy in Lošinj. Convinced a sojourn in such a place could only do them good, ailing Austrians began to visit Lošinj: the first villas and hotels were built on ² ikat Peninsula, and it soon became a fashionable winter health resort. The same Hara³iᵃ initiated a 10-year reforestation scheme, planting the area behind town with dense pinewoods. Since then Mali Lošinj has never really looked back. Today it lives primarily from tourism, though there is still a shipyard producing small motorboats.

**Background**

Kvarner

**Sights**   There is little here of great cultural note, but if you're interested in art be sure to catch the **Umjetničke Zbirke** combining two private art collections donated to the town. That of the local art historian, Andro Vid Mihičić (1896-1992), is refreshingly modern, featuring 87 works of Croatian 20th-century painting and sculpture. The other collection, formerly belonging to the Italian Piperata family, consists of 27 paintings, mainly romantic landscapes produced between the 16th and 18th centuries by Venetian artists, along with several works by Dutch and French painters. ■ *Summer Mon-Sat 0900-1200 and 1900-2100. Winter Mon-Sat 1000-1200. 10Kn. Vladimira Gortana 35, T231884.*

The best place for swimming is **Čikat**, where a coastal path west of town leads past a series of concrete bathing areas and pebble beaches, backed by villas, hotels and summer cafés.

**Sleeping**   **L** *Villa Diana*, Čikat uvala bb, T232055, F231904, www.jadranka.hr  Overlooking Čikat Bay, 2 km west of town, this villa was renovated in 2001 to provide 8 luxury en-suite rooms with modern furnishing. The excellent restaurant, with an open-air terrace shaded by pine trees, is frequented by residents and non-residents alike. **D** *Hotel Alhambra*, Čikat uvala bb, T232022, F232042, www.jadranka.hr  Also overlooking Čikat Bay, 3 km west of town, this old pink villa offers 29 peaceful rooms with simple modern furnishing. In summer the restaurant works on a terrace shaded by palms. Pets welcome. The agency *Capelli* at Kadin bb in Mali Lošinj, T231582, www.capelli-tourist.hr, specialize in private accommodation on both the islands of Lošinj and Cres.

**Eating**   **Mid-range to expensive**  *Corrado*, Sv Marije 1, Mali Lošinj, T232487. This is the best place to try traditional Lošinj fare such as *gulaš od junjetine* (lamb goulash). The owner is a cook and fisherman, so you can also expect top class seafood dishes: stuffed squid, and scampi with pasta. See also *Villa Diana* above. **Mid-range**  *Artatore*, Artatore 132, Uvala Artatore, 7 km north of Mali Lošinj, T232932. This restaurant is especially popular with yachters, who moor up in front of the terrace overlooking the bay. The owner does the cooking himself: his top dishes are *škampi rižot* (shrimp risotto), *jastog s rezancima* (lobster with pasta) and *ribe na žaru* (barbecued fish). **Cheap** *Pizzeria Draga*, Braće Vidulića 77, T231132. This friendly, bustling restaurant offers a range of pasta dishes and salads at lunchtime, adding to the menu a vast choice of delicious brick-oven baked pizzas in the evening. There's a large covered terrace area so you can eat out even if it rains. Closed mid-Jan to mid-Feb.

**Festivals**   *International underwater spear fishing contest*, **New Year's Day**. *Lošinj regatta*, **early-Aug**.

**Sport**   **Diving**  *DSC Lošinj*, based in Rijeka at Šetalište XIII divizije 28, T219111, www.diver.hr, organize a diving school here from **early-Apr** to **mid-Nov**.

**Transport**   **Boat**  *Jadrolinija*, T231765, run a once-weekly ferry service **Zadar** to Mali Lošinj (5 hrs 20 mins), stopping at **Olib**, **Silba** and **Premuda** en route. The boat leaves Zadar early morning to arrive in Mali Lošinj early afternoon, then returns to Zadar for the late evening the same day. *Lošinjska Plovidba*, based at Privalaka bb in Mali Lošinj, T231524, www.losinj plov.hr, operate a summer service from **Pula** to **Zadar**, stopping at **Unije**, Mali Lošinj and Silba en route. The boat leaves Zadar 5 times a week, and extends the route from Pula to Koper (in Slovenia) once a week.

**Bus**  Three buses run daily from **Rijeka** to Mali Lošinj (3½ hrs), passing through **Cres Town** and **Osor** en route. In addition, 5 local buses daily cover the route from **Cres Town** to Mali Lošinj (1 hr). *Autotrans* can supply bus times, T231110.

**Car hire**  *Avis*, Privlaka bb, T231938. **Taxi**  T231102.

**Banks**  There are several. **Communications**  Post office: Vladimir Gortana 4, Mon-Fri  **Directory**
0700-2000, Sat 0700-1400. **Medical services**  Pharmacy: Ljekarna, T231661. **Doctor**:
Dom zdravlja, T231824.

## Island of Susak

The tiny island of Susak attracts up to 700 visitors daily in peak season. In con-   *Colour map 3, grid A1*
trast to the other islands of the Adriatic, it's made up of compact sand forming a   *10 km west*
small hill (98 m) on a limestone base. Clumps of reeds protect the island from   *of Mali Lošinj*
erosion, and the locals cultivate terraces of vines, producing small quantities of
surprisingly good wine. In Italian the island is called *Sansego*, probably from the   *The majority of people*
Greek *sansegus*, meaning oregano, which also grows here in abundance. Susak's   *living on Susak*
real oddity is the unusual costume paraded by its womenfolk (today only for   *today are over 60*
special occasions): a multi-coloured embroidered miniskirt worn well above
the knee, over crimson woollen stockings and six layers of lace petticoats, so it
sticks out like a ballerina's tutu. The island's population peaked at almost 2,000
in 1936, but after the Second World War many families emigrated to the US.
Houses are gradually being sold off as holiday cottages, and a handful of bars
and restaurants work from late-April to mid-September.

The only settlement, also called **Susak**, is in two parts: the hilltop **Gornji
Selo** (Upper Village), which grew up around an 11th-century Benedictine
monastery (no longer standing), and **Donji Selo** (Lower Village) on the east
coast, which serves as the island's port. From Donji Selo, 120 steps lead up to
the Church of St Nicholas (Crkva Sv Nikole) built in 1770, the year the monastery closed. Inside, *Veli Bog* is a 12th-century crucifix that was reputedly
washed up on the island by the sea: local superstition predicts catastrophe
should it ever leave the church.

**Mid-range**  *Bistro Megi*, Susak 19a, T239140. Close to the port, the menu at this infor-  **Eating**
mal eatery is limited to barbecued fish and steaks, salads, pancakes and locally produced wine.

Through summer it's possible to take a day trip to the island, with **boats** leaving each  **Transport**
morning from Mali Lošinj harbour.

## Veli Lošinj

Veli Lošinj is a compact, little fishing town of pastel-coloured houses built   *Phone code: 051*
around a narrow bay. It's quieter and more authentic than its neighbour, but   *Colour map 3, grid A1*
still has a few things worth seeing, a modest selection of decent fish restaurants   *Population: 917*
and an unusual dolphin research centre.   *4 km southeast of*
   *Mali Lošinj*

On the south side of the harbour, close to the water's edge, the late-18th-cen-  **Sights**
tury Baroque **Church of St Anthony the Abbot** houses a number of paintings
by Italian masters, notably a 15th-century *Madonna with the Child and Saints*
by the Venetian painter Bartlomeo Vivarini (1432-99). ■ *0800-1200*. Set back
from the harbour, the **Fortress Tower** was built by the Venetians in 1445 to
protect the village from pirate attacks. It is now a small museum, the show-
piece being a copy of a bronze life-size statue of an athlete found in the sea in
1999, which some scholars attribute to the renowned fourth-century BC
Greek sculptor Lysippus. ■ *Summer 0900-1200 and 1900-2100*.

▶ **Bottle-nosed dolphins**

*The bottle-nosed dolphin, the most commonly seen dolphin in zoos and aquariums, can be found along coasts worldwide, except for in the polar regions. Along the British coast, they are often sighted in the Moray Firth off Scotland and Cardigan Bay off Wales. Gregarious by nature, this dolphin tends to live in groups of up to 20 in coastal areas, though farther out to sea and in deep water groups may be as large as 200. It has a dark grey or black back and a light grey belly, and a large curved dorsal fin with a thin trailing edge that easily becomes tattered: researchers use this trait to distinguish individual dolphins. Adults vary in length from 2 m to 4 m and can weigh up to 300 kg. Males tend to be slightly larger than females, and specimens living in cold waters are often larger than those living in warmer seas. It feeds on fish, shrimps and squid, and often follows fishing boats to pick up easy food. Dolphins can communicate and identify one another with a complex range of whistles and high-pitched squeals. They also make clicking sounds, which they use for echolocation, a way of sensing and distinguishing nearby objects.*

During the late 19th century, when the island was making its name as a popular winter destination for members of the Austrian aristocracy, Karl Stephan von Hapsburg had a mansion built on the edge of town. He called it *Seewarte* (*Morska Straža* in Croatian) and had the surrounding parkland planted with exotic trees such as magnolia and eucalyptus, and evergreen firs, pines and cypresses. Today the building houses a sanatorium for the treatment of respiratory diseases.

**Sleeping**   **D** *Pansion Kaiser*, T236256, www.island-losinj.com   In an old building overlooking the harbour in the centre of Veli Lošinj, this *pansion* has 15 rooms. Breakfast is served in a romantic courtyard. **D/E** *Villa San*, T/F236527, www.island-losinj.com   In an old building in the centre of Veli Lošinj, this friendly 14-room hotel stays open all year. The hotel restaurant prides itself in catering for special diets. They also plan to open a pizzeria for summer 2003. **Youth Hostel**, OH Zlatokrila, Kaciol, T236312. Set in a lovely villa with a terrace and a garden dominated by tall palm trees, the Veli Lošinj youth hostel has 60 beds and is open May-Sep.

**Eating**   **Mid-range** *Marina*, Obala Maršala Tita 38, T236178. With dining on a seafront terrace, this restaurant specializes in tasty spaghetti with lobster, and barbecued meat and fish dishes. See also *Villa San* above.

**Dolphin Research Centre**   The environmental organization *Plavi Svijet* (*Blue World*) runs the *Adriatic Dolphin Project (ADP)* off the east coasts of Lošinj and Cres. The research team includes experts from Croatia, Italy, UK and Germany, who are currently studying 120 photo-identified bottle-nosed dolphins living in the surrounding waters. It's possible to join the team as an eco-volunteer for 12 days at their base in Veli Lošinj. Volunteers help collect data at sea (the group goes out daily by boat) and assist with data analysis in the office. Accommodation is provided with the researchers in a house in Veli Lošinj, where volunteers are also expected to contribute to cooking and cleaning. In the future, the organization is planning to set up a Lošinj Marine Education Centre. *Blue World*, Zad Bone 11, T236406, www.blue-world.org

**Transport**   Three **buses** run daily from **Rijeka** to Mali Lošinj and Veli Lošinj, passing through **Cres Town** and **Osor** en route. In addition, 5 local buses cover the route from Cres Town to

Mali Lošinj and Veli Lošinj each day. *Autotrans* can supply bus times, T231110. It's also possible to walk from Mali Lošinj to Veli Lošinj.

**Bank** There is a bank in Veli Lošinj. **Commmunications** Post office: Obala M Tita 33, Mon-Fri 0700-2000, Sat 0700-1400. **Medical services** Pharmacy: the nearest pharmacy is in Mali Lošinj. **Doctor and emergency treatment**: T236180.

**Directory**

# Island of Rab

*Rab is probably the most beautiful of all the Kvarner islands. While the wind-swept northeast side is rocky and barren with steep cliffs plummeting down to the sea, the sheltered southwest part is gently undulating and covered with dense, green* **pinewoods***. The main reason for coming here is to explore the medieval* **Rab Town***, an architectural treasure perched on a walled peninsula, rising high above the sea. There are also some blissful stretches of sandy* **beach** *on the northern coast, so you can combine sightseeing with swimming and sunbathing, not to mention the excellent* **fish restaurants***. Rab is a particularly popular destination for Zagrebians, being one of the easiest islands to access from the capital.*

*Phone code: 051*
*Colour map 3,*
*grid A1/2*
*Population: 9,480*
*20 km south of the*
*island of Krk*

Kvarner

## Ins and outs

Two buses daily run direct from Rijeka to Rab Town (the ferry crossing is included in the price of the ticket). There is also a twice-weekly ferry from Rijeka to Rab Town, but the most frequent ferry service from the mainland runs from Jablanac (3 km off main coastal road) to Mišnjak (8 km from Rab Town) several times daily. From the neighbouring islands, there is a once-daily ferry service from Lun on Pag to Rab Town, and a summer service from Baška on Krk to Lopar (13 km from Rab Town).

**Getting there**
*See Transport, page
169, for further details*

Through summer a local bus runs every 30 mins from Rab Town to Lopar; the service is slightly reduced in winter. In summer, taxi boats transport visitors from Rab Town to nearby beaches along the coast. Alternatively, you can rent a motorboat and explore the island's shoreline independently.

**Getting around**

The tourist office is in the old town, Trg Municipium Arbe 8, T771111, www.tzg-rab.hr

**Tourist office**

## Rab Town

With four elegant bell towers lining the crest of a narrow peninsula, viewed from the sea the night-time silhouette of Rab Town is poetically compared to a giant sailing boat with four slender masts. The old town is compact and well-preserved, and can be divided into two parts: the medieval stone cottages of **Kaldanac**, on the tip of the peninsula, where the early Roman settlement was located, and **Varoš**, which takes up the land end of the peninsula, and is made of narrow paved streets lined with elegant Gothic and Renaissance buildings, many with ornate balconies, finely carved windows and doorways topped with family coats of arms, built between the 15th and 17th centuries. Through summer, the old town sees a constant influx of tourists, though fortunately all the large hotels (except for the *International*) are located a short distance away along the coast, leaving the historic centre perfectly intact.

*Phone code: 051*
*Colour map 3, grid A2*
*Population: 554*
*in the Old Town*

**History** The Romans occupied the island in the second century BC and called it *Arba*, a name probably derived from the Illyrian *Arb*, meaning dark, green, forested. Their main settlement, on the site of Rab Town, was proclaimed a *municipium* (a self-governing municipality) in 10BC, and later passed under Byzantine rule.

During the Middle Ages, Rab enjoyed a period of freedom and prosperity, earned through the production of silk. The town was fortified in the 13th century and many fine churches constructed. However, it fell to Venice in 1409, and, despite becoming a major trading point between East and West and the port to a large merchant fleet, began to slump into economic decline. The islanders were obliged to pay the Doge an annual tax of ten pounds of silk and five pounds of gold, and the local fleet was restricted to preventing competitive trade.

During the 15th century, Rab was ravaged by two successive outbreaks of the plague. In Kaldanac, you can still see abandoned houses, with doorways and windows bricked-up in an attempt to curtail the spread of the disease. Although the local population was decimated, the church seems to have fared pretty well out of the fear aroused by such misery. When Alberto Fortis visited the island in the 18th century, he found a community of only 3,000 peasants and fishermen contributing to the stipends of 60 priests. There were also three monasteries and three convents.

In 1808, Napoleon put an end to Venetian rule and also dissolved several religious institutions. After a short period under the French, the island became part of the Austro-Hungarian Empire. During the years prior to the First World War, Rab became a favourite winter retreat for wealthy Viennese.

# Island of Rab

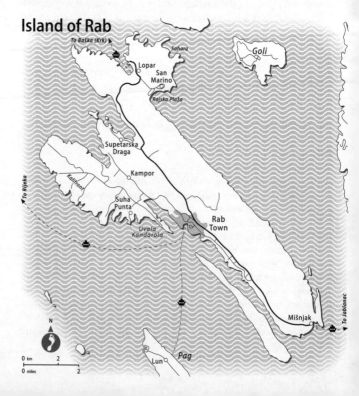

The first hotel, the *Imperial*, was built, and the green expanse of Komrčar Park was laid out. At the same time, the island was one of the first places in Europe to advocate nudism, an activity much publicized following a visit by the British king, Edward VIII, and his American fiancé, Wallace Simpson, in summer 1936. The couple apparently swam naked at Kandarola, which has remained a popular nudist beach to this day.

During the Yugoslav years, Rab Town expanded east of the port, and a number of large hotel complexes were built. Today Rab is a popular tourist resort, particularly with yachters, who moor up in the large marina next to the town port.

The compact old town is closed to traffic and can be explored in an hour's leisurely stroll. The layout is simple: three longitudinal streets, running parallel to the waterfront promenade, linked together by a series of steep alleyways. The lower street is known as **Donja Ulica**; the middle street, **Srednja Ulica**; and the upper street, **Gornji Ulica**. While the main cultural monuments are on Gornji Ulica, you'll find standard tourist haunts such as ice cream parlours and night-time bars on Srednja Ulica, where local street artists set up their easels through peak season.

**Sights**

The large paved square, **Trg Municipium Arbe**, opens out onto the seafront, half way along the peninsula. It's rimmed with a number of popular open-air cafés and the tourist office is also located here. The main monument is the **Knežev Dvor** (Rector's Palace) built between the 13th and 16th centuries, with a tall square tower and a stately balcony supported by three lions' heads sculpted in stone above the main entrance. The ground floor has been made into an art gallery, hosting exhibitions of modern art. ■ *Summer 0800-1200 and 1900-2200. Knezov Dvor.*

Standing on the highest point of the peninsula, the 12th-century Romanesque basilica, **Crkva Svete Marije Velike** (Church of St Mary the Great), was blessed by Pope Alexandar III in 1177, who happened to be passing through on his way from Zadar to Rome. Slightly squat in appearance, the façade is made up of alternating bands of pink and white stone, and decorated with two rows of six Romanesque blind arches to each side of the main portal. Above the portal, a *Pieta* featuring the Virgin holding the body of Christ was completed by the Dalmatian sculptor Petar Trogiranin in 1514. Inside, above the main altar, six slender marble columns support an ancient ciborium, which was restored in the 15th century. In front of the church, a pleasant terrace offers views over the sea. St Mary's was a cathedral until the bishopric was shut down in 1828, though locals still refer to it as the *Katedrala*. ■ *0800-1200 and 1700-2000. At the end of Ivana Rabljanina.*

A short distance from the Church of St Mary the Great, the free-standing, 13th-century **Veli Zvonik** (Great Bell Tower) is the tallest (25 m) and most beautiful of Rab's four *campanili*. You can climb to the top for spectacular views over the town and the surrounding seascapes. ■ *Summer 1000-1300 and 1900-2200. 5kn. Ivana Rabljanina.*

A Benedictine convent for the daughters of patrician families was founded here in 1020. **Crkva Sveti Andrije** (St Andrew's Church), dedicated to St Andrew, was restructured during the Renaissance, but the bell tower, dating from 1181 making it the oldest in town, has retained its Romanesque appearance. ■ *Rarely open. Ivana Rabljanina.*

Rab's second Benedictine convent, **Crkva Sv Justina** (St Justine's Church), intended for nuns from non-noble families, was consecrated in 1578. When the French dissolved it in 1808, the nuns were relocated to St Andrew's. The

Kvarner

convent church now houses the small **Muzej Sakralne Umjetnosti** (Museum of Sacral Art), displaying, among other things, an ornately decorated 13th-century silver-plated box containing the skull of St Christopher (the town's patron saint), a 15th-century Tuscan Renaissance terracotta *Our Lady with the Child*, and a mid-14th-century polyptych by Paolo Veneziano. The church bell tower, topped with an onion dome, dates from 1672. ■ *Summer 0900-1200 and 1930-2200. 5Kn. T725805. Gornja Ulica.*

Probably originating from the early Christian era, **Bazilika Sv Ivana Evandeliste** (Basilica of St John the Evangelist), now in ruins, was abandoned in the early 19th century. Today, all that remains is the 12th-century bell tower, which was restored in 1933 and stands 20 m high, offering a spectacular panorama over town. ■ *Summer 1000-1300 and 1900-2200. 5Kn. Gornja Ulica.*

Landscaped in the 1890's by Pradvoje Belija, the 16-ha **Komrčar Park** is planted with Aleppo pine, holm oak, spruce and cypress trees. A series of paths lead through the woodland to a pleasant coastal promenade with a series of rocky coves interspersed by concrete bathing areas and steps down to the sea.

The most central places to swim and sunbathe are on the west side of **Komrčar Park**. Through summer, taxi boats shuttle visitors to and from Frkanj Peninsula, close to the tourist village of **Suha Punta**, west of Rab Town, where there are plenty of secluded rocky coves backed by pinewoods, as well as the renowned nudist beach of **Kandarola**. However, Rab's best beaches are on **Lopar Peninsula** (see Excursions) on the northern tip of the island.

**Excursions**  On the northern tip of the island, the sparsely populated **peninsula of Lopar** boasts some of Croatia's sandiest beaches. There are two rather uninspiring little villages here: **Lopar** on the west coast (the departure point for summer ferries to the island of Krk) and **San Marino** on the east, which claims to be the birthplace of an early Christian stonecutter, Marinus, who fled religious persecution and settled on Mount Titano in Italy, where he founded the city state of San Marino in AD301. Next to San Marino lies Rab's largest and most popular family beach, **Rajska Plaža** (Paradise Beach), a 1.5-km stretch of sand backed by pinewoods and a string of seasonal restaurants and cafés. A 15-minute walk north of Rajska Plaža lies the nudist beach of **Stolac**, while an even more remote nudist beach, **Sahara**, is found in the peninsula's northern most bay.

**Sleeping**  **B-C** *Imperial*, Komrčar Park, T724522, F724126, www.imperial.hr  Rab Town's oldest hotel, dating back to the early 1900's, sits on the edge of the old town, amid the greenery of Komrčar Park. The rooms are modern, if rather basic, and facilities include a restaurant, 3 tennis courts and a hotel beach just 100 m away. **C** *Hotel Istra*, T724134, F724050. Overlooking the harbour, between the bus station and the old town, this 103-room hotel offers simple but comfortable accommodation, plus a ground floor café with a terrace overlooking the seafront. **C-D** *Hotel International*, T724266, F724206, www.imperial.hr  Located in the heart of the old town, this modern 130-room hotel was cleverly designed to blend into the surrounding architecture. Facilities include a restaurant, an indoor pool and a billiard hall. The agency *Katurbo*, at M Dominisa 5, T724495, www.katurbo.hr, can help you find private accommodation in Rab Town and Lopar. The website, www.otokrab.hr, also has a good selection of rooms and apartments across the island. See also *Zlatni Zalaz* below, 10 km northwest of Rab Town.

**Mid-range to expensive**  *Zlatni Zalaz*, Supertarska Draga 379, about 10 km north-   **Eating**
west of Rab Town, T775150, F775465. This highly regarded restaurant serves some of
the best food on the island. The house speciality is *janjeći but s jabukama* (leg of lamb
with apple) but there's also a good choice of fish dishes. Located in a bay overlooking a
pebble beach and backed by pinewoods, the terrace is divine. There are also 14 rooms
and four apartments to rent. Closed Jan. **Mid-range**  *Konoba Rab*, Kneza Branimira 3,
T725666. Lying in a side street running between Srednja Ulica and Gornja Ulica, this
*konoba* serves up meat and fish prepared either on a barbeque or under a *peka*. The
dining room is warm and inviting with exposed stonewalls hung with knick-knacks.
*Santa Maria*, Dinka Dokule 6, T724196. This long-standing restaurant lies in a
13th-century building in the old town with a large terrace offering stunning views over
the sea. The house specialities are *rižot fruti di mare* (seafood risotto) and *škampi na
buzaru* (shrimps in tomato).

*Rab Tournament*, **29 May** and **27 Jul**. Dating back to 1364, this medieval tournament   **Festivals**
records the defence of the town by knights with crossbows. Since 1995 it has been celebrated by a crossbow contest, with competitors in period costume. *Rapske Glazbene
Večeri* (Rab Musical Evenings), **Jun-Aug**, classical music performances by Croatian and
international musicians, staged on Thu evenings in the Church of St Mary the Great
and the Church of the Holy Cross in the old town.

**Boating**  The best way to discover the most idyllic hidden beaches is by boat. You can   **Sport**
rent small motorboats in Rab Town, T721608. **Biking**  There are a series of bike paths
on the relatively flat peninsula of Kalifront, close to Kampor, northeast of Rab Town.
You can rent mountain bikes from the agency *Katurbo*, M Dominisa 5, Banjol, the mod-
ern part of Rab Town east of the harbour, T724495, www.katurbo.hr  **Diving**  *Aqua
Sport*, Supetarska Draga 331, T776145, www.aquasport.hr  Open all year. *Moby Dick*,
Lopar 493, T775577, www.moby-dick1.com  Open Apr to Nov. **Sailing**  *ACI Marina*,
Rab Town, T724023, www.aci-club.hr 140 berths. Open mid-Mar to end-Oct. *ACI
Marina*, Supetarska Draga, on the island's northwest coast, 7 km from Rab Town,
T776268, www.aci-club.hr  270 berths. Open all year.

**Bus**  There are 2 daily from Rab Town to **Rijeka** (3 hrs 25 mins). On the island, regular   **Transport**
local buses run between Rab Town and Lopar Peninsula (30 mins). Bus station,
T724189.

**Ferry**  *Rapska Plovidba*, Stjepana Radića 3, T724122, www.rapska-plovidba.hr, run a
regular daily ferry service from **Mišnjak** on the island of Rab to **Jablanac** on the mainland (22 daily through summer, reduced gradually to 9 daily in winter, 15 mins). The
same company also run a once-daily ferry between Rab Town and **Lun** on the island of
Pag (35 mins). *Jadrolinija*, Rijeka office, T211444, run a ferry direct to Rab Town from
**Rijeka** on the mainland, departing 1430 Tue and Thu (3 hrs). The same company runs a
summer service of 5 ferries daily from **Lopar** to **Baška** on the island of Krk (50 mins).

**Taxi**  It's often possible to find a taxi at the bus station. Taxi, T724955.

**Banks**  There is a bank with an ATM behind the bus station close to the post office, and   **Directory**
on Trg Sv Kristofora at the entrance to the old town. **Communications**  Post office:
behind the bus station at Mali Palit 67, Mon-Fri 0700-2000, Sat 0700-1400. **Medical
services**  Pharmacy: in the shopping centre behind the bus station, T725401. **Doctor
and emergency treatment**: Dom zdravlja, T724094.

Kvarner

# Introducing North Dalmatia

South of Kvarner lies North Dalmatia, focusing on the port of **Zadar**, with its historic centre packed with Roman ruins, Byzantine churches and Venetian-style town houses. It was once the capital of all Dalamatia, and in nearby **Nin**, a small town built on an island accessed by a stone footbridge, the medieval Croatian royal family kept their court.

The most interesting island in the region is **Pag**, renowned for delicious salty *paški sir* (sheeps' cheese) and a long tradition of lace making. Its chief settlement, **Pag Town**, is a perfect model of renaissance urban planning, having been designed entirely by one architect, Juraj Dalmatinac.

However, North Dalmatia's main attraction, especially for yachters, has to be **Kornati National Park**, a unique seascape of almost 90 scattered islands and islets. Dry, rocky and practically devoid of vegetation, the islands are uninhabited. If you don't have your own boat, it's possible to visit them on an organized day trip, while the more adventurous might even consider renting a Robinson Crusoe style cottage here. No electricity or running water: Just sea, rocks and solitude.

Those who prefer terraferma and the sweet smell of meadows and pinewoods can retreat to **Paklenica National Park** on the seaward slopes of the rugged Velebit mountain chain – an area criss-crossed by well marked hiking paths and much loved by free climbers.

North Dalmatia

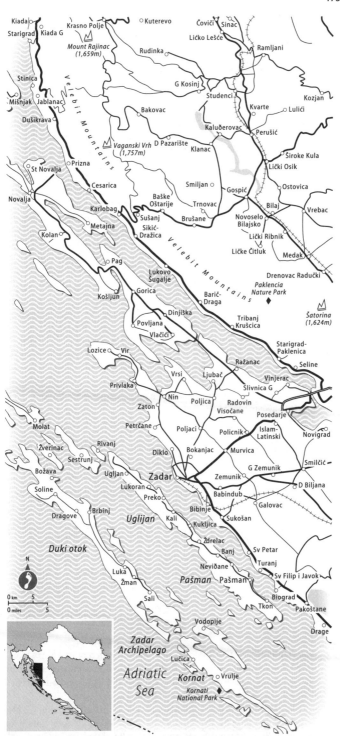

North Dalmatia

# Zadar

Phone code: 023
Colour map 3, grid B2
Population: 72,718

*Sitting compact on a rectangular peninsula, accessible only to pedestrians, the historic centre of Zadar is renowned throughout Croatia for its beautiful medieval churches, the most impressive being **St Donat**, which stands on the site of the ancient Roman forum. Close by, in the St Mary's Convent complex, **Gold and Silver of Zadar** is a stunning collection of minutely detailed Byzantine reliquaries. The narrow cobbled streets are lined with fine **Venetian-style town houses**, many converted into shops and cafés at ground level, giving the old town the buzz of a modern-day urban centre. The surrounding modern suburbs are dispersed and more difficult to negotiate: most of the hotels, restaurants and sports facilities lie 5 km along the coast at Puntamika. Before leaving, be sure to try **Maraschino**, a cherry flavoured liquor made in Zadar since 1821.*

*During the War of Independence, backed by the Serb-held Krajina territory, the city was repeatedly shelled and electricity and water supplies cut off for some time. Zadar became a hotbed of Croatian nationalism, a sentiment that still pervades to this day, despite its long history as a sophisticated multi-ethnic urban centre.*

## Ins and outs

**Getting there**
See Transport, page 180, for further details
Zadar is 190 km from Zagreb, 190 km from Rijeka, 288 km from Pula, 160 km from Split and 376 km from Dubrovnik

Through summer, *Croatia Airlines* run regular flights to and from most European capitals. The airport is at Zemunik, 7 km from the city centre. A *Croatia Airlines* airport bus leaves 60 mins before each flight, ticket 15Kn. Bus departure information, T250094.

The bus station is at Starčevića 1, a 15-min walk from the old town. Left luggage in the train station. The train station is at Starčevića 3, next to the bus station. Left luggage 0600-2000, 10Kn per piece per day.

The city port is on Liburnska Obala, immediately outside the old town walls, accessed through the Sea Gate. *Jadrolinija* run a coastal ferry from Rijeka to Dubrovnik stopping at Zadar en route, plus services to the surrounding islands.

**Getting around**
The old town lies compact on a peninsula closed to traffic, and can easily be explored on foot. However, most of the large hotels and many of the sports facilities lie at Puntamika, 5 km northwest of the centre. Puntamika can be reached by bus no5 and no8, both of which depart from outside the main bus station and stop en route close to the footbridge near the old town.

**Tourist office**
The city tourist office is at Ilije Smiljanića bb, T212222. The regional tourist office is at Leopolda Mandića 1, T315316, www.zadar.hr

**Best time to visit**
Like most cities along the coast, Zadar is at its most animated through summer, when you'll find open-air restaurants and cafés, plus a variety of outdoor cultural events in the old town.

## History

First mentioned in a Greek document from the fourth century BC as a settlement founded by the Illyrian tribe of the Liburnians, Zadar was later taken by the Romans, who called it *Jadera* and developed it into a port and fortified market town with a forum, theatre and public baths.

Following the fall of the Western Roman Empire in the fifth century, Zadar became the capital of the Byzantine *thema* (province) of Dalmatia: within the ancient walls a medieval town developed, with churches decorated with

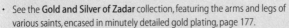

## Things to do in North Dalmatia

- See the **Gold and Silver of Zadar** collection, featuring the arms and legs of various saints, encased in minutely detailed gold plating, page 177.
- If you're in Zadar on a summer evening, attend a **classical music concert** in the ninth-century Church of St Donatus, page 176.
- Architecture enthusiasts would do well to make a pilgrimage to **Nin** to see the tiny, perfectly proportioned ninth-century **Church of the Holy Cross**, page 182.
- Buy delicious *paški sir* (sheeps' cheese) direct from a local producer on the **Island of Pag**, page 183.
- Pack a picnic, put your boots on and hike up a karst canyon in **Paklenica National Park** for stunning views over the sea and islands, page 185.
- Spend a day on a boat, sailing between the uninhabited 'moonscape' islands of **Kornati National Park**, page 189.

frescoes and mosaics, and workshops where goldsmiths crafted ornately detailed objects for religious ritual use.

In 1105 Zadar came under the Hungarian king, Koloman, and around the same time Venice, which wanted the city for its sheltered port, began a series of repeated attempts to conquer it. Upon the request of the blind Venetian Doge, Enrico Dandolo, when the Fourth Crusades set off for Constantinople in 1202, they stopped at Zadar and after a five-day siege captured and ransacked the city, an act for which Dandolo was later excommunicated by Pope Innocent III. However, Venice continued to dispute Zadar with Hungary, and in 1409 finally obtained permanent possession of the city.

By this time Zadar was the largest urban centre in Dalmatia and possessed the strongest naval fleet on the East Adriatic. So as to retain control, the Venetians rapidly curtailed all political and economic rights of its citizens. In the early 16th century, when the Ottoman Turks conquered the Zadar hinterland, the city was fortified with a system of sturdy defensive walls, and became an important stronghold for ensuring the safe passage of Venetian merchant ships up and down the Adriatic. During the 17th century, refugees from the Turkish occupied territories of Bosnia and Albania arrived in the area, and still today several villages outside Zadar have retained a local dialect heavily influenced by the Albanian language.

After the fall of Venice in 1797, Zadar came under Austria (and remained so until the Second World War except for a brief period of French rule (1805-1813)). During the 19th century the city walls were largely demolished, and new public buildings such as an army barracks and post office erected. *Hotel Bristol*, later renamed *Hotel Zagreb*, opened in 1902, hailing the birth of tourism.

At the end of the First World War, the 1920 Treaty of Rapallo awarded the city to Italy: unfortunate timing given Mussolini's rise to power in 1922. Thus when Italian fascists occupied Dalmatia in 1941, they chose Zadar as their headquarters. After Italian capitulation in September 1943, the Italian forces left, the Germans moved in, and the Allies began a brutal bombing campaign, so that by the time the Yugoslav *partizani* arrived in 1945, two-thirds of the city centre lay in rubble. Zadar was officially reunited with the rest of Yugoslavia in 1947. The Tito years saw a period of rapid reconstruction coupled with industrial development, and the building of new high-rise residential suburbs and modern tourist facilities.

North Dalmatia

## Sights

**Roman Forum**
*All the sights described in the Sights section lie within the old town on the Peninsula*

Now known as Zeleni Trg, the Forum measures 95 m x 45 m and dates from between the first century BC and the third century AD. In Roman times it served as the main market place and public meeting space: still today the city's top monuments, floodlit by night, are found here. On the northwest corner stands an ancient Roman column used as a 'pole of shame' from the Middle Ages up until 1840, where criminals were chained and exposed to public scorn and ridicule. ■ *Zeleni Trg.*

**Sv Donat (Church of St Donatus)**

Standing in the centre of the Forum, this imposing ninth-century rotonda is Zadar's best-known monument and the largest Byzantine building in Croatia. Standing 27 m high, it's a robust cylindrical structure flanked by three circular apses. Fragments of Roman stones have been incorporated into the sturdy outer walls, and inside a *matroneum* (womens' gallery) is supported by six pilasters and two Roman columns, and capped by a central dome. St Donat ceased to function as a church during the early 19th century. Today it stands empty, but due to its excellent acoustics it hosts the annual summer festival of Medieval, Renaissance and Baroque music. ■ *Apr-Oct 0800- 2000, and Jul-Aug for evening concerts. Closed Nov-Mar. Zeleni Trg.*

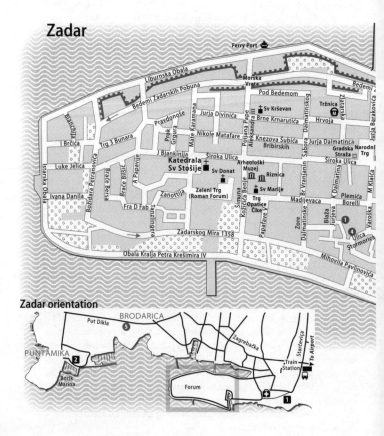

Next to Sv Donat stands the 12th-century late-Romanesque Cathedral, built on a rectangular ground plan with a splendid façade bearing three doors, a series of blind arches and two central rose windows, the lower one Romanesque and upper one Gothic. Inside you'll find a simple stone altar and finely carved wooden choir stalls from the 15th century. At the end of the left aisle, a smaller altar displays a ninth-century stone casket containing the remains of St Anastasia, to whom the cathedral is dedicated. Work on the **bell tower** began in the 15th century, though the upper three floors were completed in 1892 to drawings by the English architect T G Jackson. ■ *0800-1200 and 1700-2000. Zeleni Trg.*

**Katedrala Sv Stošije (Cathedral of St Anastasia)**
*If you have a head for heights its well worth a climb to the top of the bell tower for spectacular views over the city*

Housed in a modern concrete building close to the Forum, this museum traces local history from the Stone Age up to the late Middle Ages. The ground floor is devoted to finds from between the seventh and 12th centuries, and includes several fine examples of medieval stone carving. The first floor examines North Dalmatia under the Romans, while the second floor is given over to the Palaeolithic, Neolithic, Copper, Bronze and Iron Ages. ■ *Summer Mon-Sat 0900-1300 and 1800-2100; winter Mon-Fri 0900-1300 and 1700-1900, Sat 1000-1300. 10Kn. T250516. Trg Opatice ³ike 1, on the east side of Zeleni Trg.*

**Arheološki Muzej (Archaeological Museum)**

Close by, the early-Romanesque Church of St Mary dates back to 1066, though the present Renaissance façade was added in the 16th century and the interior stuccowork completed in 1744. The Romanesque **bell tower**, often referred to as Koloman's Tower after the 12th-century Hungaro-Croatian king, was built between 1105 and 1111. The complex was badly damaged during the Second World War, and reconstruction only completed in 1972. ■ *0800-1200 and 1700-2000. Trg Opatice ³ike.*

**Crkva Sv Marije (Church of St Mary)**

Standing next door to the Church of St Mary, the treasury houses a stunning collection known as **Zlato i Srebro Zadra** (Gold and Silver of Zadar), curated by the Benedictine nuns who live in the neighbouring Convent of St Mary. The first floor displays a horde of sumptuous reliquaries – arms and legs of various saints, encased in minutely decorated gold plating – and gold and silver processional crosses. On the second floor you'll find an equally well-displayed collection of religious paintings – look out for three panels from a 15th-century polyptych by the

**Riznica (Treasury)**

North Dalmatia

**Eating**
1 Dva Ribara
2 Foša
3 Konoba Marival
4 Konob Stomorica
5 Roko

Not to scale

■ **Sleeping**
1 Kolovare
2 Youth Hostel

Venetian artist Vittore Carpaccio (1455-1526) and a striking *Assumption of the Virgin* from 1520 by Lorenzo Luzzo. Before leaving, be sure not to miss the adjoining ground floor chapel, Crkvica Sv Nedjeljica, behind the ticket office by the main entrance. ■ *Summer Mon-Sat 1000-1300 and 1800-2000, Sun 1000-1300; winter Mon-Sat 1000-1230 and 1700-1830, Sun 1000-1230. 20Kn. T250496. Trg Opatice čike.*

**Sv Krševan (Church of St Chrysogonus)** North of the Forum, the street of Pape Aleksandra leads to the 12th-century Romanesque Church of St Chrysogonus. Strangely, the most beautiful part of the building is the exterior decoration of the apses at the back of the church, with a series of Romanesque blind arches. The church is rarely open, but if you have the chance to go inside you'll see statues of the city's four patron saints, Chrysogonus, Zoilus, Simeon and Anastasia, on the main altar. ■ *Open in Jul-Aug for evening concerts.*

**Morska Vrata (Sea Gate)** Following Pape Aleksandra beyond the Church of St Chrysogonus you will come to the Sea Gate, also known as Vrata Sv Krševana (Gate of St Chrysogonus), leading out to the **ferry port**. Originally a Roman arch, it was reconstructed by the Venetian architect Michele Sanmichele in 1560. On the landward side is a plaque commemorating the 1171 visit of Pope Alexander III, after whom the street is named. On the seaward side the gate bears a chiselled relief of the Lion of St Mark's (emblem of Venice), plus a memorial stone honouring local sailors who fought at the Battle of Lepanto (see page 223) in 1571.

**Tržnica (open-air market)** East of the Sea Gate lies the open-air fruit and vegetable market. From here, just outside the town walls, you will find a modern **footbridge**, spanning the channel and joining the peninsula to the newer part of town to the north.

**Narodni Trg** Two blocks south of the market lies Narodni Trg, which took over the role of the Forum as the city's main square in the 16th century. On the west side stands the **Gradska Straža** (City Guardhouse) from 1562 with an imposing 18th-century clock tower. On the opposite side of the square, the **Gradska Loža** is a Renaissance loggia designed by Michele Sanmichele in 1565. The open-sided front has been glazed and the interior now houses an art gallery. ■ *Mon-Fri 0900-1200 and 1700-2000, Sat 0900-1300.*

**Sv Šimuna (Church of St Simeon)** East of Narodni Trg stands the 17th-century Church of St Simeon. Inside, on the high altar, the main attraction is a magnificent 14th-century silver casket weighing 250 kg and containing the mummified body of St Simeon, one of the city's four patron saints, which is opened and displayed to the public on 8 October, St Simeon's Day. ■ *Trg Šime Budinića. Open for mass.*

**Trg Pet Bunara** East of St Simeon's Church, just within the town walls, this square is named after five identical wells, still complete with pulleys, which supplied fresh drinking water to the entire population until the late-19th century. On the edge of the square stands the pentagonal **Kapitanova Kula** (Captain's Tower), a 16th-century look out post built to observe the comings and goings of boats in the nearby channel. It was recently renovated to provide a four level gallery space with a heady spiral staircase leading all the way up to the roof terrace and stages temporary modern art exhibitions. ■ *Winter Mon-Sat 1000-1200 and 1700-1900; summer Mon-Sat 1000-1200 and 1900-2100. 5Kn. Trg Pet Bunara bb.*

South of Trg Pet Bunara stands the monumental Land Gate, which as its name **Kopnena Vrata** suggests was built as the main landside entrance to the city. Based on a classical **(Land Gate)** Roman triumphal arch, it was designed by the Italian Renaissance architect Michele Sanmicheli in 1543. The main central arch is topped by a proud Ventian Lion of St Marks, and flanked to each side by a smaller arch.

## Essentials

Unfortunately most hotels and restaurants are situated in the Borik complex at **Sleeping** Puntamika, 5 km northwest of the centre. The only hotel in the old town, *Hotel Zagreb*, ■ *on map, page 176* dating back to 1902, is currently closed and awaiting renovation, but does not look set to reopen in the near future.

**A** *Hotel Kolovara*, B Peričića 14a, T203200, F203300, www.tel.hr/hotel-kolovare-zadar Zadar's most central hotel, the 220-room *Kolovara* lies a 5-min walk from the bus and train stations. It's smart and modern, with a bar, restaurant, sauna, swimming pool and beach. **F** *Youth Hostel*, Obala kneza Trpimira 78, Borik, T331145. This friendly hostel lies 5 km from the centre, overlooking the marina in Borik. To get there, take either bus no5 or no8 from the bus station. Open all year: 35 beds in winter, 290 in summer. *Holidation.Com*, Marina Držić 39, T337143, www.holidation.com Can arrange private accommodation in Zadar. *Interalfa*, Matice dalmatinske 6, T315704, www.interalfa.hr Can arrange private accommodation on the islands of the Zadar archipelago.

**Mid-range to expensive** *Foša*, Foša 2, T314421. Close to the Land Gate, just outside **Eating** the city walls, this is probably the best centrally located fish restaurant. Pasta, risotto, ● *on map, page 176* seafood and steak are served on a lovely terrace overlooking a small harbour.

**Mid-range** *Dva Ribara*, Blaža Jurjeva 1, T213445. Most people come here to eat pizza, but it's also possible to order pasta, risotto, fish, and meat dishes. You'll find it in the old town, with a small terrace for outdoor dining in warm weather. *Konoba Marival*, Don Ive Prodana 3, T213239. Located in the old town, just off Narodni Trg, *Marival* serves up traditional Dalmatian dishes such as *škampi na buzaru* (shrimps in tomato and onion) and *miješano meso* (mixed grilled meats). *Roko*, Put Dikla 54, Brodarica, T331000. Lying on the road from the old town to Borik, this restaurant is owned by a fisherman and serves up delicious spaghetti with shrimps, and fresh lobster, on a large summer terrace.

**Cheap** *Konoba Stomorica*, Ulica Stomorica 12, T315946. In the heart of the old town, this tiny *konoba*, frequented by local fishermen, serves *girice* (small fried fish) and *pržene lignje* (fried squid) along with house wine on tap.

*Café Lovre*, Narodni Trg bb. Standing next to Gradska Straža (City Guardhouse) this is **Cafés** an ideal place to stop while sightseeing in the old town. *Central*, Široka ulica 5. A large café, popular with locals and visitors alike, with a busy open-air terrace through summer. *Kult*, Stomorica 9. A small café renowned for good rock music, frequented mainly by local students.

*Barakuda*, Obala kneza Domagoja. An open-air summer disco by the sea, located **Bars & clubs** within the Borik complex at Puntamika, 5 km from the centre. *Forum*, Marka Marulića bb, T214556. Zadar's most central nightclub, located just outside the city walls. *Gotham Multimedia Center*, M Oreškovića 1, Borik, T200289. A large modern complex combining a café (daily 1800-2400), disco (Thu-Sat winter, daily summer, 2300-0400) and cinema, a 10-min walk north of the old town, via the footbridge.

North Dalmatia

**Entertainment** **Cinemas** *Gotham Multimedia Center*, M Oreškovića 1, Borik, T200289. *Pobjeda*, Kraljskog Dalmatina 1a, T214362. **Theatre** **Hrvastsko Narodno Kazalište**, HNK (Croatian National Theatre), Široka ulica 8, T314552.

**Festivals** *Glazbene veceri u Sv Donatu* (Musical Evenings in St Donat's), **early-Jul** to **mid-Aug**. Concert office, Trg P Zoranica 1, T315807, www.hinet.hr Medieval, Renaissance and Baroque music concerts staged inside the churches of St Donat, St Chrysogonus, St Michael, St Simeon and the Franciscan Monastery. Held annually since 1960. *Zadarsko Kazalšno Ljeto* (Zadar Theatre Summer), **mid-Jul to mid-Aug**. Open-air theatrical performances in historic sites around town. Organized by the HNK (see above). *Zadar Snova* (Zadar Dreams), **late-Jun to early-Jul**. Alternative open-air theatre festival.

**Shopping** **Tržnica**, open-air fruit and vegetable market in the old town, open daily until 1600.

**Sport** **Biking** *Super Nova*, Obala kneza Branimira 2a, on the seafront, across the footbridge from the old town, T311010, rent bikes on a daily basis, which may be a good option if you're staying outside the centre at Puntamika. **Diving** *Zadar Sub*, Dubrovačka 20a, T214848, www.zadarsub.hr, run a diving centre at Sali on the island of Dugi Otok. **Sailing** There are 2 marinas in Zadar. *Borik Marina*, Kneza Domogoja bb, T331018, with 200 berths, and *Tankerkomerc Marina*, Ivana Meštrovica 2, T332700, with 300 berths. **Tennis** *Tennis Club Zadar*, Sutomiška 1, between the old town and Borik, T332022.

**Tour operators** *Atlas*, Branmirova Obala 12, T235850, www.atlas-croatia.com, organize one-day excursions to Šibenik and the waterfalls of Krka National Park, plus boat trips to the islands of Kornati National Park. *Croatia Express*, Široka ulica bb, T211660, www.croatiaexpress.com, provide public transport information and tickets for the entire country. *Generalturist*, Obala kneza Branimira 1, T318997, www.generalturist.com One of the of largest Croatian travel agencies, *Generalturist* specialize in tailor-made trips both with and without guides.

**Transport** **Air** Through summer, there are regular flights to and from **Amsterdam**, **Berlin**, **Brussels**, **Dusseldorf**, **Frankfurt**, **Istanbul**, **London** (Gatwick and Heathrow), **Munich**, **Paris**, **Prague**, **Skopje**, **Tel Aviv**, **Warsaw**, **Vienna**, **Zagreb** and **Zurich**. The number of destinations and the frequency of flights are reduced in winter. Zadar Airport, T205800.

**Bus** Internal services include 20 buses daily to **Zagreb** (5½ hrs); 11 to **Rijeka** in Kvarner (4½ hrs); 3 to **Pula** (7 hrs) and 16 to **Split** (3½ hrs). There are also daily international bus lines to **Ljubljana** (Slovenia), **Trieste** (Italy) and **Munich** (Germany). Buses depart several times a week for various other destinations in Germany and Austria. For all information about buses to and from Zadar, T211555.

**Car hire** *Avis*, *Hotel Kolovare*, B Peričića 14, T311360, www.avis.hr and *Budget*, Branimirova obala 1, T313681, www.budget.hr

*Schedules vary from day to day and season to season, so you need to check times with their ticket office* **Ferry** *Jadrolinija*, T254800, www.jadrolinija.hr, run overnight ferries to **Ancona** (Italy) several times per week, 8 hrs. Days and times vary from month to month, check at the ticket office for details. *Mia Tours*, Vrata Sv Krševana (Sea Gate), T254300, www.miatours.hr, run a hydrofoil service to **Ancona** (Italy) through summer, 3 hrs. *Lošinjska Plovidba*, Splitska 2/4, Rijeka, T (051) 319000, www.losinjska-plovidba.hr, operate a ferry mid-Jun to mid-Sep from **Koper** (Slovenia) to Zadar, stopping at **Pula**,

North Dalmatia

Unije, **Mali Losinj** and **Silba** en route (no cars taken to Unije or Silba). Tickets can be bought in Zadar from *Jadro* agent, Poljana Natka Nodila, T251052. *Jadrolinija* runs a regular overnight coastal service between **Rijeka** and **Dubrovnik**, stopping at **Zadar**, **Split**, **Stari Grad** (island of Hvar), **Korčula** and **Sobra** (island of Mljet) en route. Through winter the service is reduced to 2 departures a week. The same company also runs daily ferry services connecting Zadar to the nearby islands of **Ugljan**, **Dugi Otok**, **Olib**, **Iž**, **Rava**, **Premuda**, **Mali Lošinj**, **Sestrunj**, **Molat** and **Ist**.

**Taxi**  Liburnska obala, in front of the ferry port, T251400.

**Train**  There are 3 trains daily to Knin, from where it is possible to take connecting trains to **Zagreb** and **Split**, though this may imply a long wait. Zadar train station, T212555. National train information, T 060 333444, www.hznet.hr

**Airlines offices**  *Croatia Airlines*, Poljana Natka Nodila 7, T250101. **Communications**  Internet cafés: *Jet Net Internet Point*, Tržnica, in the old town. Large internet café on the 1st floor above the covered market. Mon-Sat 0800-2000. **Post offices**: the main post office is at Kralja S Držislava 1, Mon-Sat 0700-2100. **Telephone**: if you prefer to telephone from a peaceful phone booth, rather than calling on the street, go to one of the Post offices (see above). Otherwise, you'll find numerous phone kiosks around town. **Medical services**  Doctors and hospitals: General Hospital Zadar, at Bože Peričića 5, between the old town and the bus station, T315677. **Pharmacies**: all pharmacies are marked by a glowing green cross. *Ljekarna Donat*, T211264, Braće Vranjina bb usually works 24 hrs, non-stop. If it is not open, there will be a notice on the door saying which pharmacy to go to. **Useful telephone numbers**  Ambulance 94; Fire 93; Police 92.

**Directory**

*North Dalmatia*

# Nin

Backed by a flat, fertile hinterland, the old town of Nin is wonderful, sitting compact on a small island (500 m x 500 m) jutting out into a lagoon and joined to the mainland by a 70-m long pedestrian stone bridge which brings you directly to the town gate, built between the 15th and 18th centuries. The medieval churches are Nin's main attraction, the best known being the tiny but perfectly proportioned ninth-century Church of the Holy Cross. Today there are minimum tourist facilities. Most visitors arrive from Zadar, or stay in the purpose-built package resort of Zaton, 2 km to the south, where there are some decent stretches of sand and pebble beaches, and warm, shallow water for bathing.

*Phone code: 023*
*Colour map 3, grid B2*
*Population: 4,603*

**Getting there**  On the regional road to the small island of Vir, 17 km north of Zadar, Nin can comfortably be visited as a half-day trip from Zadar. **Getting around**  There are no street names in the old town, but being small and compact all the sights are easily explored in a couple of hours. **Tourist office**  At Zadarska bb, close to main road, above the old town, T264280, www.grad-nin.de

**Ins & outs**
*See Transport, page 182, for further details*

Built on what was originally a peninsula, Nin was first settled by the Illyrians and later developed into a relatively prosperous town, known as *Aenona*, under the Romans. Between the ninth and 12th centuries it became the first political, religious and cultural centre of feudal Croatia: seven Croatian kings were crowned here, and Nin was the seat of a bishop, whose jurisdiction stretched over the entire Croatian territory of that time.

**History**

In 1328 the town came under Venice, and a canal dug, converting the peninsula into an island joined to the mainland by a bridge. From the 16th century onwards, constant fighting between Venice and the Turks, coupled with several serious outbreaks of malaria, gradually depleted the population and Nin declined into relative obscurity.

**Sights** From the town gate, a central thoroughfare runs the length of the island. Half way along it stands the 18th-century **Crkva Sv Anzelma** (Church of St Anselmo) with a neighbouring treasury. Inside you'll find a small but precious collection of gold and silver religious objects, such as the ninth-century casket of St Marcela, ornately crafted jewellery and several finely decorated reliquaries. Close by stands a statue of Grgur Ninski, the notorious ninth-century Bishop of Nin, created by Ivan Meštrović (1883-1962), identical to the one in Split, only smaller. ■ *0900-1200. 10Kn.*

Just off the main street, to the right of the Church of St Anselmo, is the tiny, ninth-century, whitewashed **Crkva Sv Križa** (Church of the Holy Cross). It is based on the plan of a Greek cross and topped by a central dome. A perfect example of Dalmatian pre-Romanesque architecture, the British architect Thomas Graham Jackson, who visited Nin in 1887, hailed it "the smallest cathedral in the Christian world". It's normally kept locked: the interior is quite bare, but if you'd like to see inside try asking for the key at the Archaeological Museum.

The small **Arheološka Muzej** (Archaeological Museum) is well laid out and the collection concentrates on local Roman finds, though pride of place is taken by an early Croatian baptismal font carved from block marble, incorporating a slender pedestal supporting a finely decorated hexagonal bowl. The piece on show here is a copy, with the original now kept in the Archaeological Museum in Split. ■ *Winter 0900-1200, summer 0900-1200 and 1800-2100. 10Kn. T264160.*

Perched on a small hill just outside Nin, the tiny 11th-century **Crkva Sv Nikole** (Church of St Nicholas), built on a clove-leaf plan, once held the tombs of several early Croatian kings, now on show in Zadar Archaeological Museum. The octagonal watchtower was added in the 16th century, as a defence post against the Ottoman Turks. Unfortunately it's seldom open, but merits inspection from the outside if you are interested in medieval architecture. ■ *Prahulje, 1 km from Nin, on the road to Zadar.*

**Eating** **Mid-range** *Stara Kužina*, close to the tip of the island, at the opposite end from the town gate. This typical Dalmatian *konoba*, complete with rough stonewalls decorated with old fishing tools and a wooden beamed ceiling, serves excellent fresh fish and shellfish prepared over an open-fire, along with a steady stream of local wine. Open late-Apr to early-Oct for food. Drinks only through winter.

**Transport** Hourly bus from **Zadar**, departing 0600-2000.

# Island of Pag

*Long and skinny, rocky and uncultivated, its sparse pastures, scented with wild sage, support sheep farming with twice as many sheep on the island as people. The island is known throughout the country for its excellent* paški sir *(Pag cheese) made from sheep's milk and succulent* janjetina *(roast lamb). Several fertile valleys are given over to* **vineyards**, *producing two local dry white wines, the golden coloured Žutica and the light, crisp Gegić. The chief settlement is the picturesque 15th-century* **Pag Town**, *with a long tradition of salt production and lace making, while the main tourist destination is* **Novalja**, *a recently developed, commericalized seaside resort with some decent pebble beaches.*

*Phone code: 023 and 053*
*Colour map 3, grid A2*
*Population: 7,685*
*The island is 63 km long*

**Getting there**  Pag is joined to the mainland by a 300-m-long road bridge on its southeast tip. There are 6 buses daily from Zadar and 2 from Rijeka, both arriving in the chief settlement, Pag Town. There are regular ferries from Prizna on the mainland to Žigljen on Pag, plus a once-daily ferry service from Rab Town on the neighbouring island of Rab to Lun on the north tip of Pag. **Getting around**  A scenic regional road runs the length of the island, joining all the main settlements. A local bus service between Pag Town and Novalja runs twice daily. Alternatively you can hire a bike. **Tourist office**  The tourist office in Pag Town is at Ulica od Spitala bb, T/F611301, www.pag.hr  For the Novalja tourist office, T661404, www.novalja.hr

*Ins and outs*
*See Transport, page 184, for further information*

**North Dalmatia**

## Pag Town

Located at the southeast end of Pag Bay, at the mouth of a narrow channel leading to a shallow salt lake, Pag Town is the island's chief economic and administrative centre since its founding in the 15th century. Although there are no notable beaches here, and the surrounding landscape is somewhat dreary, the old town is a gem of Renaissance architecture, as well as the best place to buy locally produced sheep's cheese and handmade lace.

*Phone code: 023*
*Colour map 3, grid A2*
*Population: 2,701*

The original settlement, now abandoned, lies 3 km south of present-day Pag Town. Granted the status of a free royal town in 1244 by King Bela IV, it quickly became a prosperous trading centre, its wealth based on the production of salt, and indeed a vast expanse of salt pans, overlooked by the 12th-century Crkva Sv Marije (Church of St Mary) can still be seen there today. The island came under Venice in 1403, and in 1443, as the danger of a Turkish invasion looked ever more likely, plans were drawn up for a new fortified centre. The renowned architect and sculptor Juraj Dalmatinac (also responsible for Šibenik Cathedral) masterminded the project, which took several decades to build. A grid of narrow streets, centring on a main square with a Cathedral and Rector's Palace, were to be enclosed by sturdy walls and ten towers.

*Background*

Today the complex remains well intact, though the walls have largely gone. On the main square, **Trg Kralja Petra Krešimira IV**, you can see the 15th-century parish church of **Sv Marije** (St Mary's), which although it was never awarded the status of cathedral remains a proud monument based on

*Sights*

the form of a three-nave Romanesque basilica, with a fine façade featuring a Renaissance rose window above an elegant Gothic portal. Café life centres on the main square, while much of the post-1960's tourist development such as hotels, apartments and restaurants lie west of town, overlooking a family beach, with shallow water suitable for kids.

**Sleeping** **B** *Valentino*, A Danielli 2, T611131, www.valentino-pag.com You can't get more central than this. *Valentino* offers 5 luxury apartments, complete with beamed ceilings, bathrooms with hydro-massage showers, and kitchenettes, overlooking the main square. There's also a bar on the ground floor. *Maricom*, S Radića 8, T612266, can help you find rooms and apartments to rent in Pag Town. **D** *Hotel Restoran Biser*, A G Matoša 8, T611333, F612224. Overlooking the sea, a 15-min walk west of the centre, this modern white building conceals 20 comfortable rooms, each with a bathroom, TV and balcony, plus a large, highly regarded restaurant serving delicious *paška janjetina ispod peke* (Pag lamb prepared under a *peka*) and offering great views back over town. Pets welcome.

**Eating** **Expensive to mid-range** *Hotel Restoran Biser*, see above. **Mid-range** *Natale*, S Radića 2, T611194. Lying close to the harbour, this small restaurant specializes in barbecued fish and Pag lamb, which you might round off with *palačinke* (pancakes). Pizzas are also available.

**Shopping** Next to the church, on the main square, the local lace-making school (founded in 1906) have opened a small gallery displaying items such as **tablecloths** and **bed linens** made of Pag lace. Summer 2000-2200. T611017. The best place to buy *paški sir*, a hard, salty cheese similar to the Italian *pecorino*, is at *Paška Sirvana*, Trg Kralja Petra Krešimira IV.

**Transport** Six **buses** depart daily from **Zadar**, crossing Pag Bridge then driving 20 km along the island to arrive in **Pag Town**. There are also 2 buses daily from **Rijeka**, which use the Prizna-Žiglen 20-min ferry crossing and then drive south along the island to **Pag Town**.

**Directory** **Post office** Golija bb, Mon-Fri 0700-2000, Sat 0700-1400.

## Novalja

*Phone code: 053*
*Colour map 3, grid A2*
*Population: 2,078;*
*20 km northwest*
*of Pag Town*

In a sheltered cove backed by pinewoods, lies Novalja, Pag's largest and busiest resort. Pristine clear emerald seawater and a number of bays with fine pebble beaches make it the best place for sunbathing on the island, while sports and entertainment facilities compensate in part for its lack of cultural attractions. The one sight you might check out is the 1,024-m-long underground **Roman aqueduct**. Visitors are offered raincoats and crash helmets with lamps at the entrance to this dark underground tunnel, where even in mid summer temperatures do not rise above 15°C. Some 3 km north of Novalja lies the peaceful fishing village of **Stara Novalja**, hidden away at the end of a 5-km-long channel, happily protected from the prevailing winds, and backed by vine-covered slopes. The most popular bathing areas are the pebble beaches of *Zrće* and *Straško*, lying a short distance south of Novalja.

**Sleeping** **C** *Hotel Loža*, Trg Loža 1, Novalja, T661315, F661304, www.turistdd.hr Bang in the centre of town, this unassuming but comfortable modern hotel offers 40 rooms, each with satellite TV and a minibar. There's also a ground floor café with a summer terrace overlooking the seafront. Novalja-based agencies *Navalija Kompas*, Primorska bb, T661215, www.navalija-kompas.hr and *Sunturist*, Krančevićeva bb, T661211, www.sunturist.hr, can help you find private accommodation on the island.

**Mid-range** *Restaurant Stefani*, Petra Krešimira IV 28, Novalja, T66167. In the centre of **Eating**
Novalja, *Stefani* is popular with locals and visitors alike who come here to savour fresh
seafood and lamb, along with local specialities such as snails and dried octopus. Pizza
makes a cheap option. *Sv Marija*, Stara Novalja bb, T661655. Popular with yachters, *Sv Marija* serves up *paški sir* (sheeps' cheese), *janjetina* (roast lamb), fresh fish and local
wine at tables on a summer terrace overlooking the sea in Satra Novalja. For a spot of
wine tasting, *Taverna Boškanic*, Stara Novalja, perched on a hillside above Stara
Novalja, is a homely *taverna* serving local wine and *rakija*, along with platters of *pršut*
(smoked ham), *paški sir* (sheeps' cheese) and *slane srdele* (salted sardines). It's also possible to buy bottles and cheese to take home.

*Aquarius Club*, Zrće Beach, Novalja. Through summer, open-air drinking and dancing **Club**
by the sea, with regular live concerts given by popular Croatian musicians.

**Diving**  *Nautilus*, Kunera 31, Stara Novalja, T651285.  **Sport**

There are 2 **buses** daily from **Pag Town** to Novalja. *Jadrolinija*, Zadar office, T (023) **Transport**
254800, run regular **ferries** (18 daily in winter, 22 in summer) from **Prizna** on the mainland to **Žigljen** on Pag. From **Žigljen**, it is just 5 km to Novalja. *Rapska Plovidba*, Rab
office, T (051) 724122, run a once-daily ferry from **Rab Town**, on the island of Rab, to
**Lun**, which lies on a narrow peninsula 20 km northwest of Novalja.

# Paklenica National Park

Lying on the southeast slopes of the Velebit Mountains, which itself is 145 km *Phone code: 023*
long and designated a nature park, the national park covers 100 sq km and *Colour map 3,*
runs for 20 km along the Riviera, combining coastal and mountain scenery, *grid A2/3*
making it a haven for hikers and free-climbers. The lower levels are covered *42 km north of Zadar*
with beech forests, which gradually give way to pines, dramatic rocky out-
crops, scanty mountain meadows and scree slopes.

The best starting point for exploring Paklenica National Park is the seaside town of **Ins & outs**
Starigrad Paklenica, overlooking the narrow *Velebitski Kanal* (Velebit Channel). The *See Transport, page*
national park office lies at the entrance to the park at Jadranska cesta bb, Starigrad *186, for further details*
Paklenica, T369202, www.tel.hr/paklenica, and can supply visitors with maps of the
walking paths and information about mountain refuges.

The most popular walking route leads up the impressive karst canyon of **Sights**
**Velika Paklenica**, which is 10 km long and up to 400 m deep, and runs from
the highest peaks down to the sea. The path starts about 4 km inland from
the park entrance at Starigrad Paklenica. Passing a couple of mountain refuges a stiff climb will bring you to the 1757 m peak of **Vaganski Vrh**, the
highest point on southern Velebit, offering stunning views over the sea and
islands. This walk requires an entire day, and you should only set out armed
with good hiking boots and a plentiful supply of water. Alternatively, a little
way up the gorge, a secondary path branches off to the right, leading to
**Anića Kuk**, a bizarre 721 m vertical rock form and a popular training
ground for free-climbers since the 1930's. From here the path continues,
passing through a dense forest, and eventually arrives at a height of 550 m,
where you will find **Manita Peć**, a 500-m-long illuminated cave, filled with

*North Dalmatia*

stalactites and stalagmites, which can be visited as part of a guided tour (ask at the national park office for details). A final stretch of path brings you to the 800 m peak of **Vidakov Kuk**.

The gorge is home to birds of prey such as peregrine vultures and sparrow-hawks, while bears and wild boars are occasionally sighted on the more remote areas of Velebit.

**Sleeping** **D** *Hotel Vicko*, Joze Dokoze 20, Starigrad Paklenica, T/F369304, www.hotel-vicko.hr
**& eating** A comfortable, modern hotel with 50 beds and a pleasant restaurant with a summer terrace shaded by pine trees. Pets welcome. **E** *Rajna*, Jadranska cesta 105, Starigrad Paklenica, T369130, F369888. Popular with Croatian and foreign climbers and walkers thanks to its location close to the national park entrance, *Rajna* offers 10 guest rooms (most with balconies) and a highly regarded restaurant serving up a range of fish and meat dishes. The house speciality is *rižot s morskim plodovima* (sea-food risotto).

**Tours** The national park can organize individual half-day and full-day **guided tours** of the park, which cost 300Kn and 600Kn respectively, and should be arranged one week in advance. Special **bird watching tours**, in the company of a qualified ornithologist, will also be available as of summer 2003, for groups of 5 to 10 people, half day or full day (the price of these tours has yet to be decided). Bird watchers must bring their own equipment, eg binoculars and cameras. Regular organized **visits to the cave** depart from the national park office at Starigrad Paklenica at 1000 and return at 1300 on the following days: Apr Sat; May and Oct, Wed and Sat; Jun and Sep, Mon, Wed and Sat; Jul and Aug daily. Price 30Kn.

**Transport** All buses running along the coastal road from **Zadar** to **Rijeka** stop in Stari-grad Paklenica.

## Dugi Otok and the Zadar Archipelago

*Phone code: 023*
*Colour map 3, grid*
*B2/3*
*Population: 1,820*

Dugi Otok, translating literally to 'Long Island', is the largest of a scattering of islands and islets that make up the Zadar Archipelago. Running 43 km from northwest to southeast, and never wider than 4.6 km, it's a rugged, sparsely populated place, which seems to have passed through the centuries with few notable events. The island's villages lie along the northeast coast, looking back towards the mainland, while the southwest side, opening on to the sea, is made up of steep cliffs and a series of small inlets. A scenic road runs the length of the island from **Veli Rat** in the northwest, passing through Božava, Brbinj and Zaglav to arrive in the chief settlement, **Sali** in the south-east. The main attractions lie at the extremities of the island: **Telašćica Nature Park** on the southern tip, and **Sakarun** bay in the north. However, tourist facilities are minimal, and public transport limited, so you really need a car to get around.

Between Dugi Otok and Zadar lie the similarly long and skinny, but not quite as rugged or dramatic, islands of **Ugljan** and **Pašman**, which are joined together by a bridge and are connected to Zadar and Biograd-na-Moru by regular ferry services. Now almost a suburb of Zadar, many locals have sum-mer houses here, though there is little cultural or recreational interest to the passing traveller.

**Getting there** The year through, regular ferries operate from Zadar to Brbinj, and from Zadar to Sali and Zaglav. If you're thinking of taking a car to Dugi Otok, remember that the ferry for Brbinj carries vehicles, but that the boat for Sali and Zaglav is for foot passengers only, and that the only petrol station on the island is in Zaglav.

**Ins & outs**
*See Transport, page 188, for further details*

**Getting around** The main road runs the length of the island from Veli Rat to Sali. Buses are few and far between: a local bus meets incoming ferries at Brbinj, taking passengers to Božava and Veli Rat on the northern end of the island; likewise, another local bus connects Sali, Zaglav and Luka to correspond with incoming and outgoing ferries on the southern end of the island. But, for now, Veli Rat and Sali are only connected by a once weekly bus, leaving the northern and southern ends of Dugi Otok somewhat divorced from one another.

The best place for swimming and sunbathing is **Sakarun**, a white pebble beach in a large sheltered bay, lying between Božava and Veli Rat on the northern tip of the island. Dugi Otok's most developed resort is **Božava** (population 127), an old stone fishing village built around a pretty harbour with a quay where yachts can moor up. On the edge of the village, overlooking the sea, lies a modern hotel complex with eating and sports facilities. West from here, **Veli Rat** (population 83) is a sleepy seaside village which dates back to Roman times.

**North Dugi Otok**

Dugi Otok's largest settlement is **Sali** (population 769), which takes its name, first mentioned in 1105, from the former saltpans. Built around a sheltered bay, it also has a long history of fishing, though today the locals are gradually moving towards tourism, with the main attraction being **Telašćica Nature Park**, 3 km to the south. A natural extension of the Kornati, Telašćica is an 8.6-km-long bay surrounded by pinewoods and steep sided cliffs of up to 166 m, with countless secluded coves ideal for bathing. Close by, a 2-km-long saltwater lake, **Jezero Mira**, contains water several degrees warmer than the sea and is said to have therapeutic properties. Most people arrive in Telašćica by boat, either private yacht or as part of an organized excursion to the Kornati, but it's also possible to walk through the olive groves from Sali.

**South Dugi Otok**

**North Dalmatia**

**C** *Hotel Božava*, Božava, T377684, F377682. This sprawling white modern hotel complex overlooking the sea offers 120 basic guest rooms. Facilities include a bar, restaurant, swimming pool and seaside bathing area. Pets welcome. Open mid-Jun to mid-Sep. *Veli Rat Lighthouse*, contact *Adriatica Net*, Selska 34, Zagreb, T01 3644461, F3644463, www.adriatica.net Lying 3 km from the small village of Veli Rat, this mid-19th-century lighthouse has been converted to provide 2 apartments, sleeping 3 and 4. Accessible by car, it lies close to a decent pebble beach and is backed by pine trees. The Zadar-based agency *Marlin Tours*, R K Jeretova 3, T305919, can help you find private accommodation on the island.

**Sleeping**

**Mid-range** *Restoran Kornat*, Sali, T377049. In the centre of Sali, this large restaurant serves up traditional Dalmatian meat and fish dishes and good choice of wines on an open-air terrace, May-Oct. *Restoran Roko*, Zaglav, T377182. A small restaurant in Zaglav where the owner-cook serves barbecued fish and meat dishes prepared under a *peka*, May-Oct.

**Eating**

Sport  **Diving** *Kornati Diver*, Zaglav, T377167, www.kornati-diver.com *Hotel Božava Diving Club*, Božava, T377619. **Sailing**  Although there are no marinas on the island, Telašćica Bay is a popular sheltered place to put down anchor. Zaglav is the only place on the island, and the nearest place to the Kornati, for petrol.

Transport  *Jadrolinija*, Zadar office, T254800, operate a ferry service from Zadar to Brbinj, with 2 crossings daily through winter and 3 in summer. They also run a boat (foot passengers only) from Zadar to Sali, calling en route at Zaglav, departing once daily through winter and twice daily in summer.

## Biograd-na-Moru

*Phone code: 023*
*Colour map 3, grid B3*
*Population: 5,259*

Overlooking the Pašman Channel, 20 km southeast of Zadar, the package resort of Biograd offers little of cultural interest, though its proximity to the Kornati islands make it an important landmark for yachters, with two marinas and several charter companies hiring sailing boats on a weekly basis.

Historically, Biograd's greatest moment passed in 1102, when the Hungarian king, Koloman, was crowned King of Croatia and Dalmatia here, following the *Pacta Conventa*, an agreement between Croatian nobles and the Hungarian state. Sadly nothing of the medieval town remains, having been devastated by the Venetians in 1125. Although it was later rebuilt, it was destroyed once again by the townspeople themselves as they retreated from the Turks in 1646. Today it's a fairly unremarkable place, made up largely of the standard concrete block summer houses that were built along the coast during the tourist boom of the 1970's.

Behind Biograd lies **Vransko Jezero**, Croatia's largest lake: one of the country's few colonies of herons can be spotted in the ornithological reserve on the northwest shore. And last but not least, you will pass through Biograd if planning to visit the islands of Pašman and Ugljan: a regular *Jadrolinija* ferry service connects the town to Tkon on Pašman, which in turn is connected to Ugljan by a bridge.

Eating  **Cheap to mid-range**  *Restoran Guste*, Kralja Petra Svačića bb, T383025. A range of reasonably priced fish and seafood dishes, plus a children's menu with goodies such as *pljeskavica sa pomfritom* (beef burger and chips), are served at simple wooden tables and benches on a summer terrace.

Sport  **Bird-watching**  For information about visits to the ornithological reserve on Vransko Jezero contact the nature park office, Kralja Petra Svačića 2, Biograd, T383181, www.vransko-jezero.hr **Diving** *Albamaris*, T385435, www.albamaris-divecenter.de *Bougainville Diving*, T385900, www.bougainville.nl **Sailing** *Marina Kornati*, T383800. 600 berths, open all year. *Marina Šangulin*, T385020. 200 berths, open all year. The following charter companies are based in Biograd: *Full Team*, Ivana Mazuranića 7, T384502; *Gomar*, Splitska 21, T314807 and 384508, www.gomar.hr and *Sangulin*, Kraljice Jelene 3, T383738.

Tour operators  *Andea*, Kralja Petra Svačića 19, T383507, www.andea.org, organizes one-day boat trips to the islands of Kornati National Park.

Transport  All **buses** covering the coastal stretch from **Zadar** to **Šibenik** stop in Biograd.

# Kornati National Park

Lying parallel to the mainland coast midway between Zadar and Šibenik, *Colour map 3,* Kornati National Park covers an area 35 km long and 13 km wide, containing *grid B2/3* 89 islands, islets and reefs. Declared a national park in 1980 due to its wealth of underwater life and its unique natural beauty, the area is made up of crystal clear blue sea and a scattering of eerie 'moonscape' islands supporting scanty vegetation.

Although the Kornati are best explored by private sailing boat, they can also be visited **Ins & outs** as part of an organized day trip, arranged by private agencies operating from Zadar, *See Transport, page* Biograd-na-Moru, Murter, Vodice and Šibenik (see respective sections for details). *190, for further details* Entrance to the park costs 50Kn, which will be included in the price of the trip if you arrive as part of a group. If you're travelling by private boat, you should pay at any one of a number of kiosks scattered through the park from Jun-Sep, or at the national park head office in Murter, which operates the year through. Kornati National Park office is based in Murter (see page 258), Butina 2, T (022) 434662, www.kornati.hr

Having no fresh water sources and little fertile land, the Kornati passed **Sights** through the centuries with minimum human intervention. During the 17th century, Zadar noble families, with the blessing of the Venetians, used the islands for sheep rearing, employing serfs from Murter as shepherds. Later the *Murterini* bought rights to 90% of the Kornati, and continued to use them for seasonal farming; grazing sheep, cultivating olives, grapes and figs, and keeping bees (there are few wild animals here other than lizards). They also built some 300 simple stone cottages, mainly in sheltered coves, which they used as temporary homes when fishing or tending the land. Today many of these cottages, still without running water and electricity, have been turned over to tourism, and are available for rent through the summer months, often with a small boat included, as Robinson Crusoe retreats: amusingly enough, the 're-turn-to-nature' idea appeals particularly to affluent city folk (see Sleeping).

The largest island, Kornat, is 25 km long and up to 2.4 km wide. Travelling along the west coast by boat you'll pass a series of dramatic cliffs plummeting 100 m down to the sea, punctuated by small coves, many with pleasant sheltered beaches, and here and there an informal summer restaurant serving fresh fish at tables by the water's edge.

As they have never been truly inhabited, many of the smaller islets have no name, though you may come across amusing references to *Klobučar* (Hatmaker), *Balun* (Ball), *Košara* (Basket) or *Mrtvac* (Dead Man): according to local legend, when cross-questioned by Austro-Hungarian surveyors, the people of Murter invented these peculiar names in jest, and they have remained ever since.

Camping within Kornati National Park is strictly forbidden. The Murter-based agencies **Sleeping** *Coronata*, ōrtava Ratova 17, T (022) 435089, www.coronata.hr and *Kornat Turist*, Hrvatskih vladara 2, T (022) 435854/5, www.kornatturist.hr both have a selection of Robinson Crusoe type accommodation: simply furnished cottages with gas lighting and water from a well, no cars, no shops, and probably no neighbours.

North Dalmatia

**Eating**

*The restaurants listed here are all found on the west coast of the largest island, Kornat*

**Mid-range**  *Restoran Beban*, Uvala Gujka (Gujak Cove), T (099) 475739 (mob). *Beban* is one of the few restaurants in the area to offer *janjetina* (roast lamb), as well as *brodet* (fish stew), seafood and barbecued fish, from mid-Apr to early-Oct. *Restoran Quattro*, Uvala Strižnja (Strižnja Cove), T (022) 435187. *Quattro* offers a decent range of Dalmatian meat and fish dishes, from early-May to late-Oct. *Restoran Solana*, Uvala Šipnate (Šipnata Cove), T (022) 435433. A tiny eatery with seating for just 30 people and a menu including seafood risotto, barbecued fish, steaks, and pancakes. Open early-Jun to mid-Sep. *Restoran Strižnja,* Uvala Strižnja (Strižnja Cove), no phone. Close by to *Restoran Quattro*, *Strižnja* serves up seafood risotto and pasta dishes, *brodet* (fish stew), seafood and barbecued fish, from early-May to early-Oct.

**Sport**

**Diving**  Within the park diving it is restricted to organized groups. Although there are no sub-aqua clubs based on the Kornati, the following local clubs can arrange dives here: *Albamaris*, Biograd-na-Moru, T(023) 385435, www.albamaris-divecenter.de *Aquanaut*, Murter, T(022) 434988, www.aquanaut.ingob.com *Bougainville Diving*, Biograd-na-Moru, T(023) 385900, www.bougainville.nl *Neptun-Sub*, Šibenik, T(022) 331444, www.neptun.sub.hr *Odysseus Diving*, Šibenik, T(022) 577733, www.odysseusdiving-sibenik.hr *Zadar Sub*, Zadar, T(023) 214848 www.zadarsub.hr

**Sailing**  Setting down anchor around the Kornati is restricted to 16 designated coves. **ACI Marina** at Piškera, within the national park, T 099 470009 (mob), open mid-Mar to late-Oct, 150 berths. Facilities include water and power supplies, a restaurant, telephone, toilets and showers, and a grocery. The nearest gas station is in Zaglav on Dugi Otok (19.5 km). **ACI Marina** at Žut, just outside the national park, to the northeast, T (099) 470028 (mob), open mid-Mar to late-Oct, 120 berths. Facilities include water and power supplies, a restaurant, telephone, toilets and showers, and a grocery. The nearest gas station is in Zaglav on Dugi Otok (13 km).

**Transport**  There are no ferries to the Kornati. The only way to arrive is as part of an organized tour group or by private boat.

North Dalmatia

# Introducing Central Dalmatia

More mountainous and less developed than the northern regions, Central Dalmatia is home to several of Croatia's most beautiful medieval coastal towns, and some of its worst hotels. The main cultural and economic pulse is **Split**. Overlooking the blue waters of the Adriatic and backed by the rugged **Dinaric Mountains**, it is one of the most extraordinary places of the late Roman world. Today the **Roman palace** is filled with elegant Venetian-Gothic town houses and ringed by high-rise suburbs, which some find daunting, and others find strangely exhilarating. With a busy port and regular ferry and catamaran services, it's a perfect point of arrival if you're coming from Italy, and a good launching pad if you intend to explore the surrounding islands.

Central Dalmatia

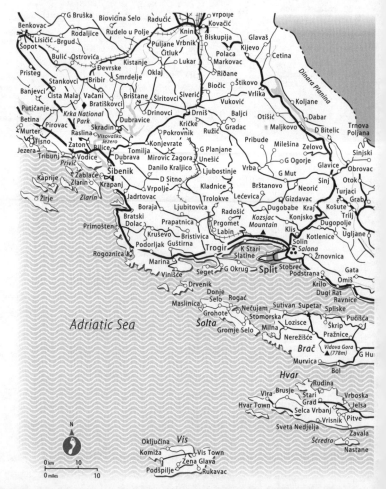

The nearest, and probably the least appealing island is **Brač**. Its best-known resort, **Bol**, heaves with tourists through July and August, each one eager to find a space for their beach towel on the undeniably stunning Zlatni Rat beach. Outside peak season, however, it's well worth the trip, and can be combined with a hike up to **Vidova Gora**, the highest peak on all the Adriatic islands.

For many people the most beautiful island is **Hvar**, and its capital, **Hvar Town**, now has the unenviable honour of being Croatia's most hip resort. Built around a small harbour and backed by a hilltop fortress, the old town is made up of winding cobbled streets, which converge on a vast piazza (the biggest in Dalmatia), overlooked by trendy late-night bars and several excellent restaurants. The rest of the island falls away into a wilderness of lavender fields and vineyards.

Further out to sea lies **Vis**, Croatia's most distant inhabited island and a place that, for now at least, has been spared of commercial tourism. Its two main settlements, **Vis Town** and **Komiža**, are popular with yachters and offer a selection of authentic fish restaurants and wine cellars, but for that reason are fast becoming known as desirable destinations.

Back on the mainland, north of Split lies the little medieval town of **Trogir**, and further north still Dalmatia's second largest city **Šibenik**, with its magnificent 15th-century cathedral and soaring unemployment. Nearby **Krka National Park** conceals a series of dramatic waterfalls, hemmed in on each side by steep wooded slopes. South of Split, the **Makarska Rivijera** offers a string of decent pebble beaches and making a good starting point for hiking up **Mount Biokovo** in spring and autumn.

Central Dalmatia

## Things to do in Central Dalmatia

- Spend a day in Split exploring Diocletian's **Roman Palace**, page 197.
- Also in Split, visit the **Meštrović Gallery** to see the works of Croatia's greatest modern sculptor, page 204.
- Soak up the sun on **Zlatni Rat beach** on the island of Brač, page 241.
- Stay a night in **Hvar Town**, on Hvar, currently Dalmatia's most fashionable resort, page 221.
- Check out **Modra Spilja** (Blue Cave) on the island of Biševo, near Vis, page 237.
- Visit **Krka National Park**, near Šibenik, where a series of spectacular waterfalls thunder through a steep-sided, wooded valley, page 255.

# Split

*Phone code: 021*
*Colour map 3, grid C5*
*Population: 188,694*

*Split is Croatia's second largest city, after Zagreb, and the main point of arrival for visitors to Dalmatia. Unfortunately, in the past Split was regarded as a transit centre rather than a destination in itself, and consequently suffers from a dearth of good hotels and restaurants. However, if you do decide to stay, you'll undoubtedly be impressed by the extraordinary mix of the old and the new: magnificent ancient buildings, romantic cobbled back streets, lively open-air seaside cafés and a vibrant nightlife.*

*Outside the historic centre there are some lovely **coastal paths**, each side of town, so you can explore the whole place on foot. A 15-minute walk from the centre rises **Marjan Hill** – a nature reserve planted with pine forests, palms, algaves and cacti – offering a wonderful panorama over the city rooftops, the sea and the surrounding islands. You'll find a number of well-equipped **marinas**, where charter companies hire out yachts for those who wish to explore the region in the best way possible, by sailing boat.*

## Ins and outs

**Getting there**
*See Transport, page 209, for further details*

*Split is 365 km from Zagreb, 448 km from Pula, 350 km from Rijeka and 216 km from Dubrovnik*

Through summer there are regular flights from most European capitals. The airport is at Kaštela, 25 km from the city centre. The airport bus leaves 1½ hrs before each flight, 30Kn. For bus departure information, T203305. The city **port** is on Obala kneza domogoj, a 10-min walk from the palace walls. *Jadrolinija, SEM* and *Adriatica* run regular overnight ferries to Ancona (Italy), departing daily at 2100 through summer. The *Jadrolinija* coastal ferry from Rijeka to Dubrovnik stops at Split en route. *Jadrolinija* and *SEM* operate ferry and catamaran services to the islands of Šolta, Brač, Hvar, Vis, Korčula and Lastovo. The bus station is on Obala kneza Domogoja 12, next to the train station. There are regular services to the major cities in Croatia and to nearby European cities. The train station is on Obala kneza Domogoja 10, a 5-min walk from the city centre, in front of the port. There are services to Zagreb, Knin and Šibenik.

**Getting around**
The historic centre, where the city's main sights are found, is contained within the walls of Diocletian's Palace which is closed to traffic. A pleasant 20-min stroll along the seafront will bring you to the Museum of Croatian Archaeological Monuments and the Meštrović Gallery. Alternatively, bus no 12 from Sv Frane (Church of St Francis) opposite Trg Republike, at the end of the Riva, runs every 40 mins along Šetalište Ivana Meštrovića, to Bene recreation centre at the end of Marjan Peninsula, passing both the Mestrovic Gallery and the Museum of Croatian Archaeological Monuments en route.

## Arriving at night

◀

Both the airport and bus station are perfectly safe if you arrive late at night. All incoming Croatia Airlines flights are met by an airport bus, which will transport passengers to the city centre. Charter companies with incoming flights usually arrange their own bus transfers. All reputable hotels have someone on duty through the night – book ahead and let them know that you are arriving late. In summer, bars in the centre and along the seafront remain open till at least 0200, so you'll still find the city reasonably animated if you arrive late. All ferry and catamaran services to Split arrive during the day or early evening.

The main Tourist Information Centre (TIC), T342606, www.visitsplit.com, is in Crkvica Sv Roka (the former chapel of St Rocco) on Peristil. The Tourist Guide Service, for guided tours, is also on Peristil. The Turisticki Biro, T342544, at Obala Hrvatskog narodnog preporoda 12, on the seafront, is the place to go to find out about private accommodation. **Tourist information centres**

Being a busy port town, Split sees people coming and going the year through. The major cultural event, the *Split Summer Festival*, takes place from mid-Jul to mid-Aug. During this period the city becomes extremely crowded, with tourists from all over the world coming to see Split itself, and passing through on their way to the islands. **Best time to visit**

The climate remains reasonably mild through winter. Temperatures very rarely fall below freezing, and it's quite feasible to drink morning coffee on the seafront in Jan, even though the surrounding mountains are often snow-covered between Dec and Mar. Having said this, Split is probably best visited in spring or autumn, when temperatures are neither too hot nor too chilly, and most tourist attractions and facilities are working.

## History

According to the 10th-century Byzantine Emperor, Constantine VII, the name Split is a contraction of *Spalatum*, from *palatium*, meaning 'Palace'. However, contemporary scholars believe that the name is more likely to have derived from the Greek name for the area, *Aspalathos*, after broom, the flowering shrub that colours the surrounding hills yellow in spring time.

Although this second theory suggests the Greeks may have had a settlement here, the founding of Split is generally recognized as 295, the year Roman Emperor Diocletian ordered the building of a vast palace in his native Dalmatia. He chose this site due to its undeniable splendour, and its proximity to *Salona*, the largest Roman settlement in Dalmatia at the time and his presumed birthplace. In 305, when the palace was completed, the emperor resigned from his position in Nikomedia (present day Izmir, in Turkey) and retired to his beloved homeland, where he lived the life of a near god – which indeed he believed himself to be – until his death in 313.

Over the following decades, various Roman rulers used the palace as a retreat, and the penultimate Western Roman Emperor, Julius Nepos, lived here after having been overthrown in 475. However, by the late sixth century the palace had fallen into abandon.

Life returned in 615, when refugees from *Salona* – which had been sacked by tribes of Avars and Slavs – found shelter within the palace walls, and divided up the vast imperial apartments and underground substructure into modest living quarters. They brought with them the bones of their saint, Duje (Domnius), the former Bishop of Salona, and ironically placed them in the

Central Dalmatia

## 24 hours in the city

Begin the day in true Split style, with a 'wake-me-up' coffee on the palm-lined **Riva** (seafront). Spend the morning within the walls of **Diocletian's Palace**, contemplating the Roman Peristil, climbing the Cathedral **bell tower**, and checking out the stalls on the **Pazar** (open-air fruit and vegetable market) and **Ribarnica** (covered fish market). If you're truly hungry stop for lunch at *Pizzeria Galija*. Otherwise, pick up a freshly made sandwich at *Rizzo*, and walk along the seafront past the ACI marina to the gardens of **Sustipan**, and picnic in the shade of the cypress trees.

After lunch, visit the **Meštrović Gallery** and the **Holy Cross Chapel**, to see the works of Croatia's best-known modern sculptor. Hike back to town through the pinewoods of **Marjan Nature Reserve**, passing the churches of **Sv Jere** and **Sv Nikola** en route, and stop for a drink at *Vidilica Café*, where you have great views over the city rooftops and the harbour.

Return to the centre through the winding cobbled streets of **Varoš**. If the *Summer Festival* is in progress, be sure not to miss the open-air evening opera on Peristil. Either before or after the performance, head for dinner at *Kod Jose*, an old-fashioned Dalmatian 'konoba' serving excellent fish and seafood, which should be accompanied by generous quantities of local wine. Finish with a nightcap, either in the candle lit courtyard at *Ghetto Club* within the palace walls, or at *Club Tropicana* on Bačvice Bay, overlooking the sea. If you still have energy *Metropolis* is where you can go for the sounds of commercial, techno and rock.

late-emperor's mausoleum – Diocletian had violently opposed Christianity and had himself ordered the execution of the bishop. By the 11th century the settlement had spread beyond the ancient walls, and during the 14th century, an urban conglomeration west of the palace was fortified, thus doubling the city area.

Split came under Venice from 1420 to 1797, a period of increased trade – as a gateway to the Balkan interior Split became one of the Adriatic's main trading ports – coupled with the ever-growing fear of an Ottoman invasion. The trade boom led to economic well-being and a wealth of cultural activity – local architects, notably Juraj Dalmatinac, endowed the city with beautiful Venetian-Gothic palaces, and writers, such as the poet Marko Marulic, began producing sophisticated Croatian-language literature. The Ottoman threat led the construction of an elaborate defence-system – in the 17th century the entire city was surrounded by polygonal fortifications with projecting bastions. With the fall of Venice, the Hapsburgs ruled the city from 1813 to 1918, and connected it overland with Central Europe and the rest of the Austro-Hungarian Empire by the construction of the Split-Zagreb-Vienna railway line.

After the First World War, Split entered the Kingdom of Serbs, Croats and Slovenes (later renamed the Kingdom of Yugoslavia). As Zadar, formerly Dalmatia's official capital, had been awarded to Italy, Split took over as the region's economic and administrative centre. This period was also important creatively, with the sculptor Ivan Meštrović, painter Emanuel Vidović and poet Tin Uljevic all representing Split on the Yugoslav cultural scene.

The Second World War saw Split under occupation, first by Italy, then Germany, and the Allies caused further destruction through bombing raids aimed at 'liberation'. German occupation ended when Partisan units entered

Split in October 1944, and in 1945 Federal Yugoslavia was born. The post-war years, under Tito, saw increased industrialization, with the expansion of the shipyards and the cement factory. This brought about an influx of workers from other parts of the country, which in turn led to the building of high-rise apartment blocks in the suburbs.

During the war of independence Split was attacked only once – in 1991 the Yugoslav Navy (who had their main base here) briefly shelled the city from sea, but there were no serious consequences. However, economically and socially the city suffered from the complete collapse of the manufacturing and tourist industries, the exodus of many educated citizens, the arrival of countless refugees and inevitable political corruption. A decade later, unemployment remains a major problem, though factories are gradually reopening and tourism is back on its feet.

# Sights

## Within the walls of the Diocletian's Palace

The heart of the city lies within the massive walls of the palace, a splendid third-century structure combining the qualities of an imperial villa and a Roman garrison. Rectangular in plan, this monumental edifice measures approximately 215 m by 180 m, with walls 2 m thick and 25 m high. Each of the four outer walls bears a gate: **Zlatna Vrata** (Golden Gate), **Željezna Vrata** (Iron Gate), **Srebrena Vrata** (Silver Gate) and **Mjedna Vrata** (Bronze Gate). Originally, there were two main streets: the Decumanus, a transversal street running east-west from Srebrena Vrata to Željezna Vrata, and the Cardo, a longitudinal street running from the main entrance, Zlatna Vrata. Both streets were colonnaded, and intersected at the central public meeting space, Peristil. On the east side of Peristil lay the mausoleum, and on the west, Jupiter's Temple. Diocletian's imperial apartments were located on the south side of the palace, overlooking the sea, while the servants and soldiers quarters were on the north side, overlooking the main land entrance. The stone used to build the palace came from the nearby quarries of Brač and Trogir, while the architects themselves may well have originated from the east – the names *Filotas* and *Zotikos* have been found, engraved in Greek within the palace walls.

From the early Middle Ages onwards, new buildings were erected within the palace, so that the original Roman layout has been largely obscured. The first detailed plans and drawings of how it must have once looked were published in 1764, by the Scottish neoclassical architect, Robert Adam, in *The Ruins of the Palace of the Emperor Diocletian at Spalato in Dalmatia*. Adam, who is generally regarded as the greatest British architect of the 18th century, was fascinated by the scale and quality of Diocletian's building projects, and stayed in Split for five weeks in 1757 to investigate the palace. By asking permission to enter people's houses and inspecting their walls, he managed to trace the original Roman structure through the medieval buildings. No easy task – the Venetian governor of the time suspected the Scot of spying and nearly had him deported. Fortunately Adam completed his research, and the space and symmetry of Diocletian's Palace is said to have inspired some of his greatest buildings, which in turn became models for neoclassical architects throughout Europe.

*In 1979 the complex was listed as a UNESCO World Heritage Site. Excavation and restoration work is still being carried out*

Central Dalmatia

**Podrum (Underground chambers)** The south façade of the palace, which once rose directly from the sea, is now beside the coastal promenade lined with cafés and palm trees, officially called Obala Hrvatskog narodnog preporoda, but better known to locals as the **Riva** (seafront). From here **Mjedna Vrata** (Bronze Gate) – where Roman ships would once have docked – leads into the Podrum. According to the Byzantine Emperor Constantine VII (905-59), Diocletian used this vast space as a prison, "in which he cruelly confined the saints whom he tormented". Today, most of this labyrinth of vaulted underground halls remains closed except for special events such as craft fairs and concerts. However, through daylight hours the main passageway, lined with stalls selling handmade souvenirs, is kept open and leads directly onto Peristil.
■ *0600-2300. Between Obala Hrvatskog narodnog preporoda and Peristil.*

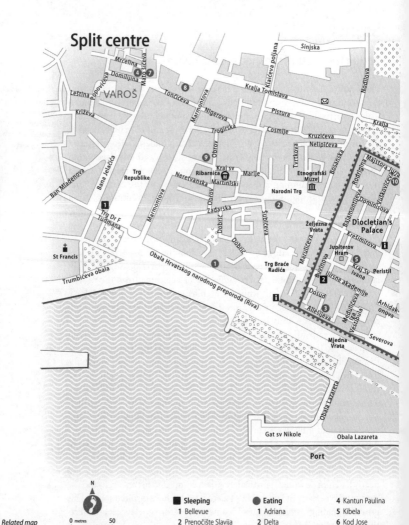

# Split centre

*Central Dalmatia*

**Sleeping**
1 Bellevue
2 Prenočište Slavija

**Eating**
1 Adriana
2 Delta
3 Dioklecijan

4 Kantun Paulina
5 Kibela
6 Kod Jose
7 Pizzeria Galija

*Related map*
*Split, page 204*

0 metres 50
0 yards 50

From Roman times up to the present day, this spacious central courtyard has been the main public meeting place within the palace walls. It is here that Diocletian would have made his public appearances – probably flanked by a guard, and dressed in an elaborately decorated silk toga – and his subjects would have kneeled or even prostrated themselves before him.

**Peristil (Peristyle)**
*Each year from mid-July to mid-August, Peristil becomes an impressive open-air stage, hosting classical music and opera as part of the Split Summer Festival*

The two longer sides of the square are lined with marble columns, topped by Corinthian capitals and richly ornamented cornices linked by arches. On the east side stands Diocletian's mausoleum (now the Cathedral), guarded by a black granite Egyptian sphinx dating back to 1500BC. On the west side, the Roman arches have been incorporated into the late 15th-century Grisogono- Cipci Palace, now housing *Luxor Café*. Some architectural critics have compared this particular building to Andrea Palladio's 16th-century *Palazzo di Giustizia* (Palace of Justice) in Vicenza, and it could be that the Italian architect was influenced by sketches of Peristil, known to be in his possession.

At the south end of the square, immediately above the podrum exit, four columns mark the monumental arched gateway to the **Vestibule**, a domed space that served as the main entrance into Diocletian's private living quarters. To each side of the gate lies a 16th-century chapel: one now houses a small art gallery, and the other the Tourist Guide Service. At the opposite end of Peristil stands the small Renaissance *Crkvica Sv Roka* (Chapel of St Rocco) from 1516, now the Tourist Information Centre.

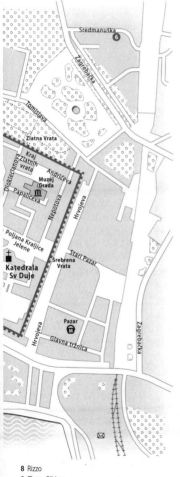

Diocletian's **mausoleum**, an octagonal structure surrounded by 24 columns, now forms the main body of Split's Cathedral. Before the third century, to prevent the spread of disease, dead bodies (no matter how illustrious) were disposed of outside city walls. However, Diocletian had raised the Emperor's status to that of divine, so as an 'immortal' he was to be an exception. Upon his death, he was laid to rest here, though his body later mysteriously disappeared. During the seventh century, refugees from *Salona* converted the mausoleum into an early Christian church, ironically dedicating it to Sv Duje, after Bishop Domnius of Salona, who Diocletian had beheaded in 304 for sowing the seeds of Christianity.

**Katedral Sveti Duje (Cathedral of St Domnius)**

In 1214, local sculptor Andrije Buvina carved the wooden Cathedral

**8** Rizzo
**9** Zlatna Ribica
**10** Zlatna Vrata Pizzeria

▶ ## A sportsman from Split

*"The trouble with me is that every match I play against five opponents: umpire, crowd, ball boys, court, and myself".*
Goran Ivanišević

One of the best-loved bad boys of tennis (known for shouting and swearing at umpires, insulting linesmen and lineswomen, smashing rackets and kicking the net), Ivanišević was born in Split on 13 September 1971. He started playing at the age of seven (and also claims to have broken his first racket the same year) at Firule Tennis Club above Bačvice Bay. A natural sportsman, he turned professional at 17. His powerful left-handed serve and aggressive style saw him scale the ranks to be rated ninth best player in the world by 1990. Around this time, his sister was diagnosed with cancer, from which she has since recovered, inspiring Goran to put extra energy into the game to raise money for her medical treatment. By 1992, the year he carried the Croatian flag at the Olympics in Barcelona, from which he brought home bronze medals from both the singles and doubles, he was ranked second in the world. But the victory he most wanted, and the one he always failed to grab, was the Wimbledon Cup. He reached the final in 1992 and lost to Andre Agassi, and reached it again in 1994 and 1998, losing both times to Pete Sampras. By 2001, almost considered a has-been, he received a wild card to play once more at

the Lawn Tennis Championship. Referred to as a "one-shot wonder" by the BBC commentator and former Wimbledon champion John McEnroe at the beginning of the tournament, and rated as a 125/1 outsider by the bookies, he stunned fans and colleagues by knocking out rival after rival, to make it once more to the semi-final, this time versus Tim Henman. As usual, neither his mother nor girlfriend was among the spectators (apparently they make him nervous), but his firmest supporter, his father, was there to watch him play from start to finish. He made it through 6-3, 3-6, 6-3, 2-6, 9-7, and in a moving speech dedicated his win to a dear friend, the late Dražen Petrović, the NBA basketball player from Šibenik who was tragically killed in a car crash in Germany in 1993.

Back in his hometown of Split, the ships in the harbour blasted their sirens and children let off firecrackers, and the following night more than 100,000 people gathered to give him a massive welcome home party on the seafront, with music and dancing into the early hours. At present he is building a luxury villa overlooking the sea close to the Museum of Croatian Archaeological Monuments. He spends his summer holidays cruising around the Dalmatian islands on a 20-m yacht, and rumour has it that when he retires he plans to open a tennis school in Split.

**doors** (now kept behind glass screens in the main entrance). They are quite magnificent, ornamented with reliefs portraying 28 scenes from the life of Christ.

The interior space is round in plan: eight columns with Corinthian capitals support a central dome (symbolizing the Emperor's divine nature), which would originally have been decorated with golden mosaics. To the left as you enter, stands a 13th-century hexagonal **Romanesque stone pulpit**, with richly carved decoration. To each side of the main altar lies a gothic chapel. To the left is *Kapela Sv Staša* (Chapel of St Anastasius), executed by Juraj Dalmatinac in 1448 and dedicated to the martyr and the co-protector of Split, a clothmerchant from *Aquileia*, near present-day Venice. St Anastasius moved to *Salona* in Dalmatia and painted a cross on the door of his shop. As Christianity was outlawed at that time (AD304), he was arrested and drowned, thrown into the River Jadro a millstone around his neck. *Kapela Sv*

Dujma (Chapel of St Domnius) stands to the right, completed by Bonino of Milan in 1427 and dedicated to the equally unfortunate Bishop Domnius.

In front of the main entrance, the elegant 60-m Romanesque-gothic **belltower** was constructed in stages between the 12th and 16th centuries, but then collapsed at the end of the 19th century and had to be rebuilt in 1908. If you have a good head for heights, climb to the top for a bird's-eye view of the palace layout. ■ *Cathedral daily 0800-1200, 1630-1900. Bell tower daily, May-Sep 0900- 1900, Oct-Apr 0900-1200. 5Kn. Peristil.*

Leaving Peristil by the dark, narrow passageway of Kraj Sv Ivana you come to Jupiterov Hram, which would originally have stood in its own courtyard, directly facing Diocletian's mausoleum across the Peristil. Jupiter was the ruler of the Gods, and Diocletian proclaimed himself Jupiter's earthly representative to Rome.

**Jupiterov Hram (Jupiter's Temple)**

During the Middle Ages the temple was converted into a baptistery. Inside, beneath a beautifully coffered barrel vault, an 11th-century baptismal font is carved with a stone relief showing a medieval ruler, possibly the Croatian King Zvonimir, seated on a throne. ■ *Admission upon request. Ask at the Tourist Guide Service on Peristil.*

East of Peristil stands Srebrena Vrata (Silver Gate), leading onto Pazar, the colourful open-air fruit and vegetable **market**, held daily just outside the palace walls. It's well worth a look to size up the season's fresh produce: broccoli, spinach, wild asparagus and strawberries in spring; tomatoes, red peppers, peaches and melons in summer; grapes, pomegranates and walnuts in autumn, and cabbages, potatoes and oranges in winter. Thankfully the supermarket culture has yet to reach Dalmatia, and the only way to shop is to buy local seasonal produce, which means that while choice may be limited, quality is assured. ■ *Mon-Sat 0700-1300, Sun 0700-1100.*

**Pazar**

**Central Dalmatia**

The 15th-century Papaliᵃ Palace, designed by Juraj Dalmatinac, is one of the city's finest examples of Venetian-Gothic architecture, with typical elements of a courtyard and ground-floor loggia, and an outer staircase leading up to the first floor. Inside there's a collection of medieval weaponry, and the dining room on the first floor is furnished just as it would have been when the Papaliᵃ family lived here, giving a good picture of 15th-century aristocratic lifestyle. On the ground floor you'll probably also find a collection of oil paintings donated to the city by local artist Emanuel Vidoviᵃ (1870-1953), though it is due to be moved to a new permanent exhibition space, the Emanuel Vidoviᵃ Gallery, sometime in the future. ■ *Jul-Aug 0900-1200 and 1800-2100, Sep-Jun Tue-Fri 0900-1600, Sat-Sun 1000-1200. 10Kn. T341240. Papaliceva 1.*

**Muzej Grada (City Museum)**

This, the largest and most monumental of the four palace gates, originally opened onto the road to the nearby Roman settlement of *Salona* (see page 214). It was walled up during the 14th century, and only uncovered again during the 19th. Just outside the gate stands a colossal bronze statue of Grgur Ninski (Bishop Gregory of Nin) by Ivan Meštroviᵃ. The ninth-century Bishop campaigned for the use of the Slav language in the Croatian Church, as opposed to Latin, thus infuriating Rome. The statue of him was created in 1929 and placed on Peristil (where its proportions must have been daunting) to mark the 1,000th anniversary of the Split Synod. Under Italian occupation in 1941, the statue was seen as a symbol of Croatian nationalism and promptly removed. It was re-erected here in 1957.

**Zlatna Vrata (Golden Gate)**

*Touch the big toe on the left foot of the bronze statue of Grgur Ninski, which is considered a good luck charm, and has been worn gold by hopeful passers-by*

## The historic centre west of the palace walls

During the 13th and the 14th centuries, the town spread outside the Roman walls. A second centre developed west of the palace, and was in turn fortified in the 14th century. From then on, Peristil remained the focus of ecclesiastic activity, while Narodni Trg became the city's municipal centre.

**Narodni Trg (People's Square)** From Peristil, Krešmirova leads to **Željezna Vrata** (Iron Gate) in the western wall of the palace, linking the 'old' and 'new' parts of the historic centre. Beyond the gate lies Narodni Trg, better known to locals as *Pjaca*, from the Italian, 'piazza'. Paved with gleaming white marble, this is contemporary Split's main square, and you'll find a number of open-air cafés here, where you can happily sit and watch the world go by.

In the middle of the square stands the former Town Hall, constructed under Venice in 1443, and easily recognized by its three pointed Gothic arches. Inside lies Croatia's oldest **Etnografski Muzej** (Ethnographic Museum) founded in 1910 and displaying folk costumes from Dalmatia. ■ *Mon-Fri 1000-1500. 10Kn. T344164. Narodni Trg 1.*

**Trg Braće Radića (Radic Brothers' Square)** From Narodni Trg, Šubićeva leads south to Trg Braće Radića, better known to locals as **Vocni Trg** (Fruit Square) after the open-air market that used to be held here. In the centre of the square stands a statue of the local poet Marko Marulić (1450-1524), completed by Ivan Meštrović in 1924. **Hrvojeva Kula** (Hrvoje's Tower), an octagonal tower, now housing the tiny *AS Café*, is the remains of a 15th-century Venetian citadel, closing the square from the seafront.

**Ribarnica (Fish Market)** West of Narodni Trg lies the Ribarnica, where you'll find a daily selection of locally caught fresh fish and seafood. ■ *Mon-Sat 0700-1300, Sun 0700-1100. Kraj Sv Marije.*

**Varoš** West of the centre, built into the hill leading up to Marjan lies Varoš, a labyrinth of winding cobbled streets and traditional Dalmatian stone cottages, dating back to the 17th century. The oldest church in Varoš is the tiny 12th-century **Romanesque Sv Nikola** (St Nicholas), hidden away in the side street of Stagnja.

## Outside the historic centre

**Arheološki Muzej (Archaeological Museum)** A 10-minute walk north of the palace walls lies the Arheološki Muzej, founded in 1820, and in its present location since 1921. You'll find a well-displayed collection of Roman artefacts from *Salona* – jewellery, ceramics, glassware and coins – plus a few Greek pieces from *Issa*, on the island of Vis. Heavier stone objects such as sarcophagi are on show outdoors in the arcaded courtyard and leafy gardens. ■ *Tue-Sun 0900-1400. 20Kn. T318714, Zrinjsko-Frankopanska 25.*

**Pomorski Muzej (Maritime Museum)** A 10-minute walk east of the palace walls, past the old stone cottages of Radunica, brings you to Gripe Fortress, built by the Venitians as part of the 17th-century city fortification system against the possibility of an Ottoman invasion. Inside lies the Pomorski Muzej, entertaining enough even for those who know little about shipping. There are two distinct sections, one dedicated to naval war and the other to naval trading. You'll see scale models of ships, sailing equipment and a fine collection of early 20th-century naval paintings

## Diocletian the Builder   ◀

*Diocletian initiated a number of extraordinarily grandiose building projects. His best-known surviving monument is probably the* Terme di Diocleziano *(Diocletian Baths) in Rome. In 298, almost a century after Caracalla had given the Eternal City his gargantuan baths, Diocletian, who was at that time based in Nicomedia, decided to outshine his imperial predecessor by commissioning Rome's largest and most luxurious bathing establishment. Between 300 and 305, ten thousand Christian prisoners were used as forced labour to construct this massive edifice, comprising mosaic floors and marble façades, and covering 13 hectares (32 acres). It was designed to accommodate 3,000 bathers, and included hot baths, steam baths and cold baths, plus dressing rooms, gymnasiums, meeting rooms, libraries and gardens.*

*In the draft introduction to The Ruins of the Palace of the Emperor Diocletian at Spalato in Dalmatia, the 18th century Scottish neoclassical architect Robert Adam explains that he was particularly fascinated by Diocletian, "Not only from his*

*Baths at Rome, but from the accounts of his extraordinary expenses bestowed on building, at Nicomedia, Milan, Palmyra and many other places of his Empire".*

*And Lactantius, a professor of Literature appointed by Diocletian in Nicomedia, writes of the Emperor's extravagance in building, "Diocletian had a limitless passion for building, which led to an equally limitless scouring of the provinces to raise workers, craftsmen, wagons, and whatever is necessary for building operations. Here he built basilicas, there a circus, a mint, an arms-factory, here he built a house for his wife, there one for his daughter. Suddenly a great part of the city [Nicomedia] was destroyed, and all the inhabitants started to migrate with their wives and children, as if the city had been captured by the enemy. And when these buildings had been completed and the provinces ruined in the process, he would say: 'They have not been built rightly; they must be done in another way'. They then had to be pulled down and altered – perhaps only to come down a second time."*

Central Dalmatia

by Alexander Kircher. Of particular note are the world's first torpedoes, made in Rijeka in 1866, designed by a Croat, Ivan Blaž Lupis, and manufactured by an Englishman, Robert Whitehead. ■ *Tue-Sun 0900-1300 and 1800-2100. 15Kn. T347346, Glagoljaška 18.*

West of the historic centre, a 15-minute uphill hike through Varoš brings you to *Vidilica Café*, where an ample terrace offers panoramic views over the city. From here you can begin to explore Marjan, a nature reserve planted with Aleppo pines, holm oak, cypresses and Mediterranean shrubs such as rosemary and broom, located on a compact peninsula, 3.5 km long. From Vidilica, a path along the south side of Majan leads to the 13th-century Romanesque church of **Sv Nikola** (St Nicholas), and further on still to the 15th-century church of **Sv Jere** (St Jerome), built on the remains of an ancient temple.

**Marjan**
*Nearby is a medieval cave hermitage carved into the cliffs. Each year in April the Marjan Cup free-climbing contest is held here*

The highest peak, **Telegrin**, rises 178 m and offers panoramic views of Trogir and Čiovo to the west, Kozjak, Mosor, Kaštela Bay, Solin and Klis to the north, as well as the islands of Šolta, Brač, Hvar and Vis to the south. At the western tip of Marjan lies **Bene**, a recreation area with a family beach and sports facilities, overlooking the sea and backed by pinewoods.

The gardens of Sustipan, planted with elegant cypress trees and dotted with park benches, offers memorable views out to sea, and over the ACI Marina back to town. A Benedictine monastery was established here in the 11th

**Sustipan**

century, only to be abandoned 300 years later. The foundations of the early medieval church of **Sv Stipe** (St Stephen) can still be seen; in 1814 a second church was constructed amid the ruins, with fragments from the earlier structure built into the new walls. The centrepiece to the gardens is a curious neo-classical pavilion, erected by the French in the 19th century, when Split spent a brief period under Napoleon's Illyrian Provinces.

**Muzej Hrvatskih Arheoloških Spomenika (Museum of Croatian Archaeological Monuments)** West of town, overlooking the sea and sheltered to the north by Marjan Hill, lies the upmarket residential area of Meje. Here you'll find the museum, a modern three-story building opened in 1975, displaying early Croatian religious art from between the seventh and 12th centuries. The most interesting exhibits are fine stone carvings decorated with plaitwork design, reminiscent of the geometric patterns typical of Celtic art. In the garden stand several *stećci*, monolithic stone tombs dating back to the cult of the Bogomils, an anti-imperial sect that developed in the Balkans during the 10th century. ■ *Tue-Sat 0900-1600, Sun 0900-1200. 15Kn. T358420. Šetalište Ivana Meštrovića bb, overlooking the sea, 2 km west of the centre.*

**Galerija Meštrović (Meštrović Gallery)** Close by lies one of Split's most delightful cultural institutions: the Galerija Meštrović. Croatian sculptor Ivan Meštrović designed this monumental villa in the early 1930's, and used it as his summer residence and studio until fleeing the country during the Second World War. On display in the villa and the garden are almost 200 sculptures and reliefs, in wood, marble, stone and bronze, created between the begining of the century and 1946. The entrance ticket is also valid for the **Holy Cross Chapel** within Kaštelet, a 17th-century complex bought by Meštrović in 1932, situated 100 m down the road at Šetalište Ivana Meštrovića 39. Here you can see a cycle of New Testament bas-relief wood carvings, considered by many to be Meštrović's finest work. ■ *Jun-Sep Tue-Sat 1000-1800, Sun 1000-1400; Oct-May Tue-Sat 1000-1600, Sun 1000-1400. 15Kn. T358450, Šetalište Ivana Meštrovića 46.*

*Central Dalmatia*

## Split

*Detail map*
*A Split centre,*
*page 198*

0 metres 200
0 yards 200

■ Sleeping
1 Consul

2 Jadran
3 Marjan

4 Park

Locals generally prefer to go to the islands. However, the main city beach at **Beaches** Bacvica is clean and functional (if not very romantic); it is possible to rent a sun-bed and umbrella, and there are showers and a plethora of (rather noisy) bars. Bene, on the tip of Marjan Peninsula, offers a number of small, secluded rocky coves backed by pine trees; there are also showers and a pleasant bar for refreshments.

# Essentials

Due to the lack of good central hotels and restaurants, finding a place to eat and sleep in high season can be quite a challenge. Book a room as far in advance as possible to be assured of a place to stay. **Turisčki Biro**, Obala Hrvatskog narodnog preporoda 12, T342544, can arrange private accommodation in Split and the surrounding area.

## Sleeping

**A Hotel Park**, Hatzeov Perivoj 3, overlooking Bačvice Bay, a 10-min walk east of the pal- **Outside** ace walls, T406400, F406401, www.hotelpark-split.hr  In a 1920's building with a gar- **the walls** den and palm-lined terrace overlooking the sea, this hotel's 54 rooms are smart and ▪ on map, below modern following extensive renovation work completed in 2001. Facilities include a restaurant, meeting room, sauna and massage. **A Hotel Split**, Put Trstenika 19, over-looking the sea, a 25-min walk east of the centre, T303111, F303011, www.hotel split.hr  A white modern building hosting 135 rooms, each with a balcony and full modern comforts. Facilities include a hotel beach, outdoor pool, gym, sauna and mas-sage, plus a business centre and 4 function rooms.

**B Hotel Consul**, Trščanska 34, just off Domovinskog Rata, a 10-min walk from the cen-tre, T486080, F486079, www.hotel-consul.net  Situated in a leafy side street in a quiet residential area, this 17-room hotel is modern and comfortable. It's some distance from

Central Dalmatia

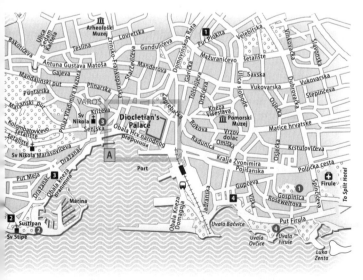

● **Eating**       2 Jugo       4 Šumica
1 Boban       3 Konoba Varoš

the sea, but there's a pretty summer terrace out front. **B** *Hotel Bellevue*, Bana Josipa Jelačića 2, overlooking Trg Republike, T585655, F362383. Located in a 19th-century building overlooking the seafront, this hotel is often criticized for being musty and poorly maintained. However, it's central and reasonably comfortable, and there's a pleasant old-fashioned café on the ground floor.

**C** *Hotel Marjan*, Obala Kneza Branimira 8, a 10-min walk west of the centre, overlooking the sea, T399211, F399210, www.hotel-marjan.com  Once the pride of the city, this modern tower block looks almost ready for demolition. However, the 106 rooms still in use are comfortable and well-equipped, and the staff friendly. All rooms have balconies, but you pay a little extra for a sea view. **C** *Hotel Jadran*, Sustipanjska Put 23, overlooking Uvala Zvončac, an enjoyable 15-min walk west of the centre, T398622, F398586. A pleasant but basic 1970's hotel overlooking the sea, close to the gardens of Sveti Stipan. In summer, guests have the use of a large outdoor swimming pool.

**Within the palace walls**
■ *on map, page 198*

**E** *Prenočište Slavija*, Buvinova 2, within the walls of Diocletian's Palace, T347053. This is the only hotel within the city walls. Standards are extremely basic, but the location more than makes up for it, if you don't mind the noise from the surrounding bars.

## Eating

**Outside the palace walls**
● *on map, page 204*

**Expensive**  *Restaurant Boban*, Hektoroviceva 49, off Spiničićeva, a couple of blocks back from Luka Zenta (Zenta Bay), T543300, www.restaurant-boban.com  Dating back to the 1970's, *Boban* is often cited as the best restaurant in town. Through summer, excellent fresh seafood dishes are served up on a leafy terrace. In winter, the rather kitsch dining room – black and silver chrome furnishing with violet table linens – comes into use. *Šumica*, Put Firula 6, T389897. Set in pinewoods overlooking Bačvice Bay, *Šumica* pulls the black-BMW crowd. The house speciality is tagliatelli with salmon and scampi, and popular meat dishes include barbecued steak, beef stroganoff and veal escalopes. Indoors the atmosphere tends to be over formal, but outdoor tables below the pine trees offer a blissful sea breeze.

**Mid-range**  *Adriana*, Obala Hrvatskog narodnog preporoda 6, T344079. A large and boisterous restaurant in the centre, with an ample terrace overlooking the seafront. Popular dishes include *rižot fruta di mare* (seafood risotto), *pohani sir* (cheese fried in breadcrumbs), *frigane lignje* (fried squid) and *ražnjiči* (kebabs). It gets unbelievably crowded in summer, and the music is often rather loud. *Kod Jose*, Sredmanuška 4, just outside the palace walls, close to Zlatna Vrata, T347397. Highly recommended, this typical Dalmatian *konobar* combines rough stonewalls, heavy wooden tables and candlelight. Top dishes are the risottos and fresh fish – the choice changes daily so you'll need to ask to see what is on offer. The waiters deserve a special mention for their discretion. *Konoba Varoš*, Ban Mladenova 7, between the centre and Marjan. T396138. Less atmospheric than *Kod Jose*, though some believe the food to be better here. The walls are decorated with seascapes and paintings of ships, and the ceiling hung with fishing nets. *Restoran Jugo*, close to *Hotel Jadran*, between the gardens of Sveti Stipan and the ACI Marina, T398900. Worth the 15-min walk from the centre for its summer terrace overlooking the marina, with a fantastic view of the city behind. Serves up passable Dalmatian dishes plus pizza.

**Cheap**  *Pizzeria Galija*, Tončićeva 12, T347932. Lying close to the fish market, *Galija* reputedly does the best pizzas in town. The informal atmosphere – wooden tables and benches, draught beer and wine by the glass – make it popular with locals. The owner, Željko Jerkov, is an Olympic gold medal winning basketball player. *Zlatna Ribica*, Kraj

Sv Marije 8, next to the fish market. A simple bar working Mon-Fri until 2000 and Sat until 1400, this is the place to eat *girice* (small fried fish) or *frigane ligne* (fried squid), accompanied by a glass of *bevanda* (half white wine, half water).

**Seriously cheap**  *Delta*, Narodni Trg 3 (main square). Bakery selling *pita sa sirom* (cheese in filo pastry), croissants, cakes and pastries. *Kantun Paulina*, Matosica 1, opposite *Galija Pizzeria*. The place to come for take-away *čevapčići*, a Bosnian meat speciality similar to kebabs. *Rizzo*, Tončićeva 6. Excellent sandwich bar, hidden away between the fish market and *Galija Pizzeria*. Oven-warm bread buns are filled with cheese, salami, tuna and salad of your choice.

**Cheap**  *Zlatna Vrata Pizzeria*, Majstora Jurja, close to Zlatna Vrata, T341834. Set in a magical Renaissance courtyard within the palace walls, this pizzeria turns out tasty pizzas, pasta dishes and a range of generous salads featuring tuna, chicken and feta. Try for a table outside: the interior is disappointing. *Dioklecijan* (Tri Volta), Dosud 9. No phone. Known affectionately as Tri Volta, after the 3 arches on the terrace that form part of the palace walls, this bar is popular with local fishermen. You can get *merenda* here the year through: early morning helpings of hearty dishes such as *gulaš* (goulash) and *tripice* (tripe). During summer the menu is refined and extended to cater for tourists. *Kibela*, Kraj Sv Ivana 5, in front of Jupiter's Temple, T346205. Hidden away in a narrow passageway off Peristil, this small family-run bar serves up simple *merenda* at lunchtime. During winter, the house speciality is *fažol sa kobasicom* (beans and sausage).

**Within the walls**
● *on map, page 198*

*Café Bellevue*, Trg Repubike. Old-fashioned café with summer terrace. *Luxor*, Peristil. Ideal stopping place while sightseeing, bang in front of the Cathedral. *Teak Caffe*, Majstora Jurja 11, close to *Zlatna Vrata* (Golden Gate). Currently 'in' with locals, the smart interior comprises rough stone walls and polished woodwork, and there are several tables outside in summer.

**Cafés**

## Bars and clubs

*Ghetto Club*, Dosud 10. The alternative crowd meet here for drinks, occasional exhibitions and performances. Through summer tables spill outside into a delightful candlelit courtyard. *Puls 2*, Buvinina 1, opposite Prenočište Slavija. Probably still the most 'in' bar for the mainstream 16-25 age group. Industrial interior with thumping techno music, crowded summer terrace outside.

**Within the palace walls**

*Jungle*, Uvala Zvončac, close to ACI marina, west of the palace walls. Popular bar with loud music and a terrace overlooking the sea, open until 0300 through summer. *Ovcice*, 5-min walk east of Kupalište Bačvice, east of the city centre, www.ovcice.hr Pleasant terrace café overlooking the sea, open until 0100. In summer you can hire an umbrella and sun-bed on the pebble beach during the day. *Pivnica Klara*, Kavanjinova 5, 10-min walk north of the palace walls. Good place for a beer, especially in summer when there are tables under the trees in the walled garden. *Tropic Club Equador*, Kupalište Bačvice (bb), T323574. First-floor café with great views over the sea. Pricey cocktails, Caribbean music and fake palms – undeniably pretentious but cheerful and fun. Clubs include: *Discovery*, Kupalište Bačvice. A big, new club occupying an underground space below the Bačvice seafront cafés. Closed Jun-Sep. *Metropolis*, Matice Hrvatska 1, T305110. Decent mix of commercial, techno and rock, with occasional live concerts. *Missisipi*, Osječka bb, T314788. Techno still dominates in this mainstream club. *Shakespeare*, Cvjetna 1, T519492. Popular club on 2 levels, with a summer terrace overlooking the sea.

**Outside the palace walls**

Central Dalmatia

## Entertainment

**Cinemas** *Kino Bačvice*, open-air summer cinema under the pine trees, in a garden above Uvala Bačvice (Bačvice Bay). The following are central cinemas that work the year through: *Central*, Trg Gaje Bulata bb, T342940; *Karaman*, Ilićev prilaz 3, T342141; *Tesla*, Kralja Tomislava 15, T585715 and *Marjan*, Trg Republike 1, T347838.

**Theatre &** *Hrvastsko Narodno Kazalište*, HNK (Croatian National Theatre), Trg Gaje Bulata, **classical music** T585999, www.hnk-split.hr   Responsible for organizing the *Summer Festival*.

## Festivals

*Karnivale* (Carnival), **Shrove Tuesday**. Locals dress up in *maskera* (masks and costumes) and an evening procession culminates with the burning of Krnjo (an effigy made to resemble a contemporary political figure) on the Riva (seafront), thus relieving citizens of the past year's sins. *Sudamje* (Feast of St Domnius), **May 7**. Celebrates the patron saint of Split, whose bones go on display for a week in the Cathedral. Local public holiday, with stands selling handmade wooden objects and basketry on the Riva. *Split Summer Festival*, **mid-Jul to mid-Aug**. Founded in 1954, the festival hosts opera, theatre and dance at open-air venues within the walls of Diocletian's Roman Palace. The highlight is *Aida* on Peristil. For information check out the website, www.hnk-split.hr   *Splitska Luda Noč* (Split Mad Night), **mid-Sep**. A night of live music on the Riva – a binge of eating, drinking and dancing bring the summer season to its official end.

## Shopping

*Algoritum*, Bajamontijeva 2, close to Srebrena Vrata, between Peristil and Narodni Trg, T348030, is the best **bookshop** for foreign language publications, including novels, travel guides and maps. *Croata*, Mihovilova Širina 7, overlooking Trg Brace Radica (Vocni trg), T346336, www.croata.hr   Sells original Croatian **ties** in presentation boxes, along with a history of the tie. *Pazar*, colourful **open-air market** just outside the palace walls, with stalls selling fruit and vegetables, plus clothes and leather goods. *Vinoteka Bouquet*, Obala hrvatskog preporoda 3, on the seafront, T348031, is a tiny shop well-stocked with the best **Croatian wines**, plus some truffle and olive oil products. *Vinoteka Sv Martin*, Majstora Jurja 17, close to Zlatna Vrata, T343430, another tiny store filled with quality Croatian wines, olive oils and truffle conserves, plus natural soaps and cosmetic oils from Dalmatia.

## Sport

**Diving**  *Issa*, T536806, www.diving.hr/idc  Run this centre on the island of Vis. *Ocean*, T312198, www.ocean.hr  *Kronmar*, T470509, www.scuba.diving.hr  On the island of Mljet. **Hiking and climbing**  *Croatian Mountaineering Association Mosor*, Marmontova 2, T431131. Organize Sun morning walking trips up to the peak of Mosor (1339 m), and free-climbing on Marjan. **Sailing**  **ACI Marina**, Uvala Baluni bb, T398599, www.aci-club.hr  1 km southwest of city centre, near Sustipan Peninsula. 360 berths, open all year. Charter companies based in the Split ACI marina include: *Bav Adria Yachting*, T361712, www.bavadria.com  *Nautika Centar Nava*, T398430, www.navaboats.com  *Euromarine*, T398420, www.euromarine.hr  *Pivatus Yachting*, T321300, www.pivatus.hr  *Ultra*, T398980, www.ultrasailing.hr  **Tennis**  *Tennis Club Split*, Put Firule, close to Bačvice Bay, T389576. Visitors welcome, 40Kn/hr. Wimbledon 2001 champion, Goran Ivaniševic, learnt to play here.

# Tour operators

*Atlas*, Nepotova 4, T343055, www.atlas-croatia.com  Organize 1-day excursions to Dubrovnik, Šibenik and Krka, *Salona* (Solin), Plitvice National Park, Bol, Hvar and Biševo, plus rafting trips on the River Cetina, near Omiš. *Generalturist*, Obala Lazareta 3, T345183, www.generalturist.com  One of the largest Croatian travel agencies, *Generalturist* specialize in tailor-made trips both with and without guides, pilgrimage tours and yacht charters.

# Transport

**Bus**  Local buses serve the city suburbs and surrounding towns of **Trogir** (40 mins), **Salona** (Solin) (30 mins), **Klis** (35 mins) and **Omis** (40 mins), all of which make pleasant day trips from Split. **Taxi**  The 2 main taxi ranks lie at each end of the Riva (Obala hrvatskog preporoda), in front of the market and in front of *Hotel Bellevue*. *Radio taxi*, T970.

**Local**

**Air**  Through summer, there are regular flights to and from **Amsterdam**, **Berlin**, **Brussels**, **Dubrovnik**, **Dusseldorf**, **Frankfurt**, **Istanbul**, **London** (Gatwick and Heathrow), **Ljubljana**, **Manchester**, **Munich**, **Paris**, **Prague**, **Pula**, **Rome**, **Skopje**, **Tel Aviv**, **Warsaw**, **Vienna**, **Zagreb** and **Zurich**. The number of destinations and the frequency of flights are reduced in winter. **Split Airport**, Kaštela, T203171 (information), T203218 (lost and found), www.split-airport.tel.hr  Airport bus service, T203305.

**Long distance**

**Bus**  Internal services include about 30 buses daily to **Zagreb** (7 hrs); 14 to **Zadar** in North Dalmatia (3½ hrs); 12 buses daily to **Rijeka** in Kvarner (8 hrs) and 12 to **Dubrovnik** in South Dalmatia (4 hrs). There are also daily international bus lines to **Ljubljana** (Slovenia), **Trieste** (Italy) and **Munich** and **Stuttgart** (Germany). Buses depart once a week for **Vienna** (Austria), and for **London** (UK) via **Paris** (France). For all information about buses to and from Split, T338483. Left luggage 0430-2200, 15Kn per piece per day.

**Car hire**  *Avis*, www.avis.hr, at the airport (T895320), and in the centre at *Hotel Marjan*, Obala Kneza Branimira (T342934); *Budget*, www.budget.hr, at the airport (T203151) and in the centre at *Hotel Marjan*, Obala Kneza Branimira (T345700); *Hertz*, www.hertz.hr, at the airport (T895230) and in the centre at Tomica stine 9 (T360455); *Mack* (www.mack- concord.hr) at *Hotel Split*, Put Ttrstenik 19 (T303008).

**Ferry**  *Jadrolinija* run a regular overnight coastal service from between **Rijeka** and **Dubrovnik**, stopping at **Zadar**, **Split**, **Stari Grad** (island of Hvar), **Korčula** and **Sobra** (island of Mljet) en route. Through winter the service is reduced to 2 departures a week. *Jadrolinija* also run daily ferry services connecting Split to the islands on **Mljet**, **Brač**, **Hvar**, **Vis**, **Korčula** and **Lastovo** the year through. Schedules vary from day to day and season to season, so you need to check times with their ticket office. *SEM* run a daily catamaran service connecting Split to the **island of Vis** the year through. In summer, they also run catamarans to the neighbouring islands, but schedules vary from day to day, so you need to check with their ticket office. *Jadrolinija*, *SEM* and *Adriatic* all run overnight ferries to **Ancona** (Italy), departing from Split at 2100 and arriving in Ancona at 0700 the following day. The same vessels depart 2100 from Ancona to arrive in Split at 0700. Through summer these services operate almost every day, in winter they are reduced slightly. *SNAV*, an Italian company, run a daily high-speed catamaran service between **Split** and **Ancona** (Italy) from Jun to Sep. The catamaran departs from Split at

*Jadrolinjia T338333;*
*SEM T338292;*
*Adriatica T338335;*
*SNAV Croatia Jet*
*T322252*

Central Dalmatia

1700 and arrives in Ancona at 2100. The same vessel departs from Ancona at 1100 and arrives in Split at 1500.

**Train** Internal services includes 4 trains daily to and from **Zagreb** (7 hrs by day, 9½ hrs by night); 5 trains daily to **Knin** (2 hrs) and 5 trains daily to **Šibenik** (2 hrs, change at Perković). Split train station, T338535. National train information, T060 333444, www.hznet.hr  Left luggage 0700-2200, 10Kn per piece per day.

## Directory

**Airlines offices** *Adria Airways*, Obala kneza Domagoja bb, T338445. *Croatia Airlines*, Obala hrvatskog narodnog preporoda 9, T362997. *ČSA*, Dominisova 10, T343422. *Lufthansa*, Generalturist office, Obala Lazareta 3, T345183. **Communications** Internet: *Internet Club Issa*, Dobrić 12, between Trg Braće Radića (Voćni Trg) and the covered fish market, within the palace walls, T341050. 0900-2300. **Post office**: the main post office is at Obala kneza domogoja, near bus station and ferry port, and is open daily 0700-2000. The central post office is at Kralja Tomislava, north of the palace walls, and is open Mon-Fri 0700-2000 and Sat 0700-1300. **Telephone**: if you prefer to telephone from a peaceful phone booth, rather than calling on the street, go to one of the post offices (see above). Otherwise, you'll find phone kiosks on the seafront. **Consulates** **Denmark**, Supilova 10, T358488; **Finland**, Vukovarska 6, T591068; **Germany**, Obala hrvatskog narodnog preporoda 10/II, T362114; **Great Britain**, Obala hrvatskog narodnog preporoda 10/III, T341464; **Italy**, Obala hrvatskog narodnog preporoda 10/II, T348155; **Netherlands**, Zagrebačka 35, T585770; **Slovenia**, Obala hrvatskog narodnog preporoda 3, T364468; **Spain**, Dioklecijanova 1/II, T589471; **Sweden**, Branimirova obala 16, T302620. **Medical services** Doctors and hospitals: *Hospital Firule*, Spinčićeva 1, a 15-min walk east of the centre, T556111 (24 hr casualty). **Pharmacies**: all pharmacies are marked by a glowing green cross. *Dobri* at Gunduliceva 52 (T341190) and *Lučac* at Pupačićeva 4, T533188, alternate as non-stop 24 hr pharmacies. **Libraries** British Consulate, Obala hrvatskog narodnog preporoda 10, T341464. Small library operated by the British Council. **City Library Marko Marulić**, Tolstojeva 32, T343913. **Useful numbers** Ambulance 94. Fire 93. Police 92.

# Trogir

Phone code: 021
Colour map 3, grid C5
Population: 12,995
27 km west of Split

*Medieval Trogir, just off the main coastal road, sits compact on a small island, connected to the mainland by one bridge and tied to the outlying island of Čiovo by a second. It's a quiet, lonely place through winter, but swarms with visitors on warm summer evenings. Once protected by city walls, a labyrinth of narrow cobbled streets twists its way between the **medieval town houses** bringing you out on to a splendid main square, overlooked by a monumental **Romanesque Cathedral**. In 1997, Trogir was listed a UNESCO World Heritage Site. It is well worth a visit.*

*The south-facing seafront promenade is lined with cafés and restaurants, and there are also a couple of good, reasonably priced hotels. Just across the narrow Trogir Channel, on the island of **Čiovo**, a well-equipped marina makes a base for several companies chartering yachts.*

Ins & outs
See Transport, page
214, for further details
**Getting there**  There are regular buses running from Split to Trogir. **Getting around** Small enough to get around by foot. **Tourist office**  The town tourist office is at Obala Bana Berislavića 12, T881412, www.dalmacija.net/trogir.htm

# History

Trogir was founded in the third century BC by Greeks colonists from *Issa* (on the island of Vis) who named it *Tragurion*. From AD78 Tragurium flourished as a Roman port, and after the fall of the Western Roman Empire, it became part of Byzantium. Thanks to its island location, it was saved a similar fate to nearby *Salona*, which was devastated by rampaging Avar and Slav tribes during the seventh century, but in 1123 it was almost completely demolished by the Saracens. However, successful trade relations throughout the Mediterranean had brought the citizens of Trogir a certain affluence, and they soon rebuilt their city, adding to it a splendid Romanesque Cathedral, built from fine local stone, described by Rebecca West in *Black Lamb and Grey Falcon*, as "the colour of rich crumbling shortbread". In 1242, when King Bela IV found temporary refuge here as he fled the Tatars, he would have seen the almost-completed Cathedral, minus the bell tower, which was added later. Over the following centuries Trogir became one of the most important cultural centres in Dalmatia. In June 1420, after a bloody battle, the city was taken by Venice – a conquest that met continual resistance from the people of Trogir, who having been born into an independent city with its own glorious past resented being governed by outsiders. The Venetians took tough measures, sending in specially imported language teachers to instruct the nobles, and forcing local families to change their names to Venetian equivalents – Čubranović, for example became Cipriani. However, Trogir remained a hive of artistic activity, with renowned architects and sculptors such as Nikola Firentinac and Andrija Aleši living and working here during the second half of the 15th century. The Venetians, ever fearful of the possibility of a Turkish invasion, reinforced the city walls, adding St Mark's Tower and Kamerlengo Fortress. The Turks never succeeded in taking Trogir, but the devastation they caused in the surrounding hinterland led the city into economic decline during the 17th century. Upon the fall of Venice in 1797, Trogir passed to Austria, and then spent a brief period spent under Napoleon's Illyrian Provinces. This too met with local opposition, and the French condemned several of the town leaders to death after a failed uprising. After a final phase under Austria, Trogir entered the Kingdom of Yugoslavia in 1918.

In 1932, an unfortunate affair led Trogir and the rest of Yugoslavia into a diplomatic scuffle with Italy. Apparently a relief of the Venetian Lion, hung in the town loggia in Trogir, has been badly disfigured in an act of 'anti-Italian' vandalism. Mussolini, who was rising to power in Italy and coveted this particular part of the Dalmatian coast, caught wind of the affair and took umbrage. Anti-Yugoslav demonstrations were held in Italy, and Mussolini announced chillingly, "The lions of Trogir are destroyed, but in their destruction they stand stronger than ever as a living symbol and a certain promise". The Yugoslav Government was obliged to deliver a formal apology. Nine years later, with the outbreak of the Second World War, Trogir was occupied by Italian soldiers. Under Tito, the economy picked up significantly during the 1970's with most of the population working in shipbuilding and tourism, and a suburb grew up on the neighbouring island of Čiovo. Today the small shipyard lies all-but-abandoned, but tourism has taken off once more.

Central Dalmatia

## Sights

**Kopnena Vrata (Land Gate)** The city walls were constructed under Venice during the 15th century. However, the main entrance into Trogir, the Land Gate, was rebuilt in late-Renaissance style during the 17th century. Above the arch stands a statue of Sv Ivan Trogirski (St John of Trogir, also often referred to by the Italian version of his name, Giovanni Orsini), a 12th-century Bishop and one of the city's two patron saints.

**Muzej Grada Trogira (City Museum)** Standing just inside the walls, close to the Land Gate, the rather dull city museum is housed within the Baroque Garagnin-Fanfogna Palace. There's a small lapidarium on the ground floor displaying various Greek and Roman finds, while the first floor is given over to 18th-century furniture and a collection of city documents. ■ *Summer 0900-1200 and 1800-2100. 10Kn. T881406, Gradska Vrata 4.*

**Katedrala Sveti Lovrijenac (Cathedral of St Lawrence)**
*You can climb to the top for stunning views across the ancient rooftops*

Undoubtedly Trogir's most remarkable building, this triple-nave Romanesque basilica is one of the most perfect examples of medieval architecture in the country. Work began in 1213, and the main core of the building was completed in 1250, well before the arrival of the Venetians.

The main portal, sheltered within a spacious vestibule edged by a marble banquette, is adorned with elaborately detailed Romanesque sculpture by Master Radovan. The great door is flanked by a pair of burly lions that form pedestals for figures of Adam and Eve. Around the portal, scenes from the Bible are mixed with references to every day peasant life, in an extraordinary orgy of saints, apostles, animals and grotesques. Still within the vestibule, to the left of the portal lies a Baptistery dating from 1467, the most important preserved work by Andrija Aleši (who also completed the delightful Baptistery of Šibenik Cathedral). Inside, above the altar, check out the relief of St Jerolim and the Cave.

The Cathedral itself is dimly lit, the main sight being the **Kapela Sv Ivana** (Chapel of St John), to the left of the main aisle. Considered one of the most beautiful Renaissance monuments in Dalmatia, it was built in 1480 by Nikolo Firentinac (who also worked on Šibenik Cathedral). Below a barrel-vaulted ceiling, statues of Mary, Christ, the saints and the apostles watch over a sarcophagus, on which lies the figure of St John of Trogir (Giovanni Orsini). The building of the elegant bell tower began in the early 15th century, and took place in successive stages – the first two storeys are Gothic, while the third and final level, in Renaissance style, was completed in 1610.

■ *0800-1200 and 1630-1900. Trg Ivana Pavla II.*

**Čipiko Palace (Čipiko Palace)** Standing opposite the main entrance to the Cathedral, this was once the home of the Čipikos, Trogir's leading noble family during the 15th century. It's of special note for the delicately carved Venetian-Gothic triple window with pointed arches, completed by Adrija Aleši in 1457. Within the main entrance (which is usually open) stands a giant wooden cockerel, a trophy taken from the prow of a Turkish ship at the Battle of Lepanto (see page 223) in 1571. Seven Dalmatian cities were each ordered to send a galleon to fight in this decisive battle, where the Turkish navy suffered a defeat it never fully recovered from. The Trogir crew was captained by Alviz Čipiko. ■ *Trg Ivana Pavla II.*

**Loža (Loggia) & clock tower** Across the square, the 15th-century loggia would originally have been used as a court. The stone table where judges once sat is still there, and behind it

*Central Dalmatia*

there's a wall relief, appropriately portraying *Justice*, by Nikola Firentinac from 1471. In contrast, the back wall bears a 1950's modernist equestrian relief by Ivan Meštrović, portraying *Ban Berislavić*, a native of Trogir who became Ban of Croatia and Bishop of Zagreb, and eventually died in battle against the Turks in 1520. Close by stands the town clock tower, once part of the small Renaissance church of St Sebastian. ■ *Trg Ivana Pavla II.*

**Samostan Sv Nikole (Convent of St Nicholas)** Behind the loggia stands the Benedictine Convent of St Nicholas, founded in 1064 but rebuilt during the 16th century. The nuns here look after a collection known as the *Zbirka Umjetnin Kairos*, with the centrepiece being a remarkable third-century BC Greek marble relief of Kairos, the god of opportunity. There's also an ancient Greek inscription built into the cloister walls. ■ *Summer 0900-1200 and 1600-1900; winter by appointment. 10Kn. T881631. Gradska ulica 2.*

**Kaštel Kamerlengo (Kamerlengo Fortress)** Perched on the southwest corner of the island, overlooking the sea, this impressive fortress was built by the Venetians as part of the improved city fortification system in 1430. On summer evenings, the internal courtyard becomes an open-air cinema. Just north of the fortress stands Kula Sv Marka (St Mark's Tower), built at the same time. ■ *Jun-Sep, Mon-Sat 0900-2000. 10Kn.*

**Marmontov Paviljon (Marmont's Pavilion)** Lying close to the fortress, on the western tip of the island, before the sea level dropped this small neoclassical gazebo used to rise directly from the water. It dates from the period spent under Napoleon's Illyrian Provinces. Napoleon's right hand man in Dalmatia, General Marmont, loved the place and used to play cards here and watch the sunset.

## Essentials

*Central Dalmatia*

**Sleeping** C *Hotel Fontana*, Obrov 1, T885744, F885755. On the seafront overlooking Trogir Channel, this old building has been tastefully modernized to accommodate 13 guest rooms (several with jacuzzis) plus a suite. The same management run the popular *Restaurant Fontana*. D *Concordia*, Obala bana Berislavića 22, T885400, F885401, www.tel.hr/concordia-hotel Close to *Hotel Fontana*, in an 18th-century town house overlooking Trogir Channel, *Concordia* has 14 comfortable rooms.

**Eating** **Expensive** *Restaurant Fontana*, Obrov 1, T884811. This highly esteemed restaurant has tables outside on a waterfront terrace through summer. The fish and seafood dishes can be pricey, but pizza makes a cheap option. **Cheap** *Škrapa*, Augustina Kazotića, no phone. Popular with locals and visitors alike, *Škrapa* serves up large platters of delicious *frigne ligne* (fried squid) and *ribice* (small fried fish). It's informal and fun, with heavy wooden tables and benches both indoors and out.

**Bars & clubs**   *F1*, large techno-orientated nightclub, 5 km out of town. Fri and Sat open until 0500. *Intermezzo Cyber Café Bar*, Ribarska 3. Popular café on the seafront, large summer terrace, open daily until 0300. Internet.

**Festivals**   *Trogir Summer Festival*, **early-Jul to late-Aug**, features classical and folk music concerts, staged in the Cathedral and Kamerlengo Fortress, and at various open-air venues around town.

**Sport**   **Diving** *Trogir Diving Center*, Pod Luku 1, Okrug Gornji, 4 km from Trogir, T886299, www.tel.hr/trogir-dc **Sailing** ACI Marina, Čiovo, T881544, www.aci-club.hr Across the bridge, a 10-min walk from the centre of Trogir. 180 berths, open all year. Charter companies based here include *Aventur*, T882388, www.aventur@aventur-agency.com and *Lucis Charter*, T885464.

**Transport**   A regular local **bus** service runs from Split to Trogir every 30 mins, 0600-2200 (40 mins). **Coaches** running along the coast between Split and Šibenik also stop here. Trogir bus station T881405. Split **airport** is located just 2 km from Trogir.

## Salona

*Phone code: 021*
*Colour map 3, grid C5*
*Population: 19,011*
*6 km inland*
*from Split*

At the foot of Kozjak Mountain, Salona is the most important archaeological sight on Croatia. As the largest Roman settlement on the Dalmatian coast, during the third century it is said to have had a population approaching 60,000. Today the site is rather poorly maintained, due to lack of funds, and most of the important finds are in the Archaeological Museum in Split. However, with a bit of imagination you can visualise how it must once have looked as a prosperous Roman settlement, backed by rugged mountains and facing out towards the sea. In some ways it's the very lack of upkeep and 'sanitization' that give it this special atmosphere of having been abandoned. The modern town of Solin, which has grown up southeast of ancient Salona, is of little great interest, being no more than a suburb of Split.

**Ins & outs**
*See Transport,*
*page 216,*
*for details*

Tusculum, at the entrance to the archaeological site, serves as a small information centre. Here you can pick up a plan of the site and buy postcards. The Salona site is open daily, Jun-Sep 0700-1900, Oct-May 0900-1500. 10Kn. The Solin town tourist office is at S Radića 42, T210048, www.solin.hr and www.dalmacija.net/solin.htm

**History**   Salona was probably founded by Greeks colonists from *Issa* (on the island of Vis) in the fourth century BC, later becoming a Greek-Illyrian settlement. The Greek geographer and historian, Strabon (63BC-AD24), mentions Salona as the harbour of the Illyrian *Delmata* tribe. In the first century BC, it was conquered by the Romans, and went on to become their most important base in Dalmatia. Public buildings were erected, with a forum serving as the centre of the region's public, political and religious life, and a large *terme* (baths). During the third century, under Diocletian (who was probably born here, though he governed from Nicomedia, present-day Izmir in Turkey) Salona expanded further. An influx of immigrants arrived from the east, bringing with them various oriental religions. Findings on the site prove that Isis (the goddess of fertility and motherhood, originating from Egypt and later adopted by the Greeks); Cybele (the goddess of nature and fertility, originating from Asia Minor and later becoming the Roman 'Great Mother of the Gods') and Mithras (the Persian god of light) were all worshipped here.

Christianity arrived in mid-third century through Bishop Verantius, who came from Rome with the mission of spreading the religion throughout Dalmatia. However, in 304 Diocletian ordered the execution of all Christian bishops, and Domnius, the first Bishop of Salona, along with other Christian leaders of the time, probably met his end in the amphitheatre. Less than a decade later, the Edict of Milan, passed in 313, legalized Christianity. A powerful Christian community rapidly developed in Salona, and in the early fifth century Salona's Bishop became the Metropolitan of the province of Dalmatia. Many churches were built on the Salona site, and the centre moved from the Forum to what is now Manastirine, where a basilica was built over the site of Domnius's grave. In the sixth century Salona became part of the Byzantine Empire under Justinian (the son of Slavonian peasants, born near present-day Skopje in Macedonia). Salona was destroyed by Avars and Slavs in 614, and the surviving inhabitants fled for shelter within the walls of Diocletian's Palace, where they founded Split.

Since then, ancient Salona has lain in ruins. Much of what remained was deliberately destroyed in the 17th century by Venetian generals, to prevent the Turks, who had already captured nearby Klis, from taking refuge here. And in the 18th century, British historian Edward Gibbon wrote, "*A miserable village still preserves the name of Salona; but so late as the sixteenth century the remains of a theatre, and a confused prospect of broken arches and marble columns, continued to attest to its ancient splendour*".

The site, by this time overgrown with vineyards and olive trees, was excavated during the late 19th century by Father Frane Bulić (1846-1934) from Split, and most of the finds were transferred to the Archaeological Museum in his hometown.

On the road between Split and Salona, you will pass the **Roman aqueduct** to your right. Built by Diocletian during the third century, it was 9 km long and conducted water from the spring of the River Jadro on the slopes of Mosor, all the way down to the palace. It was renewed in 1879 and is still partly in use today.

**Tusculum** (Father Frane Bulić Memorial Museum) is a two-storey house commissioned by Father Frane Bulić in 1898 as a base for archaeologists working on the site. Various stone finds such as inscriptions and statues were built into the façade. On the ground floor there's a memorial room to Bulić, displaying his furniture and documenting his work. The garden features a charming pathway flanked by columns and capitals of various styles found on the site, now overgrown with climbing roses and honeysuckle. ■ *Opening hours as for the rest of the site. T212900. Put Starina bb, Manastirine, left of the main entrance.*

**Manastirine**, immediately south of the entrance, is the place where the early Christians buried their martyrs, notably Bishop Domnius. It subsequently became a place of worship, and countless sarcophagi were placed around the Bishop's tomb. In the early fifth century a triple-nave basilica, measuring 48 m by 21 m was built over the site. The foundations, sections of the crumbling walls and several sarcophagi can still be seen today. In 1934, Bulić was buried to the west of the site, in an area surrounded by cypresses.

Built into a hillside in the northwest corner of the site stands Salona's most impressive building, an elliptical **amphitheatre** from the late second century. It was designed to seat 18,000 spectators, and **gladiators** and wild animals, and later Christians, would have fought here. In the sixth century, Byzantine Emperor Justinian banned gladiator fights, and it was probably used instead for religious and defensive purposes.

Sights

Central Dalmatia

**Festivals** *Ethno Music Festival*, **late-Jul**, 3-day open-air event attracting musicians from as far a field as Ireland, Spain, Israel and Iran.

**Transport** Local **buses** leave from Trg Gaje Bulata (opposite the National Theatre) in Split, every 20 mins, 0700-2200, for Salona (30 mins).

## Klis

*Phone code: 021*
*Colour map 3, grid C5*
*Population: 2,557*

Just 9 km inland from Split, the sleepy village of Klis nestles on the south-facing slopes between the mountains of Kozjak (779 m) and Mosor (1339 m). Historically it's known for its medieval hilltop fortress, once the site of many gruelling battles, but today an all-but-abandoned monument offering romantic views over the sea at sunset. Locally, Klis is also esteemed for its down- to-earth restaurants serving *janjetina* – you can't miss them, each one has a whole lamb turning on a spit by the roadside.

**Sights** Today many of the original families from Klis have moved to Split but keep weekend cottages here, while the elderly people who have remained run small-holdings with goats, chickens and orchards. Klis is divided into three distinct parts: **Klis-Varoš**, below the fortress; **Klis-Grlo**, behind the fortress, separated from Klis-Varoš by a tunnel, and **Klis-Megdan**, by the main entrance to the fortress.

*Kružić and his*
*men have not*
*been forgotten:*
*the local football*
*team is called NK*
*Uskok, in tribute*
*to their struggle*
*against the Turks*

The **Tvrdava** (Fortress), set on rocky mass 340 m above sea level, was probably first settled in the first century BC by the Illyrian tribe of the *Delmata*, who were particularly fond of hard-to-reach hilltop sites. During the ninth century, it became a seat of the medieval Croatian Kings, and subsequently passed to the Hapsburgs. Lying on the borders between Austro-Hungary, Venetian Dalmatia and the rapidly expanding Ottoman Empire, and overlooking a mountain pass traversed by lucrative trade routes leading from the coast inland to Bosnia, this was a vital strategic base. The Hapsburgs thus established a garrison here, under the command of Captain Peter Kružić. His army was made up primarily of Uskoks (see page 149) – a notorious Slav people who had fled the Turks in the east and obtained permission to stay in the Hapsburg territories, without being subjected to taxes, on the condition that they provided military service. During the early 16th century, the Ottoman Turks, who had already taken nearby Sinj, laid siege upon Klis several times, but Kružić and his men held them off. Finally in 1537 the Uskoks were defeated: details of the events are recorded in heroic ballads, concluding with Kružić being captured, having his throat slit and his head mounted on a pole. The Turks thus established *Klisko-lički sandjak* (Klis-Lika county), stretching from Bosnia in the east to Skradin (near Šibenik) and Klis in the west. This turn of events spread terror along the coast – the fear of falling under Ottoman dominance became an ongoing preoccupation. In 1648, the fortress was eventually captured by the Venetians, and a village grew up below its ramparts. Built into the south face of a rocky mass and barely discernable as a man-made structure from a distance, the present day aspect of the stone fortress dates from restructuring work carried out by the Venetians in the 17th century. The grassy ramparts offer spectacular views down to the sea and an impressive sunset over the islands. ■ *Summer Tue-Sun. 0900-1900. 10Kn.*

The oldest remaining building is a former Turkish mosque, though the Venetians pulled down the minaret and promptly converted it into a church.

*Restaurant Perlica*, Grlo 3, T240004. Although there are 3 restaurants serving up **Eating**
*janjetina* (roast lamb) in Klis Grlo, this is possibly the best – people from the surrounding area drive for miles to eat here. Open day and night, Feb-Dec.

18 local daily **buses** depart from Split for Sinj (35 mins), passing through Klis-Varoš en **Transport**
route. There is also a less frequent service from Split to Klis-Megdan.

## Sinj

Sinj, set in a broad valley, close to the River Cetina, is a provincial market town    *Phone code: 021*
with a sizeable Croatian Army base. There's nothing much to see here, but the    *Colour map 3, grid B5*
spectacular *sinjksa alka* – a medieval riding tournament – assures the town    *Population: 25,373*
national media coverage at least once a year. It's also a popular pilgrimage    *34 km inland*
centre, thanks to a supposedly miraculous painting of the Virgin.    *from Split*

Sinj came under various local noble families until being captured by the Otto-    **History**
man Turks in 1513. The *raja* (non-muslims) fared pretty badly at the time,
and there are countless stories of the atrocities suffered by the local population. The town was finally liberated by the Venetian army in 1686.

The most prominent event in Sinj's history dates back to the early 18th century. On 7 August 1715, a massive Turkish offensive, led by Mehmed Paša and
comprising several thousand soldiers, hit the town for a second time. A local
contingent of just 700 men managed to hold off the army for over a week,
finally seeing the complete withdrawal of the Turks on Assumption Day,
15 August. The event is now celebrated by the annual *Sinjska Alka*. Sinj's main
period of expansion occurred under the Hapsburgs during the 19th century.

The miraculous *Sinjska Gospa* (Our Lady of Sinj), a painting of the Virgin    **Sights**
Mary by an unknown 16th-century Venetian artist, takes pride of place inside
the parish church **Crkva Gospa Sinjska** (Church of Our Lady of Sinj), which
is part of the Franciscan monastery complex. The painting formerly belonged
to the Franciscans in Rama, Bosnia, during which time it became apparent
that it was able to perform miracles. It was transferred to the monastery in Sinj
in 1687, and its reputation was only boosted by the Ottoman defeat of 1715 –
apparently local women had prayed to the Virgin and the Sinj victory was in
part attributed to the magical powers of the painting. As a way of thanks, the
town's military officers had a golden crown made to adorn the *Sinjska Gospa*,
which was put in place by the Archbishop of Split in 1716. Today this is one of
Croatia's best-known pilgrimage sites. Each year on Assumption Day, 15
August, the painting is ceremoniously paraded around town, and thousands
of people from all over the country walk, some for miles and some barefoot, to
pay their respects to the Virgin. ■ *0630-1200 and 1700-1900 (for mass).*
*Šetalište Alojzije Stepanica 1.*

**D** *Hotel Alkar*, Vrlička bb, T824488, F824505. Modern 3-storey white concrete hotel    **Sleeping**
with comfortable rooms, close to the tourist office. If you plan to stay here the weekend
of the *Alka*, book well in advance.

**Midrange** *Konoba Ispod Ure*, Istarska 2, T822229. Located in the centre of town, this    **Eating**
restaurant serves a wide choice of Croatian dishes, including the local speciality,
*arambašići* (cabbage leaves stuffed with minced meat and rice), better known in other
parts of the country as *sarma*.

Central Dalmatia

**Festivals**    *Sinjska Alka*, staged on the first Sun in **Aug**, commemorates the 1715 victory over the Turks. It's a colourful and entertaining affair, with whole roast lamb turning on spits, a brass band, competitors in traditional costume (blue uniforms with silver buttons and tall fur hats) and around 15,000 spectators. The competition, which has taken place for almost 300 years, starts at 1500 and involves *alkari* (mounted knights) riding at full gallop carrying 3-m long jousts, with the goal of spearing an *alka* (small metal ring) suspended at a height of 3.32 m. The winner, who becomes a local hero for the following 12 months, receives a cash prize, plus a silver shield and sword. For further information check out the website, www.alka.hr (in English).

*Assumption Day*, **15 Aug**. Religious pilgrims flock to town, some ailing and in hope of a miraculous cure, to pay their respects to the *Sinjksa Gospe*.

**Transport**    18 local **buses** daily from Split (1 hr). Long-distance buses, taking the inland route Split-Zagreb, also pass through Sinj.

## Omiš

*Phone code: 021*
*Colour map 3, grid C5*
*Population: 15,472*
*On the E65 coastal road, 28 km southeast of Split*

Where the River Cetina emerges from a dramatic gorge to meet the sea, lies Omiš. Many people pass straight through, but closer inspection reveals a pleasant market town with alleys of old stone houses and a port, overlooked by a hilltop fortress backed by the spectacular Omiška Dinara Mountains. Omiš makes an ideal base for exploring the Cetina Gorge, where various agencies organize adventure sports such as rafting, canoeing and kayaking, and there are also a couple of highly regarded riverside restaurants.

**Ins & outs**    **Getting there** Frequent buses run from Split and there are connections with
*See Transport,*    Makarska and Dubrovnik. **Getting around** Taxi boats run up and down the river from
*page 220, for*    the bridge in town through summer. **Tourist office** The town tourist office is at Trg
*further details*    Kneza Miroslava bb, T/F861350, www.dalmacija.net/omis.htm

**History**    Omiš's main claim to fame is having been the base of a fearsome band of medieval pirates. Thanks to the deep gorge carved out by the River Cetina, they were able to cause havoc on the Adriatic, raiding Byzantine and Venetian ships then taking refuge upriver out of sight. A water wall at the mouth of the Cetina prevented larger ships from pursuing them, and the pirates themselves used a secret route, closed by chains. The frequent plundering of local monasteries, coupled with the raid of a Crusader ship in 1221, even caused the wrath of Rome. Pope Honorius III invited the cities of Split and Dubrovnik to launch an attack on Omiš, but the pirates remained undeterred. Shortly afterwards Omiš was ordered to burn all its vessels – a contract was signed but the agreement never fulfilled. The looting continued right up until 1444, when the town was taken by Venice. The Ottoman Turks attacked Omiš unsuccessfully in 1498, but managed to capture it in 1537, and governed until 1684, when it passed back to Venice.

**Sights**    Built as part of the 16th-century fortification system set up by Venice against the Turks, the well-preserved little **fortress** stands on a hill 311 m above town. It's a steep pull up, but well worth it for the spectacular views.

The oldest surviving structure in town, is the tiny 10th-century church of **Crkva Sv Petar** (Church of St Peter), measuring just 6 m by 11 m. It is one of loveliest pre-Romanesque buildings in Dalmatia, and clearly shows the influence of Byzantine style on early Croatian architecture. It's all-but-new appearance is explained by restoration work carried out during the 1960's. It lies north of town across the river, on the right bank of the Cetina, in an area known as Priko. ■ *Closed, but worth viewing from the outside.*

The River Cetina rises east of Knin (see page 261), at first running through a gentle valley of green meadows, which in turn becomes a dramatic landscape of spectacular *karst* formations, the **Cetina Gorge**. The last stretch cuts a high-sided canyon between the mountains of Mosor and Biokovo, to meet the sea at Omiš. A series of rapids make the river ideal for rafting, canoeing and kayaking, while the sheer-faced cliffs attract free-climbing enthusiasts. Riverside restaurants serve up freshwater specialities such as trout, eels and frogs, making a welcome change from the omnipresent seafood of the coast.

There's a colourful fruit and vegetable **market** under the trees on the side of the main road, and one block away is **Knezova Kačića**, a peaceful cobbled street linking the old east and west town gates. At the east end stands the 17th-century parish church, where the annual *Dalmatian Klapa Festival* takes place.

There's a town beach just south of the centre, though it's somewhat spoilt by the nearby traffic. Altogether more relaxing beaches lie at **Duce**, 3 km west of Omiš, and at **Ruskamen**, 6 km to the southeast. Ruskamen is a lovely pebble beach backed by pines with a stretch reserved for nudists, and also claims to be the best place in the area for windsurfing.

**Sleeping**

*Active Holidays*, Knezova Kačića bb, T/F863015, www.activeholidays-croatia.com, can help you find private accommodation.

**Eating**

**Mid-range** *Radmanove Mlinice*, T862073. Lying on the banks of the River Cetina, 6 km upstream from Omiš, this old watermill was once the home of the Radman family. Today it's a pleasant garden restaurant serving local *pastrva* (trout) and *janjetina* (roast lamb) at tables under the trees. Open Apr-Oct. *Restoran Kaštil Slanica*, Slanica bb, T861783. Lying 4 km upstream from Omiš, this riverside restaurant specializes in *žabji kraci* (frog's legs), *jegulje* (eels) and *janjetina* (roast lamb), while the bread comes freshly baked from a *peka*. They also rent canoes on an hourly basis.

**Cheap** *Konoba u Našeg Marina*, Knezova Kačića bb, T861328. In the centre of Omiš, the rough wooden furniture in this tiny *konoba* creates a rustic atmosphere. They do local wine along with platters of *sir* (cheese), *pršut* (ham) and *slane srdele* (salted sardines), and can also prepare meals under a *peka* if you request a day in advance. Open all year, 0800-1200 and 1700-2400.

**Festivals**

*Dalmatian Klapa Festival*, Jul. This 3-week competitive *klapa* festival was founded in 1967 with the aim of both preserving this traditional form of harmony singing (see Background, page 335) and promoting new songs. In 2002 it attracted 80 groups comprising over a thousand singers. Performances are held on Trg Sv Mihovila, Trg Stjepana Radica and inside the parish church. For further information contact *Festival Dalmatinskih Klapa Omis*, Ivana Katušića 5, T861015, www.fdk.hr (in Croatian only).

**Sport**

**Adventure sports** *Active Holidays doo*, Knezova Kacica bb, T/F863015, www.active holidays-croatia.com, organize rafting, free-climbing, paragliding, windsurfing and scuba-diving in Omiš and the surrounding area. *Atlas*, Nepotova 4, Split, T343055, www.atlas-croatia.com, run full-day guided rafting expeditions on the River Cetina. They also organize 1-week adventure sports packages including canoeing, mountain biking, rafting, kayaking, horse riding and fishing in the Cetina Valley, Mar-Oct. **Diving** *Almissa*, Put Borka 53, T(099)-526801 (mob), www.ssi.hr

*Central Dalmatia*

**Transport**   Local **buses** run from **Split** to Omiš every 30 mins taking 40 mins. Coaches south-bound from Split, heading for **Makarska** and **Dubrovnik**, also stop in Omiš. Through summer small private **boats** run 6 km up the River Cetina from Omiš bridge, dropping visitors at the 2 restaurants. Expect to pay 30Kn per person.

# Island of Hvar

*Phone code: 021*
*Colour map 3,*
*grid C5/6*
*Population: 8,286*
*68 km from*
*east to west*

*A long, thin island, Hvar is an island of **vineyards** and **lavender fields**, old **Venetian coastal villages** with an altogether slower, more pleasurable way of life. The most popular, and by far and away the most charming, resort is **Hvar Town**. Close by, all grouped together on the western end of the island, lie **Stari Grad**, **Jelsa** and **Vrboska**. The eastern end of Hvar is sparsely populated and offers little of cultural interest. If you really want to get away from it all, head for the emerald green waters and sun-scorched slopes of the south coast.*

**Ins & outs**   **Getting there**   There are regular ferries from Split from the island's main port, Stari
*See Transport,*   Grad. **Getting around**   There are several buses daily between Hvar Town, Stari Grad
*pages 226 and 227,*   and Jelsa. If you are staying for a while, however, it would be worth hiring a car. The
*for further details*   area between Stari Grad and Jelsa is reasonably flat, making biking an option (mountain bikes are available for rent in Jelsa). The landscape behind Hvar Town is pretty
steep though so not well suited to biking. **Tourist office**   In Hvar Town at Trg Sv
Stjepana 16, T741059, www.dalmacija.net/hvar and www.hvar.hr

**History**   It was first settled by ancient Greeks from the Aegean island of Paros, who
founded Pharos (present-day Stari Grad) in the fourth century BC. When the
capital moved from Pharos in the 13th century, the new centre was named
*Civitas Nova* (New Town) while Pharos became *Civitas Vetus*, meaning 'Old
Town', or in Croatian, Stari Grad. The name Pharos mutated to Hvar, which
later came to be used for both *Civitas Nova* (present-day Hvar Town) and for
the entire island.

From 1420 to 1797 Hvar came under Venice. The 15th and 16th centuries
saw a degree of prosperity owed principally to shipping, which could have
been greater still had the Venetians not limited the tonnage allowed to the
island. During this period Hvar gave Croatian literature two prominent writers, Hanibal Lučić (1485-1553) from Hvar Town, and Petar Hektorović
(1487-1572) from Stari Grad. The sons of noble families were educated in
Italy, though Hvar remained an island in the true sense of the word. Regular

## Island of Hvar

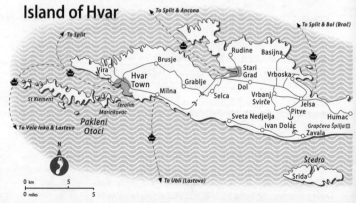

*Related map*
*Hvar Town,*
*page 222*

boat connections with the mainland and surfaced roads between the island's towns and villages did not come into being until the second half of the 19th century.

The first tourists on Hvar were Austrians, who were sent to convalesce in Hvar Town as early as 1870. One hundred years later, as part of Yugoslavia, a number of large hotel complexes were constructed just outside the old town centre along the coast, and the island became known as the Croatian Madiera.

## Hvar Town

Located on the southwest coast of Hvar, Hvar Town is probably Croatia's most fashionable resort. Old stone houses are built into the slopes of three hills surrounding a bay, with the highest peak crowned by a Venetian fortress, which is floodlit by night. Café life centres on the magnificent main square, giving directly onto the harbour and backed by a 16th-century cathedral. The bay is protected from the open sea to the south by the scattered **Pakleni Otoci** (Pakleni Islets), covered with dense pine forests and rimmed by rocky shores offering secluded coves for bathing. Hvar Town is a favourite retreat of the Croatian president, Stipe Mesiᵃ, and from July to late-August (when it's almost unbearably crowded) various illustrious characters moor their yachts up here – Goran Ivaniševiᵃ, Luciano Benetton and Bernie Eccleston, to name but a few.

*Phone code: 021*
*Colour map 3, grid C5*
*Population: 4,138*
*39 km south of Split*

Although people had probably lived on this site for centuries, the settlement only became a true town in 1278, when the Venetians (during a brief period of occupation) encouraged people from Pharos (present-day Stari Grad) to relocate around this southwest facing bay, which they considered a more suitable centre, as it could be better defended in the event of an attack. In the same year, the area known as Grad, north of the main square, was surrounded by protective walls, and the first public buildings were erected. Later, south of the square, the more humble quarter of Burg developed.

**History**

In 1420, the town came under Venice for a second time, and rapidly became one of the wealthiest centres in Dalmatia. The Venetians used it as port of call for trade ships travelling to and from the Orient, and also set up the headquarters of their Adriatic fleet here. Cultural life flourished, and many fine buildings were erected. However, in 1571, during the run up to the Battle of Lepanto, much of the town was devastated in a Turkish onslaught led by Uluz Ali; thus the buildings here today date almost exclusively from the late-16th century onwards.

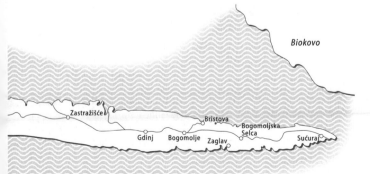

In 1610, in an act unique for its time, an agreement was signed declaring nobles and commoners politically equal and giving people of all social classes the same right to participate in administration. From then on, for a short period, years were counted from that date onwards: the inscription on the entrance to the theatre bears witness to this.

Hvar Town was first promoted as a seaside and health resort when the *Hygiene Society of Hvar* was founded in 1868. Its main selling point was a mild climate – it receives more hours of sunshine per year than any other place on the Adriatic – and fresh sea air. During the 1970's, a publicity stunt was launched offering visitors free hotel accommodation if it snowed (which has been known to happen), and the same promise holds true today.

**Sights** **Trg Sv Stjepan** (St Stephen's Square) is the largest piazza in Dalmatia and dates back to the 13th century. The east end is backed by the cathedral, while the west end opens out onto the **Mandrac**, an enclosed harbour for small boats, which in turn gives onto the bay. The paving dates from 1780 and in the centre stands a well from 1520. Today many of the old buildings lining the square house popular cafés, restaurants and galleries at street level.

The bishopric was originally founded in Stari Grad in 1147, but relocated to Hvar Town when it took over as the political and cultural centre in the 13th century. **Katedrala Sv Stjepan** (St Stephen's Cathedral), providing a majestic backdrop to the main square, is a three-aisled basilica built in stages between the 16th and 17th centuries on the foundations of an earlier monastery, to produce a trefoil façade standing in perfect harmony with a four-storey bell tower. ■ *0700-1200 and 1700-1900. In summer it sometimes stays open all day. Trg Sv Stjepana bb.*

The **Venetian Loža** (Loggia) and **clock tower** was reconstructed in high- Renaissance style after the former loggia was damaged during the Turkish onslaught of 1571. It was used as a café from 1868 to 1971, and then incorporated into the *Hotel Palace* to form an elegant salon. The clock tower was part of the Governor's Palace – from which the *Hotel Palace* takes its name, though the original building was destroyed in 1571 – and the clock was added in the 19th century. ■ *Trg Sv Stjepana bb.*

Lying on the south corner of the main square, looking onto the harbour, the **Arsenal i Kazalište** (arsenal and municipal theatre) is easily identified by its huge front arch, which allowed Venetian galleys to dock inside for repair work. It dates back to the 13th century, but was reconstructed after damage caused by the Turks in 1571. The upper floor

**Hvar Town**

Sleeping ■
1 Fortica
2 Palace
3 Slavija

Eating ●
1 Bacchus
2 Gostionica Junior
3 Macondo
4 Pape
5 Zlatna Školjka

0 metres 50
0 yards 50

## Battle of Lepanto

*During the late-16th century, as the possibility of Ottoman expansion westwards became ever more real, the Holy League, an alliance of Spain, Venice, Genoa and the Papal States, massed a huge fleet on the Adriatic in the hope of halting Turkish progress. The eventual confrontation took place on 7 October, 1571, in the Gulf of Lepanto, near Corfu. The League's forces, made up of 200 galleys (including seven from Dalmatia, one apiece from the towns of Zadar, Šibenik, Split, Trogir, Krk, Rab and Hvar), were well outnumbered by the Ottoman Turkish fleet, which counted over 270 ships. The battle was one of the bloodiest in naval history, with both sides losing countless vessels and thousands of men. The Holy*

*League won, achieving their first victory over the Ottoman Empire. However, although the Ottoman navy was seriously depleted, they managed to keep their hold over much of the Balkan peninsula for the following three centuries.*

*In the lead up to the battle, Uluz Ali, the Ottoman Bey of Algiers, gathered a fleet of 80 galleys and staged a diversionary attack on the island of Hvar on 17 August 1571. The first settlement to be attacked was Hvar Town, after which the Turks sailed round the island and carried out similar offences on Stari Grad, Vrboska and Jelsa. Having wreaked havoc, they set sail south and joined the rest of the Ottoman fleet near Corfu.*

houses the Galerija Arsenal, displaying a collection of paintings by local artists, plus the *Zvir* (Beast), a wooden prow in the form of a dragon, formerly mounted on the front of the town galleon, one of seven ships to represent Dalmatia at the Battle of Lepanto. Passing through the gallery one arrives at the Kazalište, which opened in 1612 and welcomed all citizens regardless of their social standing, making it one of the first institutions of its kind in Europe. An inscription on the entrance door reads *Anno secundo pacis* (The Second Year of Peace) which was 1612 in the new system of counting years, temporarily established after the agreement of 1610. The interior was refurbished in 1803, and is still used for performances today. ■ *Summer 0900-1200, 1900-2100; Winter 1000-1200. 10Kn. Trg Sv Stjepana bb, T741009.*

South of the centre, a pleasant seafront path leads past a series of small Baroque chapels, built by the commander of the Adriatic fleet, Marin Capello, in 1720, to arrive at the **Franjevački Samostan** (Franciscan Monastery). The main core of the complex was built between 1461 and 1471, and walled in 1545. It was damaged by the Turks in 1571, but reconstructed in 1574. One enters through a charming 15th-century cloister – used for classical music concerts during the summer festival – to arrive at the former refectory, now a museum. The most impressive piece on show is undoubtedly the *Last Supper*, a vast 17th-century canvas by an unknown Venetian artist, measuring 2.5 m by 8 m. The refectory opens onto a beautiful garden, with a magnificent 300-year-old cypress tree, overlooking the sea. The monastery church, **Gospa od Milosti** (Our Lady of Mercy), also dates from the 15th century and bears a relief *Madonna and Child*, attributed to Nicola Firentinac, above the main portal. Inside, set into the floor in front of the main altar, lies the tombstone of the local poet Hanibal Lučić1. ■ *Summer 1000-1200 and 1700-1900; Winter 1000-1200. 10Kn. T741123.*

On the north side of the main square, set back from the other buildings, stands the rather eerie 15th-century **Hektorović House**. It was left unfinished after the writer's death, but the Venetian-Gothic windows are among the most beautiful example of Venetian architecture on the island. The street

Central Dalmatia

leading off the square, past the house, forms several flights of stone steps, conducting one through the area known as Grad to the hilltop castle. A couple of blocks up, on the left, lies the **Benediktinski Samostan** (Benedictine Convent). Inside there's a Baroque chapel and a display of lace, made by the nuns. ■ *Summer 0900-1100 and 1600-1900. 10Kn. 3 Ulica Nikole Karkovica.*

Above Grad, a winding footpath leads through a garden of dense Mediterranean planting, to arrive at the **Fortica** (Fortress). A medieval castle once stood here, though the present structure was erected by the Venetians in 1557, and the ochre-coloured barracks added by the Austrian military authorities during the 19th century. From the ramparts, you have fantastic views down onto the town and harbour, and out across the sea to the Pakleni Islets. There's a small **Amphora Collection**, consisting mainly of pieces salvaged in the 1970's from a Roman shipwreck close to the island of Palagruža, and a suitably dark and dingy **Zatvor** (Prison), accessed down a flight of steep stone steps. Up top, you'll also find a restaurant and snack bar, and several rooms providing overnight accommodation (see Sleeping below). ■ *Summer 0800-2400; winter by appointment. 10Kn. T741816.*

There is a **beach** in the town itself. More pleasant are those on the islands near by. The coastal path west of town leads to a south-facing bay with a pleasant pebble beach, now unfortunately dominated by the vast modern *Hotel Amfora* complex. During the late-19th century the Austro-Hungarians set up a bathing establishment here, complete with prim changing huts and showers, but the 'Victorian' charm of the place has been somewhat spoilt by the 1970's monster behind. You're better off taking a taxi boat (they depart regularly from the harbour through summer costing 10Kn) to the nearby **Pakleni Otoci**, a group of small uninhabited covered with pinewoods, and rimmed by rocks interspersed with secluded pebble beaches. The name 'Pakleni' comes from *paklina*, meaning pine resin. The nearest island, **Jerolim**, is predominantly nudist, and has a good informal eatery with a shady terrace, serving salads and barbecued dishes daily till 1830, to coincide with the last boat back to town. The next island, **Marinkovac**, has two pleasant bays: Uvala Stipanska, overlooked by a couple of restaurants, and Ždrilica. The next and largest island, **St Klement**, is known for its particularly lush vegetation. There's an ACI marina on the north side, while a wide bay with a popular beach called Palmižana (from *spalmare*, 'to spread' in Italian – this is where wooden boats used to be pulled up out of the water and coated with pine resin) lies on the south side. Taxi boats also run from the harbour to the village of **Milna**, on the coast 6 km east of Hvar Town, where there's a decent pebble beach.

**Sleeping**
■ *on map, page 222*

**AL** *Hotel Palace*, Trg Sv Stjepana, T741966, F742420, www.suncanihvar.hr Commanding a prime site, on the edge of the main square, overlooking the harbour, the 76-room palace has an indoor-heated swimming pool, massage and sauna. Internet available in the reception. **A** *Hotel Slavija*, Obala Oslobodenja, T741820, F741147, www.suncanihvar.hr This old stone building, opposite the ferry quay, offers 57 comfortable rooms. On the ground floor there's a restaurant, pizzeria and café with a large seafront terrace.

**B** *Hotel Podstine*, Pod Stine, T741118, F741899, www.podstine.com Located on the coast, a 20-min walk west of the main square, this peaceful family-run hotel has a lovely terrace restaurant by a pebble beach, backed by palms and pine trees. There are 17 rooms, each with a sea view, plus 1 apartment. **C** *Fortica*, T098-567541 (mob). Within the fortress walls, part of the barracks has been converted to make 6 double rooms, each with an en-suite bathroom and sea view, available for rent through summer.

*SEM Marina Travel Agent*, based in Split, T338219, www.sem-marina.hr, can help you find private accommodation in Hvar Town. It's also worth checking out www.hvar.hr for apartments to let on the island.

**Mid-range to expensive**  *Macondo*, Groda bb, T742850. This excellent fish restaurant lies in a narrow alleyway between the main square and the fortress. In summer there are several tables outside, while the indoor space has a large open fire and is hung with discreet modern art. Start with scampi pâté, followed by a platter of mixed fried fish, and round off with a glass of homemade *orahovica* (*rakija* made from walnuts). The food and service are practically faultless, but you may have to queue for a table. *Zlatna Školjka*, Petra Hektorovića 8, no phone. This *Slow Food* eatery serves local specialities rarely found in restaurants, such as *kožji sir iz ulja* (goat's cheese in olive oil). There's also a good range of unusually creative dishes – try the *sotirana janjetina u kiselom umaku od aroma plodova* (lamb stew with aromatic herbs). Open Jun-Sep. *Pape*, Ulica Pučkog Ustanka bb, T742309. The main plus here is the terrace, high above the ferry quay, offering fine views down to the harbour. There's the usual choice of fish and seafood, plus Balkan meat specialities such as *muckalica* (spicy stew with peppers, onions and paprika) and *Čevapčići* (minced meat kebabs).

**Eating**
● *on map, page 222*

**Cheap**  *Gostionica Junior*, Uliča Puckog Ustanka bb, T742069. According to locals, this is the best place in town to eat *gregada* (fish stew prepared with potato and onions). Run by a family of fishermen, it's a small, informal eatery, with a few tables outside on a cobbled street. *Bacchus*, Trg Sv Stjepana bb, T742251. With a terrace overlooking the main square, this is the best place to go for a reasonably priced steak. It's popular with locals, and stays open all year.

*Carpe Diem*, Riva bb, T742369, www.carpe-diem-hvar.com  Trendy cocktail bar with oriental furniture and a plant-filled summer terrace overlooking the sea. Through peak season, when it stays open until 0300, it's so popular they have two bouncers outside, controlling the people waiting to get in. *Cofein*, Trg Sv Stjepana bb. Overlooking the main square, this popular bar has outside tables almost the year round. Indoors, on an upper level, there's a small lounge with funky modernist armchairs. Open until 0300 through summer.

**Bars**
*Through winter there are no clubs in Hvar Town, so people drive to Mlin, page 229, in Jelsa*

In summer, *Veneranda*, a multimedia centre with an open-air **cinema**, **concerts** and **dancing** until 0500, is the most popular nightspot on the island. It lies above the coastal path west of town, set in the 16th-century Greek Orthodox Monastery of St Veneranda, which was dissolved and turned into a fortified military complex by the French in 1807. More recently, it was reconstructed and arranged as an open-air theatre in 1953, with latest additions including a cocktail bar in the former church. For the older generation, *Fortica* offers evening barbecues plus **ballroom dancing** on the terrace until midnight.

**Entertainment**

*International New Year Regatta*, 1 Jan, *Dalmatia Cup International Regatta*, early-May, Zadar to Dubrovnik, stopping in Hvar Town en route, *Hvar Summer Festival*, Jul-Aug. Various open-air cultural performances, with the main attraction being the classical music concerts held in the cloisters of a Franciscan Monastery, each evening at 2130, tickets 30Kn.

**Festivals**

**Diving**  *Jurgovan Diving Centre*, close to *Hotel Amfora*, T742490 www.jurgovan.com
**Sailing**  The official **ACI Marina** is at Palmižana, on the island of St Klement, 3.5 km from Hvar, T744995, www.aci-club.hr  It has 160 berths and a couple of good restaurants, and is open mid-Mar to end-Oct. However, many visitors want to be in Hvar

**Sport**

*Central Dalmatia*

Town itself. If you arrive in the bay by late-afternoon, it is possible to moor up along the seafront, though through peak season it does get unbelievably crowded.

**Transport** **Local** If you plan to stay for more than several days it could be worth hiring a **car**: *Atlas*, T741911; *Peligrini*, T742743 and *Luka Rent*, T742946. There is usually a **taxi** and/or minibus taxi available at the bus station in Hvar Town, T741450/741445. **Long distance** *Jadrolinija*, T741132, run regular **ferries** to **Split** from the island's main port, **Stari Grad** (2 hrs), 20 km east of Hvar Town. **Buses** from **Hvar Town** to Stari Grad (35 mins) are scheduled to coincide with the ferries. *Jadrolinija* also operate a once-daily catamaran service, running from Split to Ubli on the island of Lastovo, stopping at Hvar Town en route. It departs from Split for Lastovo in the early afternoon, then passes Hvar Town again on the return journey early the following morning, 50 mins.

**Directory** **Banks** There are several banks and ATMs along the sea front and on the main square in Hvar Town. **Communications** Post office: Obala bb, Mon-Fri 0800-2000, Sat 0800-1300. **Medical services** Doctor and emergency treatment: Trg Sv Stjepana (main square), T741111, Mon-Sat, 0700-2100. **Pharmacy**: Trg Sv Stjepana (main square), T741002, Mon-Sat 0800-2030.

## Stari Grad

*Phone code: 052*
*Colour map 3, grid C5*
*Population: 2,187*

This is the island's oldest settlement and chief ferry port. It's a more relaxed, slightly less swish, resort than Hvar Town, with an easy-going village atmosphere. There aren't many great beaches though and little of cultural interest other than the 16th-century Hektorović House. Most of the buildings in the old part of town date from the 16th and 17th centuries – the best examples can be seen on Škor, a picturesque square enclosed by Baroque houses. The town tourist office is at Nova Riva 2, T765763.

**History** In 385BC, Greeks from the Aegean island of Paros founded Pharos. Their arrival was recorded later, possibly in slightly exaggerated form, by the Sicilian-born Greek historian Diodorus Siculus (90-21BC): "This year the Parians, who had settled Pharos, allowed the previous barbarian inhabitants to remain unharmed in an exceedingly well fortified place, while they themselves founded a city by the sea and built a wall around it. Later, however, the old barbarian inhabitants of the island took offence at the presence of the Greeks and called in the Illyrians of the opposite mainland. These to a number of more than 10,000, crossed over to Pharos in many small boats, wrought havoc, and slew many Greeks. But the Governor of Lissus (*Issa*, present-day Vis) appointed by Dionysius sailed with a good number of *triremes* [three-banked galleys] against the light craft of the Illyrians sinking some and capturing others, and slew more than 5,000 of the barbarians, while taking some 2,000 captive." Little of the original Greek settlement remains today, other than the 11-m long **Cyclop's Wall**, made up of massive stone blocks, that can be traced through some of the buildings on the south side of the bay.

During medieval times, the town continued to hold its position as the island's main centre, and a bishopric was founded here in 1147. However, when the Venetians encouraged citizens to relocate to Hvar Town in 1278, Stari Grad sunk into a period of stagnation, from which has never really recovered.

In the early 19th century the port was expanded to facilitate the export of wine from the island, and during the 1970's, several large hotels were built on the north side of the bay, bringing Stari Grad into the package tourism market. In May 2003, a local crew from Stari Grad will set sail on a 700-mile journey to the Greek island of Paros, in the hope of establishing future cultural connections with their mother town. Details about the expedition can be found at www.stari-grad-faros.hr/expedition

Stari Grad's best-loved building is the **Tvrdalj** (Hektorović House), on the south side of the bay, in the old part of town, set back about 100 m from the seafront. It originally came right up to the coast, until the front square was added in the 19th century. It's an unusual fortified residence, built by the local poet, Petar Hektorović (1487-1572) in 1520, as a home for him and his friends, and also as a place of refuge for the entire town, in the event of a Turkish invasion. Hektorović was an aristocratic landowner, who had been educated in Italy and went on to become one of Dalmatia's most prominent Renaissance poets. Much of his work celebrated the lifestyle of local fishermen and peasants – his best-known work is *Ribanje i ribarsko prigovaranje* (Fishing and Fishermen's Conversations) in which he describes a fishing trip around the neighbouring islands. Tvrdalj's centrepiece is a long rectangular fishpond, surrounded by a fine cloister, around which the living quarters, domestic area and servant quarters are arranged. On the south side of the complex, there's a walled garden where Hektorović cultivated both indigenous Mediterranean and exotic plants. ■ *Summer 1000-1300 and 1700-2000; winter by request. 15Kn.*

Also on the south side of bay, a short distance east of Tvrdalj, several blocks in from the seafront, stands the **Dominikanski Samostan** (Dominican Monastery). Founded in 1482, it was fortified after the Turkish attack of 1571. Inside there's a museum, with a number of ancient Greek tombstones from Pharos, plus a collection of paintings, the most notable being *Oplakivanje Krista* (The Mourning of Christ) by the 16th-century Venetian Mannerist, Jacopo Tintoretto (1512-94). The old man in the top right corner of the painting is said to be Hektorović. The monastery church was built in 1893 on the site of a much older sanctuary, and next to the altar, set into the floor, lies Hektorović's tomb. ■ *Summer 1000-1300 and 1700-2000; winter by request.*

A pleasant coastal path along the north side of the bay leads to the main **beach**, just before *Hotel Helios*. Beyond the hotel lies a rocky stretch of coast backed by pines, also offering reasonable access to the water.

**Sights**
*The walls of the interior of Hektorović House bear many plaques, with witty and philosophical inscriptions in both Croatian and Latin*

**Sleeping**

All of Stari Grad's hotels are big modern commercial establishments, located on the north side of the bay. You're better off looking for private accommodation, which is plentiful and of a high standard. Ask at the tourist office for details, or check out www.hvar.hr

**Eating**

**Mid-range** *Eremitaž*, Priko, no phone. Overlooking the sea on the north side of the bay, close to the main beach, this old stone building was once the quarantine, back in the days when trade ships returning from the east would stop here. The menu features typical Dalmatian fish and seafood. *Jurin Podrum*, Donja Kola, T765804. This small family-run restaurant specializes in fish and seafood. Try the tagliatelli with scampi and mushrooms, and a carafe of the house white. In the summer, they have several tables outside.

**Festivals**

*Stari Grad Summer Festival*, Jul-Aug. Open-air theatre and music, including *klapa* performances. *Faros Marathon*, last weekend of Aug. International long distance swimming competition, 15 km from town to the end of the bay and back. First swum in the 1970's, in 2002 it attracted 50 competitors, from as far afield as Russia and France.

**Transport**

Stari Grad port lies 2 km southwest of town, with a local **bus** laid on for all incoming and outgoing ferries. *Jadrolinija*, T765048, run a regular service from **Split** (2 hrs), with

Central Dalmatia

an average 5 **ferries** per day in summer and 3 ferries per day in winter. Schedules vary from day to day, so you need to check times with their ticket office. Through summer, *SEM* ferries travelling between **Split** and **Ancona** (Italy) stop in Stari Grad a couple of times a week – check with their ticket office for the exact days.

**Directory** **Banks** There are a couple of banks and ATMs in Hvar Town. **Communications** Post office: Ulica Braće Biancini 2, Mon-Fri 0800-1500, Sat 0800-1300. **Medical services** Pharmacy: T765061 (ask here if you need a doctor).

## Jelsa

*Phone code: 021*
*Colour map 3, grid C5*
*Population: 1,798*
*10 km east of*
*Stari Grad*

Jelsa is a lively fishing town and seaside resort, built around a natural harbour. Everyday life focuses on the 19th-century seafront promenade, lined with cheerful cafés and pizzerias, while to each side of the bay, dense pine woods have been used to conceal a number of large hotel complexes, built during the 1970's. The town tourist office is on the seafront at Mala Banda bb, T761017.

**Sights** Looking onto the *Hvarski Kanal* (Hvar Channel) and facing Bol on the island of Brač, with distant views of Makarska and Mount Biokovo on the mainland to the northeast, Jelsa was founded in the 14th century as the port for Pitve, a semi-abandoned village lying 2 km inland. There's not much of cultural interest here, but it makes a cheap option to staying in Hvar Town, and offers several decent beaches and a series of bike paths. It's also the only place on the island to have a nightclub working 12 months a year.

During the 16th century, **Trg Sv Ivana**, a square lined with Renaissance and Baroque houses, many of which now accommodate cafés and shops at street level, was constructed close to the seafront. Just off the square stands the pretty miniature **Baroque Crkva Sv Ivana** (Church of St John), and inland from here lies an old quarter with stone houses and winding cobbled streets built into the hillside. The quay and the buildings lining the bay date from the 19th century, when the local shipping industry flourished. During the 1970's, Jelsa turned to tourism, as several large hotels were constructed along the coast to the edge of town.

West of the centre, a lovely 4-km road follows the coast, winding its way through pinewoods, to **Vrboska**, making an perfect afternoon walk or bike ride. The most central place for a swim lies just west of town, where rocks and concrete bathing areas give easy access to the water. However, the best beaches are found beyond Vrboska, on **Glavica Peninsula**, and on the small island of **Zečevo**, where there's a nudist beach. Through summer, you can reach both Glavica and Zečevo by taxi boat from Jelsa harbour.

**Excursions** Recorded by the ancient Greeks in the third century BC as the Illyrian settlement of *Pityeia*, **Pitve**, a picturesque, semi-abandoned village of old stone houses is built into the hillside 2 km southwest of Jelsa, just before the tunnel leading to the south side of the island. Few people live here the year round, though several buildings have been tastefully renovated to make holiday houses.

Even if you don't have private transport, it's worth walking along the country road from Jelsa to eat at *Konoba Kod Komina,* a delightful *konoba*, with its splendid terrace surrounded by grapevines and lemon trees. Fish and meat dishes are prepared over an open fire (*komin* means 'fire place') and served with home-grown vegetables, salads, and excellent house wine. ■ *Jun to Sep.*

East of Jelsa, a poorly maintained local road leads all the way to Sučuraj, on the eastern tip of the island. If you follow this road for 8 km, you'll see a sign to the right for **Humac**. Walk the final 400 m along a rough track, to arrive at a romantic cluster of abandoned stone houses, founded as a temporary dwelling for shepherds in the 15th and 16th centuries. No one lives here anymore, but during summer it's possible to eat at the unforgettable *Konoba Humac*.

A 30-minute walk from Humac lies **Grapčeva Špilja**, a vast chamber of underground stalactites and stalagmites, with traces of human civilization from the third millennium BC. Through summer you can visit the cave with a guide. Contact Jelsa tourist office for details.

At *Konoba Humac*, in Humac, there's no electricity so everything is cooked as it would have been over a century ago: under a *peka* or on a *roštilj*. The bread is homemade and the cheese, salad and wine locally produced. You can't get much more authentic than this. ■ *Jun to Sep.*

**Sleeping**

Most of the hotels are modern commercial establishments outside the centre of town. You're better off looking for private accommodation, which is plentiful and of a high standard. *Globus Tours*, Strossmayerova Setaliste bb, T761995, www.globus-tours.hr, can help you find rooms and apartments.

**Eating**

*See Excursions, above, for some recommended places to eat around the town*

**Mid-range to expensive** *Taverna Arsenal*, Mala banda bb, T762000. The 18th-century shipyard warehouse has been refurbished to house a sophisticated restaurant, decorated with paintings of ships that were built here during the 19th century. Fish and seafood top the menu, though they also do a good steak. Open Easter to late-Sep. **Mid-range** *Restoran Vinerija Huljić*, Kod Crkve bb, T761409. Close to the parish church, this small *vineria* serves excellent wine made by the Huljić family, along with a selection of authentic local dishes prepared under a *peka*. There's outdoor seating on an attractive stone terrace. Open Jun-Sep.

**Clubs**

*Mlin* is hidden away in a side street in the heart of town – you'll hear it before you see it. It's small but fun, stays open all year, and gets incredibly crowded in summer.

**Festivals**

*Carrying of the Holy Cross*, night before **Good Friday**. Jelsa, Pitve, Vrisnik, Svirče, Vrbanj and Vrboska – 6 neighbouring villages – take part in an all-night procession. At 2200, a group leaves from each parish church, led by a much-honoured (and hopefully very strong) young man carrying a wooden cross. The parties pass through each of the other villages in turn, to return to their respective churches for sunrise on Good Friday morning. *Fešta Vina* (Wine Festival), **Jul**. What used to be an authentic local celebration has turned into a bit of a tourist gimmick, but it's still a good excuse for indulging in the area's plentiful wine supply.

**Sport**

**Biking** Being quite flat, the surrounding area is ideal for cycling. A network of narrow country roads, linking nearby villages, have been designated as 'bike paths' by the local tourist board, though they are still open to cars. You can rent a bike, or moped, from Globus Tours at Strossmayerova Setaliste bb, T761995, www.globus-tours.hr **Diving** *Divecentar Jelsa*, T761822, www.tauchinjelsa.de

**Transport**

*Jadrolinija* (no Jelsa office, for information contact Split office, T338333) run a daily **catamaran** service from Jelsa to Split (1½ hrs), calling at **Bol** on the island of Brač en route. The **boat** departs from Jelsa at 0600 to arrive in Split at 0730, then leaves Split at 1600 to return to Jelsa for 1730. In addition, regular **ferries** run between **Stari Grad** and **Split**. Local **buses** from Jelsa to **Stari Grad** (20 mins) are scheduled to coincide with the ferries.

Central Dalmatia

**Directory** **Banks** There are a couple of banks and ATMs in Hvar Town. **Communications** Post office: *Strossmeyerov*, Šetalište 33, Mon-Fri 0800-1400, Sat 0800-1300. **Medical services** Pharmacy: T761108 (ask here if you need a doctor).

## Vrboska

*Phone code: 021*
*Colour map 3, grid C5*
*Population: 526*
*4 km west of Jelsa*

This pretty fishing village is built around a long 'S' shaped inlet and merits a visit for its unusual fortified church and carefully laid out fishing museum. It's not a place you'd particularly choose to stay long, unless you're travelling by yacht – there's an excellent marina – or setting up a tent in the naturist camp. The town tourist office is at Riva bb, T774137, and works early-May to late-September. Out of season, contact the tourist office in Jelsa for further information.

**History**   Vrboska's protected waters have served as a refuge for ships since Greco-Roman times. However, the town itself was not founded until the 15th century, when it became the harbour for the inland village of Vrbanj. Typical Dalmatian stone houses line each side of the narrow channel, connected by three small bridges, and to the north lie several fine Renaissance and Baroque *palazzi*, constructed by the local nobility. Vrboska suffered the fate of neighbouring coastal towns in 1571, when it was invaded by the Turks, in the run up to the Battle of Lepanto. Through the centuries that followed, fishing became an increasingly lucrative activity, until it was usurped by tourism in the 1970's.

**Sights**   Located on the south side of the channel, on the hillside above the seafront, **Crkva Sv Marije (Church of St Mary)** is quite unique. Its original structure dates from the 15th century, but it was fortified in 1575, after the Turkish attack of 1571, so as to create a refuge for the townspeople, should the same thing happen again. In the apse, a tombstone laid into the floor and dated 1737 bears a chilling inscription: *Ne differas amice – hodie mihi cras tibi* (You won't be different friend – Me today, you tomorrow). ■ *Jul-Aug 1000-1200 and 1800-2000.*

The 15th-century **Crkva Sv Lovrinac (Church of St Lawrence)**, which was enlarged and took on its Baroque appearance during the 17th century, is home to several invaluable works of art by Venetian masters, notably a series of three paintings above the main altar, depicting St Lawrence, St John the Baptist and St Nicholas. Experts now attribute these works to Paolo Veronese (1528-88) though locally they were long believed to have been created by Tiziano Vecellio, better known as Titian (1485-1576). ■ *Jul-Aug 1000-1200 and 1800-2000.*

The small but informative **Ribarski Muzej (Fishing Museum)** speaks of the town's long tradition of fishing. Under Venice, Vrboska began producing salted sardines for the crews of the Empire's galleons, on long-distance hauls to the Orient. Local men would go out on the open sea to fish, while the women worked from home, cleaning sardines and preserving them between layers of rock salt. The museum displays the equipment they used, amid a setting of suggestive reconstructions of how people's homes would have looked at that time. ■ *Jul-Aug 1000-1200 and 1900-2200.*

The best beaches are on **Glavica Peninsula**, some 2 km northeast of town. Through high season, taxi boats leave from the harbour, taking visitors to and from the island of Zečevo, which is given over to nudist bathing.

*Camping Nudist*, T774034, F774187. A walled campsite giving onto the sea, with **Sleeping**
space for up to 1,000 guests. *Škojić*, Riva bb, set in an old-fashioned courtyard garden **& eating**
in the centre of Vrboska, just back from the seafront, this restaurant is known for excellent pizza.

**Sailing** *ACI Marina*, Vrboska, 21463 Hvar, T774018, www.aci-club.hr 85 berths. **Sport**
Open all year.

Vrboska is linked to **Stari Grad** (15 mins) and **Jelsa** (10 mins) by local **bus**, which have **Transport**
**ferry** and **catamaran** links to the mainland (see relevant sections).

## South side of Hvar

Viewed from the water, much of the south coast of Hvar is made up of vertical *Phone code: 021*
cliffs plummeting down to the sea. However, the 8-km stretch between *Colour map 3, grid C4*
**Zavala** and **Sveta Nedjelja** offers a series of pebble beaches backed by steep
hillsides planted with quality vineyards. Thanks to its inaccessibility – it can
only be reached by boat, or through a long, narrow road tunnel running
below the overlying peaks – this particular part of the island remains a world
unto its own. There are no hotels and little in the way of tourist facilities, but
there are a couple of good places to eat and sleep, and if you're lucky, you'll
chance upon a number of **idyllic coves**, **stunning views** out to the open sea
and not a soul in sight. There is no tourist village on the south side of Hvar.
The tourist office in Hvar Town can help provide information.

Separated from the north side of the island by a 600 m high plateau, the tiny **Background**
coastal settlements of Zavala, Ivan Dolac and Sveta Nedelja have passed
through the centuries in a state of relative isolation. In the past, families from
Jelsa and the surrounding villages on the north of the island kept vineyards
here, trekking over the hills by donkey during the warmer months to tend the
vines and reap an annual harvest. The south-facing slopes afford the vines maximum
benefit of the sun, resulting in an excellent full-bodied red, while the
cooler north-facing slopes are better suited to the production of white wine.

During the 1960's, the Yugoslav army constructed a 1,400-m long tunnel
through the overlying plateau, finally making year-round access possible.
However, the tunnel is narrow and unlit – only one car can pass through at a
time, and there is no traffic control system at either end. It is possible to pass
through by motorbike, but riding a bicycle or walking are certainly not
recommended.

Plans to construct a road from Dubovica, on the south coast east of Hvar
Town, to Sveta Nedjelja have been in the pipeline for decades, but (thankfully)
it has yet to be approved by the powers that be.

Lying east of the tunnel, 6 km from Jelsa, Zavala is a slightly sprawling coastal **Zavala**
village, much of which has been constructed over the last couple of decades.
It's not a particularly attractive place, but there's a decent pebble beach. See
also Sleeping and eating, page 232.

Lying west of the tunnel, 6 km from Jelsa, Ivan Dolac is a small stone village **Ivan Dolac**
built into the hillside above the sea. The excellent red wine, *Ivan Dolac*, produced
by Podrum Plančić, comes from here. Worth checking out is the roadside
chapel from 1901, with a plaque above the door (in Croatian) reading:
"In honour of the Mother of God, this church was built by Ivan Carić, the son

*Central Dalmatia*

of late Juraj. Rot and mildew have affected the grapes since 1852. There have been hard times. Root parasite has been passed down from Zadar and the grapevine is perishing. People, stop insulting God, and turn to the Blessed Virgin Mary! May God Almighty protect you from these three curses. 1901".

**Sveta Nedjelja** Some 4 km west of Ivan Dolac, nestling into the hillside below the island's highest peak, Sv Nikola (626 m), is Sveta Nedjelja. A cluster of old stone houses, making up the original village, lie 1.5 km back from the sea. In the hillside behind, the gaping entrance to a cave accommodates a small church, *Gospe Snijega* (Virgin of the Snow), founded in the 15th century by Augustian monks who kept a retreat within the cave until 1787. Today locals live mainly from wine making, and the name Sveta Nedjelja is now synonomous with the vineyards and wine cellars of the Plenković family. Below the village, a winding road leads through pinewoods down to the coast, where a number of holiday houses have been built in recent years. There's no natural harbour, but a small marina is currently under construction. See also Sleeping and eating, page 232.

**Islet of Šćedro** This small island, just off the mainland, is still more isolated. It is visited almost exclusively by sailing boats, though in high season it's possible to get there by taxi boat from Zavala. In the larger bay, **Luka Lovišće**, you'll find a number of good summer restaurants, while the smaller bay, **Uvala Mostir**, is overlooked by the remains of a 15th-century Dominican monastery, and is also home to a pleasant informal eatery. It's possible to walk right across the island, taking any one of a series of paths that run through the pinewoods, to arrive on the south coast, rimmed by rocks and a number of pleasant pebble beaches. There is a small restaurant here. *Mostir*, Uvala Mostir, run by a family from the island of Hvar, who live here most of the year. It serves fresh fish, home-grown salad and local wine at tables on a shady terrace. ■ *Getting there: in high season taxi boats run to and from Zavala.*

*Lying 3,000 m from the coast, it is particularly popular with yachters due to two sheltered bays on the north side*

**Wine cellars** **Podrum Plančić** is a family-run wine cellar, which has been in business since 1919. It offers wine tasting and bottles for sale. Try the dry white, *Bogdanuša*, and the velvety-red, *Ivan Dolac*. ■ *Vrbanj. T768030, www.plancic.com*

*You can taste and buy these wines here, direct from the producer*

    **Zlatan Otok** is a highly successful wine cellar best known for its red, *Zlatan Plavac*, and white, *Zlatan Otok*, which are exported as far afield as California. ■ *Sveta Nedjelja, T745709.*

**Sleeping** **D** *Pansion Skalinada*, Zavala, T767019, F767010. This 14-room *pansion* offers comfort-
**& eating** able, modern accommodation. The restaurant, mid-range, serves home-made food and wine on a large summer terrace, beside a pleasant pebble beach. Open mid-May to late-Sep. **E** *Tamaris*, Sveta Nedjelja, T745733. This family-run, mid-range restaurant serves up excellent fresh fish and seafood dishes, plus good local wine, on an ample stone terrace immediately above the sea. They also have a number of rooms to let. Open late-May to early-Oct.

**Transport** Local **buses** do not run through the tunnel as it is too narrow. However, during the school term, a minibus transports children to and from **Jelsa** a couple of times a day, and visitors are welcome to jump aboard if there is space. Ask at the Jelsa tourist office for details. During the school summer holiday, late-Jun to early-Sep, the only way to pass through the tunnel is by private transport.

Central Dalmatia

# Island of Vis

*Closed to foreigners until 1989 due to the presence of a Yugoslav naval base, Croatia's most distant inhabited island was spared the commercial brand of tourism that flourished along much of the Adriatic during the 1970's. It's now rapidly developing into a discreet but rather upmarket destination, thanks to its wild, rugged landscapes and the insight it offers into the way people once lived throughout Dalmatia. The two main settlements, **Vis Town** and **Komiža**, both lie on the coast, while there are also about a dozen semi-abandoned inland villages. There is limited holiday accommodation, but the restaurants are truly wonderful, the **wines**, notably the white Vugava and the red Viški Plavac, are organically produced, and there are several peaceful **beaches** where you can soak up the sun and swim in crystal clean waters, said to be among the cleanest in the Adriatic.*

*Phone code: 021*
*Colour map 3, grid C4*
*Population: 3,637*

**Getting there** After years of apparent isolation, the Croatian government recently subsidised a fast catamaran service to the mainland, so it's now possible for people to live in Vis and work in Split. During summer, tourists also travel to and from the island in ever growing numbers. **Getting around** There are several buses daily between Vis Town and Komiža, but no service to the villages of Rukavac and Milna on the southeast coast (locals are very good about offering lifts if they see you walking, and so are Italian tourists who turn up with 4WD jeeps). **Tourist office** In Vis Town, Šetalište Stare Isse 5, T/F711144, www.dalmacija.net and www.dalmatianet.com

**Ins & outs**
*See Transport, pages 236 and 238, for further details*

Vis was first settled by the Greeks in the fourth century BC, when Dionysius the Elder, tyrant of Syracuse, probably attracted by the island's natural water sources, founded Issa. It soon became an independent city-state, forged its own coins and founded colonies in Lumbarda on Korčula, and Trogir on the mainland.

**History**

From the mid-15th to the late 18th century, Vis came under Venice, then spent a brief period of time during the early 19th century under the British, who saw it as an ideal base from which to confront Napoleon's Adriatic hold, and also introduced the game of cricket, a peculiarity which has remained until this day. In 1815 Austria took over, and fought and won the most famous sea battle of the 19th century just off the northern coast of Vis, when the Italian navy launched an offensive aimed at capturing the island. The population peaked at over 10,000 in 1910, but since then there's been a slow process of depopulation.

During the Second World War, Vis was occupied by Italians troops from 1941 to 1943, and many of the islander's women and children were evacuated to Egypt. In the summer of 1944 it became the headquarters of the Partisan movement, with Marshal Tito temporarily lodging in a cave, still known as **Titova Splija** (Tito's Cave), on the south side of Hum. As of January 1944 the British also set up a naval and air base on the island, from which they supplied the Partisans, attacked German-held territories throughout Dalmatia, and also organized a meeting between Tito and the head of the royalist Yugoslav government in exile.

## Island of Vis

## Vis Town

Phone code: 021
Colour map 3, grid C4
Population: 1,960
56 km southwest
of Split

On the north coast of Vis, this is the island's largest town and chief port. It actually grew out of two separate settlements, so today a 3-km string of buildings, ranging from humble fishermen's cottages to noble Baroque villas, hugs the large sheltered bay. To the east lies **Kut**, a picturesque 16th-century residential quarter, and to the west **Luka**, where you'll find the ferry quay and tourist office, as well as another conglomeration of typical Dalmatian stone cottages and a proud **Franciscan Monastery** jutting out on a small peninsula. The entire scene is backed by craggy hills, promising the wild, unspoilt landscapes of the interior. Through summer, yachts moor up along the seafront, their crews drawn by Vis's authentic fish restaurants and fine wines.

**History**

The ancient Greeks founded Issa, their first colony in Dalmatia, on the slopes above the northwest part of the bay, in 389BC. Unfortunately there's not much left of it today, but excavations have unearthed finds now on display in the archaeological museums in both Split and Vis itself. The Romans moved in later, and built a theatre on Prirov Peninsula, the walls of which can still be traced, having been incorporated into the 16th-century Franciscan Monastery that now stands on the same spot. The present settlement developed when Luka and Kut were joined by the building of Gospa od Spilica (Church of Our Lady of Spilice) in 1512. During the centuries that followed, under Venice, several aristocratic families from the island of Hvar built summer villas here, and in the 17th century the town was fortified with four towers.

From 1811 to 1814, during the Napoleonic Wars, the British took Vis as a base for their Adriatic fleet, and built two forts, St George and Wellington (both of which are now in ruins), to protect the entrance to the bay. Close by, on an islet just east of the bay, rises Hoste Lighthouse, built in 1873 and named after Captain William Hoste.

West of Kut, a small British naval cemetery, surrounded by high walls and kept locked, dates back to 1812, and pays tribute to the British who fell here, both in the Napoleonic Wars and later in the Second World War. During the Yugoslav years, when the island was closed to foreigners, exception was made for surviving British war veterans, who made an annual pilgrimage every September. A few, by now well into their 80's, still return to meet with former comrades.

**Sights**

Through August, evening classical music concerts are held in the courtyard of the Town Museum

Lying within the walls of a **16th-century Venetian fortress**, the Gradski Muzej (Town Museum) and Gospina Baterija (Our Lady's Battery) were added by the Austrians in 1842. The upper floor now houses the Archaeological Collection Issa, an enlightening display of Greek finds from Issa, including a fourth-century BC bronze head of a goddess (either Aphrodite or Arthemide, scholars have yet to decide which), plus vases and amphorae. The ground floor is devoted to the life and customs of the island: period furniture, fishing and wine-making tools are on show, and there's a section highlighting the island's role during the Second World War when Tito set up the partisan base here. ■ *Jun-Sep Tue-Sun 0900-1300 and 1700-1900, Oct-May Tue-Sun 0900-1300. 10Kn. T344574, Šetalište Viški Boj 12.*

**Beaches around**

The main beach lies west of town, beyond Luka, in front of *Hotel Issa*, where it's also possible to rent motorboats. The more peaceful pebble beach of **Grandovac** lies east of town, beyond Kut, behind *Vila Češka*, where there's a small waterside bar serving drinks, salty snacks and *palacinke* (pancakes). If

Central Dalmatia

you have your own transport, you could drive across the island to **Rukavac** on the southeast coast. It's a peculiar place, not so much a village as a cluster of holiday houses, built mainly by Slovenians who arrive during summer and make up the major part of a seasonal community. Here **Uvala Rukavac** (Rukavac Bay) offers a small pebble beach, while **Uvala Srebrena** (Silver Bay) is overlooked by a dramatic series of rocky ledges stepping down to the water and backed by pinewoods. Close by, the hamlet of **Milna** has a decent sand beach in **Uvala Zaglav**, accessed by a 10-minute walk along the coast. It's particularly suitable for families, as the water is shallow and the sea bed smooth, making it possible for children to enjoy. There's also an excellent little restaurant, Zoglov, serving delicious lunchtime snacks.

**Sleeping**

**C** *Hotel Paula*, Petra Hektorovica 2, Kut, T/F711362. Hidden away in a cobbled side street, this pleasant family-run hotel has 12 smart, modern rooms. Downstairs there's a small fish restaurant, with tables on a walled terrace. Open Apr-Oct. **C** *Tamaris*, Šetalište Apolonija Zanelle 5, T711350. Located in the centre of town, overlooking the seafront promenade, this late 19th-century building has been converted into a basic but comfortable 27-room hotel. Open all year. *SEM Marina Travel Agent*, based in Split, T338219, www.sem-marina.hr, can help you find private accommodation in Vis Town.

**Eating**

**Mid-range to expensive** *Villa Kaliopa*, V Nazora 32, Kut, T711755. Lying close to the Town Museum, this enchanting restaurant is set in the walled garden of a Renaissance villa. The menu changes daily, depending on what fresh products are available. Dinner here is an event in itself, and worth dressing up for.

**Mid-range** *Konoba Vatrica*, Kralja Krešimira IV bb, Kut. T711574. With an ample vine-covered terrace on the seafront in Kut, this restaurant gets incredibly busy in summer. Guests sit at heavy wooden tables, to a feast of barbecued fish and meat dishes. Open all year. *Težok*, Kralja Krešimira IV bb, Kut, T711271. A few doors down from *Vatrica*, this informal eatery serves up slightly cheaper 'blue fish' such as *tunj* (tuna), plus the local favourite *brodet* (fish stew) at tables overlooking the harbour. *Stoncica*, Uvala Stoncica, T711669. A simple fish restaurant lying in a beautiful secluded bay, several kilometres east of Vis Town. The best way to arrive here is by boat, but it's also possible to hike along a rough track from Kut. Open Jun-Sep.

**Cheap** *Bufet Vis*, Obala Sv Jurja 32, no phone. Here you can eat as the locals do at home – a slap-up dinner of barbecued *srdele* (sardines), accompanied by fresh salad. It's opposite the ferry quay, with just half a dozen tables overlooking the sea, so you may have to queue for a place.

**Seriously cheap** *Pekara Kolderaj*, Trg Klapavica 1. A bakery selling delicious *viška pogaca*, the local version of Italian *focaccia*, filled with tomato, onion and anchovies.

**Wine bars & wine shops**

*Peronospora Blues*, Obala Sv Jurja bb. A vineria and gallery with outdoor seating in a romantic courtyard. Try the excellent *Plavac Mali*, a red wine produced by the owner, served with platters of ham and cheese. It's also possible to buy bottles to take home. *Roki's*, Obala Sv Jurja bb. A small shop selling wines produced by the Roki family. They also run *Konoba Roki's*, preparing meals for visitors at their home at Plisko Polje, on the 'old road' between Vis and Komiža. If you don't have transport, call first and they'll come and pick you up, T714004 (English spoken). *Vitis Vis*, Augusta Šenoa 4, set back off the *Riva*, next to the *Ribarnica* (covered fish market). A small shop selling wines and an assortment of *rakija* – *travarica*, *rogoš* and *mirta* – produced by the Lipanović family.

Central Dalmatia

**Entertainment**  **Cinema**  *Ljetno Kino*, open-air cinema, **Jul-Aug**. Projections start at 2115, ticket 15Kn.

**Sport**  **Diving**  *Dodoro Diving Tours*, T711311, www.dodoro-diving.com   Organize half-day diving trips for up to 12 people, plus weekends. Five tours with accommodation and meals included. **Sailing**  There is no official marina in Vis, but it is possible to moor up along the seafront in both Luka and Kut, where electricity and water supplies are available.

**Transport**  *Jadrolinija*, T711032, run a regular service from **Split**, with an average 3 **ferries** per day in summer and 2 ferries per day in winter (2½ hrs). Schedules vary from day to day, so you need to check times with their ticket office. *SEM* run a daily **catamaran** service from Vis to **Split**, departing from the island at 0700 and leaving Split for the return journey at 1800 in winter and 2030 in summer (1½ hrs). This service is designed to accommodate the islanders rather than people from the mainland, so it means you have to stay a couple of nights to make it really worthwhile.

**Directory**  **Banks**  There is a bank with an ATM on the seafront. **Communications**  Post office: Obala Sv Jurja 18, Mon-Fri 0800-2000, Sat 0800-1300. **Medical services**  Doctor and emergency treatment: Dom zdravlja Vis, Poljana Svetog Duha 10, T711633. **Pharmacy**: Ljekarna Vis, Vukovarska 2, T711434.

## Komiža

*Phone code: 021*
*Colour map 3, grid C5*
*Population: 1,677*
*18 km southwest of Vis Town*

On the west coast of Vis, this friendly fishing village is built around a small harbour. Old stone buildings with wooden shutters and terracotta-tiled roofs line a series of narrow alleys, each of which runs down to the seafront, where locals of all generations meet for morning coffee, conduct their evening promenade and put the world to rights. Above the village, from the weather-beaten slopes of **Hum Hill**, a 13th-century monastery surveys the open waters of the Adriatic and the outlying **islet of Biševo**, home to *Modra Spilj* (**Blue Cave**). Through winter 20 or so wooden fishing boats animate the harbour, but come summer elegant yachts from all parts of Europe pay call here. It's probably one of the most unspoilt places on all the islands in a fantastic setting and with excellent restaurants.

**Background**
*There are said to be more people originating from Komiža in San Pedro, California, than there are on the island itself*

Although Benedictine monks from the islet of Biševo had set up a base here already in the 13th century, it was not until the 16th century that the settlement really began to develop. With a natural harbour giving onto well-stocked sea, people lived primarily from fishing, using a unique wooden boat known as a *falkuša*, tapered at both the bow and the stern, with a large triangular sail mounted diagonally to the mast. They were small but seaworthy boats, and local fishermen were known to follow shoals of sardines across the Mediterranean as far as Spain. In 1890, a sardine canning factory was set up here, the first processing plant of its sort in Dalmatia. Komiža sardines were exported to various parts of Europe, and even as far afield as Canada and the USA.

During the early 20th century families began emigrating to America. Some of them, accompanied by their children and grandchildren, still return to their native home each summer. The people who have remained here continue to live primarily from winemaking, seafaring and fishing (though the sardine stocks are now sadly depleted), along with the more recent addition of tourism. The local tipple is *rogoš*, a type of *rakija* flavoured with carob, which grows in abundance on the surrounding hills.

**Ribarski Muzej** (Fishing Museum) is housed within Komuna, a Venetian tower erected in 1585. The main attraction here is the last existing ship-wrecked *falkuša*, built in 1925. On the first floor, a collection of fishermen's equipment, including delicately woven nets, rope knots and old sardine tins celebrates the town's once-prosperous fishing industry. All exhibits are labelled in the Komiža dialect, which most Croatians, even Dalmatians, fail to understand. ■ *Jun-Sep. 1700-2200. 10Kn. Riva bb.*

**Sights**
You can climb to the top of the tower for great views over the harbour below

**Samostan Sv Nikola** (Monastery and Church of Sv Nikola) is perched on the hillside above town and set amid terraces of vines and olives. This fortified monastery was founded in the 13th century by Benedictine monks who fled their former abbey on the islet of Biševo, following a series of pirate raids. Each year on St Nicholas Day, 6 December, the ceremonial burning of a fishing boat takes place in front of the church. ■ *Closed to the public, but well worth the walk up for the view down onto town.*

**Gospa Gusarica** (Church of Our Lady of the Pirates) overlooks the main beach, close to *Hotel Biševo*. This Renaissance building consists of three single-nave churches, each of the same size, connected by interior arches. The oldest is the middle church, dating from the 16th century, while the side churches were added during the 17th and 18th centuries. ■ *0700-1200 and 1700-1900.*

**Modra Spilja** (Blue Cave), on the east coast of the islet of Biševo, 5 km southwest of Komiža, is often compared to the Blue Cave on Capri, Italy. Some 24 m long, 12 m wide and with water 10-20 m deep, sunlight enters the cave through a submerged side entrance, passes through the water and reflects off the seabed, casting the interior in a magnificent shade of blue. Small boats ferry visitors in and out to see this natural wonder. You can visit the cave as part of an organized day trip from Komiža. Excursions are planned so you enter the cave around midday, when the light is at its best, then continue to the west side of Biševo for a few hours in **Porat Uvala** (Porat Bay), where there's a pleasant sand beach and a couple of simple restaurants. ■ *Boats depart at 0900 from the harbour, and return at 1700. Enquire at Komiža tourist office for further details. Expect to pay 80Kn per person.*

**Central Dalmatia**

**D** *Hotel Biševo*, Ribarska 72, T713095, F713098. Komiža's only hotel, the *Biševo*, is a modern structure overlooking the pebble beach west of the centre. Comfortable but not particularly romantic, and it tends to be invaded by tour groups. The Komiža-based agencies, *Darlić and Darlić*, Riva 13, T713760, and *Srebrena Tours*, Ribarska 6, T713668, can help you find private accommodation. *SEM Marina Travel Agent*, Split, T338219, www.sem-marina.hr, also have a list of apartments and rooms to let in Komiža. *Palagruža Lighthouse*, 70 km south of Komiža. Contact Adriatica Net, Selska 34, Zagreb, T(01)3644461, F3644463, www.adriatica.net This lighthouse is on the small, uninhabited island of Palagruža, which makes up part of the Vis archipelago. On a hill 90 m above the sea, in the centre of the island, it dates from 1875 and has recently been converted to 2 apartments, each sleeping 4 people. There's a wonderful beach, but not a soul in sight, so you have to take your own provisions. Rentals are on a 1-week basis, Sat to Sat, with transfers by boat arranged from either Split or Korčula.

**Sleeping**

**Mid-range to expensive** *Konoba Bako*, Gunduliceva 1, T713008. This informal and friendly seafood restaurant lies in a tiny bay with tables right up to the water's edge. The indoor dining area has rough stonewalls and a pool stocked with fresh fish and lobster, and amphorae. *Konoba Jastožera,* Gunduliceva 6, T713407. Newly opened in 2002, this restaurant is based in the former town lobster-pot house. The interior has been beautifully refurbished with tables set on wooden platforms above the water,

**Eating**

and small boats can still enter the central space. Needless to say, the house speciality is lobster.

**Mid-range** *Konoba Porat*, Uvala Porat, on the islet of Biševo. If you spend a day on Biševo, call here for delicious *brodet sa polentom* (fish stew with polenta). They also have a cut-price 3-course daily menu. Open early-Jun to mid-Sep.

**Cheap** *Pizzeria Hum*, Riva bb. Overlooking the seafront promenade, the menu here is limited to octopus salad, pizza and delicious warm tuna sandwiches. Inside there's a billiard table, making it a popular haunt for local teenagers.

**Seriously cheap** *Pekara Kolderaj*, Trg Kralja Tomislava 1. The place to buy fresh *komižka pogača*, a flat bread filled with tomato, onion and anchovies. Open until 0200 through summer. *Hajduk*, Riva 25. A small café serving delicious homemade *krafne* (doughnuts), often still warm, ideal for breakfast with a coffee overlooking the harbour.

**Bars** There are several bars (and cafés) along the Riva (seafront), with the main concentration being at the west end on a small piazza known as *Škor*, where you can drink until the early hours of the morning.

**Festivals** *Ribarski Noč* (Fishermen's Night), first Sat in **Aug**. Live music, local wine and barbequed sardines on the Riva. Sv Nikola (St Nicholas' Day), 6 Dec. The ceremonial burning of a fishing boat takes place at 1100 in front of St Nicholas ' Church.

**Shopping** *Podrum Komiña*, Riva 13. A warehouse selling locally produced wine and *rakija*, including the Komiña speciality, *rogoš*. *Roki's*, Ribarska 23. A small shop selling wines produced by the Roki family.

**Sport** **Diving** *Issa Diving Centre*, Ribarska 91, T713651, www.diving.hr/idc Offer diving courses and trips to a shipwreck and to *Modra Spilja*, as well as night diving. Apr-Oct. **Sailing** There is no official marina in Komiža, but it is possible to moor up along the quay at the far end of the harbour, where electricity and water supplies are available. The 3-day National Day Regatta, Split-Komi ža-Split, is held each year in late May.

**Transport** The island's main port lies in Vis Town. From there, a local **bus** connects incoming **ferry** and **catamaran** services to Komiža (20 mins).

**Directory** **Banks** There is a bank with an ATM on the seafront. **Communications** Post office: Hrvatskih Mućenika bb, Mon-Fri 0800-1400, Sat 0800-1300. **Medical services** Doctor and emergency treatment: Dom zdravlja, T713122. **Pharmacy**: *Ljekarna Komiža*, Podšpiljska bb, T713445.

# Island of Brač

*Phone code: 021*
*Colour map 3, grid C5/6*
*Population: 8,388*

*As the closest island to Split and the only island in Dalmatia with an airport, Brač has the advantage of being easily accessible but the disadvantage of having lost a degree of its island identity due to its proximity to the mainland. The island's top destination is* **Bol**, *home to the lovely beach of* **Zlatni Rat**, *presided over by* **Vidova Gora**, *the highest peak on any of the Adriatic islands. Bol is crawling with tourists through July and August, but if you manage to visit outside peak season it's still well worth it for the fantastic beach. The small coastal town of* **Pučišća** *has long been known for its quarries, which have supplied quality stone for renowned* *buildings such as Diocletian's Palace in Split, Liverpool Cathedral in the UK and the White House in Washington, US.*

**Getting there** There are regular ferries from Split to Supetar (12 daily summer, 7 winter). **Getting around** Local buses then cover the routes across the island from Supetar to Bol and Supetar to Milna, but the times vary through the year, so it's worth checking with the tourist office in advance. **Tourist office** Supetar's tourist office is at Trg Jakšica 17, T630551, www.supertar.hr Bol's tourist office is at Porat bolskih pomoraca bb, T635638, www.bol.hr Milna's tourist office is on the seafront at Riva bb, T/F636233, www.dalmacija.net/milna

**Ins & outs**
*See Transport, pages 240, 243 and 244, for further details*

## Background

The ancient Greeks never settled here, probably due to the lack of fresh water sources. The first inhabitants were Illyrians, who built hilltop forts, followed by the Slavs in the seventh century, who adapted the Illyrian's inland sites to form small isolated villages, where they lived from farming.

During the Middle Ages, pirates from Omiš subjected the island to frequent raids, a factor that only reinforced the logic of the inland settlements. However, when Venice took over in 1420, the pirate problem was resolved and the islanders gradually began to move down to the north coast, though no towns of great cultural significance were to emerge. During the 15th century, an epidemic decimated much of the population, and many of the old villages were burnt in an attempt to stamp out disease. However, over the next 100 years, numbers were boosted by a steady influx of refugees from the mainland interior, who fled to Brač in preference to coming under Ottoman rule. Up until 1815, the island's chief administrative centre was the inland town of Nerežišca. After that date it transferred to Supetar.

The island's population peaked in 1900 at 24,408. Winemaking and the production of olive oil were the main sources of livelihood, and the first wine co-operative in Dalmatia was founded in Bol around this time. However, in the early 20th century, *phylloxera* (a disease that destroyed countless vineyards along the Adriatic) swept across the island, causing many families to abandon the land and emigrate for the Americas, notably to Chile. Farming here has never really recovered, and still today, only one-sixth of the land is used for the potentially lucrative cultivation of vines and olive groves. The tide of fortune turned once again in the 1960's, as tourism brought prosperity to Brač.

## Supetar

This is the island's largest town and chief ferry port. While the bulk of foreigners pass straight through, on their way to the more prestigious resort of Bol, many families from the mainland have summer homes in Supetar itself. It's a pleasant enough place, with the old town focusing on a crescent-shaped harbour, and a decent bathing area, backed by several large hotels, west of the centre. There is little of cultural interest here, though the town cemetery is noted for its beautifully carved tombstones.

*Phone code: 021*
*Colour map 3, grid C5*
*Population: 3,889*
*14 km from Split*

Findings such as ancient sarcophagi and traces of mosaics on St Nicholas peninsula, where the graveyard lies, suggest that the Romans were here. However, the present settlement was not founded until the 16th century, when people from Nerežišća, lying 8 km inland, began to use it as their harbour. They named the place Supetar, after an old chapel dedicated to St Peter (Sveti Petar

**Background**

in Croatian), no longer in existence. The town's main period of development took place during the 18th and 19th centuries, and in 1815 Supetar took over from Nerežišća as the island's administrative centre.

**Sights**  The most interesting monument here is the **cemetery**, located on the wooded cape of St Nicholas. The noted sculptor, **Ivan Rendić** (1849-1932), was from Supetar, and wealthy local families of his time commissioned him to create personalized tombs, ranging from whimsical Art Nouveau gravestones to more substantial Byzantine mausoleums. Strangely, the most prominent monument, the large *Mausoleum of the Petrinović Family*, is not by Rendić, but by Tomo Rosandić (1875-1958) from Split. During the Tito years, Supetar became a popular seaside resort and a large modern hotel complex was built on the coast, west of the centre.

**Sleeping**  **D** *Villa Britanida*, T/F631038. This friendly 30-room hotel lies in a modern building surrounded by palm trees a short distance east of the centre, close to the ferry port. There's an ample terrace with a restaurant serving typical Dalmatian seafood and meat dishes. Open all year. *Supetar Tours*, Porat 27, T631066, can help you find private accommodation.

**Eating**  **Mid-range**  *Vinotoka*, Jobova 6, T630969. Said by locals to be one of the best restaurants on the island, *Vinotoka* lies a couple of blocks back from the bay. Fresh fish and shellfish top the menu, with most dishes prepared outside on a *roštilj* (barbecue). **Cheap to mid-range**  *Dolac*, Ulica Petra Jakšića 8. Just off the bay, in the centre of town, *Dolac* offers a standard choice of meat and fish dishes. They also do a cut-price daily menu, including soup, a main course and side salad, for 40Kn.

**Sports**  **Diving**  *Kaktus*, Put Plive 4, T630421. Based in the *Kaktus Hotel* sports complex, *Kaktus* organizes scuba diving courses and diving trips. **Tennis**  *Hotel Kaktus* sports complex has 8 tennis courts and is open to non-residents.

**Transport**  **Air**  The small airport of Brač, T648615, lies 30 km from Supetar and works summer only. Through high season there are once-weekly flights from **Amsterdam**, **Berlin**, **Frankfurt**, **London** (Heathrow), **Munich**, **Paris**, **Prague**, **Warsaw**, **Vienna**, **Zagreb** and **Zurich**. An airport bus transports passengers to and from various destinations on the island. **Boat**  *Jadrolinija*, T631357, run a regular service from **Split**, with an average 12 ferries per day in summer and 7 ferries per day in winter (1½ hrs). Schedules vary from day to day, so you need to check times with their ticket office.

# Islands of Brač & Šolta

**Banks** There are several banks and ATMs in the town. **Communications** Post office: Vlačica 13, Mon-Fri 0700-2000, Sat 0700-1300. **Medical services** Pharmacy: T640025.

## Bol

On the south coast of Brač, Bol is home to Croatia's most-photographed beach, the spectacular **Zlatni Rat**. This once-upon-a-time idyllic little fishing village has somewhat lost its charm due to the rampant success brought upon it by its beach, but if you can visit outside peak season, it's more than worth the trip. Zlatni Rat is also Croatia's number one site for **windsurfing**, and with the heady heights of **Vidova Gora** mountain surging up behind the coastal strip, it's also a great place for hiking or mountain biking. A little way down the coast, **Pustinja Blaca**, an impressive 16th-century monastery built into the cliff face, can be visited by boat.

*Phone code: 021*
*Colour map 3, grid C5*
*Population: 1,478*
*35 km south*
*of Supetar*

Traces of *villae rusticae* and early Christian sarcophagi show that there was some sort of community here back in Roman times. In fact, Bol claims to be the oldest settlement on the island, though whatever used to stand here was destroyed during a Saracen raid in the ninth century.

    About 600 years later, Dominican monks set up a monastery on the small promontory overlooking the sea, and during the 17th century, as the islanders began to move down from the interior and build settlements along the coast, the present-day village came into being.

    For centuries the people of Bol lived from farming, winemaking and fishing, then in 1963, tourism began. During the 1970's, a string of large hotels were built along the seaside promenade leading from the village to the beach, and Bol soon established itself as one of the country's top resorts. Today it remains a popular destination for package tours; countless agencies organize day trips to and from Bol, and along the waterfront you'll see more signs in German, English, Polish and Czech than Croatian.

**Background**

*Central Dalmatia*

A pleasant tree-lined promenade leads from the village of Bol to the renowned beach, **Zlatni Rat** (Golden Cape). An extraordinary geographical feature, it's composed of fine shingle and runs 500 m perpendicular to the coast, moving and changing its shape slightly from season to season, depending on local winds and currents. It's a perfect beach for children as the water is shallow and the seabed easy on their feet. A cluster of pines at the top end of the cape offer respite from the sun, and there's also a bar here selling cold drinks and snacks.

**Sights**

■ *Getting there: walk along a tree-lined promenade, overlooked by the big package hotels (discreetly hidden by the trees), 2 km. There are no buses but it's a pleasurable walk.* As well as Zlatni Rat there's a stretch reserved for nudists, known as **Paklina**, just 200 m west of the cape. On the east side of Bol, there's a slightly more peaceful pebble beach next to the Domican monastery.

    **Branislav Dešković Gallery** was founded by Branislav Dešković, a native of Brač and keen animal

sculptor. It lies inside a charming Baroque building on the seafront. The collection concentrates on 20th-century Croatian artists who have been inspired by Dalmatia, and includes work by sculptors Ivan Rendić and Ivan Meštrović, and expressionist painter Edo Murtić. ■ *Jul-Aug 1800-2400. Porat bolskih pomoraca bb, close to the tourist office.*

**Dominikanski Samostan** (Dominican Monastery), lying on the eastern edge of the village, overlooking the sea, was founded in 1475. The monks keep a museum, exhibiting a vast collection of coins, notably from the ancient Greek settlements of *Pharos* (Stari Grad on Hvar) and *Issa* (Vis Town on Vis), plus amphorae, Creto-Venetian icons, and an outstanding *Madonna with Child* attributed to the Venetian Mannerist painter Tintoretto (1518-1594). The complex is set in charming gardens and it's possible to stay here overnight (see Sleeping). ■ *Early-May to late-Sep. 1000-1200 and 1700-2000, 10Kn.*

**Excursions** The highest peak on all the Croatian islands, **Vidova Gora** offers a bird's-eye picture of Zlatna Rat and Bol, plus distant views of Hvar, Vis, Pelješac Peninsula and Korčula. Through summer, a small *konoba* serves visitors *pršut* (ham), *sir* (cheese), *janjetina* (roast lamb) and local wine. It's possible to walk or bike up, though the less athletic might opt for a tour by minibus. Enquire at Bol tourist office for details.

A pleasant 5-km walk west of Bol brings you to the coastal hamlet of **Murvica**. Just 200 m above this tiny settlement, the **Drakonjina Spilja** (Dragon's Cave) is a 20-m long cavern, divided into four halls by a series of walls. The first hall is decorated with bizarre reliefs, carved into the stone, depicting dragons and other fabulous creatures. It's said to be the work of the monks from Blaca. The cave is kept locked, but if you ask at Bol tourist office they can arrange for someone to open it for you.

*If you don't fancy the full hike, it's possible to reach Blaca bay by boat from the harbour in Bol – just as the monks used to do*

From Murvica, a further 8 km west along the coast lies **Pustinja Blaca** (Blaca Hermitage). From here, a 2-km uphill hike brings you to this hermitage, an impressive monastery complex built into the cliffside. The hermitage was founded by monks from Poljica, on the mainland, who fled here to escape the Turks in 1550. Originally they took shelter in a cave, subsequently building the church (completed in 1588) and hermitage, and later opening a printing press and a school for children from nearby hamlets (now abandoned). The last monk to live here, Father Niko Miličević Mladi, was a keen astrologer. He set up an **observatory** in 1926, and besides his astronomical tools, left behind a collection of old clocks. Visitors can see these, along with the old-fashioned kitchen, an armoury and a display of period furniture. *Atlas* at Rudina 12, T635233, organize trips.

**Sleeping** Three large pricey package hotels, the *Borak*, *Elaphusa* and *Bretanide*, lie between the village and the beach. **A** *Hotel Ivan*, David cesta 11a, T640888, F640846, www.hotel-ivan.com In the centre of Bol, this traditional Dalmatian house has been converted into a luxury hotel set in a walled garden. There are 16 suites, each with a kitchen and balcony, and 16 guest rooms. Facilities include an outdoor swimming pool, gym, massage and restaurant. **B** *Hotel Kaštil*, Frane Radića 1, T635995, F635997. This old stone building overlooking the harbour offers 32 simple but comfortable guest rooms. It has its own restaurant, on a 1st-floor terrace above the sea. **F** *Dominican Monastery*, Glavica, T778000. From Easter to early Oct, it is possible to rent rooms and apartments in the monastery. Breakfast, lunch and dinner are also available. An extra 25% rate for a shower. *Boltours*, Vladimira Nazora 18, T635693, www.boltours.com, can help you find private accommodation. They also rent scooters, bikes and boats, and organize scuba diving, surfing and tennis courses.

**Mid-range**  *Gušt*, Frane Radic 14, T635911. In an old stone building in the centre of
Bol, this small restaurant offers a good range of fish and lobster dishes, as well as
*janjetina* (roast lamb) and *pašticada* (beef stew). There are a few tables outside on the
terrace, but you may have to queue for a place.

**Eating**

**Cheap to mid-range**  *Ribarska Kućica*, T635144. The coastal path east of the centre
leads to this informal eatery, with tables next to the sea. Fish and seafood are on offer,
while pizza makes a cheaper option. It's popular with locals and works all year, staying
open until 0200 through summer.

*Faces Club*, Bol, T635410, www.mastersfaces.com  One of the largest open-air discos
in the country. *Faces* is owned by footballer Igor Štimac, formerly of West Ham United
and the Croatian national team.

**Entertainment**

**Diving**  *Big Blue*, Podan Glavice 2, T635614, www.big-blue-sport.hr, organize diving
courses and trips. **Hiking**  *Behind Bol*, Vidova Gora stands 778 m high. It's possible to
reach the peak following a marked footpath from the village (see Excursions). Be sure
to wear decent walking boots and take plenty of water. Ascent 2½ hrs, descent 2 hrs.
**Mountain biking**  *Big Blue*, Podan Glavice 2, T635614, www.big-blue-sport.hr, rent
mountain bikes and organize biking expeditions to Vidova Gora and Blaca Hermitage
(see Excursions), with an optional shuttle service to shorten the ride. **Tennis**  *Zlatni
Rat* (Tennis Centre), T635222. Lying close to the beach, this vast complex comprises 20
clay courts, 8 of which are floodlit. Coaching is available, and raquets and balls can be
hired. The annual one-week WTA Ladies' Open is held here, late-Apr to early-May.
**Windsurfing**  *Big Blue*, Podan Glavice 2, T/635614, www.big-blue-sport.hr, organize
windsurfing courses and rental equipment.

**Sports**

**Air**  The small airport of Brač (see Transport, page 240, for details) lies 10 km from
Bol. **Boat**  *Jadrolinija* (no Bol office, for information contact Split office, T338333) run a
daily catamaran service from **Jelsa** on the island of Hvar to **Split**, calling at Bol en route.
The boat departs from Bol at 0630 to arrive in Split at 0730, then leaves Split at 1600 to
arrive in Bol at 1700. In addition, regular ferries run between the island's main port,
**Supetar**, and **Split**. Local buses from Bol to Supetar are scheduled to coincide with the
ferries (50 mins).

**Transport**

**Banks**  There are several banks and ATMs in the town. **Communications**  Post offices:
Uz Pjacu 5, Mon-Fri 0800-1400, Sat 0800-1300. **Medical services**  Pharmacy: T635987.

**Directory**

# Milna

In a deep, sheltered bay, Milna is found on the southwest corner of Brač. It's a
restful fishing village with a seafront promenade built around a deep curving
harbour. A centuries-old retreat for ships, due to its sheltered waters, it's still
popular with sailing boats today, and offers Brač's only year-round marina for
yachts. If you're travelling from Split by private boat, Milna makes an ideal
first port of call on the way out to the surrounding islands.

*Phone code: 021*
*Colour map 3, grid C5*
*Population: 1,100*
*18 km from Supetar*

Many a Roman galley in distress must have taken shelter in this protected
bay, and for centuries shepherds from the island's interior are said to have
wintered their flocks here, finding respite from the icy *bura* wind and capturing the late-day sun. However, the village itself only came into being in the late
16th century, when it was settled by families from the inland town of
Nerežišća. People lived from fishing, sailing and winemaking, and Milna
quickly grew into a prosperous little place. The late-Baroque Church of Our

Lady of the Annunciation was erected in 1783, when only 500 people lived here, though the church's grandeur gives the impression of a place of considerable status. In 1806, at the time of the Napoleonic wars, Milna served as the island's capital during a brief period of Russian occupation. By the late 19th century, there were 2,500 inhabitants and two shipyards, and Milna was producing a greater tonnage of ships than the far larger city of Split. Sadly, over the last 100 years, many families have emigrated and Milna has seen a rapid process of depopulation. Today there's just one medium-sized hotel here, and recent talk of constructing a special beach for disabled children has been quashed, as the project failed to meet the approval of the local council. A pleasant coastal path leads to the main public beach, about 2 km from the centre, on the north side of the bay.

**Sleeping & eating**   **E** *Hotel Milna*, T636116, F636550. A typical 1970's building, on the south side of the bay, just a 10-min walk from the centre, *Hotel Milna* offers basic but comfortable rooms and a small private beach. Open early-May to late-Sep. *Fontana*, Riva bb, T636285. The only restaurant in the village to stay open all year, *Fontana* serves up passable risotto, pasta and *frigane ligne* (fried squid) on a large summer terrace overlooking a small square, just off the seafront. Mid-range. Several local families let out rooms and tastefully refurbished apartments – Milna tourist office for details.

**Sport**   **Sailing**  **ACI Marina**, Milna, T636306, www.aci-club.hr  170 berths. Open all year.

**Transport**   *Jadrolinija*, T631357, run regular **ferries** between **Supetar** and **Split**. Local **buses** from Milna to Supetar are scheduled to coincide with the ferries (30 mins). In addition, through summer, *SEM* run a weekend **catamaran** service, departing from **Split** Fri 1500 and Sun 1945, and returning from Milna Fri 1600 and Sun 2030.

## Island of Šolta

*Phone code: 021*
*Colour map 3,*
*grid C4/5*
*Population: 1,500*
*16 km southwest*
*of Split*

Šolta, separated from the mainland by the *Splitski Kanal* (Split Channel), has never been a particularly popular destination. The few Croatians who visit the island generally have some family connection here, and the only tourist development to be found is a modern holiday village, used as a children's camp through summer. However, if you have your own boat, the south side of Šolta offers steep cliffs punctured by a number of pleasant coves, perfect for putting down anchor and bathing, while Maslinica, on the western tip of the island, even warrants an overnight stop. The chief town, Grohote, lies inland, while the other major settlements line the north and west coast.

**Background**   It's a long-standing joke with little girls in Split; 'If you're naughty you'll end up marrying a man from Šolta'. There's nothing particularly horrid about the place, it's just rather desolate and slightly neglected. No great towns were ever founded here, and the *karst* landscape supports scanty pastures. Grapes, olives, figs and almonds grow well enough, but are produced in modest quantities, just enough for the local population.

In Roman times, ships would take shelter in Nečujam Bay on the north side of the island, where Emperor Diocletian had a fish farm, and when Roman *Salona* was sacked in the seventh century, some of the survivors took refuge on Šolta. Like most of the surrounding islands, Šolta came under Venice from 1420 to 1797, though even then it remained a sleepy backwater, with few eventful moments other than the arrival of a group of refugees from mainland Klis, following the village's capture by the Turks in 1537.

The islanders have a reputation for keeping themselves to themselves, and remain aloof from mainland politics. Traditionally communism was well supported here, and several partisan monuments bearing the red star can still be seen, unlike on the mainland where most were demolished during the recent war of independence.

**Sights**

The island's main port is **Rogač**, which grew up during the 18th century as the harbour to Grohote, lying 2 km inland. There's little of interest here, but local buses connect Rogač to the surrounding villages, with the timetable corresponding to incoming and outgoing boat services.

Lying practically in the centre of the island, **Grohote** is Šolta's chief town, and this is where you'll find services such as the post office, school, doctor's surgery and fire brigade. Most of Grohote has been rebuilt over the last three decades, though a quarter of abandoned stone houses to the south of town give a picture of how it once looked.

Some 9 km west of Rogač, perched on the western tip of the island, is **Maslinica**. It's indisputably Šolta's prettiest village – 18th-century fishermen's cottages surround three sides of a narrow bay, protected from the open sea to the west by the scattered islets of the Maslinica archipelago, creating a particularly memorable scene at sunset.

On the south side of the bay, the impressive **Dvor Conte Alberti** (Count Alberti's Castle) dates from 1708. During Tito's time it served as a hotel, but since Croatia gained independence it's one of many state properties to have been privatized. A German businessman has bought it for his own private use, with plans to open a restaurant on the ground floor.

Behind the villages, modern holiday houses are dispersed through the pinewoods to each side of the bay, and there's a decent pebble beach, **Tepli Bok**, as well as several secluded coves for bathing. Small yachts can moor up in the harbour along the seafront, and just south of Maslinica, **Uvala Šešula** is a sheltered bay offering safe overnight anchorage.

**Nečujam**, 7 km east of Rogač, is a deep bay backed by a modern holiday complex of 200 small whitewashed villas, set amid a dense pinewoods. The focal point is a long pebble beach, and the complex encompasses tennis courts, boat rentals, a restaurant, disco and post office. It's open late-May to late-September, and managed by *Šoltatours* (see Sleeping). From mid-June to late-August most of the place is taken over as a children's summer camp. Nečujam means literally 'I can't hear'. This goes back to the original Latin name, *Vallis Surda* (Deaf Cove), probably in reference to the numerous small coves that surround the bay, making communication from one point to another all but impossible.

**Stomorska**, 10 km east of Rogač, is a sleepy fishing village made up of 18th-century terracotta-roofed cottages, built around a small bay, with a nearby pebble beach.

**Sleeping & eating**

*SEM Marina Travel Agent*, based in Split, T338219, www.sem-marina.hr, can help you find private accommodation on Šolta. *Šoltatours*, T475259, www.soltatours.com, manage the holiday village of Nečujam, and can also help you find houses and apartments to rent across the island. *Konoba Saskinja*, Riva bb, Maslinica, is a cheap to mid-range restaurant with a pleasant terrace overlooking the harbour. This old stone building accommodates a *konoba* serving coffee and drinks through the morning, and offering a standard choice of barbecued meat and fish, plus pasta and risotto dishes, for lunch and dinner.

Central Dalmatia

Transport  *Jadrolinija* (no Šolta office, for information contact the Split office, T338333) run a regular **ferry** service from Rogač to **Split**, with an average 5 ferries per day in summer and 3 per day in winter (1 hr). In addition, *SEM* run a daily **catamaran** service, designed for islanders working on the mainland, departing from Rogač at 0700 and leaving Split for the return journey at 2030 (30 mins). Local **buses** connect the surrounding villages to Rogač, to correspond with incoming and outgoing boat lines.

# Makarska

*Phone code: 021*
*Colour map 3, grid C6*
*Population: 13,716*
*67 km southeast of*
*Split, on the E65*
*coastal road*

*Makarska combines the qualities of an old-fashioned Dalmatian port town and a modern-day tourist resort. The setting is impressive – a palm-lined seafront promenade is built around a large cove, protected from the open sea by a wooded peninsula to the southwest, and sheltered from the cold bura wind by the craggy limestone heights of Mount Biokovo to the northeast. Through summer it makes a perfect base for holidaying on the beaches of the so-called **Makarska Rivijera**, while keen walkers are drawn to the rugged landscapes and rural villages of **Biokovo Nature Park** during spring and autumn. Makarska is popular with SAGA – the only travel agency that continued operating in Croatia through the 1990's – but come summer it's overrun with young visitors and families from all over Europe, who are drawn by it pleasant beaches, vibrant nightlife and reasonably priced accommodation.*

Ins & outs  **Getting there** There are about 20 buses daily from Split to Makarska and around
*See Transport,* 12 daily from Dubrovnik. **Getting around** Makarska is very small and you can easily
*page 249, for* explore the place on foot. The seafront promenade is closed to traffic, as are the cob-
*further details* bled streets of the old town. **Tourist office** The town tourist office is at Obala Kralja Tomislava 16, T616288, www.makarska.hr

## History

Makarska was founded as the Roman *Mucurum*, though the original settlement was devastated by the Goths in 548. It was next mentioned in 950 by the Byzantine Emperor, Constantine VII, in *De Administrando Imperio* (On Imperial Administration). Describing the coastal strip running from the River Cetina in the north to the River Neretva in the south, an area he referred to as *Pagania*, he noted four *castrum* (fortified towns): *Berullia* (Brela), *Mokron* (Makarska), *Ostrok* (Zaostrog) and *Labinetza* (Lapčan, present-day Gradac).

This entire territory later fell to the Ottoman Turks, who captured Makarska in 1499 and established it as a port and administrative centre. During the mid-16th century, the *Emir* (local governor), ordered that the town be fortified, and paintings from that time depict three towers connected by sturdy walls, sadly no longer in existence.

The Turks were pushed out in 1646, though locals did not fully recognize subsequent Venetian rule until 1681. However, under Venice the economy thrived, and the centre of Makarska gained its present-day appearance during the 18th century, when the Baroque Crkva Sv Marko (Church of St Mark) was erected at the top end of Kačićeva Trg, the main square, around which wealthy local merchants built elegant town houses.

Tourism has a long tradition here; the first hotel was built in 1914, under the Austrians, and the *Society for the Beautification of the Town* was founded in 1922. In 1962, a terrible earthquake caused considerable damage to Makarska and the surrounding villages, but just a decade later it became a popular holiday destination. As the economy boomed, more hotels were constructed along the coast, and locals built increasingly larger houses with rooms and apartments to let to summer vacationers.

## Sights

Founded in the 16th century by monks from Bosnia, who the Ottoman Turks granted special permission to build a religious home just outside the town walls, the original monastery was burnt down in the late 17th century, so the building's present appearance, with a lovely central cloister, dates largely from 1671. The main reason for visiting the complex is to see the Shell Museum, a well-presented collection of over 3,000 shells from all over the world. It was initiated in 1963 by Fra Jure Radic (1920-90), a nature-loving monk who also founded the Botanical Garden at Kotišina (see Excursions, Biokovo Nature Park). ■ *Summer 1000-1200 and 1700-1900. 10Kn. T611256.*

**Franjevački Samostan (Franciscan Monastery) & Muzej Malakološki (Shell Museum)**

Lying 100 m off the coastal road, 2 km northwest of Makarska, this delightful sanctuary is set in a cave next to a glade amid pinewoods. It was founded in 1908, due to its resemblance to the shrine at Lourdes in France. A small chapel, called **Our Lady of Lourdes**, was built in the opening to the cave, and an open-air altar erected in the meadow before it. Masses are held daily at 1500 through winter and 1700 in summer. The main pilgrimage days are 11 February, 25 March, 15 August and 7 and 8 September.

**Veprič**

## Excursions

Behind Makarska, a network of narrow country lanes and signed footpaths lead through vineyards and olive groves to the semi-abandoned stone hamlets of Makar (1 km northeast), Veliko Brdo (3 km north) and Kotišina (3 km east), each of which lie on the border of Park Prirode Biokovo (Biokovo Nature Park). These settlements were badly damaged by the 1962 earthquake. Residents subsequently moved down to Makarska, though some families still keep weekend homes and small-holdings here.

**Veliko Brdo & Kotišina**

Just above Kotišina, you'll find the enchanting Kotišina Botanical Gardens, an informal rockery established in 1984, displaying indigenous plant species, each marked with its Latin name. Above the gardens stands **Kaštel**, a 16th-century hideaway built into the cliff face, where locals took refuge from the Turks. Over the main entrance, note several small stone channels, intended for pouring hot oil over would-be attackers.

**Kotišina Botanical Gardens**

Once within the park, the *karst* landscape becomes increasingly barren, with scanty pastures and bare limestone rocks supporting only the hardiest indigenous species, such as herds of chamois goats and mouflon sheep. A number of mountain huts provide basic overnight accommodation during the hiking season. From Makar, a well-marked trail leads to the peak of **Vošac** (1440 m), which can be walked in 3½ hours, while another trail departs from Kotišina to reach the same peak in five hours. From Vošac, the terrain becomes increasingly rocky, though hardened hikers can attempt a final 1½ hour pull to the highest peak, **Sveti Jure** (1760 m). The summit is capped by a slightly disheartening radio and TV transmitter, while its namesake, the tiny stone chapel of Sv Jure, lies close by, but remains closed for most of the year. However, the views are breathtaking, and on a clear day it is

**Park Prirode Biokovo (Biokovo Nature Park)**

possible to see across the sea to Montegargano in Italy to the southwest, and inland to the hills around Sarajevo in Bosnia to the northeast. See Eating, below for *Vrata Biokova* restaurant.

■ *Getting there: you can hike to the park or less athletic visitors can reach Sveti Jure by private transport from Makarska (31 km), taking the road for Vrgorac then swinging sharp left for the park. The head office is in Makarska, T616924, www.biokovo.com However, they offer very limited assistance, and you're better off contacting the Makarska-based* Biokovo Activ Holidays, *T611688, an agency running organized tours of the mountain, both on foot or by jeep. They can also give you up-to-date information about which mountain huts are open.*

## Essentials

**Sleeping**   **C** *Hotel Biokovo*, Obala Kralja Tomislava bb, T615244, F615081, www.hotelbiokovo.hr Comprising 55 rooms and 5 apartments, this pleasant old-fashioned hotel lies in the centre of town, has a ground floor café and restaurant giving onto the seaside promenade. Open all year. Pets welcome. *Sv Petar Lighthouse*. Contact *Adriatica Net*, Selska 34, Zagreb, T3644461, F3644463, www.adriatica.net Built in 1884, on the peninsula of Sv Petar, at the entrance to Makarska Bay, this lighthouse has been refurbished to create an apartment sleeping 6. It lies close to the main beach, just 800 m from town, and is accessed by an asphalt road. *Mariva Turist Agency*, Obala kralja Tomislava 15a, T615264, www.marivaturist.hr, can help you find private accommodation in Makarska and villages along the Makarska Rivijera.

**Eating**   **Mid-range**   *Restoran Susvid*, Kačićev Trg 9, T612732. Overlooking the main square, this restaurant serves excellent barbecued fish and carefully prepared vegetable and salad side dishes. It stays open all year. *Stari Mlin*, Prvosvibanjska 43, T611509. Housed in an 18th-century Baroque building, a few blocks back from the seafront, *Stari Mlin* specializes in fish and seafood. The cavernous interior is warm and cosy through winter, while a large vine-covered terrace comes into use through summer. Closed Sun. *Vrata Biokova*, Park Prirode Biokovo, T613902, www.makarska.hr/vratabiokova Some 15 km from Makarska and 897 m above sea level, this farmhouse restaurant specializes in typical rural cooking. Firm favourites are the lamb, veal and chicken dishes prepared under a *peka*, though for these you should call one day in advance. Visitors are welcome to take a look at the farm animals – horses, donkeys, sheep and goats – making this an amusing outing for children. Open early-May to mid-Oct.

**Café**   *Café Hotel Biokovo*, Obala Kralja Tomislava bb. With a spacious terrace beside the seafront promenade, this café is popular with locals and non-residents as well as people staying in the hotel.

**Club**   *Grotta*, Setaliste Sv Petra. Open-air summer nightclub on the peninsula of Sv Petar, overlooking the sea.

**Entertainment**   *Ljetno Kino*, Kralja Tomislava 8, T612280. Open-air summer **cinema** in a walled garden, just off the seafront.

**Festivals**   *Makarska Summer Festival*, mid-**Jul** to late-**Aug**, open-air concerts of *klapa*, folk music and Croatian pop bands. *Sveti Jure* (St George's Day), last Sat in **Jul**. Pilgrims walk up to the small chapel of Sv Jure on Mount Biokovo, where a special mass is held.

**Sports**   **Diving**   *More-Sub*, Kralja P Krešimira 43, T611727. **Tennis**   *Tennis Centre Posejdon*, Put Cvitacke bb, T617044. This modern tennis centre, comprising 6 outdoor clay courts and 2 indoor courts, is often used for big tennis tournaments. It's situated close to the main beach, and visitors are welcome to play here. Expect to pay 55Kn per hr. **Walking**  Well-marked paths lead to several peaks on Mount Biokovo (see Excursions, page 247.

**Transport**

**Bus**  About 20 buses per day run between **Split** and Makarska (1 hr 10 mins), many of them on long distance hauls along the coast between **Rijeka** and **Dubrovnik**. Makarska bus station lies on the main road above town, T612333. **Ferry**  *Jadrolinija* (no Makarska office, for information contact Split office, T338333) run a ferry service from Makarska to **Sumartin** (30 mins) on the eastern tip of the island of Brač, with an average 5 ferries per day in summer and 3 ferries per day in winter.

**Directory**

**Communications**  Post office: Trg 4 Svibanj bb, Mon-Fri 0800-2000, Sat 0800-1300. **Medical services**  Doctor and emergency treatment: Dom zdravlja, T612033. **Pharmacy:** Ljekarna, T611227.

## Makarska Rivijera

Apart from Makarska itself, none of the resorts offer much of cultural interest, though their pebble beaches, clean sea and large modern hotels cater well enough for visitors who simply want to swim and sunbathe. The 60-km strip of coast runs from Brela in the north to Gradac in the south.

*Local buses running along the coast stop in all the towns mentioned*

Baška Voda, 9 km northwest of Makarska, is made up of a string of large modern hotels, restaurants and pizzerias on the seafront. From here, a pleasant coastal path leads north to Brela and south to Makarska both of which are within walking or biking distance. Families from Bast, a pretty hillside village of slate-roof cottages 2 km to the east, founded Baška Voda in the late 17th century, after the Ottoman Turks had left the region. The harbour dates back to 1912, and during the 1930's tourism began with the opening of the *Hotel Slavija*. The tourist office is at Obala Sv Nikole 71, T620713, www.baskavoda.hr

**Baška Voda**

**Sleeping and eating**  **C** *Hotel Slavija*, Obala Sv Nikole 71, T620155. Baška Voda's oldest hotel, dating back to the 1930's, is set in a terraced garden overlooking a narrow pebble beach. Ask for a room with a balcony and sea view. Open mid-May to mid-Sep. *Restaurant King*, Iza Placa 3, T620640. This friendly little restaurant is known locally for good fresh fish and seafood. Open for dinner only. Mid-range.

At Brela, a 2-km stretch of pebble beaches, interspersed by rocky outcrops and small harbours, is backed by agave and scented pinewoods. The town was founded in the 19th century, when families from Gornja Brela, on the lower slopes of Biokovo, moved down to the coast. Organized tourism began in 1937, when the first hotels were built along the seaside promenade, and although they have since multiplied, Brela still prides itself with being less commercial than its neighbours. It's possible to walk or bike along the coastal path all the way to Makarska, passing through Baška Voda en route. Brela tourist office is at Obala Kneza Domagoja, T618337, www.brela.hr

**Brela**

*Most Dalmatians consider Brela, 5 km up the coast from Baška Voda, to be the loveliest of all the Makarska Rivijera resorts*

**Sleeping and eating**  **D** *Hotel Berulia*, Brela, T603599, F619005. Renovated in 2002, this 153-room modern hotel is set amid a pinewood, a short distance back from the beach. Facilities include an indoor pool, a fitness centre with sauna and massage and a restaurant and café with an open-air terrace. Renovated *Konoba Feral*, Obala kneza

Central Dalmatia

Domagoja, T618909. Guests sit at rustic tables and benches on a terrace next to the beach, while the owner-cook serves up local seafood dishes such as *brodet* (fish stew) and house wine by the carafe. Cheap to mid-range.

**Tučepi** Lying 5 km southeast of Makarska, the scattered hamlets of Gornji Tučepi – Podpeć, Čovići, Srida Sela, Šimići and Podstup – nestle on the lower slopes of Biokovo. Their history dates back centuries, though since the 18th century they have seen a gradual process of depopulation, as families began moving down to Tučepi-Kraj, a 4-km long sprawling resort along the coast. Like Makarska, Tučepi offers decent pebble beaches plus a series of footpaths leading up to Biokovo Nature Park. Tučepi tourist office is at Kraj 46, T623100, www.tucepi.com

**Sleeping B** *Hotel Kaštelet*, Dracevica 35, Tučepi-Kraj, T623305. The 18th-century summer home of Don Klement Grubišic, a notorious local priest, has been converted to provide 20 guest rooms. It's managed by the neighbouring *Hotel Alga*, and works late-Apr to early-Oct. *Ratours*, Donji Ratac 24, T623169, www.ratours.com, specialize in private accommodation in Tučepi, and also organize excursions to Split, Korčula and Hvar. **F** *Restoran Pansion Jeny*, Gornji Tučepi 49, T623704, www.makarska.com/jeny Located on the lower slopes of Biokova, just 3 km from Makarska and 2 km from the nature park, this unassuming modern building is home to an excellent restaurant. Local ingredients are used to create beautifully presented dishes. A sophisticated version of Dalmatian cooking, influenced by Italian and French cuisine. They also offer overnight accommodation with a hearty cooked breakfast.

**Eating** *Restoran Postup*, Tučepi-Kraj, T623531. With a summer terrace overlooking the marina, this friendly eatery serves up delicious *salata od hobotnice* (octopus salad) and *ribe na žaru* (barbecued fish). They also do a cut-price daily fixed-menu, and a special vegetarian plate. Open all year.

**Sport** Sailing: *Marina Tučepi*, Raj bb, T601112. 70 berths, open all year.

**Zaostrog** Some 37 km southeast of Makarska, Zaostrog, like its neighbours, grew up from an older settlement (deserted after the 1962 earthquake) located on the slopes of Biokovo. The first building on the coast was the Franciscan Monastery dating from 1468, where monks kept the Catholic faith alive during Ottoman occupation. Inside, there's a small museum and a charming cloistered courtyard. Zaostrog itself is an unspoilt village with a good pebble beach backed by pinewoods and olive groves. There's only one hotel, but locals rent rooms to visitors.

**Gradac** Located 42 km southeast of Makarska, Gradac marks the end of the Rivijera. The newer part of town lies just off the main coastal road, perched on a triangular peninsular jutting out to sea. There's a popular pebble beach, Gornja Vala, south of town, while the original settlement of Gradac, built into the hillside above the coast, has a watchtower from 1661, built to defend the area against the Turks.

**Sleeping and eating C** *Hotel Marco Polo*, Obala 15, Gradac, T/F697502, www.hotel-marcopolo.com This rather non-descript modern building conceals a friendly family-run hotel with 18 rooms and a pleasant terrace restaurant giving onto a pebble beach. *Konoba Naše Malo Misto*, Starin Porat, Gradac, T697374. On the seafront, this traditional Dalmatian *konoba* specialises in fish and seafood.

# Šibenik

*In a protected channel, at the mouth of the River Krka, the medieval part of Šibenik is a warren of steep winding alleyways and terracotta rooftop houses, built into a hillside below the remains of a* **Venetian fortress**. *Close to the sea-front, the city's main sight is the monumental* **Renaissance Cathedral of St Jacob**, *which is included on the UNESCO list of World Heritage Sites.*

*From the small harbour, local ferries enter the open sea through a narrow channel, stopping at the peaceful islands of* **Zlarin** *and* **Prvić**, *before continuing to the nearby mainland resort of* **Vodice**. *On the edge of town, disused factories and sprawling modern suburbs reveal a period of 20th-century industrial development followed by economic collapse caused by the war. Šibenik is not well-geared towards tourists – most visitors to the area stay in Vodice – but you can happily devote half a day to the historic centre, and it makes a good starting point for a visit to* **Krka National Park**.

*Phone code: 022*
*Colour map 3, grid B4*
*Population: 51,553*
*300 km from Zagreb,*
*403 km from Pula, 300*
*km from Rijeka, 74 km*
*from Zadar, 75 km*
*from Split, and 291 km*
*from Dubrovnik*

## Ins and outs

There are good bus and train links with the main cities in Croatia and from surrounding countries. The bus station is at Draga bb, on the seafront, a 5-min walk from the city centre. Left luggage 0630-2100, 10Kn per piece per day. The train station is at Milete bb, south of the bus station, a 10-min walk from the city centre. There's no left luggage.

**Getting there**
*See Transport, page 254, for further details*

The historic centre occupies a small area, concentrated on the hillside below the fortress. It can only be explored on foot, as the winding cobbled alleyways are too narrow to allow traffic – be sure to wear comfortable walking shoes.

**Getting around**

The city tourist office is at Ulica Fausta Vrančića 18, T212075. The county tourist office is at Fra N Ružića bb, T212346.

**Tourist office**

As it's not really a tourist destination, life in Šibenik continues at its own pace the year through, with little seasonal variation. If you're planning on visiting Krka National Park, the woods are at their most beautiful in spring and autumn, when the river is also quite swollen, making the waterfalls all the more impressive. However, one of the greatest pleasures at Krka is swimming, which is only possible in midsummer as the water is icy cold the rest of the year.

**Best time to visit**

Central Dalmatia

## Background

Unlike other major cities along the East Adriatic coast – such as Zadar, Trogir and Split – which were established by Greeks and Romans, Šibenik was founded by Slavs. It was first documented in a Royal Charter issued by the Croatian king, Petar Krešimir IV, in 1066. In 1298, it gained the status of town, and was described as a settlement of triangular plan, with a hilltop fortress (present-day Sv Ana) overlooking a quarter of tightly packed stone houses built into a hillside (present-day Gradina).

In 1412, following three years of strong local resistance, Šibenik fell to Venice. Over the following three centuries, lucrative trade, conducted between the Ottoman-held hinterland and the Venetian port, brought material wealth coupled with a surge of creative activity. Inspired by the beauty of the cathedral in nearby Trogir (see page 212), the people of Šibenik set about building a similar yet even grander monument, and the Cathedral of St Jacob, sponsored by local citizens of all social classes, was erected. Not so well documented but even more innovative for its time, several decades later, the local scientist Faust Vrančić (1551-1617) published *Machinae Novea*, in which he anticipated the invention of the parachute.

During the 20th century, under Yugoslavia, Šibenik expanded into a busy industrial centre, with a large aluminium factory, metal works and a shipyard, drawing workers from all corners of the country. The war of the 1990's saw the city in a complex situation, as its mixed population of Croats and Serbs were driven to internal conflict. The result, a decade later, is a situation of social and economic depression, industrial collapse and high unemployment.

## Sights

**Katedrala Sv Jakova (Cathedral of St Jacob)**
*Take a look at the intricately sculptured portals and the wonderful baptistery*

Built over an entire century, between 1431 and 1536, this splendid cathedral was constructed in several distinct stages. The result, combining a mix of late-Gothic and Renaissance styles, is a three-aisle basilica based on the plan of a Latin cross, with a trefoil façade and cupola. The project was initiated by Venetian architects, who worked here for 10 years. They were responsible for the ornate Gothic portals – the main door portraying *The Last Judgement*, surrounded by the twelve Apostles and crowned by a portrait of Christ, and the side door, the *Entrance to Paradise*, guarded to either side by a lion, one carrying Adam and the other Eve. In 1441, Juraj Dalmatinac, a Dalmatian from Zadar, who had trained as an architect in Venice, took over. He proposed a far grander edifice, a three-aisle basilica topped by an octagonal cupola, introducing the newly emerging Renaissance style. He also created one of the building's best loved features – a frieze running around the outer walls, made up of 74 faces, some moustachioed, some turbaned, said to be those citizens too stingy to contribute to the cost of the building. Sadly, Dalmatinac died in 1473, before his masterpiece was completed. The final works were conducted by one of his pupils, Nikola Fiorentinac, who oversaw the mounting of the cupola and the construction of the vaulted roof, employing a unique system of interlocking monolithic stone slabs cut to shape.

The baptistery was designed by Dalmatinac but completed by another of his pupils, Andrija Aleši, an Albanian from Durres. It lies to the right of the main altar, and is accessed by a short flight of stone steps. It is an enchanting space, with decorative stonework carved fine as lace. The final stone of the building was laid in 1536, and in 1555 it was dedicated to St Jacob.

In front of the cathedral, opposite the main portal, stands a bronze statue of Dalmatinac, by the 20th-century sculptor, Ivan Meštrović.

■ *0900-1900. Trg Republike Hrvatske.*

**Šibenski Muzej (Šibenik Museum)**

Immediately behind the cathedral stands the late-Renaissance *Kneževa Palača* (Rector's Palace), built in Venetian times as the residence of the city governor. Today it houses a rather dull museum, displaying archaeological finds from Šibenik and the surrounding area and a number of 15th-century religious icons. ■ *Summer 1000-1300 and 1900-2200; winter closed. 10Kn. T213880. Gradska Vrata 3.*

Opposite the Cathedral stands the Old Loggia, which served as the seat of the town council under Venice. It was built between 1533 and 1542, to a design by the Venetian Mannerist architect, Michele Sanmicheli. Badly damaged during the Second World War, it was subsequently restored, and the ground level now houses a restaurant, with tables outside in the arched portico through summer. ■ *Trg Republike Hrvatske 1.*

**Gradska Vijecnica (Old Town Hall)**

Perched on the hilltop above Gradina, the medieval quarter of town, this fortress merits a visit for the spectacular view it offers over the terracotta rooftops and out across the sea. Orientated towards the west, it's particularly evocative at sunset. It's the city's oldest defensive structure, though what you see today – little more than crumbling ramparts – dates back to the 16th century. From the Cathedral follow any one of the steep winding streets up through the medieval quarter, to arrive at the hilltop fortress.

**Tvrdava Sv Ana (St Anne's Fortress)**

Locals recommend going to the nearby islands of **Zlarin** and **Prvić**, where the water is crystal clear and perfect for swimming. Otherwise, the beaches in front of the *Hotel Solaris* complex, 3 km south of town, are probably the best.

**Beaches**

## Essentials

Accommodation in the city centre is limited (if you're arriving late and planning on staying here arrange a place to sleep in advance). Few visitors choose to stay in Šibenik itself, with the nearby seaside resort of Vodice offering plentiful accommodation and a more salubrious environment for holiday-makers. In the past there was a Youth Hostel in Šibenik, but it is now closed and looks unlikely to reopen in the near future. **C** *Jadran Hotel*, Obala Oslobodjenje 52, T212644. Located in the centre of town on the seafront promenade, just a 5-min walk from the bus station, this 70-room 1970's hotel provides simple but comfortable accommodation. Open all year. *Nik*, A Supuka 5, T338550, www.nik.hr, can help you find private accommodation in the Šibenik area, including Vodice, Primošten, and the small islands of Zlarin and Prvić. They also arrange excursions to the nearby national parks of Krka and Kornati.

**Sleeping**

**Mid-range to expensive** *Gradska Vijećnica*, Trg Republike Hrvatske 1, T213605. Commanding a prime site, with tables on the main square opposite the Cathedral, this restaurant is based in the 16th-century Venetian Town Hall. The house speciality is *paprika punjena sirom* (peppers stuffed with cheese). *Uzorita*, Bana Jelačića 50, T213660. Šibenik's best-known restaurant, dating back to 1898, lies a 20-min walk northeast of the centre and specializes in seafood. The dining room is done out in traditional Dalmatian style with exposed stonewalls, beamed ceilings and heavy wooden furniture. In summer, tables spill out into a romantic courtyard. *Zlatna Ribica*, K Spuňvara 46, Brodarica, on the coast 8 km south of Šibenik, T350300, www.zlatna-ribica.hr Said by many to be the best fish restaurant in the area, the house speciality here is *punjeni oslic* (hake stuffed with spinach and olives). The summer terrace offers views across the sea to the small island of Krapanj, and there is live music on Fri and Sat night. The same management run the neighbouring *Zlatna Ribica Pansion* (T350695), with 16 pleasant double rooms and 2 apartments. Open all year .

**Eating**

**Seriously cheap** *Tržnica*, the open-air market just above the bus station, is the best place to shop for a cheap snack, with several kiosks selling fresh *burek* (filo pastry filled with either cheese or meat).

**Cafés** The seafront promenade, Obala Oslobodjenje and Obala prvoboraca, is lined with busy cafés with outdoor seating.

**Entertainment** *Šibensko Kazalište*, the **theatre**, Kralja Zvonimira 1, T213123. *Kino*, a **cinema**, at Obala Oslobodjenje, next to *Hotel Jadran*, T212870. *Hacijenda*, Magistrala bb, on the road between Šibenik and Vodice is the biggest **nightclub** for miles. Open-air, summer only.

**Festivals** *Medunarodni dječji festival* (International Children's Festival), **late-Jun** to **early-Jul**. Founded in 1958, this 2-week event is organized by Šibenik Theatre and features children's music, drama and puppet theatre.

**Sport** **Diving** *Neptun-Sub*, Draga 4, T331444, www.neptun.sub.hr *Odysseus Diving*, Spardici 1 T577733, www.odysseusdiving-sibenik.hr **Sailing** *Marina Solaris*, *Hotel Solaris* complex, 3 km south of town, T364000. 305 berths, open all year.

**Tour operators** *Atlas Šibenik*, Trg Republike Hrvatske 2, T330232, www.atlas-croatia.com, arrange various excursions throughout the country, including day trips to the nearby national parks of Krka and Kornati. *Croatia Express*, Fra Jerolim Milete 24, T333669, www.croatiaexpress.com, provide public transport information and tickets for the entire country. *Nik*, A Supuka 5, T338550, www.nik.hr, arrange excursions to the nearby national parks of Krka and Kornati.

**Transport** **Bus** Internal services include about 13 buses daily to **Zagreb** (6 hrs); 34 to **Split** (1½ hrs); 3 to Pula in **Istria** (8½ hrs) and 12 to Rijeka in **Kvarner** (6½ hrs). There are also daily international bus lines to **Ljubljana** (Slovenia), **Trieste** (Italy) and **Munich** (Germany). Buses depart several times a week for various other destinations in Germany and Austria. For additional information about buses to and from Šibenik, T212087.

**Ferry** *Jadrolinija*, T213468, run a daily ferry service between **Šibenik** and **Vodice** (total 1 hr), with boats stopping at the islands of **Prvić** and **Zlarin** en route. Schedules vary from day to day and season to season.

**Train** Internal services include 2 trains daily to and from **Zagreb** (7½ hrs); 5 trains daily to **Knin** (1½ hrs) and 5 trains daily to **Split** (2 hrs). Some services require a change at Perković. Šibenik train station, T333699. National train information, T060 333444, www.hznet.hr

**Directory** **Communications** **Post office**: the main post office is at Vladimira Nazora 51, a 5-min walk from the bus station. **Telephone**: if you prefer to telephone from a peaceful phone booth, rather than calling on the street, go to one of the post offices (see above). Otherwise, you'll find phone kiosks on the seafront. **Medical services** Doctors and hospitals: **Bolnica** (Hospital), on Stjepana Radica, a 15-min walk southeast of the centre, T246246, (24-hr casualty). **Pharmacies**: all pharmacies are marked by a glowing green cross. *Ljekarna Varoš*, Kralj Zvonimira 31, T212249, on the main road, a 10-min walk east of the centre, often works 24 hrs, non-stop. If it is not open, there will be a notice on the door saying which pharmacy to go to. **Useful numbers** Ambulance 94; Fire 93; Police 92.

# Skradin and Krka National Park

The picturesque small town of Skradin lies at the point where the Krka River enters a long sea channel. Backed by dense woodland and directly on the waterfront, Skradin's old stone houses and two church spires (one Roman Catholic, the other Orthodox) appear the epitome of peace and harmony. However, less than a decade ago this was the front-line between the Croat-dominated municipality of Šibenik and the Serb-controlled are of Krajina. Many families fled, though thankfully the town suffered little structural damage. Over the last couple of years Skradin has re-established itself as a popular tourist destination, with an excellent marina and a number of good fish restaurants overlooking the harbour. The main reason for coming here though is to catch a boat up to the Krka National Park. The town tourist office is at Obala Bana Šubića 1, T771306, www.skradin.hr

*Phone code: 022*
*Colour map 3, grid B4*
*Population: 3,986*
*16 km north of Šibenik*

Skradin was founded as *Scardona* by the Romans in the third century BC, but met the fate of other early settlements when tribes of Avars and Slavs rampaged along the East Adriatic coast during the seventh century. It was conquered by the Turks in 1522, who held onto it until 1684, when it passed to Venice. Tourism began here during the 1960's, when the Krka Falls area became a popular place for camping. Since the national park was established in 1985, camping has been prohibited, but a regular boat now shuttles day-trippers up river from Skradin 4.5 km to the park's main entrance a Skradinski buk.

**Background**

**Vinarija Bedrica**, in the centre of town, is a family-run wine cellar dating back to1722. The interior is tastefully arranged with wooden barrels and old-fashioned wine-making equipment. The owner lives in the same building, and is happy to open the *vinerija* for visitors interested in sampling and purchasing his wine, *rakija* and *prošek*. ■ *Fra Luje Maruna 14. T771095.*

**Skradin**

Beginning a short distance southwest of Knin, see page 261, and following the course of the River Krka almost to Skradin, the national park encompasses a steep sided, wooded canyon and a series of seven waterfalls. The main entrance lies close to **Skradinski buk**, the park's most spectacular falls, made up of a series of 17 cascades plunging over 40 m into a wide emerald-green basin, ideal for bathing. Next to the falls, a sheltered meadow, bordered by woods, offers an idyllic spot for sunbathing and picnicking. Above Skradinski buk, a series of wooden bridges and well-marked footpaths lead to the next falls, **Roški slap**, 10 km to the north. If you don't fancy the hike, it's possible to catch a second national park boat, which runs several times a day, shuttling visitors between the two falls and calling en route at the 15th-century **Visovac Samostan** (Visovac Monastery) perched on a small island in the middle of **Visovačko Jezero** (Visovac Lake). ■ *Summer 0800-2000; winter 0900-1700. 60Kn. National park boats leave from Skradin for Skradinski Buk on the hour, departing for the return journey on the half hour (25 mins). The cost of the boat ride is included in the entrance ticket. The National Park office is in Šibenik at Trg Ivana Pavla II 5, T217720, www.npkrka.hr*

**Krka National Park**

Central Dalmatia

**Sleeping**  **D** *Hotel Skradinski Buk*, Burinovac bb, T771771. Opened in 2002, this family-run hotel lies in a carefully renovated old stone building in the centre of Skradin. There are 28 rooms, and a 3rd-floor terrace offering views down onto the River Krka. Alternatively, Skradin tourist office can help you find private accommodation in town.

**Eating**  **Mid-range to expensive** *Konoba Toni*, Trgovačka 46, T771177. *Toni* specializes in traditional Dalmatian dishes such as *brudet sa purom* (fish stew with polenta) prepared over an open-fire, and lamb and veal cooked under a *peka*. Guests are welcome to take a look inside the old-fashioned kitchen, to watch the food being made. Open late-Mar to late-Dec. *Zlatne školjke*, Grgura Ninskog 9, T771022. Located in an old stone house with a summer terrace overlooking ACI Marina, this restaurant is best known for *crni rižot* (black risotto), *špageti s plodovima mora* (spaghetti with seafood) and *riba na žaru* (barbecued fish). Open all year.

**Sport**  **Sailing** *ACI Marina*, T771365, www.aci-club.hr, 200 berths. Open all year. Private vessels are not allowed upstream of *Skradinski Most* (Skradin Bridge). Skradin Marina is a popular place for keeping wooden boats through winter, as the combination of fresh water (from the river) and seawater prevent wood from premature ageing.

**Transport**  Local **buses** run 5 times daily between **Šibenik** and Skradin (25 mins). In addition, several travel agencies operate all-inclusive day trips to the national park, by **boat**, from **Šibenik** and **Vodice**.

## Islands of Zlarin and Prvić

*Phone code: 022*
*Colour map 3, grid B4*
*Population: 729*

The tiny islands of Zlarin and Prvić lie just a short ferry ride away from Šibenik and Vodice, making a restful escape from urban life. Both are car-free and offer crystal clear water for swimming.

**Zlarin**  Lying a 30-minute ferry ride from Šibenik, this tiny island is roughly 6 km long and 2 km wide. The sole settlement, also called Zlarin, is built around a deep bay, with a palm-lined seafront promenade overlooked by old stone houses and an 18th-century Baroque parish church. During the Middle Ages, Zlarin was owned by the Šibenik chapter, and for six centuries, the islanders lived from one trade alone: collecting coral. Still today, it is possible to buy coral necklaces and earrings from the so-called *Muzej Koralja* (Coral Museum), more a shop than an exhibition space.

Antony Maglica, the designer of the Mag-Lite (the torch used by astronauts and deep-sea explorers) and founder of the California-based company, *Mag Instrument*, originated from Zlarin.

**Sleeping and eating**  **C** *Hotel Koralj*, Zlarin, T553747. This small hotel has 20 guest rooms and a restaurant. It stays open all year, but is often pre-booked Jul-Aug. The agency **Nik**, www.nik.hr, at A Supuka 5 in Šibenik, T338550, can help you find private accommodation on Zlarin, while their branch at Artina bb in Vodice, T441730, has a list of rooms and apartments to rent on Prvić.

**Prvić**  Lying a 10-minute boat ride from Vodice, Prvić has two settlements, Prvić Luka and Šepurine, and the local ferry stops at both. Šepurine, home to about 220 residents, is a pretty west-facing village, made up of traditional Dalmatian stone houses, dominated by a waterside church with a bell tower and onion dome. From Šepurine, a pleasant footpath (a 15-minute walk) leads across the island to the slightly smaller Prvić Luka, with 170 inhabitants. Luka, built

*Central Dalmatia*

around a deep southeast-facing bay, is popular with yachters and has a couple of harbourside restaurants.

Historically the islanders lived from farming (keeping sheep and goats which grazed freely on the nearby small uninhabited islands), fishing and producing olive oil and wine. Today tourism is slowly taking over, though many families still make their own wine, and if you're lucky enough to be offered some, be sure to try it – somewhere between a white and a rosé, it has a specific musky taste of rocky soil exposed to hours of endless sunshine.

**Sleeping and eating** The agency *Nik* can help finding private accommodation. See Sleeping and eating, above. *Punta*, Prvić Luka, T (098) 266274 (mob). This small friendly restaurant serves up fish and seafood dishes at tables on a terrace overlooking the bay. Open Easter to early-Oct. *Ribarski Dvor*, Šepurine, T448511. White washed walls and a beamed ceiling hung with fishing nets lend a rustic atmosphere to *Ribarski Dvor*, where guests tuck into classic Dalmatian fish and meat dishes. Open early-May to early-Oct.

**Transport** *Jadrolinija* (contact Šibenik office, T213468, for information) run several **ferries** daily between **Šibenik** and **Vodice** (total 1 hr), with boats stopping en route at **Zlarin** (on Zlarin), and **Šepurine** and **Prvić Luka** (on Prvić).

# Vodice

Vodice was once a quiet fishing village built around a small square with an 18th-century parish church. Then came along the tourist boom of the 1970's. Since then, a number of high-rise hotels have sprung up, many of the old buildings along the seafront have been converted into seasonal cafés, restaurants and pizzerias, and in summer the place is inundated with people from all over Europe. However, it has by no means lost its charm, and it's a far more cheerful place to stay than Šibenik – in fact, people from Šibenik often come here for a night out. Despite its success as a seaside resort, Vodice offers little in the way of good beaches. The coastal path north of town is lined with concrete bathing areas giving easy access to the water, though locals would sooner take a ferry to the small island of Prvić for a day on the beach. The well-equipped marina, immediately in front of the old town, is a popular port of call with sailing boats, and there are a couple of large charter companies based here. The town tourist office is at Jurićev Ive-Cota 10, T443888, www.vodice.hr

*Phone code: 022*
*Colour map 3, grid B3*
*Population: 9,407*
*11 km northwest of Šibenik*

*Central Dalmatia*

**Sleeping** The majority of the hotels are large, modern, commercial establishments. You're better off looking for private accommodation, which is plentiful and of a high standard. The agency *Nik*, Artina bb, T441730, www.nik.hr, has a list of rooms and apartments to rent in Vodice and the surrounding area.

**Eating** **Mid-range to expensive** *Santa Maria Restaurant Pizzeria*, Kamila Pamukovića 9, T443319. Although you probably didn't come to Dalmatia to eat Mexican, this is the one place you might be tempted to do so. The interior comprises a split-level space with wooden floors and beamed ceilings, decorated with a fascinating array of traditional sailing equipment and South American folk objects. People from the surrounding area drive for miles to sample the houses specialities, *paella* and *tortillas*. Open all year.

**Mid-range** *Restoran Adria*, Obala matice Hrvatska 8, T441543. Located on the seafront in the cente of town, this popular restuarant serves up carefully presented seafood and charcoal-grilled meat dishes. There's also a good choice of desserts. Open Apr-Oct.

**Entertainment** *Hacijenda*, Magistrala bb, just outside town. Vast open-air **nightclub**, summer only.

**Sport** **Boating** You'll find small motorboats for rent on the seafront. Expect to pay 400Kn for a full-day, or 250Kn for a half-day. **Diving** *Dive In*, V Lisinskog 2, T440468. **Sailing** ACI **Marina**, T 443086, www.aci-club.hr, is located in the centre of town. 415 berths, open all year. The following charter companies are based here: *Adriatic Yacht Club*, Artina bb, T443221, and *FDO-Nav Centar doo*, Artina bb, T443221.

**Tours** *Vodicanka-Tours*, Ive Cace 8, T451488. Www.vodicanka.com, organize day trips by boat to the national parks of Krka and Kornati, as well as guided bus trips to Šibenik, Primošten and Split.

**Transport** Frequent **buses** running along the coastal road between Šibenik and **Zadar** (20 mins) stop in Vodice. *Jadrolinija* (no Vodice office, contact Šibenik office T213468 for information) run a daily **ferry** service between Vodice and Šibenik (total 1 hr), with boats stopping at the islands of Prvić and Zlarin en route.

## Island of Murter

*Phone code: 022*
*Colour map 3, grid B3*
*Population: 2,075*
*30 km northwest of Šibenik; 50 km southeast of Zadar*

The small island of Murter is joined to the mainland by a 38-m bridge, spanning the Murter Channel at Tisno. With scanty pastures and a handful of minor settlements it's not a particularly attractive place, but lying close to the scattered islands of the Kornati archipelago, it's a popular launching pad for visits to the Kornati National Park. Confusingly, although the national park office is located in Murter Town, in the county of Šibenik, the park itself lies largely within the waters of North Dalmatia, see page 189, and thus falls under the county of Zadar.

**Ins & outs**
*See Transport, page 259, for further details*

**Getting there** The 5 buses running daily from Šibenik to Murter Town. **Getting around** These buses zig-zag their way across the island to pass through the various settlements. It's an easy 2-km walk along the (not very attractive) seafront from Murter Town to Betina. **Tourist office** The town tourist office is at Rudina bb, T434995, www.tzo-murter.hr Kornati National Park office, at Butina 2, T434662, www.kornati.hr, is responsible for protecting the natural environment within the park, and provides very limited information of use to tourists.

**Sights** **Murter Town**, known as Veliko Selo (Big Village) until 1715, dates back to the 13th century. The *Murterini* (people from Murter) traditionally lived from fishing the waters of the Kornati and cultivating olives, figs and vines on the closest islets. Tourism began in 1930, when the so-called Czech Villa was built in Slanica Bay 1 km away on the southwest coast, and today the same site boasts the island's most popular beach, overlooked by the modern *Hotel Colentum* complex. Through summer, the quay in Murter Town is busy with private agents, plying organized boat-trips to the Kornati, usually with a fish lunch thrown in.

Murter Town straggles east along the coast to merge with **Betina**, said to have been founded in the 16th century by mainland refugees seeking shelter from the Turks. Its narrow cobbled streets meander their way uphill to a 17th-century parish church, dedicated to St Francis. On the east side of the island, giving onto the Murterski Kanal (Murter Channel) lies the village of **Jezera**. Today it is home to a well-equipped ACI marina, and the base for a renowned summer sailing school.

While on the island, those interested in seafaring should look out for *gajete*, old-fashioned Murter fishing boats pointed at both the bow and the stern and usually painted white and blue. Today, the Murter **shipyard** is one of the few remaining places in Dalmatia to have kept alive the tradition of constructing wooden boats.

The best **beaches** lie southwest of Murter Town, between Uvala Slanica (Slanica Bay) and Uvala Cigrada (Cigrada Bay), and are well within walking distance. Slanica Bay, backed by a row of noisy beachside bars and a big hotel, is rather commercial and gets very busy. If you're in search of a more relaxed atmosphere, you're better off following Pod Raduc, a coastal road giving onto a rocky shoreline, to Cigrada Bay, where there's a lovely peaceful beach overlooked by a couple of discreet restaurants.

**Sleeping**

The Murter-based agencies *Coronata*, Žrtava Ratova 17, T435089, www.coronata.hr and *Kornat Turist*, Hrvatskih vladara 2, T435854/5, www.kornatturist.hr, both have a selection of Robinson Crusoe-type accommodation – simply furnished cottages with basic amenities, but no electricity or running water – on the Kornati islands. *Prišnjak Lighthouse*, contact *Adriatica Net*, Selska 34, Zagreb, T01-3644461, F3644463, www.adriatica.net   Located on the islet of Prišnjak, just 300 m from the northwest tip of the island of Murter, this lighthouse has been tastefully renovated to provide a spacious apartment sleeping 4.

**Eating**

**Mid-range** *Tic Tac*, Hrokešina 5, Murter Town, T435230. Lying in the Hramina quarter of town, in a narrow side street leading down to the harbour, this popular restaurant offers the standard selection of seafood pasta and risotto dishes, barbecued fish and meat, plus an unusual favourite, tuna *sushi*. *Konoba Stari Mlin*, Trg Španjolskog Borca Dragutinina Bilica bb, Betina. With exposed stonewalls and rustic wooden furniture, this typical Dalmatian *konoba* is a great place to enjoy local wine, along with a range of savoury eats, well into the early hours. Open late-May to early-Oct, 2000-0300.

**Cheap** *Lantana*, Uvala Čigrada, 2 km south of Murter, no phone. Overlooking Čigrada Bay, this wooden beach hut offers delicious cheap snacks such as *salata od hobotnice* (octopus salad) and *pohani škampi* (scampi in breadcrumbs) daily through summer, 1000-2300. Tables are arranged on a series of levels, below the shade of a bamboo canopy. There's good music all day, and live concerts by the sea at night, 2300-0300.

**Sport**

**Boating** *Eseker Tours*, Mainova bb, Murter Town, T435669, www.esekertours.hr, have a wide range of speedboats and motorized rubber dinghies for hire on a daily basis – ideal for those who wish to visit the Kornati islands without having to tag along with a tour group. **Diving** *Aquanaut*, Jurija Dalmatinca 1, Murter Town, T434988, www.aquanaut.ingob.com   **Sailing** *Hramina Marina*, Put Gradine bb, Murter Town, T434411. 350 berths, open all year. *Betina Marina*, Trg na moru 1, Betina, T434996. 180 berths, open all year. The British charter company *Activity Holidays*, www.activity-holidays.co.uk, have a fleet based here. *ACI Marina*, Jezera, T439315, www.aci-club.hr 200 berths, open all year. From late-Mar to early-Nov, the Adriatic Nautical Academy (ANA) run a sailing school here, with intensive courses at all levels for pupils from various parts of Europe. For further information, contact the administrative office in Opatija, T (051)711967, www.sailing-ana.hr

**Transport**

Five local **buses** run daily from Šibenik to Murter Town, passing through Vodice en route (45 mins).

## Primošten

Seen from a distance Primošten is enchanting. Lying just off the main coastal road, it is a cluster of old stone houses packed tightly on a small island joined to the mainland by a bridge. Closer inspection reveals a place not quite so magical as one first imagined. There's little of cultural interest here, though a couple of hours exploring the town's narrow winding streets and stopping for a bite to eat or a drink are certainly not ill spent.

Story has it that the island was settled by refugees from Bosnia, who fled to the coast after the Ottoman Turks conquered their land in the late 15th century. During the 16th century, a bridge was built, connecting the island to the mainland, and from then on the settlement became known as Primošten (from *primostiti*, meaning 'to bridge over').

Today Primošten is best-known for *Babić*, an excellent full-bodied red **wine** produced in vineyards on the slopes of the nearby mainland. Driving along the coast you can't miss them – the stony land has been cleared into small square plots of the most amazing geometrical precision, with each unit surrounded by dry stonewalls. **Jurlinovi Dvori**, a wine cellar lying a short distance inland, is a complex of 16th-century farm buildings which have been carefully restored to form a small ethnological museum. There's a *konoba* where you can taste local *Babić* wine, served with black olives, cheese and smoked ham. ■ *Draga, 5 km from Primošten. T574106. www.jurlinovidvori.com* The best **beaches** are in the nearby coves of Vela Raduca and Mala Raduca.

The town tourist office is at T Rudina Biskupa J Arnerica 2, T571111, www.primosten.hr ('under construction', Croatian only).

**Sleeping** Most of the hotels are big modern commercial establishments, situated along the mainland coast. You're far better off looking for private accommodation, which is plentiful and of a high standard. *Daltours*, Dalmatinska 7a, T571572, www.daltours.com and *Nik*, Raduca 1, T571200, www.nik.hr, can both help you find rooms or an apartment.

**Eating** **Mid-range to expensive** *Restoran Dalmacija*, Put Murve 15, T570009. This highly regarded restaurant is located in the old town, with a lovely summer terrace surrounded by traditional stone cottages. Seafood and fish top the menu; try the delicious *fondi sa hobotnicom* (octopus fondue). Closed 1 Dec-3 Jan. **Mid-range** *Šaricevi Dvori*, Šupljak bb, Primošten Burnji, 4 km from Primošten, T571197. Set amid fields a short distance from the coast, this romantic old stone building has been converted into an informal eatery. The menu focuses on typical Dalmatian fare such as *brodetto* (fish stew), and *hobotnica* (octopus) and *janjetina* (lamb) prepared under a *peka* (for which you need to call one day in advance). If you are without private transport and don't fancy the walk, call and someone will come and pick you up by minibus.

**Entertainment** *Aurora Club*, www.auroraclub.hr, located 1 km from the old town, is one of the largest **discos** in Dalmatia. Open mid-Jun to early-Sep.

**Sport** **Diving** *Plavi Val*, Splitska 5, T (091) 5163776 (mob), www.plavival.com **Sailing** *Kremik Marina*, Splitska 24, T570068. 265 berths, open all year. The charter company *Nauticki Klub Primošten*, T571222, www.ncp.hr, is based here.

**Transport** Frequent **buses** running along the coastal road between **Split** and **Šibenik** stop in the new part of Primošten, above the coast (30 mins from Šibenik, an hour from Split). From here, it's just a 100-m walk down to the historic centre, on the former island.

# Knin

On the main road and rail routes between Zagreb and Split, Knin is built around the remains of an impressive hilltop fortress. During the 1990's, the town hit the news as capital of the self-declared *Serbian Autonomous Region of Krajina*, and the traumatic events that followed left it all but abandoned. Today this once, prosperous industrial centre is struggling to re-establish itself, but with vacant factories, soaring unemployment and a population made up largely of refugees, it has some way to go. It's by no means geared up to tourists, but if you're passing through and have time to spare, the fortress merits a visit.

*Phone code: 022*
*Colour map 3, grid B4*
*Population: 15,190*
*56 km northeast of Šibenik*

Guarding Kninska Vrata (Knin Gateway), a natural passage between the Dalmatian coast and the inland territories, Knin Fortress was built in the 10th century and was established as the seat of the early Croatian royalty. A town and parish grew up on the flat plain below, and in the 11th century, Knin became the seat of a bishop. The fortress was occupied by the Turks from 1522 to 1688, marking a watch point on the western border of the Ottoman Empire.

**Background**

During the Tito years, Knin saw a period of rapid industrialization, as metal works, wood works and factories producing building materials and textiles were set up. It also became the headquarters of a large Yugoslav army base. By 1990, with a population of around 40,000, approximately 90% of the town's population were Serbs, who also held a marked majority in the surrounding inland region, known as *Kninska Krajina*. With the onset of animosity between Croats and Serbs in the early 1990's, the Serbs effectively cut the country in two by establishing an autonomous 'republic' (1991-95) and blocking major transport routes between Zagreb and Dalmatia. In early August 1995, the Croatian army (with US backing) carried out *Oluja* (Operation Storm) and the resulting fall of Knin marked the collapse of the *Serbian Autonomous Region of Krajina*. On 26 August of the same year, the much-televised *Vlak Slobode* (Freedom Train), with a jubilant President Franjo Tudman aboard, was the first train to run from Zagreb to Split after a five-year lull. It stopped at Knin, but by this time the town was virtually deserted, tens of thousands of Serbs having fled the region. Many houses were quickly filled with Croatian refugees from Bosnia, though the present government is trying to encourage Serb families to return.

Once the biggest fortress in Dalmatia, **Tvrdava** is made up of impressive walls and grassy ramparts perched upon Sveti Spas, a rocky limestone hill in the centre of town. It is divided into three areas, joined together by drawbridges. The oldest and lowest part lies to the north of the complex, while the middle and upper areas were constructed later, sometime during the Middle Ages. The ramparts were reinforced in the early 18th century. On 5 August 1995, following *Oluja*, the Croatian army hoisted the red and white chequer-board flag above the fortress, and the next day Tudman was on the spot to bless the Croatian victory and declare the region liberated. A restaurant within the walls is currently closed, but may reopen for summer 2003. ■ *0700-sunset. 10Kn. T662151.*

**Sights**

Driving between Šibenik and Knin, the main road passes through the unremarkable market town of Drniš. Some 9 km east of here lies the village of Otavice, where the **Meštrović Mausoleum** can be found, the childhood home of Croatia's best-known 20th-century sculptor, Ivan Meštrović (see

**Excursions**

*Central Dalmatia*

page 330). In 1926 he designed this splendid mausoleum – a stone cube topped with a dome and an interior decorated with art nouveau style religious reliefs – for his family. He emigrated to the US in 1942, but upon his death in 1962 his last wish was that he be buried here. Around 2,000 people and 16 members of the clergy attended the funeral. ■ *Tue-Sun. Summer 0800-1100 and 1700-2000; winter 1000-1400. T872630.*

**Sleeping** **D** *Hotel Mihovil*, Vrpolje bb, T/F662416. Lying 2 km northeast of town, on the road
**& eating** heading for Bosnia Herzegovina, this hotel offers 26 basic but comfortable rooms and
the only notable restaurant in the area. Open all year.

**Transport** **Bus** 10 buses per day run between Knin and **Šibenik** (1 hr 20 mins) and 17 per day
between Knin and **Zagreb** (about 5 hrs). Knin bus station lies next to the train station,
T661005. **Train** Services includes 4 trains daily to and from **Zagreb** (5½ hrs); 5 to **Split**
(2 hrs) and 5 to Šibenik (1½ hr, with a change at Perkovic). Knin train station, T663722.
National train information, T060-333444, www.hznet.hr

# Introducing South Dalmatia

The southern most region of Croatia, South Dalmatia is a long, thin, coastal strip backed by the dramatic **Dinaric Alps**, which form the natural border with Bosnia Herzegovina. Urban life centres on the former city-republic of **Dubrovnik**, an architect's dream contained within ancient defensive walls, facing out to sea and packed with Baroque churches, elegant 17th-century town houses, well-stocked museums and open-air cafés.

A two-hour ferry ride west of the city lies the **island of Mljet**, one-third of which is a national park, where indigenous pine forests cover the steep slopes before reaching two interconnected salt-water lakes, one home to an island capped by a 12th-century monastery. As most visitors arrive as part of an organized day trip, if you decide to stay the night you'll have the place (almost) to yourself. Be sure to try the lobster – Mljet's culinary speciality.

Further west still, **Lastovo** is one of Croatia's most remote and least visited islands, where you can escape the crowds, wallow in unspoilt nature and listen to the locals' bizarre and amusing tales of the island's history.

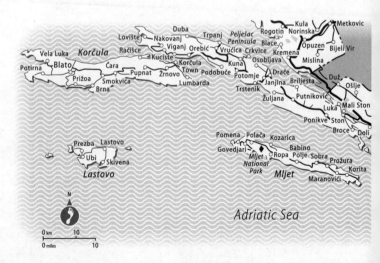

The region's most-visited island is **Korčula**, with **Korčula Town** (often described as a smaller version of Dubrovnik) renowned for its fine cathedral and regular evening performances of the medieval moreška sword dance.

The neighbouring village of **Lumbarda** is backed by the Grk vineyards, which in turn are criss-crossed by a network of narrow lanes: pick the right route and you'll arrive on a blissful south-facing sand beach. The easiest way to reach Korčula from Dubrovnik is to travel the length of the mountainous **Pelješac Peninisula** by bus. If you have time to spare, jump off at one of several roadside wine cellars, where you can sample the locally produced reds, Dingač and Pelješac, regarded by many as Croatia's most sophisticated wines.

South Dalmatia

## Things to do in South Dalmatia

- Walk a full circuit of Dubrovnik's **medieval city walls**, commanding panoramic views over the city rooftops and out to sea, page 269.
- If you're in Dubrovnik during the *Summer Festival*, be sure to attend an open-air theatrical performance or classical music concert, page 277.
- Eat fresh local oysters at a restaurant overlooking the harbour in **Ston** on Pelješac Peninsula, page 301.
- Visit one of the **Pelješac wine cellars** to try Dingač, Croatia's most esteemed red wine, page 298.
- Watch a performance of the **Moreška medieval sword dance** in Korčula Town, page 285.
- Swim in **Veliki Jezero**, a lake surrounded by pine covered slopes, on the island of Mljet, page 296.

# Dubrovnik

Phone code: 020
Colour map 4, grid B3
Population: 43,770

*Backed by rugged limestone mountains and jutting out into the Adriatic Sea, Dubrovnik is one of the world's finest and best-preserved fortified cities. Its gargantuan walls and medieval fortress towers enclose the historic centre, filled with terracotta roof town houses and monuments such as the **15th-century Rector's Palace**, two **monasteries** with cloistered gardens and several fine **Baroque churches** with copper domes. The old town is traversed by the main pedestrian promenade, **Placa**, paved with glistening white limestone and lined with open-air cafés and small boutiques. In 1979, the city became a UNESCO World Heritage Site.*

*Tourism has a long history here and the museums, churches, hotels and restaurants are all well geared to foreign visitors. Today, after the 10-year lull caused by the war, Dubrovnik is once again considered one of Europe's most exclusive destinations. Cruise ships en route from Venice to the Greek islands stop here, and it's also a major base for charter companies hiring out yachts in South Dalmatia.*

## Ins and outs

**Getting there**
*See Transport, page 278, for further details*

*581 km from Zagreb, 664 km from Pula, 566 km from Rijeka and 216 km from Split*

Through summer there are regular flights to most European capitals. The airport is at Cilipi, 21 km from the city centre. Airport buses run to and from the airport, 25Kn. Bus departure information, T773232. The bus station is at Put Republike 19, a 15-min walk west of the old town. There is no railway to Dubrovnik. The city port lies at Gruñ, 3 km west of the old town. *Jadrolinija* run an international ferry to Bari, in Italy, plus a regular coastal service to Rijeka, stopping at Sobra (island of Mljet), Korčula, Stari Grad (island of Hvar), Split and Zadar en route. The same company operates local ferry services to the nearby islands of Koločep, Lopud, Šipan and Mljet.

**Getting around**
Dubrovnik's main sights are concentrated in the pedestrian old town, within the medieval fortifications and can easily be seen by foot. There are no hotels inside the walls, though the more upmarket establishments lie within easy walking distance of the old town, on the coastal road east of the centre. The larger modern hotels are found on Lapad Peninsula, 3 km west from the centre, and can be reached by buses no 1 and no 8 (both of which run from Pile Gate to Gruž Harbour) disembarking at Stanica Lapad.

## Arriving at night

Both the airport and bus station are perfectly safe if you arrive late at night. All incoming Croatia Airlines flights are met by an airport bus, which transports passengers to the city centre. Charter companies with incoming flights usually arrange their own bus transfers. All reputable hotels have someone on duty through the night – book ahead and let them know that you are arriving late. All ferry services to Dubrovnik arrive during the day or early evening.

The main tourist information centre, T427591, www.dubrovnik.laus.hr, is at Dr Ante Starčevića 7, opposite *Hotel Imperial* (currently closed) just outside Pile Gate. Mon-Fri 0800-2000, Sat-Sun 0900-1300. For guided tours of the city visitors should contact *Atlas* travel agency, see page 278. **Tourist offices**

Dubrovnik is undoubtedly at its most animated between mid-Jul and mid-Aug when the *Summer Festival* is in full-swing: troupes of actors and musicians from all parts of the world arrive in town, along with a plethora of holiday makers and cultural visitors – all great fun but it does get very busy and prices go up accordingly. The city's churches and museums are open the year through, and during winter – when you can expect clear blue skies, mellow sunshine and an icy bite to the air – Dubrovnik can be quite enchanting. However, if you're looking to avoid the crowds but still have the possibility of sunbathing and a swim, try to visit in Jun or Oct. **Climate**

## History

The city was founded in the early seventh century, when the nearby Greco-Roman *Epidaurum* (present-day Cavtat, see page 281) was overrun by tribes of Avars and Slavs. Refugees fled north and took refuge on a small rocky island, which they named Laus, and later Ragusa. In the years that followed, the Slavs founded a separate settlement on the mainland hillside opposite the island, and called it Dubrovnik (from *dubrava* meaning 'oak woods'). In the 12th century the narrow channel separating Ragusa and Dubrovnik was filled in, and the two settlements became one, which was known as Ragusa until 1918.

For 450 years (1358-1808), Ragusa was a powerful independent Republic, which kept its freedom by paying off potential rulers: first the Hungarian king, then, after the defeat of Hungary by the Turks at the Battle of Mohacs in 1526, the Ottoman Sultan. It owed its wealth to shipping, becoming the main outlet for silver, lead, wool and leather from the hinterland regions of Bosnia and Serbia, and carrying grain, spices, cotton and salt from Epirus (present-day northwest Greece), Syria and Egypt to Sicily, France and Spain.

As prosperity grew, so did the republic's territory, and by the late-15th century it boasted approximately 120 km of mainland coast, extending from Neum in the north to the Bay of Kotor (in present-day Montenegro) to the south. Its possessions included the island of Lastovo (as of 1252), the Pelješac Peninsula (1333) and the island of Mljet (1345). It also took the islands of Korčula, Brač and Hvar in 1414, but was forced to release them to its arch-rival, Venice, in 1417.

The republic was remarkably sophisticated for its time: the first pharmacy opened in 1317; an old people's home was founded in 1347; slave trading was abolished in 1418 and an orphanage for abandoned and illegitimate babies opened in 1432.

South Dalmatia

## 24 hours in the city

After morning coffee at an open-air café on **Placa**, begin exploring Dubrovnik by walking a complete circuit of the sturdy **city walls**, marking the perimeter of the old town and offering spectacular views over the city rooftops and out to sea.

Mid-morning visit the **Rector's Palace**, a fine Gothic-Renaissance building and home to the **City Museum**, where you can get some idea about how people lived under the Republic of Ragusa.

Afterwards, shop for a picnic at the **open-air market** on Gunduliceva Poljana, and take a taxi-boat from the old port to the **Island of Lokrum**, where you can swim and enjoy a picnic lunch in the shade of the pine trees.

Return to town for late afternoon, and either check out the **Dominican Monastery** and the **city's church**, or, if you're beginning to tire of religious art, visit the **Aquarium** and **Rupe Museum**.

If the *Summer Festival* is in progress, get tickets to an open-air evening concert or theatre production For dinner, head for *Kamenica* on Gunduliceva Poljana (where the morning market is held) and tuck into a feast of fresh seafood and local wine. Close the evening with a nightcap at the *Hard Jazz Café Trubadour*, just round the corner on Buniceva Poljana, where you may even catch a live jazz performance on the piazza. Or, during summer, go to *Divinae Folie*, on Lapad Peninsula, the place to go for open-air dancing into the early hours.

The chief citizen was the Rector, who had to be over 50, and was elected for only a month at a time after which he could not stand for re-election for at least two years. His role was primarily symbolic, while power was held by the Grand Council (made up exclusively of members of the local nobility) and the Senate (a consultative body made up of 45 invited members over the age of 40). The Archbishop of Dubrovnik had to be a foreigner (usually an Italian), a law intended to keep politics and religion apart. Senior officers in the army and navy were members of the nobility, while the increasingly prosperous middle class were traders.

Ragusa's strength lay not in its military power, but in its diplomatic cunning. The republic remained neutral throughout the ongoing international conflicts between Christians and Muslims, and by the Pope's consent was permitted to continue trade with the Levant.

By the 16th century, Ragusa's Golden Age, it had one of the world's greatest merchant fleets, with over 180 ships and 4,000 sailors voyaging back and forth across the Mediterranean and the Black Sea, and consulates in over 50 foreign ports, including Naples, Malta, Lisbon, Corfu, Constantinople, Tunis and Alexandria. During this period, inspired by the Italian Renaissance, the republic became the birthplace of Croatian literature, lead by local writers such as the dramatist Marin Držic (1508-67) and the poet Ivan Gundulic (1589-1638).

In 1667, the city was hit by a severe earthquake, killing an estimated 5,000 inhabitants and levelling most of the splendid Gothic and Renaissance buildings. The city walls survived the disaster and the basic urban layout remained; new buildings were erected in a rather more sober Baroque style.

French troops entered the city in 1806, and in 1808 the Republic lost its independence and was incorporated into Napoleon's Illyrian Provinces. In 1918 it officially became known as Dubrovnik. During the 20th century, as part of Yugoslavia, the city developed into a well-known and much-loved tourist destination.

◀

## City under siege

*In the early 1990's, when the war for independence broke out, Yugoslav forces placed the city under siege. From November 1991 to May 1992, the ancient fortifications stood up to bombardments and fortunately none of the main monuments were seriously damaged, though many of the terracotta rooftops were blasted to fragments. The international media pounced on the story, and ironically it was the plight of Dubrovnik that turned world opinion*

*against Belgrade, even though less glamorous cities, such as Vukovar in Eastern Slavonia (see page 96), were suffering far worse devastation and bloodshed. During the second half of the 1990's, money poured in from all over world and today thanks to careful restoration work (costing an estimated US$10 million), few traces of war damage remain and Dubrovnik is once again a fashionable, high-class holiday resort.*

# Sights

There are two gates into the city walls – **Pile Gate** is to the west. During the time of the Republic, they were closed each evening at 1800 and reopened at 0600 the next morning; the keys were kept under the custody of the Rector. Pile Gate, as it stands today, combines a stone bridge, a wooden drawbridge on chains, and an outer Renaissance portal from 1537 followed by a Gothic inner gate from 1460. A niche above the outer portal contains a 15th-century statue of St Blaise (the city's patron saint), while a niche above the interior gate bears a 20th-century figure of the same saint, by Ivan Meštrović.

**Vrata od Pila (Pile Gate)**
*The name Pile comes from the Greek pili meaning 'gate'*

The walls, as they stand today, follow a ground plan laid down in the 13th century. However, the fall of Constantinople to the Turks in 1453 sent panic waves throughout the Balkans, and Ragusa hastily appointed the renowned Renaissance architect, Michelozzo di Bartolomeo (1396-1472) from Florence, to further reinforce the city fortifications with towers and bastions. On average the walls are 24 m high and up to 3 m thick on the seaward side, 6 m on the inland side. To walk the full circuit, 2 km, you should allow at least one hour. ■ *May-Sep 0900-1900, Oct-Apr 0900-1500. 15Kn. To reach the walls, climb the steps immediately to your left after passing through Pile Gate.*

**Gradske Zidine (City Walls)**
*The highlight of any visit to Dubrovnik has to be a walk around the city walls*

South Dalmatia

Located in the square just inside Pile Gate, this polygonal fountain was part of the city's water supply system, designed by the Neapolitan builder Onofrio de la Cava to bring water from the River Dubrovačka 20 km away. It was completed in 1444. Topped with a dome, water runs from 16 spouting masks around the sides of the fountain. Originally it would have been decorated with ornate sculptures, which were unfortunately destroyed during the earthquake of 1667. ■ *Poljana Paska Milicevica.*

**Velika Onofrio Fontana (Onofrio's Greater Fountain)**

Up until the 12th century Placa (also known as Stradun) was a shallow sea channel, separating the island of Laus from the mainland. After it was filled in, it continued to divide the city socially for several centuries, with the nobility living in the area south of Placa, while the commoners lived on the hillside to the north. It forms the main thoroughfare through the old town, running 300 m from Pile Gate to Ploče Gate. The glistening white limestone paving dates from 1468, though the stone buildings to each side were constructed

**Placa**

after the earthquake of 1667. While the upper levels were residential, the ground floors were used as shops, many displaying the characteristic *na koljeno* frontage (*na koljeno* translates literally to 'like a knee', which Croatians use to say 'L-shaped' relating here to a particular architectural feature of shop fronts, with a door and window in a single frame spanned by a semicircular arch so that the door can be kept closed and goods handed over the sills serving as counters). Still today Placa serves as the city's main public gathering place, where locals conduct their morning and evening promenades and meet at open-air cafés.

**Franjevačka Samostan (Franciscan Monastery)** The monastery complex centres on a delightful cloister from 1360 – late-Romanesque arcades supported by double columns, each crowned with a set of grotesque figures, beside an internal garden filled with palms and Mediterranean shrubs. There's a small museum displaying early laboratory equipment, ceramic bowls and old medical books from the pharmacy, founded by the monks in 1318 and said to be the oldest institution of its kind in Europe. ■ *0900-1500. 5Kn. T321410, Placa 2.*

**Sinagoga (Synagogue)** Claiming to be the oldest surviving synagogue in the Balkans and the third oldest in Europe (after those in Prague, the Czech Republic, and Toledo, Spain), this tiny place of worship was founded in the 15th century on the second floor of a 13th-century Gothic town house. The interior was redecorated in Baroque style in the 17th century, and the blue ceiling painted with stars added in the 19th.

Dubrovnik's Jewish community, first mentioned in 1352, grew in number after 1492 following the expulsion of Jews from Spain, and increased still further with a subsequent banishment from southern Italy in 1514. As of 1546,

## Dubrovnik centre

Related map Dubrovnik orientation, page 272

0 metres 50
0 yards 50

● Eating
1 Atlas Club Nautika
2 Buffet Škola

3 Dundo Maroje
4 Jadran
5 Kamenica

6 Marco Polo
7 Mea Culpa
8 Steak House Domino

## Sveti Vlaho (St Blaise)

*St Blaise, the former Bishop of Sebaste (present-day Sivas in Turkey), lost his life during a late anti-Christian campaign conducted by the Romans in AD 316 (although the Edict of Milan, officially allowing Christians the freedom to practise their religion, had been passed in AD 313, in certain parts of the Empire they were still subject to persecution for some time). As well as a spiritual leader, Blaise was a physician, who, according to legend, miraculously saved the life of a child who*

*was choking on a fish bone. Still today, those suffering from ailments of the throat pray to St Blaise for a cure. He was made the patron saint of Dubrovnik in 972, having appeared to the rector of the cathedral in a dream, warning of an imminent Venetian attack and thus saving the city. The bearded figure of St Blaise, holding a mitre and pastoral staff, was featured on coins and seals of the Republic, as well as the flag.*

local Jews were obliged to live in a ghetto, established along today's *Žudioska* (formerly Via del Ghetto). The community peaked in 1830 with 260 members, though today there are only about 40 Jews living in the city. ■ *Sat-Sun 1000-1300. Free. Žudioska 5.*

**Palača Sponza (Sponza Palace)** *This is one of the few buildings to survive the 1667 earthquake*

Lying at the west end of Placa, this palace was designed by Paskoje Miličević in 1522 and displays a blend of Renaissance arches on the lower level and Venetian-Gothic windows on the first floor. Through the centuries it has been used as a customs office and the city mint (Ragusa minted its own money, a convertible currency known as the *perpera*) though it now houses the state archives. The ground floor is open for temporary exhibitions, and during the *Summer Festival* concerts take place in the internal courtyard. ■ *0900-1400. Free (ground floor only). T321032, Luža.*

**Dominikanski Samostan (Dominican Monastery)**

Lying behind the Sponza Palace, in a passageway leading to Ploce Gate, the Dominican Monastery centres on a 15th-century late-Gothic cloister, designed by the Florentine architect Michelozzo di Bartolomeo (1396-1472) and planted with orange trees. The east wing of the complex houses a museum exhibiting 15th- and 16th-century religious paintings by members of the Dubrovnik School – notably a triptych featuring the *Virgin and Child* by Nikola Božidarevic and a polyptych centring on the *Baptism of Christ* by Lovro Dobričević – as well as works by the city's goldsmiths and reliquaries collected by the monks through the centuries. The rather plain interior of the monastery church is worth a look in for the *Miracle of St Dominic* by Vlaho Bukovac (1855-1922), a local painter from Cavtat. See page 281. ■ *Summer 0900-1800; winter 0900-1500. 10Kn. T321423, Sv Dominika 4.*

**Vrata od Ploča (Ploce Gate)**

The main entrance into the old town from the east, Ploce, like Pile Gate, combines a 15th-century stone bridge with a wooden drawbridge and a stone arch bearing a statue of St Blaise.

**Lazareti**

Just outside the walls, overlooking the sea close to Ploče Gate, this complex of brick sheds beside a central courtyard was built as a quarantine centre in the 16th century. Both land and sea travellers were obliged to check in here and stay for a period of up to 40 days before being granted permission to enter the city. Today the buildings are used for occasional cultural events and there are plans to set up a number of artists' studios here.

South Dalmatia

**Crkva Svetog Vlaha (Church of St Blaise)** Lying opposite the Sponza Palace, this 18th-century Baroque church, built between 1705 and 1717, replaced an earlier 14th-century structure destroyed by fire following the earthquake of 1667. It is dedicated to the city's patron saint, St Blaise, and on the high altar stands a silver statue of him, holding a model of the city from the 16th century, which is paraded around town each year on 3 February, the Day of St Blaise. The stained-glass windows, a feature rarely seen in churches in southern Europe, were added in the 1970's. Each year, May and June and September and October, performances of folk music and dancing are held in front of the church. They begin on Sunday at 1100. ■ *0800-1200 and 1630-1900. Luža.*

**Knežev Dvor (Rector's Palace)** Lying behind the Church of St Blaise, this is the building where the citizen holding the one-month term as Rector was obliged to reside during his time in office; he could only leave for official business and his family remained in their own home.

The original 15th-century building was damaged first by a gunpowder explosion, later by a fire and then by the 1667 earthquake, so that the structure as it stands today, with an arcaded loggia and an internal courtyard, shows a combination of late-Gothic and early-Renaissance styles.

In the **central courtyard** (where classical music concerts are held during the *Summer Festival*) stands a bust of Miho Pracat (1528-1607), a powerful merchant and ship owner from the nearby island of Lopud, who left his wealth to the republic for charitable purposes when he died. When the bust was erected in 1638, he became the only man to be honoured in such a way – the production of statues of local personalities was generally forbidden to prevent the cult of hero worship. Next to the courtyard are a series of large rooms where the Great Council and Senate held their meetings; over the entrance to the meeting halls a plaque reads *Obliti privatorum publica curate* (Forget private affairs, and get on with public matters).

South Dalmatia

# Dubrovnik orientation

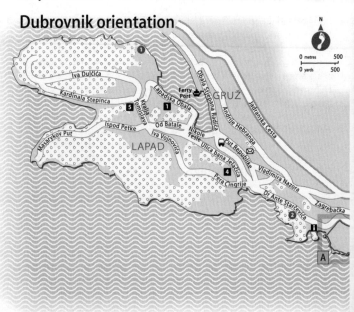

Detail map
A Dubrovnik centre, page 270

Upstairs, the Rector's living quarters now accommodate the **Gradski Muzej** (City Museum), offering an idea of how people once lived in the Republic of Ragusa. Exhibits include paintings by Venetian and Dalmatian artists, period furniture, costumes and a curious collection of clocks, each one stopped at 17.45, the hour Napoleon's men took the city on 31 January 1806, symbolizing the fall of the republic.

■ *Summer 0900-1900; winter Mon-Sat 0900-1400. 15Kn. T321497, Pred Dvorom 3.*

Each morning, Monday to Saturday, an open-air fruit and vegetable **market** sets up on Gundulićeva Poljana, west of the Rector's Palace. Come sunset, the market stalls are packed away and several restaurants put out tables in their place. In the middle of the square stands a bronze statue of the Ragusan writer Ivan Gundulić (1589-1638), completed by Ivan Rendić in 1892. Gundulić is best known for his epic poem *Osman* (1626), describing the Poles' victory over the Turks, and the four sides of the stone pedestal upon which the statue is mounted are decorated with reliefs of scenes from the poem.

**Gundulićeva Poljana**

The original 12th-century cathedral, said to have been sponsored in part by Richard the Lionheart of England out of gratitude for having been saved from a shipwreck on the nearby island of Lokrum on his return from the Crusades in 1192, was destroyed in the 1667 earthquake. What you see today is a splendid Baroque structure with three aisles and cupola, designed by Andrea Buffalini of Rome in 1671. The light but rather bare interior contains a number of paintings, notably a large polyptych above the main alter depicting *The Assumption of Our Lady*, attributed to the Venetian master, Titian (1485-1576). Adjoining the cathedral, the rich Treasury displays 138 gold and silver reliquaries, originating primarily from the East and brought to the city by the local seafarers. Pride of place is held by the skull of St Blaise in the form of a bejewelled Byzantine crown; an arm and a leg of the saint are also on show, likewise encased in elaborately decorated golden plating. ■ *0900-1200 and 1500-1900. 10Kn (Treasury). Poljana Marina Držica.*

**Katedrala (Cathedral)**

South Dalmatia

■ Sleeping
1 Lapad
2 Villa Dubrovnik
3 Villa Orsula
4 Youth Hostel
5 Zagreb

● Eating
1 Orsan
2 Tovjerna Sesame

The St John's Fortress complex, behind the Cathedral, guards the entrance to the old city port. At night, the port used to be closed by stretching a chain from the fortress to Kaše, a breakwater built in the 15th century. The ground floor of the fortress now houses the aquarium, where several salt water pools and 27 well-lit tanks display an impressive variety of Adriatic fish including ray and small sharks, and other underwater life such as octopus, sponges and urchins. ■ *Summer 1000-1800; winter Mon-Sat 0900-1300. 15Kn. T427937, Tvrdja Sv Ivana (St John's Fortress), Damjana Jude 2.*

**Akvarij (Aquarium)**

**Pomorski Muzej (Maritime Museum)** Above the Aquarium, on the first floor of St John's Fortress, this museum traces Dubrovnik's development into one of the world's most important sea faring nations, with exhibits including intricately detailed model ships, as well as engine room equipment, sailors' uniforms, paintings and maps. There are also smaller sections dedicated to the age of steam, Second World War, and sailing and navigation techniques. ■ *Tue-Sun 0900-1400. 15Kn. T426465, Tvrdja Sv Ivana (St John's Fortress), Damjana Jude 2.*

**Jezuitska crkva i samostan (Jesuit Church & Monastery)** Completed in 1725, Dubrovnik's largest church was modelled on the Baroque Il Gesu in Rome, which was designed by Giacomo da Vignola in the mid 16th century. To reach it, follow Uz Jezuite and climb an imposing stair-case dating from 1738, often compared to Rome's Spanish Steps. Next to the church stands the Jesuit College where many illustrious citizens, such as the mathematician and philosopher Ruder Bošković (1711-87), were educated. ■ *0900-1200 and 1500-1900. Poljana R Boškovića.*

**Muzej Rupe (Rupe Museum)** The republic kept an ample supply of grain as a safe measure against siege or famine. This museum is housed in the city's main grain deposit, a vast storage space with 15 deep cisterns carved into the rock (*rupe* means 'holes') during the 16th century. The building itself is more impressive than the exhibition, which consists of an ethnological collection displaying folk costumes and local handcrafts. ■ *Summer 0900-1900; winter 0900-1400. 10Kn. T323018, Od Rupa.*

**Kuća Marina Držica (Marin Držić's House)** This memorial museum is dedicated to the life and work of the writer Marin Držić (1508-67), whose best known script, *Dundo Maroje* (Uncle Maroje), a comedy, was performed throughout western Europe. The 40-minute audio-visual presentation (available in either Croatian or English) gives an enlightening glimpse into Ragusan society during the Renaissance. ■ *Summer 0900-1900; winter Mon-Sat 0900-1400. 10Kn. T323242, Siroka 7.*

**Muzej pravo-slavne crkve (Orthodox Church Museum)** Next door to the Orthodox Church, built in 1877, stands the Orthodox Church Museum, with a collection of 77 religious icons, originating largely from the island of Crete and the Bay of Kotor (a short distance down the coast in Montenegro) and painted between the 15th and 19th centuries. ■ *Mon-Sat 0900-1300. 10Kn. T426260, Od Puca 8.*

**Islet of Lokrum & other beaches** East of the city walls, just 700 m from the old port, the small, lush island of Lokrum which has some good places to swim. A **Benedictine Monastery** was founded here in 1023, and legend has it that when French authorities began closing down religious institutions in the early 19th century, local Benedictines placed a curse upon anyone who should try to possess Lokrum. A succession of subsequent owners died mysterious and horrific deaths, one being the unfortu-nate Archduke Maximilian von Hapsburg, who bought the island in 1859, only to be taken prisoner and shot in Mexico in 1867. Before departing, Maximilian built a **summer home** here, set amid a **Botanical Garden** filled with exotic plants and peacocks, which can still be seen today. Even now, locals remain superstitious about Lokrum, and while it is a popular bathing area during day-light hours, no one stays on the island after sunset. The best beaches lie on the southwest side of the island, where there's also a small saltwater lake (usually a few degrees warmer than the sea), and beyond it an area reserved for nudists. ■ *Getting there: through summer, regular taxi boats shuttle visitors back and forth from the old port; expect to pay 25Kn for a return ticket.*

The main bathing area on Lapad Peninsula is **Lapad Cove**, where a pebble beach lies in a deep bay, close to *Hotel Zagreb*.

# Essentials

## Sleeping

There's a lack of good cheap hotels in Dubrovnik. If you decide to really splash out, then go for one of the top-notch establishments overlooking the sea, just east of the town walls. The mid-range hotels, mainly of the package variety, lie on Lapad Peninsula, 3 km from the centre. However, your best bet for reasonably priced and good standard accommodation, near to town, is to rent a room or apartment through an agency. Renting a room is also the only way to stay within the city walls.

■ *on map, page 272*
*See inside cover for price codes*

**LL** *Villa Orsula*, Put Frana Supila 14, 600 m east of the old town, T440555, F423465, www.hoteli-argentina.hr  Set in a 1930's villa, this is Dubrovnik's most prestigious hotel. The exquisitely furnished 12 rooms and 3 suites offer magnificent views of the old town, and at the front a terraced garden leads down to a private bathing area – a concrete platform giving access to the sea for the hotel residents only. Guests have access to the *Hotel Argentina* swimming pool, sauna, massage and tennis courts, which come under the same management.

**L** *Villa Dubrovnik*, V Bukovaca 6, T422933, F423465, www.villa-dubrovnik.hr  Built into a cliff above a small bay and private bathing area, this white modernist building offers 40 light and airy rooms looking out to sea. A pleasant 20-min walk above the coast brings you to the city walls, though you may prefer to use the complimentary hotel shuttle boat. Prices drop considerably through low season.

**B** *Hotel Lapad*, Lapadska Obala 37, on Lapad Peninsula, overlooking Gruž harbour, 3 km from the old town, T432922, F417230, www.hotel-lapad.hr  Set in a late-19th-century building, this 193-room hotel has an outdoor swimming pool, a hairdressers, newspaper and tobacco shop, plus a hotel boat service to nearby beaches through summer. It stays open all year and offers cut prices through low season.

**C** *Hotel Zagreb*, Šetalište kralja Zvonimira 27, on Lapad Peninsula, 4 km from the old town, T436136, F436006. Housed in a 3-storey neo-Classical building erected in 1922, this hotel is set in gardens with palm trees, close to Lapad Cove and its popular pebble beach. The 20 rooms are basic but comfortable. There's a small restaurant serving Dalmatian specialities and vegetarian dishes.

**G** *Youth Hostel*, V Sagrestana 3 (side street off Ulica bana Jelačića), T423241. Indisputably the best youth hostel in Croatia, and maybe one of the finest in Europe. It lies a 10-min walk from the bus station, has 82 beds and stays open all year.

The following agencies can help you find private accommodation: *Dubrovnik Servis*, Setaliste kralja Zvonimira 10, T436004, www.dubrovnikservis.com; *Dubrovnik Travel*, Gruška obala 1, T313024, www.dubrovniktravel.com; *Dubrovnik Turist*, Put Republike 7, T356969, www.dubrovnikturist.hr; *Elite Travel*, Put Republike 7, T358200, www.elite.hr

South Dalmatia

## Eating

**Expensive**

● on maps, pages 270 and 272 See inside cover for price codes

*Atlas Club Nautika*, Brsalje 3, T442526, www.laus.hr/nautika  Said by many to be the best restaurant in Dubrovnik, this rather formal establishment occupies the 19th-century Dubrovnik Nautical Academy building just outside the town walls, close to Pile Gate. There's an excellent choice of fresh shellfish, lobster, fish and meat dishes, making it a popular choice for business lunches and celebrations. *Jadran*, Poljana Plaska Miličevića 1, T323403. Set in the lovely cobblestone courtyard of the former Convent of St Clare (dissolved by Napoleon in 1808), opposite Onofrio's Greater Fountain, close to Pile Gate, *Jadran* serves up a full range of Dalmatian meat and fish dishes. Open mid-Feb to mid-Nov. **Steak House Domino**, Od Domina 6, T432832. A perfect choice if you've exhausted your appetite for fish and seafood. It lies in the old town and occupies an unusual double-height space with rough stonewalls and a wrought iron spiral staircase. In summer it's also possible to eat outside.

**Mid-range** *Dundo Maroje*, Kovačka bb, T321445. Lying in a side street running between Placa and Prijeko, despite its somewhat kitsch pink interior locals recommend *Dundo Maroje* for reasonably priced seafood dishes. Closed late-Dec to mid-Jan. **Marco Polo**, Lučarica 6, T323719. Located in a side street behind the Church of St Blaise, the dining room here is tiny, but through summer tables spill out onto a pretty courtyard, making it an old-time favourite of visiting actors and musicians. Seafood predominates, with *crni rižot* (black risotto in cuttlefish ink) a popular choice. **Tovjerna Sesame**, Dante Alighieria bb, side street off Dr Ante Starčevića, T412910. Lying just outside the city walls, close to Pile Gate, this romantic eatery is a perfect venue for a light supper over a bottle of good wine. The menu features platters of cheeses and cold meats, truffle dishes and an enticing variety of creative salads.

**Cheap** *Kamenica*, Gundulićeva Poljana 8, no phone. Overlooking the open-air market within the town walls, *Kamenica* is a down-to-earth eatery much loved by locals for its fresh oysters and simple seafood dishes. The platters of *girice* (small fried fish) and *pržene lignje* (fried squid) make a delicious lunchtime snack. Open all year, but closes at 2000 through winter. **Mea Culpa**, Za Rokom 3, T424819. Locals recommend *Mea Culpa* for the best pizza in town. It lies within the city walls, is open daily until midnight, and has tables outside on the cobbled street through summer. Closed late-Dec to mid-Jan. *Orsan*, Ivana Zajca 2, Lapad, T435933. This family-run restaurant lies on Lapad Peninsula, with a pleasant, leafy terrace overlooking Gruž Harbour. Favourite dishes are *salata od hobotnice* (octopus salad), *svježa morska riba* (fresh fish) and *rozata* (a Dubrovnik desert similar to crème caramel).

**Seriously cheap** *Buffet Škola*, Antuninska ulica bb. Lying in a narrow side street between Placa and Pirjeko, this family-run sandwich bar is known far beyond Dubrovnik. Sandwiches come in delicious homemade bread, filled with locally produced *sir iz ulja* (cheese in oil), *pršut* (dried ham) and tomatoes from the villages of nearby Konavle.

**Cafés** Placa is lined with a number of popular street cafés, all of similar ambience and price-range. The one establishment worth a special mention is **Gradska Kavana**, an old-fashioned café with an ample summer terrace looking onto Luža Square, at the east end of Placa. It occupies the former Arsenal building, where the republic's ships were built and serviced.

**Bars & clubs** *Bebap*, Kneza Damjana Jude. Lying in the narrow street leading to Aquarium, in the old town, *Bebap* is one of the few bars within the walls to stay open after midnight the year round. It also hosts occasional live concerts.  **Otok**, Pobijana 8.

Alternative cultural centre, in the old town, behind the Cathedral, with a late-night bar and occasional concerts, some staged at Lazareti, see page 271, east of Ploce Gate. *Hard Jazz Café Trubadour*, Bunićeva Poljana. Fashionable bar, in the old town, with a large summer terrace and wicker chairs. Occasional live jazz concerts on a small stage outside. *Divinae Folie*, Put V Lisinskog, T435677, www.divinaefollie2.com Open-air Italian-run disco on Lapad Peninsula, working mid-Jun to early-Sep. *Esperanza*, Put Republike 3, close to the bus station. Popular club playing a mix of techno and disco music, with occasional concerts featuring Croatian bands.

## Entertainment

**Theatre**  Marin Dr ica Theatre, Pred Dvorom 3, T321419. Most performances in Croatian, apart from occasional foreign theatre groups on tour. **Orchestra  Dubrovacki Simfoniski Orkestar** (Dubrovnik Symphony Orchestra), Dr Ante Starčevića 29. Also known as the 'Festival Orchestra'. Slavica, Dr Ante Starčevića 42, a 10-min walk west of Pile Gate, open-air summer cinema in a walled garden above the sea.

## Festivals

*Sveti Vlaho* (Feast of St Blaise), **3 Feb**. Celebrates the patron saint of Dubrovnik. A ceremonial holy service is held in front of the Cathedral at 1000, followed by a religious procession around town at 1130, with the remains of St Blaise, in the form of relics, taking pride of place. During the time of the republic, those prisoners who did not present a threat to public safety were released on this day to participate in the festivities.

*Dubrovnik Summer Festival*, **mid-Jul to mid-Aug**. Founded in 1950, this highly acclaimed international festival hosts drama, ballet, concerts and opera at open-air venues within the city walls. Shakespeare's *Hamlet* staged on Lovrijenac Fortress is one of the most popular performances. For information check out the website, www.dubrovnik-festival.hr

*Quarantine*, **late-Aug to early-Sep**. International multimedia festival founded in 1996, featuring evening performances of contemporary theatre, dance, music and film at the Lazareti. For information check out the website, www.karantena.mi2.hr

## Shopping

*Algoritam*, Placa 8, T322044. The best **bookshop** for foreign language publications, including novels, travel guides and maps. *Dubrovačka Kuča*, Svetog Dominika bb, near Ploce Gate. T322092. Tastefully laid out small shop stocking the best **Croatian wines**, *rakija*, olive oil and truffle products. There's also a picture gallery upstairs.

## Sport

**Diving**  *Dubrovnik Travel Scuba Diving*, Gruška obala 1, T311733 www.dubrovniktravel.com; *Navis*, Copocubana beach, T420876. **Sailing** ACI Marina, Mokošica, 3 km from Gruž harbour and 6 km from the old town. T455020 or 455021. 450 berths. Open all year. The charter company *TA Atlas*, Brsalje 17, T442222, is based here. **Tennis** Hotels *Argentina*, *Splendid* and *Adriatic* all have tennis courts where non-residents are welcome to play.

South Dalmatia

## Tour operators

*Atlas*, Cira Carića 3, T442222, www.atlas-croatia.com, organize guided tours of the city, as well as excursions by bus to Trtsteno, Ston and the Pelješac vineyards, and by hydrofoil to the islands of Mljet or Korčula, plus yacht charters from Dubrovnik and Split. **Dubrovnik Travel**, Gruška obala 1, T311733, www.dubrovniktravel.com, organize accommodation, car hire, boat hire (motor boats and yachts) and diving in the Dubrovnik area. **Generalturist**, F Supila 9, T432974, www.generalturist.com One of the largest Croatian travel agencies, *Generalturist* specialize in tailor-made trips both with and without guides, pilgrimage tours and yacht charters.

## Transport

Local  **Taxi**  The main taxi ranks lie just outside the town gates of Pile and Ploce, and at Gruž Harbour and the bus station.

Long distance  **Air**  Through summer, there are regular international flights to and from **Amsterdam**, **Berlin**, **Brussels**, **Dusseldorf**, **Frankfurt**, **Istanbul**, **London** (Gatwick and Heathrow), **Manchester**, **Munich**, **Osijek**, **Paris**, **Prague**, **Rome**, **Skopje**, **Tel Aviv**, **Warsaw**, **Vienna** and **Zurich**. Internal flights link Dubrovnik with **Pula**, **Split** and **Zagreb**. The number of destinations and the frequency of flights are reduced in winter. Dubrovnik Airport, T773377 (information), T773328 (lost and found), www.airport-dubrovnik.hr Airport bus service T773232.

**Bus**  Internal services include 6 buses daily to **Zagreb** (10½ hrs); 12 buses to **Split** in Central Dalmatia (about 4 hrs); 5 buses daily to **Rijeka** in Kvarner (about 12 hrs); and 1 bus to **Pula** in Istria (about 14 hrs). There is also a daily bus to **Trieste** (Italy). Buses depart 3 times a week for **Frankfurt** (Germany). For all information about buses to and from Dubrovnik, T357088. Left luggage costs 10Kn per item, open 0600-2100.

**Car hire**  *Avis* is in the city centre at V Nazora 9, T422043, www.avis.hr; *Budget*, T773290, is at the airport, www.budget.hr, and in the city centre at Obala Stjepana Radica 20, T418997; *Hertz*, www.hertz.hr, is at the airport, T771568, and in the city centre at F Supila 5, T425000, and *Mack*, www.mack-concord.hr, is in the city centre at F Supila 3, T423747.

**Ferry**  *Jadrolinija*, T418000, run a regular overnight coastal service between **Rijeka** and Dubrovnik, stopping at **Zadar**, **Split**, **Stari Grad** (island of Hvar), **Korčula** and **Sobra** (island of Mljet) en route. Through winter the service is reduced to 2 departures a week. *Jadrolinija* also run daily ferry services connecting Dubrovnik to the islands of **Koločep**, **Lopud** and **Šipan**, departing 3 times daily Mon-Sat and twice daily Sun, and connecting Dubrovnik to **Sobra** on the island of Mljet, departing twice daily through summer and once daily in winter (1 hr 50 mins). In addition, the same company run a ferry to **Bari** (Italy), departing 5 times per week (2 overnight services and 3 daytime services) through summer, but just once a week through winter (9 hrs by night, 6 hrs by day).

**Train**  As there is no railway line south of Split, Dubrovnik is not connected to the rest of the country by train.

## Directory

**Airlines offices** *Croatia Airlines*, Brsalje 9, T413776/7, www.croatiaairlines.hr
**Banks** There are banks with ATMs on the Placa, and close to the bus station and ferry

port and inside the airport. **Communications** Internet cafés: *DuNet Club*, Put Republike 7, T356894. *Internet Klub Planet*, Dr Ante Starčevića 41, T425524, www.planet-dubrovnik.hr  **Post offices**: the main post office is at Put Republike 28, close to the bus station, and is open Mon-Fri 0800-2100. The most central post office is at Dr Ante Starčevića 2, just outside the city walls, opposite Pile Gate, open Mon-Fri 0800-1500. **Telephone**: it is possible to make calls from either of the above post offices, or from the blue public telephone kiosks dotted round town. **Consulates** British, Buničeva Poljana 3, T324598. **Danish**, Od Svetog Mihalja 1, T356733. **Netherlands**, Od Svetog Mihalja 1, T356141. **Medical services** General Hospital, Roka Mišetića bb, T431777 (24 hr casualty). **Pharmacies** All pharmacies are marked by a glowing green cross. *Gruž* at Gruška obala (T418900) and *Kod Zvonika* on Stradun (T428656) alternate as non-stop 24-hr pharmacies. **Useful telephone numbers** Ambulance 94; Fire 93; Police 92.

## Trsteno Arboretum

The small village of Trsteno lies on the main coastal road. Its 16th-century Renaissance arboretum, one of the oldest and most beautiful landscaped parks in Croatia, makes it a pleasant outing the year through, though the trees and planting are at their most attractive in spring and autumn. *Colour map 4, grid B2 24 km northwest of Dubrovnik*

The 25.5-ha park, laid out in the grounds of a Renaissance villa belonging to the Gucetic family, was designed to emphasize its magnificent cliff top setting: a series of terraces tumble down to the sea, offering stunning views over Trsteno's harbour and out across the water to the Elafiti islands, see below.

Traditionally the men of Trsteno were sailors, and wherever they went in the world they would collect seeds and saplings for the Gucetic gardens. Today, the arboretum contains pines from Japan, palms from Mexico and cypress trees from various parts of the Mediterranean, as well as pomegranate, almond and lemon trees, and exotic climbing plants such as intoxicating perfumed sweet jasmine and delicate passion flowers. Pride of place is taken by a 500-year old plane tree, with a 12 m circumference and boughs so massive that one of them has to be supported by a concrete pillar.

Behind the villa stands an ornate water garden from 1736, featuring a grotto presided over by Baroque statues of Neptune and two nymphs, and a pool fed with crystal clear water from a trickling stream.

On 2 and 3 October 1991, during the war of independence, the arboretum was shelled from the sea and part of the pinewoods was consumed by fire. However, careful restoration work has covered up the worst of the damage, and today Trsteno still evokes the sophisticated lifestyle of Renaissance Dubrovnik.

■ *Summer 0800-1800; winter 0800-1600. 12Kn. T751019, Trsteno. Getting there: all buses heading north up the coast from Dubrovnik stop in Trsteno though you should tell the driver in advance otherwise he may drive straight on (45 mins).*

## Elafiti Islands

Recently nominated as one of Croatia's 'undiscovered paradises', the tiny, car-free Elafiti Islands are just a short ferry ride from Dubrovnik. The three larger islands of Koločep, Lopud and Šipan offer unspoilt nature just a stone's throw away from the city. Pinewoods and scented shrubs such as rosemary and sage cover the island – the natural vegetation has been largely untouched, apart from on the inland area of Šipan, where there are cultivated fields of grape vines and olive trees. Being car free, the pace of life here is wonderfully slow and easy going. Through summer a number of reasonably priced *Phone code: 020 Colour map 4, grid B2 Population: 879*

South Dalmatia

no-frills fish restaurants open up on the islands, but if you plan to visit for a day's exploring out of season, be sure to pack a picnic as you're unlikely to find anything working.

**Ins & outs**
*See Transport, page 281, for further details*

**Getting there** There are several ferries a day from Dubrovnik to the main islands. **Getting around** Cars are banned from the islands and there are no vehicles apart from a few old farm tractors on Šipan. The only way visitors can get around is on foot, but seeing as the islands are so tiny, this is hardly a problem if you don't mind walking. **Tourist office** There are no tourist offices on any of the islands, but the Dubrovnik County tourist board, T324222, can provide basic information.

**History** The name Elafiti is said to stem from the Greek word *elafos*, meaning deer. Some scholars believe that in ancient times deer may have grazed here; others attribute the name to the shape of the islands. In 1272 the Elafiti came under the Republic of Ragusa (Dubrovnik). Initially they were governed by a Rector based on Šipan, but as of 1669 the centre was relocated to Lopud, with the Rector dividing his time between Lopud and Šipan, spending three months on each. During the 15th and 16th centuries, Dubrovnik aristocracy built modest summer villas and small chapels on the islands, and Franciscan monks used to gather medical herbs for use in the pharmacy in Dubrovnik. In 1571, in the lead up to the Battle of Lepanto (see page 223), the Ottoman Turks ransacked the Elafiti, after which a series of defence towers and fortifications were built in case of future raids. During the Tito years a couple of modern hotels were constructed, one on Koločep and one on Lopud, but there was no large scale development.

**Koločep** Lying 7 km northwest of Gruž harbour, Koločep, with a population of 174, is the smallest of the inhabited Elafiti islands. There are two settlements: the port of **Donje Čelo** on the northwest coast and **Gornje Čelo** on the southeast side, which are linked by a pleasant footpath, shaded by pine trees. The best beach, overlooked by a large modern hotel in Donje Čelo, is of sand; there are also several secluded pebble beaches, some given over to nudism. Historically the islanders lived from diving for coral, exploiting the nearby reef of Sv Andrija.

**Sleeping and eating  C** *Hotel Koločep*, T757025, F757027. A hotel complex consisting of 8 white villas built into a pine-covered hillside overlooking the beach in Donje Čelo. Facilities include a restaurant, swimming pool and water sports. Open early-May to late-Oct. 151 rooms. *Sv Andrija Lighthouse*, Island of Sv Andrije. Contact *Adriatica Net*, Selska 34, Zagreb, T01-3644461, F3644463, www.adriatica.net This tiny island (400 m x 80 m), 9 km west of Dubrovnik, 4 km from Koločep and 3 km from Lopud, has a rocky shoreline and is covered by sparse vegetation and pines. The lighthouse, from 1873, has been refurbished to form a 4-room apartment sleeping 8. There are no supply boats, so you need to take a week's provisions.

**Lopud** The island of Lopud is home to 269 residents. It's 12 km northwest of Gruž and 4½ km long and 2 km wide. The sole village, also called Lopud, is made up of old stone houses built around the edge of a wide northwest-facing bay, with a view of Suđurađ on Šipun across the water.

Guarding the entrance to the harbour, on the north side of the bay, stands a semi-derelict 15th-century **Franciscan monastery**. The oldest part of the building centres on an arcaded internal courtyard from 1483; during the 16th century the complex was fortified to provide a place of refuge for the entire population in the case of an attack. It was recently purchased by

Francesca von Hapsburg, Archduchess of Austria, who plans to restore it to its former glory, and will keep part of it for her own personal use, while opening the rest to the public.

Close by, the abandoned and roofless **Rector's Palace** is easily recognised by its fine triple Gothic windows. In stark contrast, on the south side of the bay stands the colossal *Lafodia Hotel* complex, erected in the 1980's.

From Lopud a footpath (15-minute walking time) leads across the island, passing through lush vegetation scented with sage and rosemary to **Šunj**, a south facing cove with a generous stretch of sand beach and a couple of summer restaurants.

**Sleeping and eating  C** *Hotel Lafodia*, Lopud, T759014, F759026. This gargantuan complex lies on the edge of town, overlooking the bay. There are 196 rooms, and basic dining and sports facilities. Pets welcome. Open Apr-Oct.

Šipan, the largest of the Elafiti Islands, is 9 km long and with a width of just **Šipan** over 2½ km. The main settlements, **Šipanska Luka** (on the northwest coast) and **Sudurad** (on the southeast coast) are both built at the end of deep narrow inlets and account for a total population of 436. Šipanska Luka has a palm-lined seafront overlooked by old stone buildings and the island's only hotel – there is a decent beach a short distance from the centre. Sudurad is a sleepy fishing village with several small Renaissance villas and a pair of 16th-century watchtowers set back from the harbour. The two villages lie at opposite ends of **Šipansko Polje**, a fertile valley planted with olive trees and grape vines, and are connected by a 5-km asphalt road and a network of hiking paths.

**Sleeping and eating  C** *Hotel Šipan*, Šipanska Luka, T758000, F758004, www.sipan hotel.com  This 3-storey white building lies on the edge of town, overlooking the seafront promenade. There are 83 rooms, a bar and restaurant. Pets welcome. Open mid-May to mid-Oct.

**Transport**  *Jadrolinija* (contact Dubrovnik office, T418000 for information) run several **ferries** daily between Gruň harbour in **Dubrovnik** and **Luka Šipanska** (total 1¾ hrs), with boats stopping at Koločep (25 mins), Lopud (50 mins) and Suđurađ (1 hr 10 mins) en route.

## Cavtat

This attractive fishing village is Croatia's southern most seaside resort. Built around a 'U' shaped bay, protected to each side by a peninsula, the old town centres on a seafront promenade lined with bars and restaurants and a row of palms. Most of the hotels are located north of town, set amid lush Mediterranean vegetation, overlooking a second bay. The town tourist office is at Tiha 3.

*Phone code: 020*
*Colour map 4, grid B3*
*Population: 2,015*
*17 km southeast of Dubrovnik*

Founded by ancient Greeks from *Issa* (on the island of Vis), the settlement **History** was originally called *Epidauros*. In 228BC, it was taken by the Romans, only to be devastated at the beginning of the seventh century by rampaging tribes of Avars and Slavs. The name Cavtat originates from *Civitas Vetus*, as Roman refugees in the newly established Ragusa (present-day Dubrovnik) used to call their former home.

The area was incorporated into the Republic of Dubrovnik during the 15th century, Cavtat was rebuilt and walled, and a Rector installed to govern

South Dalmatia

the town and the rural hinterland region known as Konavle. Tourism began in the early 1900's under Austro-Hungary; during the 1980's several large hotel complexes were erected and Cavtat turned into a popular package resort. For a year from October 1991, Cavtat was occupied by the JNA (Yugoslav Peoples' Army). The town suffered minimal material damage, though many houses in the villages of Konavle were looted and burnt during this period.

**Sights** Housed within the 16th-century Renaissance *Knežev Dvor* (Rector's Palace), the **Baltazar Bogišic Collection** includes drawings by Croatian and foreign artists and an impressive canvas, *Carnival in Cavtat*, by Vlaho Bukovac. There is also a lapidarium with Roman stone pieces from the first century AD and a display of old coins, some from the Republic of Ragusa (Dubrovnik). ■ *0900-1300. 10Kn. T478556. Obala Ante Starčevića 18.*

The birthplace of the realist painter, Vlaho Bukovac (1855-1922), has been turned into the **Vlaho Bukovac Gallery**. Bukovac spent most of his years abroad: studying in Paris, visiting England and painting portraits of various aristocrats, and later becoming a professor at the Academy of Art in Prague. However, from time to time he returned to Cavtat, and used this late 18th-century stone building as an atelier. In 1964 it was converted into a gallery displaying a collection of his paintings, drawings, furniture and mementoes. It was closed for refurbishment through 2002, but should reopen in spring 2003. ■ *Summer 0900-1300 and 1700-2100; winter 0900-1300. 10Kn. T478646. Riva bb.*

The impressive white stone **Račić Mausoleum**, designed by the sculptor Ivan Meštrović in 1921, stands on the highest point of the town cemetery, on Rat Peninsula. It was built in place of a 15th-century church, which was demolished after the Bishop of Dubrovnik granted that the site could be used to create a tomb for the Račićs, a family of wealthy ship owners. An octagonal structure with a cupola, it is made of white stone from the island of Brač. The entrance features a pair of art nouveaux style caryatids (statues of female figures, used as columns to support the porch) and impressive bronze doors. The interior is decorated with reliefs of angels and birds in scenes symbolizing the three stages of life: birth, fate and death. Meštrović built the mausoleum to keep his promise to Marija Račić, who was rumoured to have been his lover. The bronze bell, hanging from the cupola, is inscribed with a touching epitaph, 'Know the mystery of love and thou shalt solve the mystery of death and believe that life is eternal'. ■ *Summer Mon-Sat 1000-1200 and 1800-2000, Sun 1000-1200. Winter by appointment.*

The best **beaches** lie in the bay east of the centre, where most of the package hotels are located, and west of town, below the gargantuan (but very expensive) *Hotel Croatia.*

**Sleeping** D *Hotel Supetar*, Dr Ante Starčevića, T478278, F478770. In an old stone building 200 m from the seafront, this basic but welcoming hotel has 29 rooms, a private beach, and a restaurant and summer terrace. Pets welcome. *Adriatica*, Trumbićev Put 3, T478713, can help you find private accommodation. Alternatively, check out the website, www.dubrovnik-online.com, for rooms and apartments available for rent.

**Eating** **Mid-range to expensive** *Leut*, Trumbićev Put 11, T478477. In business for over 30 years, this excellent fish restaurant lies in the centre of town, with a large summer terrace overlooking the seafront. The house speciality is scampi cream risotto. Closed Jan. Out of town, 18 km east of Cavtat, is *Konavoski Dvori*, Ljuta, Konavle, T791039. This highly regarded restaurant lies beside a working watermill on the River Ljuta. It's best known for authentic regional specialities such as fresh trout, and lamb baked under a *peka*, see page 43. The idyllic rural setting and waitresses dressed in traditional Konavali costume make it a popular destination for tour groups.

*Cavtat Summer Festival*, Jul-Aug, features an unusual mix of *klapa* concerts, see page 335, and waterpolo contests.  **Festivals**

**Diving**  *Atlas*, Trumbićev Put 2, T479031, www.atlas-croatia.com, organize 6-day div-  **Sport** ing holidays based in Cavtat. *Diving Centre Epidaurum*, Šetalište Žal bb, T471444, www.epidaurum-diving-cavtat.hr, organize diving trips to several caves, a shipwreck, and a large underwater archaeological site filled with amphorae.

Cavtat lies just 2 km from Dubrovnik **airport**. The town is connected to **Dubrovnik** by an  **Transport** hourly regional **bus** (40 mins). Through summer, **water taxis** shuttle tourists back and forth between Cavtat and Dubrovnik. The journey takes about 40 mins, expect to pay 30Kn one-way.

# Island of Korčula

*This long skinny island is green and hilly, with some of the steeper north-facing slopes covered with dense pine forests. The coastline is rocky and indented, with several small coves on the south side offering secluded pebble beaches. People from the seaside towns and villages live mainly from fishing and tourism, while those from the inland settlements cultivate vineyards and olive groves to produce quality white wine and olive oil.*

**Getting there**  The island is connected to Split on the mainland by a once-daily catama-  **Ins & outs** ran service, and a once-daily ferry service, both running to Vela Luka. In addition, there  *See Transport,* are several ferries daily from Orebić on Pelješac Peninsula to Dominče (2 km from Korčula  *page 288, for* Town), and from Orebić to Korčula Town (foot passengers only). A once-daily bus service  *further details* runs from Dubrovnik to Korčula Town. **Getting around**  From Mon to Fri, 5 local buses run the length of the island, 32 km long and 8 km across at its widest point, from Korčula Town to Vela Luka, stopping at Smokvice, Čara and Blato en route. **Tourist office**  The tourist office is housed in the 16th-century loggia at Obala Dr Franje Tudmana bb, on the seafront next to *Hotel Korčula*. T715701, www.Korcula. net, in Korčula Town.

Korčula was once covered with dense pine forest, leading the ancient Greeks  **Background** to call it *Kerkyra Melaina*, or 'Black Corfu'. In fact, it had been inhabited in Neolithic times, as early as 6500BC, as finds from Vela Spilja (Big Cave) in

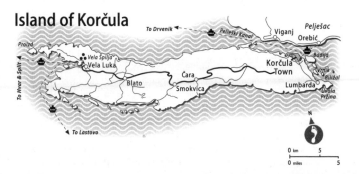

**Island of Korčula**

*South Dalmatia*

Vela Luka prove. The first Greeks to arrive were from Cnidos (on the Aegean coast in present-day southwest Turkey), and it seems they lived in relative peace with the local Illyrian tribes, neither attempting to conquer nor assimilate them, but dividing land rights with them, as recorded by a fourth-century BC stone inscription found in Lumbarda.

Between the 10th and 18th centuries the island came under Venice several times, and with arch-rivals the Republic of Dubrovnik and the Ottoman Empire in close proximity, *La Serenissima* did all it could to fortify and defend its main base here, the tiny yet culturally advanced Korčula Town. During the 13th century, the legendary Venetian explorer, Marco Polo, made history with his epic journeys through the Orient. Historians are undecided as to where he originated from, but many believe he was born in Korčula Town, and an old stone building open to the public is said to have been his family home. Other attractions include a medieval sword dance (known as the *Moreška* in Korčula Town and the *Kumpanjija* in Blato), which is performed regularly through summer for tourists, plus a selection of excellent local white wines, *Grk* from Lumbarda and *Pošip* from the inland villages of Smokvica and Cara.

Finally, there is an interesting British connection. Fitzroy Maclean of Dunconnel (1911-96), the Scottish politician, soldier, adventurer and writer, had a house in Korčula Town, the only property owned by a foreigner in former Yugoslavia. During the Second World War, as a member of the SAS, Maclean was parachuted into various parts of Dalmatia and Bosnia, and acted as Churchill's personal envoy at meetings between Tito (then head of the partisan movement) and representatives of the royalist Yugoslav government in exile, which took place on the island of Vis, see page 233, in summer 1944. Later he served as the key link between Tito and the British and American governments, levering support for the Yugoslav state. Maclean and his adventures are said to have inspired Ian Flemming's *James Bond* novels.

## Korčula Town

*Phone code: 020*
*Colour map 4, inset*
*Population: 3,126*

Lying on the northeast coast of the island, medieval Korčula Town is often referred to as a 'mini-Dubrovnik'. A compact cluster of terracotta roof houses perched graciously above the sea on a peninsula fortified with walls and round towers, the same elements are here, but concentrated into a far smaller space, no more than the size of a modern football stadium. The town is backed by hills covered with pinewoods, and faces onto a narrow sea channel offering views of the tall mountainous peaks of Pelješac in the distance. Large modern hotels have been built a short distance from centre, leaving the historic core as an open-air museum and making Korčula one of the most popular resorts on the islands, second only to Hvar. The main cultural attraction is the *Moreška*, a medieval sword dance performed in the old town on summer evenings.

**History**

*The town claims to have been the birthplace of the great discoverer, Marco Polo; some historians agree that this may be true, as the Venetians recruited many sea captains from Dalmatia*

Legend has it that Korčula was founded by the Trojan hero Antenor in the 12th century BC, though there is no material evidence to back up such claims. The Venetians arrived here during the 10th century, and came and went several times over the next 800 years, their final and most significant period of dominance being 1420-1797. The buildings they left behind are comparable to those in *La Serenissima* itself: Jan Morris, in *The Venetian Empire*, refers to Korčula as "one of the most Venetian of all its [Venice's] sea ports".

Korčula grew up as an extraordinarily compact settlement, built on a small but strategically important peninsula, controlling the passage of ships through the 1270 m wide *Pelješki Kanal* (Pelješac Channel) between the island

## Fighting feet

*The Moreška (from morisco, meaning 'Moorish' in Spanish) came to Korčula via Italy in the 16th century. It originated in Spain in the 12th century, where it was inspired by the struggle of Spanish Christians against the Moors; on the East Adriatic, it was simply adapted to represent the ongoing fight of local Christians against the Turks.*

*Over the centuries the text, music and pattern of the dance have been altered and shortened, but the central story remains: Bula, a beautiful Muslim maiden, has been kidnapped by the Black Knight, and her sweetheart, the White Knight, comes to her rescue. The performance begins with the Black Knight (dressed in black) dragging Bula in chains, and the maiden crying out against his amorous proposals. The White Knight (confusingly, dressed in red) and his army then arrive, as do the Black Knight's army, ready to defend their leader. The two Knights hurl insults at one another, then cross their swords, and the dance begins. Their armies are pulled into the confrontation, with soldiers clashing swords in pairs within a circle, to the accompaniment of a brass band. The pace of the music gradually accelerates (in the past, performers were often wounded and had to replaced by reserves during the dance), with the black soldiers facing outwards and the circle contracting as they retreat inwards from the white army. Finally, all the black soldiers fall to the ground, the Black Knight surrenders, and the White Knight frees Bula from her chains and kisses her.*

*In the past, various versions of the dance were found throughout the Mediterranean, where they were probably used as much as an exercise for swordsmen as for entertainment. It also reached Northern Europe, and could well be the forerunner to English Morris dancing, where wooden poles are used instead of swords.*

and the mainland. It was walled in the 13th century, further fortified during the 15th, and for defence reasons dwellings were not permitted beyond the medieval perimeter until the 18th century. Extremely advanced for its time, a town statute was written in 1214, laying down strict rules about communal life, urban layout and human values (eg slavery was banned). The most important period of artistic development, during the 15th and 16th centuries, bequeathed the town with many fine Gothic and Renaissance buildings, and Korčula became renowned for its skilled stone masons (notably members of the Andrijic family) and the high quality of its stone, quarried on the nearby island of Vrnik (which was also used on Diocletian's ancient Roman palace in Split (see page 197) and the sixth-century Byzantine Hagia Sofia in Constantinople (present-day Istanbul)). At its peak, in the early 16th century, the town could accommodate around 6,000, but the population was seriously depleted by the plague in 1529.

The first hotel opened in 1912, under Austro-Hungary, attracting European gentry and intellectuals. During the 1970's, larger hotels were constructed on the edge of town, and Korčula entered the commercial market.

Close to the main ferry quay, **Kopnena Vrata** (Land Gate) is the principal entrance to the old town. A sweeping flight of steps lead up to the 15th-century Revelin tower, a crenellated quadrangular structure forming an arched gateway into the historic centre. A plaque bearing a relief of the winged Lion of St Mark, the symbol of Venice, is mounted above the arch. From here, Korčulanskog Statuta runs the length of the tiny peninsula, with narrow streets branching off at odd angles to form a herring-bone pattern,

**Sights**

*The old town is small and compact and can be explored in an hour or so, though you will need more time to check out the museums*

South Dalmatia

# ▶ Tales of the East

*Tales of the exotic landscapes and highly refined lifestyles of the Orient first arrived in medieval Europe through* The Travels of Marco Polo, *a best-selling travelogue of its time, which later inspired Christopher Columbus and Vasco da Gama in their voyages of discovery.*

*At the age of 17, Polo, accompanied by his father and uncle, both of whom were Venetian merchants, travelled overland to China along the Silk Route, passing through the mountains and deserts of Persia, and then across the Gobi desert, to arrive, three years later, at the court of the great Mongol Emperor Kublai Khan.*

*Polo entered the Emperor's diplomatic service, acting as his agent on missions to many parts of the Mongolian Empire for the next 17 years, visiting, or at least gaining extensive knowledge about, Siam (present-day Thailand), Japan, Java, Cochin China (now part of Vietnam), Ceylon (present-day Sri Lanka), Tibet, India, and Burma (present-day Myanmar). Some 24 years after their journey began, the*

*Polos returned to Venice, laden with jewels, gold and silk, and eager to recount the extraordinary tales of what they had seen.*

*In 1298, as a captain in the Venetian fleet, Marco (along with several thousand other sailors) was taken prisoner during a sea battle against the Genoese close to Lumbarda, off the island of Korčula. During a year in prison in Genoa, he dictated the memoirs of his magnificent journeys to a fellow prisoner and romantic novelist, Rusticello of Pisa.*

*Although the subsequent book met with commercial success, it was heavily criticized for exaggeration and whimsy, and it was only several centuries later, when future travellers to the East were able to confirm Polo's descriptions, that it was regarded as an accurate account (though to this day, the giant birds capable of carrying elephants remain something of an anomaly).*

*On his deathbed, Polo declared, "I have only told the half of what I saw".*
*(1254-1324)*

ingeniously preventing local winds from blowing through the heart of town. Through summer, the Moreška sword dance is performed in a walled garden to the left of the Land Gate. ■ *May-Sep Mon and Thu 2100. 50Kn.*

Built of warm yellow-grey stone, Korčula's much admired Gothic-Renaissance **Katedrala Sv Marka** (Cathedral of St Mark) opens out on to Strossmayer Trg, the main square, in the heart of the old town. The Romanesque portal, by Bonino of Milano in 1412 (also responsible for the Chapel of St Domnius in Split cathedral) is flanked by finely carved figures of Adam and Eve and topped with a statue of St Mark. The composition of the façade is completed with a central rose window. Inside, above the main altar stands a 15th-century ciborium (a canopy supported by four columns), carved by the local stonemason Marko Andrijić, who introduced the Renaissance style to the city. Beneath the ciborium, on the main altar, a 19th-century gilt sarcophagus holds the relics of St Theodore (the city's protector) brought to Korčula in 1736. Above it, the painting *St Mark with St Bartholomew and St Jerome* is an early work by the esteemed Venetian Mannerist, Tintoretto (1518-94). In the southern nave lies a curious collection of cannon balls and gruesome looking weapons used against the Ottomans Turks. Above them, set in a gold frame, hangs a 13th-century icon, *Our Lady with the Child*, formerly kept in the Franciscan church on the island of Badija. When a Turkish fleet, commanded by the Algerian viceroy Uluz-Ali, attacked the town on 15 August, 1571, children and the elderly prayed to the icon for divine intervention. Miraculously, a ferocious storm broke, destroying several galleys and causing others to retreat (they continued up the coast and went on to devastate Hvar instead). Also in the southern nave is an *Annunciation* attributed to Tintoretto, while in the apse, a painting above the altar depicting the *Holy Trinity* is the work of another Venetian artist, Leandro Bassano (1557-1622). ■ *Summer 0700-2100; winter 0700-1900. Strossmayerov Trg.*

Next door to the cathedral, on the first floor of the 17th-century Renaissance-Baroque Bishop's Palace, lies the town treasury, **Opatska Riznica** (Abbey Treasury). An impressive collection of icons and religious paintings includes an outstanding polyptych *Our Lady with Saints* by Blaž Jurjev Trogiranin, a prolific Dalmatian painter, also known as Blasius Pictor (1412-48). Other objects on display are gold and silver chalices, mass vestments (garments worn by the clergy), ancient coins and a necklace donated to Korčula by Mother Theresa, which had been given to her by the town of Calcutta when she won the Nobel Peace prize in 1979. ■ *Summer 0900-1900; winter by appointment. Strossmayerov Trg.*

Opposite the cathedral, the 16th-century Renaissance Gabrielis Palace now houses the **Gradski Muzej** (Town Museum). Exhibits include a copy of the fourth-century BC Greek *Lumbardska Psefizma*, see page 289, Roman ceramics and a section devoted to local shipbuilding. The interior itself gives some idea of how local aristocrats lived between the 16th and 17th centuries, and on the top floor the old kitchen is replete with stone pots and cookery utensils from that era. ■ *Apr-Jun and Sep-Oct 1000-1400; Jul-Aug 0900-2200; winter by appointment. 10Kn. T711420.*

Tucked away in a side street in the southeast part of the old town, the **Galerija Ikona** (Ikon Museum) contains a display of Cretan School icons painted between the 14th and 17th centuries. They arrived in Korčula during the Candian Wars (1645-69), when the town sent a galley to aid the Venetian fleet in its unsuccessful battle against the Turks for the possession of the Greek island of Crete. ■ *Summer 1000-1300 and 1800-2000; winter closed. 8Kn. Trg Svih Svetih.*

Next to the icon gallery stands the **Crkva Svih Svetih** (Church of All Saints). It was founded in the 13th century, making it the town's first parish church, though its present appearance dates from 300 or 400 years later. Inside, to the right of the altar is a polyptych *Our Lady the Co-redeemer* by Blaž Jurjev Trogiranin, and to the left hangs a large 15th-century Cretan crucifix, a magnificent combination of wood-engraving, painting and gilding. The coffered ceiling is decorated with biblical scenes by the Dalmatian Baroque painter Tripo Kokolja (1661-1713). ■ *Summer 1000-1300 and 1800-2000; winter closed. Trg Svih Svetih.*

Northeast of the main square, behind the cathedral, stand the modest home and watchtower of the Depolo family, **Kuca Marca Pola** (Marco Polo House). Local myth has it that Marco Polo, the legendary 13th-century traveller, was born here, though the present building was constructed several hundred years after his death. However, it's an amusing enough oddity, and is also an ideal point of reference for tracking down the town's best restaurant (see Eating). ■ *Summer 0900-1300 and 1700-1900; winter closed. 10Kn.*

A 10-minute walk west of the centre, along the seafront, brings you to the **Memorial Collection of Maksimilijan Vanka**, the villa-turned-museum of Maksimilijan Vanka's presenting a cross-section of his drawings and paintings and showing his development from Art Nouveau and expressionism through to constructivism. Vanka (Zagreb 1889-Puerto Vallorta, Mexico 1963) is an important name in modern Croatian painting. He divided his early years between Korčula and Zagreb, where he taught at the Academy of Art. In 1936 he emigrated to the United States; his best known works are the frescoes in the Church of St Nicholas, in Millvale, Pittsburgh. ■ *Summer daily 0900-1200 and 1800-2100, winter closed. 10Kn. Put Sv. Nikole bb.*

The main town **beach** lies east of the centre, in front of *Hotel Marco Polo*. However, it gets very busy, so you're better off visiting the tiny island of Badija or the neighbouring village of Lumbarda, see page 289. **Badija**, where a beautiful 14th-century Franciscan monastery has been converted into a residential sports centre (see Sleeping), is a wooded islet criss-crossed by paths leading to a series of pebble beaches, one reserved for nudists. ■ *Through summer, regular taxi boats run to the island from the main ferry harbour, 15 mins.*

**Sleeping**   **B** *Hotel Korčula*, Obala bb, T/F711078. Erected in 1871 and originally used as a café, this building was converted to become the island's first hotel in 1912. Today the only hotel in the centre, it has 20 simple but comfortable rooms, a restaurant and a glorious west-facing seafront terrace, ideal for watching the sunset. **G** *TSC Badija*, island of Badija, accessible by taxi boat (see above). T711115. The 14th-century Franciscan Monastery has been converted into a residential sports centre, with 61 rooms sleeping 240, a restaurant, and facilities for basketball, handball, tennis and swimming. Through summer it's often pre-booked by school groups, but if you call in advance there may be a spare room. Open May-Sep. *Marco Polo Tours*, Biline 5, T715400, www.korcula.com, can help you find private accommodation.

**Eating**   **Mid-range** *Adio Mare*, Svetog Roka, T711253. This unforgettable restaurant lies in a narrow side street in the old town, close to Marco Polo's House. It's kept the same down-to-earth menu, including *pašta-fažol* (beans and pasta), *brodet* (fish stew served with polenta) and *pašticada* (beef stewed in prošek and prunes, served with gnocchi), since it opened in 1974. There's an open-plan kitchen, so you can watch the cooks at work. Open mid-Apr to early-Oct. *Morski Konjic*, Stari Grad 47a, T711642. Located in the old town, practically on the tip of the peninsula, this tiny eatery serves up delicious *punjene paprika* (stuffed peppers) and a limited range of meat and fish dishes. There are just a couple of tables inside, and 6 outside, so you may have wait for a place.

**Cheap** *Planjak*, Plokata 19 Travnja 1914 bb, no phone. Friendly and totally unpretentious, *Planjak* is popular with locals and visitors alike and stays open all year. Tables are set out on a shaded terrace overlooking a small square behind the port. The menu features standard Balkan fare such as *frigane lignje* (fried squid), *ražnići* (kebabs) and *palacinke* (pancakes).

**Festivals**   *Dan Grada* (St Theodore's Day), **29 Jul**, local holiday celebrated by mass in the cathedral and an evening performance of the *moreška* sword dance.

**Sport**   **Biking**   The surrounding area is reasonably flat and lends itself to biking – Lumbarda is just 6 km away, and there's a pleasant coastal path west of town, leading to several small bays. Bikes are available for hire from *Hotel Marco Polo*. **Boating**   *Rent a Dir* at Obala Hrvatskih Mornara bb, T711908, www.korcula-rent.com, rent speed boats on a daily basis, as well as cars, mopeds and motorbikes. **Diving**   *Dupin Diving Centre*, PP101, Korčula, T716247 and T098 812496 (mob), croatia_diving@hotmail.com Englishman Steve Collett opened a diving school (the only one in Croatia recognized by the *British Sub-Aqua Club*, BSAC), based at *Hotel Bon Repos*. He lives in Korčula and can arrange diving trips all year. **Sailing**   *ACI Marina*, T711661, www.aci-club.hr Located in a small cove just east of the old town. 135 berths.

**Transport**   **Bus**   A once-daily bus service links Korčula to **Dubrovnik** (3½ hrs), with buses leaving the island at 0630 to arrive in the city around 1000, then departing at 1500 to arrive back at 1830. A local bus runs the length of the island to Vela Luka, 5 times daily (1½ hrs), stopping at **Smokvice**, **Cara** and **Blato** en route. Korčula bus station, T711216.

**Ferry** *Jadrolinija*, T715410, run a regular ferry service, winter 9 times daily, summer 14 times, from **Domince** (2 hrs 10 mins), 2 km from Korčula Town and served by a connecting bus, to **Orebić** on Pelješac Peninsula. *Mediteranska Plovidba*, T711156, run a passenger service from Korčula Town to **Orebić**, with 10 ferries daily through summer, 5 in winter. The same company also run a once-daily summer service from Korčula to **Drvenik** on the mainland, just south of Makarska. Their boats depart from the quay opposite *Hotel Korčula*.

**Communications** Internet: *Tino Computers Cyber Café*, overlooking ACI Marina, Šetalište F Kršinića bb, T716188, www.tinocomputers.hr      **Directory**

# Lumbarda

Lying at the eastern tip of the island, just 6 km southeast of Korčula Town, the tiny village of Lumbarda is best known for its idyllic sand beach and surrounding vineyards, which produce a dry white wine, *Grk*. Today, a narrow road lined with mulberry trees leads from the village through vineyards planted with *Grk* vines, which some experts consider indigenous to Dalmatia, while others, due to its name, conclude that it must have arrived here during ancient times from Greece. Whatever its origin, it grows particularly well in the area's fine reddish sandy soil.

*Phone code: 020*
*Colour map 4, inset*
*Population: 1,221*

The *Lumbardska Psefizma*, a fourth-century BC inscription carved in stone, was found here. Proof of early Greek settlement on this site, it records a decree regarding land distribution, and includes the names of Greek and Illyrian families living here at the time. Today the original is in the Archaeological Museum in Zagreb, but you can see a copy at the Town Museum in Korčula, see page 287. The settlement was later abandoned, probably due to lack of defense and fear of pirates, but grew up again during the 16th century, as a village of stonecutters and seafarers who quarried and transported stone from the nearby island of Vrnik.

**Background**

**South Dalmatia**

There's little of cultural interest here, though the village itself is a pleasant enough place, strung around a north-facing bay, lined with fish restaurants, cafés and rooms to let. Roads through the vineyards criss-cross the eastern tip of the island, bringing you to a number of small family beaches. The island's most popular bathing spot is the south-facing sand beach of *Pržina*, backed by a fast food kiosk and bar, 2 km south of Lumbarda. A short distance east of Lumbarda lies the north facing beach of *Bili Žal*, made up of white stones beaten smooth by the water, and overlooked by a tumble-down old stone building which has been converted into a rustic restaurant. A short distance east of *Bili Žal* lies a rocky stretch reserved for nudists.

**Sights**

There is just 1 hotel, a modern package place sleeping 162. Private accommodation is the best option. In Orebić, the agency *Orebić Tours*, Bana Jelačića 84A, T713367, can help you find private accommodation here.

**Sleeping**

**Mid-range** *Konoba Zure*, Lumbarda 239, T712008. Everything on offer at this family-run restaurant is homemade; there's no fixed menu (the choice changes from day to day) but you can look forward to delights such as octopus stew and lobster with

**Eating**

spaghetti, and a plentiful supply of the locally produced *Grk*. Guests sit at wooden tables in a walled garden, and are offered a complimentary glass of *travarica* upon arrival.

**Sport**  **Diving**  *MM Sub*, T712288, www.mm-sub.hr

**Transport**  Through summer, hourly local **buses** connect Lumbarda and Korčula Town (20 mins). You can also **cycle** here from Korčula Town, just 6 km away,

## Vela Luka

*Phone code: 020*  Located in a 7-km long bay at the western end of Korčula, Vela Luka is the sec-
*Colour map 4, inset*  ond largest settlement on all the Croatian islands, after Mali Lošinj. It's also
*Population: 4,380*  Korčula's main port, with ferry connections to Split on the mainland and the neighbouring islands of Hvar and Lastovo. It's not a particularly attractive place and there's little of cultural interest, but it makes a good starting point for exploring the island.

**Background**  Built around a west-facing bay and backed by gently sloping hills, Vela Luka is often referred to as the 'oldest and youngest town on Korčula': the oldest because of prehistoric finds discovered in a nearby cave; the youngest because it only really developed from the 19th century onwards. And while Korčula Town has a somewhat aristocratic past, Dalmatians consider Vela Luka a 'town of fishermen and peasants'. During the 20th century, a couple of small factories opened up here: *Jadranka* sardine canning factory and *Greben* shipyard, both of which are still functioning. The people of Vela Luka are renowned for their fine voices, and the town has a number of *klapa* singing groups. In the 1960's, the Kalos health resort opened in Kale cove, on the north side of the bay, promoting the use of marine mud (called *liman*) for the treatment of rheumatic diseases. Vela Luka's final oddity is its system of marking streets. They are not named, but numbered. Ulica 1, Ulica 2 etc, just like in New York, as locals point out wryly.

**Sights**  **Kulturni Centar** (Cultural centre) hosts contemporary art exhibitions, as well as having its own collection, including an undated work by the British sculptor Henry Moore (1898-1986). Also on display are prehistoric finds from *Vela Spilja* (see below). ■ *Summer 0800-1200 and 1600- 2000. T813001.*

Located on a hillside 3 km east of town, the **Vela Spilja** (Big Cave) is 53 m long and 20 m high. Finds dating back to 6500BC, now on display in the *Kulturni Centar* (see above), prove that it was inhabited in Neolithic times. In summer 2002 a *klapa* concert, attended by an audience of 500, was held inside the cave, and there are plans to repeat this in the future. Formerly the cave entrance was left open, but as of 2003 it will be kept shut, with restricted visiting hours during the tourist season.

The main town beach is on the north side of the bay, in front of *Hotel Posejdon*. However, the best place for bathing is on the tiny island of Proizd, 6 km from town, where you'll find lush vegetation, white pebble beaches (with an area reserved for nudists) and crystal-clear water. There's also an informal eatery, *Restoran Proizd*, in Uvala Perna (Perna Bay), serving up a choice of seafood and grilled meats (0900-1800). ■ *Boats for Proizd depart from the town harbour three times daily, return ticket 20Kn, 30 min.*

**Sleeping**  **E** *Hotel Dalmacija*, Obala 4/broj 21, T812022, www.suncorporation.hr  In an old stone building overlooking the ferry quay, this 23-room hotel has a pleasant terrace bar and restaurant out front. ***Pločica Lighthouse***, Island of Polčica. Contact *Adriatica Net*, Selska 34, Zagreb. T01-3644461, F3644463, www.adriatica.net  Between the islands of Korčula and Hvar, 20 km from Vela Luka, the lighthouse on this tiny island has been converted into 2 apartments, one sleeping 8, the other 6. There is no lighthouse keeper here so guests are totally alone. Scuba diving trips can be organized upon request. ***SEM Marina Travel Agent***, based in Split, T021-338219, www.sem-marina.hr, can help you find private accommodation in Vela Luka.

**Cheap to mid-range**  *Feral*, Obala 2 bb, T813045. This friendly, informal fish restaurant serves fresh mussels and oysters from Pelješac, as well as a choice of pasta, risotto and fish dishes. It's popular with locals, and although there's no terrace the open-sided 1st-floor dining room is light and airy and offers views over the bay. ***Hotel Dalmacija***, listed above, has a good restaurant. **Eating**

*Annual rowing competition*, **24 Jun**, regatta in honour of St John. Competitors row from Gradine to Vela Luka (3 km). In 2002 the competition attracted about 25 boats and 2,000 spectators. ***Summer Klapa Festival***, **Aug**, twice weekly evening *klapa* concerts on the square in front of the 19th-century parish church, set back a short distance from the seafront. **Festivals**

**Posejdon Croatia Divers**, *Hotel Posejdon*, Obala 1/42, T813508, www.croatiadivers.com This scuba diving school runs courses and tours, and also rents motorized rubber dinghies on a daily basis. **Sport**

**Buses** from Vela Luka to **Korčula Town** coincide with the above boat services. In addition, Mon-Fri, there are 5 local buses daily to **Korčula Town**, passing through **Blato**, **Cara** and **Smokvice** en route (1½ hrs). **Transport**

**Ferry**  *Jadrolinija* (T812015) operates a once-daily catamaran service, running from Split on the mainland to Ubli on the island of Lastovo, stopping at Vela Luka en route. It departs from Split for Lastovo in the early afternoon, then passes Vela Luka again on the return journey early the following morning, 1¾ hrs. The same company also runs a daily ferry service covering the same route, departing from Split mid-afternoon, 2 hrs 40 mins.

## Blato

The inland town of Blato lies in a fertile valley on the main road running the length of the island from Vela Luka (7 km) to Korčula Town (38 km). There is nothing on offer for tourists, but it is the economic and administrative centre of the island and the second largest town after Vela Luka. The centre is traversed by a 1-km long avenue of lime trees, and the oldest part of town is made up of 17th- and 18th-century stone houses, many unfortunately abandoned or empty. Like many other places on the Croatian islands, Blato suffers from depopulation: while the present population stands around 3,700, there are now about 15,000 people claiming to originate from Blato living in Sydney, Australia. South of town, a steep winding road (served by a sporadic bus service) leads to the south side of island, where you'll find a number of small but pleasant pebble beaches and several villages, the most popular being **Priñba** and **Priščapac**, offering rooms to let by the sea. *Colour map 4, inset*

If you do have to stay here for sometime, worth taking a peek at, one street back from the main road, is the raised piazza, known as **Plokata**, overlooked by the 17th-century All Saints' Church. Inside, there is a chapel dedicated to Sv

Vincenza (St Vincent, the town's protector) later constructed to house the bones of the saint, which were returned here by the consent of Pope Pius VI (1775-99). Opposite the church is an open-sided loggia from 1700.

Each year on 28 April, St Vincent's Day, the *Kumpanjija* sword dance (similar to the *Moreška* in Korčula) is performed here.

**Sleeping & eating** There is only one hotel in Blato, a run-down 1950's building, which is still open though it has little business. **Mid-range** *Zlinje*, one street back from the main road, close to Plokata, T851323. From the street, an arched gateway leads to this traditional *konoba* with a flagstone floor and heavy wooden furniture. The menu features a range of barbecued meat and fish dishes, but you might come here solely to taste quality local wines: reds from Pelješac and whites from Korčula, as well as *rakija* made from carob and walnut, all of which are on sale in presentation boxes. *Giča*, on the road between Blato and the south side of the island, T851644. This easy-going agrotourism restaurant lies in an old stone building set amid olive groves, 200 m off the road. Everything on offer is homemade, from the bread and wine to the *janjetina* (spit-roast lamb) and lamb, chicken and octopus prepared under a *peka*. There are a few goats and a donkey to amuse the kids. Open non-stop Jul-Aug, also on demand in Jun and Sep.

# Island of Lastovo

*Phone code: 020*
*Colour map 4, inset*
*Population: 835*
*80 km southeast of Split and 80 km west of Dubrovnik*

*This is Croatia's second most isolated inhabited island (after Vis). Like Vis, due to its remoteness, it was chosen as a Yugoslav military base, and therefore closed to foreigners from 1976 to 1989. Fortunately this blocked all commercial tourist development and today it is undoubtedly one of the most unspoilt islands on the Adriatic, with dense **pinewoods** punctuated by meticulously cultivated **farmland**, an indented **coastline** with several sheltered **bays**, and only one true settlement, the charming semi-abandoned **Lastovo Town**, made up of old stone houses built prior to the turn of the 20th century.*

*Today, despite a serious problem of depopulation, life goes on. If you visit in springtime you'll see a veritable troop of elderly women (plus the occasional donkey) hard at work in the fields. Lastovo is self-sufficient in fruit and vegetables even though only 35% of potential farmland is currently under cultivation. A network of footpaths criss-cross the island, passing through fields, woods and lush vegetation scented with sage, rosemary and mint, making walking a pleasurable pursuit. And the islanders will assure you that there are no poisonous snakes – according to local myth, several centuries ago a priest saw an adder here and cursed it, after which all the island's snakes threw themselves into the sea.*

**Ins & outs**
*See Transport, page 295, for further details*

**Getting there** A fast catamaran service to the mainland, subsidized by the Croatian government, was recently set up. Although Lastovo comes under Dubrovnik county council administration, the islanders requested a connection with Split instead, so it's now physically linked to Central Dalmatia, though it's geographically part of South Dalmatia. **Getting around** A sporadic bus service runs from one end of the island to the other. **Tourist office** In Lastovo Town, opposite the bus stop on the hill above town, T801018, www.lastovo.net

**Island of Lastovo**

South Dalmatia

# History

First settled by Illyrians, the island was known to the ancient Greeks and Romans as *Ladesta*. Archaeological digs have unearthed fragments of ceramic vessels, proving early trade links between the Illyrians and Greeks from the island of Vis, and the remains of Roman *villae rusticae* from the first century. The first important reference to the island dates from the year 1000, when the Doge of Venice, Pietro Oreolo II, ordered the burning of the wooden houses of Lastovo, following a series of raids on Venetian merchant ships. It seems the islanders lived primarily from piracy, and with several concealed harbours ideal for hiding ships they had a perfect base. However, over the next two centuries, they gave up villainous activity on the high seas and turned to the more peaceful activity of farming – the land on Lastovo is exceptionally fertile and the *polje* (fields) in the flat valley bottoms lend themselves to the cultivation of vines and olives, as well as a variety of seasonal fruit and vegetables.

In 1252 the island chose to unite with Dubrovnik, though it kept its own administration for a couple of centuries longer. The town statute, written in 1310, included a number of unusual laws: people from Hvar were banned from the island and 'foreigners' were allowed to stay for a maximum of eight days. In 1486 the Republic of Dubrovnik pressurized Lastovo into giving up its autonomy, and immediately imposed heavy taxes, compulsory military service and even built a prison. By 1602 the situation had become so bad that the islanders staged a revolt and sent an envoy to Venice, asking for assistance against the Republic. Venice subsequently occupied the island in 1603, but handed it back to Dubrovnik in 1606. Lastovo's history then followed the course of the rest of the Republic up until the end of the First World War, when it was awarded to Italy (along with Istria, Zadar and the islands of Cres and Lošinj). Under the Italian name of *Lagosta*, the economy improved and the population increased, peaking at 1,940 in 1936. Many of the older islanders still speak good Italian, as it was the official language until Lastovo was reunited with the rest of Yugoslavia in 1947.

Ubli, an insignificant cluster of modern buildings and the island's main ferry port, lies on the south coast. Founded as a fishing village in 1936 by Mussolini, when the island was under Italy, it was initially populated with fishermen from Istria. However, after just one year they packed up and left, so *Il Duce* sent a community of Italians from the island of Ponza, close to Rome, instead. There's nothing much to see, but from here a pleasant 3-km coastal road leads to Uvala Pasadur (Pasadur Bay), where you'll find the island's only hotel.

**Ubli**

**Sleeping**  **D** *Hotel Ladesta*, Ulava Pasadur bb, 3 km north of Ubli, T/F805014. Formerly known as *Hotel Solitudo*, this white modern 80-room hotel is backed by pinewoods and lies opposite the small island of Prežba, linked to Lastovo by a bridge. Current renovation work should be completed for summer 2003. Facilities include a restaurant, bar and diving centre. Pets welcome.

**Eating**  Mid-range: *Konoba Malo Lago*, Uvala Pasadur bb, T805002. Part of the *Hotel Ladesta* complex, this restaurant has a summer terrace overlooking Prežba. The menu features fresh fish, lobster and lamb dishes, plus local wine.

**Bars**  *Lounge Lizard*, opposite the ferry quay, is a simple bar where locals waiting for a boat meet for early morning coffee or an evening beer. It's possible to rent mountain bikes here (see Sport).

South Dalmatia

## Lastovo Town and around

*10 km northeast of Ubli and about 1 km inland from the north coast, Lastovo Town lies 86 m above sea level*

This once wealthy community is made up of closely packed old stone houses, built into a south facing slope, forming an amphitheatre-like space focusing on carefully tended allotment gardens in the fertile valley below. The buildings date from the 15th century onwards (before which they would have been wooden) and are noted for their unusual chimneys, strangely similar to minarets. A series of steep cobbled paths wind their way between the houses, and to the east side of town stand the 15th-century parish church of *Sv Kuzme i Sv Damjana* (St Cossimo and St Damian) and a pretty open-sided loggia. Above town, perched on a triangular hill known as Glavica, is *Kašćel*, a fortress erected by the French in 1810, now used as a meteorological station and worth the climb up for its breath taking views.

There are three north-facing bays within walking distance of town: **Lučica** (1 km), a tiny harbour made up of a dozen or so old stone fisherman's cottages, most of which have been restored and are now used as holiday homes; **Sv Mihovil** (1.5 km) where you'll find a large quay suitable for yachts, a summer bar and open-air disco by the water's edge, and the tiny 14th-century chapel of Sv Mihovil (St Micheal); and **Zaklopatica** (3 km), a large sheltered harbour, popular with yachters, overlooked by a string of modern summer houses and a good fish restaurant. In addition, a 7-km walk south of Lastovo Town will bring you to **Skrivena Luka**, called 'hidden bay' as it cannot be seen from the sea. A 3-km road runs the perimeter of the bay, passing a number of simple holiday cottages and a few summer restaurants, and the entrance to the bay is capped by a lighthouse, available for rent on a weekly basis (see Sleeping).

If you want to **swim**, the closest place to Lastovo Town is the bay of **Sv Mihovil**, where there's a large concrete quay offering easy access to the water and a rocky coastal strip shaded by pinewoods. Better still, through summer locals transport visitors by boat to the Lastovcici (an archipelago of over 40 islets lying northeast of Lastovo) usually stopping at the tiny uninhabited island of Saplun where there's a secluded cove with a blissful sand beach.

**Sleeping**

*The tourist office in Lastovo Town can help you find rooms and apartments to rent on the island*

*Struga Lighthouse*, Lastovo. Contact *Adriatica Net*, Selska 34, Zagreb, T01-3644461, F3644463, www.adriatica.net Perched 70 m above the sea, on a peninsula at the entrance into Skrivena Luka, this lighthouse dating from 1839 has been converted into 2 apartments, one sleeping 6, the other sleeping 4. It lies about 7 km from Latsovo Town and can be reached by a rough track. *Sušac Lighthouse*, island of Sušac. Contact *Adriatica Net*, Selska 34, Zagreb. T01-3644461, F3644463, www.adriatica.net Lying 21 km west of Lastovo and 37 km south of Hvar, this uninhabited island is criss-crossed by footpaths and has several pleasant bays for bathing. The lighthouse, on the edge of a steep cliff offering wonderful views, was built in 1878 and has recently been converted into 2 apartments, each sleeping 4.

**Eating**

*If you opt for private accommodation outside high season you'll probably be offered the possibility of half or full board, as the island's restaurants shut down for winter*

**Mid-range to expensive** *Konoba Triton*, Zaklopatica, T801161. Unanimously considered the best restaurant on the island, *Triton* is popular with yachters, who moor up directly in front of the summer terrace overlooking Zaklopatica bay. The owner catches fresh fish daily, and has several apartments to rent upstairs.

**Mid-range** *Konoba Bač*vara, Lastovo Town, T801057. Hidden away in an old stone building in the lower part of town this traditional *konoba* serves up fresh seafood through high season. *Konoba Portorus*, Skrivena Luka, T801261. With tables set out on a terrace overlooking the 'hidden bay', this simple eatery attracts people with smaller boats (the water is shallow here), who can moor up outside and hop ashore for a meal.

*Mamilo*, Lastovo Town. The town's only bar lies opposite the bus stop on the hill above town. Open all year. Through summer a late-night bar and open-air disco overlooking the sea operate in Sv Mihovil bay, 1.5 km north of Lastovo Town.

**Bars & clubs**

*Karneval* (Carnival), **Shrove Tuesday**. Locals make a straw figurine, known as *Poklad*, who is tied to a rope and hoisted up and down the hill in the centre of town 3 times, with fireworks attached to his boots. He is then put on a donkey and taken to the square in front of the parish church where he is burnt. The festivities then commence.

**Festivals**

**Diving** *Diving Centre Ronilački Raj*, Pasadur bb, Ubli, T805179, www.diving-para-dise.net **Mountain biking** It is possible to rent mountain bikes from the *Lounge Lizard bar* in Ubli, T805149. Expect to pay 70Kn for 24 hrs. **Sailing** There are no official marinas on the island, but yachts can moor up along the quays in the protected bays of Skrivena Luka and Zaklopatica.

**Sport**

**Bus** These run from **Ubli** to **Lastovo Town** to coincide with incoming and outgoing boat services. During summer, early-Jul to mid-Sep, they run all the way to **Skrivena Luka**. **Ferry** *Jadrolinija*, T805175, operate a once-daily catamaran service, running from **Split** on the mainland to **Ubli**, stopping at **Hvar Town** (island of Hvar) and **Vela Luka** (island of Korčula) en route. It departs from Split for Lastovo in the early afternoon, and makes the return journey very early the following morning. 2¾ hrs. The same company also run a once-daily ferry service covering the same route. It departs from Split mid-afternoon to arrive in Lastovo in the evening, and makes the return journey very early the following morning. 4¾ hrs.

**Transport**

**Banks** There is 1 bank (but no ATM) opposite the tourist office. Mon-Fri 0800-1330.

**Directory**

# Island of Mljet

*Mljet, the southernmost of the Croatian islands, is an island of steep rocky slopes and dense pine forests. The western third is a national park and within it lies one of the country's most photographed sights: a proud but lonely **12th-century monastery** perched on a small island in the middle of an emerald saltwater lake. Through the passing of the centuries, Mljet has remained something of a backwater. No great towns ever grew up here, and today it is home to half a dozen small villages, linked by a single road running the length of the island. Depopulation is a serious problem; the number of people living here has halved over the last 50 years. However, each summer Mljet is rediscovered by a steady flow of nature lovers, discerning travellers and escapists – recent visitors include **Prince Charles** and **Steven Spielberg**. The island isn't geared towards tourism – most arrive on organized day trips from Dubrovnik, and few remain overnight – but its natural beauty and lack of commercial development make it a wonderful escape for those in search of peace and tranquility.*

*Phone code: 020
Colour map 4,
grid B1/2
Population: 1,111
27 km west of
Dubrovnik, 38 km long
and an average
width of 3 km*

**Getting there** To reach the park, if you're arriving in Sobra by ferry from Dubrovnik, take the connecting bus that runs the length of the island and drops visitors directly at the National Park headquarters in Pristanište, overlooking Veliko Jezero. **Getting around** A bus runs the length of the island to coincide with incoming and outging ferries (from Sobra to the national park and back). There is no other service on the island. Within the park visitors can walk or rent bikes to get around. **Tourist office** In Polače, T744086. National Park Office is at Pristanište 2, T744041, www.np-mljet.hr

**Ins & outs**
*See Transport,
page 298, for
further details*

## History

Scholars of Greek mythology have yet to identify the lost island of *Ogygia*, where the nymph Calypso seduced Odysseus (Lat Ulysses) on his epic journey back to Ithaca from Troy, as narrated in Homer's *Odyssey*. However, the island of Mljet may well have been home to the nymph's cave, where the Greek hero was held for seven years which passed like seven days.

What we do know for certain is that Mljet was originally inhabited by Illyrian pirates, before being taken by the Romans in 35BC, who used it as a place of exile. Their main base was present-day Polače, where they built a palace (the name Polače is derived from the Croatian *palača*, meaning palace) overlooking Uvala Polače, a deep bay offering safe anchorage to ships during storms.

In 1151, the Kings of Bosnia, who ruled the island during medieval times, gave it to Benedictine monks from Montegargano in Puglia, Italy. They built a monastery on the islet in the middle of a lake at the west end of the island, and from this safe haven exerted feudal power over the islanders, subjecting them to hefty taxes in return for religious enlightenment. As of 1345, Mljet was incorporated into the Republic of Dubrovnik, and governed by a Rector who resided in the inland village of Babino Polje.

## Sights

**Nacionalni Park Mljeta (Mljet National Park)**

*Before you begin exploring, call at the park headquarters in Pristanište, overlooking Veliko Jezero, where you can buy a detailed map*

In 1960 the western third of the island was declared a national park to protect the indigenous forest of Aleppo pines and holm oaks. Covering an area of 31 sq km, the densely forested park centres on two magnificent interconnected saltwater lakes, **Malo Jezero** (Little Lake) and **Veliko Jezero** (Big Lake). From Pristanište, National Park boats shuttle visitors back and forth to **Otočić Svete Marije** (St Mary's Islet) with its charming 12th-century **Benedictine Monastery**, in the middle of Veliko Jezero. The church and cloister, now in a poor state of repair, have retained their original Apulian-Romanesque features, though much of the building was reconstructed in Renaissance style in the 16th century. The monks who lived here wielded considerable power until the monastery was dissolved when Dubrovnik fell to Napoleon in 1808. During the Tito years it was used as a hotel, but has since been returned to the Diocese of Dubrovnik, though the ground floor continues to function as a summer restaurant, with tables outside overlooking the lake. There are various rumours about foreign business tycoons wanting to buy the complex, though a sale looks unlikely.

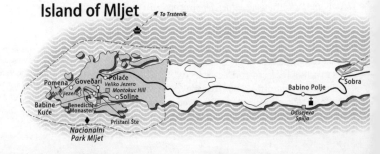

# Island of Mljet

*To Trstenik*

Pomena · Govedari · Polače · *Veliko Jezero* · *Montokuc Hill* · Soline · Babino Polje · Sobra · Babine Kuće · Benedictine Monastery · Pristani Šte · *Odisejeva Spilja* · *Malo Jezero* · Nacionalni Park Mljet

*(South Dalmatia — vertical side text)*

The park is ideal for those who enjoy **walking** or mountain **biking**: a network of paths criss-cross their way through the forests, and a 9-km trail runs around the perimeter of the two lakes. Southeast of Veliko Jezero, a steep winding path leads to the highest point within the park, **Montokuc** (253 m), offering great views over Pelješac Peninsula and the island of Korčula to the north. For **swimming**, the best bathing areas lie on **Solominji Rat**, just south of **Mali Most**, the bridge over the channel that connects the two lakes. From the bridge, you can watch the current change direction every six hours, due to the ebb and flow of the tide. Also within the park, **Veliko Jezero** and **Mali Jezero** offer an extended bathing season, the temperature of the water being 4°C warmer than that of the open sea.

It's possible to stay overnight within the park. The prettiest places are undoubtedly **Babine Kuće**, a cluster of old stone houses on the edge of Veliko Jezero, and **Soline**, just south of Veliko Jezero, overlooking the sea channel. However, they offer limited accommodation and if you're here in high season it's far easier to find a place in **Pomena**, where the modern *Hotel Odisej* (see below) overlooks Uvala Pomena (Pomena Bay), just a 15-minute walk from Malo Jezero. Alternatively, **Polace**, where you'll find the tourist office and the remains of a fourth-century Roman palace, has a number of rooms and apartments giving onto Uvala Polace (Polace Bay), a 45-minute walk from Pristanište. Last but not least, the inland village of **Goveđari**, on the hillside behind Veliko Jezero, was built during the late-18th century for workers on the Benedictine estates, and today several houses have been converted into holiday homes.

■ *Entrance tickets to the park cost 55Kn in summer, 40Kn for the rest of the year. This can be paid at any one of a number of wooden kiosks within the grounds. But if you stay overnight, this fee is included in the price of your accommodation.*

On the southeastern tip of the island lies Saplunara (from the Latin *sabalum* meaning 'sand'), a protected cove with South Dalmatia's most spectacular sand beach. Close by, in a small, scattered settlement of the same name (population 32), several families let rooms and apartments through summer. There are also a handful of down-to-earth seasonal fish restaurants. A 20-minute walk from Saplunara lies **Blace**, a 1-km long stretch of sand, facing south onto the open sea and backed by pines, popular with nudists.

**Saplunara**

Lying on the south coast, below the inland village of Babino Polje, this is the cave where Odysseus is said to have been held captive by the nymph Calypso. Through summer, *Hotel Odisej* in Pomena organize trips to the cave by boat.

**Odisejeva Spilja (Odysseus' Cave)**

South Dalmatia

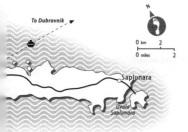

## Essentials

Due to the lack of development facilities are limited. There is 1 hotel, a limited selection of private accommodation and several waterside restaurants serving fresh lobster, for which the island is renowned.

**Sleeping** **B/C** *Hotel Odisej*, Pomena, T744022, F744042, www.hotelodisej.hr  Lying within the national park, a pleasant 15-min walk from Malo Jezero, this cluster of modern white buildings, overlooking Pomena Bay, is Mljet's only hotel. The best rooms each have a balcony, sea view, a/c, TV and minibar. In Dubrovnik, *Dubrovnik Travel* at Gruška Obala 1, T313024, www.dubrovniktravel.com, and *Kompas Južni Jadran* at Stjepana Radica 34, T419804, can arrange private accommodation on Mljet.

**Eating** **Expensive to mid-range** *Nine*, Pomena 6, T744037. Overlooking the seafront in Pomena, this restaurant is popular with the yachting fraternity, who are drawn here by its excellent lobster dishes. The live lobsters are kept in wells outside, and fished out upon request. Open mid-Apr to late-Sep.

**Mid-range** *Mali Raj*, Babine Kuće 3, T744115. This informal *konoba* serves up a typical range of Dalmatian eats. *Mali Raj* means 'little paradise': take a table on the summer terrace overlooking Veliko Jezero, and you'll agree it lives up to its name. Open mid-Apr to late-Sep. *Melita*, Otočić Sv Marije, T744145. Located on the islet of St Mary, in the middle of Veliko Jezero, this smart restaurant serves up a fine selection of barbecued meat and fish dishes. A restaurant boat shuttles guests back and forth from Pristanište. Open mid-Apr to late-Sep.

**Sports** **Bikes** Mountain bikes can be rented from *Hotel Odisej*. Expect to pay 15Kn per hr or 90Kn per day. **Boating** Kayaks and canoes can be rented at Mali Most, the bridge between the 2 lakes. Expect to pay 20Kn per hr or 100Kn per day. **Diving** Kromnar from Split, T021-470509, www.scuba.diving.hr, run the *Odyssey Diving Centre* based at *Hotel Odisej* in Pomena through summer. **Sailing** There are no marinas on the island, but yachts can moor up along the quays in the protected bays of Pomena and Polace.

**Transport** *Jadrolinija* (contact the Dubrovnik office, T418000, for details) run a once daily **ferry** service from **Dubrovnik** (summer departure Mon-Sat 1400, Sun 2030) to **Sobra**. 2 hrs. A connecting **bus** then runs across the island from **Sobra** to **Pomena** (1 hr), within the national park. *SEM* (contact the Split office, T021-338292, for details) run a summer ferry service, mid-Jun to mid-Sep, twice daily from **Trstenik** on Pelješac Peninsula directly to Polače within the national park (1 hr 20 mins). *Atlas*, Ćira Carića 3, Dubrovnik, T442222, www.atlas-croatia.com, organize day trips from Dubrovnik to Mljet by hydro-foil, 3 times per week, May-Oct.

# Pelješac Peninsula

*Colour map 4,*
*grid B1/B2*
*46 km northwest*
*of Dubrovnik*

*Forking out from the mainland, this long skinny mountainous peninsula stretches almost 90 km from end to end. High above the coast, a single road runs its entire length, linking a succession of pretty hamlets and offering fine views out over the sea, with the islands of Mljet, Lastovo and Korčula clearly visible in the distance. In the past, fear of pirates meant that most settlements developed on the south-facing slopes, and it was only from the 18th century onwards that any sizeable villages grew up along the coast. Today, its relative lack of*

*development and isolation from the mainland give Pelješac something of an
island identity, and most Croatians know it purely for its red wines, **Postup** and
**Dingac** – which are truly excellent and can be tasted at some of the larger **vineyards**, which open their cellars to the public through summer. However, many
visitors travelling by bus between Dubrovnik and Korčula pass straight over
Pelješac, missing out on its wine cellars, as well as its two most charming seaside
towns, **Ston** and **Orebić**.*

**Getting there and around**  Two buses daily, one from Korčula Town and the other
from Orebić, run the length of the peninsula on their way to Dubrovnik. There is no
separate local service. **Tourist office** The tourist office is at Trg Mimbeli bb, Orebić,
T/F713718. There is also one at Ston.

**Ins & outs**
*See Transport, pages
300 and 302, for
further details*

## Orebić

Lying close to the western tip of Pelješac Peninsula, Orebić is linked to Ston
by a 67-km road, which runs much of its length high above the coast, passing
through the Dingač vineyards. It's become Pelješac's top resort, thanks to its
fine beaches and attractive centre. In the past, it produced many able sea
captains, and when they retired they built villas here, which you can still see
today, with gardens of palms, and orange, lemon and almond trees. The
town is protected from the cold *bura* wind by the dramatic heights of Sv Ilija
Hill (961 m), whose south-facing slopes are dotted with pinewoods,
cypresses and agaves. From here it's just 2 km across the Pelješki Kanal
(Pelješac Channel) to the island of Korčula: the two coasts are linked by a
regular ferry service, making it possible for the people of Orebić to pop over
to Korčula for an evening out.

*Phone code: 020
Colour map 4, grid B1
Population: 1,949*

The town took the name Orebić, after a family of local sea captains, during
the 16th century; before this date it had been known as *Trstenica*. As part of
the Republic of Dubrovnik it was governed by a local Rector and had
very restricted dealings with neighbouring Korčula, which was at that time
under Venice.

**Background**

The town's greatest period of prosperity began in 1865, when locals
founded their own shipping company, *Associazione Marittima di Sabioncello
(AMS)*. It had 33 impressive wooden sailing ships (each with a Biblical name
from the Old Testament) and covered sea routes all the way to North America. However, it was a short-lived affair; it closed down in 1887, when steamers
began replacing wind-driven ships.

Today, thanks to its pleasant climate and south-facing beaches, Orebić
lives primarily from tourism. It makes a cheap alternative to the more
upmarket resort of Korčula Town, with which it is connected by a frequent
ferry service.

A pleasant walk through dense pinewoods brings you to the charming
Gothic-Renaissance **Franjevačka Samostan** (Franciscan Monastery),
perched on a craggy cliff 152 m above the sea, 2 km west of Orebić. It was
built in the late-15th century by Franciscan monks, who chose this site for its
vista onto the sea channel and surrounding islands. At that time nearby
Korčula was under Dubrovnik's arch-rival, Venice. The monks constructed
a loggia and terrace, which they used as a vantage point to spy on Venetian
galleys; at the first sign of trouble they would send a warning to Dubrovnik
by mounted messenger. 'Friendly' ships would let out three blasts of the

**Sights**

South Dalmatia

siren as they passed below the monastery, to which the Franciscans would reply with a peal of the church bells. Inside the monastery you can see a fine collection of religious paintings, notably the *Gospa od Angela* (Our Lady of the Angels), a Byzantine icon said to protect sailors from shipwreck. There are also several votive paintings dedicated to the Virgin Mary, commissioned by local seamen who survived danger on the ocean. ■ *Summer 0800-1200 and 1600-1900.*

Set in a typical old stone villa with a courtyard garden, the small **Pomorski Muzej** (Maritime Museum) displays maps, pictures of ships and navigational equipment related to Orebić's maritime past. ■ *Summer 0800-1200 and 1600-1900. Trg Mimbeli 12.*

Nearby **beaches** include Trstenica, a 1,500-m stretch of pebble beach, about a 15-minute walk east of the port. There is also a nearby nudist beach called Ostupa.

The **Podrum Bartulovića** is a welcoming, family-run **wine cellar** offering wine tasting sessions accompanied by *pršut* (ham), *sir* (cheese) and *slane srdele* (salt sardines) in a beautifully restored traditional *konoba*. If you call in advance they can arrange something more substantial than these snacks. ■ *Easter to late-Oct 0900-1900. T742346. Getting there: on road between Ston and Orebić. Catch a local bus or alternatively, Wine Tours, run by Atlas in Dubrovnik, often stop here for lunch.*

**Sleeping**  Orebić is home to 4 large impersonal package hotels; you're probably better off contacting either *Orebić Tours* at Bana Jelacica 84A in Orebić, T713367, or *Dubrovnik Travel* at Gruška Obala 1 in Dubrovnik, T313024, www.dubrovniktravel.hr, both of which can help you find rooms and apartments to rent. Alternatively, check out the website, www.dubrovnik-online.com, for private accommodation on Pelješac.

**Eating**  **Mid-range** *Mlinica Taverna*, Joza Šunja bb, T713886. Occupying an old mill, this popular taverna specializes in meals prepared under a *peka*, see page 43, which need to be ordered a day in advance, though more simple dishes can be eaten without prior notice. *Mlinica Taverna* opens for dinner only. ***Restoran Vrgorac***, Perna 24, Kućište, T719152. Situated 4 km west of Orebić, on the road for Vinganj, this family-run restaurant offers good home cooking and a cosy atmosphere. Favourite dishes include *brodet* (fish stew) and *punjene paprike* (stuffed peppers). Open for lunch and dinner the year through.

**Sport**  **Diving** *Orebeach Club*, Mokalo bb, T713985, www.orebeach-club.com, organise diving trips, water-skiing and jet-skiing. **Hiking** A well-marked footpath leads from the Franciscan Monastery up to the peak of Sv Ilija (walking time 3 hrs) offering stunning views across the channel to Korčula and beyond – on a clear day it's even possible to see Italy. **Windsurfing** The small village of Viganj, www.viganj.net, 7 km west of Orebić, is one of the country's top windsurfing sites.

**Transport**  **Bus** An early morning bus leaves from Orebić to Dubrovnik (0500, Mon-Fri, 3 hrs); if you miss it, you can still catch the bus from Korčula Town to Dubrovnik, which passes through Orebić around 0720 daily. **Ferry** Regular ferries connect Orebić to the nearby island of Korčula, 15 mins (see Transport, page 288, for details).

# Ston

This fortified settlement is made up of two towns, Veli Ston and Mali Ston. It was founded when Dubrovnik took control of Pelješac in 1333, and soon became the Republic's second most important centre. Lying on opposite sides of the peninsular, each with its own bay, the two towns are linked by several kilometres of well-preserved walls, effectively controlling land access onto Pelješac. Today Ston is known for oyster and mussel farming, and most visitors come here especially to eat at one of several excellent seafood restaurants. If you decide to stay overnight, there are also a couple of romantic old-fashioned hotels. You can explore the area in a few hours; from Veli Ston, Mali Ston is just a 15-minute walk over the hill.

*Phone code: 020*
*Colour map 4, grid B2*
*Population: 693*
*(Veli Ston 528;*
*Mali Ston 165)*
*8 km along Pelješac*
*Peninsula and 54 km*
*northwest of*
*Dubrovnik*

**Sights**

Between 1333 and 1506, under the auspices of great Dubrovnik architects such as Paskoje Milicevic (who designed the Sponza Palace, see page 271), the two towns were each individually fortified and then connected by a further fortification system, to produce one of the most interesting defence structures on the Adriatic. Originally there was a total 5.5-km length of **walls** observed by 40 **towers**, of which 3 km of walls and 20 towers remain today.

On the south side of the peninsular, facing onto *Stonski Kanal*, **Veli Ston** is surrounded by walls forming an irregular pentagon, stretching from the coast up the hillside above town. Within the fortifications, Gothic and Renaissance buildings from the 14th and 15th centuries are laid out on a formal grid, and include the former Rector's Palace, the Bishop's Palace and a Franciscan Monastery. The monastery complex centres on a pretty 14th-century Gothic-Renaissance cloister and the Romanesque-Gothic church of **St Nicholas**, containing works of art such as a large painted crucifix by Blaž Jurjev Trogiranin (1412-48) and a Gothic wooden statue of St Nicholas. There are no official opening hours, but if you telephone in advance (T754474) the nuns are happy to accept visitors. Below town lies an expanse of saltpans, which once covered more than 400 sq km and provided the Republic of Dubrovnik with one third of its annual revenue.

Perched on a hilltop west of Veli Ston, the interior of this tiny pre-Romanesque church, Sv Mihajlo (St Michael), is decorated with 12th-century frescoes. It's kept locked, but if you ask at the tourist office they will give you the key.

The smaller twin town of Mali Ston, 1 km northeast of Veli Ston, on the north side of the peninsula can be reached in 15 minutes on foot, following the walls. It's a compact settlement of old stone houses laid out on a grid pattern and enclosed within rectangular ramparts, with a pleasant harbour front where you'll find several eateries serving locally grown oysters and mussels. The long narrow channel of *Malostonski Zaljev*, between the mainland and the peninsula, contains a mix of fresh water (from the River Neretva) and saltwater, ideal for cultivating shellfish. Fort Koruna, built on the hillside above town in 1347, offers great views over the channel.

The best place for swimming is *Prapratna Uvala*, where there's a pleasant pebble beach backed by olive trees, 3 km from Veli Ston.

**South Dalmatia**

**Sleeping**

**B** *Hotel Ostrea*, Mali Ston, T754556, F754575, www.ostrea.hr This former mill has been restored to form a small luxury hotel, with 9 rooms and one suite, all with parquet flooring and antique furniture. Through summer, breakfast is served on a pleasant terrace. Open all year. **E** *Hotel Ston*, Placa 1, Veli Ston, T754703, F754001. This simple but comfortable hotel is an old stone building in the centre of town. There are 30 rooms, each with a telephone, TV and minibar. Pets welcome. Open all year.

**Eating**    **Mid-range to expensive** *Kapetanova Kuca*, Mali Ston, T754264. This highly regarded restaurant draws connoisseurs from all over Croatia. The house speciality is fresh oysters, but there's also a good choice of seafood risotto and pasta dishes, plus fresh fish. It's run by the same family that own the nearby *Hotel Ostrea* (see Sleeping).

**Festivals**    *Ston Summer Festival*, **late-Jul to late-Aug**. Open-air evening music and theatre in the centre of Veli Ston, given partial coverage by Croatian television.

**Transport**    There are 2 **buses** daily from Ston to Dubrovnik, 1 hr 40 mins, one early morning and the other at midday. Likewise, 2 buses daily run the route from Ston to Orebić, 1 hr 20 mins, one early morning and the other mid-afternoon.

# History

By Domagoj Mijan

## Prehistoric times

The area that is today Croatia was inhabited as long ago as the Stone Age. One of the sites with the oldest traces of man is the cave of Sandalja, near Pula, where a 1,000,000-year-old human tooth was found. The other notable Stone Age site is a cave on the hill of Hušnjak, near Krapina, where the Croatian scientist Dragutin Gorjanović-Kramberger unearthed 30,000-year-old Neanderthal remains in the late 19th century. Traces of Neanderthal hunter-gatherers from the period preceding the last Ice Age have also been discovered in the cave of Veternica, near Zagreb, and in Vindija, near Varaždin.

During the late Stone Age, climatic and geographical factors caused a cultural division between Pannonian Croatia and Mediterranean Croatia, which were to have repercussions on the region's later history. The Adriatic Coast with its hinterland up to the Dinaric Mountains came mainly under the influence of Mediterranean cultures, while the plains of northern Croatia were influenced by the Central European-Danubic cultures. Sites from this period include the cave of Grabac on the island of Hvar, where engravings of boats on fragments of a ceramic dish, dating from around 2500 BC, prove that man had already taken to the sea. At the same time, Neolithic people belonging to the Starčević culture in northern Croatia had begun building simple huts of wood and mud.

## Bronze age

The Bronze Age began here in the late fourth century BC following the arrival of the first groups of Indo-Europeans, settlers from the East who knew how to work metal. The most famous site from this period is Vučedol, near Vukovar in Eastern Slavonia, where objects such as ornamental ceramic dishes, tools and weapons have been unearthed. The best known find is the Vučedol Dove, which was associated symbolically with the rebirth of Croatia in 1991 when the area of Vukovar was exposed to some of worst fighting and bloodshed of the war for independence. In northern Croatia, several urn-fields (burial sites where cremated bodies were placed in an urn with a lid, which was buried in a circular pit) have been discovered. These people probably worshipped the sun, and were part of a culture that spread across Central Europe at that time.

Along the Adriatic Coast and its hinterland, this period witnessed the appearance of predecessors to the Illyrian tribes of the Liburnians, Histri, Japodians and Delmati, who built simple hilltop settlements fortified with stonewalls, in the manner of the Greek acropolis. DNA analysis has proved that a certain number of families living on the islands of Brač, Hvar and Korčula today are direct descendents of these peoples. Later, people living south of the River Sava were known as Illyrians, while those north of the river were referred to as Pannonians. The Celts arrived in Slavonia in the fourth century BC, assimilated with the Pannonians and spread aspects of Celtic culture such as the potter's wheel and ironwork.

## Greek colonization

The Greeks started colonizing the coast in the fourth century BC. The first settlement, Issa, was founded by inhabitants of the Greek colony of Syracuse (Sicily) on the island of Vis, and included a theatre with a capacity for 3,000 spectators. Issa later became independent, and founded several more colonies such as Tragurion (present-day Trogir), Epetion (Stobreč) and Lumbarda (on the island of Korčula). Local Illyrians traded jewellery, metalwork, glassware, salt, wine and oil with the Greeks, and thus Greek colonization induced the development of craftsmanship, the building of towns and a more sophisticated form of farming.

## The arrival of the Romans

Mid-third century BC the southern tribes united to form an Illyrian state under the leadership of the Ardedians, a people renowned for piracy. Under King Agron the Illyrian state encompassed South Dalmatia, part of Herzegovina, Montenegro and Albania, with its centre in Skodra (present-day Shkodar in Albania). Feeling threatened by Illyrian expansion, the Greeks called the Romans for help. In the meantime King Agron died, and his place was taken by Queen Teuta, who managed the throne in the name of her under-aged son. When Roman messengers arrived to ask Teuta to curtail piracy they were promptly put to death, causing the beginning of a series of wars between the Romans and the Illyrians. After three wars fought between 229 and 167 BC, the Illyrian state was defeated and its territory turned into the Roman province of Illyricum.

The Roman Liburnia, which was a fast and powerful ship powered by two banks of oarsmen, was built on the original model of those used by Liburnian pirates, and the majority of sailors in the Roman military navy originated from Illyricum. It's worth mentioning that testimonies of Greek and Roman writers of that time claim that the Liburnians kept a matriarchal society.

The Illyrian tribe of the Histri was conquered in 177 BC, when the Romans took their last point of resistance, the fortified city of Nesactium (present-day Nezakcij near Pula) and the last Histrian king, Elio, and his soldiers chose death rather than surrender. In the following decades the Romans gradually expanded the borders of Illyricum up to the River Danube, and the territory was divided on two provinces: Pannonia and Dalmatia. The capitals of these two provinces were Poetovio (in present-day Slovenia), and Salona (present-day Solin, near Split), which is said to have had a population of 60,000, a figure only attained by modern-day Split in the year 1960. During later administrative divisions, Pannonia was divided into four smaller provinces, and Dalmatia into two.

## Culture during Roman times

The first Romans that came to these parts were traders and soldiers. Legions built military camps that soon developed into centres of Roman culture. In the Roman military camp near Sinj, a Roman stone monument presents the world's oldest illustration of football. Besides fortresses, the Roman army built roads, bridges and aqueducts, which stimulated the arrival of civilians who were attracted by the possibility of expanding trade and colonization. This lead to the development of the inland towns of Siscia (present-day Sisak) and Sirmium (present-day Srijemska Mitrovica), and the coastal towns of Pola (Pula), Senia (Senj), Jader (Zadar), Salona (Solin), Narona (Vid near Metković) and Epidaurum (Cavtat). Among the distinguished citizens, two mayors were elected in each town, who had full Roman rights and acted as the main bonds in spreading Roman influence. The Romans built roads so as make military intervention possible and to improve trade and communications. The two most important routes both linked Aquileus (Aquileia) in northeast Italy to Byzantium (present-day Istanbul), one passing through Emona (Ljubljana), Poetovia (Ptuj) and across Pannonia to Singidunum (Beograd) and Naissu (Niš), while the other ran south along the coast through Dalmatia and then veered east to join the Via Egnatia (Egnatian Way) through Epirus (mainland Greece).

Croatia's best preserved Roman monuments are the Arena (amphitheatre) and the Forum with the Temple of Augustus in Pula, and Diocletian's Palace in Split.

## Christianity

Christianity arrived early in this part of the world. Apparently St Paul sent his disciple Titus to the area to spread the new religion, and St Paul himself was shipwrecked close to the island of Mljet. The oldest diocese in the country was probably Salona (Solin), and its founder was the martyr Venancius, who died around AD 257. The Bishop of Salona, later known as St Gaius, was elected Pope in Rome in AD 283. After the 'Edict of Milan', which legalized Christianity, Salona became the seat of the Archbishop of Dalmatia, and its importance is testified by numerous archaeological finds on the site.

Along the coast, Christian centres also developed in Epidaurum (Cavtat), Jadera (Zadar), Parentium (Poreč) and Pola (Pula). In Pannonia the main Christian centres were Sirmium (Srijemska Mitrovica), Cibalia (Vinkovci), Mursa (Osijek) and Siscia (Sisak). Many early Christians died for their belief, with the greatest persecution taking place under Emperor Diocletian.

## The end of the Roman Empire

When the Roman Empire was divided into the Eastern and Western Empires in 395 – a division that was to have far-reaching consequences for the later history of the Balkans – Dalmatia fell within the West. With the fall of the Western Empire in 476, the region became part of the Ostrogoth state of Theodoric the Great, until the Byzantine emperor Justinian I conquered the Ostrogoths in 555, and it was made a Byzantine province. During the second half of the sixth century, it was invaded by tribes of Slavs and Avars, and by 600 they had reached the most western point in their migration, Istria. They also travelled south through Dalmatia, where they demolished Salona.

According to the Byzantine Emperor and historian Constantine Porphyrogenitus, the Croats were invited to present-day Croatia by Emperor Heraclius (575-641) to expel the Avars. This they did, also defeating other Slavic tribes, and they soon became at the dominant force in the former Roman province of Dalmatia.

## The origin of Croats

The name Hrvat (Croat) has been used by two other Slavic tribes, besides today's Croats – the so-called White Croats in Poland, who populated the area around the River Vistula, with their centre in Krakow (Pope John Paul II comes from these parts) and the Croats of the northeast region of the Czech Republic. Other smaller groups who also called themselves Croats have been traced in Slovenia, Slovakia, Montenegro, Macedonia and even in Greece.

In the 14th century, the name Croat was applied to people living in the area south of Petrova Gora Mountain (which forms the natural border between Slovenia and Croatia), and from the 15th century onwards the name spread north as far as the River Sava, and later beyond it.

Science has not entirely defined the origin and the meaning of the name Croat. In the early 20th century, two stone tablets were found near the ancient city of Tanais, close to the Sea of Avoz (between Russia and Ukraine), bearing Greek inscriptions which mentioned an archon (chief magistrate) Horoathos or Horuathos – a name very close to Hrvat (Croat).

Many linguists believe that the name Hrvat is of Iranian origin, and that the Croats conquered the Slavs gradually but took their language, so that today Croatian belongs, without a doubt, to the Slavic group of languages. Recent genetic research verifies the theory that Croats came from Iran, as up to 50% of the inhabitants of the Croatian coast and the mountains that rise behind it carry these genes. Alternatively, it is possible that the Illyrians were of Iranian origin and later assimilated with the Croats.

## Towns in Dalmatia

In the seventh century, citizens of Salona fled the rampaging tribes of Avras and Slavs, and took refuge within the walls of Diocletian's Palace, converting the late-Emperor's mausoleum into a cathedral. During the Middle Ages the geographical term Dalmatia narrowed, and instead of referring to the great Roman province of Dalmatia the name was applied to a few isolated islands and coastal towns populated by families of Roman descent, while the hinterland was taken by the Croats. Interestingly, all these towns, apart from Split, were built on peninsulas so they could be well defended against attack, and belonged to Byzantine theme (province) of Dalmatia. According to Constantine Porphyrogenitus this province included the coastal towns of Zadar, Trogir, Split, Dubrovnik and Kotor, and the towns of Krk, Rab and Osor on the islands. The greatest military forces of the time – the Byzantine Empire, the Franks, Arabs, Hungarians, Normans and Venetians – all fought for the control of these towns, which was essential for control over the Adriatic, and ruling the Adriatic was a strategic point for control of the Mediterranean, the economic, political and cultural centre of Europe in the Middle Ages. The strategic importance of these towns lay in the fact that the Eastern Adriatic boasted good sea currents and, with its indented coastline, provided shelter and safe ports essential for medieval ships. Due to its position in Europe, Croatia gained great international importance, which proved in fact to be a great burden, as it had to invest everything it could in obtaining and maintaining its independence.

## The development of the Croatian state

The Croats were the only Slav nation fortunate enough to have settled on the culturally rich Roman Mediterranean. Very few written documents exist regarding their early years in the region, though around the year 800 we have evidence of one Duke Višeslav, whose court was based in Nin (near Zadar, in North Dalmatia).

Around the same time, the Byzantines and the Franks came into conflict over Dalmatia. Charlemagne (768-814), the Frankish king, who also held the title Emperor of the Western Roman Empire, and Michael Rangabus (811-13), the Byzantine Emperor, eventually signed a peace treaty in 812, in which Byzantium would hold onto the Roman coastal towns of Dalmatia, on the condition of acknowledging Charlemagne's imperial title and leaving continental Croatia to the Franks.

Between 819 and 822, led by Duke Ljudevit, tribes in south Pannonia staged an unsuccessful rebellion against the Franks and their cruelty. During this uprising, Borna, Duke of Dalmatia and Liburnia, sided with the Franks, and thus became the beneficiary of the victory over Ljudevit, who was killed in 823. In the same year, a certain Trpimir made a contribution to the Split Archdiocese, and in a document recording this called himself the Duke of Croatia (Dux Croatorum).

Croatian territory covered the hinterland of the coastal towns of Zadar, Trogir and Split, but did not actually include these towns. It stretched south as far as the River Cetina (near Omiš), and east into central and western Bosnia. To the north it included Lika and Krbava, which were governed by a Ban (governor or viceroy) and later it also covered the province of Istria. When the Croatian rulers were at their height, Pannonia, between the River Drava and Gvozd Mountain, was part of Croatia, but during periods of weak central authority Pannonia lead a life of its own.

Trpimir, Duke of Croatia (845-64), is deemed as the founder of the dynasty that the country until the end of the 11th century. He expressed a patrimonial perception of the state, considering the entire territory as his own personal property and surrounded himself with a council of hand-picked counts (župani), who were each responsible for a county (županije), to help him rule.

Trpimir's successor, Domagoj (864-76), built up Croatia's naval strength and came into conflict with Venice over the control of the Adriatic, which is why the Venetians called him the worst Duke of Croatia. After Domagoj, Zdeslav (878-79) came to power, but he was assassinated and succeeded by Branimir (879-82) who was loyal to the Pope, and obtained the first international recognition of Croatia from Pope John VIII.

At that time the 'Apostles of the Slavs', the brothers Methodius and Cyril, were requested by the Byzantine emperor to invent an alphabet that could be modified for Slavic languages and would thereby spread the Byzantine influence among these people. The papacy, worried about the strengthening of Byzantium, wanted to keep Croatia under Rome's watch.

Around the same time, an agreement known as a *tributum pacis* was drawn up between the Byzantine emperor Basil I and the Croatian ruler, stating that Dalmatian towns would pay 710 golden coins to the Croatian ruler instead of to the head of the Dalmatian theme so as to be able to work their fields in peace. It is most likely that at the same time the Venetians also started paying tribute to the Croatian rulers so as to have safe naval passage along the Croatian coast.

## Tomislav, the first Croatian king

The following century is linked with Tomislav's reign (910-28). He started his rule as a *dux* (duke) but changed his title to that of *rex* (king) around 925. For his achievements in the wars against the Bulgarians, the Byzantine emperor Romanus Lacapenosus awarded him control over the Dalmatian towns and the title of 'proconsul' so he could rule them in the name of the Byzantine Empire.

During Tomislav's rule, two state-church assemblies took place in Split, one in 925 and the other in 927-28. Only a century earlier it would have been beyond imagination that a Croatian ruler should preside over a church council in the Roman city of Split. In Europe at that time, the church wielded such material wealth and political influence that rulers did not interfere directly with church matters. Croatia had its own independent bishop in Nin who had no connection with the other bishops in the Dalmatian cities. Now that Byzantine Dalmatia and coastal Croatia were united under the authority of a single ruler (though each area had its own administration and laws), bishops in Dalmatia saw a unique opportunity to spread their jurisdiction, and by doing so increase their income, which up until then depended solely on the towns. Bishop Gregory of Nin, whose monument stands in front of the Zlatna Vrata (Golden Gate) entrance to Diocletian's Palace in Split, wanted to preserve the diocese of Nin, the use of glagolitic and the Slav liturgy. But the Bishops of Dalmatia won the day, and the diocese of Nin was abolished and its jurisdiction divided between the Dalmatian dioceses.

Tomislav defeated the Hungarians and united Coastal and Pannonian Croatia. The attack of the Bulgarian emperor Simeon on Croatia ended with a Bulgarian defeat. Constantine Porphyrogenitus records that during Tomislav's reign, Croatia was divided into the following administrative counties (županije): Livno, Cetina, Imotski, Pliva, Pset, the coastal county, Bribir, Nin and Sidra, while a Ban ruled Lika and Krbava.

The period of Croatian history after Tomislav's death is unclear due to lack of historical sources, and the number of people living on Croatian territory at that time is uncertain. Constantine Porphyrogenitus claimed that during Tomislav's reign Croatia had an army of 100,000 infantry, 60,000 horsemen and 5,000 sailors with 80 large ships and 100 smaller ships. This number is unusually high considering the size or the territory and can only be explained by the fact that all free residents (ie non-slaves) were probably seen as warriors, and thus counted as members of the army. In comparison, the Venetian fleet had only 200 ships, and the Byzantines 300, and these were said to be the strongest fleets in Europe.

## Venetian claims to Dalmatia

However, in the year 1000, the Doge of Venice, Peter Orseolo, led a successful campaign to gain control over the Dalmatian coastal towns, which were subsequently forced to acknowledge Venetian rule and honour Orseolo with the title Dux Dalmatiae. Although these towns were later reclaimed by the Croatian crown, this was to be only the first of many attempts by Venice to take Dalmatia.

## Allegiance to Rome

In 1054 the 'Great Schism', the break between Eastern and Western Christian churches, took place, and the border between the Eastern and Western Roman Empires, drawn up by Theodosius in AD 395, became the border between the Roman Catholic and Orthodox churches. The east Adriatic, bisected by this border, was of direct interest to both the pope in Rome and the patriarch in Constantinople, and the papacy was eager to keep Croatia under the Catholic wing.

During the rule of Petar Krešimir IV (1058-74), two church councils met in Split, proclaiming sanctions against clergy who served sermons in the Croatian language, had beards, were married or in any other way resembled the Eastern Church. Krešimir was recognized as the King of Dalmatia and Croatia by the pope, and thus the Byzantine theme of Dalmatia was truly united with Croatia. Krešimir was not only just a Byzantine official like Tomislav and Tomislav's successors, he was the absolute leader of the entire region.

## The last Croatian kings

However, soon after his death a conflict blew up, provoked by the Normans, Venetians, Byzantines, Hungarians and the pope in Rome, who all hoped to gain control over Croatia and Dalmatia. The result of this was that Zvonimir, the former Ban (governor or viceroy) at the time of Petar Krešimir, succeeded to the throne in 1075 and took the title King of Croatia and Dalmatia. Zvonimir was chosen thanks to the support of Pope Gregory VII, and in return he placed the country under papal sovereignty. He was linked to the Hungarian dynasty Arpadović through his wife Jelena, who was a sister of the Hungarian king Ladislas. Legend says that Zvonimir left the Croats with a curse that they would not have their own king for one thousand years.

After Zvonimir, Stjepan Trpimirović ruled for a short time, but he was too weak to put an end to difficult internal problems. This chaos was used by the Hungarian Arpadović Dynasty, with some assistance from the pope, to take control of Croatia and Dalmatia and finally fulfil their long desire to open up their land-locked territories with access to the sea. Rome favoured the Arpadovics, and thus in 1091 the Hungarian king Ladislas came to Slavonia and claimed the right of his sister Jelena (widow of Zvonimir) to Croatia and Dalmatia. Ladislas succeeded in taking Pannonian (which from then on became known as Slavonia), and in 1094 he founded a diocese in Zagreb, but he had no luck in conquering the hills of coastal Croatia. In 1097, his successor to the throne, Koloman, defeated the last Croatian king Petar on Gvozd Mountain, which was later renamed Petrova Gora (Petar's Mountain).

In 1102, with the signing of the Pacta Conventa the heads of the 12 most powerful Croatian families recognized Koloman as their leader, and accompanied him to Biograd-na-Moru (near Zadar) where he was crowned King of Croatia and Dalmatia.

## The Hungarian crown

The Hungarian Arpadović family, like the other royal dynasties that ruled Croatia, did not gain their crown through military occupation but with the approval of the Croatian nobility. In spite of this, each royal house that ruled the country treated it as a province in their kingdom, and not as an equal subject.

Croatian history from 1102 until 1991 finds the country divided into three large administrative areas that had little contact with each other – Croatia, Slavonia and Dalmatia – under foreign rulers such as the Arpadović Dynasty as of 1102, the Anjou dynasty as of 1301, the Habsburgs from 1527 and the Karadjordjević Dynasty from 1918. In theory this was the free choice of Croatian nobility (the people with a say in politics), but in reality it was somewhat different.

Under each foreign ruler, the Croatian nobility requested that the union should be between two equal partners, and that it should have the character of a personal or individual union. However, each dynasty, upon settling in Croatia, insisted on a real or actual union. Personal union is when both countries concerned retain autonomy in internal affairs and are linked by the persona of the ruler – the best examples of this are the countries of the Commonwealth that recognize the Queen of England as their ruler, but govern their own internal and foreign political matters. Real union is when a king has the power to make laws and the countries under him have limited local autonomy.

The Croats were misfortunate in that every time they gave their independence to foreign royalty, they then had to claim back their historical rights from them. Croatia could oppose the ruling dynasties when it still had great noble families such as the Frankopans and the Subić-Zrinskis who were powerful enough to oppose the king. But with the loss of territory upon the arrival of the Turks and the extinction of the Frankopans and the Subić-Zrinskis, and with the increase in the number of rulers in Europe (absolute monarchy), this freedom was decreased. Until the French revolution the conflict between the ruler and the nobility was a conflict between a narrow class of people, but later with the growth of a national consciousness it became a conflict between entire nations.

The change of dynasty had far-reaching consequences for Croatia. Most of the national territory – Croatia, Dalmatia, Slavonia, and the county of Neretva (south of the River Cetina) – was united under the Arpadovićs, but in spite of this there were significant differences between these regions. The dualism of Croatia and Dalmatia continued, while medieval Slavonia and the county of Neretva each developed separately.

The Hungaro-Croatian alliance was positive, as the two countries would later work together to oppose the process of Germanization in the region. The Arpadović Dynasty considered themselves the heirs of the Croatian rulers in the patrimonial-feudal sense, and from the time of King Koloman onwards they were the supreme owners of the entire territory, and at the same time the direct owners of those lands that were not the legal property of free men. The special position Croatia had in this Hungaro-Croatian union was incarnated in the persona of a Ban (governor or viceroy).

## Croatian nobility

After 1180 the king's power weakened and the transformation of royal counties into fiefs, or noble counties, began. The first such feudal donation took place in 1193 when Bčla III gave Bartol Duke of Krk possession of the County of Modrus, making Bartol a hereditary Count, whose descendants would inherit his lands. From that date onwards, the donation of fiefs to feudal noblemen became more frequent, and a new landed noble class developed. These noblemen commanded complete administrative, juridical and economical power over their lands and subjects (serfs), of which they were master, free of interference from the royal count. Such feudal families included the Counts of Krk, Vinodol, Modrulj (later known as the Frankopans), Bribir (the Šubić family), Cetina (the Nelipčić family), Omis (Kačić), Krbava (Kurjaković).

## The sacking of Zadar

In 1190, Zadar, which was the largest town in Dalmatia, scored a naval victory over the Venetian fleet near Osor (island of Cres) and also fought off a subsequent attack by the Venetian duke Dandolo in 1194. Victory over the Venetian navy, which at that time was one of the world's leading forces, proves that Zadar was a force to reckoned with at that time. The French writer of Crusade chronicles, Geoffroi de Villehardouin, recorded that "there was not a bigger and richer town than Zadar". In 1202, the blind Venetian duke Enrico Dandolo persuaded members of the Fourth Crusade to pay their way to the Holy land by conquering Zadar, which was one of the richest towns on the Mediterranean at that time.

## Founding of the Sabor

By excessive donations of feudal estates, the king's juridical and economical power weakened. The situation climaxed at the time of Andrew II (1203-35), when the feudal nobility gained certain privileges on the king's account through a charter known as the Golden Bull (1222), an agreement very similar to the English Magna Carta from 1215.

The 13th century saw the king's patrimonial power further diminished with the forming of the Sabor (parliament), where nobles would meet to discuss matters of national importance. The first meetings were held in Zagreb and attended only by nobles from Slavonia.

Also at that time, several towns in Slavonia, such as Vukovar, Virovitica, Petrinja and Samobor, which were mainly settlements of foreign craftsmen and merchants, attained autonomy. These towns were granted certain privileges by the king: they were free from the power of the local count; they could write their own laws and they practiced their own form of government.

## A short history of Dalmatian communities

In 1107, five years after rest of Croatia had done so, the coastal towns of Dalmatia recognized Koloman as their king, and he return granted them a certain autonomy. The first town to receive a charter was Trogir, which soon became a model for those of other Dalmatian towns. According to this charter, citizens of Trogir were obliged to recognize the supreme power of the king and to give him two-thirds of all customs fees, and in return they were granted autonomy in all other aspects of town life. The Hungarian kings gave greater privileges to the Dalmatian towns than to Hungarian towns as they needed them for their access to the sea.

Around this time, many towns began drawing up their own statutes: first was the statute of Korčula in 1265; then Dubrovnik in 1272; Zadar and the island of Brač in 1305; Split in 1312; Trogir in 1322 and Hvar in 1331. These statutes laid down urban planning regulations and measures to fight the plague epidemics that were rife in Europe. Consequently, each of these communities had a sewerage system and a communal watchmen, at a time when in the cities of France and England people were still throwing rubbish out of their windows onto the street. Pigs were forbidden inside the Dalmatian communities, while in western European towns they were used as communal watchmen. The statutes also regulated ecological problems such as the amount of fish that was caught and number of trees that were chopped. Communal matters were decided through secret votes (using small marbles), although the right to vote was confined to the local aristocracy. Juridical decisions were logical and righteous: a party that lost a case would have to pay for it, and foreigners were judged on the basis of reciprocity. In short, each town and its immediate surroundings was a community that had its own clerks, physicians, pharmacists, judges, teachers and solicitors. Even though we cannot say that life in these communities was democratic in the sense of the word today, it is clear a written statute meant a certain degree of progress.

## The Anjou dynasty

The Mongol invasion of 1241-42 left Croatia and Hungary devastated and impoverished. It also rapidly liquidated the king's power and strengthened that of the feudal nobility and the Ban (viceroy), who substituted the king and became the political exponent of the nobles.

At the turn of the 14th century, the Hungarian Anjou dynasty succeeded to the throne with the help of the Croatia's most powerful family, the Šubićs, who had installed themselves as hereditary Bans. Both Carl (1301-42) and Ludovic (1342-82) ruled without parliament, but the riots and conflicts between local noblemen left the country in a state of turmoil. Venice took advantage of the situation to gain control of the Dalmatian coastal towns of Šibenik and Trogir (1322), Split (1327) and Nin (1329).

In 1408, Ladislas of Anjou sold his rights to Zadar and its surroundings to Venice for 100,000 golden coins, and by 1420 La Serenissima had control of the entire coast from Zadar to Dubrovnik, much of which it would retain until 1797. The loss of Dalmatia severely weakened the position of Croatia.

## The city-republic of Dubrovnik

The town was founded in the seventh century on a site known to the Romans as Ragusium. Dubrovnik came under the protection of the Byzantine Empire until 1205, after which it came under the Venetian Republic. Dubrovnik liberated itself from Venetian protection in 1358 and from that moment onwards its rise to glory began. Even though the town recognized the authority of the Hungaro-Croatian king, in reality it became an independent city-republic. The term Republic was used for the first time on in 1430. Due to the fall of the Hungaro-Croatian kingdom and Turkish hegemony, Dubrovnik recognized the authority of the Turkish Sultan to whom it paid a fee of 12,500 golden coins.

Later the Habsburg dynasty became stronger and the Turks weakened, so in 1684 Dubrovnik made a contract with the Habsburgs, agreeing to an annual tribute of 500 golden coins, an act which revived the protection of the Hungaro-Croatian crown, whose successors were the Habsburgs. Dubrovnik continued to pay a fee to the Turkish Sultan too. The French brought about the end of the Republic in 1808, 11 years after the fall of Dubrovnik's greatest rival, Venice.

During its golden years, Dubrovnik developed diplomacy to the extent that no country before and after has ever managed. This was essential, as sitting between the mountains and the sea it was surrounded by the Ottoman Empire landwards and Venice seawards. It achieved the impossible and maintained it. Dubrovnik aristocracy cherished the Republic and put it above their own interests. Their motto was "With everyone nicely, with everyone carefully". The secrets they discovered in the courts of the Christian rulers they would sell to the Turks, and visa-versa, they would sell similar information to the Christian rulers. This was their position between the East and the West. In a way, Josip Broz Tito continued this policy and passed it on to the Non-aligned Countries during the Cold War.

In 1377, Dubrovnik was one of the first places in Europe to open an organized quarantine as protection against the plague. Following this model, other European towns founded similar quarantines: Marseille in 1378, and Venice in 1403. In 1570, the

Republic's fleet numbered 180 ships with a total capacity of 56,810 tonnes, worth almost 700,000 golden coins: For some time, tiny Dubrovnik had the third largest merchant fleet in Europe. In the early-16th century, the city started building the biggest ships in the world at that time, with capacities of up to 2,050 tonnes. The English language testified this fact by assigning the term argosy (from the Latin name for Dubrovnik, Ragusa) to any large merchant ship.

It is worth mentioning that from the 16th century up until the end of the Republic, merchants from Dubrovnik had their place on the London stock market. It must be mentioned that Dubrovnik as a city-republic reached a far more distinctive structure on its small territory than it's much wealthier rival Venice. Dubrovnik, unlike Venice, was not surrounded by the rich Paduan valley but by the rocky Herzegovinian mountains, and had to apply its resources optimally to achieve success. However, in the mid-16th century, with the rise in importance of the Americas, the centre of economic power in Europe shifted from the Mediterranean to the countries overlooking the Atlantic Ocean, and Dubrovnik was pushed into recession.

## Ottoman expansion

Having lost Dalmatia to Venice, Croatian political life was reduced to the region of Slavonia (formerly known as Pannonia). By this time, the term Slavonia was applied further to the east, while the name Croatia was moved from Dalmatia northwards to the area between Gvozd Mountain and the River Drava.

It was at this time that the Ottoman Turks began expanding towards Croatia. The Holy Roman Emperor and King of Hungary, Sigismund I (1387-1437) organized a crusade against the Turks, but was defeated at the Battle of Nicopolis in 1396. It was an evil omen that signified forthcoming wars between Croatia and the Ottoman Empire that would last for centuries. Sigismund's negligence and his absence from the country brought about the disintegration of his authority – the aristocracy began oppressing the lower nobility, fights between themselves and against the king. Disunited Croatian society in these feudal conditions spent all its efforts on internal conflicts and was unable to fight the Turks.

Conditions were even worse during the reigns of Albrecht Habsburg (1438-39) and Vladislav (1440-44), who was also King of Poland. The more competent Matthias Corvinus (1458-90), who aspired to establishing a Central Europe kingdom that would counterbalance the Turks (a role that was later played by the Habsburg monarchy), tried unsuccessfully to enforce order in the country and protect it from the Turks.

After the fall of neighbouring Bosnia in 1463, the Croatian borderlands lay open to Turkish attack. Attempts to organize defence by setting up borderline military camps in 1435 were unsuccessful. The first defeat took place in the battle on the field of Krbava near Udbina in Lika in 1493 where the Turks achieved a great victory over the Croatian army. Constant Turkish attacks on Croatian lands brought great disruption to the country. Peoples from the east (Serbia and Bosnia) fled the Turks, seeking refuge in Croatia, and these migrations affected food production, resulting in poverty and famine. Croatia's western neighbours, namely Venice and the Habsburgs, recognized the danger for their own countries and started worrying about how to defend Croatia in order to defend themselves. But these measures were not enough. By the end of the 15th century, conflicts between the ruling Hungaro-Croatian aristocracy culminated in the aristocracy opposing the king and the lower nobility, and the burghers opposing the clergy. In 1526, a catastrophic defeat of the Hungarian army by the Turks at the Battle of Mohacs opened the problem of electing a new king, as Louis II had somewhat ignominiously drowned in a river as he tried to escape the battle.

Background

## The arrival of the Habsburgs

There were two aspirers to the throne: the Hungarian aristocrat Ivan Zapolja, who originated from Slavonia, and Ferdinand Habsburg. The Croatian nobles thought that Ferdinand would give them better support against the Turks than Zapolja, so they elected him as king at a meeting in the town of Cetin on 1 January 1527. But on 6 January 1527, the Slavonian nobles elected Zapolja as king, resulting in fights between the followers of the respective potential leaders. The conflict ended with the death of Zapolja in 1540. This was how Ferdinand Habsburg became the leader of Croatia, Dalmatia and Slavonia, and the entire territory absorbed into the Holy Roman Empire of the German people. At the time the Habsburgs were the kings of Czech, Hungary, Spain, the Netherlands, Naples and even the rulers of Mexico.

## The Krajina

In defence of the Turks, the krajina (military border) was established in the 16th century. In 1578, with the approval Vienna, work began to build Karlovac as a nucleus of defence against the Turks – Turkish skulls were thrown into the foundation of Karlovac as a sign of the mood of the times. Other defence posts were later built to the south and east. To guard these positions, a special borderline army was formed, made up largely of Vlahi, Orthodox Serb cattle farmers who were fleeing the Turks from the east. By this time the Habsburgs were over-riding the authority of the ban (Croatian governor) and the sabor (Croatian parliament), and the Krajina was put under German officers who took their orders directly from Vienna and Graz.

## Defending the country against the Turks

The rule of the first Habsburgs, Ferdinand (1527-64), Maximillian (1564-76) and Rudolph (1576-1608) was devoted to defending the region against the Turks. When the Turks took Klis in 1537, they effectively had control over the entire Dalmatian hinterland all the way south to the River Neretva, leaving Dalmatia divided between Venice and the Ottoman Empire. In October of the same year, the Turks defeated Ferdinand's armies at Gorjan (near Djakovo), and thus opened their way to the Croatian lands in the west. Croatia, under the authority of the Ban, was "the remains of the remains of what it once was" (*reliquiae reliquiarum olim incliti regni Croatiae*). Ferdinand, using the excuse of installing better defence, centralized the government into his own hands in order to constitute a unified monarchy.

The Turks achieved their greatest victories at the time of Sultan Suleiman the Magnificent (ruled 1520-66). On his campaign against Vienna, his army was detained by the Croatian Ban, Count Nikola Zrinski, and his army at Szeged (southern Hungary). Even though Szeged was eventually conquered in 1566, Zrinski's heroic defenders aroused doubts about Turkish invincibility and also indicated the turning point that was to come. One hundred years after the disaster on Krbava field, the Turks suffered a defeat near Sisak in 1593, marking the beginning of a 13-year war against Croatia and Hungary. This war ended with a peace treaty in Zitva-Torok (on the Danube, near Komarn in present-day Czech Republic) in 1606, and was a clear symptom of the decline of Turkish power. During the first half of the 17th century, following this satisfactory peace treaty, the Croatian nobles considered that the krajina (military border) had fulfilled its task, and they demanded that it should come back under the authority of the Croatian Ban.

## Re-organization of the Krajina

The Krajina had physically divided Croatian territory in two, which made national integration very difficult. The Emperor's Court in Vienna had double reasons not to disband the troops of the military border: on one hand, the military border was an infinite source of cheap, well-trained and true soldiers, and on the other hand, Vienna feared that national integration would strengthen the Croatian aristocracy. These soldiers saved the Habsburg monarchy from a revolution of nearly all its citizens in 1848. The Habsburgs decided to train the border soldiers better, provide them with new uniforms at low cost and send them to battlefields all over Europe to serve their interests.

## The Habsburgs tighten their control

During the 200-year fight to hold back the Turks, Croatia lost not only three-quarters of its territory, but also the same number of its population. People either died in battle, or were captured by the Turks and taken away without a trace to be used as slaves. The survivors moved to the north and the west of the country, and even beyond its borders. The aristocracy also migrated, with the Šubić-Bribirski family, the Draškovićs, Kukuljevićs and Vranicanis all moving northwards, thus displacing the centre of the Croatian state from Coastal Croatia to Upper Croatia. The history of other European peoples shows similar example of movements of central authority from the south to the north during foreign invasions: from Kiev to Moscow after the Mongolian invasion in Russia, and from Raša to Belgrade in Serbia. The clergy, knights and military government encouraged these migrations.

Two Croatian aristocratic families in particular distinguished themselves in the wars against the Turks: the Frankopans and Zrinskis. These two families were related by blood, and also by similar political beliefs. In the 17th century, Petar Zrniski, together with a group of Hungarian aristocrats, lead a diplomatic mission to free Croatia of Habsburg domination. But the conspiracy was soon discovered and the court in Vienna sentenced Petar Zrinski and his brother-in-law Franjo Frankopan to the guillotine. They were executed on 30 Apr 1671, and their extensive estates were confiscated on behalf of the court chamber, ie the Habsburgs.

By 1718, Croatia had reclaimed all of Slavonia, a part of Srijem, Banovina, Kordun, Lika and Krbava from the Turks. These lands were immediately claimed by Vienna, even though in theory they should have been placed under the jurisdiction of the Croatian parliament and the Ban. But the Habsburgs did not want to strengthen Croatia, so on the pretext of having been won in war, they were placed instead under military authority, effectively becoming a constituent part of the krajina. The Habsburgs also started to give away large estates in the liberated and recently acquired Slavonia to foreign (German and Hungarian) families, such as the Odescalchis, Eltzes, Normans and Trenks, to the obvious detriment of the Croatian nobility. Therefore, the Croatian parliament started to lose its importance, and less and less noblemen participated in its meetings, attending the Hungarian parliaments instead, where they solved Hungaro-Croatian matters together with the Hungarian nobles.

Ironically, with the expulsion of the Turks, Croatia's position became even more uncomfortable, as the Habsburgs tightened their grip on the country. By this time a sizeable Serbian population (of the Orthodox faith) were living in Croatia, and when Russia began to show interest in the situation, the so-called Eastern Question evolved: when the Turks finally left the Balkans, who would rule, Catholic Austria or Orthodox Russia? Later this would be one of the causes of the escalation towards the First World War.

## Germanization

The Habsburg's power gradually strengthened under Marie Thèrése (1740-80) and Joseph II (1780-90), and with them came a process of increased Germanization. Marie Thèrése employed centralistic rule; governing from 1764 without the parliament and issuing her own laws, pleasing Croats one moment and Hungarians the next. In 1745 she joined Slavonia and Croatia under a combined administrative unit as a reward for the contribution Croatian soldiers had made to various wars the Habsburgs were participating in. However, in 1779 she eliminated the work of the Croatian regency council, handing its affairs to the Hungarian council, effectively erasing any type of Croatian independence.

In 1784, Marie Thèrése's son, Joseph II, ordered Croatian clerics to learn the German language within a three year period. This lead to considerable protest, as the official language in Croatia and Hungary at that time was Latin. However, the emperor went ahead with his plans and in 1786 he ordered that all administration should be carried out in German.

This decision opened a Pandora's Box of national problems that eventually resulted in the fall of the monarchy. For the first time ever, the national question became the priority issue.

## Hungarianization

Meanwhile, a great surprise was install for the Croatian representatives at the Hungaro-Croatian parliament in Buda (part of present-day Budapest). Instead of Joseph's decision on German being the official language, the Hungarians proposed that Hungarian should be the official language of Banska Croatia (the area of Croatia under the Ban). However, in the upper house of parliament, where Croatian representatives had a right to veto, the proposal was declined and Latin remained the official language.

By this time the Hungarians were making claims that Slavonia was part of Hungary: indeed, a Hungarian nationalist movement was developing, which planned to establish a compact Hungarian nation all the way from the Carpathian Mountains to the Adriatic Sea.

## Venetian rule in Dalmatia

By the mid 16th century, the Turks had conquered all of Dalmatia apart from the islands and the coastal cities of Zadar, Šibenik, Trogir and Split, leaving more or less the area that had been the Byzantine theme of Dalmatia in the early Middle Ages to Venice. During the Candian War (1645-69) Venice conquered a narrow territory from Novigrad to the River Neretva together with Poljica and the Makarska coastline. Following the war against the Turks (1682-99) in which Poland, the Habsburgs and Russia all participated on the Venetian side, Venice extended it territories to Ravni Kotari and the towns of Knin, Sinj and Vrgorac. The Venetians applied the name Dalmatia to all these parts, including the hinterland, which had once been the centre of the Croatian kingdom, with towns such as Knin, Benkovac and Sinj. Venice, just like the Habsburgs, declined to return territories liberated from the Turks to the Croatian aristocracy, but held onto these lands itself instead.

In 1718, the peace treaty of Požarevac awarded Venice the hinterland territory up to the Dinara mountains, the area around Imotski, one half of the gulf of Boka Kotorska (in present-day Montenegro) and the area to each side of Dubrovnik, thus threatening the Republic's 100-year independence.

However, the citizens of Dubrovnik were very skilful diplomats, and not wanting the Venetians as neighbours they gave the area to the north around Klek (present-day Neum) and the area south around Sutorina (close to Herceg Novi in Montenegro) to the Turks, thus forming a buffer-zone between the Republic and the Venetian Empire.

This was later to cause great difficulties in defining the geographical limits of Croatia. The borders of today's Croatia were drawn up according to the peace treaty in Požarevac. As Bosnia and Herzegovina remained under the Ottoman Turks until 1878, part of the territory of medieval Croatia is now western Bosnia, and the area around Klek (present-day Neum) has been awarded to Bosnia as access to the sea, thus cutting across the Croatian coast. Croatian nationalists have always resented this: during the war of the 1990s Tudjman described Croatia as a croissant-shaped country that needed a filling.

## Napoleon's Illyrian Provinces

Dalmatia remained within these borders under Venetian government until the demise of Venice in 1797, when the peace treaty of Campoformio handed Dalmatia to the Habsburgs. In this inconvenient position, the country entered the period of the French Revolution and Napoleonic Wars. In 1806, Napoleon took Dalmatia, bringing to the region a series of progressive reforms, but also imposing hefty taxes and recruiting local men to participate in his army and navy. In 1809, Napoleon united Dalmatia with parts of Slovenia and Croatia, calling the new region the Provinces Illyriennes (Illyrian Provinces), as it was believed at that time that all South Slavs were of Illyrian descent. During the Napoleonic Wars, the English navy defeated the French fleet near Vis, and subsequently took the island from 1811 to 1815, using it as an important strategic base on the Adriatic. After Napoleon's downfall in 1815, Dalmatia came back under the Habsburgs.

## Illyrian Movement

In 1827, the parliament in Zagreb passed a law making the Hungarian language obligatory in all secondary schools in Croatia. However, by this time new political aspirations were blossoming in Croatia, lead by the so-called Illyrian Movement, founded by Ljudevit Gaj (1806-72). Gaj believed that unification of the South Slavs (Croats and Serbs) was the best way to oppose the increasing Germanization and Hungarianization of the region under Austro-Hungary, and aimed at doing this through a reawakening of the national consciousness, primarily through language and literature.

Besides the Illyrians, a pro-Hungarian party also existed in Croatia, made up mainly of knights, who wanted union with Hungary. Understandably, these two parties came into strong conflict. The pro-Hungarians accused the Illyrians of acting on the behalf of Russia, and the name Illyrian was thus prohibition in 1843. In its place, Gaj's movement was renamed the National Party.

The National Party rapidly gained popularity on county assemblies and as a counter-Hungarian wing in the parliament. Meanwhile, the revolutions that swept across Europe in 1848 gave further impetus to the movement. The ideas the Illyrians cherished were expressed in so-called 'Demands of the People' that were announced and accepted on 25 March 1848. These included the union of Dalmatia, Slavonia and the Krajina (military border), the institution of Croatian as the official language, and the foundation of a Croatian people's army.

The National Party also voted for Josip Jelačić as Ban (governor), and he instated on 4 June 1848. Croatia was now in a difficult position because the revolutionary movement in Hungary refused any possible agreement with the Croats: The Hungarian revolutionary leader, Lajos Kossuth, famously said "Where is Croatia, I do not see it on the map?" In September 1847, Jelačić thus lead his army into battle with the Hungarian revolutionaries, in the defence of both Croatia and the Habsburgs. Not that he was protecting the empire, but rather he hoped that by so doing he would be able to procure certain favours from the Austrians.

As the situation became more complicated than had been expected, in December 1848 Emperor Ferdinand abdicated in favour of his teenage son Franz-Josef I. With the revolution in Hungary finally over (with the help of the Russian Tsar) Jelačić's dream of a 'Slavic Austria' also ended. In August 1849, the Habsburgs returned to their old ways, with Emperor Franz-Josef I eliminating the new constitution he had formulated and together with his minister Alexander Bach imposing a centralistic-absolutistic regime accompanied by Germanization that eliminated all political freedom. "While the Magyars received absolutism as a punishment, the Croats got it as a reward" became a common expression at the time.

One of the National Party's demands that was eventually implemented was the integration of the Krajina (military border) into Croatia in 1881, which extended Croatian territory by one-third. This brought a considerable Serb population into the sphere of Croatian politics, a situation that was immediately abused by the new pro-Hungarian Ban, Khuen Hedervary (1883-1903), who played off the ongoing competition between Croats and Serbs to weaken the Slav position by inciting conflicts between them. At his time there were 103 Serb representatives in the Croatian parliament, of whom 101 were pro-Hungarian.

On 16 May 1895, during a state visit by Francis Joseph, the Hungarian flag was burnt in Zagreb, reflecting a mood of discontent. Soon after that, the Croatian Peasants Party, led by Stjepan Radić, entered the Croatian political scene: It represented a sizable force, as about 80% of the population were peasants at that time. All the progressive parties united themselves into one party in 1902, and the so-called Croatian Question, dealing with the destiny of Austro-Hungarian Slavs and the monarchy, came more and more to the centre of politics.

Meanwhile, in Serbia, King Alexander, of the pro-German Obrenović dynasty, was assassinated in 1903, and substituted by Petar, of the Karadjordjević dynasty, which was more orientated towards Russia, French and Britain. The change of dynasty brought about opposition to the Austro-Hungarian Empire within Serbia, and many Serbs in Croatia also stopped supporting Hungary, and switched their interests instead to building closer ties with the Croats.

A series of events, culminating with the assassination of the Austrian Archduke in Sarajevo (organized by a Serbian movement known as the Black Hand, without the knowledge of the Serbian king) led to entire region into the First World War (1914-18).

## The First World War

During the First World War, the centre of Croatian politics was moved outside the country with the exiled Yugoslav Committee, which represented the Yugoslavian people under the Austro-Hungarian monarchy, and aimed to unify all the South Slav countries in the Balkans into one nation.

A very important event, which somehow inspired the idea of a new South Slav nation, was an agreement between the allied forces of the Triple Entente (Britain, France and Russia) and Italy. Formulated in 1915 and known as the London Agreement, it promised a large part of the Croatian coast to Italy, provided that Rome entered the war on the Allied side. Thus in 1918, Croatia (which was on the losing side) encountered two problems: it was threatened by the Kingdom of Serbia from the east and the Kingdom of Italy from the west, and both these countries were on the winning side, and both possessed documents in which a part of Croatian territory was granted to them.

## Kingdom of Serbs, Croats and Slovenes

At the end of the First World War, other European countries such as Poland, the Baltic countries, Finland and Czechoslovakia formed their own states, but this option was not open to Croatia. The Croats therefore seized the solution of forming a new South Slav country, and their neighbours, Serbs and Slovenians, agreed. After the military collapse of the monarchy on 29 October 1918, the Croatian parliament made a resolution to break all relations with Austro-Hungary and announced that Dalmatia, Croatia and Slavonia, together with the independent city-state of Rijeka, would enter a new State of Slovenians, Croats and Serbs. On 1 December 1918 this unification was officially announced in Belgrade and the new Kingdom of Serbs, Croats and Slovenes was formed. The leader of the Serbian military delegation responsible for the unification was Dušan Šimović. The only person to oppose the unification was Stjepan Radić, leader of the Croatian Peasant's Party, who said to the Croatian delegation before their journey to Belgrade, "Do not rush yourselves like geese in the fog".

The basic problem with the unification was that it was done unconditionally, leaving Croatia with little state autonomy. The other problem was that peoples with different cultural and legal traditions, and no prior experience of living together in one state, now united themselves. It was like trying to building a house from the roof downwards rather than from the foundations. The unification came about not only due to the aspiration of South Slavic intellectuals from within the country, but also through the interest of France and Britain to disable German influence and the Bolshevik ideal. Already on 5 Dec of the same year the first bloody conflict between members of the People's Guard and the Zagreb garrison took place on the main square in Zagreb, spelling the trouble that lay ahead. Meanwhile, the Treaty of Rapallo was signed in order to arrange the borders between the Kingdom of Italy and the Kingdom of Serbs, Croats and Slovenes. Istria, the islands of Cres, Lošinj, Lastovo and Palagruža, the city of Zadar and part of Slovenia were all awarded to Italy, effectively placing over 500,000 Croats and Slovenes under Italian rule.

In 1921, on St Vitus Day (28 June), parliament voted for a constitution that was centralistic, and as such could not satisfy the Croats, who were determined to keep some sort of autonomy. The Croatian Peasant's Party opposed the move and tried to obtain the support of several Western European countries, but they approved the politics of Belgrade.

Thus in 1927, the Croatian Peasant's Party, lead by Radić, together with the Independent Democratic Party, lead by Svetozar Pribićević, formed a political coalition named the Peasant's-Democratic Coalition. Svetozar Pribićević was a Serbian politician from Croatia who initially supported Yugoslavian centralism, and was one of the people responsible for the unconditional unification, for which he had been awarded the position of Minister of Internal Affairs. However, he was later disheartened and changed his views. Realizing that there was a danger that the Serbs in Croatia might unite with the Croats, extremist politicians from Belgrade made the radical move of shooting at members of the Croatian Peasant's Party in the parliament on 20 June 1928. Two members of the party were killed, and Stjepan Radić later died of the wounds he had received.

## Kingdom of Yugoslavia

King Aleksandar used the assassination to dismiss the parliament on 6 January 1929, to abolish the constitution and to set up a royal dictatorship in order "to save the people from parliamentary troubles." In the same year the king signed a law by which he changed the country's name to the Kingdom to Yugoslavia, meaning the 'Kingdom of the South Slavs', and divided the country into nine governmental regions. The use of the terms Croat, Serb and Slovene, together with their national flags, was prohibited. Exception was made for the Serbian flag, on the grounds that it was also the flag of the Serbian Orthodox Church. In 1931, the king announced the new constitution of the Kingdom of Yugoslavia, without a parliamentary vote.

Background

The police became ever more powerful. Public demonstrators were likely to be shot, and by law the family of the deceased had to pay for the bullet. By this time, around 90% of all higher governmental official were Serbs, and out of 165 generals, 161 were Serbs and only two Croats. Out of reaction to the regime, the Bosnian-Croat Ante Paveliæ founded the Ustaša movement, which stood for military action against the Kingdom of Yugoslavia, and was supported by extremists in Italy and Hungary. On 9 October 1934, members of this movement assassinated King Aleksandar in Marseille while on an official visit to France. After Aleksandar's death, Duke Pavle Karadjordjeviæ was installed as a regent to lead the country in the name of the underage king, Peter.

## The Second World War

Even though Duke Pavle was strongly opposed to the Germans, the Kingdom was surrounded by Axis Powers, and he therefore decided to join them under reasonable conditions. In reply to a message from the American president, Franklin Roosevelt, that Yugoslavia should not approach the Germans, the Duke said "It's easy for you big nations a long way away to tell the smaller ones what to do." Two days later, on 27 March 1941, a military putsch took place in Belgrade, organized and paid for with 100,000 pounds in gold by the British secret services.

Once the regency had been removed from power, a new government, led by General Dušan Šimović, was formed. Already on 6 April 1941, Germany and Italy attacked the Kingdom. On 10 April, in Zagreb, the Independent State of Croatia (NDH) was proclaimed, with Ante Pavelić as leader. The Germans thought that Vlatko Maček should stand as president, but he believed that the Allied forces would eventually win and therefore refused the position.

Croatia's independence was at first met with high hopes by the majority of Croats, but when the government gave a large part of the coast to Italy, and began persecuting Serbs, Jews and Gypsies, this support suddenly vanished. The country was divided into two spheres: the south was governed by Italians, and the north by Germans.

As a reaction, the Partisan movement was founded, made up mainly of Croats, Serbs from Croatia, and Slovenians. As the terror enforced by the Italians, Germans and the government increased, so the number of partisans increased. Even though the movement was mainly organised by Communists, members of the Croatian Peasant's Party also participated. As of 1937, the leader of the outlawed Communist Party had been Josip Broz, and he now became the organizer of the largest antifascist movement in occupied Europe.

In 1943, the Zemaljsko antifašističko vijeće narodnog oslobodjenja Hrvatske (Territorial Antifascist Council for the Liberation of Croatia) or ZAVNOH, was formed. Italy capitulated on 8 September 1943, and at the following ZAVNOH assembly it was decided that both the Treaty of Rapallo from 1920 and the Treaty of Rome from 1941, through which Italy had taken possession of much of the Croatian coast, should be abolished.

Initially, the Allied forces only acknowledged the Yugoslav royal government in exile, based in London, but later the British were the first to help the partisans, having been persuaded by Winston Churchill, who even sent his son as a military agent to Tito. That was how the British established a strong military base on the island of Vis, where still today there is a British military cemetery. Vis was for some time the capital of liberated Yugoslavia and it was here, on 14 June 1944, that the first meeting between Tito and Šubašić, the representative of the Yugoslav government in exile, took place.

Since Tito was the military victor in the war, all possible agreements between the two of them were unsuccessful. At the beginning of 1945 there was a conference in Yalta in which three great leaders participated, and the well-known division of interests in a liberated Europe was agreed between Stalin and Churchill. Their interests in Yugoslavia were divided 50%-50%.

Germany capitulated on 9 May 1945, bringing about the end to the Independent State of Croatia. Together with the military retreat, many pro-Ustaša civilians also tried to leave the country, frightened of possible revenge attacks. When they reached Austria, they were turned back by the British army, and regardless of whether they were soldiers or civilians, they were handed over to the partisans and killed on the field of Bleiburg.

As usual in history, when the number of war casualties comes into question, the sum of people killed varied depending on who one asks. After WWII, the Yugoslavian government sent a report (for obtaining war reparations) to an international committee in which they stated that 1,700,000 people had been killed. But many people believe that the real number was around 1,000,000. Estimates regarding how many people died in the infamous concentration camp of Jasenovac vary from 700,000 to 60,000.

## Tito's Yugoslavia

The Federal People's Republic of Yugoslavia was proclaimed on 29 November 1945, supposedly organized as a federal and socialist country of people with equal rights. It was made up of six republics (Slovenia, Croatia, Serbia, Montenegro, Macedonia, and Bosnia and Herzegovina), and unlike the other countries of Eastern Europe, did not acknowledge Stalin as holding absolute power, as the Yugoslav partisans had liberated the country from the Germans by themselves.

This snubbing of Stalin resulted in conflict between the Soviet Informburo and the Yugoslavian Communist Party in the spring of 1948. Tito consequently broke with Stalin, and many Yugoslav communists who supported Stalin ended up in prison.

Yugoslavia now found itself as a barrier between the Eastern and Western blocks. Tito thus decided to strengthen relations with his western allies (America and Britain) and thereby received humanitarian help from them: Truman's eggs. Yugoslavia wanted to find a midway between the Communist east and the capitalist west, and began the so-called self-management organisations.

Thus, in 1949, in Solin, near Split, Yugoslavia's first worker's council was formed. By 1950 self-management had been proven a viable scheme, a third way between the free-enterprise of the west and the state planning and state economy of the Soviet block. To put it simply, firms were managed by the workers themselves through a workers' council, which had the power to determine production, to decide on the distribution of profit and to build homes for their workers.

Post-war reconstruction was rapid and optimistic. Increased industrialization brought about mass migration from rural areas to the cities, and modern high-rise suburbs sprung up. Public health and education were well funded, and living standards rose significantly. Tourism began developing along the Adriatic coast in the 1960s, bringing with it foreign currency. All this was conducted under the ideal of 'Brotherhood and Unity', a motto Tito coined to stress the importance of holding the country together and suppressing individual nationalist aspirations.

However, the richer republics (Croatia and Slovenia) soon began to object to having to pay hefty taxes to Belgrade for investment in the less developed parts of the country. This, plus the fact that national feelings could not be openly expressed, gradually lead to a silent discontent that culminated in the so-called 'Croatian Spring' of 1971. Those who participated in the event asked for greater autonomy for Croatia, greater cultural freedom, and for the foreign currencies received from tourism and earned by Croats working abroad to stay in the republic. Some communist officials from Croatia of that time also participated in this movement. By the end of 1971 Tito decided that it had all gone too far and the movement was suppressed. However, some results were gained in 1973 when the Socialistic Federal Republic of Yugoslavia introduced a new constitution by which the individual republics' sovereignty was strengthened and their right to eventual independence was acknowledged.

On 4 May 1980, Josip Broz Tito, the persona who had held Yugoslavia together for almost four decades, died in Ljubljana. The respect he had gained abroad was illustrated by the extraordinary line up of world statesmen who attended his funeral, said to have been the largest gathering of its kind in history. Due to his policy of non-alignment and skilful manoeuvres between the East and West, Yugoslavia had gained greater importance and more loans than a country of such proportions and economic development objectively deserved. Tito left behind the proposal of a rotating presidency, where by each republic would take a turn at leading the country for one year. But as only a charismatic persona such as Tito himself could hold so many different interests and people on one leash, future problems were in store.

## Milošević rises to power

In the late 1980s, the appearance of Albanian nationalism on Kosovo gave a good excuse for the program for a Greater Serbia, which was the idea that all Serbs should live in one country. It was a continuation of the Serbian nationalist politics from the 19th century, which aimed to make the country the leading force in the Balkans. Having seized the presidency in Serbia, in 1988 Slobodan Milošević deposed the communist leaders of Vojvodina, Kosovo and Montenegro, and in 1989 he made amendments to the Serbian constitution, thereby eliminating the autonomy of the provinces of Vojvodina and Kosovo.

The year 1989 saw the fall of the Berlin Wall and the demise of Communist regimes throughout the countries of Eastern Europe followed the disintegration of the USSR. In a way it was a case of history repeating itself, just as in 1918, when a succession of new independent countries were founded following the fall of an Empire. This time, Croatia did not want to miss the opportunity.

Attempts by the Croatian economist Ante Marković and the Reformed Communists to save Yugoslavia seemed destined to fail from the start, mainly because of Slobodan Milošević. In spring 1990, the Croatian Democratic Union (HDZ), lead by Franjo Tudjman, won the elections in Croatia on a nationalist manifesto. The Assembly met for the first time on 30 May 1990, and Tudjman was elected president. However, already in August, Serbs in Knin began rebelling against the Croatian state, fearing that they would be marginalized by its nationalist agenda.

During the first months of 1991, the presidents of the six republics of Yugoslavia conducted negotiations about the governmental structure of Yugoslavia. Croatia and Slovenia wanted a confederation, while Milošević insisted on a firm federation, even though he knew it would be unacceptable to the others. In May 1991, a referendum for independence and sovereignty was held in Croatia, with 93% of those who attended voting in favour (the turn out was 82%). The Croatian parliament declared Croatia an independent state on 25 June 1991, the same day as Slovenia.

## Descent into war

Already at the end of June, the Yugoslavian People's Army (JNA) was sent in to Slovenia, but fighting there lasted only several days as the country was not a target of Milošević's expansionism, having no significant Serbian minority. However, the war then transferred to Croatia, where Milošević was more than eager to defend the 600,000 strong Serbian community, who were mainly concentrated in the old Krajina zones. Local Serbs worked together with the JNA, who were confronted by poorly armed Croatian policemen and voluntary soldiers. Much of the former Krajina came under Serb control in the so-called Log Revolution (trees were felled and placed across roads to literally block access to the region), and the Republic of the Serbian Krajina was declared, effectively cutting off one-third of the country. Basically the Serbs said that if the Croat could claim independence from Belgrade, then they wanted independence from Zagreb.

Serbian TV, Milošević's main propaganda tool, predicted the resurgence of the Independent State of Croatia (NDH), spreading fear among Serbs of a return to the Second World War style persecution. Likewise Croatian TV broadcast horrific stories of Serbian barbarianism and the evils of Communism. The seeds of ethnic hatred had been sown, and it became increasingly impossible to distinguish the truth from the lies.

Since negotiations with the mediation of the European Union proved unsuccessful, the Croatian parliament broke off all relations with Yugoslavia on 8 October 1991. Also in October, the JNA and Montenegrin forces placed Dubrovnik under a six-month siege, and in November, after heroic resistance by the Croats, the Serbs managed to take Vukovar in eastern Slavonia in the bloodiest and cruellest fighting the war would see.

## The closing stages

Members of the EU, with much persuasion from Germany and the Vatican, recognized Croatia's independence on 15 January 1992. The JNA left Serb-occupied territories, which remained however in the hands of the self-proclaimed Republic of the Serbian Krajina, and in March 1992 UN peacekeepers were sent in to oversee the situation. Isolated incidents of ethnic violence continued, but all out fighting had stopped. On 22 May 1992 Croatia became a member of the United Nations.

Under Clinton, the US began sending in American military advisors to train the Croatian army. In early May 1995, with American blessing, in the military operation Blijesak (Lightning), Croatian forces attacked a Serb-held enclave in western Slavonia. The Serbs were forced to evacuate the region, giving the Croatian army a victory and considerably reducing the Croatian territory controlled by the Serbs.

Then, in August, with the military operation Oluja (Storm) Serb-held areas of North Dalmatia, Banovina, Kordun and Lika were liberated. The fall of the Republic of the Serbian Krajina was officially announced when Croatian soldiers hoisted the red and white chequer-board flag above Knin Fortress. A mass exodus of Serbian families ensued, with most fleeing to neighbouring Bosnia and to Serbia-proper.

Through the Erdut Agreement, the area of eastern Slavonia with Vukovar and Baranja was placed under UN control, until being reintegrated into Croatian territory in January 1998.

# Modern Croatia

Once hostilities were over, it was time to pick up the pieces. Despite having delivered the country its long desired independence, Tudjman and the ruling HDZ party rapidly lost popularity. The international community accused the Croatian state of interfering with Bosnia (Tudjman had set up an embarrassing allegiance with Bosnian Croats), media manipulation, an appalling human rights record, and the failure to comply with The Hague over war crimes. During the war, Tudjman's upholding of conservative values such as the family, the church and the nation had been enough to keep many people happy.

But after several years of peace, it became apparent that the entire national economy had been undermined, and that nothing would improve until there was a complete change in policy. A new elite class had emerged – those close to the HDZ who had been awarded hefty slices of state property for their loyalty, and those who had made fast money out of black market dealings during the war. The rest of society remained impoverished – unemployment was rife, and even those who had jobs seldom saw their monthly pay cheque on time.

Tudjman died in Zagreb on 10 December 1999, following a long illness. The HDZ immediately set about trying to organise a convincing election campaign, but the Croatian public had already lost faith. At the elections on 4 January 2000 a new centre-left six party coalition won, with the two largest parties, the Social Democratic Party (SDP) and the Croatian Social Liberal Party (HSLS) together taking 56% of the vote, and the HDZ scoring only 24%. Former communists Ivica Račan and Stipe Mesić were sworn in as Croatia's Prime Minister and President.

The new government promised to steer the country towards Europe, increase regional co-operation, speed up national reconciliation and introduce something closer to democracy. However, despite much improved relations with Serbia, by the close of 2002 only an estimated 110,000 of the 350,000 displaced Croatian Serbs had returned to their old homes, most of these were elderly people from rural villages. Human Rights Watch attributed this slow progress to problems over property (many Serb homes were destroyed or occupied by other people during the war), unemployment and fear of discrimination.

Another worrying issue has been Croatia's failure to hand over indicted war criminals to the Criminal Tribunal for the Former Yugoslavia (ICTY) in The Hague. Key figures such as General Ante Gotovina (indicted for crimes during and after Operation Storm in 1995) and General Janko Bobetkin (accused of crimes against Croatian Serbs in 1993) are still at large. The present government has, however, stepped up domestic prosecution for war crimes committed between 1991 and 1995, and is currently conducting cases at home and hoping to take over certain cases from the ICTY.

On the plus side, the present government has done much to improve Croatia's image abroad, and has renounced the 'special relationship' with Bosnian Croats, which had been set up during the Tudjman era. And in October 2001, Croatia took a step closer to membership in the European Union (EU) after Prime Minister Račan signed a Stabilization and Association Agreement (SAA) with the EU: Croatia now hopes to enter the EU along with Bulgaria and Romania in 2007.

# Economy

The war and its after effects had a devastating effect on the Croatian economy, especially in the industrial sector. Shipbuilding and maritime transport, in which former-Yugoslavia held the third position in the world economy (and which were mainly concentrated along the Croatian coast) faced a sharp decline. Some 35,000 Croatian sailors now work on foreign ships. Recently, however, shipbuilding has seen a slight recovery.

Privatization began in earnest after the war, though it is still not complete. The power generation sector, oil industry and the majority of hotels are still under state ownership, though the financial sector has been completely privatized and 90% of banks are now owned by foreign investors.

At the end of summer 2002, the average short-term interest rate on the Kuna fell below 10% and the embarrassing memories of summer 1996, when it peaked at 25%, faded. Since the Kuna's introduction as a national currency in 1994, the stability of the exchange rate Kuna-German Deutschmark was constantly maintained, and now stability is monitored against the euro. From March 2002 to December 2002 currency oscillations ranged from 7.30-7.40Kn to 1 euro.

The Croatian trade deficit is constantly growing, though it is being compensated for in part by money transfers from Croats living abroad, sailors working for foreign companies, and from income from tourism: 80% of deposits in Croatian banks are in euros.

Trade contributes to 36% of the Croatian GDP, and manufacturing industries 31%. The GDP growth rate is estimated at 4.5% and is expected to be maintained through 2003. Industrial production grew by 9.3% between October 2001 and October 2002, and the strongest Croatian companies, such as pharmaceutical company PLIVA and the food processor PODRAVKA are present on the world market.

However, the costs of the state represent a major burden on the economy. The war and its after-effects have lead to a drastic rise in unemployment. In 1980 the employment rate was 5.5%, in 1989 8%. Today it stands at 22%. The number of retired persons has risen to 1,100,000.

In 2002 Croatia joined the Central European Free Trade Association and signed a contract for potential entry to the EU. Croatian GDP stands at US$5000 per capita, exceeding that of many of the Eastern European countries that will become EU members as early as 2004.

According to international economic analysts, low labour costs, a skilled work force and natural resources represent the country's top assets. The biggest potential lies in the tourism sector with a growth rate of 5.4% in 2002, higher than any other Mediterranean country. The introduction of the euro has made Croatia more attractive to EU citizens, and while such clean sea cannot be found anywhere else in Europe, it is worth mentioning that, paradoxical though it may seem given the country's recent history, Croatia is probably the safest destination on the Mediterranean.

Croatia's greatest resource is its well-preserved natural environment. The decline of the industrial sector as a result of the war meant that already an ecologically clean country, became even cleaner. the high proportion of fertile land per capita gives the country the potential of producing large quantities of healthy food. Land and property prices are still much lower than in the EU. Croatia obtains 45% of its power supply from hydro-electric power plants, and could potentially provide for its energy needs from renewable sources such as wind and sun. Drinking water is abundant and tap water is drinkable through out the country.

A motorway linking Zagreb and Split is currently under construction: by the end of June 2003, 315 km should be completed, and the entire project finished by summer 2005. The Zagreb to Rijeka motorway should be completed in the same year. The Zagreb-Split connection will increase tourism in the region, while the Zagreb-Rijeka road will link the country's largest port to the Danube basin, giving it distinct advantages over the Adriatic ports of Trieste and Koper, as the port of Rijeka boasts deeper water allowing for larger ships. Foreign debt has reached US$13.6 billion, which is still less than 60% of GDP. This increase is due to trade deficit, variations in the exchange rate of the euro against the US$, and the expense of constructing the new motorways.

Background

# Culture

## Architecture

### Classical

The finest remaining buildings from Roman times can be seen in the cities of Pula and Split. In the former, the oldest significant monument is a first-century BC triumphal arch, known as the Arch of the Sergi. It was built to celebrate the role of three high ranking military officers from the Sergi family at the Battle of Actium in 31BC, and upon their return home they would have marched through it into the walled city, leading their triumphant soldiers. Made up of a single arch flanked with slender columns with Corinthian capitals, it is ornamented with base reliefs of dolphins, a sphinx and a griffon, and an eagle struggling with a snake. Originally it would have been topped with statues of the three generals. Italian Renaissance architects Palladio and Michelangelo were obviously suitably impressed by it, as both sketched it on their travels. Close by, the present day main square was once the forum, and of the principal public buildings that stood here, the first-century AD Temple of Augustus remains intact. Typically designed to be viewed from the front, it is elevated on a high base with steps leading up to an open portico supported by six tall columns. Located outside the former walls, Pula's best known Roman building is the colossal first-century AD amphitheatre, which was built to host gladiator fights and could accommodate up to 22,000 spectators, making it the sixth largest building surviving Roman amphitheatre in the world.

Moving south down the coast, Split grew up within the 25-m high walls of a unique third-century palace, commissioned by Emperor Diocletian as a retirement residence. Combining the qualities of a Roman garrison and an imperial villa, this vast structure is based on a rectangular ground plan measuring 215 m by 180 m, and contains various individual monuments such as an octagonal mausoleum (now the cathedral) and a classical temple dedicated to Jupiter (now a baptistery). British and French architects and artists first acknowledged its magnificence during the 18th century when many visited it as part of the Grand Tour: it is said to have inspired the Scottish architect Robert Adam in some of his finest neo-Classical projects upon his return to the UK.

Six kilometres inland from Split, the archaeological site of Salona was once the largest Roman urban centre in Croatia, with an estimated population of 60,000 in the third century AD. Sadly it was devastated in the seventh century: today only the ruins remain.

## Byzantine

During the sixth century the coastal region came under Byzantium. Architecturally, the Byzantine Empire is best known for its magnificent Christian basilicas, and the most outstanding example in Croatia is Euphrasius Basilica in Poreč. Built under the rule of Emperor Justinian (483-565AD), during the same period as Hagia Sophia in Constantinople (present-day Istanbul), this complex comprises a central atrium, with an octagonal baptistery to one side, and opposite it the basilica itself, where the central aisle focuses on a main apse decorated with splendid golden mosaics.

## Pre-Romanesque

The Croats arrived in the region in the seventh century and gradually began taking on the Christian faith. Between the ninth and 11th centuries about 150 small pre-Romanesque churches, often referred to as early Croatian churches, were built, mainly along the coast. Byzantine influence is apparent in their geometric massing, though they tend towards minimum decoration, limited to finely carved stonework ornamented with plait-design motifs reminiscent of Celtic art. The most perfect example is the tiny ninth century Holy Cross in Nin, based on the plan of a Greek cross, while the largest and most imposing is the monumental ninth-century rotonda St Donat's in Zadar, based on a circular ground plan with three semi-circular apses. You can see an excellent collection of early Croatian church stonework in the Croatian Museum of Archaeological Monuments in Split.

## Romanesque

The 12th century saw the dawn of the Romanesque age, which was marked by imposing cathedrals, generally made up of triple naves with semi-circular apses, and ornate facades featuring blind arches. The most beautiful – the Cathedral of St Anastasia and the Church of St Chrysogonus – are in Zadar, though other notables examples include the Cathedral of Our Lady of the Assumption in Krk Town, the Church of St Mary the

Great (which was a cathedral until 1828) in Rab Town, and the portal of the Cathedral of St Lawrence in Trogir, which was carved by the outstanding Dalmatian sculptor Master Radovan in the early 13th century. Unfortunately, Croatia's two most important Romanesque cathedrals were destroyed – the one in Zagreb by the Tartars in 1242, and the one in Dubrovnik by the 1667 earthquake – and subsequently rebuilt in later styles.

## Venetian Gothic

When Venice began colonizing the east Adriatic Coast, it brought with it the so-called Venetian Gothic style, characterized by the pointed arch and rib vaulting. The style is apparent in 15th- and 16th-century churches and houses in Istria and Dalmatia, such as the finely carved portal of Korčula Cathedral by Bonino from Milan, and the triple pointed-arch windows of the Čipko Palace in Trogir by Andrea Aleši. It is often seen mixed with more severe Renaissance elements, most notably in the work of Juraj Dalmatinac on Šibenik Cathedral (see below), hence the term Gothic-Renaissance.

## Renaissance

The Renaissance, which started in Italy, marked a revival of Roman civilization, not just in art and architecture but in an entire set of values. The movement is normally said to have dawned in Croatia in 1441, when Juraj Dalmatinac, a builder from Zadar who had trained for a short time in Venice, began work on Šibenik Cathedral. Although he did not live to see it completed, the later work was carried out by two of his pupils, Nikola Firentinac and Andrija Aleši. Dalmatinac also drew up the urban plan for Pag Town in 1443, and worked on other noted projects such as the Chapel of St Anastasius in Split Cathedral and Minčeta Fortress in Dubrovnik. You can see a 20th-century statue of Dalmatinac, by Ivan Meštrović, in front of Šibenik Cathedral.

The Renaissance continued developing along the coast, in areas not under the Turks, until the end of the 16th century. During this period many towns were fortified with defensive walls and towers, the best examples being Dubrovnik, Korčula and Hvar.

Increased wealth, plus the ideals of Renaissance philosophy, lead to the construction of more sophisticated houses, with refined details such as carved doors and window frames, balconies with balustrades, stone wash basins, decorated fireplaces and built in cupboards. People became interested in the relationship between man and nature: houses were set in gardens with arcaded covered walkways, fountains and stone benches, the best examples being Tvrdalj in Stari Grad on the island of Hvar, and Trsteno Arboretum near Dubrovnik, both from the 16th century.

Also worth a mention here is Lucijano Vranjanin, a Croat born near Zadar in the 15th century. He spent most of his life in Italy, where he was known as Luciano Laurana, and built several notable early Renaissance palaces, the best known being the Ducal Palace in Urbino.

## Islamic

When the Ottoman Turks moved into Slavonia they brought with them the Muslim faith. Many mosques were built, but few locals converted to Islam, so that when the Turks were finally driven out, the mosques were largely destroyed – a situation quite different to that in neighbouring Bosnia, where still today there is a sizeable Muslim population. One of the very few remaining mosques in Croatia can be seen in Đakovo, though the minaret was pulled down and it was converted into the Catholic Church of all Saints when the Turks left in 1687.

## Baroque

Regarded as a symbol of western civilization, and therefore the antithesis of Ottoman culture, the Baroque style flourished in northern Croatia during the late 17th and 18th centuries. The Jesuits, who played an important part in reinforcing the Roman Catholic faith in areas threatened by the Turks, were responsible for introducing the grandiose, curvilinear Baroque style to the region. As the Turks were gradually pushed out, many buildings were constructed, reconstructed or extended in Baroque style.

Today, the best-preserved Baroque town centre is in Varaždin – tragically Vukovar, formerly regarded as the finest Baroque town in Croatia, was all but devastated during the war for independence during the 1990's. Other notable examples can be found in Osijek – the 18th-century Tvrdja complex – and in Dubrovnik – the Cathedral from 1671 and the Jesuit Church from 1725, both designed by Italian architects during reconstruction following the earthquake of 1667.

## Eclectic

During the 19th century, eclectic design – the revival and reinterpretation of past styles – was popular throughout Europe. In Zagreb, the buildings of Donji Grad, constructed when the region was under Austro-Hungary, mix various elements from classical, Gothic and baroque periods. The most prolific architect in north Croatian at this time was Herman Bolle (1845-1926). Born in Koln, Germany, he participated in the construction of about 140 buildings in Croatia, including Zagreb Cathedral, Mirogoj Cemetery and the Museum of Arts and Crafts, all in Zagreb.

## Vienna Secession

By the close of the 19th century, artists and architects in various parts of Europe were rebelling against the decadence of eclectic buildings and the pomp and formality of older styles, and searching instead for more pure and functional forms. In German-speaking countries this current was known as Jugendstil, and in France as Art Nouveau. In 1897 in Vienna, a group of visual artists founded a movement, which became known as the Vienna Secession. The architects involved strove to give simple geometric forms to their buildings, while working in close collaboration with artists, who provided discreet, elegant details such as frescoes and mosaics. The best examples of this style in Croatia, which was still part of the Austro-Hungarian Empire at the time, are Villa Santa Maria, Villa Frappart and Villa Magnolia, all designed by the Austrian architect Carl Seidl and found in Lovran, close to Opatija. In Osijek, Europska Avenue is lined with fine Vienna Secession buildings by local architects.

## Modernism

There are very few examples of quality modernist architecture in Croatia, though the ideals of the modern movement were held dear by the socialist state during the second half of the 20th century. The resulting buildings are primarily high-rise apartment blocks, most of which are light and airy with large balconies, and vast hotel complexes that sprung up along the coast, which are rather impersonal but functional and comfortable.

## Restoration

Croatia's wealth of historic monuments and well-preserved town centres are obviously a source of national pride and an important element in the country's tourist industry.

In 1979, the historic centres of Dubrovnik and Split were designated UNESCO world heritage sites, in 1997 Trogir and Euphrasius Basilica in Poreč followed, and in 2000 Šibenik Cathedral was added. These sites are thereby entitled to various degrees of international funding for restoration work. Careful refurbishment projects are currently underway on many other historic buildings, and most city centre damage caused by the recent war has been fully repaired. Visiting Dubrovnik, it is difficult to believe the city was held under a six-month siege in 1992. In addition, local people have began to re-evaluate the importance of folk architecture, and stone farm buildings and cottages in Dalmatia and Istria are also finally being lovingly restored and preserved for future generations.

# Art

Passing through the centuries under a series of foreign rulers, Croatia has had little opportunity to develop its own artistic movements. The rich and powerful have always been more interested in the works coming directly out of the empire they represented, being it Venice, Turkey or Austro-Hungary. Those Croats who did become successful artists were mainly educated abroad and often remained outside of the country for most of their lives. However, here is brief summary of notable Croatian painters and sculptors.

## Painting

The first notable Croatian movements emerged during the 15th century. In the wealthy and culturally advanced city of Dubrovnik, a group of painters inspired by Italian Gothic art and the Byzantine tradition became known as the Dubrovnik School. Unfortunately few of their works have been preserved – mainly due to the destructive earthquake of 1667 – but **Blaž Jurjev Trogiranin** (also known as Blasius Pictor) from Trogir and **Lovro Dobričević** from Kotor (present-day Montenegro) can be singled out. They produced a wealth of icons and ornate polyptychs featuring religious scenes, both for Catholic and Orthodox churches, using rich blues, greens and reds often against a golden background. Today you can see examples of Trogiranin's work in Korčula Town – a polyptych Our Lady with Saints in the Abbey Treasuy and a polyptych Our Lady the Co-redeemer in the Church of All Saints. Several outstanding pieces by Dobričević are on display in the Dominican Monastery in Dubrovnik.

In the north of the country, in Istria, a more humble school of fresco painting emerged, best represented by the works of **Vincent of Kastav** in St Mary's Church in Beram, near Pazin. Painted in 1474, this extraordinary cycle consists of 40 paintings depicting events from the life of Christ, figures of individual saints and scenes such as the Adoration of the Kings and the Dance Macabre. Full of religious symbolism it was intended as a Bible for the illiterate, being both amusing and easy to relate to, for those who could not read the scriptures. The frescoes were covered over by plaster during reconstruction in the early 18th century and only rediscovered in 1913 – today their colours are muted and subtle, with shades of rusty red, ochre, blue and green.

The year 1498 saw the birth of one of Croatia's finest painters, **Julije Klović**. He grew up in Vinodol, near Rijeka, then moved to Italy where he was known as Don Giulio Clovio Croata and became one of the most important Renaissance miniaturists. He painted for the Pope and the Medici family, and today has works in the Uffizi Gallery in Florence, the Louvre in Paris and the British Museum in London. He tutored the Cretan artist El Greco while in Rome, who painted a portrait of him, now on show in the Museo di Capodimonte in Naples.

The next big name in Croatian art is the realist painter **Vlaho Bukovac** (1855-1922). Born in Cavtat, he studied in Paris and also spent some time in England, where he executed portraits of various aristocratic families, into which he was received as a friend and guest: His Potiphar's Wife was exhibited in the Royal Academy of London. From 1903 to 1922 he was a professor at the Academy of Art in Prague. The house were he was born in Cavtat has been turned into a gallery displaying a collection of his paintings and drawing.

Split's greatest painter is generally acknowledged to be **Emanuel Vidović** (1870-1953). He studied in Venice then moved back to Split, where he would work outdoors, making colourful sketches, then return to his studio to rework his impressions on large canvasses, often producing dark, hazy paintings with a slightly haunting atmosphere. He especially loved the neighbouring city of Trogir, and executed several painting of the interiors of the cathedrals in Split and Trogir. There are plans to open a Vidović Gallery in Split with about 70 paintings donated to the city by his family.

The one movement in painting which is unique to Croatia is the **Hlebine School**, which developed in the village of Hlebine, close to Koprivinca, in the 1930's. It evolved when Professor Krsto Hegedušić (1901-71) met the self-taught painter **Ivan Generalić** (1914-92), was highly impressed by his works and exhibited them as part of the Zemlja group in Zagreb and Sofia (Bulgaria). Generalić then went on to tutor a whole group of local farmers, who produced a vast range of naive works, typically depicting scenes from everyday rural life using bright colours painted on glass. Altogether about 200 artists make up the group, including Ivan's son Josip Generalić, Franjo Mraz and Mirko Virius. You can see their works in Koprivnica Gallery, Hlebine Art Gallery and the Croatian Naïve Art Museum in Zagreb.

A Croatian artist well-known in the US is **Maximiliano Vanka** (1889-1963). Born in Zagreb, he studied at the Academy of Fine Arts there, where he later became a professor of painting. He exhibited throughout Europe and obtained the Palme Academique of the French Legion of Honour. In 1936 he moved to the US, where his best known works are the murals in the Church of St Nicholas, in Millvale, Pittsburgh, which depict traditional Catholic scenes as well as reflecting the lives and spirituality of the Croatian immigrant community. Although many of his works have remained in the US, you can see a collection of his drawings and paintings in the delightful Memorial Museum Maximilian Vanka in Korčula Town.

For many people, Croatia's most outstanding 20th-century artist is **Edo Murtić**. Born in 1921 in Velika Pisanica near Bjelovar in inland Croatia, he grew up in Zagreb where he also studied art. During the Second World War he designed posters and illustrated books connected to the Partisan liberation movement. After the war he visited New York, where he met American abstract expressionists such as Jackson Pollock, and completed a cycle of paintings called Impressions of America. During the 1960's and 1970's he was one of the masters of European abstract art, painting vast canvasses with mighty bold strokes and daring colours. In the 1980's his works became less abstract, featuring recognisable Mediterranean landscapes. He has paintings in the Tate Gallery in London and MOMA in New York, and lives and works in Vrsar and Zagreb.

## Sculpture

The church was the main sponsor of sculptors until the 20th century, when the state realized the powerful messages that can be put across through public works of art. Nearly all the most noted sculptors came from Dalmatia, where they worked predominantly in local stone.

The first individual artists to have been recorded in the history of Croatian sculpture were working in Romanesque style during the 13th century: **Master Radovan**, who completed the magnificent main portal of Trogir Cathedral, and **Andrea Buvina** who carved the well-preserved wooden doors to Split Cathedral.

During the 15th century, with the dawn of the Renaissance, some important artists combined the skills of architecture and sculpture, notably **Juraj Dalmatinac**, who was responsible for the 74 heads cut in stone that make up a freize on the exterior of Šibenik Cathedral, and his pupil **Andrea Aleši**, who completed the delicately carved baptistery in the same building.

Moving forward to the 19th century, **Ivan Rendić** (1849-1932), who was born in Supetar on the island of Brač, was highly respected for the tombs and grave stones he designed for the local upper classes. He also executed several statues of prominent historic figures.

However, the country's best known and most prolific sculptor was **Ivan Mestrović** (1883-1962). Born into a peasant family from the Dalmatian hinterland, he was sent to work with a stonecutter in Split, where he showed considerable skill and was thus sent to study at Art Academy in Vienna, financed by a Viennese mine owner. Although he did not like his professor, he had great respect for the noted Austrian architect Otto Wagner, who also taught there, and soon became influenced by the Vienna Secession movement. He also met Rodin in Vienna, who inspired him to travel in Italy and France, and then to settle in Paris, where he became internationally renowned. He then spent several years in Rome, mixing with members of the Italian Futurist movement such as Ungaretti and de Chirico, and in 1911 he won first prize at an international exhibition in Rome, where critics hailed he the best sculptor since the Renaissance. During the First World War he spent some time in England where he staged a one-man exhibition at the Victoria and Albert Museum in London. After the First World War he returned to his homeland, taking a house in Zagreb – which is now open to the public as the Meštrović Atelier – and designing a villa in Split, today the Meštrović Gallery. However, at the beginning of the Second World War he was imprisoned by the fascist Ustaše, and it was only through intervention of his friends in Italy, including the Pope, that he managed to leave the country. He spent the rest of his life in the USA, but upon his death his body was returned to Croatia where he was buried in the family mausoleum as he had requested. Today he has pieces in stone, bronze and wood on exhibition in the Tate Gallery in London and the Uffizi in Florence. In several Croatian towns you can see bronze statues of important local cultural figures, such as Grgur Ninski and Marko Marulić in Split and Juraj Dalmatinac in Šibenik, which he created as public works. In the US his best known outdoor piece is Indians in Grand Central Park, Chicago.

During his career Meštrović took several pupils, and one of them, **Antun Augustinčić** (1900-79) went on to have great success. Under Tito, Augustinčić became the official state artist of Yugoslavia, creating many large bronze pieces with typical socialist themes such as the Heroic Worker. His best known work is *Peace*, on display in the gardens in front of the United Nations building in New York. In the Augustinčić Gallery, in his native town of Klanjec in Zagorje, you can see a fine display of his works.

# Literature

Going back to the Middle Ages, Croatian writing consisted mainly of Church manuscripts, histories, legal codes and some poetry. It was not until the 16th and 17th centuries, despite highly unfavourable conditions of foreign occupation and ongoing battles with the Turks, that literature really began to develop, with writers publishing works in both Latin and Croatian.

## Renaissance

The father of Croatian literature is generally considered to be **Marko Marulić** (1450-1524) a poet and prose writer born in the Dalmatian city of Split, which was then under Venice. You can see a 20th-century statue of him, portrayed as a thin serious man with a beard, by Ivan Meštrović on Voćni Trg in Split.

Influenced by medieval Catholic theology, Marulić believed that suffering was brought upon us by our own sins, and that real happiness could only be found through knowledge of God and the performing of good deeds. Disillusioned by local bishops, most of whom had scandalous lifestyles, Marulić became a recluse and even retreated for two years to the island of Šolta. Seeing the Ottoman onslaught as punishment, he called for repentance, and sent a dramatic letter to Pope Hadrian VI asking for help against the Turks. His best known piece is the epic poem *Judita* from 1501, the first printed literary work in Croatian (written in the ćakavian dialect). Inspired by the biblical tale of Judith (who killed the Assyrian general Holofernes) it was a plea for the national struggle against the Turks. The message was that with God's help, they could be overcome. Another significant work by Marulić, which was read throughout Europe, was *Quinquaginta parabolae*, written in Latin and published in Venice in 1510: it was a collection of 50 allegorical stories about peasants and fishermen, each with a religious message.

Two noted writers who followed soon after Marulić where **Hanibal Lucić** (1485-1553) and **Petar Hektorović** (1487-1572), both from the island of Hvar. Lucić wrote the first secular drama in Croatian, *Robinja* (The Female Slave), while Hektorović was a poet who examined the classic Renaissance themes of nature and its beauty in most of his works, as well as the wisdom of lower classes, despite having been born into a noble family. His best known work is *Ribarenje i ribarsko prigovaranje* (Fishing and Fishermen's Conversations) from 1556, in which he recounts the tale of a three-day fishing trip to the islands of Brač and Šolta in the company of two local fishermen. Hektorović's former home, Tvrdalj, a beautiful Renaissance residence he built in Stari Grad, is open to the public.

Another writer who took the beauty of nature as his central theme was **Petar Zoranić** (1509-69), from Nin near Zadar, who wrote the idyllic novel *Planine* (The Mountains) in 1536, inspired by the rocky slopes of Velebit.

Around the same time, an important literary movement was developing in Dubrovnik, thanks to the number of young nobles who studied in Padua, and thus had first-hand knowledge of the Italian Renaissance. The city found its best interpreter in the dramatist Marin Držić (1508-1567) who wrote bawdy comedies about the problems of society and contemporary lifestyles, and is often regarded as the Croatian Shakespeare. His best known work is the comedy *Dundo Maroje* (Uncle Maroje) from 1550, which was performed throughout Western Europe, and can still be seen at the Dubrovnik Summer Festival today. Držić's house in Dubrovnik has been turned into a memorial museum and is open to the public.

While the forementioned authors were already writing in Croatian, many Croatian scholars continued to write in Latin, both at home and abroad. One of the most interesting is the inventor, philosopher and lexicographer, Faust Vrančić (1551-1617) from Šibenik. In 1595 he published the *Dictionarium quinque nobilissimorum Europae linguarum Latinae, Italicae, Germanicae, Dalmaticae et Ungaricae*, a dictionary of the 'five most noble languages', which included Latin, Greek, German, Hungarian and Croatian, or Dalmatian as it was referred to here. This was the first dictionary to include Croatian. Another work worth mentioning by Vrančić was the highly eccentric *Machinae Novae*, in which he used sketches and text (in Latin) to describe outlandish inventions including a parachute. In later life he withdrew to Rome and became a Pauline monk.

Another 17th-century intellectual concerned about the evolution of the Croatian language was the Jesuit monk **Bartol Kašić** (1575-1650) from the island of Pag, who wrote the first Croatian grammar book *Osnove ilirskog jezika* (The Basics of Illyrian language), which was published in Rome in 1604. Kašić suggested that the štokavian dialect should be the standard language.

In 1612 the first permanent public theatre in Europe opened in Hvar Town on the island of Hvar, a revolutionary idea of its time, as everyone, regardless of their social standing, was welcome to attend performances.

## Baroque

The most distinguished Baroque writers were from Dubrovnik, and the best known of these was the poet **Ivan Gundulić** (1589-1638). Gundulić's greatest works, clearly reflecting the city-republic's strong spirit of freedom, are the stirring epic poem Osman from 1626, describing the Poles' 1621 victory over the Turks, and the play Dubravka from 1628. It is worth mentioning here that Gundulić and other Dubrovnik authors wrote in the štokavian dialect, which during the 17th century became regarded as the accepted form of Croatian by writers throughout Dalmatia, paving the way for a uniform standard Croatian language that was to be realized in the 19th century. You can see a statue of Gundulić, by the Dalmatian sculptor Ivan Rendić, on Gundulićeva Poljana in Dubrovnik.

In the 18th century, a book that played a very important role in the awakening of the national consciousness was *Razgovor ugodni naroda slovinskoga* (A pleasant conversation of the Slav people) from 1756, written by the Franciscan monk **Andrija Kačić Miošić** (1704-60). It was so popular that almost every house in Dalmatia had a copy and it was known affectionately as *Pismaricom* (The Song-book).

Also during the 18th century, foreign intellectuals became fascinated by the epic folk poems of inland Dalmatia, which were traditionally recited by a bard to the accompaniment of a musical instrument. The man responsible for their diffusion was **Alberto Fortis** (1741-1803), an Italian priest from Padua, whose journeys and research were financed in part by the Scottish Lord, John Stuart, Count of Bute – who also encouraged the study of folk songs in the British Isles. Fortis travelled through Dalmatia between 1770 and 1774, exploring the way of life of the Vlahi (inhabitants of the Dalmatian hinterland, who he referred to by their Venetian name, *Morlacchi*) collecting and studying their heroic poems, which he recorded in his internationally acclaimed *Viaggi in Dalmazia* (Travels into Dalmatia) from 1774, which was translated into English and French in 1778. Here he talks about the primitive customs of the Vlahi– describing them in a rather patronising tone as noble savages – and also mentions the tensions between them and the sophisticated urbanites of the Dalmatian coastal towns, a socio-regional divide which still exists today. Fortis also translated the most famous Croatian ballad, *Hasanaginica* (The Wife of Asan Aga), a heroic tale of the region's ongoing battles between Christians and Turks, into Italian. This work was to have great influence on Romanticism throughout Europe, subsequently being translated into German by Goethe in 1778 and then into English by Sir Walter Scott.

## Illyrian Movement

The next historical landmark for the evolution of Croatian literature was the founding of the Illyrian Movement by *Ljudevit Gaj* (1809-72) from Krapina in Zagorje. Aimed at the union of South Slavs (ie Croats and Serbs) within the Austro-Hungarian federation, members of the movement believed that the Slav tongue should be acknowledged as the official language within these regions, and that it should find a uniform standard form. Gaj thus published *Kratka osnova hrvatsko slavenskoga pravopisanja* (The Basics of Croato-Slavic Orthography) in 1830, in which he proposed writing the palatals - ć, č, š and ž – according to the Czech model. Thanks to the efforts of the Illyrian Movement, a standard language based on the štokavian dialect with etymological orthography was introduced in 1836. You can see a monument of Gaj, by Ivan Rendič, on the main square in Krapina.

Background

Literary works coming out of the Illyrian Movement were suffused with Romanticism and nationalism as can be seen in the patriotic and reflective lyrics of **Petar Preradović** (1818-1872), a soldier and poet of Serbian origin who gave his name to Trg Petra Preradovića in Zagreb, where you can see a statue of him. Here it is also worth mentioning **Antun Mihanović** (1796-1861), a poet from Klanjec in Zagorje, who wrote Lijepa Naša, the words to the Croatian national anthem. In Northern Croatia, patriotic-romantic themes prevailed into the late 19th century, with their main exponent being the poet, dramatist, journalist and critic **August Šenoa** (1838-81).

## 20th century

The 20th century is marked by the works of Zagreb-born **Miroslav Krleža** (1893-1981), a harsh critic of bourgeois society and fore-runner of existentialism whose best known novel is *Povratak Filipa Latinovicza* (The Return of Philip Latinowicz), which was translated into several European languages, including English. Another writer held dear to the socialist intellectuals of the Tito period was **Vladimir Nazor**, (1876-1949) from Bobovišća on the island of Brač, who lived most of his life in Istria. During the Second World War, Nazor joined the Partizans at the age of 66, and his best known work is *Veli Jože*, the story of a giant from the Istrian hill town of Motovun, who was captured by the Venetians and used as a slave.

Regarding the Yugoslav years, it is also necessary to mention **Ivo Andrić** (1892-1975) who won the 1961 Nobel Prize for Literature. He originated from Travnik in Bosnia, which was then under Austro-Hungary control, and although he officially declared himself a Serb (and lived most of his later life in Belgrade), some Croats like to include him among the ranks of Croatian literary figures – in any case, the language he was writing in at the time was Serbo-Croatian. Andrić's favourite theme was life in Bosnia under the Turks and the cultural effect of living in a region where East meets West, and he had an unrivalled skill of portraying the peculiarities of human nature through the narration of everyday situations. His two greatest novels were *Na Drini cuprija* (The Bridge on the Drina) and *Travnička hronika* (Bosnian Story), and he also wrote several collections of touching and amusing short stories.

More recently, the most highly regarded Croatian writers have been those living outside the country. Many of them, such as **Dubravka Ugrešić**, author of *The Museum of Unconditional Surrender and Culture of Lies*, were critical of the political situation and the rise in nationalism that took place in Croatia through the 1990's.

Finally, it is worth mentioning that during the second half of the 20th century, writers in Croatia and indeed in all of Eastern Europe, had a far more important role in society than those in Western Europe, and were often active in political movements, writing both for and against the state.

# Language

Croatian belongs to the South Slavic branch of the Slavic group of languages – a similar language is spoken by Serbs, Montenegrins and Bosnians. While the latter three speak only the štokavian dialect, Croats speak štokavian, kajkavian and ćakavian. The names of these dialects are derived from the interrogative relative pronoun 'what', being spoken either as 'kaj', 'ća' or 'što'. Kajkavian is mainly spoken in northwest Croatia (but not in Istria), while ćakavian can be heard on all the Dalmatian islands (except Mljet) and along the Dalmatian coast near Zadar and Split. Croats in other parts of Croatia, as well as in Bosnia and Herzegovina, western parts of Vojvodina (in Serbia) and Boka Kotorska (in Montenegro) speak the štokavian dialect. Since it is the official variant taught in schools, štokavian is also spoken in kajkavian and ćakavian parts of the country.

The area where these dialects were spoken was far larger before the Turkish wars, which caused mass migrations. As a result of these population movements, today there are Croatian minorities in Burgenland (Austria), Slovakia, Moravia (Czech Republic) and the region of Molise (Italy), where the older variant of the Croatian language has been preserved.

Croatian is almost identical to Serbian, the main difference being that Croats, who are mainly Catholic, write in Latin script, while Serbs, who are predominantly Orthodox, use the Cyrillic script. Variations in grammar, spelling and pronunciation are comparable to differences between British English and American English.

During the Tito years it became normal to refer to the common language as Serbo-Croatian, though Croatian nationalists always had a problem with this, feeling their Croatian identity somehow undermined: they preferred to call the language Croato-Serbian, or even just 'Croatian'. More recently, during the war of the 1990's, Croatian nationalists tried to exaggerate to differences between Croatian and Serbian, reviving archaic expressions and even inventing new words. President Tudjman insisted the new words should be used on radio, television and in schools, but in reality relatively few are in common usage today.

# Music

Croatian traditional music has a rich variety of performing styles, repertoires and instruments, reflecting the country's geographical position, turbulent history and variety of cultural spheres. Each region has its own unique musical style and characteristic instruments.

## Folk music

The best-known form of Croatian traditional music is rural dance music performed by a **tamburica** ensemble. A long-necked string instrument related to the Russian balalaika, the Ukrainian bandura and the Italian mandolin, the tamburica is considered the Croatian national folk instrument and one of the country's hallmarks. Its name originates from Turkish and it made its first appearance in Bosnia during the 14th century, when the region was part of the Ottoman Empire. Its popularity spread to other Slavic countries, including Croatia, primarily to the region of Slavonia and Baranja. Today the largest tambura festivals are the *Golden Strings of Slavonia* held in Požega in September and the *Croatian Tambura Music Festival* held in Osijek in May.

Other traditional instruments, which slightly lost popularity during the 20th century due to the success of the tamburica, include the **gajde** (bagpipe) also played in Slavonia; the **diplica** (a simple, ancient wind instrument) still played in Baranja; the **trontole** (drone zither) and **cimbal** (dulcimer) played in Međimurje (notably in the Čakovec area), and the **žvegla**, **fajfa**, and **dvojnice** (all types of flute), which were once popular in the Central Croatia. In the regions of Istria and Kvarner (notably on the island of Krk) traditional woodwind instruments such as the **sopile**, **mih** and **šurle** are still very popular.

In Dalmatia, special place is taken by so-called *klapa* singing; songs performed by ensembles of between five and eight vocalist, without instrumental accompaniment. *Klapa* – which in Dalmatian dialect means company or group – traditionally consists only of male voices, but nowadays many female-only and mixed ensembles have emerged, with a varying number of members. Nevertheless, its basic characteristic and distinction remain solely vocal harmony singing, only rarely discreetly and quietly accompanied by instruments. A special annual festival of amateur singers, the *Dalmatian Klapa Festival*, takes place in July in Omiš, near Split. Over the last 20 years, this festival has grown into a cultural institution of great importance and reputation.

Background

## Classical music

In the history of Croatian music, it is necessary to mention church music, with the first known manuscripts dating back to the 11th century. Some Christmas folk songs, of which there are more than 500, can be traced back to the 12th century, and are still sung today. Christmas carols vary considerably from region to region, and can have a dozen different melodies.

The Glagolitic chant is a type of church music, which was first mentioned in 1177, when Pope Alexander III visited the city of Zadar. It represents a unique phenomenon in the history of European music and has three basic components: Gregorian coral, Croatian folklore and Byzantine church music. It is still preserved on some of the Croatian islands, notably during the *Za Križem* (Carrying of the Holy Cross), an all night procession staged on the night before Good Friday on the island of Hvar.

The Croatian people are very proud of having two excellent Renaissance composers: **Julije Skjavetić** (Schiavetti) and **Ivan Lukačić**, both of whom lived in Šibenik during the 16th century. Their compositions, as well as other performances of medieval, Renaissance and baroque music, are the core of the *Music Evenings* in St Donat's annual summer festival held in Zadar. The festival attracts well-known European ensembles, which also perform masterpieces from their own countries.

Having several famous opera composers makes Croatia one of only three Slavic nations (besides Czechs and Russians) who have their own national operas. The first Croatian opera *Ljubav i zloba* (Love and Malice) was composed by **Vatroslav Lisinski** in 1846. Operas composed by **Ivan Zajc** (1832-1914) and **Jakov Gotovac** (1895-1982) have been performed in concert halls throughout the world, the best knowm being Gotovac's *Ero s onoga svijeta* which has been translated into nine languages and performed in about 80 countries. Renowned females opera singers from Croatia include **Milka Trnina** (1863-1941) who performed in the first Tosca at Covent Garden, **Maja Strozzi-Pecic** (1881-1962) and **Zinka Kunc-Milanov** (1906-89).

Today probably the most famous Croatian musician is the pianist **Ivo Pogorelić** (born in Belgrade in 1958) who has performed with leading orchestras all over the world. Tickets for his solo performances are invariably completely sold out, and over the last decade he has given many charity concerts in aid of the countries of former-Yugoslavia, leading UNESCO to name him an 'Ambassador of Goodwill' in 1998. Another up-and-coming pianist is **Maksim Mrvica** (born in Šibenik in 1975) who won the Nicolai Rubinstein International Competition of Pianists in Paris in 1999, and the International Pianist Competition Pontoise in Paris in 2001.

Other world renowned contemporary Croatian musicians include the cellist **Valter Despalj**, born in Zadar in 1947, who has performed at venues all over the world, including the Royal Festival Hall in London, and was the Dubrovnik Summer Festival musical director from 1996 to 2000. His star pupil, **Monika Leskovar**, a Croat born in Germany in 1981, won the prestigious Chaikovsky Competition in Japan in 1995, took second prize at the 1998 Eurovision contest for young instrumentalists and won the 1999 Roberto Caruana competition in Milan.

Notable young guitarists include the brother and sister **Viktor and Ana Vidović**, born in Karlovac in 1973 and 1980 respectively. At the age of only 18, Ana won the 1998 International Guitarist Competition in Spain. Another promising young guitarist is **Marko Belenić**, who at the age of 20 shared first prize at the 2002 Young Concert Artists competition in New York.

The Croatian national anthem is *Lijepa naša domovino* (Our Beautiful Homeland). The verses were written by the Croatian poet **Antun Mihanović** (1796-1861) and the music composed by **Josip Runjanin** (1821-78), a Serb born in Croatia. The song was first sung as the national anthem at an exhibition held by the Croatian-Slavonian Economic Society in Zagreb in 1891.

# Land and environment

## Geography

Croatia is a boomerang-shaped country with a total surface area of 56,690 sq km, making it about three-quarters the size of Scotland. It lies on the east coast of the Adriatic and serves as the main gateway from the Mediterranean to Eastern Europe, bordering Slovenia in the northwest, Hungary in the north, Serbia in the northeast, Bosnia and Herzegovina in the east and Montenegro in the extreme south. It has 1,778 km of indented mainland coastline and over a thousand islands and islets, of which 67 are inhabited.

The territory is made of flat plains, low mountains, the mainland coast and numerous offshore islands, and can be broken down into three regions: the Pannonian Basin, the Dinaric Mountains and the Adriatic Coast.

### Pannonian Basin

The gently undulating hills and expansive flat plains between the River Drava to the north (forming a natural border with Hungary), the River Danube to the east (border with Serbia) and the River Sava to the south (border with Bosnia and Herzegovina) were historically known as Pannonia, which was later renamed Slavonia. This is a region of extremely fertile agricultural land, producing wheat, corn, sugar beet and sunflowers, with lush pastures and vineyards on the hills to the north. Moving west towards Zagreb, the so-called Peri-Pannonian area is made up of low hills and pastureland suitable for livestock, which gradually gives way to industry as one nears the capital.

### Dinaric Mountains

The rugged Dinaric Alps extend 640 km along the east coast of the Adriatic Sea from the Isonzo River in northeast Italy to north Albania. A narrow belt running from northwest to southeast, they mark the natural border between the west of Bosnia and Herzegovina and Croatia, and form a barrier to travel from the coast to the interior, as there are no natural passes. They are composed of limestone and dolomite, easily eroded sedimentary rocks which give rise to karst forms such as sinkholes and caves. The region is sparsely populated and supports scanty cereal production, some small orchards and vineyards, livestock breeding and dairy farming. The highest peak is also called Dinara, and reaches 1,831 m.

### Adriatic Coast

The partially submerged western slopes of the Dinaric Alps form the numerous bays, gulfs, inlets and offshore islands along the Croatian Coast. The coast extends from the northwest to the southeast, following the basic extension of the Dinaric system. Between Rijeka (Kvarner) and Šibenik (Central Dalmatia), the islands run parallel to the coast, and are separated by channels, which are interlinked by straits. Southeast from here, between Split and Dubrovnik, the islands of Ćiovo, Šolta, Hvar, Brač, Korčula, Vis, Lastovo and Mljet extend from the west to the east. The largest island is Krk; other sizeable islands include Cres, Brač, Hvar, Pag and Korčula. The Croatian coastal area may further be divided into the northern (Istria and Kvarner) and southern (Dalmatia) parts. The coastal areas and offshore islands grow olives, citrus fruits and vegetables.

Background

## Climate

Croatia lies halfway between the North Pole and the Equator. The Pannonian basin displays a continental climate, the Adriatic coast a Mediterranean climate. In the Pannonia region, winter temperatures average 0°C, and summer temperatures 22°C. Along the coast, winter temperatures average 2°C in the north and 9°C in the south, with summer temperatures between 24°C and 26°C respectively. The sunniest place is said to be Hvar Town, which has 2,718 hours of sunshine a year: in comparison, Nice in the south of France has 2,706 sunny hours. In the Dinaric mountains, in areas over 1500m, winter temperatures average -6°C and summer temperatures 18°C.

The average annual rainfall ranges between 600 mm and 3,850 mm. The mountainous regions of Gorski Kotar, Biokovo and Velebit have the heaviest rainfall (3,850 mm) while the lowest rainfall is found in the eastern parts of the country (600 mm).

# Wildlife and vegetation

Croatia's contrasting geographic regions afford a wide variety of natural vegetation. Approximately 35% of the country is forested. The common oak predominates in the low hills on the northern edge of the Pannonian basin, while the indigenous forests and grasslands of the eastern part have been largely felled and turned into arable land, the one exception being the wetlands of Kopački Rit, which have been preserved as a nature park. The Dinaric Mountains are quite barren in parts, though lower altitudes of up to 1200 m support dispersed forests of beech and fir, while individual specimens of spruce, sycamore and elm can be found in the same belt. In areas over 1200 m, the sub-alpine beech dominates. The area along the Adriatic coast and the islands are covered with sub-Mediterranean and Mediterranean vegetation. Evergreen forests of holm oak and Aleppo pine, as well as macchia, are typical of the coastal belt and the islands. Some of the islands, notably Pag and the Kornati, display typical karst features and are relatively barren, but for feather grass and sage.

There are some 380 protected animal species in Croatia, the largest and most impressive being the brown bear, the wild boar and the wolf, all of which are occasionally sighted in Risnjak, Paklenica and Plitvice national parks. The deer, wildcat and lynx are also present in Risnjak, while the otter is sometimes spotted in Plitvice. The seaward slopes of the Dinaric mountains, notably Velebit and Biokovo, are populated by small flocks of mouflon and chamois. Large birds of prey such as Eurasion griffon vultures and peregrine vultures can be occasionally be found in seawards facing cliffs and gorges, while wading birds such as storks and herons are seasonal visitors to the inland wetlands of Kopački Rit and Losinjsko Polje nature parks. Various species of whales and dolphins swim in the Adriatic.

## National parks

The richest and most fascinating areas of natural beauty have been designated national parks. To enter them, visitors are required to pay an entry fee, which goes towards their upkeep. Each park has an information office providing a basic introduction to the area's flora and fauna, plus maps. Three of the national parks (Kornati, Brijuni and Mljet) are on islands, two centre on systems of waterfalls (Plitvice and Krka), and the others are mountainous.

National park websites: Risnjak, www.risnjak.hr; Brijuni, www.np-brijuni.hr; Plitvice, www.np-plitvicka-jezera.hr; Paklenice, www.paklenica.hr; Krka, www.npkrka.hr; Kornati, www.kornati.hr; and Mljet, www.np-mljet.hr

# Books

The books listed below are non-fictional and reference guides. For the best of Croatian fiction and poetry, see Croatian Literature, on page 331.

## History, politics and culture

**Glenny, Misha**, *The Fall of Yugoslavia* (1996) Penguin and *The Balkans: Nationalism, War and the Great Powers*, 1804-1999 (2001) Penguin. Both these books give detailed and readable analysis of the history and politics of the wider Balkan region, with many relevant references to Croatia.

**Judah, Tim**, *The Serbs: History, Myth and the Destruction of Yugoslavia* (1997) Yale University Press. A scholarly but lively account of the last six centuries of Serbian history.

**Morris, Jan**, *The Venetian Empire* (1990) Penguin. Includes an excellent chapter about the Venetian port towns along the Croatian coast.

**Silber, Laura and Little, Allan**, *The Death of Yugoslavia* (1996) Penguin Group and BBC Worldwide Ltd. Based on the BBC documentary of the same name, this book gives a step-by-step account of the lead up to hostilities and the war itself.

**Stavrianos, Leften Stavros**, *The Balkans Since 1453* (3rd edition, 2000) New York University Press. Although it was written back in 1958, this book gives an excellent introduction to the Ottoman Empire, tracing Balkan history from the fall of Constantinople up to the close of the Second World War.

**Tanner, Marcus**, *Croatia: A Nation Forged in War* (1997) Yale University Press. Offers one of the best general accounts of Croatian history, tracing events from the arrival of the Slavs up to the 1990's.

## Tito biographies

**Maclean, Fitzroy**, *Josip Broz Tito*, a pictorial biography (1980) McGraw-Hill, New York. Photos covering Tito's years as the leader of Yugoslavia.

**Ridley, Jasper**, *Tito* (1994). Constable, London. An excellent general biography, written with hindsight following the break up of Yugoslavia.

## Travelogues and memoirs

**Murphy, Dervla**, *Through the Embers of Chaos: Balkan Journeys* (2002) John Murray. Murphy on a bike, exploring the current situation in the countries of former-Yugoslavia.

**West, Rebecca**, *Black Lamb & Grey Falcon* (1942) Macmillan, London. Describes a journey through Yugoslavia in 1937. The first section of the book deals with the writer's experiences in Croatia at that time.

Background

# Cinema

Before the 1990s, cinema was strong in Yugoslavia, with three Yugoslav films receiving Oscar nominations: *Cesta duga godinu dana* (The Road One Year Long, 1958), Deveti krug (Ninth Circle, 1960) and *Bitka na Neretvi* (The Battle of Neretva, 1969). This was probably due to in part to the fact that Tito loved cinema – especially westerns – and always attended the annual *Pula Film Festival*. While Serbia was noted for black comedies and films about the Partisans, Croatia built up a firm reputation for animation, with the Zagreb School of Animated Film gaining international renown, not least when the Zagreb director Dušan Vukotić won the 1961 Oscar for animation with Ersatz (*The Substitute*).

With the break up of Yugoslavia and Tudjman's rise to power, cinema in Croatia went into a decline. Funding was short, and in any case avant-garde expression had no place in the new country of conservative ideals.

Things are improving. Croatia's most promising young director is Vinko Brešan. His *Kako je poèeo rat na mom otoku* (How the War Started on My Island, 1996), filmed in Šibenik, Primošten and Zagreb, takes a comic look at the tragic events of the recent war and was extremely well received by the Croatian public. This was followed by *Maršal* (Marshal Tito's Spirit, 1999), set in Nin near Zadar, which also had success at home and was shown at the Berlin Film Festival.

During the war for independence, many artists and intellectuals left the country, one being the actor Rade Serbedzija, who now lives in London. A Serb born in Lika in Croatia in 1946, he had already been acknowledged as Yugoslavia's top actor during the 1980s, but as ethnic tensions were aroused in 1991, he was told that he was no longer a member of the Society of Drama Artists of Croatia and was asked to withdraw his membership card. His first big international success came with *Before the Rain* (1994) directed by Milcho Manchevski, in which he played a Macedonian photographer working in London. The film itself, which is stunning, won the *Leone d'Oro at Venice Film Festival* and Serbedzija received the Critics' Award for the Best Actor. In Broken English (1996) he plays the role of a Croat who has fled the country due to the war and settled in New Zealand, while in the Italian production *La Tregua* (The Truce, 1997) he is a Second World War Greek prisoner of war. His latest films have come out of Hollywood: he starred as the Russian crime boss in *The Saint* (1997), the eccentric owner of the Rainbow Costume Shop in Stanley Kubrik's *Eye's Wide Shut* (1999) and the Russian scientist in *Mission Impossible II* (2000).

The best known young Croatian actor today is probably Goran Višnjić, who was born in Šibenik in 1972. Educated at the Academy of Dramatic Arts in Zagreb, he first gained the attention of the Croatian public at the age of 21 as Laertes in Hamlet at the Dubrovnik Summer Festival. Then, in the minor role of a translator-driver for a team of British war correspondents in Micheal Winterbottom's *Welcome to Sarajevo* (1997), he was noticed by Hollywood, and Madonna. He then took a minor role in *The Peacemaker* (1997), a spy-thriller starring George Clooney and Nikole Kidman, in which a group of Bosnian-Croatian terrorists get hold of a nuclear warhead from Russia, and plan to bomb New York out of revenge for international interference in the recent Yugoslav war. The following year he featured in Madonna's video *The Power of Goodbye*, and played Kidman's abusive East European boyfriend in *Practical Magic* (1998). When George Clooney left the hospital drama ER in 1999, Višnjić took over as Dr Luka Kovac, a Croatian immigrant to the US. In 2000 he was voted one of the world's 50 Most Beautiful people by People magazine. His recent films include *Committed* (2000), *The Deep End* (2001) and *Doctor Sleep* (2001). He now lives in Los Angeles, US, but returns to Cratia regularly, occasionally taking a role in the Dubrovnik Film Festival.

# Useful words and phrases

Croatian is difficult to learn unless you already have some knowledge of another Slavic language. However with a few basics your visit will be all the more enjoyable, and once you have spent some time in the country you will pick up more words.

Remember that each region has its own dialect. As a general rule, places along the coast use a fair smattering of Italian (or to be more precise, Venetian) terms, while in the north of the country you will hear words borrowed directly from German. For information about self-study packs, and Croatian language courses in Croatia itself, see page 22.

## General pronunciation

Every letter is pronounced, so Croatian is spoken as it is written. Besides the five standard vowels (a, e, i, o, u) the letter r also acts as a vowel when it appears between two consonants, or as the first letter in a word followed by a consonant so, the first syllable of the word Hrvat sounds like her in English will a rolled r.

There are also eight letters that are not found in the English alphabet:

Č as the ch in cheap
ž as the j in jug
Š as the sh in sheep
š as the s in leisure
Ć as the t in future
Đ as d in duke (can also be written as Dj)
Lj as the lli in million
Nj as the ni in onion

## Greetings, courtesies

Hello  *Bog*
Good morning  *Dobro jutro*
Good afternoon  *Dobar dan*
Good night  *Laku noć*
Goodbye  *Dovidjenja*
See you later  *Vidimo se kasnije*
How are you?  *Kako ste?*
Pleased to meet you  *Drago mi je*
Please  *Molim*

Thank you  *Hvala*
Yes  *Da*
No  *Ne*
Excuse me  *Oprostite*
I do not understand  *Ne razumijem*
Please speak more slowly  *Molim Vas govorite sporije*
What is your name?  *Kako se zovete?*
Go away!  *Odlazi!*

## Basic questions

Where is_?  *Gdje je_?*
How much does it cost?  *Koliko košta?*
How much is it?  *Koliko je ovo?*
When?  *Kada?*
When does the bus leave?
*Kada polazi/kreće autobus?*
Does it take long?  *Da li to dugo traje*

When does the bus arrive?
*Kada dolazi/stiže autobus?*
Why?  *Zašto?*
What for?  *Zbog čega?*
What time is it?  *Koliko je sati?*
How do I get to_?  *Kako mogu stići do_?*
Is this the way to the church?
*Je li ovo put do crkve?*

## Basics

Entrance  *Ulaz*
Exit  *Izlaz*
Bathroom/toilet  *WC* (pronounced
'vey tsey')
Police  *Policija*
Hotel  *Hotel*
Restaurant  *Restoran*
Post office  *Pošta*

Telephone  *Telefon*
Bank  *Banka*
Exchange office  *Mjenjačnica*
Exchange rate  *Tečaj*
Notes/coins  *Papirnati novac/kovanice*
Travellers' cheques  *Putni čekovi*
Cash  *Gotovina*

## Getting around

On the left/right  *Lijevodesno*
Straight on  *Ravno*
Second street on the left
*Druga ulica lijevo*
To walk  *Hodati*
Bus station  *Autobusni kolodvor*
Railway station  *Eljeznički kolodvor*

Bus  *Autobus*
Train  *Vlak*
Aeroplane  *Avion*
First/second class  *Prvi/drugi razred*
Ticket  *Karta*
Ticket office  *Agencija za prodaj karata*
Bus stop  *Autobusna stanica*

## Accommodation

Do you have a room for the night?
*Imate li slobodnu sobu za noćas*
Room  *Soba*
Single/double room  *Jednokrevetna soba/*
*dvokrevetna soba*
With private bathroom  *Soba sa kupatilom*

Shower  *Tuš*
Sheets  *Plahte*
Blankets  *Deke/pokrivači*
Pillows  *Jastuci*
Toilet paper  *Toaletni papir*
Key  *Ključ*

## Shops

Bakery  *Pekara*
Book shop  *Knjižara*
Butchers  *Mesnica*
Cake shop  *Slastičarna*
Chemists  *Apoteka/ljekarna*

Fishmongers  *Ribarnica*
Market  *Tržnica*
Hairdresser's  *Frizer*
Newsagents/tobacconist  *Trafika/kiosk*
Travel agent  *Putnička agencija*

## Sightseeing

Cathedral  *Katedrala*
Church  *Crkva*
Garden  *Vrt*
Museum  *Muzej*

Art gallery  *Galerija umjetnina*
Tourist information centre  *Turistički ured*
Town hall  *Gradska vijećnica*
Closed for holiday  *Zatvoreno zbog praznika*

## Sports

Beach  *Pla a*
Swimming pool  *Bazen*
Tennis court  *Teniski teren*
Sailing boat  *Jedrilica*

Diving club  *Ronilački klub*
Hiking path  *Pješačka staza*
Mountain refuge  *Planinarski dom*

# Days, months and time

Day *Dan*
Week *Tjedan*
Month *Mjesec*

Monday *Ponedjeljak*
Tuesday *Utorak*
Wednesday *Srijeda*
Thursday *Četvrtak*
Friday *Petak*
Saturday *Subota*
Sunday *Nedjelja*

January *Siječanj*
February *Veljača*
March *Oñujak*
April *Travanj*
May *Svibanj*
June *Lipanj*
July *Srpanj*

August *Kolovoz*
September *Rujan*
October *Listopad*
November *Studeni*
December *Prosinac*

At one o'clock *U jedan sat*
At half past two *U dva i trideset/ u pola tri* (North Croatia) *U dva i pol* (Dalmatia)
At a quarter to three *U petnaest do tri/ tri manje kvarat* (Dalmatia)
It's one o'clock *Jedan je sat*
It's seven o'clock *Sedam je sati*
It's twenty past six *Šest i dvadeset je*
It's five to nine *Pet do devet je* (North Croatia)/ *devet manje pet* (Dalmatia)
In ten minutes *Za deset minuta*
Five hours *Pet sati*

# Numbers

0 *nula*
1 *jedan*
2 *dva*
3 *tri*
4 *četiri*
5 *pet*
6 *šest*
7 *sedam*
8 *osam*
9 *devet*
10 *deset*
11 *jedanaest*
12 *dvanaest*
13 *trinaest*
14 *četrnaest*
15 *petnaest*
16 *šestnaest*
17 *sedamnaest*
18 *osamnaest*
19 *devetnaest*

20 *dvadeset*
21 *dvadeset i jedan*
22 *dvadeset i dva*
30 *trideset*
31 *trideset i jedan*
40 *četrdeset*
50 *pedeset*
60 *šezdeset*
70 *sedamdeset*
80 *osamdeset*
90 *devedeset*
100 *sto*
101 *sto i jedan*
102 *sto i dva*
200 *dvjesto*
500 *petsto*
700 *sedamsto*
900 *devetsto*
1000 *tisuću*
1001 *tisuću i jedan*

# Eating out

Do you have a table? *Imate li stol?*
Can we have the menu? *Molim vas, moemo li dobiti jelovnik*
Can we have the bill? *Molim vas, možemo li dobiti racun?*
Breakfast *Doručak*
Lunch *Ručak*

Dinner *Večera*
Meal *Jelo*
Drink *Piće*
Jelovnik *Menu*
ivjeli! *Cheers!*
Račun *Bill*

# Food glossary

## Snacks
*Burek sa mesom*  Filo pastry filled with minced meat and onions
*Burek sa sirom*  Filo pastry filled with curd cheese
*Ćevapčići*  Meat rissoles served in pitta bread
*Ribice*  Tiny fried fish (similar to whitebait)

## Meat and meat dishes
*Grah sa kobasicom*  Beans and sausages
*Gulaš*  Goulash
*Janjetina*  Whole spit-roast lamb
*Kulen*  Salami spiced with paprika (Slavonian speciality)
*Meso na žaru*  Barbecued meat
*Miješano meso*  Mixed grilled meats
*Odojak*  Whole spit-roast suckling pig
*Pasticada*  Beef stewed in wine (Dalmatian speciality)
*Piletina*  Chicken
*Pršut*  Smoked ham (Istrian and Dalmatian speciality)
*Punjene paprike*  Stuffed peppers (with meat)
*Purica z mlincima i štrukle*  Roast turkey with savoury pastry (Zagorje speciality)
*Ramsteak*  Rump steak
*Ražnjići*  Kebabs (normally pork)
*Sarma*  Cabbage leaves stuffed with meat and rice

## Fish and seafood
*Bijela riba*  'White' fish (eg mullet, bass, bream, John Dory)
*Brudet*  Fish stew (Dalmatian speciality, with sea fish)
*Crni rižot*  Black risotto (prepared with cuttlefish ink)
*Dagnje*  Mussels (various names in different regions)
*Fiš paprikaš*  Fish stew (Slavonian speciality, with freshwater fish)
*Jastog*  Lobster
*Ostrige*  Oysters
*Plava riba*  'Blue' fish (eg tuna, mackerel, sardines)
*Pržene lignje*  Fried squid
*Riba na žaru*  Barbecued fish
*Rižot frutti di mare*  Seafood risotto
*Rižot sa škampima*  Shrimp risotto
*Salata od hobotnice*  Octopus salad
*Škampi na buzaru*  Shrimps in garlic and white wine
*Školjke na buzaru*  Shells in garlic and white wine
*Slana srdela*  Salted sardines
*Špageti frutti di mare*  Spaghetti with seafood

Footnotes

## Side dishes
*Blitva*  Swiss chard
*Krumpir*  Boiled potatoes
*Mješana salata*  Mixed salad (usually lettuce, cucmber and tomato)
*Njoki*  Gnocchi
*Pomfrit*  Chips
*Riňa*  Rice
*Špinat*  Spinach
*Zelena salata*  Green salad (lettuce)

## Sweets
*Baklava*  Layers of filo pastry and walnuts drenched in syrup
*Palačinke*  Pancakes
*Roňata*  Creme caramel (Dubrovnik speciality)
*Sladoled*  Ice cream

## Fruit
*Breskva*  peach
*Jabuka*  apple
*Lubenica*  melon
*Marelica*  apricot
*Naranča*  orange

## Miscellaneous
*Ajvar*  Relish made from aubergines and peppers
*Juha*  Soup
*Kajmak*  Clotted sour cream
*Maslinovo ulje*  Olive oil
*Ocat*  Vinegar
*Papar*  Pepper
*Paški sir*  Sheeps' cheese from the island of Pag
*Sol*  Salt
*Štrukli*  Baked cheese dumplings (Zagorje speciality)
*Tartufi*  Truffles (Istrian speciality)

## Drinks
*Bijelo vino*  White wine
*Crno vino*  Red wine
*Gazirana mineralna voda*  Sparkling mineral water
*Negazirana mineralna voda*  Still mineral water
*Pivo*  Beer
*Rakija*  Spirit
*Tamno pivo*  Stout (dark beer)
*Travarica*  Spirit flavoured with herbs
*Voda*  Water

# Index

Footnotes

# Shorts

# Advertisers index

# Map index

Footnotes

# Map symbols

## Roads and travel
— Main road
— Other road
- - - Track
······ Footpath
⊢■ Railway with station

## Water features
🌊 River
⬭ Lake
🌊 Ocean
⚓ Ferry

## Cities and towns
▫ Sight
🔢 Sleeping
❶ Eating
▭ Building
═ Main through route
═ Main street
═ Minor street

◫ Pedestrianized street
Σ Ⅹ Tunnel
→ One way street
⋈ Bridge
⊡ Park, garden, stadium
⫿ Steps
▬ Fortified wall
✈ Airport
🚌 Bus station
✚ Hospital
🏪 Market
🏛 Museum
✉ Post office
🛈 Tourist office
✝ ♠ Cathedral, church
✡ Synagogue
Ⓐ Detail map

## Other symbols
♦ National park/wildlife reserve
❀ Viewing point

# Credits

**Text editor:** Stephanie Lambe
**Map editor:** Sarah Sorensen

**Publishers:** James Dawson and
Patrick Dawson
**Editorial director:** Rachel Fielding
**Editorial:** Alan Murphy, Sarah
Thorowgood, Claire Boobbyer,
Felicity Laughton, Caroline Lascom,
Davina Rungasamy, Laura Dixon
**Production:** Jo Morgan, Mark Thomas
**Cartography:** Claire Benison, Kevin
Feeney, Robert Lunn
**Design:** Mytton Williams
**Marketing and publicity:**
Rosemary Dawson, La-Ree Miners
**Advertising:** Debbie Wylde,
Lorraine Horler
**Finance and administration:**
Sharon Hughes, Elizabeth Taylor,
Leona Bailey

## Maps
Black and white maps:
PCGraphics (UK) Ltd
Colour map: Kevin Feeney, Footprint

## Photography credits
**Front cover:** Hans Georg Roth/
Corbis UK Ltd
**Back cover:** Alamy
**Inside colour section:** Alamy; Art Direc-
tors and TRIP; gettyone Stone

## Print
Manufactured in Italy by LegoPrint
Pulp from sustainable forests

### Publishing information
Footprint Croatia Handbook
1st edition
© Footprint Handbooks Ltd
May 2003

ISBN 1 903471 53 2
CIP DATA: A catalogue record for this
book is available from the British Library

® Footprint Handbooks and the Footprint
mark are a registered trademark of
Footprint Handbooks Ltd

### Published by
### Footprint Handbooks
6 Riverside Court
Lower Bristol Road
Bath BA2 3DZ, UK
T +44 (0)1225 469141
F +44 (0)1225 469461
E discover@footprintbooks.com
www.footprintbooks.com

### Distributed in the USA by
Publishers Group West

Neither the black and white nor coloured
maps are intended to have any political
significance.

Every effort has been made to ensure that
the facts in this Handbook are accurate.
However, travellers should still obtain
advice from consulates, airlines etc about
travel and visa requirements before
travelling. The authors and publishers
cannot accept responsibility for
any loss, injury or inconvenience
however caused.

# Acknowledgements

Jane would like to thank all those who helped with the research for this book, especially Željka Dubravica and Renata Janeković from the Croatian National Tourist Board; Vjenceslav Vlahov in Zagreb; Đurđa Somođi, Rudi Grula and Gordan Vrbanec in Čakovec; Vesna Jovičić in Pula; Radmila Paliska in Labin; Gordana Perić in Zadar; and Ivana Rakić in Lastovo.

Thanks are also due to the special contributors: Domagoj Mijan (who wrote the History section) and Goran Vuletić (who translated it), Sanja Kuvačić (who wrote the Music section) and Dr Charlie Easmon (for adapting the Health section).

A special mention goes to Dejan Dobrota for agreeing to embark on many an impromptu journey, by bus, ferry, bicycle and sailing boat.

Jane would also like to thank the team at Footprint for all their efforts and patience, especially Stephane Lambe.

# Footprint feedback

We try as hard as we can to make each Footprint Handbook as
up-to-date and accurate as possible but, of course, things always
change. Many people write to us - with corrections, new information,
or simply comments.

If you want to let us know about an experience or adventure –
hair-raising or mundane, good or bad, exciting or boring – we would
be delighted to hear from you. Please give us as precise information
as possible, quoting the edition number (you'll find it on the front
cover) and page number of the Handbook you are using.

Your help will be greatly appreciated. In return we will send you
details about our special guidebook offer.
Email Footprint at:
**cro1_online@footprintbooks.com**

or write to:
**Elizabeth Taylor**
**Footprint Handbooks**
**6 Riverside Court, Lower Bristol Road**
**Bath BA2 3DZ UK**

## www.footprintbooks.com

**Dip in and keep on the pulse with what Footprint are
up to online.**

- Latest Footprint releases
- Entertaining travel articles
  and news updates
- Extensive destination
  information for inspiration
  and trip planning
- Monthly competitions
- Easy ways to buy Footprint
  guides

Footnotes

# Complete title listing

**Footprint publish travel guides to over 120 countries worldwide. Each guide is packed with practical, concise and colourful information for everybody from first-time travellers to travel aficionados. The list is growing fast and current titles are noted below.**

**Available from all good bookshops**

**www.footprintbooks.com**

## Latin America & Caribbean

Argentina Handbook
Barbados (P)
Bolivia Handbook
Brazil Handbook
Caribbean Islands Handbook
Central America & Mexico
 Handbook
Chile Handbook
Colombia Handbook
Costa Rica Handbook
Cuba Handbook
Cusco & the Inca Trail Handbook
Dominican Republic Handbook
Ecuador & Galápagos Handbook
Guatemala Handbook
Havana (P)
Mexico Handbook
Nicaragua Handbook
Peru Handbook
Rio de Janeiro Handbook
South American Handbook
Venezuela Handbook

## North America

Western Canada Handbook

## Africa

Cape Town (P)
East Africa Handbook
Libya Handbook
Marrakech & the High Atlas
 Handbook
Morocco Handbook
Namibia Handbook
South Africa Handbook
Tunisia Handbook
Uganda Handbook

(P) denotes pocket Handbook

## Middle East

Egypt Handbook
Israel Handbook
Jordan Handbook
Syria & Lebanon Handbook

## Australasia

Australia Handbook
New Zealand Handbook
Sydney (P)
West Coast
   Australia Handbook

## Asia

Bali Handbook
Bangkok & the Beaches
   Handbook
Cambodia Handbook
Goa Handbook
India Handbook
Indian Himalaya Handbook
Indonesia Handbook
Laos Handbook
Malaysia Handbook
Myanmar (Burma) Handbook
Nepal Handbook
Pakistan Handbook
Rajasthan Handbook
Singapore Handbook
South India Handbook
Sri Lanka Handbook
Sumatra Handbook
Thailand Handbook
Tibet Handbook
Vietnam Handbook

## Europe

Andalucía Handbook
Barcelona Handbook
Berlin (P)
Bilbao (P)
Bologna (P)
Copenhagen (P)
Croatia Handbook
Dublin Handbook
Dublin (P)
Edinburgh Handbook
Edinburgh (P)
England Handbook
Glasgow Handbook
Ireland Handbook
London Handbook
Madrid (P)
Naples (P)
Northern Spain Handbook
Paris (P)
Reykjavik (P)
Scotland Handbook
Scotland Highlands & Islands
Handbook
Spain Handbook
Turkey Handbook

## Also available

Traveller's Handbook (WEXAS)
Traveller's Healthbook (WEXAS)
Traveller's Internet Guide (WEXAS)

Footnotes

# For a different view of Europe, take a Footprint

**New pocket Handbook series:**
**Bilbao, Bologna, Copenhagen, Madrid, Naples, Berlin,**
**Reykjavik, Dublin, Edinburgh.** Also available: Cape Town,
Havana, Barbados, Sydney, Vancouver

**Discover so much more...**
Listings driven, forward looking and up-to-date. Focuses on what's
going on right now. Contemporary, stylish, and innovative
approach providing quality travel information.

# Zagreb
### CROATIA

Zagreb, old Croatian metropolis, is the oldest and the most significant administrative, cultural, industrial, commercial, scientific and university centre of the Republic of Croatia.

Nowadays the Croatian metropolis consist of three municipal parts: the historical, mediaeval core of the Upper Town, the Lover Town which was subjected to progress and growth in the second half of the 19th century and in the interwar years, and of New Zagreb, the new part of the city where modern housing developments are being built, thus pushing the city limits over the river Sava.

Zagreb is the city with the fascinating, old and well-preserved historical central part covered by the patina of the Middle Ages and marked by the atmosphere characteristic of Central Europe.

The new, modern Zagreb has grown beside the medieval walls and towers, baroque palaces, old mansions and valuable memorials of the feudal past of Kaptol and Gradec.

Of course, the contemporary world has thoroughly changed the world of the past but all its traces have remained outstandingly preserved, especially on Kaptol and in the Upper Town.

Through numerous cultural events, theatrical performances, exhibitions in the Museum and gallery Klovićevi dvori, in the unique Mimara Museum and in very many other museums, galleries and s h o w - r o o m s, Z a g r e b attracts its inhabitants as well as its guests.

A lively atmosphere indeed pervades the city throughout the year, and especially is it vivacious when various international cultural, economic sports and other kinds of events take place.

### Zagreb Tourist Board

www.zagreb-touristinfo.hr e-mail: info@zagreb-touristinfo.hr

# Croatia

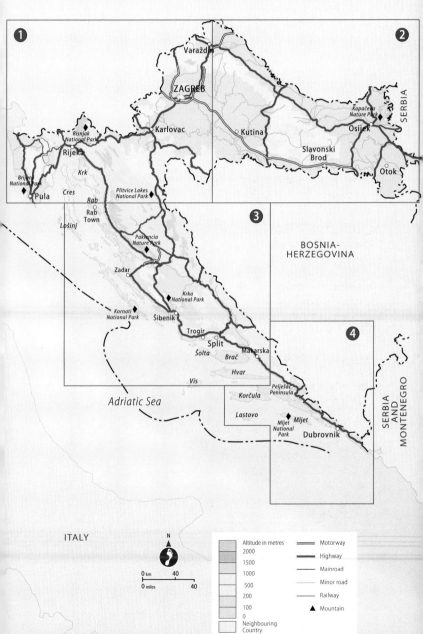

SLOVENIA

HUNGARY

**1**

**2**

Varaždin

ZAGREB

SERBIA

Kopačeva
Nature Park

Risnjak
National Park

Karlovac

Kutina

Osijek

Rijeka

Slavonski
Brod

Krk

Brijuni
National Park

Cres

Plitvice Lakes
National Park

Otok

Pula

Rab

Rab
Town

**3**

Lošinj

Paklenica
Nature Park

BOSNIA-
HERZEGOVINA

Zadar

Krka
National Park

Kornati
National Park

Šibenik

Trogir

**4**

Split

Makarska

Šolta

Brač

SERBIA
AND
MONTENEGRO

Hvar

Vis

Pelješac
Peninsula

*Adriatic Sea*

Korčula

Lastovo

Mljet
National
Park

Mljet

Dubrovnik

ITALY

N

| | Altitude in metres | | Motorway |
|---|---|---|---|
| | 2000 | | Highway |
| | 1500 | | Mainroad |
| | 1000 | | Minor road |
| | 500 | | Railway |
| | 200 | ▲ | Mountain |
| | 100 | | |
| | 0 | | |
| | Neighbouring Country | | |

0 km   40
0 miles   40

Map 2

BOSNIA-
HERZEGOVINA

HUNGARY

N

0 km        10
0 miles     10

Udvar  Doboševica
        Topolje
Kneževo    Batina
        Draž
        Zmajevac
    Branjin Vrh      Suza
Beli Manastir
Baranjsko-    Bolman    Kneževi-
Petrovo Selo          Vinogradi
Belišće          Zlatna
    Grabovac      Greda
N Čeminac  Čeminac
        Lug
Nard    Švajcernica  Vardarac  Kopačeva
Valpovo  Petrijevci    Darda      Nature Park
                Blilje
Šljivoševci        Josipovac  Kopačevo
Benicanci  Harkanovci
    Bizovac      Osijek
Klokočevci  Breznica        Sarvaš
Đurđenovac  Našička  Vučkovac  Čepin    Alimaš
D Motičina  Markova  Lug Suboticki      Dali    Erdut
Našićki          Ovačara
Našica    Podgorač  Cepinski  Ivanovac  Antunovac  Vera
Gradac        Martinci  Vladisavci  Ernestinova  Klisa  Trpinja
        Budimci  Vuka    Laslovo  Bobota
Gradište          Hrastin      Korog
            Gorjani  Široke Polje      Pačetin
                Koritna  Markušica  Tordinci  Borovo
Ruševo    Satnica  Viškovci  Semeljci  Kesinci  Gaboš  Ostrovo  Bršadin  Vukovar
dina Rijeka  Đakovačka      Jarmina    Nuštar  Petrovci
        Selci  Koševac  St Mikanovci        Sotin
Podcrkavlje  Đakovačka  Đakovo        Vinkovci  Neglosiavci
Klokočevl  Kondrić          Mirkovci  Stari Jankovoi  Opatovac
Bukovlje  Trnava  Budrovci  Rokovci    Slakovci  Orolik  Šarengrad  Ilok
Podvinsko  Vrpolje  Strizivojna  Andrijaševci      Bapska
Trnjani D Andrijevci      Černa    Privlaka  Komletinci  Tovarnik
Slavonski  Garčin  V Kopanica  Gundinci        Otok
Brod  Sredanci      Gradište    Podgrađe
Oprisavci          Babina Greda
Kuti Trnjanski    Županja        Apševci
Donja Peprrina              Lipovac
            Bošnjaci
                Podgajci  Soljani
                Posavski
                Rajevo  Drenovci
                Selo
                Gunja
                Račinovci

Moslavina
Podr
Vilijevo
Krčenik    Donje  D Miholjac
Moslavački  Rakitovica  Svali Đurad
Kapelna  Miholjačk
    Poreč  Ömkovci
Magadenovac  Marijanci
Donje Predrijevo
Boksić
hovica        Lavanjska Varoš
Ferikanci
žluk
žije
jevo
krež

SERBIA

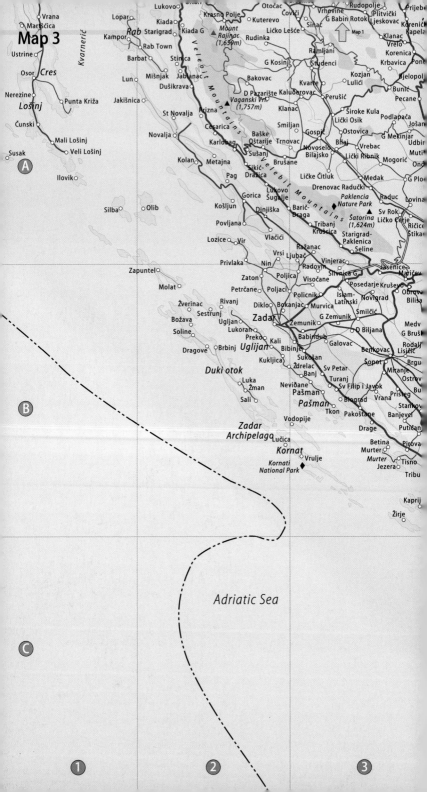

# Map 4

Map 3

stranje
kvičič
G Vinjani
Imotski
Podbablje

**A**
Runović

Aniči

okovo untain

Kozica

Stilja
G Igrane
Ravča

Igrane
Vrgorac
Crveni Grm
Živogosce
V Prolog
olje
M Prolog
Drvenik
Zaostrog
Podaca
Šućuraj
Staševica
Gradac
Bačina
Peračko Blato
Ploče
Metkovic
Duba
Rogotin
Kula
Nakovanj
Trpanj
Pelješac
Peninsula
Blace
Norinska
Opuzen
Bijeli Vir
Vigani
Orebić
Vručica
Crkvice
Kremena
uciste
Kuna
Osobljava
Mislina
Korčula
Town
Podobuče
Potomje
Drače
Zrnovo
Janjina
Briljesta
Lumbarda
Trstenik
Duž
Žuljana
Ošlje
Trnovica
Putnikovic
Luka
Mali Ston
Ponikve
Ston
Čepikuče
Broce
Doli
Baniči

**B**
Pomena
Polača
Kozarica
Siano
Govedjari
Ropa
G Majkovi
Mljet
Sobra
Prožura
Šip Luka
Steno
Osojnik
National
Babino
Korita
Flafiti
Sv Đurad
Orašac
Park
Polje
Maranovici
Islands
Lopud
Zeton
Mokošica
Koločep
Lapad
Dubac
Gruz Bigat
**Dubrovnik**
Srebreno
Lokrum
Kupari Mlini
Sravca
*Adriatic Sea*
Uskopje
Cavtat
Dubravka
Cilipi
Gruda
Popovici
Vodovada
Radovčiči
Pločice
Molunat
Prevla

BOSNIA-HERZEGOVINA

N

0 km    10
0 miles    10

see inset map

**C**
Lovište
Duba
Nakovanj
Vigani
Vela Luka
Račišce
Orebić
*Korčula*
Kuciste
**Blato**
Cara
Pupnat
Korčula
Town
Potirna
Smokvica
Zrnovo
Prižoa
Brna
Lumbarda

*Kopište*
Prezba
Lastovo
*Lastovo*
Ubi
Skivena

1        2        3